Portrait of Whittier by Albert Gallatin Hoit, 1846, Whittier Home, Amesbury, Mass.

John Greenleaf Whittier:
A Biography
by
Roland H. Woodwell

Printed in Ward Hill, Haverhill, Massachusetts
by DBL Commercial Printers

Foreword

A photograph of John Greenleaf Whittier was on a small easel on the marble-topped parlor table in my childhood home. I was told that Whittier was a distant relative of mine. Perhaps my interest in his life and writings was already faintly stirring. When in 1924 I began what became forty-three years of teaching in the town where he had lived during the larger part of his life, I thought that it would be interesting to collect facts about him and perhaps to put them together, although I was not at all aware of his importance in the events, the thoughts, and the emotions of the Nineteenth Century.

The result is an old-fashioned biography, without "interpretation" or "theme."

There seems to be evidence that Whittier has something to say to the Twentieth Century in the willingness of so many people to make his life and writings better known. Many of these people have died, and probably did not know how helpful they had been. They include hundreds of my pupils and former pupils, older people who had known Whittier personally, and others whom I had never met but who patiently and carefully answered my letters. Carroll A. Wilson and C. Marshall Taylor, collectors of Whittier material, gave a great deal of help and encouragement.

I am grateful to the Librarians at Amesbury, Haverhill, and Newburyport Public Libraries, Boston Atheneum, Essex Institute, Harvard College Library, and Massachusetts Historical Society. T. Franklin Currier, while working on the *Bibliography of John Greenleaf Whittier*, Harvard University Press 1937, answered many questions and gave valuable advice. The Whittier Home Association of Amesbury gave me unlimited access to the books and papers at the Amesbury home of Whittier, and Mrs. Frieda Marion, when curator there, continued the work begun by her predecessor Mrs. Ruth Hill of cataloging items, some of which had remained undiscovered since Whittier's time, and placed them where I could use them.

When Professor John B. Pickard of the University of Florida was preparing his three-volume *Letters of John Greenleaf Whittier*, Harvard University Press, 1975, he permitted me to keep closely in touch with his work and to have copies of scores of letters in his file. Without this help my book would never have been finished.

Finally, this book would never have been published without the sponsorship of the Trustees of the John Greenleaf Whittier Homestead, Haverhill, Massachusetts. I am grateful for their confidence in my work.

I am also grateful for the kindness and patience of Mr. and Mrs. Donald C. Freeman, whose help in proof-reading and other details of publication has prevented errors and has resulted in a volume, which is accurate, and, I hope, will be of value to scholars in the future. Donald P. Wright has been helpful in supplying information from his extensive knowledge of persons and publications and from his collection of portraits of Whittier and of illustrations for Whittier's poems.

Also of invaluable assistance in collecting and identifying photographs were Howard Curtis, Director, and Gregory Laing of Haverhill Public Library.

My appreciation to Mrs. Frances Dowd, who in the last stages of the book — the printing — served as a courier to transfer batches of proof between Haverhill and Amesbury.

Contents

List of Illustrations

Unless otherwise credited, the illustrations are from the Whittier
Collection at Haverhill Public Library and were used by permission of the trustees. All illustrations except the Hoit portrait and
author's photo were copied and printed at the library by Michael
J. DeMatteo, staff photographer.

I

1807 - 28

John Greenleaf Whittier was born December 17, 1807, in a farmhouse built by his great-great grandfather about 1688.

Thomas Whittier came from England to Massachusetts when he was eighteen, lived briefly in Salisbury (now Amesbury) and Newbury, and laid out a farm and built a log house in the frontier wilderness on the edge of the new town of Haverhill in 1647. He was sixty when he built the two-and-a half story house which was to be the scene of "Snow-Bound" and consequently one of the most photographed houses in America.

In John Greenleaf Whittier's boyhood the house and farm were little changed from Thomas Whittier's time. On the north and east were miles of woodland. On the west was a pasture with a few oak and walnut trees. The house faced the south, with its east end toward the road. The front windows looked out on a little brook which flowed from a blueberry swamp and wound through a belt of beeches and black birches to a larger stream called Country Brook. Beyond the brook was a wooded hill. There were the usual farm buildings, a barn behind the house, a corn house, a piggery, and a small building across the road where shoes were made during the winter.[1]

This farm supported four adults and four children. It was owned jointly by John Greenleaf Whittier's father, John, and his Uncle Moses, who had mortgaged the farm to buy out the other heirs. John Whittier was forty-seven when his second child and first son, known in the family as Greenleaf, was born. Before his marriage he had made long trading trips through New Hampshire to Canada. He had delayed marrying until he was reasonably certain of being able to support a family on the farm. His wife, Abigail, was twenty-eight. Her sister Mercy lived with them. The other children were Mary, a year older than Greenleaf, Matthew Franklin, five years younger, and Elizabeth, eight years younger.

The farm land was poor. Whittier once said that when he succeeded in getting fifty bushels of corn from a half acre it cost all that the corn was worth to do it. Daisies sometimes overran and ruined the mowing fields. Frugality was necessary, and the children as well as the adults had to work indoors and out. One of Greenleaf's duties, which he did not enjoy, was milking seven cows.[2] But the family was safely above the bitter poverty of the poorest New England farmers. There was some additional income from the sale of ship timber. When Greenleaf was ten years old two and a quarter acres of meadow were bought in his name to be added to the farm,[3] and a new barn was built on the other side of the road. The children could not have thought of themselves as poor; the Whittiers owned the only chaise in the neighborhood.[4]

The children could enjoy the security that comes from a father held in high regard in the community. In spite of having no church connections to help him politically and living a long way from the center of the town, John Whittier was elected or appointed to a list of public offices: selectman, assessor, and member of budget committee, district school committee, and a committee to inspect bridges.

Whittier described his father in "Snow-Bound" as prompt and decisive, one who did not waste breath in needless talk, but he had a sense of humor and could talk well when there was leisure and occasion. He gave lively accounts of his trips to Canada, including the time when he was with a party of horsemen who met a tribe of friendly Indians on the shore of Lake Memphremagog. All of the Indians were drunk except one who was kept busy preventing the others from rolling into the lake or otherwise getting into trouble. When John Whittier asked him if he never got drunk he replied that he got drunk sometimes but "Me keep watch this time; next time me get drunk." One of Elizabeth's schoolmates remembered him as a fine-looking old man who always had a pleasant word for everybody. He held himself well, with good poise of head and shoulders.

Whittier's affection for his mother was deep and life-long. Elizabeth's schoolmate described Abigail Whittier as high-spirited, and she was capable of firm and decisive action. But she was kind. Tramps — then called "stragglers" — who called at the farmhouse were well treated. When she refused food and shelter to a black-bearded Italian whose dark appearance frightened her, she soon relented and sent Greenleaf to bring him back to supper, bed, and breakfast, thinking, "What if a son of mine was in a strange land?" One day she took Greenleaf with her when she called on a sick woman whom she pitied and whom the other neighbors would not visit because she was regarded as wicked. He never forgot the incident and mentioned it only a few weeks before his death. Her sympathies were not confined to the neighborhood. She told her children about the kidnapping of negro children, knowing that their sympathies would go more surely to unfortunates of their own age. From his mother's goodness and compassion the boy got the concept of God's goodness and compassion.[5]

The bachelor uncle Moses Whittier knew all about birds and animals and could tell about them so vividly that an imaginative boy listening in front of the fireplace would think that he was seeing them himself. He knew where the best pickerel were to be found, and Greenleaf was willing to work hard on summer days hoeing corn or raking hay because when his work was finished he could go fishing with Uncle Moses. Although Whittier, looking back through the years, described him as simple and guileless, he appraised the ways of men with native shrewdness. When the boy jubilantly exclaimed,

"I've got a fish" just before the fish got away, and refused to be comforted, Uncle Moses rebaited the hook, urged the boy to try again, and advised, "Never brag of catching a fish until he is on dry ground. I've seen older folks doing that in more ways than one, and so making fools of themselves. It's of no use to boast of anything until it's done, nor then either, for it speaks for itself."[6]

Aunt Mercy Hussey kept a youthful spirit and a sense of romance heightened by an incident in her youth. Late one night, as she was sitting alone in the kitchen, she felt an urge to go to the window where she thought that she saw her lover, whom she supposed to be in New York, riding toward the house. From the porch window she saw him turn as if to dismount at the step. When she opened the door he had disappeared. She then recalled that she had heard no sound of hoofs. After some days she received a letter telling her that her lover had died at the time when she had the vision. But she did not spend the rest of her life in idle sentimentalizing. She worked as a practical nurse and she baked excellent squash pies.[7]

Greenleaf enjoyed much of the outdoor life on the farm. Going barefooted in the summer was fun — most of the time. But it wasn't so pleasant when he had to rake wild meadow grass, a thin, sharp-edged grass that the young live-stock would eat in the winter when they were really hungry. The boy's bare feet stumbled over rough hassocks and sank into black mud, with the chance of stepping on a watersnake or adder or even a black snake. But the meadows were also places where bobolinks sang, bullfrogs croaked, fog rose and drifted in summer moonlight, and fireflies flashed their signals.

The small brook near the house seemed to the children to be speaking to them in an almost human tone, and it was a good place to set water wheels. Along the banks of Country Brook were wildflowers from early spring to late fall, and for the hot summer days there were bathing pools with clear water and white sand. In the spring the children enjoyed watching the sheep-washing in the brook.

Like other country boys, Greenleaf liked to swing on birch trees and to hunt for eggs in the barn. He liked the oxen best of the farm animals. One day his favorite ox, old Ben, amused him by coming to the window of the house while a Friends Meeting was being held there, listening with apparent interest to a woman speaker, but racing toward the barn when a harsh-voiced elder began to speak.

In the fall, when he went to drive the cows home from pasture, he would fill his pockets with nuts which he and the other children would crack on the horse block near the gate in the wall. One cold morning he climbed a nut tree and had got near the top when the branches that he was standing on gave way. He seized a small branch, which broke, and he started to fall. Under the tree was a pile of stones. Death, heaven, home, friends flashed through his mind, and then he was stopped with a jerk that almost dislocated his shoulder. He had caught hold of a branch strong enough to support his weight.

Hemlock branches which the boys got from a grove a half mile from the house were used as brooms. When they were dry they were thrown on the wood burning in the fireplace, and the crackling fusillade suggested a great battle — even to Quaker children.

The Whittier children had the pleasurable excitement of being afraid of something. Neighbors told them stories about witches and ghosts. One evening a woman came to the house badly frightened by a headless ghost that she had seen as she passed Country Bridge. Greenleaf and some other boys agreed to go there on a moonlight night, and he bravely asserted that he would run onto the bridge and call for the ghost. When they came to the bridge his courage failed him but he kept his promise, shouted for the ghost to appear, and then ran as fast as he could.

The stellar witchcraft attraction was Aunt Mose, who lived about two miles away and whose nephew, Aaron Chase, was Whittier's schoolmate. She was popularly supposed to be in league with Satan, who did not properly reward her devotion: she was poor, bent with rheumatism, and dependent on charity which was given by people who were afraid of her. She was accused of interfering with the making of butter and of snuffing out candles at huskings and quilting parties. She once went before a justice of the peace and swore that she was not a witch. Greenleaf was still afraid of her when he was ten years old, and his fears were increased when he saw Gallows Hill in Danvers and the skeleton of a tree on which, he was told, witches had been hanged.

Greenleaf did not have the physical vigor expected of country boys. His first memory, he once said, was a sick headache, and it is not surprising that he did not enjoy old-fashioned boiled dinners, which he once described as "cabbage, onions, beets, potatoes, turnips, carrots all boiled up together and turned out into a great dish all in a heap, with a great greasy piece of meat in the middle." He suffered more than most boys from the cold. His boyhood was before the time of woolen underwear, and the only difference between summer and winter clothing, he once said, was a muffler or mittens on the coldest days.

A compensation for lack of physical vigor was a sensitive awareness of country sights, sounds, and odors. He once remarked that if he had ever written anything worth remembering, the credit was partly due to the beautiful scenery around him in his childhood. As an old man he remembered his early enjoyment of the fragrance of new-mown hay. The odor of sweet fern as he slowly climbed a hill near Asquam Lake in 1883 took him suddenly back to his boyhood and he saw the pond shining through the trees and the rising mist showing the line of the river and heard the summer sounds of leaves and bees and birds.[8]

Quakers did more travelling than Congregationalists or Baptists, who were strongly local and self-governing. Quakers were organized in Monthly, Quarterly, and Yearly Meetings. The meeting in Amesbury which the Whittiers attended was called a Preparative Meeting and was part of the Seabrook, New Hampshire, Monthly Meeting and the Salem, Massachusetts, Quarterly Meeting. Greenleaf saw Gallows Hill in Danvers when his parents took him to Salem Quarterly Meeting. This travelling now seems too short a distance to deserve the name, but an observant child could learn that there were places and people different from those that he saw every day.

During the weeks and months when the Whittier children did not go far from home, there were visitors who made life interesting. The "stragglers" who received food and shelter at the farmhouse were often amusing or pathetic. Whittier described some of them in "Yankee Gypsies": the black-eyed woman with silent, impassive face, frozen rigid by some great wrong or sin; the herb-gatherer who called himself a doctor and who counterfeited lameness; the man with the huge pack — what horrible thing was in it?; Jonathan Plummer of Newburyport, "Lord" Timothy Dexter's poet laureate; Rev. Benjamin Bell, once pastor of the prosperous and important First Church in Amesbury but now fallen on evil days, sober only when he lacked money for drink, but always grave, decorous, and gentlemanly as he held religious meetings in the schoolhouse.[9] Greenleaf's love of poetry was strengthened by hearing a wandering Scotchman sing the Songs of Burns, which were already familiar to him from their reading by one of his schoolteachers — fortunately, because music was forbidden in the Whittiers' as in most Quaker households. Another straggler sang a humorous ballad, stayed over night, and departed the next day with the village doctor's horse.

There were other visitors of a somewhat higher type. Uncle Nathaniel Whittier came annually on his way to Yearly Meeting, "tall, plain, and drab-clothed — an Israelite indeed in whom was no guile." Another elderly relative told the story of the Haunted House at Hampton, New Hampshire, which Whittier remembered and used in "The New Wife and the Old."

William Forster, who has been described as "that passionate lover of human freedom, that high-souled, almost Franciscan saint," visited the Whittiers on his first journey in the United States, probably in the fall of 1822. Whittier was then at the impressionable age of fourteen, too young to understand all that Forster said, but not too young to receive an impression of purity and goodness which warned and guided him in emotional crises.[10]

A cousin, Mary Emerson Smith, was a visitor at a farm where Greenleaf helped with the chores. She found her country cousin interesting and succeeded in bringing out what Whittier called "the powers of my own mind, the mysteries of my own spirit." She seemed to him glorious in the aura of boarding school and knowledge of grammar and philosophy and mineralogy and French and high acquaintance with society and her ability to talk. He was not in love with her, he said positively some years later, but might have been if she had not gone to live in Cincinnati, where Daniel Webster saw her and described her as one of the finest girls that he had seen west of the Alleghany.

Greenleaf Weld, nephew and adopted son of Dr. Elias Weld, the doctor described in "Snow-Bound," was a frequent visitor at the Whittiers', often bringing books from Dr. Weld's Library. Both boys were shy and did not become intimate friends. But Greenleaf's shyness did not keep him from playing with Dr. Weld's niece Sally, a friend of Greenleaf's older sister Mary. He had evidently absorbed the Quaker injunction of plainness of dress and the counsel against "Ribbonds, Knots, and Ruffles upon Women's Heads" and criticized her bonnet because it had a knot of ribbon and a flower.[11]

Harriet Livermore was the "half-feared, half-welcomed" guest described in "Snow-Bound." She was a frequent visitor at the Whittiers' when she was about twenty-five, dark eyed, striking in appearance, brilliant, and a good conversationalist. But unhappily she was telling the truth when she said of herself, "I was never endued with any natural equanimity, moderation or sweetness. I was always called passionate from my earliest remembrance." She had once struck a girl for not admitting that Harriet's father was the handsomest man in the world.

It is not recorded that Harriet resorted to any violence while at the Whittiers', probably during the brief period of her interest in the Society of Friends. The Quakers can hardly have been eager to have her join them; in a burst of anger during a quarrel at a Quaker's house she knocked down a Quaker with a piece of wood.

Harriet Livermore performed one important service for Greenleaf: she corrected his pronunciation. She was well qualified to do this. She had attended Atkinson Academy, and after hearing her preach a sermon in Congress George H. Briggs, later a Governor of Massachusetts, wrote that he had heard but few better models of public speaking.[12]

The school that the Whittier children attended was half a mile down the road, standing partly in the road and partly in a pasture, a small unpainted wooden building with three small windows. Beside it was a still smaller building that looked like a sentry box but was doubtless an outdoor privy. Before the schoolhouse was built or when it was being repaired, rooms in nearby houses were used. One was in the house of Daniel Ela on Corliss Road, where a rough board partition with cracks and knotholes let the pupils hear the quarrels going on in the kitchen. In winter the walk to school on zero days in homespun clothing through snow broken only by tracks of sleighs and ox-sleds ended in a schoolroom that was not really warm until noon. Greenleaf had to take his turn building the fire — and before he could do that he had to dig the wood out of the snow.

The school had one room, with pupils of all ages and one teacher. No teacher stayed long. Some were Dartmouth College students earning a little money for their next term's tuition. One of them was recorded as receiving food, lodging, and $27.69 for the annual term of twelve weeks — perhaps as much as he was worth. With a few exceptions, Whittier said, they were not worth much.

One of the exceptions was George Haskell, the teacher described in "Snow-Bound." He was delightfully boyish but studious. He became a physician and helped found a college and an industrial school.

Joshua Coffin, Greenleaf's first teacher, boarded at the Whittiers'. He was different from many teachers at the time who regarded corporal punishment as conventional procedure. He had the knack of arousing pupil interest by humorous storytelling. Whittier felt under life-long obligation to him. Coffin lent him a copy of Burns' poems when he was fourteen. He later recalled that when he was in the field mowing the early hay, he would stop work and forget the unmown hay while he read Burns in the shade of a maple tree and found the glory of the commonplace and the worth of man. There is some imaginative interpretation here: Whittier's first poems show the influence of authors quite different from Burns and none of these poems is local except "The Tale of the Merrimac," the style of which resembles Samuel Woodworth's a great deal and Burns' not at all. But there is no doubt that he read the poems and liked them. A volume of Burns given to him by James F. Otis in 1830 contains many of his pencil markings.

An incident in the school became the subject of one of Whittier's most popular poems. It moved Oliver Wendell Holmes to tears and it led Henry Wadsworth Longfellow to remark, "There is something more in education than is set down in the school books." The poem, "In School Days," told of the girl who was sorry that she had defeated the boy in a spelling match.

"Because, you see, I love you."

When Whittier was old and some children asked him if the story was true he replied that it was quite likely there was some truth in it.[13] He told Helen Keller that he was the boy and that the girl's name was Sally.

In spite of poor and inadequate schooling, he had become something other than a crude, ignorant country boy when he began to write poetry in his late teens. These early verses were poor products; they had no real originality, they revealed no hidden depths, they were fashionably sentimental, and their wording was prosaic or conventionally poetic — as he once said, he learned to rhyme before he learned to think. But they were better than the average teen-ager could do today, with the help of three or four times the schooling that Whittier had. He could visualize an object or scene from hearing or reading about it and describe it clearly and at times vividly. The meter was regular, if monotonous and imitative; he wrote four poems in anapestic tetrameter quatrains echoing "The Old Oaken Bucket." They show a surprisingly wide range of information: muleteers in Iberia; Petrarch in an orange grove on the Rhone; the heroism and suffering of the Irish, O'Neil, Fitzgerald, Emmet; the life of Alexander I; Louis XVI; the Crusades; Putnam and Stark.

Many of the facts and much of the inspiration came from reading. He read for hours at a little table in the center of the east front room and took time out to read when he worked on the farm. He remembered what he read and entered into it, achieving the communion which is better than communication.

There were so few books in the house that he could list most of them in a rhymed catalogue of thirty-four lines.

Some of them were good. On Sunday afternoon his mother and the children would read the Bible together —[14] and when he came to read it himself he liked best the stories about wars and battles. Among his early poems were three paraphrases of Bible passages: Micah IV 3, Baruch V ("The Restoration") and Psalm 137 — the first of these, the beating of swords into ploughshares, being perhaps a repentent corrective to his un-Quakerly interest in war.

Another book was one that all boys in good families were expected to read, *Pilgrim's Progress*, which, as George Bernard Shaw once remarked, has the best fights of any book in the English language. Whittier was like other boys that read the book: Mr. Greatheart was his favorite character, and he enjoyed horrifying himself by looking at the picture of Appolyon, "horned, hoofed, scaly, and fire-breathing, his caudal extremity twisted tight with rage, illustrating the tremendous encounter of Christian in the valley, where Appolyon straddles over the whole breadth of the way."[15]

In his rhymed catalog he treated Rollin's *Ancient History of the Egyptians, Carthaginians, Asyrians, Medes and Persians, Grecians and Macedonians* unkindly:

How Rollins [sic] to obtain the cash
Wrote a dull history of trash.

A few years later, however, a passage in it inspired the poem "Pericles", which is introduced by a quotation from Volume III. He probably read the History and remembered a good deal of it. Educators did not share his expressed opinion of it; it lasted well over a century as a text-book.

There were a few Quaker books. One was Robert Barclay's *Apology*, which Whittier often referred to in his later years as basic in the religion of the Friends, although there is no direct evidence that he read it as a child. He read Thomas Chalkley's *Journal*, his interest in it aroused by stories from it told by his mother on winter evenings: he pondered over it "with deep and quiet joy".[16]

Another book in which Whittier's mother found stories to tell was William Sewel's *History of the Rise, Increase, and Progress of the Christian People Called Quakers*. Although Whittier referred to it in "Snow-Bound" as a book of "faith fire-winged with martyrdom," some of the incidents are lively and amusing. In the account of James Nayler, about whom Whittier wrote a prose essay in 1846, Sewel tells of three women who knelt before Nayler in Exeter Prison and kissed his feet and later spread their scarfs and handkerchiefs before him as he rode along the muddy road to Bristol. Thomas Ibbitt, who prophesied the 1666 Great Fire of London a few days before it occurred, was so exalted when his prophecy came true that he stood in front of the fire with his arms outspread in the belief that he could stop it. Two men hostile to Quakers got punished in ways that obviously pleased Sewel. An Independent minister, cursing the Quaker "inner light" in his pulpit, evidently became overexcited and suffered a stroke, and although revived by having "strong waters" poured into him, was "mopish" and never recovered his senses. A cruel jailer who forced a ninety-year-old blind Quaker to sit up three nights in a chair had horrid pangs of conscience when dying of spotted fever.

Another Quaker book was Thomas Clarkson's *Portraiture of Quakerism*. Whittier referred to Clarkson in an early poem, "Benevolence". Twenty years later he wrote to Clarkson, who he said had perhaps never heard of him, praising Clarkson's interest in Anti-Slavery.[17]

The only book of poetry the family owned was Thomas Ellwood's *Davideis*. Ellwood was the first person to read Milton's "Paradise Lost," but he did not absorb any of Milton's poetic excellence, and Whittier could not have got much help from it except perhaps a sense of meter. As Walter Scott once pointed out, "There is a period in youth when the power of numbers has a more strong effect on ear and imagination than in more advanced life."

There was one novel in the house, *The Coquette or History of Eliza Wharton*. Greenleaf found it on the top of a high chest of drawers, wrapped in a napkin, where Aunt Mercy had hidden it to keep it out of the hands of the children. A half century later he described it as "a poor enough sort of fiction — a tame affair, scarcely readable," but he lived with its story for months, imagining the gay and courtly Major Sanford dancing with the beautiful heroine, and her dignified lover rebuking her for her faithlessness.[18]

He found some old Congressional Reports in the attic, and in the midst of the dullness of most of the debates he discovered the speeches of John Randolph, which were often lively reading: "The Greeks were pirates in the days of Agamemnon — they were pirates before his time, and they will always be pirates."[19]

Greenleaf probably read all of the books in the house. There were eighteen biographies — from their number it may be assumed that they were brief and inexpensive. There were four travel books and four religious books besides those already mentioned.

Books could be borrowed from kindly people. As an old man, Whittier recalled walking miles through snow and rain to borrow a book. Dr. Weld sent books to the Whittier house by his adopted son and found time to talk to Greenleaf about them. It was after he had talked about Milton and Thomson that the boy attempted, as he later described it, "to bring a few words to rhyme and measure."[20]

It must have been even earlier that he read Gray's "Elegy" and Cowper's "Lament for the Royal George." He was too young to understand them, but he felt their power, and their phrases became part of his being: "cool sequestered shade" in one of his earliest poems, "The Brothers," is evidently an echo of Gray's "cool sequestered vale." He read some of Byron's poetry — from his "Byron" in *The Free Press* December 2, 1826, it would seem that he had read a good deal of it, and while the poem was filled with cliches and was painfully moral about Byron's sins, it showed enthusiasm. He read John Pierpont's *Airs of Palestine*. He read at least some of Ossian's poetry; and while he derived "The Song of Peace" from it, and with its pledge that to peace

A bard unknown to fame
Would dedicate his minstrelsy

he admitted later that he followed "Ossian over Mervan's battlefields, exulting in the vulture - screams of the blind scald over his fallen enemies." Farther still from his own surroundings was Stephen Harvey's translation of Juvenal's Ninth Satire, which was quoted, with one inaccuracy, in the poem beginning "I envy not the station gained." "Paulowna" was based on a pathetic incident in Eugene Labaume's *A Circumstantial Narrative of the Campaign in Russia.*[21]

Newspapers were then a real source of education. Sports and comics had not been thought of and there was little local news but a great deal of what would now be found in magazines. It was in the Haverhill paper that Whittier read and, as he later said, "responded to" the simple verses of Robert Dinsmore. It was probably in the same paper that he read, at the age of twelve or thirteen, a speech by William Plumer, Jr., which he reread thirty years later.[22] Newspaper items about slavery must have added to the feelings aroused by other influences. One such item was in the *Essex Patriot*, Haverhill, August 11, 1821:

A negro woman belonging to Ratcliff Pointeur (Maryland) being informed that she had been sold to the negro buyers, first cut the throat of her child and afterwards her own — their bodies were found a few days afterward near home.

There are Anti-Slavery lines in two of the earliest poems, "Benevolence" and "The Tale of the Merrimac."

Whittier's parents attended the Friends Meeting in Amesbury on Sundays and Thursdays, and he went in his turn; there wasn't room for all four children in the chaise. The family did not sit together in the meeting: the men were on one side and the women and children on the other. There was no Sunday School, no children's sermon, and no activities for children. The changes that were later to make some Friends meetings no different from other Evangelical Protestant services had not begun, and the meeting was unprogrammed and without leadership. There were long periods of silence — and they must have seemed very long to a child. There was no music and, in theory at least, no planned speaking. However, Whittier never said that he objected to going to the meeting except for the cold drive followed by an hour in an unheated room.

It is unlikely that there was much effective speaking at Amesbury Friends Meeting unless there were visiting ministers present. As is usual in unprogrammed meetings, secular and religious, the eccentrics probably did more than their share of the talking and at least succeeded in amusing the children. One of them was Abram Morrison, whom the Amesbury Meeting had hesitated for eight years to admit to membership but who had now become an elder and sat in one of the seats facing the congregation. There was only half-checked smiling among the children when, evidently at the time of President Monroe's visit to Amesbury in 1817, Morrison exhorted the young people not to go after

 . . . . . Elephants,
 Learned pigs, and presidents
 And the likes

as Whittier quoted him in "Abram Morrison."

Quakers resembled other Protestant sects of the time except Episcopalians in paying no attention to religious holidays, and children missed all the color and poetry that earlier generations had enjoyed in England. Whittier had never heard of Christmas until he was about fifteen.[23]

Whittier's youthful acceptance of the peace principles of the Quakers was traditionary rather than the result of serious convincement. He also accepted the belief, common to all New England Christians, in a future life to which one looked forward with happy confidence and he expressed it in the sentimental clichés of his contemporaries:

 Look beyond the narrow mansion
 Bound by the silent tomb
 To the bright and fair expansion
 Of a world of endless bloom.

He smiled at the queer old-fashioned clothes that the Quaker wore,

 . . . . . . His hat-brim resembling the wing
 Of the bird which old Sinbad the warrior saw,

the roundabout fashion of his coat, and his vest with long pocket flaps, but these could be overlooked since the Quaker had meekness, truth, and compassion — the first of his many references to the simple fundamentals of the Friends which it seemed to him in later years were often forgotten in the search for new ways.[24]

Whittier's early poems changed the course of his life. Two newspaper editors were impressed by verses written by a young farmer and went out of their way to urge that he get more education. The first was William Lloyd Garrison.

Whittier's sister Mary, without his knowledge, sent one of his poems, "The Exile's Departure," to Garrison's *Free Press* in Newburyport, signing it "W. Haverhill, June 1, 1826." Whittier's father was a subscriber to the paper, and Whittier was surprised and delighted to see his poem in the paper which the post rider tossed to him as he was working with his father mending a stone wall. Three days later Mary sent "The Deity," and then a poem every week until the middle of September. Garrison's curiosity was aroused, and after asking the post rider where the poems came from, he drove to East Haverhill, accompanied by a woman friend. Whittier was crawling under the barn in pursuit of a hen that had stolen a nest when his sister Mary told him that there were visitors waiting to see him. He succeeded in getting into the house without being seen and hurriedly changed his clothes, in his haste putting on a pair of trousers that came scarcely to his ankles.

Garrison urged that the boy have further education, but his father thought that it couldn't be done: there simply wasn't any money. But the idea was put into the minds of father and son.

Garrison sold the "*Free Press*" and Whittier's weekly poem was then sent to the *Haverhill Gazette* (later, for a time, called the *Essex Gazette*), whose editor, Abijah W. Thayer, visited the Whittiers for the same purpose as Garrison and with greater success. He had one talking point that Garrison had not had: an academy was to be opened in Haverhill, and Thayer said that Greenleaf might live at the Thayer house. But the problem of money remained. Tuition was to be four dollars a term: "genteel board" in Haverhill was from $1.50 to $2.00 a week.

The solution was shoemaking. Leonard Johnson, later a shoe manufacturer in Haverhill, who worked on the Whittier farm in the summer and did shoemaking in the winter, offered to teach Whittier to make a plain turned slipper. The work was done in the small shop across the road from the house. Here Whittier sat on a low bench with a little drawer at the side in which he kept paper and poems that he composed as he worked.

Among others working in the shop was John Hoit, who was learning the shoemaker's trade and was living with the Whittiers. One day Whittier wrote a poem for him. Over fifty years later Hoit tried to recall the first stanza and thought that it was this:

"It was from the Port of Holy head, for Holland we did steer: we had not long lost site of our dear native place, Before not far astern a vessel we espied, and she quickly gave us chase."

He also remembered that Whittier wrote a poem when he had to leave the shop to thresh grain because a neighbor who had agreed to help with this work had failed to appear.[25] This poem has never been found. If he had seriously accepted the principle that poetry should be indigenous, as he said in recalling the effect of his first reading of Burns, he would have sent this poem to the *Gazette* instead of one of the poems that had nothing to do with East Haverhill or farm life.

The picture of a shoemaker-poet had a popular appeal which it has never wholly lost. James Otis, a nephew of Harrison Grey Otis, heard that some verses that he had seen in a newspaper had been written by a shoemaker-boy in Haverhill. He went to Haverhill and introduced himself to Whittier, and they spent the day wandering over the hills and on the shore of the Merrimac, talking about literary matters. A century later the Harvard University Hymnal, 1926, referred to Whittier as "farm boy and shoemaker." Whittier conscientiously tried to correct the impression: "I did not work at shoemaking except some few experiments in the winter between 16 and 18," he wrote in 1871 — the years obviously being incorrect. However, he learned the trade well enough to remember it a long time; he tried his hand at it, perhaps just to see if he did remember it, forty years later.[26]

Enough money was earned and saved, and an arrangement was made to pay part of his board with food from the farm.[27] Whittier was ready to enter the Academy, which was to open April 30, and to live in Haverhill in surroundings quite different from his farm home. Haverhill was busy and prosperous, with three hundred houses, including "elegant residences" on Water Street, four brick buildings, forty stores, a shipyard, and a distillery — destined to close, to the delight of Whittier and Thayer. Best of all, there would soon be a circulating library. The town was no longer isolated from the big world: a beautiful new bridge had just been built, and a stagecoach company which owned one hundred twenty horses maintained a schedule of nine trips weekly to Boston, while a branch line to Newburyport connected with a through line to Quebec.

The Academy building was on Winter Street, from which open fields sloped down to the river. It was of graceful Georgian design, two stories high, with two classrooms on the first floor and an auditorium on the second. There were twelve trustees, five of them clergymen and all of them local except Thomas West, who later lived in Haverhill and was president of the new railroad from Haverhill to Boston.[28]

On opening day, April 30, a procession of trustees, proprietors, "literary and professional gentlemen," town officers, and interested citizens formed at the Academy and marched at two o'clock to the First Church nearby for the long and elaborate exercises which were the fashion of the time.[29] Marching in the procession was John Greenleaf Whittier, whose local reputation was already such that he had been asked to write the ode for the occasion. He was shyly blushing with an overwhelming sense of the honor; with him marched the seventy-year-old Robert Dinsmore of Windham, New Hampshire, farmer-poet and deacon of the church, a little unsteady in consequence of the "brick in his hat" which Whittier explained as "a highly descriptive euphemism for drunk."[30]

The exercises proceeded, with an address three quarters of an hour long by Leverett Saltonstall, prayers by two clergymen of nearby towns, and music by local choirs and other musicians of Haverhill and Bradford. Whittier's ode, beginning "Hail, Star of Science: Come forth in thy splendor" was sung by John Crowell, leader of the Baptist choir. Whittier evidently got suggestions from the Boat Song in Scott's "The Lady of the Lake." The stanza form was the same. Both poems began by hailing something; in the Boat Song the pine symbolic of Roderigh Dhu was to bourgeon and grow, while in Whittier's Ode laurels of science (knowledge) were to grow greenly.

The school opened for business the next day, with a faculty of four and an enrollment of ninety.

The Preceptor (Headmaster) was Oliver Carleton, Dartmouth '24, who had been a tutor at Dartmouth the previous year. He had one quality quite necessary in a new school: he could inspire fear. One of the other teachers said that if pupils did not sit perfectly still during the morning exercises, "he would give them a look enough to take the breath from their bodies." He was evidently a good classroom teacher. He later taught for many years in a private school in Salem. One of his pupils there (Leverett Saltonstall, Harvard 1844) reported that Carleton's boys rarely failed to enter college with honor. He took a great interest in his boys and they respected him, in spite of some rural ways of action and speech. To a boy who leaned his head on his hand resting on his desk he gazed fiercely for a few seconds; then, pointing toward him and waving his arm up and down, he shouted, "What are you nursing your head for up in yonder corner? Get up and attend to your business or I'll heave the grammar and dictionary at you."

The Preceptress was Arethusa Hall, twenty-five years old, who had studied one year at Westfield Seminary, had taught the previous year at Greenland, New Hampshire, and had recently been studying French at Portsmouth. Whittier's recollections of her in the last year of his life were pleasant: she won the affection of her pupils and was earnest and faithful in the work she loved.

Except for opening exercises and French class, taught by Miss Hall, the girls and boys were kept separate. Of the boys she remembered only Whittier, who was introduced to her by James H. Duncan, Secretary and Treasurer of the trustees, as "a young man who often at the shoemaker's bench had hammered out fine verse." She remembered him as an earnest student who received much attention from the girls, who wanted him to write poems in their autograph albums.[31]

Whittier's two terms at the Academy seemed, as he looked back on them in old age, to have been among the happiest years of his life. The list of books used does not sound inspiring, but some of them at least were in fields that were new to him. One wonders how such varied subject matter was handled by such a small faculty. The list was as follows: *American First Class Book, National Reader, National Tutor, Colburn's Sequel, Adam's Improved Arithmetic, Walsh's Arithmetic, Colburn's Algebra, Simpson's Euclid, Flint's Surveying, Vose's Astronomy, Morse's Geography, Worcester's History with Charts, Conversations on Chemistry, Conversations on Natural Philosophy, Blair's Rhetoric, Hodge's Logic, Upham's Intellectual Text Book.*

Although Whittier was one of the older students, he was not above occasional playfulness. The boy who sat in front of him sometimes had his hair pulled or his ear pinched. Sometimes his slate circulated through the classroom with verses that he had written in idle or inattentive moments.[32]

At the Thayers' was another student, Harriet Plumer, and across the street in Jonathan K. Smith's house were two others, his daughter Mary White Smith and Evelina Bray of Marblehead. Whittier was not too shy to walk to school with the three girls: Mary White Smith with bright red hair, Evelina Bray with dark brown hair, and Harriet Plumer. One morning Evelina Bray's veil was blown off; it lodged on a barn door and then on a branch. Whittier handed Evelina the verses that he had written about it. His social life, however, was not limited to walks to and from school. There was one event that he remembered five years later. "Do you ever think of the old Academy: Do you recollect our walk from Whittier's party?" he wrote to Mary Emerson Smith. One of the girls at the Academy remembered another incident. She gave him a glass of cider with red pepper in it, but "by a swift, adroit movement and a still more adroit excuse he made himself master of the situation, outwitting my mischievous intent with an air of innocence which the twinkle in his eye only belied.[33]

Among the pupils at the Academy, who varied in age from ten to twenty-five, were some of higher social and cultural level than the young people of his neighborhood or of the Friends Meeting in Amesbury. Harriet Minot was the daughter of Judge Stephen Minot of Haverhill. After her mother's death she was at the head of her father's household and the center of a group of intelligent, friendly young people. She was early interested in Anti-Slavery. She was a life-long friend of Whittier and his sister Elizabeth, with whom she became acquainted when Elizabeth attended the academy. Her correspondence with Whittier is lively and interesting.

Another girl of whom he had pleasant memories was Nellie Senter of Center Harbor, New Hampshire, where Whittier spent part of his summers for several years. He remembered her, he told a boy working at the Senter House, as one of the most charming women he had ever met.[34]

Mary Marsh was one of the girls who succeeded in getting Whittier to write in their albums. He wrote the dedication, which began with a rather labored wish that her album might not contain anything that was not virtuous.

He also wrote two pieces of blank verse for her. One was a prosaic, platitudinous answer to her request that he portray her character. The other explained that he had meant age in a complimentary sense when he said, as she had been told, that she must be older than she would acknowledge. It concluded with an un-Quaker-like threat: if her informers were male

> I should be apt
> To take them as I would mischievous boys
> And shake their heads together.[35]

Two years later Whittier half believed that he fell in love with one of the girls with whom he walked to school, Evelina Bray, whom he described as "a first-rate scholar and a pretty girl." She was seventeen years old, a tall brunette, with a good deal of beauty of form, feature, and coloring. A miniature at the Whittier Home, Amesbury, shows her with smooth curls and a crown of roses; one may suspect that she was not unaware of her good looks. Both Mary Emerson Smith and Mrs. Thayer believed that she fell in love with Whittier; the former also believed that Whittier, being by nature affectionate and kindly, could not reject her attentions. One cannot avoid the suspicion that Mary Emerson Smith, to whom Whittier wrote exceedingly sentimental letters a year later, did not like to think of Evelina Bray as a predecessor in his affection. Mrs. Thayer's opinion was that Whittier was much attracted by Evelina's beauty but had no deep affection for her.[36]

The first term of the Academy ended July 31 with an oral examination of the students before the trustees and others. The writer of a letter in the *Haverhill Gazette* reported that the results were satisfactory and, contrary to the custom at most academies, the examinations had not been rehearsed in advance.

Evelina continued at the Academy during the summer term, which ended in November. Then, according to Evelina Bray's account in a letter to Whittier's authorized biographer Samuel T. Pickard, she called at the Thayers' to say goodbye to Mrs. Thayer, bringing a pamphlet in which a note was enclosed. The note was to Whittier, who opportunely was present, and according to Evelina, it was "the answer to the question he had propounded for my consideration. In it he said 'Remember that my peace of mind depends upon your answer.' "

The implication, accepted by Pickard and others, is of course that Whittier had proposed marriage. This interpretation must be questioned. The letter to Pickard is one of a series written in Evelina's old age, and others in the series definitely show that her mind was wandering. There is also no denying that Whittier in his youth wrote letters expressing more sentiment than he felt — but perhaps no more than he liked to think that he felt. He may have written or said enough to make Evelina, who was only seventeen, think that he was offering her his heart. She obviously enjoyed thinking so when she was old.

At Whittier's home in Amesbury there is a clipping from the *Hartford Times* December 16, 1886: "Mr. Whittier is naturally one who would be among the last to shun the life of the domestic affections; and it is revealing no secret to say that his lonely bachelor life has been due to an early disappointment in an affair of the heart. He loved too sincerely to be able, at any aftertime, to transfer the heart he had thus in the morning of his years so unavailingly placed on the altar of his first and only love." In the margin is one word in Whittier's writing: "Nonsense". It was perhaps similar nonsense that once drove him to say to one of the Amesbury Friends that he had never been refused by any woman.[37]

If there was any one factor that kept his half-in-love state from developing into the wholly-in-love, it may have been unhappy marriages in the Whittier family. "I quite agree with thee that the Whittiers don't take to marriage," he once wrote. "Their matrimonial infelicities have troubled me ever since I was a boy."[38] He once remarked that he was glad that he had never married and added, "Matrimony doesn't seem to have agreed with any of my family. I should be sorry for the woman who should marry me."[39] There is no way of knowing what unhappy Whittier marriages he observed in his boyhood. From his early manhood to the end of his life the Whittier family was never wholly free from them: his brother, his sister Mary, and Mary's two children.

Evelina Bray did not return to Haverhill Academy for the 1828 terms, and one day when Whittier was at Salem Quarterly Meeting of Friends he walked to Marblehead to call on her. In one of her letters to Pickard she wrote, "A shy and sensitive [sic] little girl — I was under feal [sic] of the older ones at home at that time — I did not receive him," but the disapproval of the older members of the family did not keep her from going with Whittier on an unchaperoned walk to the seashore and the old fort. The call and the walk were repeated two years later.[40] These walks supplied the material in 1874 for "A Sea Dream," parts of which are Whittier at his best. It is obviously not autobiography: the singer that tells of the girl and the seashore is not a poet but a business man whose song hints of an emotional life hidden beneath the life of trade. Nor did Evelina Bray resemble the girl in the poem who died young and remained "evermore the same"; Whittier knew that she had not died in girlhood. In 1839 he sent her a copy of his poems which she acknowledged fifteen months later in a very formal letter signed "your affectionate sister."

But in the autumn of 1827 Whittier had no time for sentimentalizing, even if he had felt so inclined. Money must be found if he was to return to Haverhill Academy in the spring, and he applied for and received the position of teacher in the one-room school of the West School District of Amesbury, known as the Birch Meadow School, in what is now in the town of Merrimac. The term began November 19 and lasted twelve weeks.

18

The experience was not pleasant. A year later he was able to look back
on it with some humor but with no lessening of dislike. The memory of it
was like a horrible dream, and rather than earn his living by teaching he would
prefer to be a tin peddler or sell essences from door to door.

His comment on an article criticizing flogging in schools was that a
schoolmaster's irritability is justified by his miseries, of which the cold was
a conspicuous one for Whittier. "Let the editor of the *Palladium* fancy to
himself the situation of an unfortunate pedagogue, surrounded by a few dozen
ragged, graceless urchins crowding to the old, rickety stove, where the poor
man has taken his station, to avoid the keen breeze, which comes whistling
through the crannies of the building, fresh from the northeast; and we are
fully persuaded he would acknowledge that the trial was too much for human
patience. We speak understandingly of this business and we have charity and
sympathy for all who are obliged to take the birchen rod of discipline. A
decent flagellation does no harm to the scholar, and is equal to a gymnastic
exercise for the instructor."

He was bothered by the mathematical puzzles which the older boys
challenged him to solve. He could not have found the only recorded cur-
riculum requirement disagreeable: that the most advanced students should
read in the Bible at least once a day.

He survived all this and had enough interest in one of his pupils, Giles
Kelley, the only one studying Latin, to give him a Latin grammar.

At the concluding half-day oral examination of the pupils by the school
committee, which included the Rev. Dr. Peter Eaton, minister of the Second
Church in Amesbury (Harvard 1818, Andover Theological Seminary 1826),
his pupils answered "pretty clever", and Whittier's own speech to his pupils
had, he said, "the very pulpit flavor" with the addition of a Quaker touch:
　　. . . . . Doubtless something of the quaver
　　of Monthly Meeting.

With the forty-five dollars that he had earned, he returned to Haverhill
Academy for another six months. The school enrollment had reached ninety-
eight and there was a new faculty member, the Assistant Preceptress Mary
Nesmith, and although Whittier saw her only a few times, he was pleased
with her.[41]

Through all these months, nothing could keep him from writing verses.
The flow continued at its former rate, a poem or two every week, most of
them appearing in the *Essex Gazette* and a few in the *Boston Statesman*.

Some of these poems showed direct influence of other poets. "Sable stole"
in "The Convent" was a borrowing, perhaps subconsciously, from "Il
Penseroso," which he may have read along with "Paradise Lost." "The
Minstrel" was in couplets and may have been suggested by Scott's "Lay of
the Last Minstrel." The Scottish dialect "Song" beginning

> "Gae an' leave me — let no sadness
> Shade that bonnie e'e o' thine."

had the tone of Burns' love-and-loss poems. His reading of Byron is indicated by his "Lines, Written after reading Lord Byron's Description of Tempest among the Alps"; the form of "The Outlaw" resembled "The Prisoner of Chillon." Bryant's "Thanatopsis" was evidently in Whittier's mind when he wrote the twenty-five lines of blank verse based on Job III 19.

His opposition to war, even if only traditional sentiment, was still a favorite theme and found expression in more extreme statements than any that he made in later life. "Lines, Written after Reading 'The Warrior's Song' Published in the Memorial of 1827" asserted that the soldier cannot sleep in peaceful death, and the concluding lines of "The Burial of the Warrior," prophesied that the grave would be haunted by the victims of his strife. The poem that he remembered sixty years later as best indicating his peace feeling,[42] perhaps because of its hope for the future, was "The Warrior," in which he reproached Christians for honoring the soldier and reminded them of a voice that had hushed "the stormy things of earth" and whispered "an earnest of the peace to come."

His firm belief in life after death, which had appeared in earlier poems and was to appear in many later ones, was in "Eve at the Burial of Abel," where its presence can be explained only if one assumes much more than is stated or implied in the Book of Genesis:

> He is not here — the soul hath sought
> Its native home in Heaven.

Whittier later said truthfully that he was no enemy of Catholics,[43] but like most Protestants of his time he had a dismal view of convent life. A convent, as described in "The Convent," was a prison of the soul, a tomb of the living where bigotry chilled the heart's powers of gratitude and love. Religion, the poem argued, should be brighter, and instead of ritual and "ostentatious sign" people could learn of purity and Heaven by meeting out of doors where "sounding breeze" replaced the "organ's lofty swell." Criticism of ritual and especially of church music reappeared in some of his best known and best-loved religious poems.

It was an age of sentimentality of the melancholy order and Whittier's verse at this time was often in the stream of fashion. In a rather confused figure he welcomed the New Year of 1828:

> Though few the joys that rest on me
> From off thy passing wing.[44]

The sailor that died at sea rested in peace

> Although his mansion, chill and deep
> Shall ne'er by weeping friends be trod.[45]

A poem written to Mrs. Susan Prescott Hatch after the death of a young son exhorted the mother not to weep for her child

> Since life hath naught to recompense
> The woes that throng its way.[46]

A poem addressed to the Merrimac River concluded:

> . . . . . All around
> Is hallowed by those fond remembrances
> Which tell of boyhood's pleasure and steal in
> Upon the ruined years of after life
> Like home born music on the wand'rer's ear.[47]

Whittier was quite able, however, to see the absurdity of sentimental verses. "The First Attempt" told of an author's first poem, which by soaring upon "its chainless wing" beyond sublimity

> Attained the true ridiculous

by telling of murdered men, love-sick maids, and discontented ghosts. "Midnight Thoughts" began with a rhapsodical description of stars and moon but broke off to say that the truth was that there wasn't any moon and if there were it would be shining not on trees and hills but on the smoke-blackened old distillery. In "The Maying" he told the girls that May Day was a lovely time "to search the fields for leaf and flower" and if in so doing they left parts of their torn garments behind

> . . . . . That which once attracted beaux
> May fright away marauding crows.

A different type of humor was in "To the Author of the Ode to Satan," the author being George Croly, whose *Salathiel* was a popular historical romance that Whittier later admired. He asked how the author could know so much about the infernal den unless he had been there and concluded that there was danger in the author's friendly attitude toward Satan: earthly kings liked to keep their flatterers near them, and Satan might do the same to him.

One effect of Whittier's education at the Academy was his seeing the values in New England legends. A poem based on an Indian legend appeared in the *Essex Gazette* July 28, 1827, beginning "Yes! brightly does the sunlight fall." The legend that there were spirits living in the White Mountains that would destroy anyone who ventured into their territory reappeared three years later in "The White Mountains" in Whittier's first published volume, *Legends of New England*.

Another Indian poem written in 1827 was "The Pawnee Brave," an improbable story of a young Indian who rescued a girl about to be burned at the stake while the Indians who were about to do the burning looked on admiringly and made friends with him. The poetry is no better than the narrative: much of it is prosaic and filled with clichés. However unsatisfactory these poems are, Whittier was among the earliest American writers to see possibilities in Indian material. Cooper's *The Last of the Mohicans* had been written only the year before.

Interest in common people, peace, and freedom appeared in "The Ruin" in which Whittier concluded that he did not wish the days returned when the castle was at its height of splendor:

> No — for the peasant's lowly shed
> Has more endearing charms for me,
> Since there has peace her blessing spread,
> And there is truth and liberty.

In poetic quality the verses of this period show some advance over those of his pre-Academy days. "To the Memory of Chatterton," in the *Boston Statesman* January 18, 1828, was better than "To the Memory of Chatterton Who Died Aged 17" written in 1825.[48] It had better use of figures and was more coherent and concrete. The 1825 lines:

> It raised in thee the rash intent
> To mingle with the silent dead

became in 1828

> When wishing death and reckless how
> The conqueror dealt his final blow,
> Too lost to hope, too blind to fear,
> Thy hand itself assumed his spear!

The 1828 poem had no such tortured metaphor as these lines in 1825:

> And when the storm of fortune prey'd
> Upon thy heart.

Whittier's reputation as a poet was now extending beyond Haverhill. Poems printed in the *Boston Statesman*, edited by his relative Nathaniel Greene and important enough to be printed in three editions, were introduced by laudatory comments such as "the following lines are from the pen of genius — from a young man who has given many decided proofs in the Haverhill paper of a talent that only needs the trimming hand of care to make it shine one of the brightest lights in our poetical firmament.[49]

In the *Essex Gazette* January 19, 1828, was the announcement of a plan to publish a volume of Whittier's poetry, the profits of which would help him obtain a classical education. The volume was to be sold by subscription. "He is a worthy member of the Society of Friends," it was explained, "and it is hoped that from them the volume will receive a liberal patronage." A prospectus had been sent to Philadelphia, where Quakers were more numerous and more wealthy than in Essex County, and had come back with orders for twenty-two copies. However, five hundred were needed for publication, and this number was evidently not obtained.

Whittier Birthplace painting from a sketch by Obed R. Fowler, 1849. (Courtesy of Haverhill Public Library)

Corliss Hill School, Whittier Road, Haverhill.

View of Haverhill, c.1830. Lithograph originally used in Mirick's *History of Haverhill*, 1831.

Haverhill Academy. (Photograph c.1870)

24

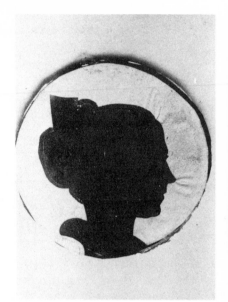

Aunt Mercy Hussey (c.1783-1846). Silhouette. (Courtesy of Whittier Home, Amesbury)

Evelina Bray (1810-1895). Miniature by John S. Porter, 1828. (Courtesy of Whittier Home, Amesbury)

Harriet Livermore (1788-1867). (Courtesy of Whittier Home, Amesbury)

Oliver Carleton (1801-1882).

II
1829 - 31

When his second term at the Academy ended, Whittier began to take stock of himself and his prospects. He described himself as tall — he was five feet ten — dark-complexioned and rather ordinary looking — he was rather better-looking than that — "bashful, yet proud as any poet should be," and concluded "I have much reason to be thankful that I am as I am." But away from the Academy and the girls who admired his verses he no longer thought that he could be happy in poverty if he could win fame by his poetry. He felt like using the pile of manuscripts in his bedroom as a burnt offering of love-sick poetry to the shrine of common sense. He must get down to business, be a man, and take up farming.

A month later he had given up the idea of farming and was looking for advice. He was certain that he would not be contented to be a shoemaker and equally certain that he could not demean himself by going through college on charity and borrowed money, ending with a paralyzing load of debt, especially since the professions were overcrowded. He had no intention of trying to earn a living by writing, which would mean struggling with debts and then returning to his "original insignificance" — perhaps thinking of Burns' unhappy last years — where the tinsel of classical honors would aggravate his misfortune. To what could he turn? School teaching? Anything rather than that.[1]

In this mood he readily accepted an offer that came at the suggestion of William Lloyd Garrison to be editor of the *National Philanthropist*, a temperance weekly published in Boston. He had commended Garrison for dedicating his *Journal of the Times* to temperance as well as opposition to slavery and war and had enrolled himself in the movement by a letter in the *Haverhill Gazette*.[2] He knew that the cause was unpopular and that showing in their true colors "those vices which endanger the community" was a thankless task, "but we cannot stifle the still, small voice of conscience. It will whisper amid our security and demand why we stand idle and unconcerned, while the work of destruction goes on around us." In his reaction against poetry he had rather be a reformer than a poet, to be remembered like Howard, Wilberforce, or Clarkson rather than like Byron.[3]

His chief purpose, however, was to have regular employment and to earn money, and he offered no objection when a change in management made him editor of the *American Manufacturer* instead of the *National Philanthropist*. Both papers were weeklies published by a Baptist minister, William Collier, and his son, William R. Collier, and contained almost identical material except that the leading article in the Thursday *Manufacturer* on an economic or industrial topic was replaced in the Friday *Philanthropist* by one on temperance.

Whittier began his work on the *Manufacturer* early in January, 1829. He lived with the Colliers at 30 Federal Street and saved half of his salary of nine dollars a week to help pay the mortgage on the farm. Whittier remembered the elder Collier fifty years later as "a very excellent man — advanced in years but zealous in every good cause and work." Whittier's acquaintance with Abijah Thayer had given him an opportunity to learn something about the work of an editor, and he was successful with the *Manufacturer*. He wrote to Thayer February 6 that the paper was doing very well "thanks to the gullibility of the public,"[4] and when he resigned seven months later he could report that patronage had been better than expected.

As the name of the paper implied, its purpose was to help New England manufacturing, which was growing rapidly — and sometimes over-expanding — by the use of water power. Whittier argued that manufacturing establishments did not corrupt morals; manufacturers knew that morality and industry among employees were necessary for efficiency. The business depression had not been caused by manufacturing, although there had been losses when "needy and desperate adventurers" had gone into it; there had also been losses in other business, including mercantile, which too many young men had gone into because they thought that it was "genteel."

The chief need of the young manufacturing interests was tariffs which would protect them from competition by established manufacturies in Europe. Whittier argued this point in poetry and prose, attacking a statement in the *Liverpool Advertiser* that the only true policy for America was entire freedom of trade by sarcastically urging:

Let the eagle that soars with the wing of the storm —
The bird of our country, his wanderings check:
Bend lowly in homage the pride of his form,
That the foot of the lion may rest on his neck.

The threat of exclusion of American products from English ports in retaliation for a tariff was of no importance, Whittier pointed out, because the only product exported to England in any amount was cotton. The South was uniting to overthrow the tariff and manufacturing; if it succeeded, the country would become like Poland, poor, beggarly, and dependent.

The wishes of the manufacturers would have a better chance if Henry Clay were President, and Whittier became an enthusiastic Clay man. Clay, he said, was consistent and a friend to the whole country; his enemies feared him because they knew that he would expose their misdeeds and they consequently tried to blacken and vilify his character.

Whittier's enthusiasm for Clay and manufacturing aroused his interest in factory workers — "mechanics," as they were then called. Clay and manufacturing seemed to him part of a movement toward democracy; aristocratic arrogance was being humbled, and mechanics as well as farmers need not hang their heads when the rich man passed in his carriage. In a series of editorials addressed "To the Young Mechanics of New England" he said that he had once been a mechanic himself and that before mechanics lay the path to honor, profit, and distinction which had been followed by Benjamin Franklin and Jacob Perkins. While their rise to wealth might not be as rapid as in trade, it would be less speculative, and if peace of mind and domestic felicity were objects, no one had a better chance of getting them than the mechanics. At their service were libraries in almost every village. He did not fail to add words of counsel: mechanics should work hard and avoid extravagance, gambling, and intemperance.

One of the new industries that Whittier looked upon with favor was to be short-lived. The "silk fever" was beginning in Essex County, and the *Manufacturer* had frequent references to the possibility of growing mulberry trees and raising silk worms. From other sources we know that it was being tried in Amesbury, where Thomas Bailey had five thousand trees and one hundred thousand worms until vandals destroyed nearly all of them.[5] Later, across the river in East Bradford, Gardner B. Perry, Congregational minister and Abolitionist, set out mulberry trees which flourished for a time. He died happy in the success of his project; the trees died the next winter.

President-elect Jackson, the *Manufacturer* reported February 19, was on his way to Washington, travelling twenty-five miles a day in a private carriage drawn by four beautiful grays. But a new day in travel was at hand, and an editorial approved the proposal to build a railway from Boston to the Hudson River over which "the tide of wealth and successful enterprize will pour in like a torrent." The automobile, which would become the victorious rival of the railroad, was already racing along the highways, covering as many miles in two hours as Jackson was covering in a day — that is, if the road was level: it was Gurney's steam coach, which travelled thirteen miles an hour with eighteen passengers on a level road.

There were occasional references to causes in which Whittier was to have a life-long interest. "The Dagon of Intemperance is tottering to its fall," he announced February 19 in reporting the first anniversary meeting of the Society for the Promotion of Temperance in Essex, North District. Indians, as usual, were being forced to move to less desirable territory: nine hundred Creeks had just passed through Pike County, Alabama. An indignant editorial July 16 attacked imprisonment for debt, asking if it was consistent to celebrate Independence Day, when "the thunder of artillery bursts from every hill top, and the shout of the reckless multitude echoes from every hamlet, to boast of freedom, while the groans of incarcerated thousands are ascending to the ear of Eternal justice." Garrison was to use this same theme in a poem, and a few years later it would be in Whittier's "The Prisoner for Debt" with its unforgettable line: "God made the old man poor." A review of John Neal's *Rachel Dyer* gave Whittier a chance to say good things about Quakers, and a report of a church being built in Montreal at a cost of more than half a million dollars led him to ask: "When will men learn that this 'pomp and circumstance' of *their* religion has no foundation in the pure precepts of Christianity?" He reminded his readers that early Christians condemned war and that during the first and second centuries there were no Christian soldiers.

The abolition of slavery would be first in the list of causes in Whittier's life and in the reform movements of the second quarter of the nineteenth century. The slave trade, which had been illegal since 1808, first aroused the reformers. An article in the *Manufacturer* January 29 mentioned a slave ship on the way to the New Orleans market, and another on June 4 told that the British ship-of-war *Sybille* had captured ships carrying 2686 slaves. In the issue of July 2 "The Capture of a Slave Ship" anticipated Whittier's poem "The Slave Ships" written five years later: the crew of a slave ship captured on the coast of Africa, without a captain and unable to navigate, had decided to throw their slaves overboard if they did not fall in with a ship that day.

The whole question of slavery was rapidly becoming a national issue. An editorial in the *Manufacturer* February 26 commended Garrison's *Journal of the Times* for its attack on politicans who had bowed down to the South and had "acted in direct opposition to the wishes of a free and enlightened people, just rising in the peculiar majesty of a righteous cause, and pronouncing in a voice, whose tones shall yet deepen into thunder, the important declaration, that 'all men are born free and equal.' "

The *Manufacturer's* announcement April 2 that Garrison had given up his position on the *Journal of the Times* and was to devote his time to the Anti-Slavery cause was followed on June 18 by the news that the Congregational churches of Boston had asked him to speak about the work of the American Colonization Society at a union meeting of these churches on July 4 at Park Street Church. The Colonization Society, which Abolitionists were later to attack as bitterly as slavery itself, was still looked upon with favor. The item in the *Manufacturer* January 29 about slaves being taken to New Orleans also mentioned a ship sailing to Liberia and contributions to the Colonization Society. The society consisted of respectable, kindly, middle-of-the-road people who thought that the best approach to the negro problem was to take free negroes to Africa where the colony of Liberia had been formed for them in 1822 and help them to engage in trade and agriculture and to govern themselves. The *Manufacturer* on June 25 quoted from the second annual report of the Connecticut Colonization Society that there were now fourteen hundred negroes in Liberia.

But Garrison was planning to do something quite different from what he had been engaged to do. He was to attack slavery itself — as Whittier knew: the speech had been shown to him page by page as it was being written.[6] He prepared the audience for it in an editorial, "Fourth of July," also in the June 25 *Manufacturer*. "It is time that the truth were spoken, although its every tone should fall like a thunderbolt upon our criminal slumber. Let the great sin of the nation be exposed, and avoided *now*, or the tremendous catalogue of its horrors will ere long be written upon the overthrown temple of our republic, in letters of blood."

Whittier was in the audience at Park Street Church and reported a successful performance. Garrison's "whole soul seemed poured into his stirring language." Whittier was in sympathy with Garrison's propositions: (1) that slaves are entitled to the prayers, sympathies and charities of the American people; (2) that since non-slave-holding states are involved in the guilt of slavery by their allegiance to the Constitution and would be called on to help suppress slave insurrections, they have a right to object to it and a duty to assist in its overthrow; (3) that the condition of the negroes is no justification for the continuing of slavery, nor is it an argument against our interfering with it, even if it means "collision with the slaveholders"; (4) that "education and freedom will do for our colored population what they will effect for any other race of men — reclaim the ignorant from darkness, and the vicious from crime — and make them useful, intelligent, and peaceable citizens".

Whittier's interest in these causes had not crowded out his love of books. He continued to read Scott's Waverley novels with boyish enthusiasm. Many years later he confessed that he had been bewitched by them.[7] But he did not wholly forget his Quaker principles and was forced to criticize Scott's war-like spirit and to lament that the "fascination of glowing narrative and masterly delineation of character" often turned the reader's sympathies to the wrong side.

It is rather surprising that Whittier gave unqualified approval to another romance that had numerous battle scenes, George Croly's *Salathiel*, which he called a "wild and dream-like story" and the "most powerfully wrought narrative" that he had ever read. One incident in it inspired his poem "The Fire Ship."[8]

He was reading Byron's poetry, as he read Scott's novels, "with an interest which chained us to his pages." But when he thought it over later, he "turned, in disgust and horror, from the polluted shrine of our idolatry, like one who has offered up at the feet of some veiled skeleton the burning vows of love." He had no such feeling when he read the women poets: Lydia H. Sigourney, whose poetry he thought remarkable for strength and correctness, and Felicia Hemans, whose "chastened purity" he would not "exchange for all the midnight incantation of Byron." Whittier was, however, not enthusiastic about Letitia E. Landon, who, he said, had not been "sufficiently careful to check the outpourings of deep and passionate feeling" — an opinion which he reversed a year later.

Whittier was aware of the low state of American poetry, which he thought contained little that was likely to survive and, although it had spots of sentiment and beauty, lacked sternness and concentration. The cause of the "imbecility of our poetry" he believed to be the low standards of literary criticism: the literary magazines were too timid and too dependent to speak with firmness and truth. He was disappointed in Samuel Kettell's three-volume *Specimens of American Poetry* but liked one poem in it, "The Buccaneer" by Richard Henry Dana, which he thought had more originality than any other American poem.

Whittier's editorial duties left him a good deal of free time. He continued to write poems which he sent to various papers as well as using some of them in the *Manufacturer*. Only six of these ever appeared in any collection of his poems, and two of these are in the Appendix to the Riverside Edition.[9]

The quality of his verse was little changed. There were lines that showed ability to picture a scene in specific and lively if sometimes hackeyed phrasing. There was, as has often been pointed out, conscious or unconscious imitation of Felicia Hemans and Lydia H. Sigourney. There were also echoes from early nineteenth century poets. "Ocean heaving in the moonlight's path" in "The Burial of Abner" reminds the reader of Byron's lines in "There Be None of Beauty's Daughters":

> And the midnight moon is weaving
>   Her bright chain o'er the deep:
> Whose breast is gently heaving
>   As an infant's asleep.

"The Ice Ship" in theme, pictures, and at times in phrasing suggests Coleridge's "The Ancient Mariner."

These poems were well received and were making Whittier more widely known. "The Sicilian Vespers" was in *Specimens of American Poetry* with the comment that Whittier showed "a more than common maturity of powers." The *Philadelphia Album* contained a quotation from "The Fire Ship" which the editor, Robert Morris, thought "would not dishonour the pages of Byron, Campbell, and Coleridge." Willis Gaylord Clark wrote that Whittier did him an injustice in thinking that he had been guilty of flattery: "I sincerely think that you evince more promise than all the rest of the Boston poets put together."[10]

In spite of his awareness of the low state of literary criticism, Whittier found these praises encouraging. "I have now got into notice considerably, and have correspondence with some of our first writers; and indeed with nearly all our poets," he proudly wrote to Mary Emerson Smith, and thought that he might publish a joint volume with George D. Prentice, editor of the *New England Weekly Review*. The suggestion had come from Prentice, who had just returned from a holiday "among the sweet creatures of my native hills." He had evidently found the sweetness to his taste, for before proceeding to business he asked if Whittier was so much of a Quaker "as to have any very serious objections to an occasional game of romps with a pretty country girl." He then went on to editorial matters. He was not wholly pleased with editorial life: he had made enemies by the severity of his remarks.[11] He may have been thinking of his comments on Whittier's editorial on Music in the *Manufacturer* March 12 in which Whittier said that he had rather hear the creaking of a cider mill or the music of a high pressure steam engine than "the shocking amalgamation of a choir of human voices — cracked hoarse and squalling" or the "harsh growl of the bass-viol — and the provoking squeal of the violin, imitating in the language of Burns the dying agonies of a pig under the hands of the butcher!" Prentice replied in the *Review* that if a Quaker had superintended creation there would have been no flowers, no breezes making music in the forest, and no sound of the sea. Whittier countered that he was fond of the music of nature and, furthermore, that he was proud to be a Quaker, and that if Prentice continued to quarrel with him on account of his odd notions, "he will yet have to learn that although far from being pugnacious in our general deportment, we can for his especial benefit divert ourselves of Quakerism in our papers, at least." Both young men were evidently enjoying the argument, but just to be sure that Whittier did not take it seriously Prentice next addressed him as "dear brother of mine" and said that there were people who knew that he regarded the Quakers "with more warmth of feeling than any other class of Religionists on Earth."

If Prentice had been better acquainted with Whittier, he would have known that Whittier was unlikely to have a "game of romps" with any girl, country or city. Whether his religion prevented or not, timidity did. "I was in reality a shy, timid recluse, afraid of a shadow, especially the shadow of a woman," he later wrote of himself at this time.[12] But he liked pretty girls as much as ever, he had plenty of spare time, and when he visited the Atheneum Gallery he looked at the girls more than at the pictures. "I love to watch their airy notions, notice the dark brilliancy of their fine eyes, and observe the delicate flush stealing over their cheeks," he wrote to Edwin Harriman, but assured Harriman that his heart was untouched. "I know that they are beautiful — very — but they are nothing to me, and I turn from one fair face to another, until my memory is altogether vague and indefinite. I know very well that I have nothing to do with them and at all events, they will not be likely to have anything to do with me. There — you have the history of my transgressions, if such it is, to look upon the fairest and most delicate works of God. I always did love a pretty girl. Heaven grant there is no harm in it. The worst of it is — if I ever get married I must marry a Quakeress with her bonnet like a flour dipper, and a face as long as a Tobacco yawl."[13]

The tone of this letter shows clearly enough that Whittier was like many a young man who hasn't quite grown up and who has a lively sense of humor: the girls are pretty, he likes to look at them, he can't help thinking about marriage, and he laughs at himself and at the whole situation. Then, being too bashful to get acquainted with new girls, he will write to one that he already knows and will say all kinds of things that neither he nor the girl will take seriously.

The girl that Whittier wrote to was Mary Emerson Smith, whom he had found interesting before and during his terms at Haverhill Academy. He wrote to her five days after his letter to Harriman.[14] He had written before and had destroyed the letters, he said; one may guess that if he had read this letter with his critical eye, he would have destroyed it also. He assured her that he was through with sentimentality. He knew that she would regard his suggestion that they write to each other as a wild proposal. He had heard that she was engaged. He had loved her passionately and she had not hated him: did she remember their last walk together beside the Merrimac River in the moonlight? He hated coldness, he valued her friendship, he loved her with a brotherly love, she was his "beau ideal," but he asked nothing except friendship. He had sent her the *Manufacturer*: "Sappho" was written after visiting the Atheneum Gallery where the beautiful painting of Sappho reminded him of her. "Boston ladies are not handsome." (This only five days after his letter to Harriman with its account of the pretty girls at the Atheneum Gallery!) He now wore his whiskers in the proper style (probably referring to the sideburns in the miniature by Porter.) He knew many of the literary people in Boston but did not like the coldness and formal politeness there. If she would write to him he would tell her about Boston fashions.

The letter ended abruptly. The fire bells were ringing, and like any country boy who has recently moved to the city, he was going to the fire.

Mary Emerson Smith answered his letter, and he wrote again promptly, a long, rambling letter about the past, which he thought she might laugh at. He had read her letter twenty times and thanked her from his soul for letting him regard her as a sister. They could be friends — "Let the cold, heartless world go on as it may. . . . Love — such as the heart can feel in its springtime — that deep, passionate, enduring love, which knows no ebb or flow — in fine that which ends in Matrimony, — that most terrible of all terrible words in the language — I place out of the question. And yet it sometimes seems to me that the most perfect Happiness attainable on earth results from the married state. But alas for me: I have had dreadful forebodings of my destiny. Only imagine for a moment what a ludicrous appearance I should make perched upon the 'high seats' with a Quaker intended, by the side of me — looking as demurely and as vacantly as any Simon Pure of the Society could devise, — with a bonnet not a little resembling the sugar-dippers which are used in a grocery store!'' He wished that she were in Boston — she was in Kennebunk, Maine — to go to the Atheneum Gallery and Washington Gardens with him; he did not mention the pretty girls there.[15]

A young man is not deeply or dangerously in love when he can be humorous in the midst of sentimental out-pourings. He was enjoying himself playing at being in love, putting his imagined emotions into words, and then laughing at the words and at himself. In the same mood he addressed some verses to her. They recalled the pleasant times when he strayed with her in the moonlight

> With hearts as idle as the rhymes
> With which my careless pen is playing

and after dismally assuring her that he is

> .... A wreck of being flung
> Upon a sea that darkened round me

concluded

> When married, for acquaintance sake
> Good cousin, I am sure you'll do it —
> Just send a piece of bridal cake
> And I — will write a sonnet to it.[16]

His letter of June 6 had not been answered when Whittier wrote again on July 2, claiming that his feelings were hurt. He assured her that she did not know the intensity of his feelings: "Passions that have slumbered so long in apparent lifelessness, like the fire of some partially smothered volcano, have been burning around my heart.'' After concluding the romantic section of the letter with the somewhat inconsistent suggestion that they consider themselves brother and sister, he proceeded to local gossip: the Headmaster at Haverhill Academy was reported as livelier than ever since the loss of his wife.[17]

After Whittier's death Mary Emerson Smith, who had married and lived in Covington, Kentucky, wrote to Samuel T. Pickard that she was "a little curious to know something of Greenleaf's inner life, in the thirty or forty years we only occasionally formally corresponded. Why did he never marry? I believe it was best for him, he did not.''[18] One may wish that she had explained the last statement. Perhaps with a woman's intuitive understanding she knew that Whittier was temperamentally unfitted for marriage — or perhaps it could be more accurately stated that Whittier, like many men who do not marry and some that do, was of a temperament that would have made marriage difficult, as was true of others in his family. In another letter to Pickard, Mary Emerson Smith mentioned Whittier's letters to her. "I always revered Whittier. I don't know that I ever loved him any better than I do now. What youth of twenty and twenty-one in these days would write such letters of Wisdom and Humor, so full of a pure love, without passion or prejudice, as were those he penned after he left school. *Why* I kept them I don't know. I did not read them for forty years. I knew he was unlike other young men, but I was surprised at the strength, dignity, and beauty of his life."[19]

It would be easy to conclude from the comic pictures in both the letter to Harriman and the one to Mary Emerson Smith of marriage to a Quaker with a bonnet like a flour dipper in one letter — amended to a sugar dipper in the other — that Whittier revolted against marrying a Quaker and since, according to the rule of that time, marriage to anyone else would have forced him to cease being a Quaker, he couldn't marry anybody. But a little over a year later he wrote "The Fair Quakeress," in which the girl described had everything: beauty — and Whittier reminded the reader that the great men of the world have been slaves to beautiful women — mind, soul, virtue, and warmth of passion.

After a winter in the city, Whittier was glad, when what he called the season of love, roses, and lettuce came, to stroll out into the nearby country and look at the streams and skies and clouds, but when the hot weather came in June, he found less delight in the world of nature. "What is the use of telling a man that the weather is delightful, the scenery beautiful and twenty more such worn-out phrases, when the thermometer is standing at 90 or 100 degrees above zero." At night the mosquitoes — window screens had not been invented — fastened themselves upon him "like blood-thirsty vampires."

Perhaps the summer discomforts made him irritable and ready to notice unpleasant conditions in the office of the *Manufacturer*. He was encountering shop jealousy, and was "determined to disappoint a few niggardly selfish scoundrels who have endeavoured to place themselves above me." He had had enough by August 6, when he wrote to one of his friends about his resignation, "Why should you be surprised? You know what kind of a concern it was; you know, if I mistake not, my dissatisfaction." The final amount due on his salary, $28.34, was never paid. He could leave, however, with some satisfaction in the success of the paper, which had exceeded expectation. William Lloyd Garrison, then editor of the *Genius of Universal Emancipation*, said with his usual enthusiasm that Whittier's brief editorial career had been "uncommonly brilliant."[20]

Not all newspaper comments were favorable. "The editor of the *Manufacturer* was assailed for his former employment, by a witty, but judging from the manner of the assault most abominably scurrilous paper, in Boston, called the Mercury" was stated in the *Newburyport Herald* August 7. There must have been other unkind criticisms, for Whittier wrote to John Neal, Editor of the *Portland Yankee*, asking him to tell if he disliked the enclosed poem and Whittier would give up literary efforts. "Insult has maddened me," he continued. "The friendless boy has been mocked at; and, years ago he vowed to triumph over the scorners of his boyish endeavors. With the unescapable sense of wrong burning like a volcano in the recesses of his spirit, he has striven to accomplish this vow, until his heart has grown weary in the struggle."

During the remaining months of 1829 Whittier stayed at the farm, where his father, now sixty-eight and unwell, was doubtless glad to have his help. He joined a debating club in Haverhill and was on the negative side in a debate on the topic: "Is man the superior of woman in intellect?"[21]

He continued to write the usual number of poems, none of which he thought good enough to include in the Riverside Edition except "Judith at the Tent of Holofernes," which is among "Early and Uncollected Poems" in the Appendix. One of them, however, is significant as showing a reawakened interest in Indian life and legends which had first appeared two years before in "The Pawnee Brave." "The Indian Girl's Lament," dated November 1829, was the first of a series that was continued in 1830 and culminated in Whittier's first published volume, *Legends of New England* in 1831. Although the poem is artificial and rhetorical, there are, as Professor John B. Pickard has pointed out, "moments of simple narration and dramatic emphasis that engender a pathos for vanquished Indians."[22] A possible source is Nathaniel Deering's *Carabasset, an American Tragedy in Five Acts* which Whittier reviewed in the *Essex Gazette* July 10, 1830.

The blank verse that Whittier wrote at this time was stilted and prosaic. "The Vestal" was overloaded with description of Rome at night and of the girl herself, beautiful in the moonlight, who with her lover was found dead the next morning. "Silent Worship" was at times obscure, incoherent, and prosaic. But it added to Whittier's popularity by being reprinted three times within a year.[23]

After the harvest season Whittier was not needed full time on the farm and was doubtless pleased at a chance to do more interesting work and to earn a little money. In the *Essex Gazette* December 26 Thayer announced that Whittier was to be editor, while Thayer would continue as publisher and attend to the mechanical part of the business. Whittier could live at home and, the paper being a weekly, he would not have to spend much time in the *Gazette* office.[24]

In the first issue under his direction Whittier announced that he would judge the Jackson administration fairly. He kept his promise by commending the President's course in regard to the tariff and his punishment of the duelist Hunter but criticized his partisan appointments: "the spoils system." He early hazarded the guess that the reelection of Jackson was impossible and, following the lead of Thayer in the previous year and abandoning the position he had taken in the *Manufacturer* less than a year earlier, favored John McLean for his "moral purity and political integrity." Clay, he said, had "a restless ambition whose aim has long been towards the highest office in his country." Four months later, however, the *Gazette* was definitely in the Clay camp, referring to Clay as an "upright and independent politician; the true republican; and the unwavering friend of the mechanic and the laborer." The campaign was heating up, and on June 26 the *Gazette* appealed to sectional feeling: "And will the citizens of New England tamely bow down to a Southern ruler — to one who has no feeling in common with them?" This was a departure from the one-nation sentiment in an editorial April 10 prompted by complaints from South Carolina about the Tariff of 1828. "We believe that there has never been a time since the formation of the Federal Government, when the necessity of strengthening, by mutual forebearance and mutual sacrifice, the ties which connect one portion of our country with another, has been so apparent as at the present day."

A century before the bitter young men of the 1930's thought that they had discovered that fiction could correct existing evils which the clergy had failed to correct from the pulpit, Whittier saw a chance to preach temperance through the short story. His "Henry St. Clair," a story of a man who sank under the effect of drink, won a prize of forty dollars offered by the *New York Amulet and Ladie's Literary and Religious Chronicle* for the "best moral tale which shall exhibit the deleterious consequences of vice in the most vivid colors." It had the exaggeration and melodrama that were too often found in temperance propaganda for the next hundred years and that brought ridicule upon the cause and its advocates:

"Allston! — Roger Allston!" repeated the wretch beneath me, in a voice which sounded like a shriek, as he struggled bolt upright even against the threatening pistol. "Great God! has it come to this? Hell has no pang like this meeting. Shoot!" he exclaimed, and there was a dreadful earnestness in his manner which sent the hot blood of indignation cold and ice-like upon my heart. — "Shoot! — you were once my friend — In mercy kill me!"[25]

Another cause which continued to arouse Whittier's indignation was the treatment of American Indians. Whittier had been disillusioned as to the nobility of the splendid savage when a group of Indians visited Haverhill in the fall of 1827:

I went among the rest, since you must know it,
	Eager to see those beings, whom I had
Sketched, with the gloomy fancy of a poet,
	Tall, dark, and fearless, in their bearskins clad.
I went, and saw them, all alive and real,
	And the plain truth destroyed my *beau ideal*.

Nevertheless, he saw the injustice in the treatment that Indians had received — and there was more to come. They had been regarded as independent nations in the making of treaties, but they were now to be moved to lands west of the Mississippi.[26]

Although Whittier's brother-in-law was a militia captain, Whittier attacked the militia system and its semi-annual training days (which he later ridiculed in "The Training") when a bill to reduce the duties to one assembly a year was defeated in the Legislature. He pointed out that the System was established to protect the property of the wealthy. If there were to be wars, the militia was not a suitable defense; in fact, in the American Revolution "undrilled yeomanry bore down the veterans of England."

While the abolition of slavery had not yet become the chief object of Whittier or of other Northern reformers, the lines of conflict were forming. When Samuel May, a guest speaker in a Boston church, referred to negroes in a sermon on Prejudice, the minister of the church told him that he would never be allowed in that pulpit again.[27] On May 29 the *Gazette* quoted an editorial from the Mt. Zion, Georgia, *Advertiser*, which asserted that slavery was an ordinance of Heaven which it was impious to question. This, Whittier commented in the *Gazette*, "was not only an open avowal of sentiments directly opposed to the spirit of our Republican Government, but a blasphemous and wicked attempt to sustain the iniquity of slavery." The slave States would have his sympathy and respect only as long as they recognized the evil of slavery, as many of their writers and statesmen had been doing. He believed that the vast majority of the free citizens of the slave states lamented the evil of slavery — it was in this same belief that he wrote *Justice and Expediency* three years later.

Whittier had commended William Lloyd Garrison in the *Gazette* January 23 when he reported that Garrison and Lundy were publishing the *Genius of Universal Emancipation*. In the May 29 issue he wrote in some excitement about Garrison, who was in the Baltimore jail because he was unable to pay a fine of fifty dollars for libel. Garrison had accused a Newburyport man of "being concerned in the disgraceful traffic in human flesh — in the domestic slave trade. — But the upholders of Slavery will learn that their victim possesses a spirit which no persecution can bow, no danger intimidate. — And we had rather — much rather — share the lonely cell in which he is imprisoned, than the proudest hall and the loftiest tower of those whose luxury is nourished by the blood of the slave."

The Newburyport man was Francis Todd, whose ship, according to Garrison, had carried slaves from Baltimore to New Orleans. Thirty-five years later Garrison remarked that Todd was a respected, wealthy, and influential merchant who had done what any ship owner of that day would have done.[28] Whittier did not stop with an editorial. On the strength of the support that he had given Henry Clay in the *Manufacturer* he wrote to Clay, urging him to use his influence to have Garrison released. He did not ask Clay to pay the fine and court costs, and had no clear idea of how Garrison's release could be arranged, but he reminded Clay that Garrison had been the first editor in New England to suggest him for the Presidency. Clay replied that he had written to a friend in Baltimore to look into the matter and to give such aid, in his name, as might be practicable in securing his release but had been informed by this friend that a man in New York had paid the fines and costs. The New York man was Arthur Tappan, who did not know Garrison personally but heard of his conviction.[29]

Whittier continued to be interested in contemporary literature. James Fenimore Cooper's *The Wept of Wish-Ton-Wish*, which he reviewed in the January 2 issue, seemed to him inferior to *The Pilot, The Red Rover*, and *The Pioneer*. His opinion of *The Last of the Mohicans* would be accepted by critics today; he found it a thrilling narrative of bloodshed and excitement but unrealistic: Indians were shown as heroes like Ossian, and their sagacity beyond the bounds of human probability. The women in Cooper's novels were "altogether a burdensome appendage to his narrative." Cooper had failed in character portrayal because he had looked at it calmly from a distance and had never entered into the human emotions of passion and revenge. The perfect novelist, Whittier believed, would combine Charles Brockden Brown's penetrating analysis with Cooper's description of externals.

Whittier thought that criticisms of N. P. Willis' *Fugitive Poems* had been too severe: the volume contained some beautiful passages. Nevertheless he thought that its publication was unwise; there was much boyish vanity and affectation, and one poem was scandalous. He would not wish the author "any greater punishment than to be under the necessity of reading this delicate piece of composition to an audience of intelligent and sensitive females."

Poems continued to appear almost weekly — twenty-four in six months. Six of them would appear a year later in *Legends of New England*. Except for the poem beginning "Yes! brightly does the sunlight fall" and "The Indian Girl's Lament" (later, "The Last Norridgewock"), these were Whittier's first use of New England legendary material. The only one of them which he included in the Riverside Edition was "Metacom," a story of the death of King Philip and his dying curse upon the white man. It was written in a mixture of quatrains and couplets that reminds the reader of the "Battle of Beal' an Duine" in Scott's *The Lady of the Lake*, and as Whittier said of "Mogg Megone," "suggests the idea of a big Indian in his war-paint strutting about in Sir Walter Scott's plaid." In the Riverside Edition one section is omitted which contained an echo from "Paradise Lost":

> And o'er his forehead passed the frown
> Of an archangel stricken down,
> Ruined and lost, yet chainless still —
> Weakened of power but strong of will."[30]

Of the other five, "The Murdered Lady" and "The Unquiet Sleeper" were stories of murder and ghosts. In spite of his months as a schoolteacher, Whittier's command of grammar was not yet complete: one line in "The Unquiet Sleeper" is "They buried him where his fathers laid." The stanza in "The Spectre Ship" is six lines, the second, fourth, and sixth rhyming (ballad meter with two additional lines), a form which is used in some of the high points in Coleridge's "Rime of the Ancient Mariner;" the phrasing at times also shows that the "Ancient Mariner" was in Whittier's mind as he wrote. "The Indian's Tale" tells of the contagious disease brought by the first white fishermen and traders which wiped out whole tribes near the New England coast; in spite of Whittier's disillusion from the Indians' visit to Haverhill, the poem gives a noble-savage picture of Indians:

This land of ours — this glorious land —
With all its wealth of wood and streams —
Our warriors strong of heart and hand —
Our daughters beautiful as dreams.

In contrast to his usual opinion of his early verses, Whittier thought two of the other poems of this half year good enough to include in the main section of the Riverside Edition: "The Disenthralled" and "The Crucifixion."[31]

In spite of his familiarity with "Paradise Lost," Whittier's blank verse continued to be nothing more than measured, stilted prose. "The Forsaken" was a melodramatic account of a girl who plunged a dagger into the man who had forsaken her; the situation was discussed at some length, and concluded:

She will arise
From her lorn desolation, far above
The weakness of her nature: and put on
A most unnatural energy, and nerve
Her soul for violence, even unto blood.

The germ of "The Demon of the Study," which first appeared in *The New England Magazine* five years later, was an editorial in the *Gazette* July 3. It began with a letter purported to be written to the editor complaining of a man who called just at dinner time and read the newspaper aloud, including advertisements, all in the same tone. The editor conceded that such a demon was worse than various renowned evil spirits, but having no power of exorcism he was afraid that nothing but the "miraculous fumigation of Tobit"[32] would be effective.

Whittier's poems continued to attract attention. As Thayer remarked later that year, if he "had not been absolutely puff-proof, he must long since have become dangerously inflated." *The New York Amulet and Ladie's Literary and Religious Chronicle*, which printed "The Disenthralled" April 17, said of its author: "There are few poets in the country who have risen to such a proud eminence in point of literary reputation, as the highly gifted individual, whose name heads this paragraph."

The first of Whittier's poems to be printed in England was "To the Author of the Improvisatrice" in the *London Literary Gazette* June 19. It had been sent by Willis Gaylord Clarke in a letter describing Whittier as "A young American poet-editor of great promise in the United States." Its tone was enthusiastic:

> I know thee not, high spirits; but the sympathy of thought
> Hath often to my hour of dreams thy living presence brought;
> And I feel that I could love thee with the fondness of a brother
> As the sainted ones of Paradise bear love for one another.

A year earlier Whittier had been coldly critical of "The Lost Star" by the same author, Letitia E. Landon, but in the meantime he had discovered that she was a pretty girl. Readers to-day would think that Whittier's first opinion was the right one and might even agree with Charles Lamb who said that if Letitia Landon belonged to him he "would lock her up and feed her on bread and water until she left off writing poetry."[33]

In the spring of 1830 Whittier had no apparent reason for melancholy or bitterness. But some young men feel sad without knowing why — or at least enjoy the sweetness of feeling sad and telling some kindred soul about it. Whittier wrote to George D. Prentice that he was haunted by ambition, "perhaps a very foolish desire of distinction, of applause, of fame, of what the world calls immortality" — the world which had neglected and wronged him, and whose idle praise was "less repulsive than its loud and open rebukes." Sad young men were in fashion, and Prentice printed the letter in his paper. The Byronic note may have been the result of Whittier's recent reading of Moore's life of Byron.

One project that Whittier had in mind at this time was soon abandoned. In the March 27, 1830 *Essex Gazette* he announced that he proposed to publish a history of Haverhill; he hoped that the citizens would approve and he promised that "no pains on his part will be spared to render the work worthy of their acceptance." He found, however, that research was harder work than he had supposed, and turned his material over to his friend B. L. Mirick, who published the history two years later.[34]

Whittier's father died June 11, 1830. Whittier had received a letter from George D. Prentice offering him the position of editor for six months of the *New England Weekly Review* of Hartford while Prentice was in Kentucky writing a campaign biography of Henry Clay. He accepted the offer, although Prentice's remark about the paper the year before was hardly encouraging: "The Review has a great share of publick patronage — but there are so many stingy proprietors connected with it, that the profits accruing to myself scarce afford me a respectable support."[35] Whittier's salary was eight dollars a week. He held the position nearly a year and a half.

Although he referred later to the anxieties and perplexing cares attendant upon the management of a political and literary periodical, Whittier was happy in Hartford — happier than Prentice had been. If we can believe his announcement in the *Review* he did not share Prentice's opinion of the publishers. They were "two as fine fellows as ever accommodated themselves to the whims of an editor." He admired Hartford — "its beautiful location, its majestic river — and the surpassing beauty of its surrounding scenery." In spite of his shyness, he became friendly with many interesting young people, including Frederick A. P. Barnard, afterward president of Columbia College, to whom he dedicated "Miriam" forty years later, Lydia H. Sigourney, whose poetry he had described in the *American Manufacturer* as "remarkable for strength and correctness," and two physicians who were kind and helpful, Eli Todd, to whom he dedicated "Moll Pitcher" a year later, and John C. Crane,[36] whose hearty laugh Whittier enjoyed and whom he described to his mother as "a clever young physician — who has been very kind to me ever since I have been here." Dr. Crane boarded, as did Whittier, at Jonathan Law's, "an excellent place," he assured his mother, "all the family are very, very kind. His wife is one of the very best of women; she is always ready to do anything for me." Law was scholarly and had a large library.[37] Also boarding at the Laws' were three young women, Ann Parker and Ann and Mary Miller.

Whittier began his work as editor with a lively announcement in the July 19 issue entitled "Egotism Extra": "We have wrapped our quiet and sober minded self in the lion-skin of Hercules; and the club which has done so much towards decapitating the Hydra of Jacksonism is in our hands to be applied as the plenitude of our discretion may dictate." He promised never to spoil a joke to avoid a libel suit or weaken a statement for fear of a challenge to a duel, being as a Quaker, hors de combat. He had, he said, once received a challenge from a Jackson editor who stood before him "shaking like a willow bough in a whirlwind — the very personification of an ague fit — with a countenance as white as a blank sheet of his own newspaper, before receiving its weekly pollution of blackguardism and falsehood. . . . Had we accepted the challenge, we should have been the death of the poor fellow. Pistols would never have reached him. Our courtesy would have finished him without the aid of gunpowder." He would attack Intemperance as well as Jacksonism — "an unclean pair of lubberly giants, who rely on each other for support."

Throughout his term as editor his political editorials reiterated that Henry Clay was the "Father of the American System" (the Protective Tariff) without which the manufacturing interests of the North were threatened with ruin, and was the friend and defender of the working man. He attacked Jackson for assorted reasons that would appeal to different types of voters: the Spoils System, appointment of criminals to public office, waste of public funds, Jackson's attack upon the United States Bank, his "horrible war of treachery and extermination among the half starved and naked Creeks and Seminoles." However, he approved Jackson's statements about nullification and the preservation of the Federal Union. When the dissensions in the President's

Cabinet, starting with Jackson's defense of the wife of John H. Eaton, Secretary of War, became known to the public and some of the men involved published their accounts of events and their part in them, Whittier printed the lengthy statement of Attorney-General John M. Berrien, followed by a humorous editorial, "A Roaring Lion," quoting Jackson's statement that Mrs. Eaton was "as pure and chaste as Mrs. Danielson's infant daughter," and presented the situation in a rather strained farce with Major Eaton representing Pyramus; Mrs. Eaton, Thisbe; Jackson, the lion; and Colonel Johnson, the wall.[38]

The appointment of John Randolph as ambassador to Russia where, said Whittier in the November 1 issue, he was making himself most superbly ridiculous, gave another chance for criticism of the Administration's appointments. The Administration has "disgraced our country for the sole purpose of rewarding a noisy political brawler," was his comment November 29.

The cause of Temperance got little attention. The only temperance poem written during Whittier's months in Hartford was "The Warning," not published in the *Review* but in the *Essex Gazette*. The only temperance item in the *Review* was a prose narrative, "Gertrude, a Fact" in the August 16 issue, advising women not to marry men who drank: such marriages were the "wedlock of beauty and pollution — of purity and pestilence — the binding of a breathing form of life to the loathsomeness of death." The story later won a prize of twenty dollars[39] and continued popular for several years. It was reprinted in the *Newburyport Herald* December 5, 1834.

Readers of the July 26 issue, the first under his charge to contain literary material by Whittier, must have thought that the *Review* would be a tearful affair. There was "The Forsaken Girl," a prose tale including a poem, with none of the melodrama of "The Forsaken"; the girl pined away, sang a melancholy song shortly before her death and hoped that the man would visit her grave and shed tears there. There was also a poem, "The Farewell," the words of a girl to her departing lover, and "Henry St. Clair." The last two were reprints, although "The Farewell" was noted "For the New England Weekly Review."

The melancholy tone continued August 2 with "The Indian Girl's Lament" (later entitled "The Last Norridgewock") written in 1829 but not previously published.

The deserted-female theme reappeared in the August 23 issue with "The Destiny," in which the false lover was warned that when he was enjoying the love of beautiful women

> Yet there — a spectre — ever nigh
> The injured one shall come
> And underneath love's melting eye
> Shall turn thy smile to gloom!

The emphasis on "spectre" indicated that the source of this poem was the same as that of Whittier's poem "The Spectre" in the September 13 issue of the "Review." The introductory note to "The Spectre" contained a passage from Byron's journal, quoted in Moore's life of Byron, which Whittier had read in the spring of that year, telling his dream of a dead person: "I do not like this dream — I hate its foregone conclusion. Am I to be shaken by shadows?" Whittier thought that this passage might be connected with the story that had been going the rounds of the press about a beautiful young girl who had attended Byron for nearly a year disguised as a page and then, neglected by him, attempted suicide by a dose of poison for which Byron substituted a sleeping potion. She entered the family vault, fastened the door, swallowed the supposed poison, and, unable to open the door, died of starvation. Whittier's poem had the melancholy furnishings fashionable at the time: wan moonlight through a lattice, white robes, eyes of stone.

It was not always the man's fault that the girl died. In "The Maiden's Death" (*Review*, August 29, 1831) the girl watched her lover ride away to war. When he did not return, the girl had a vision of his bier and was not surprised when a wandering soldier told her of his death. Needless to say, she soon died.

There was the usual Byronic melancholy in "My Birth Day," printed in the *Review* three days after Whittier's twenty-third birthday. The meter was the same as Byron's "Youth and Age".

Whittier must have known that this melancholy fare would not please all of his readers all the time, and he printed a pair of humorous poems which in tone and style resembled Oliver Wendell Holmes' earlier verses. "The Lean Man" ate and drank but stayed thin, like Pharaoh's kine:

> Like some wire-moved anatomy
>   He passeth by alone —
> And men will pause, as if to hear
>   The clash of bone on bone.

"The Fat Man" had a country seat, dashing greys, and costly clothes, but the girls turned from him, he complained,

> And love each needy skeleton
>   That kneels before their feet.

Another humorous poem, "The Fort of Goed Hoop" suggests Irving's *Knickerbocker's History of New York*. Whittier had read in Smith's *History of New York* of the capture of the Fort, on the point of land at the junction of Little River and Connecticut River, by Connecticut Yankees. He described the Dutch commander:

> A vast and mighty man was he — five feet
>   beneath his hat
> And six within his girdle — a prodigy of fat.

> He sat and smoked — that valiant chief —
>> while all around him lying
> The heroes of his garrison were in the sunlight
>> frying —
> Right nobly had they borne themselves on that
>> eventful day,
> While fish and fowl and sour-kraut had vanished
>> from their way.

The Yankees came from their onion fields, the Dutch walked out without a fight, and the Yankees ate the plentiful supply of food but remained as lean as before.

Sincere admiration prompted the writing of "Bolivar," which appeared in the *Review* February 21, 1831. Many years later the poem was revised and improved for inclusion in Longfellow's *Poems of Places*. In both versions there was a characteristic reference to the futility of ritual, but while in the later version there was the rather effective point that funeral pomp cannot atone

> For slander's sting, for envy's kiss, for friendship
>> hatred grown,

in the 1831 version there was the irrelevant point that the idle mockeries of funeral ceremony cannot wake the dead.

There was nothing directly about slavery in the *Review* during Whittier's editorship except a brief comment September 13, 1830, on a quotation from the *Washington Spectator* about the Slave Trade in Washington, D.C., and Whittier published nothing elsewhere at this time on slavery. But he commended William Lloyd Garrison's anti-slavery efforts. "To William Lloyd Garrison" was printed in the *Essex Gazette* and not in the *Review*. He was evidently astute enough to see that one cannot promote too many causes at the same time — something that Garrison had not learned. Whittier had been hired by the proprietors of the *Review* to support the candidacy of Henry Clay; campaigning for Abolition might have lost votes for him.

This poem showed clearly enough that Whittier believed that slaves should be freed. But just as he believed that Indians should be well treated even though his one near view of them had been disillusioning, his anti-slavery sentiment did not come from love of negroes. In a private letter he described a "frightful row" in Hartford when a negro mob rioted and knocked down every white man that they met, two of whom were badly injured. "I hate these negroes," the letter continued, "and would think favorably of John Randolph's proposition, of shooting them without ceremony. John, if you recollect, is a good marksman, and says he could shoot all his in half an hour, if the other planters would do likewise."[40] This, of course, was crude boyish humor, but the dislike of negroes was sincere.

Imprisonment for debt aroused Whittier's wrath, as it had two years before when he was editing the *Manufacturer*. In the April 25, 1831, issue he printed William Lloyd Garrison's "The Poor Debtor," which followed the same line of thought as Whittier's earlier editorial. He commented, "We trust this disgraceful relick of barbarism — this libel upon our vaunted free institutions — this shadow upon our national honor, will ere long be found among the remembered enormities as of the past. If poverty be crime, let it be so named upon our statute books." In both Garrison's poem and Whittier's "The Prisoner for Debt" written four years later, the prisoner had been a soldier and in both the question about his crime received the same answer, in more telling phrase in Whittier's "God made the old man poor" than in Garrison's

What was his crime, do you inquire?
The worst of all — 'twas poverty.

The readers who looked to the *Review* for entertainment rather than politics and causes found a varied fare in two prose contributions on September 13. "The Quilting Party" was a nostalgic account of such an affair on a farm; the girls did the quilting in the afternoon, to be free to enjoy the company of the young men in the evening when old-fashioned games were played. Whittier lamented that young men left the farms for more fashionable pursuits. At the other extreme is "The Plague-Stricken," which Whittier himself called a "raw head and bloody bones story."[41]

There were a number of interruptions during Whittier's year and a half as editor of the *Review*. Early in October 1830 he had what he called a "tremendous cold — a sort of influenza," as did many others in Hartford, including two of the women boarders at Law's, and, he wrote to his mother, they could all be unhappy together. They had taken enough herb drink "to carry a saw-mill four and twenty hours." He had even abandoned his Temperance principles and become familiar with gin-sling, brandy, and laudanum.[42] He told the readers of the *Review* that he was getting almost as lean as the editorial columns.

On December 30, 1830, Whittier and Isaac E. Crary left for New York to finish Prentice's *Biography of Henry Clay*. Charles E. Emerson of Hartford, a lawyer, was left in charge of the *Review*.

Crary was one of Whittier's more intimate acquaintances in Hartford. He was opposed to slavery at this time, but eight years later, when he was in Congress as a Representative from Michigan, he opposed the petitions for the abolition of slavery in the District of Columbia, to Whittier's surprise.[43]

The two young men went from Hartford to New Haven by stage coach. They arrived between eleven and twelve at night and found that they would have to stay at a miserable tavern in which there was only one vacant room with three beds — and there was a woman passenger who was, of course, entitled to one of them. Whittier and Crary wondered whether they could with propriety take possession of the other two. Recalling a similar situation in Sterne's *Sentimental Journey* and the author's decision that the fact that a lady occupied one bed ought not to exclude an honest gentleman from another, they made the same decision and had a comfortable night.

The voyage by boat the next day from New Haven to New York was not comfortable. The little steamer tossed "like the undulations of a drunken Dutchman." After dinner, sea-sickness was the order of the day. Whittier did not escape but recovered sooner than most of the victims and drank a glass of brandy which seemed "inclined to behave properly and keep in its place." He sat down to write a letter to Jonathan Law "in the midst of noise and jolting and swearing and that peculiarly interesting noise occasioned by pouring out the undigested materials of the recent dinner upon the floor around me." Fifty faces were "writhing like that of Laocoon in the embrace of the serpent: fifty throats opened like so many cataracts in miniature pouring out with unsparing prodigality a tide as nauseous and as fatal as that which flowed of old from the jaws of the Great Red Dragon of the Apocalypse." On one side of him was an elderly negro "bleached to a ghastly negro paleness;" on the other, a dandy wiping his soiled tights and tucking his deluged ruffles out of sight. Whittier himself was no longer interested in Mary Miller or Elizabeth Trumbull: sea-sickness had cured his lovesickness.[44]

He made good use of his steamboat experiences a few weeks later when he wrote a lively prose piece, "A Night in Long Island Sound," for the January 31 *Review*. The inventors of steamboats, he said, should be classed with the inventors of the guillotine and gunpowder. He described a sentimental girl who was quoting appropriate verses when her bonnet flew off. " 'My bonnet — oh! what shall I do? My bonnet, my bonnet!' she sobbed, bursting into tears, and wrinkling her visage into a similitude of a baked apple, she utterly refused to be comforted. 'Stop the boat! Stop the boat!' she exclaimed 'I've lost my bonnet!'

" 'And you'll lose your hair too if you don't get below,' " coolly returned the rough visaged old sailor, to whom she had addressed herself.

"There was no alternative; and she went below, like Niobe, all in tears."

The passengers spent the night on the boat a few miles below the city and arrived in New York in the morning. The city, he remembered many years later, was a comparatively small place and Brooklyn a little hamlet about the size of Amesbury.

Whittier and Crary boarded at the Tontine Hotel in Wall Street. He recalled it later as tumbledown, but he found it comfortable after his night on the Sound. There was a "noble fire" in the grate, and they spent most of the time in their room for the first few days. Whittier's thoughts were not wholly on Henry Clay: "Miss Parker I shall probably never find if I try till doomsday. It is strange what the girl means by taking herself off in this manner." He declined an invitation to attend a gay gathering of "Literati" including the actor Edwin Forrest and the writers Halleck, Wetmore, Leggett, and Frederick Stanhope Hill. He intended to keep sober until the work on Clay's biography was completed; then "once let this ugly affair be off my hands, and I will drink with the hardest skull among them"[45] — in the absence of evidence to the contrary, one suspects that this was a bit of boyish bravado.

Whittier and Crary soon found that the necessary research was a tiresome business. "We have ransacked every street; we have turned over the huge folios of every library; we have read, inquired, and written and rewritten, until our brains are in a worse state than Ovid's chaos." Whittier found time to call on Elizabeth Trumbull, who told him that Ann Parker was soon to return to Hartford. He called on Major Noah, the editor of the *Courier and Inquirer*, who had been impressed by Whittier's work on the *Review* and was surprised to find him such a young man.

Whittier returned to Hartford in time to contribute to the January 31 number of the *Review* and remained there until he went to Haverhill in March to help in the settlement of his father's estate.

His return to Haverhill after his longest absence from it up to this time renewed his interest in Essex County. He advocated the election of Caleb Cushing, differing from Thayer, now editor of the *Essex Gazette*, who had called Whittier's remarks in favor of Cushing "pretty" and "poetical." He recalled the political history of Essex County and the witchcraft delusion that had flourished there but added that "there is no part of the United States at the present time, whose inhabitants are more liberal, patriotic and intelligent than those of Essex." He found his old friends warm-hearted and the ladies as gentle and beautiful as ever and unaffected by the political tempest, although he could not claim to have added to their happiness, being no lady's man and in fact an avowed bachelor.[46]

The most important effect of Whittier's absence and return was an awareness of the poetic values in his immediate surroundings. His *Legends of New England* had appeared the previous month with but little material resulting from direct observation or local tradition. He now discovered that good material for verse could be found in the history of the neighborhood, and on a rainy afternoon he wrote "Suicide Pond," which was printed in the *Review* March 21. It described a small muddy pond in East Haverhill which was haunted by the ghost of a girl who had drowned herself there. When it was reprinted in the *Haverhill Iris* May 5, 1832, there was an explanatory note by the editor: "It is some ten or twelve years since that an amiable girl went from her place of residence, in the east parish of this town, silently and alone, on a cloudy summer evening, and drowned herself in a small muddy pond, about a quarter of a mile from where she resided. A deep mystery has always hung about her death. She was prepossessing in her looks and manners, always sane, cheerful, and apparently happy." The poem was not included in any authorized edition after 1844, and Whittier is said to have regretted calling attention to the tragedy.[47] The poem had none of the charm and lightness of touch of Whittier's later poems about Essex County. It was melodramatic and exaggerated — can one imagine that a school girl would turn pale every day as she passed the pond and that the boy driving the cows home would hurry past and stop whistling? But there were a few good details from Whittier's direct and accurate observation:

> When the night-hawk's wing dips lightly to that
>> dull and sleeping lake,
> And slow through its green and stagnant mass
>> the shoreward circles break.

Whittier was delayed in Haverhill by illness but was back in Hartford by the week of March 28. He enjoyed the spring weather by taking walks and picking wild flowers, but a small-pox vaccination resulted in fever, pains, and inflammation and he had to take laudanum to get any sleep. Late in May he went to New Haven in the hope of being benefited by the sea air. He remained about a week; the city was hot in spite of the sea breeze and the shade of elm trees, and sleep was made impossible by the suffocating atmosphere and the mosquitoes. He was well enough, however, to climb East Rock twice; the first time, he and a friend climbed the perpendicular side, struggling through loose rocks and bushes and arriving at the summit too exhausted to enjoy the view. He witnessed the crowning of the Queen of May by the girls of Mr. Andrew's High School on the estate of James A. Hillhouse, and he visited the studio of a sculptor at work on the meeting of Jephthah and his daughter.[48]

He did not return directly to Hartford but visited some southern New Hampshire mill towns, including Somersworth, Salmon Falls, and Dover, and had nothing but praise for what he saw. Where a few years ago there had been dilapidated farm houses, there were now white mansions and church spires. The people were industrious and temperate, and the churches were crowded with zealous worshippers. A few years later, when he saw the textile mills in Lowell at close range, his enthusiasm was somewhat tempered, but in 1831 he shared the general feeling of New England when mills were built. Property values increased, and young people thronged in from poor and lonely farms to earn good pay and to enjoy social life such as they had never known before. Country towns welcomed the mills as warmly as towns in the 1960's and 1970's rejoiced at the building of "industrial parks" where once were fields and woods. One of the worst features of the Industrial Revolution was not present in these New England countryside mills. There were no smoke and piles of ashes: the wheels were turned by water power.

Whittier's chief interest in the mills at the moment was the proof they furnished that Henry Clay was right: that manufacturing — and a tariff to encourage it — would bring prosperity as exports would replace imports.

While in southern New Hampshire Whittier visited the Devil's Den in

Chester and wrote "The Devil's Cave", which he did not include in any edition after 1838. It had Gothic embellishments — dwarf pines, moonlight, owls, a dark cave, an oak with boughs like a skeleton's arms, a lightning-blasted tree, ghostly gibbering and fiendish yells, bodiless hands — but it concluded on a note that showed Whittier's growing interest in legends and traditions: the cave told of the romantic past and stories and dreams remembered from childhood.

Whittier returned to Hartford, where he was pleased to be notified of his election as an honorary member of the Franklin Society of Brown University. Early in September he visited the Hanging Hills, midway between Hartford and New Haven. The path was overgrown with bushes and the guide lost his way, but Whittier reached the summit and, admitting that he was a passionate admirer of mountain scenery, gave the readers of the September 12 *Review* a description of the view, where a chasm between two crags reminded him of a line in Coleridge's "Cristabel."

Two weeks later, to his disgust, he was suffering from bad nerves. "I hate to trouble you," he wrote to Dr. Todd, "But really — I am too ill for ceremony; and must request you to call on me this evening. I passed a miserable night — and am miserable to-day. I fear I was not particular enough in my statement of my case to you yesterday — I have been so often disgusted with the minutiae of a hypochondriac, that I have neglected even important particulars."[49] He was able to continue his work on the *Review*, including a prose essay "The Hypochondriac," until October 17, when he apologized to the readers for the scarcity of material. "Well, here we have it in one word — sickness. . . . We shall pen nothing lugubrious on the subject, for we have a melancholy of our own — perfectly original, — a nondescript sorrow, which this lubberly affair of a world has nothing to do with. We will not be merry — for your mirth upon paper is a vile thing, when one is really suffering, — it is as if a malicious demon should lean over the victim upon the rack, and grin horribly a ghastly smile at his misery. Therefore — if what we have said be an apology, our readers are altogether welcome to it. Fire shall not burn out of us a word more."

It was evidently about this time that Whittier wrote a letter dated only "Thursday afternoon" to Cornelia Russ, seventeen-year-old daughter of Judge John Russ of Hartford. It is as follows:[50]

Miss Russ.

I could not leave town without asking an interview with you. I know that my proposal is abrupt — and I cannot but fear that it will be unwelcome. But you will pardon me. About to leave Hartford for a distant part of the country, I have ventured to make a demand, for which under any other circumstances I should be justly censurable. I feel that I have indeed no claims on your regard. But I would hope, almost against any evidence to the contrary, that you might not altogether discourage a feeling which has long been to me as a new existence. I would hope that in my absence from my own New England, whether in the sunny South or the "Far West," one heart would respond with my own — one bright eye grow brighter at the mention of a — name, which has never been, and I trust never will be, connected with dishonor, and which, if the Ambition which now urges onward shall continue in vigorous exercise, shall yet be known widely and well — and whose influence shall be lastingly felt.—

But this is dreaming, — and it may only call forth a smile. If so — I have too high an opinion of your honorable feelings to suppose even for a moment that you would make any use of your advantage derogatory to the character of a high-minded, and ingenuous girl—

I leave town on Saturday. Can you allow of an interview this evening or on that of Friday? If however you cannot afford me the pleasure of seeing you — I have only to resign hopes dear to me as life itself, and carry with me hereafter the curse of disappointed feeling.—

A note in answer will be waited for impatiently. At least you will not deny me this.

Yours most truly—

J. G. Whittier—

This letter is the whole story as far as it is known. Whittier still enjoyed imagining himself in love and he also enjoyed writing a sentimental letter.

Cornelia kept Whittier's letter, perhaps for the same reason that Mary Emerson Smith kept the letters to her. Whatever the situation and however it ended, there was no resentment on the part of Cornelia's father. When he sent Whittier his certificate of appointment as delegate to the National Republican convention he added a note inviting Whittier to visit him if his route passed through Hartford.

Whittier left for Haverhill after preparing material for the October 31 issue of the *Review*. Dr. Crane went to Haverhill with him and then returned to Hartford with a letter from Whittier to Jonathan Law addressed: "Mr. Law. By Asculapius Sangrador."[51] Whittier made no further contributions to the *Review*, although he did not formally end his connection with it until January 2.

The "sunny South" to which he referred in his letter to Cornelia Russ was Baltimore and Washington, where he planned to spend part of the winter. He started for Baltimore early in December as a delegate to the National Republican convention, but got only as far as Boston when he had an attack of influenza. He was in Lynn December 13 and then returned to Haverhill.[52]

The year and half in Hartford had been profitable in several ways. His pay had been small, but he seems to have saved some of it. The farmhouse was painted white and improvements made in 1832, and since his father's personal property was appraised at $624.25 and there were debts amounting to $1391.25 including a physician's bill of $76.37 for one hundred seventy-eight visits, medicine, and advice, the money could not have come from the estate. Whittier had enjoyed the friendship of congenial young people whom he was sorry to leave, with one of whom he had had the experience of drinking too much: he and Willis Gaylord Clarke drank some French cordial which was more potent than they supposed and they had considerable difficulty walking home.[53] In addition to the trips to various points in Connecticut already mentioned he had visited Tallcott Mountain and Litchfield. He had enjoyed exchanging letters with Mrs. Louisa C. Tuthill, to whom he had poured out his Byronic sentiments: "Disappointment in a thousand ways has gone over my heart and left it dust. Yet I still look forward with high anticipations. I have placed the goal of my ambition high — but with the blessing of God, it shall be reached."[54]

His editorial duties had not kept him from preparing a volume for the press. *Legends of New England*, his first book, appeared in February 1831. It contained eleven poems and seven prose narratives. Seven of the poems had already been published but none of the prose narratives had. Whittier later included two of the poems in the appendix to the *Riverside Edition* but never made further use of any of the prose pieces. In both the poetry and the prose there was little of the Whittier that we know: he said of the volume when he looked at it many years later that "it seemed like somebody else." When Samuel T. Pickard told him that he had a copy of it, Whittier told him not to print anything from it in the *Portland Transcript*, and offered to pay whatever Pickard had paid for it. Pickard gave it to him, and he destroyed it.[55] But the volume showed that Whittier had come to realize that New England had legends and traditions worth writing about; in fact, he claimed in the preface that, whatever the reception given his book, he would be satisfied if it led others to explore the traditionary lore of New England.

Whittier found most of this New England material in books and not in oral tradition. Of the six pieces dealing with Essex County legends, four were based on accounts given by Cotton Mather: "The Weird Gathering," "The Haunted House," "The Spectre Warriors," and "The Spectre Ship." One, "The Mother's Revenge," was merely the historical account of Hannah Dustin's killing and scalping her Indian captors. "The Murdered Lady" was the only Essex County item not derived directly from a book. But descriptive details were often from Whittier's own observatons; the gallows scene in "The Weird Gathering" was Whittier's memory of Gallows Hill in Salem as he had seen it in his boyhood. Of the pieces dealing with other parts of New England, Whittier stated that "A Night Among the Wolves" was from an oral tradition; there is no evidence that the others have this origin. "The Powwaw" was taken largely from Peters' *General History of Connecticut*.[56]

In his treatment of his subjects in this volume Whittier usually failed to get the moving simplicity of his later New England poems. There were too much sentimentality and Gothic machinery. An exception is "The Black Fox," which, as John B. Pickard has pointed out, has a "bare, simple diction and directness of narration that truly displays Whittier's ballad capacities. . . . Also woven within the poem are some telling imagistic constrasts: the fox's frightening blackness chills the warm red cheer of the family fire, while the open confidence of the two young hunters is dispelled by the deceptive white purity of the snow which brings isolation and death. Finally the arrival of spring is blighted by the presence of the crazed wanderer whose madness illuminates the pervasive power of evil in the world."

Moll Pitcher was partly written at Jonathan Law's house during one of Whittier's periods of illness. It had lain in fragments, he wrote to Law, staring him in the face until he sent it to the publishers to get rid of it. A week later he wrote to Mrs. Sarah J. Hale that all that he had written (evidently at Hartford) had been thrown off in a hurry "to meet the demands of that all-pitiless demon — the printer's devil" and that he had "concluded to publish only one poem of perhaps thirty pages founded upon the well-known story of Moll Pitcher, the celebrated New England Witch."[57]

Moll Pitcher of Lynn was a fortune-teller rather than a witch in the usual sense of the word and had a clientele including both the wealthy and the poor. She was well-mannered and benevolent, although Whittier's narrative gives a different impression.[58] According to Whittier, Moll Pitcher terrified a girl into insanity by predicting calamity to her lover who was at sea. The lover returned, the girl was cured, and her daughter took care of Moll Pitcher in her last illness. One source appears to have been C. W. Upham's *Lectures on Witchcraft*, which Whittier reviewed in the *Review* September 5, 1830.

In his later years Whittier had a poor opinion of "Moll Pitcher." "The pamphlet described in thy note I am ashamed to own is mine," he wrote in 1886. "I hoped it had died out of print and am rather sorry that old 'Moll' has materialized herself."[59] Nevertheless passages from it are in the *Riverside Edition*: "Extract from a New England Legend" and the first two stanzas of "Memories."

During his months at Hartford Whittier's poetry continued to be copied and admired.

But his poetry as well as his editorial work was also treated to a "tomahawk sort of satire"[60] in *Truth: A New Year's Gift for Scribblers* by William Joseph Snelling, published in Boston in 1831. It called Whittier an upstart, with wax still clinging to his fingers' ends, a Johnny Raw, unchecked by modesty, a self-appointed judge who told the nation what was right or wrong —

> Proud of some score of barely decent lines,
> Heavens, how he swells! how bright his
> genius shines!

Most of the authors of the day were treated as badly by Snelling as was Whittier. According to Oliver Wendell Holmes, the poem "made some talk for a while, and is now chiefly valuable as a kind of literary tombstone on which may be read the names of many whose renown has been buried with their bones.''

Whittier commented briefly on Snelling's poem in the *Review* January 10, 1831, calling it "a pamphlet in imitation of English Bards and Scotch Reviewers. . . . It possesses all the marks which distinguish its copy, except genius, spirit, satire, and poetry.'' He was rather more disturbed by an article in the *Hartford Times*, then edited by Gideon Welles, which he construed as an attack on him. He wrote to Welles: "Sir, if you know anything against my character, — a character dearer to me than life itself, in God's name publish it to the world, as becomes a man — but deal no longer in dark insinuations. I am a stranger here — with no wealth, save that of an honorable reputation, for which I have struggled long and wearily: and believe me Sir, I will not tamely see the only abiding hope of my existence sported with by the wanton and malicious.''[61] Welles replied that the article was reprinted from the *Charleston Mercury* and was not an attack on anybody and that he would like to be better acquainted with Whittier.

Later rendering of possibly the earliest likeness of Whittier, c.1827.

Portrait of Whittier by Robert Peckham, 1833, painted at Haverhill. (Courtesy of Whittier Birthplace, Haverhill)

Portrait of Whittier by Manasseh Cutler Torrey, 1835, painted at Hartford, CT.

Etching of Whittier by Steven Alonzo Schoff, 1888, of a portrait by Bass Otis, 1838.

View of Boston from the South Boston Bridge, c.1835; a lithograph by Deroy after a drawing by J. Milbert.

View of Hartford in 1841.

III
1832 - 33

Whittier was now giving little time and attention to poetry. The boyish exuberance which produced a poem every week had died down, and he could be amused by some of his verses. He wrote to Sarah Josepha Hale that he would try to get a few pieces to send to her for her magazine, and he could send her "The Demon Lady," written some time ago, which smacked "something of the terrible and it may be of the ridiculous."[1] He might have added that it smacked of the sentimental:

> And a bosom of love on his own reclining,
>> And tresses of gold 'mid his dark locks shining;
> And he felt her heart-pulse come and go
>> As she gave, in her yielding tenderness
> Her beautiful lips to his fervent kiss.

But the beautiful bride turned out to be a demon, and the sight in the bridal chamber the next morning was too horrible to describe: Whittier was evidently in a hurry to get to the moral, that many who are lovely without are dark within.

Whittier briefly had an ambitious plan to go to Cincinnati to start a daily newspaper, but illness interfered; he was unable to stir for three weeks, and for a week unable to see.[2] During the month of January there were few days when he could write without suffering.

His chief attention was now given to prose and politics. He thought of publishing "a series of sketches in the manner of Irving's, distinct enough however from him in style — sketches which shall illustrate some of the superstitions and peculiarities of our New Englanders — some of a grave and some of a lighter character."[3] He wrote one sketch as an experiment to see if the public liked it, but the series was not done until eleven years later when it appeared in the *United States Magazine and Democratic Review*; in 1847 it was expanded and became *The Supernaturalism of New England*.

The experimental sketch was "Powow Hill", which appeared, without the author's name, in the *New England Magazine* for May. It told of a Yankee jack-of-all-trades who was riding to his wedding when his horse went wild and carried him to the top of Powow Hill in Amesbury where, according to legend, Indian sprites gathered on April 1, and whoever blundered upon them was never heard of again. He was surrounded by dancing Indians who told him that he was to marry Pigwagitiokapog, the nymph of the tawneys, a huge squaw holding a bear cub as a lap dog. He could escape his fate only by throwing a Bible at Hobomoko, the chieftain. His intended squaw sought to cheer him by putting snuff under his nose. He felt in his pocket for his handkerchief, found a Bible which he had put there after using it to strap his razor, and threw it at Hobomoko. The ghosts fled, and he found himself alone on the hilltop as the sun was rising above the horizon.

Whittier also began a novel on a theme which was to be much on his mind in the years following the Civil War: "the reconciliation of the North and the South, — being simply an endeavor to do away with some of the prejudices which have produced enmity between the Southron and the Yankee." The style was to be midway between Laurence Sterne and Washington Irving.[4]

He earned a little money by writing. He received seven dollars and a half for "The Nervous Man," which was in the August *New England Magazine,*[5] and sixty dollars for compiling and editing *Literary Remains of John G. C. Brainard with a Sketch of His Life,* published in the summer of 1832.

Whittier had a high opinion of Brainard. He conceded that not all of Brainard's poems were excellent, but asked: "What poet of modern days has ever published a perfect volume?" and made some forceful comments about the popular British poets of the day: Byron's hurriedly written verses had "beauty wedded to deformity;" Southey "discoursed fustian" in "Joan of Arc"; Wordsworth sank into "the pathos and sentiment of an overgrown baby"; Shelley had "sickly conceits and unsubstantial theories"; and Keats' "Endymion" was "mawkish and affected." This led to a comment in line with the growing spirit of American literary independence: Brainard's poetry was wholly American. "He does not talk of palms and cypress when he should describe rough oak and sombre hemlock."

He was still an enthusiastic supporter of Henry Clay. If Clay's plan to conciliate Southern opposition to the tariff by removing the duties on items which did not compete with American manufacturers was adopted and was successful, Clay would deserve the Presidency.

Whittier was more violent against Martin Van Buren than even against Jackson and was sure that if he was nominated for Vice President and accepted, he would be defeated. Van Buren was "in the disgraceful catalogue of those exposed demagogues and baffled intriguers, who in all ages, and in all countries have been condemned to general and perpetual execration." He had arranged the election of Jackson, whose "mental weakness, untamed passions, bitter prejudices, and selfish vanity might be turned with fatal effect upon his political rivals." Jackson had been expected to retire at the end of a single term and Van Buren was to "glide quietly into a place, actually abdicated in his favor."

Jackson's veto July 10 of the bill to renew the charter of the Bank of the United States was attacked by Whittier as an example of abuse of Presidential power rather than as poor economics. In a series of articles in the *Essex Gazette* he argued that Jackson's statement that every public officer was to support the Constitution as he, not others (including the Supreme Court), understood it, was virtual nullification, and Jackson's whole tendency had been towards absolute dictation, as in the removal of officials (the "Spoils System").[6]

It was opposition to this lawless dictatorship that Whittier was asking three poet-editors to undertake when he called on them in "To a Poetical Trio in the City of Gotham" to defend liberty, law, and freedom of opinion. He named them in footnotes. They were editors of pro-Jackson papers: James Lawson,[7] William Leggett, and William Cullen Bryant, and the only music that their cracked lutes could utter was "Hurrah for Jackson." In rather prosaic lines he told them to

>Stand up like men for Liberty and Law,
>And free opinion. Check corruption's pride,
>Soothe the loud storm of fratricidal war.

If the three poets read Whittier's appeal, they must have thought that his lute was as cracked as theirs: "law" and "war" rhyme only in Yankee speech, and "been" and "pen", in another stanza, is not a good rhyme in any dialect.

Whittier's interest in politics now led him to think again about his own future. He was momentarily enjoying life on the farm. He liked the romantic location, and the house had been improved. Elizabeth, who had been at Haverhill Academy, was at home and writing poetry. He was keeping in touch with his Haverhill friends. But he could not look forward to a life of this kind. His father had held local public offices; why shouldn't he, with more education than his father, aim higher? Why not get elected to Congress?

There had been no Representative from the district for two years. Whittier's friends, according to his account, insisted upon his allowing himself to be a candidate. He professed to be astonished, but was not so bewildered as to fail to see the advantage to himself or to use some astuteness in trying to bring about his election. "It would give me an opportunity of seeing and knowing our public characters - - - - - -. It would be worth more to me *now*, young as I am, than almost any office after I had reached the meridian of life," he wrote to Edwin Harriman. But he would not be twenty-five, the age required by the Constitution, until December 17, and so he asked Harriman's help in a devious plan.

Harriman was to support Cushing at the next attempt at an election and to tell Cushing's Newburyport friends that those who had previously supported Kittredge would not present a candidate, although Whittier must have thought otherwise or he would have supposed that Cushing would be elected. Next, Cushing could ask his friends to vote for someone else for the sake of promoting peace in the district. Whittier would be nominated, the Kittredge supporters would nominate a candidate whom they would not expect to elect, Thayer, who had opposed Cushing, would support Whittier, and Whittier, who by this time would be twenty-five, could be elected. He would then be able to use the influence of his position to help his friends: "And give me once an opportunity of exercising it, my first object shall be to evince my gratitude by exertions in behalf of those who had conferred such a favor upon me"[8] thus promising to use the Spoils System which he had so vigorously attacked when Jackson used it.

Whittier did not intend to limit his political future to his own Congressional district, and wished to build a reputation farther afield. He sent Jonathan Law two of his articles on "The Veto and Its Doctrines." "If you should happen to like them — will you be good enough to notice them in the Hartford Mercury — and if you can in conscience say a few words respecting my political course in Connecticut while Editor of the Review — you will confer upon me a great favor."[9]

Whittier did not tell Cushing of his scheme, nor did Cushing inform Whittier of his intentions. After the death of his wife August 28, Cushing was no longer interested in the nomination, and when it was offered him he declined in favor of Jeremiah Nelson, who was elected in November.[10] Whittier did not write to Cushing until two months after Cushing's wife's death and then, evidently not knowing of Cushing's withdrawal, told him that Haverhill and Bradford people had thought it best that Cushing should decline the nomination unless there was reasonable hope of his election. He then defended his own course with more vigor than candor, claiming that he had been willing to be a candidate and to decline before the convention but had not had time to prepare an address. Some of Cushing's friends had tried to use these facts against him, but he insisted that his course had been consistent and honorable (it does not appear to have been either) and somewhat belligerently said that those who had tried "to fix dishonorable imputations upon a character which I value more than life itself - - - will live to repent of it."[11]

One of his worries during this year had been the cholera epidemic which had spread from Canada into the United States. In a hurried letter to I. A. Rockwell in July he had inquired about the origin of the disease, its treatment, and the number of deaths resulting from it.[12] In a letter to Mary Emerson Smith a month later he wrote that the "terrible pestilence" was within eighty miles of Haverhill. He had heard that it had reached Cincinnati, where she was living. "I can hardly believe it, but I fear we must make up our minds to confront it at some time or other, and in some place or other. And why should we fear it? It is but a portion of our destiny. The earth itself is but a universal grave; the pale stars and the sun himself are but the funeral torches which burn over desolation and decay." This led, as one would expect, to quoting the last nine lines of Bryant's "Thanatopsis." Then came: "I have sometimes thought that in a season of pestilence two kindred and loving spirits might die happy in each other's embraces, mingling together in death those souls which in life had been separated only by the perished bodies.'' From here he jumped to the report that had come to him that she was the belle of Cincinnati.[13]

Writing to Jonathan Law a few weeks later he reported that there had been five fatal cases of cholera in Boston and one case, not fatal, in Haverhill; the patient there was recovering. He was interested to notice that he was less nervous about the disease now that it was near at hand than when it first broke out in Canada: " 'Tis a singular fact in the philosophy of the human mind that in proportion as the dangers which we most fear at a distance gather closer around us, we become reckless, hardened and secure.''

He had also become hardened and secure to the experience of being — or imagining himself — in love. In the same letter to Law he wrote: " 'Tis true I am in love — just now — deeply and desperately — but these things seldom last with me more than ten days or a fortnight at the most, so that I shall soon be 'myself again'.''[14]

He settled down for a winter on the farm. Farmers then had little to do in the winter, and Whittier had plenty of time to write but no emotion to impel him to write poetry except his fear of the cholera, which prompted him to write "The Female Martyr" about a girl who died after catching the disease while caring for the sick. But he wrote long letters. One of them was to Mrs. Sigourney and contained some rather boyish self-analysis, an essay on the relation between love of man and love of God, and comments on public affairs: if the tariff was abolished, New England would suffer, but if "the blood-thirsty old man at the head of our government shall undertake to put down South Carolina with the bayonet, from that moment our Union will be broken-up never to unite again." As for himself, he had nearly taken leave of poetry; his political reputation was more influential than his poetical and he had "thrown the rough armor of rude and turbulent controversy over a keenly sensitive bosom." He had written a few prose articles.[15]

One of these prose pieces was "Passaconaway," in the *New England Magazine* February 1833. It was the sort of thing that Whittier did at greater length fifteen years later in "Leaves from Margaret Smith's Journal": historical fiction with the setting in seventeenth century New England, some historical and some fictitious characters, and the reader's sympathy directed toward a minority religious group. The hero of "Passaconaway" was a Familist; Whittier was to write "The Familist's Hymn" five years later with a long introductory note concluding: "They were unquestionably sincere in their opinions, and, whatever may have been their errors, deserve to be ranked among those who have in all ages suffered for the freedom of conscience."

In the same issue of the *New England Magazine* was an article by William Browne Oliver Peabody, "New England Superstitions." After reading it Whittier moved a step nearer to his "New England Supernaturalism" by writing an essay, also entitled "New England Superstitions," for the *New England Magazine*. He wished that someone would "embody and illustrate such passages of superstition as may be considered in any way peculiar to the New World" and listed seven topics: Haunted Houses, Ghosts, Witches, Fortune-Telling, Warnings of Death or Disaster, Spectres, and Supposed Preternatural Appearances.

He added some pages of introduction to "Confessions of a Suicide," which had been printed in the *New England Weekly Review,* and renamed it "The Opium Eater" for the March *New England Magazine.* It is unlikely that it was derived from thoughts and experiences of his own. He had almost forgotten about it when he told James T. Fields in 1849 that it might be used in an anthology.[16] He had surely forgotten its sentimentality and melodrama or he would hardly have wanted to exhume it.

By late winter he was tired of the quiet life of East Haverhill. His months in Boston and Hartford had given him a taste of life where there was something to see and do. He complained that he was "starving for newspapers"; he got one now and then from Boston and Washington but not until they were "greyheaded with age." Haverhill was "fearfully dull," he wrote to Mary Emerson Smith. "There is no visiting — no courting — no marrying nor giving in marriage. We are *nullified* as much as the tariff laws in South Carolina. Now and then we have a Temperance lecture, or by way of variety and amusement an occasional meeting of the tract society."[17] Boredom, as well as conviction, led to his reaction to a letter from William Lloyd Garrison a few weeks later.

Garrison's purpose in writing was to get Whittier to find a hall for a lecture on Abolition. He tactfully began by saying that Whittier had doubtless been busy with his "elastic, vigorous, glowing pen" and that if he made his writings as useful as they were brilliant he would be a blessing to mankind. Still leading toward the main purpose of the letter was a rhetorical appeal to Whittier to join the anti-slavery cause, which was "worthy of Gabriel — yes, the God of hosts places himself at its head. Whittier, enlist! — Your talents, zeal, influence — all are needed!" Then came the real object of the letter: would Whittier procure a meetinghouse where Garrison could lecture Sunday, March 31?[18]

Doubtless glad of something to do and something to go to, Whittier arranged for the use of the First Parish Meetinghouse. He was present at the lecture, and Garrison was pleased to see him "full of health and manly beauty." Garrison spoke to a crowded house — others besides Whittier were perhaps eager for some excitement after a long, dull winter — and "gave a most thrilling detail of cruelties practiced on the slaves in our country: and fully demonstrated to our minds the obligation of the American people to urge the *immediate* abolition of slavery."[19]

Whether from the lecture, Garrison's letter, conversation with Garrison, or all of these along with the fact that Whittier had nothing in mind at the moment that strongly interested him, he plunged deep into the Anti-Slavery movement. During the next year most of his writings, both prose and poetry, were directly or indirectly related to slavery. It remained a life-long interest, but as the years passed it ceased to dominate his thought and his writing. He spent less time turning "the crank of an opinion-mill," and the grist from the mill was not always anti-slavery or post-abolition problems.

In spite of this disparaging reference in "The Tent on the Beach" to his reform poems, he never seriously regretted his involvement in Abolition. As he looked back over his life he was glad that his early Anti-Slavery activity kept him from Robert Burns' fate: being shut up in a custom house. "If thou would'st win success," he once said to a fourteen-year-old boy, "join thyself to some unpopular but noble cause."[20]

The immediate result of his interest in Anti-Slavery was not quite so sweeping as has been believed. The flood of verse had slowed down a year earlier, and not all the weekly poems had been forceless and purposeless. Whittier did not give up all political ambitions: he was elected to the State Legislature in 1835. Still, after March 1833 his life was never again what it had been before.

IV

1833

Whittier plunged vigorously into abolition, confident of its early success. Slavery would be abolished by methods that Christians in general and Quakers in particular would approve, and the nation would be united and happy. He would show the injustice and folly of slavery so gently and firmly that even slaveholders would be convinced, and slavery would come to an end without violence. In this naive belief he dashed off a prose pamphlet *Justice and Expediency*, which was printed at the *Gazette* office and was ready for distribution in May. He paid for the printing.

The pamphlet took the stand of most Abolitionists at that time: that the Congress could and should abolish slavery in the District of Columbia and the territories (Florida and Arkansas) but that it had no right to interfere with slavery in the states. However, since immediate abolition was the only practicable and just scheme, they would try to bring it about "not with the weapons of violence and blood but with those of reason and truth, prayer to God, and entreaty to man."

The edition of five hundred copies was soon disposed of. Whittier sent one to Arthur Tappan, who ordered fifty copies, enclosed ten dollars, and asked permission to have it republished in New York. Permission was given and five thousand copies were printed at Tappan's expense. Tappan had recently ceased to support the Colonization Society, having found that the leading articles of commerce sent to Liberia were liquor, tobacco, gun powder, and balls, and having become convinced that the original purpose of the Society had been to get free negroes out of the country in order that slaves might be held in greater safety — a fact which Whittier made good use of in his pamphlet. Through the influence of Moses Brown, *Justice and Expediency* was printed in the *Providence Journal*,[1] and it was favorably reviewed in anti-slavery papers. Whittier was disappointed that it did not make more of a sensation. However, he had the satisfaction of knowing that it was taken seriously by at least one Southern editor. The Richmond *Jeffersonian and Times* printed a brief comment including the statement that the Abolition sentiment of New England was "false and fanatical." Someone gave Whittier a copy of the paper, and although it was the busy season on the farm, he took time to write two hurried letters in reply which he sent to the *Essex Register* of Salem.[2]

In the first letter a distinction was made between the legal right of the South to hold slaves, which was acknowledged, and the moral right, which it did not have. No human law could "make void or put aside the ordinance of the living God and the eternal laws of Nature. We therefore hold it to be the duty of the people of the slave-holding states to begin the work of emancipation now; that any delay must be dangerous to themselves in time and eternity, and full of injustice to their slaves and to their brethen of the free states." Let us, he said to the South, "reason together" in the "glorious sunshine of expediency and utility."

He continued in the second letter to emphasize that the leading Northern Abolitionists opposed any interference with the slave system by the Federal government because they were opposed to war of all kinds and considered that political interference by the Federal government was unconstitutional. He listed the peaceful methods that the Abolitionists would use, including the formation of Anti-Slavery societies. He again presented some of the evils of slavery and concluded with an inaccurate quotation from Milton's "Areopagitica": "Though all the winds of doctrine be let loose upon the earth, so Truth be among them, we need not fear. Let her and falsehood grapple; who ever knew her to be put to the worst in a free and open encounter?"

John Randolph had died May 24 and had included in his will an arrangement by which his slaves would be set free and cared for. Consequently Whittier no longer found him ridiculous but described him in the second letter as an eloquent statesman whose manumission of his slaves was a noble example. "Randolph of Roanoke," although not printed until 1847, was evidently written soon after Randolph's death.

One of the methods to be used by Abolitionists was "appeals from the pulpit to the consciences of men," which would be accompanied by the use of anti-slavery hymns. Whittier wrote one of these to be used at the Sabbath School Celebration at Haverhill July 4. A few weeks later, he asked Robert Cross, an Amesbury lawyer, to write one or more hymns for him.[3]

When Whittier heard of the opposition to Prudence Crandall's offer to admit negro girls to her school in Canterbury, Connecticut, he wrote a note to the *Essex Gazette* in a tone of satire such as he used later in some of his anti-slavery poems. "Never since the midnight inroad of the Windham frogs so celebrated by the 'Rev. Hugh Peters' in his veritable history of Connecticut, were the good people of that region so terribly alarmed. 'A negro has a soul, your honor!' said Corporal Trim."[4]

Whittier was not completely absorbed in Anti-Slavery — nor had it made him suddenly grown-up. While *Justice and Expediency* was being printed, a poem which he later called a "piece of literary mystification hardly excusable even in a young writer" appeared in the *New England Magazine*. "The Song of the Vermonters" was printed anonymously to see if it would be accepted as a ballad of Ethan Allen's time. It purported to be a rallying call to the men of Vermont to

Leave the harvest to rot on the field where it grows,
And the reaping of wheat for the reaping of foes.

Surprisingly, it was accepted as genuine. At a meeting of the Vermont Historical and Antiquarian Society in 1843 it was presented as a ballad composed at the time of the events that it referred to. It is hard to see why no one's suspicions were aroused. It had more obviously conscious literary effects than would be likely to occur in a ballad written in the excitement of war. Whittier acknowledged his authorship in 1858, and was sorry to find in 1877 that the poem was still alive. He explained that he had been early interested in the history of Vermont and in Ethan Allen, and he had not yet become seriously committed to the peace principles which he accepted as part of the Quaker tradition.[5]

His last prose article in the *New England Magazine* was "The Proselytes" in the September number. It was a fictional account of a conversation between William Penn and two earnest young seekers after the truth, and was mainly an exposition of the Quaker doctrine of the Inner Light and an added word about simplicity in dress. It was hardly the sort of thing that would interest readers, and the editor of the magazine, Joseph T. Buckingham, may have decided that he did not want any more of Whittier's prose articles. But there was probably another reason for his rejecting "Daniel O'Connell." Whittier himself called it "something of an incendiary concern,"[6] and Buckingham may have correctly guessed that it would be distasteful to his readers. It seems innocuous now; its emphasis was on O'Connell's "moral victory of reason over prejudice, of justice over oppression" — the sort of victory that Whittier thought could be won over slavery. But it contained a vigorous account of the unjust treatment of Catholics in Ireland. Hatred and fear of the Roman Catholic Church were still very much alive in New England,[7] and many readers would regard the article as the opening of a gate to a vicious beast about to spring, with its claws sharpened in the Massacre of St. Bartholomew and the Spanish Inquisition.

He was still interested in other causes. In September he and Abijah W. Thayer went to the State Temperance Convention at Worcester as delegates from the Haverhill Temperance Society. The Temperance cause then commanded the attention of successful and important men. Edward Everett was one of the delegates from Charlestown.[8]

He was as opposed as ever to Andrew Jackson, who was "full of egotistical authority", and Martin Van Buren was still "clinging to his skirts."[9] He said nothing about Henry Clay, whom he had turned against because of his support of the Colonization Society.

In November he was nominated as one of the four National Republican candidates for the Massachusetts Legislature from Haverhill. The National Republicans lost by a slim majority.[10]

Whittier's maturing attitude toward negroes appeared October 1 in his first poem since early summer, "Toussaint L'Ouverture." The black man who, in the slave uprising in Haiti

> . . . . . Round the white man's lordly hall
>   Trod, fierce and free

and whose bloodied arms were thrown round the white woman was the brute that the white man had made. Toussaint had been well treated by his master and consequently did not join the insurgents until he had helped his master and family to escape from the island. The moral was so obvious that it did not need the explicit presentation that Whittier gave it:

> . . . . . Kindness to the wronged is never
>   Without its excellent reward,
> Holy to human-kind and ever
>   Acceptable to God.

Life on the farm, with its outdoor work, and his interest in causes that took his mind off himself had been good for him. His health was good, he wrote to Jonathan Law in October. "The blues" had left him, and he was enjoying husking parties. He was not writing any poetry but was reading everything he could get hold of — "politics — history — rhyme — reason, etc." He had a lively interest in the affairs of his Hartford friends: Charles Emerson had been caught in the matrimonial trap and Whittier sent the congratulations of an old bachelor along with those of Benjamin Greenleaf, Emerson's teacher at Bradford Academy. In answer to Law's question, he was not married, but Eunice thought that she would be ready next year. (There is no way of knowing whether this is a serious announcement or a bit of playful humor, but it seems more likely to be the latter.)

Whittier was present at the organization meeting of an Anti-Slavery society in Haverhill, but was too busy on the farm to do any Anti-Slavery work. "I must work, or starve," he wrote, "or do worse, plunge again into the seven times heated furnace of modern politics." Still, he wished that he could go to an Anti-Slavery Convention to be held in Philadelphia, where he thought that he might have some influence among the Quakers, but he simply could not afford to go.[11]

There was less farm work after the harvest season, and Whittier, who doubtless knew that a cause must have martyrs if it is to prosper, wrote "To the Memory of Charles B. Storrs," who had died September 15. Storrs was not a victim of a mob — those would come later — but had overworked in writing and speaking for Abolition along with his duties as president of Western Reserve College. Whittier's poem prophesied that Storrs would be remembered and honored when slavery was finally abolished. The last stanzas mentioned "evil days before us," "trials yet to come," "the shadow of the prison," and "cruel martyrdom." Whittier was beginning to realize that Abolition would not be brought about as peacefully as he had hoped.

Late in the afternoon one day in November Whittier was surprised to learn that he had been elected a delegate to the Anti-Slavery Convention, with his expenses paid by Samuel E. Sewall. He was to leave the next morning.[12] He had to arrange for the care of the farm during his absence, and there was little time for sleep that night. He left Haverhill by stagecoach in the morning and arrived in Boston in the early afternoon, stayed over night at the Eastern Stage Tavern, and the next day left with William Lloyd Garrison on the New York stagecoach. At New York other delegates joined them, including one older man, Daniel Thurston, a Congregational minister from Maine. From New York to Philadelphia they economized by travelling in a second-class coach. Among the passengers were some young men whose language moved Thurston to give them some wholesome advice, to which they replied by offering him a drink.

In Philadelphia Whittier and his friends lodged at the home of Evan Lewis on Fifth Street. The few prosperous and distinguished delegates lodged at the City Hotel. Except these few, most of the sixty-two delegates were young men, very much in earnest, plainly dressed, strangers to each other, of no importance in their home towns and quite unknown in New York. They represented only a few newly-formed Anti-Slavery societies.

About forty of the delegates held an informal meeting at Evan Lewis' to make preparations for the Convention. Lewis Tappan, handsome and intellectual in appearance, presided. Whittier was appointed to a committee to get some distinguished Philadelphia citizens to preside at the Convention. After they called on two such men, were curtly refused, and were bowed out with cool politeness, they realized how little inducement the presidency of their group offered to men of importance.

The Convention met the next day, December 4. The presiding officer was Beriah Green of Oneida University, and sitting on either side of him were the two secretaries. One was Lewis Tappan and the other was Whittier, wearing a dark frock-coat with standing collar which, with his dark eyes and black whiskers, gave him somewhat of a military appearance. He had had no experience in this kind of work and did it awkwardly, but Tappan was competent enough for both.

The first business was to organize the American Anti-Slavery Society. While committees were meeting, a paper written by Whittier praising Garrison was read and followed by remarks to the same effect by Tappan and Amos A. Phelps. A constitution was adopted and Arthur Tappan was elected president, although Green continued to preside. Whittier was not an officer of the Society but took active part in the meetings. He seconded a motion of Charles W. Denison "that measures be taken to ascertain how many preachers in the United States are slave-holders" and made a motion which was seconded by Joshua Coffin, "that those literary institutions which have offered their privileges and benefits to our colored brethren deserve the thanks and patronage of the friends of abolition throughout the country."[13]

There was difficulty agreeing on a declaration of principles. Finally a sub-committee was appointed including Garrison, Samuel J. May, and Whittier. They met in the early morning in a small upstairs room in a negro's house, where Garrison read by lamplight a draft which he had prepared.[14] A few verbal changes were made, and the report was read to the Convention and accepted, again with a few verbal changes.

There was nothing in the Declaration of Sentiments that Whittier did not approve. Some of its most important points had appeared in *Justice and Expediency* and in the letters to the *Jeffersonian and Times*: that the Congress had no right to interfere with slavery in the states but should abolish it in the District of Columbia and the territories, and that it was the duty of the people of the free states to bring an end to slavery by peaceful, Constitutional methods such as organizing anti-slavery societies everywhere, using speakers, tracts, periodicals, pulpit, and press, and giving preference to the products of free labor. The Declaration was idealistic and religious in tone: "Our trust for victory is solely in God. We may be personally defeated, but our principles never. Truth, justice, reason, humanity, must and will gloriously triumph."

During the four days of the Convention Whittier found time to call on his cousins, the Wendells. They had moved two years before from Dover, New Hampshire, where Whittier's mother's family had lived, and they and Whittier probably had many friends in common. He talked a good deal, and his cousins found him entertaining, especially when he described his fear of ghosts and his dread of passing a graveyard. He failed to keep a promise to call again to get some Christmas presents that he was to take to his sister Elizabeth (Philadelphia Quakers were less strict than those in New England and observed church holidays) and the Wendells soon learned that he had returned to Haverhill.[15]

V
1834 - 35

Whittier was back on the farm, but he now found nothing picturesque or romantic about it. He and his brother had to do all the farm work; the profits from a farm on such poor land were too small to pay hired help. The women made butter and cheese and earned a little extra cash by binding shoes at three cents a pair — pay not to be despised when the Whittiers received only six cents a pound for pork and goose, seven cents a pound for spareribs, eighteen cents for butter and ten cents for cheese.[1]

He showed no signs of sinking into the narrow life and hopeless poverty of the poorer New England farms. In the evening he escaped from the dulling effect of hard physical labor by writing light popular fiction, the kind that editors would buy. Of five short stories which appeared in the *New York Mirror* three were from French sources and the other two centered about duels. He used some of his earnings to buy good clothes; an observant boy at Amesbury Friends Meeting remembered sixty years later the sensation that Whittier made as he "flashed in" upon the worshippers, tall, black-eyed and black-whiskered, dressed in "correct and Orthodox Quaker fashion of Philadelphia."[2]

Poetry was also an escape, of quite a different sort. With one exception, a lament for a dead girl, the sort of thing that he was always ready to do even for slight acquaintances, all of his poetry in 1834 had to do with slavery. It is unlikely that he was paid for it, and it simply came from the excitement of conviction. His remark a half century later about his poetry in general applies especially to these anti-slavery poems written in the first glow of his zeal for the cause: "I have never thought of myself as a poet in the sense in which we speak of the great poets. I have just said from time to time the things I had to say."[3] Of slavery he had something to say, and the intensity of his desire to say it gave his verses at times a dramatic force, as in "The Hunters of Men" and "The Slave Ships," which owed nothing to conscious poetic art. "Expostulation" was inspired by a speech by Samuel J. May and an address to the people of New England by a committee of which Charles Follen was chairman.[4] Follen had joined the New England Anti-Slavery Society after hearing a letter from Whittier to Samuel E. Sewall, who read it at the annual meeting.

But Whittier was no longer so naive as to suppose that slavery would come to an end without the use of other means than poetry and logical presentation. He wished that he could be free from work on the farm and the writing of pot-boilers. One hundred fifty dollars, he wrote to Elizur Wright, would hire a man to do his work on the farm. His practical sagacity showed itself in his idea of uniting scattered Anti-Slavery sentiment on something definite and workable, such as selecting men to the legislature who would introduce and support resolutions instructing Massachusetts members of Congress to advocate the abolition of slavery in the District of Columbia. He believed that his articles and letters had given him some influence with local politicians who could, in turn, influence politicians on higher levels.[5]

The one hundred fifty dollars was not forthcoming, but Whittier found time to be active in Anti-Slavery organizations. He headed a list of seventeen calling a meeting in the vestry of the Congregational Church to form a Haverhill Anti-Slavery Society and was elected Corresponding Secretary. He was chosen one of the secretaries at the organization meeting at Topsfield of the Essex County Anti-Slavery Society and was put on the committee to draw up a constitution. The secretaries were instructed to prepare an address. Its main points, like the other Anti-Slavery statements of these early years, were relatively gentle: Colonization was not workable; slaves should be freed but not immediately given citizenship; each state had power over slavery within its borders but the Congress had authority in the District of Columbia and the territories. Whittier himself had been emphatic on this point in a letter to the *Gazette* a month earlier. His political principles forbade him to try to abolish slavery by an unconstitutional interference with the slave-holding states. "I would place no new power in the hands of the General Government. It has already as much as is compatible with the rights of the States" — a position which might have given some reassurance even to John C. Calhoun. Most of the work of freeing slaves must be done by the States, in which already there were "multitudes" who opposed slavery.[6] This would not have been said a few years later, when Southern opposition to slavery had been pressured out of existence or driven underground.

On May 27 he was one of four delegates from the Haverhill Anti-Slavery Society to the New England Anti-Slavery Convention in Boston. The convention at Topsfield had evidently not completed the work of organization, and Whittier was one of eleven delegates from Haverhill to an Essex County Anti-Slavery Convention at Salem June 11; a Society was formed at that meeting and Whittier was elected Corresponding Secretary.[7]

Anti-Slavery people at this time had some reasons for rejoicing. The end of the Colonization Society seemed near. The number of Anti-Slavery Societies had increased in a year from three or four to about two hundred. The Underground Railroad was in operation — not far from Haverhill. Whittier's cousin Mary Whittier wrote to him from Salem that a former slave who was working to buy the freedom of his family had arranged for them to escape when his son was to be sold into another part of the country. The family had come to Salem where they were kept hidden in spite of a reward of six hundred dollars for their discovery.[8]

But in spite of what seems to us the mildness of the early Abolitionists, they were encountering, as Whittier had foreseen, opposition that was anything but mild. Charges were made to excite the public against them. It was said that they encouraged negroes to be what a later generation would call "uppity" — to ride up and down Broadway on horseback. They were accused of favoring miscegenation and telling their sons and daughters to marry negroes. Arthur Tappan was said to have divorced his wife and married a negro woman. Whittier replied to some of these charges in a letter to the *Gazette* in which he asserted that Abolitionists without exception opposed the so-called doctrine of amalgamation of races and that one of the strongest reasons for abolishing slavery was to end the process of amalgamation going on in the Slave States. To show that Colonization was not the solution to this particular problem he mentioned that a white man in Liberia had advertised for a negro wife.

A month later he thought it necessary to point out that the sentiments of Abolitionists were not contrary to the Constitution, the Federal Union, and religion, and that the argument that the Abolitionists should keep still because of the "sensitiveness of the public mind" and the "state of public feeling" was a weak one. Awareness of the state of public feeling had not silenced Jesus, Stephen, Paul, or Martin Luther.[9]

As would be expected, mobs soon went into action. On the Fourth of July in New York a large audience was at an Anti-Slavery meeting at Chatham Street Chapel. Whittier's hymn which had been written the year before for a Sabbath School Celebration in Haverhill —

On Thou! whose spirit went before
Our fathers in their weary way ——

was to be sung by a choir. The hymn was not sung. The orator of the day was drowned out by shouting and derisive cheers from a group of young men in the rear seats, and the meeting came to an abrupt end.[10] George Thompson's arrival in the United States to speak against slavery was an excuse for more excitement. He was attacked in the press as a foreign emissary. There was still anti-British sentiment left over from the War of 1812: there had been no rapid succession of other wars, cold or otherwise, as in a more sophisticated era, to distract attention from an enemy of two decades ago. There was a mob when he spoke at Lowell December 1; violence was coming closer to Haverhill.

When the fall elections came, Whittier put into practice his suggestion to Wright in February, that Anti-Slavery people try to elect men to the State Legislature who would favor resolutions instructing the Massachusetts members of Congress to vote for the abolition of slavery in the District of Columbia. He got himself elected. But before the election he tried to get Caleb Cushing, again a candidate for Congress, to commit himself on that question. He called at Cushing's house in Newburyport October 25 on his way back from a meeting of the Essex County Anti-Slavery Society at Danvers and not finding him at home left a note telling him that the Society had voted unanimously to write to candidates for Congress requesting a statement of their views on slavery and what Congress should do about it. He added a warning: if Cushing did not give a definite answer in favor of the abolition of slavery in the District of Columbia, he would lose the votes of the Anti-Slavery people. A week later, having received no reply, he tried another approach. He wrote that he had dissuaded some of Cushing's friends from asking his sentiments on that question. He had assured them that, although Cushing was friendly to Colonization and opposed to immediate Emancipation, he would work for the abolition of slavery in the District of Columbia. At this time "any formal interrogation of candidates in reference to matters of this kind is certainly to be deprecated" — just the opposite of what he had written the week before. But, he wrote, the question could not be avoided much longer. If he had correctly reported Cushing's views, he would like a letter so stating; if he had not, he asked that Cushing make no reply to this part of the letter.

Cushing's reply was that slavery and the slave trade in the District of Columbia were indefensible but that he would be "unwilling to enter Congress pledged to institute a legislative measure, either upon this or any subject of national policy and legislation, unless it were a point directly or publicly put in issue by my own constituents."[11]

In the meantime Whittier had been nominated by the Haverhill Whigs as one of their four candidates for Representative in the State Legislature (General Court). One of the four was elected at the first trial, and the other three, including Whittier, at the second election the next day. However strongly Anti-Slavery purposes entered into his decision, he had still done what he had told Garrison a year earlier he felt strongly tempted to do — "plunge again into the seven times heated furnace of modern politics." His election shows that his Anti-Slavery activities had not ended his chances of a political career. Perhaps he had not really supposed that they would; during the previous winter he had studied Constitutional Law and Political Economy.[12]

The other Representatives from Haverhill were Jacob Howe, a deputy sheriff; Jesse Smith, a farmer; and Leonard Whittier, a shoe manufacturer. Whittier does not seem to have had any close association with them. He lived in rooms connecting with those of Robert Rantoul of Gloucester at 24 Franklin Street in the Tontine Crescent at the Bulfinch Oval, which Rantoul's son described as a "beautiful oasis in the heart of Boston." The pay would not permit luxurious living; it was two dollars for each day that a Representative was present, and Whittier's poor health must have kept him from some of the ninety-two days the Legislature was in session. He was also allowed eight dollars for travel expenses to each of the two sessions.[13]

The Boston of 1835 was beginning to change from the city as Whittier had seen it when he edited the *Manufacturer* six years earlier. In fact, it could have called itself "The New Boston." A Court House was in process of construction, and blocks of buildings were soon to be built.

The House of Representatives was a large and undignified body of six hundred fifteen, one fourth of whom were absent when the Editor of the *Essex Gazette* dropped in for a visit in early September. A reporter described it in the *Northampton Courier* as "the most unwieldy and indecorous body of legislators . . . which can be found grouped together in the universe." The seats — wooden benches — rose in a semi-circle in front of the Speaker's chair. The Legislators, many of them with their hats on, sat in various positions, busying themselves with all sorts of activities. Business was transacted "in the midst of the most deafening hum of conversation, or the practical jokes with which legislators always seem to be infected."

The winter session began January 7. Whittier's two standing committee appointments were Engrossed Bills and License Laws. His first motion was a matter of conviction in which Quakers were a century in advance of other Americans. He moved that in the resolutions regarding the death of one of the House members the part providing that Representatives should wear crepe on the left arm for thirty days should be stricken out.[14] But before that, Whittier had spoken on a really important piece of business that had come before the House, one that was to reappear one hundred twenty-seven years later with acrimonious debate. On January 15 a petition was presented by Benedict Fenwick and others asking for indemnification for the destruction of an Ursuline convent in Charlestown by a mob which met with little interference by the town officials.

The excitement that led to the destruction of the convent had resulted from rumors about a book being written by a girl who had run away from the convent. These rumors startled even calm and thoughtful people, who, when the book was published, found nothing in it to get excited about.[15] After the burning of the convent the feeling in Massachusetts, even in rural districts where fear of the Catholic Church was especially strong, was horror and shame that such a thing could happen.[16] A bill "more effectually to suppress riots and to indemnify persons for injuries done thereby" had easy going — that was all in the future — but it was another matter to vote to pay an indemnity for what had already happened. It was not at all certain that horror and shame would mean approval by the voters of giving away public money. Furthermore, the Legislature was economy-minded: later in the year it voted 457 - 10 to instruct a committee to find what alterations and reductions could be made in salaries of State officials. Whittier spoke in the House — and he did not enjoy public speaking — denouncing the action of the mob and urging that an indemnity be paid, but he was in the minority. The House voted 415 - 67 to remove from the Resolves concerning the destruction of the convent the one that authorized a "gratuity" — the clause made clear that the petitioners could not claim an indemnity as a matter of right. Whittier said later that he was censured by some of his "Protestant brethren" for his activities on this question.[17]

Whittier had the majority with him, however, on another matter of conviction. A bill to incorporate the Worcester House Company was voted down 279 - 153 after an amendment had been rejected providing that the hotel should not sell liquor.

Whittier was of course favorable toward various attempts to abolish the death penalty. He moved February 25 to print fifteen hundred copies of a committee report made by his friend Robert Rantoul recommending its abolition.[18] His motion was defeated, but the House voted to print one thousand copies. Twice during the year he presented petitions favoring its abolition,[19] and he voted in favor of a motion by Rantoul, which passed, replacing the death penalty for treason against the Commonwealth by life imprisonment.

There are many tiresome hours in all legislative bodies. For Whittier there could have been little interest in the various motions and amendments on the Warren Bridge question. The Warren Bridge was a toll bridge, and there was public demand that all bridges leading into Boston should be free. Whittier's attitude was a business-like one: tolls should be used only for the repair and maintenance of the bridge, and should not be used for purchasing and making free all bridges and roads leading to Boston.

If Whittier hoped to aid the cause of Abolition in the House of Representatives, he was disappointed. There is no record of any reference to the slavery question. But he found time for Anti-Slavery activities.

He knew that the public must be stirred into attention. When Walter Henry Channing criticized the agitation tactics of Abolitionists, Whittier asked, "Why deprecate agitation, lawful, peaceful, Christian agitation? Under God has it not broken the sleep and disturbed the callous indifference of our whole country?"[20] And so he continued to work with those who were keeping the subject alive.

At a meeting of the New England Anti-Slavery Society January 8 Whittier, present by special invitation of the Board of Managers, was appointed to a committee to consider the conditions and prospects of the Society and of the *Liberator*. At a special meeting of the Board of Managers January 27 he was appointed to a committee to confer with Lydia Maria Child about a series of tracts that she wished the Society to publish entitled "Authentic Anecdotes of American Slavery" and to supervise the printing. On May 1 the Board of Managers elected him a delegate to the second annual meeting of the American Anti-Slavery Society, and later in the month he was on the Committee of Publication of the New England Anti-Slavery Convention.[21]

He was still active in the Haverhill Anti-Slavery Society and in July was elected Corresponding Secretary. He was also active in the Essex County Anti-Slavery Society and was appointed by the Board of Managers to prepare an address to the voters of the County. The address pointed out that the District of Columbia was the principal slave market of the nation and that the slave prison in Washington which money from Massachusetts had helped to pay for was used by traders to keep slaves awaiting sale.

Whittier wrote to his sister Elizabeth on April 12 that George Thompson had visited him the day before and had lectured in the afternoon to five hundred women. Sixty new members had joined the Boston Ladies Anti-Slavery Society. There was no disorder at this Boston meeting nor was there any when Thompson and Samuel May spoke at the First Anniversary Meeting of the Essex County Anti-Slavery Society two months later. But there was trouble when Thompson spoke at Lynn in August. It was thought that he had better not be in the vicinity of Lynn for a few days and should keep out of sight. He went to the Whittiers' and stayed there until he and Whittier left on Sunday August 30 to drive to Plymouth, New Hampshire, and visit Nathaniel P. Rogers. On the way they stayed over night at the home of Rogers' brother-in-law, George Kent, in Concord, arriving at Rogers' home at sunset on Monday. Whittier was always sensitive to the beauty of the outdoor world, and he noticed the way the setting sun lighted up the river, valley, and mountain. They found Rogers a delightful host — appreciative of art and nature, cordial, witty, a man that would have been at home in Ben Jonson's club at the Mermaid Tavern. Thompson thought that Rogers was the most brilliant man that he had seen in America.[22]

They stayed in Plymouth until Wednesday, and Thompson gave three lectures there without any disorder. Rural communities were less hostile to Abolition than cities and the larger towns. They drove back to Concord, where they found, to Whittier's surprise, that they were both listed to speak on Anti-Slavery.[23] But the meeting could not be held. The Selectmen had closed the Town Hall.

A crowd had collected, swearing vengeance against Abolitionists. When Whittier and two others passed by, they heard a shout of "To George Kent's and the wine in his cellar." Whittier and his companions turned back to warn Kent, but the crowd followed, insisting that Whittier, in spite of his Quaker coat, was Thompson. Then the action began, first with what Whittier called "a shower of harmless curses" and then "another equally harmless shower of stones" — harmless because the mob was too drunk to throw straight. A rotten egg, however, was better aimed, and Whittier's coat was stained beyond cleaning. Whittier and the others then took refuge in the house of William A. Kent,[24] who with the help of the Unitarian minister was able to persuade the mob that Thompson was not in the house. The mob moved up the street to George Kent's house where they shouted and clamored for the blood of Whittier and Thompson and threw a few stones. Kent was not at home, and his wife stood in the doorway and bravely and skillfully appealed to the mob. To the husbands and fathers she talked of the respect due to the privacy of a home, and she asked the wives and mothers for consideration for her sick sister.[25] Thompson was not in the house and did not return until the crowd had gone to burn his effigy, to parade, and to fire off cannon until just before sunrise. Whittier, Thompson, and a minister from Dunbarton left quietly in the early morning.

While the excitement was at its height, a young woman exclaimed, "Oh, I will die with you, Mr. Whittier!" Whittier, whose common sense never deserted him and who did not enjoy histrionics, replied, "And whatever good will that do us?" He does not seem to have worried about physical danger but had a dread of being tarred and feathered and laughed at — and the mob had the tar and feathers ready.[26]

Abolitionists have been accused of lack of skill in public relations in having Thompson represent them. Whittier did not believe that the disturbance in Concord was caused by hostility to Thompson but had been stirred up for political effect — to give the impression that the "hardworking democracy of New Hampshire was hand and glove with the slave-holding democracy of Virginia and the Carolinas" and that the fanatics had been put down by the friends of Van Buren. Whittier's belief that hostility to Thompson was not the cause of the trouble is supported by what had happened in Haverhill while Whittier and Thompson were on their way to Plymouth.

Samuel May, correctly described by Thomas Wentworth Higginson as "moderate, disarming, courteous", preached in the morning at the First Parish Meetinghouse and expected to speak there on slavery in the evening. The First Parish had become Unitarian, but the theological liberalism of Unitarians was in this instance tempered by social conservatism, and the use of the meetinghouse was refused. The Christian Union Chapel was found to be available; the newly formed Christian denomination was usually friendly toward Abolition, partly because its members were mainly poor or middle-class who often felt socially unacceptable in Congregational churches and were less opposed to anything that might disturb the existing order.

The Chapel auditorium was on the second floor and was reached by two flights of outside stairs. Elizabeth Whittier was in the audience, and when May was speaking in what she called "his peculiarly winning tones", stones were thrown at the window. He was eager to continue his address, but one of the other clergymen thought it useless to continue and the audience left. More had happened outside than Elizabeth recorded or perhaps knew.

A crowd had gathered to tear away the stairs leading to the auditorium and fire a cannon which they had dragged near the church, expecting that the audience would panic and rush out the doors without noticing that the stairs were gone. But before they could carry out this plan, Rufus Slocomb, known as "Old Sloc", rushed into the crowd. He had once been a tavern keeper and now operated a freight service to Boston: it is recorded that one day he had full loads for forty-one horses and eight oxen. A man running a business of that sort was not likely to be quiet or gentle, and Old Sloc had a loud voice and a considerable command of profanity. He used both, and the crowd lost its nerve. The audience came safely down the stairs, and May walked calmly through the crowd, escorted by Elizabeth Whittier and Harriet Minot.[27]

Whittier and Thompson returned to Haverhill where Thompson stayed for a week and spoke at a Sunday evening meeting at the schoolhouse.[28] Whittier returned to Boston and to the sessions of the House of Representatives. On October 21 he hurried down to Washington Street with other Legislators when he heard that a riot was going on at the headquarters of the Female Anti-Slavery Society, where Elizabeth was attending a meeting at which Garrison was to speak. At the moment of Whittier's arrival at the scene Garrison was being rescued from a mob which had dragged him through the streets with a rope around his body — not round his neck, as has generally been reported.[29] Whittier saw Garrison taken in a carriage to Leverett Street Jail and visited him there with Samuel J. May. Garrison invited him to share the safe lodgings that the state had provided.[30]

It was in the same month that Abolitionists in Boston had a foretaste of what would happen in Philadelphia three years later. Whittier, Garrison, May, and Isaac Knapp were at a special meeting of the Board of Managers of the New England Anti-Slavery Society when a cry of "fire!" drove them out of the office. At another special meeting a committee was appointed to prosecute the people who had vandalized the Society's offices.[31]

George Thompson was at the Whittiers' again in November. The Whittiers must have enjoyed his visits. Sarah Kimber, who spent four days with his family a few years later, said that she "could sing his praises for a week" and mentioned his "playful wit", his "delightful readings of Hemans and Byron till the witching hour of night" and the "unfailing interest of his conversation." Sarah L. Forten described him as "a most delightful and companionable person."[32] He may have had a good effect on Whittier's personality. Whittier's letters were soon to have a light touch which suggests the charm that many people found in him and that made him very different from the school-book stereotype.

On November 5 he was nominated for reelection to the Legislature and declined on the same day.[33] The reason usually given is his poor health. He surely had numerous illnesses which cannot be diagnosed from his references to them, but whatever they were, it is hard to understand why they should keep him from attending sessions of the Legislature. His frequent attendance at conventions and meetings, with the accompanying hotel meals and travel by stagecoach over rough roads or by open sleigh, would seem equally hazardous to anyone in delicate health. There was probably another reason for his declining the nomination: with his already developed political astuteness he could foresee that all the Whig candidates in Haverhill would be defeated in the election.

In national politics he was supporting Webster for the Presidency. Publicly, he prophesied success; privately, he said that the cause was hopeless. In the August 29 *Gazette* he described Webster as the candidate "not only of Massachusetts but of the tried and true friends of Constitutional Liberty all over the country;" if the citizens of Massachusetts were true to him and to the best interests of the country, he would be borne onward by the popular feeling of New England and the West beyond any of his competitors. But only five days earlier he had written to Jonathan Law, "As for political matters, the less said the better. It's all over with us. Webster will get the vote of Massachusetts and Van Buren all the rest of New England."[34]

At the age of twenty-eight, Whittier was already taken seriously by politicians, who wrote long letters to him. In December two Congressmen, Caleb Cushing and Stephen C. Phillips, wrote on the same topic, the petitions pouring in for the abolition of slavery in the District of Columbia.[35] They both urged one point: that petitions sent to Congress should, in Phillips' words, "do justice to the object in view, breathing a spirit of pure benevolence, and exhibiting the strongest facts and clearest arguments in a form of language manifestly unexceptionable," or as Cushing expressed it, "I beg of you, if any petitions are to be sent to me, that they may be brief *business papers*, free of the bitter language good Mr. G. cultivates in the *Liberator*."

Before he received Cushing's letter Whittier wrote to him that he had heard of the resolution in the House to reject all petitions for the abolition of slavery in the District. Whittier's chief concern was that the false charges against the Abolitionists should be answered by those who knew that they were not "incendiaries," "madmen", or "ignorant fanatics", that, in Whittier's words, "we are neither physically nor morally monsters — that we neither sport horns nor divide the hoof." He knew that he and Cushing differed on the ways of Abolitionists but he was confident that Cushing would be fair to them as constituents of his and reminded him that some of his best supporters in the last election had been Abolitionists.[36]

As was true throughout Whittier's entire life, whatever his activities or prominence in a wider field, he never felt that he was too important to take part in local affairs. In March 1835 he was elected one of the seven members of the General School Committee of Haverhill. The duties were not arduous. The Committee had an appropriation of two thousand dollars, which it allocated to the eleven districts of the town. In January, as a member of this Committee, Whittier signed a statement recommending Benjamin Greenleaf's *National Arithmetic*, which later went through numerous editions and was a standard textbook for many years.

After the adjournment of the Legislature Whittier returned to Haverhill and to work on the farm. He was happy to report to Thayer, now in Philadelphia, that Anti-Slavery was making good progress but not so happy to report that Haverhill was pro-Jackson and that Massachusetts was almost "Van Burenised."[37]

If Whittier looked back over the busy months of 1835 he must have wondered if he had accomplished anything worth doing. But the hours in the Legislature, many of them tiresome, had given him an intimate acquaintance with the way such bodies function, without which he could not have been the successful lobbyist that he soon became. His other activities, varied and not always successful, had at least increased his background of human experience and had brought him close to people in their strengths and weaknesses. All this would be useful to a poet who would never be far from the common man. But there had been little time or inclination for writing poetry.

Of the eight poems of the year, the four that had no connection with Anti-Slavery were derived from or were in addition to something written earlier.

"The Demon of the Study" had the same theme as the editorial "The Haunted Man" in the *Essex Gazette* July 3, 1830, and some of the details were the same.

"The Prisoner for Debt" was the third treatment of the topic, the first being Whittier's editorial in the *American Manufacturer* July 16, 1829, and the second Garrison's "The Poor Debtor" which Whittier printed in the *New England Weekly Review* April 25, 1831. "God made the old man poor" is one of Whittier's best-known lines.

"An Evening in Burmah" was the conclusion of "The Portrait" in the *Essex Gazette* in 1832, now entitled "The Missionary", a poem suggested by a passage in a letter of Henry Martyn. Martyn's work as a missionary in India, where he went in 1805 as a chaplain of the East India Company, attracted a good deal of attention. His life by John Sargent, including many quotations from his letters and journal, was printed by the American Tract Society.

"Mogg Megone", which had been started five years earlier, was put into form for publication in the *New England Magazine* in March and April. Like "Metacom", also of 1830, it dealt with an American Indian. It was largely fiction, based on Colonial journals and histories, especially Folsom's *History of Saco and Biddeford*, a copy of which was given to Whittier by Mary Emerson Smith's grandfather.[38] The first two parts only appeared at this time, with sixty lines of conclusion in place of Part III. In the preface to the edition published separately the next year Whittier said that he had aimed at realism (something that he had not done in his "The Pawnee Brave" in

1827) and that by following the "rough but natural delineations of Church, Mayhew, and Roger Williams" he had necessarily discarded much of the romance which poets and novelists had thrown around the illfated red men. But while the Indian in "Mogg Megone" is not a noble, picturesque child of nature, the incidents are not lacking in blood, love, vengeance, and remorse.

Whittier evidently approved of "Mogg Megone" as late as 1841 when he sent his last copy to Rufus Griswold, who was preparing *Poets and Poetry of America*. Later he thought otherwise. To someone who had evidently criticized the poem, he wrote in 1877, "I quite agree with thee as regards 'Mogg Megone.' But the mischief is after you have made a thing, it persists in living and following you like Mrs. Shelley's Frankenstein." A few years later he wrote to Francis H. Underwood, who was preparing a biography, "Pitch into Mogg Megone. That 'big Injun,' strutting around in Walter Scott's plaid, has no friends and deserves none,"[39] and included the same comment in the Introductory Note in the Riverside Edition.

In 1882 John Langdon Bonython of South Australia wrote to Whittier that he doubted that the real John Bonython was as described in "Mogg Megone." Whittier replied that the poem was written in his boyish days when he knew little of colonial history or anything else and had been included in his collected writings against his wishes. He continued, "I think thou art right in regard to John Bonython. I knew nothing of him save what I found in the 'History of Saco', and supposed the name and race extinct, as I never heard of the name on this side of the water. If possible, I shall have the entire poem omitted; if not, I will cheerfully add the note suggested. I thank thee for calling my attention to this matter, as I would not knowingly do injustice to any one, living or dead."[40] Whittier evidently intended to keep this promise. In a copy of Whittier's poems formerly owned by Fred Brown there is a manuscript note which never appeared in print pasted over the introduction to "Mogg Megone." "I could wish that 'Mogg Megone' might be omitted from my collected poems. It is not valuable as poetry, and the character of Bonython is overdrawn. A more careful examination of our colonial history satisfies me that he could not have been the wretch I represented him. Like too many of the colonists, he was doubtless not very scrupulous as to the ways and means of obtaining wealth and lands."

Of the four Anti-Slavery poems of the year, "The Yankee Girl" has been the most popular. Its appeal is sentimental — the humble but beautiful Northern girl who rejects the honorable proposal of the rich Southern slave-owner and tells him that she would rather be one of his slaves than his wife in a beautiful home in which could be heard

The crack of the whip and the footsteps of fear.

It was set to music by George W. Clark and printed in his *Free Soil Minstrel*,

1848, and in 1903, forty years after the abolition of slavery, it inspired a "Tone picture for the piano" by Charles Edwin Veon.

"Stanzas for the Times" (the first of four poems with this title) was a vigorous defense of freedom of speech on the subject of slavery. It resulted from a meeting in Faneuil Hall — a somewhat unsuitable place for such a meeting — in which it was argued that Anti-Slavery agitation would upset the course of business. Whittier's original introductory note contained the following: "In view of the outrages which a careful observation of the times had enabled him to forsee must spring from the false witness borne against the abolitionists by the speakers at that meeting, well might Garrison say to them, 'Sir, I consider a man who fires a city, guiltless in comparison!' " In Whittier's mature and mellower years he evidently did not care to quote such an extreme statement.

Another poem in 1835 was written in a white heat of enthusiasm that made him overlook the fact that he was commending a Jackson man. The historian George Bancroft, a convinced democrat and liberal, had entered politics as a Democrat and had started writing his histories with a strong pro-Jackson bias. However, his "Worcester Democratic Address" inspired Whittier to write the exclamatory stanzas of "To George Bancroft" in which he urged Bancroft to continue to speak for Truth and Right — for fair treatment of Labor, against imprisonment for debt, and against slavery.

George Thompson (1804-1878).   William Lloyd Garrison (1805-1879).

Garrison being mobbed by anti-abolitionists in Boston in 1835.

VI
1835 - 36

The winter of 1835-36 was Whittier's last winter among the scenes later made famous by "Snow-Bound." Except for a few days in February when he was confined to the house by what he called "palpitation of the heart" he was well enough to do the necessary farm work, feeding the cattle, teaming, and sledding. He had plenty of spare time, which he spent writing letters about Anti-Slavery and politics. He twice declined an offer from Abijah Thayer to join him in a newspaper project in Philadelphia. [1]

He was delighted when one hundred twenty legal voters in Haverhill signed a petition for the abolition of slavery in the District of Columbia and sent it to Caleb Cushing, who he thought would as soon see the "Old Enemy himself" as their petition. More petitions would be sent to Congress in 1837: "We'll haunt 'em, and torment 'em, till they behave better." The Whigs were "doneup" as a result of their bad treatment of the Anti-Slavery people. He was disappointed in the Philadelphia Quakers, however, who were supporting a military man, William Henry Harrison, the "Hero of Tippecanoe."

He wrote to Cushing February 10, discussing the question of slavery in the District of Columbia, commending a recent speech by Cushing, and counselling that Northern Whigs should not give their approval to the use of the Abolition question by Southern Whigs against Van Buren: it would force Van Buren to take pro-slavery ground. He soon wrote two more letters to Cushing, one thanking him for his defense of John Quincy Adams and the right of petition, and another letter a few days later to thank him for his account of political affairs in Washington. [2]

A letter to Edward Everett appeared in the *Essex Gazette* February 13, attacking the part of Everett's inaugural message referring to slavery which urged that "the patriotism of all classes of citizens is invoked to abstain from a discussion of the subject." The letter was written in a tone which Whittier later regretted. He could say in 1865, "I am saddened by the reflection that through the very intensity of my convictions I have done injustice to the motives of those with whom I differed." [3] But in 1836 it was not so easy to be tolerant, and any suggestion that slavery should not be openly talked about seemed to him "far fitter for the banks of the Bosphorus and the Nova than for those of the Connecticut and the Merrimack." Everett's "servile advice to obedience" he supposed was called forth by the Message of Governor McDuffie of South Carolina, which described "the patriarchal institution of slavery" as "the corner-stone of our republican edifice" and implied that the working people of the North must be "held in check by an aristocracy or reduced to the condition of slaves."

Later in the year, when he was again editing the *Gazette*, he printed "To Governor McDuffie", a vigorous piece of political satire which he did not include in the later editions of his poems. Why shouldn't Governor McDuffie regard himself as a patriarch like Isaac, Abraham, and Moses? the poem asked. He ruled a household of slaves, as they did, and perhaps had a negro concubine, a "swarthy counter-part" of Abraham's Hagar. But he needn't think that the fishermen of Marblehead, the shoe makers of Lynn, or the textile workers of Lowell would accept slavery:

> Our rocky hills and iron strand
> Are free, and shall be free forever.

It is rather surprising that Whittier, now openly devoted to Anti-Slavery, was made editor of the *Gazette*, which was political and not Abolitionist. The explanation may be that no one else with any experience in journalism would take the position for the low and uncertain pay — at the end of six months he had received only ninety dollars.[4] Erastus Brooks, who had been owner and editor of the paper, wished to get it off his hands and announced April 30 that Whittier would assume the entire editorial management while Brooks remained as proprietor until July 1, when the whole establishment would pass into the hands of Jacob Caldwell, Whittier's brother-in-law. Neither Whittier's name nor Brooks' appeared on the first page or the editorial page until Whittier's name appeared July 23. The probable explanation is that the printers continued to use the same page forms, and Whittier was too busy selling the farm, stock, and equipment and buying a house in Amesbury to notice. His brother was to be married in August to a non-Quaker, and could no longer be a member of a Friends Meeting.[5] For that reason, if for no other, he and his bride would not have enjoyed living with the others on the farm, and it would not have been practical for Whittier to carry on the farm alone. The farm was sold in April for three thousand dollars, and a small story-and-a-half house in Amesbury was bought by Whittier and his mother a month later for twelve hundred dollars.

If Whittier was to write "Snow-Bound," it was time for him to leave the farm, before boyhood memories and emotions were buried under adult experiences.

The choice of Amesbury proved to be a fortunate one. There was a flourishing Friends Meeting in Amesbury, and while Whittier was far from being a narrow sectarian, his religious faith and practice, vital parts of his life, had their roots in the way of the Friends. His love of natural beauty, not weakening even in old age — he could not imagine a hereafter without beauty — could be more satisfied in Amesbury than in most New England towns not in the hill country. When the Whittiers went to live there it would have been hard to find a spot in the town that did not have a view of a hill, a lake, a pond, or a river. The much-travelled Bayard Taylor gave it as his opinion that the view from Powow Hill possessed the most quiet beauty of any scene that he knew in the world.[6]

Whittier would not find a group of literary friends such as Longfellow found in Cambridge, but neither would he find anything that would restrict him to one segment of the community or chill him into restraint or silence. Cambridge, William Dean Howells testified, had reservations concerning Whittier: "I cannot put them into words which would not oversay them, but they were akin to those she might have refined upon in regard to Mrs. Stowe."

People in nearby more conservative towns often remarked that Amesbury people were impulsive, easily elated and easily depressed, quickly angered and quickly moved to deeds of kindness and generosity, responsive to the new and tiring quickly of the old. An Amesbury man was quoted in a court case in 1674 as saying that Amesbury men would live well as long as they had any land. Visitors noticed a friendliness and informality not always found in New England. Some of the Whittiers' Philadelphia friends who visited them in Amesbury were amused when the conductor on the train from Amesbury to Newburyport asked them if they had a good time.[7]

Social levels were less clearly defined than in most New England towns with over one hundred fifty years of history. After living fifteen years in Amesbury Whittier was happy to say, "We have no privileged class, no petty village aristocracy, proud of its own worthlessness and despising the more useful and, in all practical matters, more intelligent members of society." "The Squire's daughter danced with the milkman," according to a local historian. "Your butcher was also your church deacon and town meeting moderator."[8] When President Monroe visited the new textile mills and asked one of the superintendents who the working people were, the superintendent replied that his daughter was one of them.

Amesbury had a friendly feeling toward reform movements. A temperance society had been formed in 1829. An Anti-Slavery Society held monthly "Concerts of Prayer for the Slaves" alternately in the Baptist and Congregational vestries, and the town came to be known as a "hotbed of Abolition".[9] When the Whittiers were getting settled in their new home, Henry B. Stanton gave several lectures on Abolition. According to the local paper, "There was not the shadow of a mob or the least indication on the part of our citizens that they would like to see their fellow-citizens insulted because they chose to listen to abolition doctrines."[10] Several years later, when Wendell Phillips came to speak on Abolition, he was told that there would be no danger of a mob as long as Nahum Osgood was in the hall. He was large and muscular, and according to local legend stood at the head of the stairs when Anti-Slavery meetings were held in Franklin Hall, ready to throw anyone down stairs who threatened to make trouble, and sure of public approval in so doing.

The house that the Whittiers bought was in what was known as the Mills Village, consisting of the part of Amesbury near the falls on the Powow River and the part of Salisbury on the other side of the river. The Village had sprung up when mills were built to use the water power at the falls, and small local businesses were now being merged into combinations for textile manufacturing with outside capital. Large mills had been built, architecturally impressive, of late Georgian design. In 1836 flannel and satinet manufacture totalled $425,000.[11] New houses were being built and old houses were being moved from other parts of the town. A savings bank had been opened in 1828, and a national bank was about ready to open. Ox carts, however, still came to a market place with loads of firewood and farm wagons with produce to sell. A book store and circulating library had been opened in 1832, the manager of one of the mill companies maintained a library for his employees, and before the Public Library was opened twenty years later there were several subscription libraries, and there were two lyceums.

The Whittiers' house was one of the new houses not far from the mills.[12] It has had so many additions that there is no outward trace of the cottage as it was in 1836. When the Whittiers bought it there were four rooms on the first floor: parlor, kitchen with fireplace and brick oven, and two small bedrooms. Whittier's room was heated only from the kitchen; his mother's, by a stove connected with the central chimney. His sister Elizabeth slept in a low, partly finished room in the attic. A room was added at the rear for Aunt Mercy.

Diagonally across Friend Street was the Friends Meeting House, and directly across was an open field extending to the Powow River above the falls, and beyond the river was Powow Hill. The women of the family did the washing on the bank of the river.

During the buying and selling and moving, Whittier was vigorously promoting Abolition through the *Essex Gazette*. In a signed address "To the Public" in his first issue, May 7, he announced: "I regard the present struggle as the closing one between Liberty and Slavery in this republic." A week later he pointed out how profitable slavery had been, but there was now competition from other countries and slavery might prove a curse to the planters; in Eastern Virginia, where the soil was exhausted, the plantations were largely devoted to slave breeding. In another column he announced that he would send copies of petitions for the abolition of slavery in the District of Columbia to men in nearby towns who were favorable to that object. The next week he announced the New England Anti-Slavery convention to be held in Boston on May 24 and appealed to his readers: "We must come forward now, and reassert the doctrines of our Bill of Rights, and speak out in earnest tones in behalf of hunted and perilled Liberty." He attended the convention and reported on it the next week.

On May 31 the Essex County Anti-Slavery Society encountered difficulties in holding a meeting in Newburyport, and Whittier's indignation against what he thought to be the upper class in that city shows that it was fortunate that he was to live in a town that could not be accused of having an upper class. The committee making the arrangements had been given permission to use the Prospect Street meetinghouse, but the night before the meeting the Church Society (the business body of the church) voted otherwise. The meeting was held in the open air in front of Charles Butler's house on what is now Brown Square. Everything was harmonious and orderly, but Whittier was indignant. "As for Newburyport we shall remember it. We shall place it, as the Sandwich Islanders say, under *Taboo* until it comes to its senses. Nature has placed a bar in its harbor; let its self complacent aristocracy see to it that they do not place a more effectual one against the approach of their country friends, upon land."[13] This was a rather cruel gibe: the bar at the mouth of the Merrimac was endangering the city's foreign trade and shipbuilding, which were the foundation of its prosperity. But the people who voted against the use of the meetinghouse were not aristocrats. The wealthy ship-owners and the more prosperous among the shipbuilders and captains attended the First Church (Pleasant Street) or the First Presbyterian Church (Federal Street). Furthermore, about half the members of the Prospect Street Church had left when the aged minister, the eccentric Charles Milton, pastor since 1794, became physically and mentally infirm and refused to have a colleague to assist him.[14]

In the July 17 issue Whittier told his readers of a much more important matter, an evidence of the lengths to which the defenders of slavery would go to prevent discussion of the subject. Reuben Crandall, a physician, had just been released from the city prison in Washington where he had been held for eight months, part of the time in a cell with a maniac who had attempted to assassinate the President, on the charge of lending a copy of Whittier's *Justice and Expediency* to another physician.

Whittier wished it known that he was a non-resistant, and his comment on the escape of two slave women from the Court House in Boston foretold his attitude toward the Fugitive Slave Law: "For ourselves we deprecate any attempt of forcible resistance to the laws. As a member of the society of Friends we cannot indeed carry into execution the law which requires us to return the fugitive to the pretended master, for we believe that in so doing we should commit a great crime; but we are willing to be held accountable for our refusal to do so, before the courts of justice."

If Jacob Caldwell thought that his brother-in-law would improve the literary quality of the *Gazette* by writing poems for it, he must have been disappointed. Poetry now came to Whittier only from an Abolition impulse. During his editorship, from May 7 to December 17, he contributed only six poems, five of which were about Abolition or an Abolitionist, and the sixth, "Hymn. From the French of Lamartine," was prefaced by a note that Lamartine had recently distinguished himself by a speech in the Chamber of Deputies on the emancipation of slaves in the French colonies. The best of the lot was "A Summons," in which Whittier made skillful use of a stanza with a final iambic dimeter line. One stanza is so good that one can only lament that Whittier did not give more attention to developing the poetic techniques which he used here, consciously or not:

> From her rough coast, and isles, which hungry Ocean
> Gnaws with his surges; from the fisher's skiff,
> With white sail surging to the billows' motion
> Round rock and cliff.

"Song of the Free," in dactylic dimeter with alternate lines catalectic, seems an echo of Scott's "Gathering Song of Donald the Black."

The *Gazette* was preponderantly Anti-Slavery, but other causes were mentioned, including temperance, and in "Judge Edwards' Decision" July 23, the rights of the working man: "But to brand laborers as criminals for peaceably requiring an increase of their wages, we hold to be an outrage on the rights of man, and a disgrace to a community professing to be free."

Whittier had not lost his interest in contemporary literature: in the August 13 issue he printed Hawthorne's "Mr. Higginbotham's Catastrophe," without naming the author, with the comment that it was "one of the most amusing of its kind, and altogether natural, and graphic in its description."

But the *Gazette* had too much Abolition and too little Whig politics, and by August Dr. Jeremiah Spofford of East Bradford, active in Whig politics, had bought a half interest and was planning to take over the political part of the paper. Whittier wrote to him August 27 that he could not consistently support Governor Edward Everett for reelection and added some sound advice, that the *Gazette* should not become all-out Whig until after the election lest if the Whigs lost, the paper go down with them, and that Spofford should not take over as political editor until that time.[15] His advice was not taken; an announcement in the September 10 issue informed the subscribers that Dr. Spofford would be in charge of the political department of the paper, and a week later it was announced that Whittier would be in charge of the literary and miscellaneous department.

The columns of the *Gazette* were not closed to Anti-Slavery items. There was a notice October 22 that petitions for the Abolition of Slavery in the District of Columbia should be sent to Whittier or to William B. Dodge of Salem. But the divided editorial responsibility did not work out well, and by December 1 Whittier was convinced that there were people in Haverhill who would have nothing to do with the *Gazette* as long as he was connected with it and that Caldwell was disappointed and thought that he had acted unwisely; under these circumstances he could do nothing but resign. He assured Spofford that only a few Anti-Slavery people would drop the paper, since they believed Spofford to be a friend of "Free Discussion." (Was this a hint to Spofford that he had better be that?) He wanted it understood that he and Spofford were on good terms and he wanted nothing said publicly about his being forced to resign. He thought that the *Gazette* was making a profit of between five and six hundred dollars a year.[16] (If he was right, his brother-in-law had certainly treated him in a niggardly fashion.)

During the year he had been busy as usual in Anti-Slavery Societies, serving as Corresponding Secretary of the Essex County Society and Secretary of the Haverhill society even after moving to Amesbury. His services were appreciated at least by the women of Haverhill; the Ladies' Anti-Slavery Society paid fifteen dollars to make him a life member of the State Society.[17]

In spite of his virtuous refusal to use his position on the *Gazette* for "partizan politics" he had continued to support Cushing and Webster. In the first number of the *Gazette* after he became editor he advocated their reelection. He served as secretary at a meeting of Webster supporters September 3 and was on various committees in the Cushing campaign.[18]

"Mogg Megone" was published late in 1836, to sell at twenty-eight and thirty-seven cents in "neat cloth" or "gilt" to the trade and thirty-seven and fifty cents to the public. Whittier wrote a rather defiant introductory note: "In presenting his volume to the public, the author has not the common excuse to offer, that in so doing he has acted in accordance with the advice and solicitation of his friends. Upon a matter, in his estimation, of such trifling importance, he has not considered it necessary to consult them. With a calm conviction that whatever is worthy of notice in these pages will be fully appreciated, and whatever is of a contrary character speedily forgotten, he cheerfully resigns them to their fate. He has neither the vanity to expect, nor the folly to desire, a mere literary reputation which shall long survive him" — a sentiment which he expressed frequently in later years.

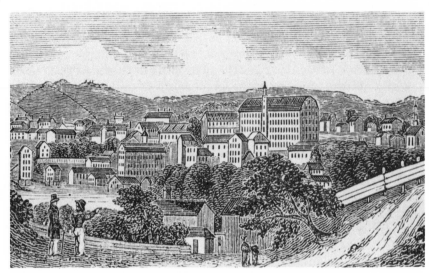

Southeast View of Mills Village in Salisbury and Amesbury, c.1839, from Barber's *Historical Collections*, 1839.

View of Amesbury, c.1850, looking toward Market Street. (Courtesy of Amesbury Public Library)

Illustration by Hammatt Billings for "Mogg Megone," which appeared in _Poems by John G. Whittier_, 1849.

VII

1837

Whittier left Amesbury for Philadelphia early in January 1837, intending to go from there to Washington to help Caleb Cushing and John Quincy Adams prepare speeches on the Right of Petition. He wrote to Adams from Philadelphia urging him and other Representatives from Massachusetts to protest against the virtual annihilation of this right but then decided not to go to Washington until after an Anti-Slavery convention in Harrisburg.[1]

There was a railroad line from Philadelphia to Harrisburg, but Whittier and three other men, Dr. Dilwyn Parish, Charles Evans, and Edward M. Davis, preferred the fun of driving in a two-horse sleigh. They left on Saturday and drove forty miles to Coatesville where they stayed over night at Lindley Coates' baronial stone house. They got to Middletown the next day, and Monday morning drove along the Susquehanna River to Harrisburg.

The convention, which was attended by many members of the Pennsylvania Legislature, lasted four days. Among the delegates were Rev. Amos A. Phelps of Boston, later associated with Whittier as one of the Corresponding Editors of the *National Era*, Lewis Tappan, and Orange Scott, whose disagreements with the Methodist Church authorities over Abolition led to the founding of the Wesleyan Methodist denomination. Whittier and others called on the Governor, Joseph Ritner, who opened the door to them himself and greeted them in German accent. Whittier's poem "Ritner", praising the Governor for his stand against slavery in his 1836 message to the Legislature, was printed a few weeks later in the *Liberator*.

Whittier and the men that he came with returned to Philadelphia by train, which took one day instead of three. They left at four in the morning and had breakfast in Lancaster, where Whittier learned how near he was to Slave territory. There was a Presbyterian negro minister at the table — a long table such as was commonly used in restaurants at that time. Someone said, "There's a nigger at the table," and the waiter pulled the chair out from under him. One of the Abolitionists demanded that a vote be taken, and it was in favor of the negro — there were fifty Abolitionists in the room. When the landlord appeared on the scene, a young Southerner drew out a pistol and brandished a dirk. The landlord dragged the negro from the table and the Abolitionists left to buy their breakfast in the markets and stores.[2]

Congress had now adopted a rule restricting debate and the Right of Petition, and Whittier gave up his plan of going to Washington. He tried unsuccessfully to find work in Philadelphia and considered another offer to edit an Anti-Slavery paper in Portland. He decided to stay a few more days in

Philadelphia although his lodgings there were not to his liking; he wrote to Elizur Wright that he was "engaged in certain scientific experiments and trying to solve certain difficult problems, as for example the following

1. What amount of coal, *without fire*, will warm a room, 12 by 13 ft.
2. If *ideas* are *things* as Bishop Berkeley supposes, what is the reason that the idea of a fire will not be a good substitute for the reality?"[3]

He was sick when he left Philadelphia on Monday, one of the coldest days of the winter, but as usual was able to endure the hardships of travel. He arrived in New York at half past five and stayed there until Thursday. The steamer left in the morning and lay off New Haven during the night because of the fog; the boat was old and over-loaded and the pumps were in use all night. The sea was rough the next day and little progress was made. Then an accident to the boat forced it to put in to New London for repairs. It arrived at Providence the next morning and Whittier and his party continued to Boston with "the celebrated Miss Ellen Tree of theatrical notoriety."

He stayed in Boston for several days lobbying for petitions that had been referred to a House committee asking the Legislature to declare that Congress had the right to abolish slavery in the District of Columbia and for other petitions protesting against a House resolution on slavery passed January 8.[4]

Whittier was also in Boston most of March lobbying with his usual adroitness. He warned Robert Rantoul that if the Democrats in the House voted against Senate-amended resolutions about slavery and the Right of Petition they would strengthen Everett and the Whig Party at the next election. Abolitionists had cut loose from party attachments and would vote for candidates who favored liberal principles and equal rights; as evidence he quoted Henry B. Stanton's denunciation of Daniel Webster at an Anti-Slavery meeting at Lynn as "craven, recreant, untrue to his professed principles and to the cause of liberty and equal rights." He digressed from Anti-Slavery long enough to urge Rantoul not to be discouraged by the vote against abolition of capital punishment and to suggest further means to promote that cause.[5]

At this point one must wonder what the Whittiers were living on unless they were spending the difference between the purchase price of the house in Amesbury and the sale price of the farm. This would have branded them, according to Yankee ideas, as improvident and not quite respectable. Whittier's royalties on *Mogg Megone* could not have amounted to much, the price being what it was and the edition a small one. He received small amounts from the Amesbury and Salisbury Anti-Slavery Society when money happened to be in the treasury.[6]

There was a chance of more profitable employment, however. There had been another offer of editorial work in Philadelphia and a rather generous offer of twelve hundred dollars a year from Portland. He was doubtful about the Maine offer. He wasn't sure that he could do a great deal of good there and he believed that the great battle of Abolition would be fought in Pennsylvania. It was his private belief that if Governor Ritner was reelected, all of the Northern states except New Hampshire and Maine would favor him for the Presidency. (Ritner was not reelected.) Also he didn't like the Maine climate. The truth probably was that he did not want to tie himself down to regular employment. He preferred to write letters and go to conventions. He wrote to John Quincy Adams inviting him to the New England Anti-Slavery Convention to be held late in May, listing the topics to be discussed, and saying that his views on any of them, especially Texas, would be welcome. He wrote a long letter to Cushing calling attention to John Quincy Adams' letters to his constituents (for which he would soon write an introduction praising Adams' almost single-handed fight in the House of Representatives for the Right of Petition). On behalf of the Essex County Anti-Slavery Society, which would meet in Amesbury April 21, he begged that Cushing would send a report on what had been done with the petitions from Essex County and concluded by tactfully thanking Cushing, an Anti-Abolitionist, for defending the character of the petitioners and the Right of Petition.[7]

Then there was a trip to New York as one of the twelve Massachusetts delegates to the Fourth Annual Meeting of the American Anti-Slavery Society in Broadway Tabernacle. His expenses were paid — fourteen dollars for travel, three dollars for board.[8] He was elected one of the seven Managers and Secretary of the Board. Signs of division were appearing in the Society. Whittier's two resolutions on the subject of political action were discussed at some length and referred to a committee consisting of Orange Scott, Garrison, Whittier, and Stanton, while Garrison's resolution was adopted, that Abolitionists ought not to organize a political party or join an existing party, but should not support any candidate who was not committed to freedom of speech and of the press, the Right of Petition, and the abolition of slavery and the slave trade in the District of Columbia and the territories and who did not oppose the admission of new Slave States to the Union.[9]

And then another convention, the Fourth New England Anti-Slavery Convention in Boston. Whittier was on the Committee on Business and presented a resolution which showed his good sense of public relations. Anti-Slavery people had been accused of threatening the existence of the Union, and it was not many years before Garrison and others did that — not with Whittier's approval. But the charges were unjustified in 1837, and Whittier met them by a resolution that since certain states, including North and South Carolina, had proposed terms to the other states as a condition for continuing the Union, it was therefore slavery and not Anti-Slavery that threatened to dissolve the Union and "nothing but the speedy abrogation of the laws which sustain slavery can save from utter annihilation that Union."[10]

While at the convention he learned that the position offered him in Maine would not materialize, at least for the present. The Panic of 1837 was making it impossible to get enough subscribers for an Anti-Slavery paper. He then went to the Yearly Meeting of the Society of Friends at Newport, Rhode Island, where to his sorrow it was voted not to permit Anti-Slavery lectures in Quaker meetinghouses. From Newport he went to New York to take a position for a few months as one of the secretaries of the American Anti-Slavery Society.[11]

The Executive Committee was not enthusiastic about Whittier's appointment. Its first choice was James Gillespie Birney, and it voted to appoint Whittier only if Birney absolutely declined. Theodore Weld, a warm personal friend of Whittier, urged Birney to take the position. Whittier, he wrote, "will never do. He has no influence in any denomination of Christians except his own and not a particle of sway over the *ministry*. Instead of carrying into the office the *confidence* of the Churches of different denominations he would be obliged to use his office to create a confidence in him. A very slow and uphill business — besides he never speaks in public — he has no talent for business and is *timid*. It would be greatly disasterous [sic] to our cause if he should be appointed."[12] Birney declined, and Whittier arrived in New York about the middle of June.

He boarded in the home of a Spaniard, a Catholic, named DeLoyo, whose brother-in-law was interested in Anti-Slavery. His board was high, he thought — six dollars and a half a week out of his monthly salary of eighty dollars. He found New York quiet; people were leaving for the country. He also found it dirty. Some parts of the city were too dirty to visit, and Boston was a perfect Shaker village for neatness compared with it. (Charles Dickens made the same comment when he was in New York five years later.) The Anti-Slavery office was near the Park and enjoyed a cool breeze. He thought at first that the city was no warmer than Amesbury, but soon there was a week that was one of the hottest that he had ever known and the sunshine fell blazing hot on the white pavements.[13]

By the Fourth of July this weather had brought on what he called his "old complaint of palpitation", but he was not too unwell to go with Theodore Weld to see the holiday celebration — thousands of people drinking, shouting, and shooting. Weld was his closest friend at this time, but he had other friends in New York: Dr. Crane, who had been so kind when he was in Hartford, and Charles Follen. He called frequently on Lucy Hooper in Brooklyn. She was twenty-three, a great-granddaughter of Robert Hooper of Marblehead, known as "King" Hooper. The Hoopers had been rich and important; Lucy's grandfather and two great-aunts had their portraits painted by Copley. Her father was somewhat less prosperous but still was able to afford a three-story house on Washington Street in Newburyport, where she had lived in her childhood. She was better educated than most girls, and somewhat of a poet. Whittier gave her a copy of *Poems Written During the Progress of the Abolition Question in the United States, Between the Years 1830 and 1838*, which he told her had been published in Boston without his knowledge or consent "full of errors and ridiculously printed, merely for *abolition purposes*," and urged her to write a long poem, which would be worth more than the "hurried sketches and 'bits of poetry' " that they and others had written. These short poems would not survive — but who cared? "But we do all care for the opinions of the good and the wise and the pure-hearted around us!" He had thought of writing a long poem himself but had been too busy. But why shouldn't she do it? He believed that she could produce in six months a poem "which would be received with general commendation on both sides of the Atlantic."[14]

From the official letters written in the summer of 1837 that now survive it is evident that he did that part of his work faithfully. Of two interesting letters incorrectly dated June 5, before his arrival in New York, one was to Henry Clay, a three-page letter asking Clay to oppose the annexation of Texas and to present and support petitions from the Society of Friends against it. He led up to the request tactfully, reminding Clay that he had once said emphatically "Slavery is all wrong" and assuring him that Abolitionists were not enemies of slave-holders and that the prayers of New England farmers would rise for a slave-holder who would advocate the rights of the colored American; the question of Slavery had reached the consciences of the religious people of the North, and Anti-Slavery societies had more than doubled in the past year, now numbering eleven hundred.[15]

The other letter with the June 5 date was to Harriet Minot. He had given her name to the Grimke sisters as one who would help them when they came to speak in Haverhill, where they were to visit Whittier's sister Mary Caldwell.

Sarah and Angelina Grimke were members of a South Carolina slave-holding family, who had become convinced that slavery was wrong and had come to the North to speak against it. Whittier had heard them at the home of Samuel Philbrick, son of a Quaker minister of Seabrook, New Hampshire, whom Whittier must have known through Monthly Meetings. He had prospered in Boston as a leather merchant and had a large house in Brookline on what is now Philbrick Road but which was then open country with a view of Boston and surrounding towns. He was treasurer of the Massachusetts Anti-Slavery Society. He arranged to have the Grimkes speak on slavery at his house to an audience of seventy women while Whittier and three other men listened. Whittier was enthusiastic: "Sarah would fill the eye with tears — Angelina moves the spirit like a trumpet-peal."

Sarah and Angelina spoke at a meeting in Haverhill July 21, where Sarah's topic was not Anti-Slavery but the rights of women. When this was reported to Whittier he wrote them a letter of sound advice containing his first strong statement against entangling Anti-Slavery with other reforms. Henry C. Wright and Garrison had done this, and it was unfair to those who gave money to pay Anti-Slavery agents or subscribed to the *Liberator*. The Grimkes did not need to argue about the rights of women; their lectures on Anti-Slavery were proofs of women's rights and duties. As for the Massachusetts Congregational Association, it could do no harm if the Grimkes did not allow its recent "splenetic and idle manifesto" to turn their attention from their great and holy purpose.[16]

Whittier himself, however, did not ignore this "manifesto", which was a letter issued by the General Association of Congregational Ministers at its Quadrennial Conference to be sent to the churches in the state. He wrote "The Pastoral Letter," which was printed in the *Liberator* October 20, reminding the clergy of the intolerance in early New England and telling them that they were trying to

> Arrest the very work of Heaven
> And bind anew the evil bands
> Which God's right arm of power hath riven.

The Congregational clergy deserved to be ridiculed for allowing the letter to go out. It was a comic example of clerical caution and self-importance. Perplexed and agitating subjects, it said, should not be forced upon a church and its Pastor. It emphasized "the importance of maintaining *that respect and deference to the Pastoral office which is enjoined in the Scripture,*" and which had been violated by having speakers come into the parish to lecture without the Pastor's consent. "Deference and subordination are essential to the happiness of society, and peculiarly so in relation of a people to their Pastor."

All that this meant, in plain language was, "Be docile, and do not talk about Anti-Slavery." The next point, with equal verbiage, was that women should not speak in public on reforms — should not "itinerate in the character of public lecturers and teachers." "The power of woman is her dependence, flowing from the consciousness of that weakness which God has given her for her protection." The Grimkes were doubtless right in thinking that this was aimed at them.

If Whittier had read the reports of the Conference he would have discovered that this letter did not express the ministers' sentiments on Anti-Slavery. They voted unanimously:

1. That the assumed right of holding fellow men in bondage, working them without wages, and buying and selling them as property, is obviously contrary to the principles of natural justice and the spirit of the gospel, offensive to God, oppressive to men, and ought to cease with the least possible delay.

2. That we approve of free and candid discussion on the subject of slavery,

and also of all other proper methods of diffusing light and promoting correct moral sentiments, which may have an influence to do away with the evil.

This vote, rather than the pastoral letter, evidently represented their attitude. The letter had been written by three Boston ministers and, in the way of conferences, was probably not listened to when it was read and was accepted as a matter of routine. One girl heard it and did not like its commands to women to keep in their place: Lucy Stone, aged nineteen, who became a leader in the Woman Suffrage movement.[17]

Whittier continued to write letters and petitions. He urged the New Hampshire Anti-Slavery Society to oppose the annexation of Texas, which, "peopled with the representatives of every penitentiary in the land — with the selected ruffianism of the Mississippi valley — the unemployed slave-drivers, the land and negro speculators of the South West — the dirk wearers of Natchez and Memphis and New Orleans — and the exiled gamblers of Vicksburg — is clamoring at the doors of our Capitol for admittance into the Union, leprous with sin, and spotted with the plague of slavery, — *where is the voice of New Hampshire*?" The question stayed in his mind and was answered in "New Hampshire" eight years later.

He sent a number of petitions to William J. Allinson and David Laing to be circulated in New Jersey, emphasizing that those dealing with the District of Columbia and Texas were most important. "We must keep Texas out of the Union," he wrote to Samuel Sewall August 8. "Give us discussion, excitement, and high feeling on this subject rather than ignorance and silence."[18]

His duties included some writing for one or more of the six serial publications of the Anti-Slavery Society. He was also assigned to the writing of *Narrative of James Williams, an American Slave, who was for several years a driver on a cotton plantation in Alabama*, which was published by the American Anti-Slavery Society the next year. James Williams — if that was his real name — said that he was a fugitive slave and told a story which the Executive Committee of the Society thought would arouse a good deal of interest. Whittier called himself the Editor of the narrative and said that while he had not been able "to present this affecting narrative in the simplicity and vivid freshness with which it fell from the lips of the narrator," he had copied Williams' manner and in some instances his exact language and had not added any comments of his own. The story was questioned by the *Alabama Beacon*, and the Executive Committee acted in a way that showed that they were really eager to get at the facts and were not fanatically devoted to their own cause. They published the charges against the book, and while evidently not discrediting the entire story, decided to withdraw it from publication. There was no question that Whittier believed that it was true when he wrote it, as did the Executive Committee.[19]

In August he wrote a preface for a pamphlet of extracts from Harriet Martineau's *Society in America* called *Views of Slavery and Emancipation*. It was published by Piercy & Reed in New York and does not seem to have had any connection with the American Anti-Slavery Society.

He was not wholly lost in his work. In a long letter to Harriet Minot he chatted about his Haverhill friends, especially a member of the Anti-Slavery Society who after a day of contention and strife could return to "the joys of his Water Street Paradise and the smiles and caresses of his amiable Eve! Oh joy of matrimony! bright dream of wedded bliss! Bachelor as I am I look upon the happiness which I may not share, as Adam looked upon the Garden after his expulsion." The French and Spanish women in New York were not as beautiful as American women. Then a sudden change: "Thee perhaps would not judge from the tone of this letter that my mind has been a good deal exercised of late on the subject of religious obligation. Yet such is the fact. The prayer of Cowper is sometimes in my mind. 'Oh, for a closer walk with God.' I feel there are too many things of the world between me and the realization of a quiet communion with the pure and Holy Spirit."[20]

Here is the first pale flame of the religious light that was to burn in a quiet glow in the poetry of his middle and later years — the verses that, often used as hymns, gave expression to the quest of millions of people for a firm faith of guidance and assurance.

Perhaps this sense of oneness with something great and eternal helped him to reply with calmness and kindness to what he called a "blowing-up" letter from Amos A. Phelps. After resigning the editorship of the *Emancipator* in June, Phelps had become Secretary of the Massachusetts Anti-Slavery Society. He was displeased with some of Whittier's statements to Henry B. Stanton which he thought reflected on him and Garrison. He asked Whittier not to pass judgment on a case about which he was not informed and not to condemn the Massachusetts Society "for getting out of a scrape into which *you* plunged us, in the best way we can. *You* sent us the Miss Grimkes — *you* saddled the Liberator upon the state society — *you* sent us Henry C. Wright with his no-family and no civil government notions." He proceeded to issue orders: Whittier must acquit the Massachusetts Society of responsibility for the Grimkes, dismiss Henry C. Wright from his agency "unless he will consent to wave [sic] promulgation of anti-government notices," and Whittier and Stanton must induce Garrison to "wave" discussion in the *Liberator* of the Sabbath, ministerial, women, and government questions.

Whittier's reply was that he loved and admired Garrison but did not wish the Massachusetts Society to be held responsible for everything that Garrison said or did. The Abolition cause needed the *Liberator*, and if it were only not connected with the Society Garrison could "blow up the clericals" as high as he pleased. The letter concluded: "In the meantime rest assured that the somewhat severe and caustic character of thy letter has not made me otherwise than thy affectionate and unswerving friend and fellow laborer."[21]

As Theodore Weld had foreseen, Whittier had not been a wholly satisfactory Secretary. Henry B. Stanton, who also liked Whittier personally,[22] now wrote to James Gillespie Birney, as Weld had done, urging him to come to New York and be one of the Secretaries. He said of Whittier: "He makes a pretty good Secretary, — is quite good at executing a plan after it is laid out to his hands, but has no power of originating, — is rather poetical in his temper, i.e. *unstable*, subject to low spirits, hypo, etc. — is a Quaker from head to foot, — is rather careless in his business habits, — in a word needs as much supervision, as to details, as a clerk. Were it not for these things, he would make an admirable Secretary; for he possesses an excellant [sic] knowledge of the whole subject of Slavery, is well acquainted with men, — with the present attitude of the public mind — has a good judgment — is apt at drafting papers (bating a little for poetry in style) etc. But, for the purposes for which we need an additional Secretary, he is not the man at all. In public estimation, he brings not an ounce of weighty influence to our committee, except among poets, and the Society of Friends. And, so far from aiding us, because he is a Quaker, that very fact would injure us. We are a little too Quaker now, in the estimation of the Conservative party."[23]

Whittier may have been told that he was not giving complete satisfaction, but it is more likely that he became tired of regular duties. He left New York August 24, after sending a farewell poem, seventy lines of heroic couplets, to Lucy Hooper and her sisters.[24] He stayed in Boston several days and, still in his mood of religious exaltation, wrote a long letter to Lucy Hooper to tell her that writing a long and elaborate poem, as he had urged her to do in his previous letter, "unless consecrated to the sacred interests of religion and humanity — would be a criminal waste of life, and abuse of the powers which God has given for his own glory and the welfare of the world. Mere intellectual renown is valueless. Do the best we can, in the matter of intellect, the Devil is wiser than any of us. The humblest and weakest follower of the meek and lowly Redeemer is more to be envied than a Voltaire, a Rousseau, or a Byron, and the lowliest teacher of that sublime philosophy which 'the wisdom of the world accounteth foolishness' is wiser and better than the prodigies of intellect, whose learning and acquirements only enable them, in the words of another, 'Sapienter descendere ad infernum' " — which he translated (it was still good manners to translate Latin for a female).

Continuing in the same strain, he criticized his *Mogg Megone,* which was, he said, "open to grave objections. It is not, I fear, calculated to do good."[25] This comment is a good illustration of a nineteenth century attitude, that literature should be, first of all, not an artistic creation but something that would do good to mankind. The poetry of Whittier's mature years was seldom free from this motive — nor were the writings of Leo Tolstoy in the latter half of his life. Tolstoy, a visitor observed, had a "well thumbed" copy of Whittier's poems on his table.[26]

Applying this same principle to Lucy Hooper, Whittier told her that the sentiment and moral of her poems were not as good as Mrs. Sigourney's from a religious point of view. Otherwise they were superior to hers — and somewhat unkindly, in view of his friendship with Mrs. Sigourney and the confidences that he had poured out to her in 1832, he said that her writings lacked originality of poetic feeling and that she said so much about babies that her book might be called "The Chronicles of the Nursery."

Whittier was in Amesbury most of the time until early the next year. During the fall he was still concerned about the *Liberator* and dissension within the Anti-Slavery ranks. He wrote a long letter to Garrison September 16 and consoled himself with the thought that if it did no good it could do no harm — it was "as pointless as a pumpkin." He wrote again a month later, lamenting that the Massachusetts Anti-Slavery Society was financially responsible for the *Liberator*, which was not under its control. He was eager to do all that he could to preserve peace, he wrote to Phelps a few days later.[27]

Abolitionists were not yet ready to name their own candidates but were trying to get regular party candidates to commit themselves in their favor — with the threat in the background of going into politics themselves. Whittier wrote to Cushing October 10 that his Newburyport friends seemed to be trying to drive Abolitionists into politics and urged him to write a letter enlarging upon his opposition to the annexation of Texas which he had mentioned in a letter to Whittier. He was sure that it would "do good". Cushing evidently thought otherwise — the letter was not written.[28]

A more direct attack of the same sort was made shortly before the election. On October 24 Whittier wrote to the twelve Senatorial candidates in Essex County asking them a number of questions. The five who did not answer were listed in the *Newburyport Herald* and the letter was printed. The first question was whether Congress ought to abolish slavery and slave trade in the district of Columbia; the second, whether they favored asking members of Congress from Massachusetts to exert their influence to get these things done; and third, whether they were opposed to the admission of any new slave state and to the annexation of Texas.[29]

Poetry had been a minor interest in 1837, but all eight poems written for publication were considered good enough to be included in the Riverside Edition. Four of them were directly or indirectly connected with Anti-Slavery. One of the others, "The Fountain," showed that he had not forgotten the discovery that he had made when he wrote "Suicide Pond" six years earlier, that "there are a good many matters connected with the history of the neighborhood which would figure well in verse." "The Fountain" was the legend of an Indian who came to look for the last time at the place where his ancestors had lived, which had now become Mills Village, and found nothing left from the past to give him happiness but the spring on the hillside. "The Familist's Hymn," like the prose sketch "Passaconaway" of 1833, showed Whittier's sympathy for the followers of Samuel Gorton, who, like the Quakers, suffered for freedom of conscience.

VIII
1838 - 39

Whittier was now in one of his periods of little interest in poetry, but he still found it useful on occasion. He wrote "Massachusetts" when he heard that the House of Representatives had refused to listen to Resolutions on Slavery by the Massachusetts Legislature presented by Cushing. The original version was much different from the one in Riverside Edition and contained references to Cushing which Whittier's later attitude toward Cushing caused him to omit, describing him as "that true spirit so eloquent and young." The last line of the poem was a quotation from one of Cushing's speeches.

He went to New York to help Elizur Wright start a quarterly magazine for the free discussion of Slavery — its columns would be open to the Pro-Slavery side of the question — one third of its space being given to literature. He asked George Bancroft to contribute, but two weeks later, after Bancroft had declined, he was already deep in another project. He was starting a series of small volumes on slavery and asked Bancroft some questions that showed that he had not learned to like research any more than when he was writing about Clay six years earlier.[1] The volumes were never written; for the next two years he was too busy for sustained writing.

He had received a letter from his friend Edward M. Davis — one of his companions on the sleigh ride to Harrisburg the year before — telling him in confidence that Benjamin Lundy might resign as editor of the *National Enquirer* of Philadelphia and asking if Whittier would like the position for three months or longer and at what pay; Lundy had been getting ten dollars a week. Arrangements were concluded by correspondence. Before going to Philadelphia he had a pleasant trip into Delaware, visiting among the Quakers and showing his social versatility by reading poetry to the girls and talking to the old people about Fox, Woolman, and Thomas Elwood. On March 13 he was in Philadelphia and enjoying himself "in the society of some most excellent people."[2]

Some of the people were old friends. He boarded for a time with the Thayers. Joshua Coffin was in Philadelphia, active in Anti-Slavery work and skillful in keeping crowds in good humor.[3]

There were pleasant evenings at the Wendells', a gathering place for young people. Isaac Wendell was a textile manufacturer. His wife was a daughter of Obadiah Whittier and hence Whittier's first cousin, but her daughters were nearer Whittier's age. Ann Elizabeth, twenty-seven, was an invalid with spinal trouble. In the evening the center table and lamp would be moved to her end of the sofa. Whittier would come in and sit at the opposite end of the sofa, tired and silent until after tea, when he would chat, often about himself, unless there were strangers present. He disliked general conversation, which he called "cross fire."

One of the young people often at the Wendells' was Elizabeth Lloyd, whom Whittier found attractive in spite of her strict Quaker bringing-up. Her sister Hannah was also among the young people at the Wendells', and Whittier had fun teasing her and Margaret Wendell. But sometimes he got teased himself; on one occasion Martha Nicholson locked him in the library because he refused to tell her something, and she once read some of his early poems aloud to his great annoyance while he walked the floor with an expression of distaste.[4]

Some of these early poems were in a copy book in which Martha's sister, Elizabeth, wrote all of Whittier's prose and verse that she could find.[5] The book was illustrated by Elizabeth Lloyd, and Whittier good-naturedly wrote some introductory lines beginning, "Sins of my luckless boyhood."

Whittier's friendship with William J. Allinson also began at the Wendells'. William and his brother Samuel were among the few Orthodox Friends who shared Whittier's views on Anti-Slavery. Others at these evening gatherings were Thomas and Elisa Earle and Whittier's cousins Moses and Joseph Cartland. Thomas Earle and Moses Cartland were useful as substitutes for Whittier in his vacations from his editorial duties.

Some comedy was provided by Benjamin S. Jones. He was quite attentive to young women, who found him amusing. He wrote poetry and produced some sentimental verses when Elizabeth Whittier gave him a bachelor button. He had a book store where Elizabeth Lloyd went to buy Whittier's 1838 *Poems* — which, strangely, he did not have and went to get, wearing a cap which had occasioned witty comments by the Nicholsons. Whittier liked him in spite of his peculiarities and thought that he had talents which his friends did not appreciate.[6]

Another house that Whittier found pleasant to visit was Abraham Pennock's on Twelfth Street. It was a large, three story house and one of the first in Philadelphia to have a furnace — which doubtless helped Whittier to enjoy his calls there on winter days. Pennock had been at one time editor of the *Philadelphia Non-Slaveholder*. He was a good deal older than Whittier, who often went to him for advice on Anti-Slavery business. As at the Wendells', a group of young people gathered in the parlor, serious in their devotion to the cause of Abolition but friendly and fun-loving. In this circle Whittier was full of mischief and once led one of the girls into a long discussion of some point in the observance of Easter which she argued with considerable warmth, not suspecting what was evident to the others, that he was doing it just for fun. Abraham Pennock's daughter Mary thought him a good conversationalist when at ease, "clear-headed, quick to see the ridiculous, satirical with the most sober face, but never unkind — a perfect gentleman."

His friendship with her was close enough to prompt a humorous comment by Rachel Healey in a letter to Whittier five years later with the news of Mary's engagement: "Now John see what thee has lost. I reckon however if all thy old sweethearts should take refuge in matrimony thee would start up anew."[7]

For a time after his arrival in Philadelphia he boarded at Joseph Healy's. The Healys were pleasant people to be with, and he spent part of his summers at their farm. But the food was pretty bad. "I didn't board with Joseph Healy, with Sarah Jonathan for cook, so long for nothing," he wrote twenty years later. "Henceforth I defy the fates in the shape of cookery."[8]

Another boarder at the Healys' was Sarah Lewis, who kept a private school and was active in the Female Anti-Slavery Society. One of her pupils was Elizabeth Neall, for whom Whittier wrote "To a Friend. On Her Return from Europe" in 1841. She was an Abolitionist and was at the Anti-Slavery Convention in Albany at which Whittier was also present in 1839. He wrote long letters to her and spent a good deal of time at her house. Sarah Lewis thought that she saw a chance for some match-making, and it was rumored that Whittier and Elizabeth Neall were engaged, but Elizabeth said firmly to her daughter many years later, "Whittier was very attentive and a good deal at the house, but he never spoke a word of love."[9]

He had his portrait painted by Bass Otis, who had a considerable reputation and painted some of the leading men of Philadelphia. Whittier would not venture to say later whether the portrait was good or not, but his friends were not enthusiastic. Joseph Sturge did not quite like it, and Ann Wendell thought that the smile was not true to life; it seemed to her that there was a similarity in the smile of all of Otis' portraits — an observation also made by more authoritative critics.[10]

His work as editor of the paper, renamed the *Pennsylvania Freeman*, and his part in Anti-Slavery activities during the next two years showed soundness of judgment along with political shrewdness and considerable knowledge of public affairs.

The first issue of the *Freeman* was dated in Quaker style "Fifth Day, Third Month, Fifteenth." Whittier promised to give his whole attention to the topic of Emancipation and to adhere to the tenets of the Pennsylvania and the American Anti-Slavery Societies. An editorial, "Democracy and Abolition," pointed out that Van Buren's supporters were not always pro-slavery; in Massachusetts and Vermont they were often Abolitionists, as was the leading Van Buren man in Rhode Island.

"Farewell of a Virginia Slave Mother," one of Whittier's most popular Anti-Slavery poems, appeared in the second issue of the *Freeman*. It successfully created an impression of the sufferings of slaves in the rice fields by a piling up of details, but for the purpose of contrast gave a pleasant picture of slavery in Virginia that was hardly good propaganda for Abolition. To remind his readers that the Colonization Society did not have the true answer to the negro problem, he printed an article describing conditions in Liberia, including slave-catching, starvation, and lack of medical care.

In the next three issues he announced regretfully that he must call Henry Clay an enemy of freedom, repeated his promise that he would not promote causes other than Abolition but somewhat inconsistently asked Abolitionists to sign memorials against the Government's treatment of the Cherokee Indians, and firmly stated his belief that Abolitionists should not form a distinct political party in which Abolition would be turned into a scramble for office and lose its hold on the hearts and consciences of religious and philanthropic people.

He took time out from his editorial duties to go to the annual business meeting of the American Anti-Slavery Society in New York, which began May 2. He offered a resolution that members and agents of Anti-Slavery Societies should not rely on physical force for protection against violence, which was defeated because it would prevent applying to civil authorities for protection against mobs — a question that would be of vital importance in Philadelphia a few days later.

Whittier returned to Philadelphia with William Lloyd Garrison, who immediately told the Anti-Slavery people that they were tame and cowardly and needed a mob to wake them up.[11]

One evening the dinner guests at Abraham Pennock's were kept waiting for one tardy guest until Mrs. Pennock was afraid that the dinner would spoil. The tardy guest was Whittier, who finally arrived with apologies; he had been writing a poem for the dedication of Pennsylvania Hall and did not want to break the thread of his thought.[12]

Pennsylvania Hall had been built by people who thought that there ought to be a place in Philadelphia where the principles of Liberty, Equality of Civil Rights, and slavery could be discussed. Its use was not limited to Anti-Slavery; the lecture hall could be hired for any purpose not of an immoral character. The building also contained offices, one of which was used by the *Pennsylvania Freeman*. The construction cost, $40,000, had been met by selling two thousand shares at twenty dollars, mainly to working people.

Whittier's "Pennsylvania Hall" was worth delaying dinner for. He had learned to use the heroic couplet with ease and dignity. The first section was the best, describing the glories of classical antiquity, whose pride gave no thought to the slave; Whittier's visual imagination gave him pictures of places and people that he had read about. In the final lines Whittier prophesied that in the happy but remote day when slavery had been abolished and the Hall was crumbling into decay, pilgrims would visit the ruin as a holy shrine.

The time when the Hall would be a ruin was not as remote as Whittier thought: it was only three days away.

The first two days of meetings passed without trouble. There was a dedicatory address by David Paul Brown, the Philadelphia lawyer whose speech at an Anti-Slavery meeting five years before at Chatham Street Chapel had been drowned out by shouts and derisive cheers. His speech this time did not please the more ardent Abolitionists, especially Garrison: Brown favored Emancipation but placed a high value on the Federal Union and advocated compensation of slave owners. There were lectures on language, meteorology, temperance, "Indian Wrongs," the Seminole War and its connection with slavery, "Future Prospects of the Human Mind," earthquakes, and physical education, and a discussion of the relative power of wealth and knowledge.

In spite of this innocuous program, feeling against the proceedings was building up. The Female Abolition Convention had voted that "Abolitionists will use their influence in having their colored friends seated promiscuously in our congregations — and that when churches are disgraced with side seats and corners, abolitionists will, as much as possible, take seats with them." This was interpreted, even by people who were shocked and pained by the destruction of the Hall, as promiscuous intermingling of blacks and whites. Actually not more than a tenth of the audiences were negroes, and there was no planned intermingling with whites; the negroes simply took vacant seats wherever they happened to be. It was reported that a negress had been escorted into the hall on the arm of a white man, who, it was later revealed, was her husband, Robert Purvis, who could easily have passed for white.[13]

There was also feeling against the part played in the meetings by women. "Instead of attending useless discussions and listening to itinerant lecturers," the *Philadelphia National Gazette* suggested, "let them read at home." Trouble started when Angelina Grimke was speaking at an evening meeting which, as it happened, was not under the direction of the Managers of the Hall or of the Anti-Slavery Society. Daniel Neall was presiding, and Whittier was seated on the platform. Stones were thrown against the windows but were stopped by inside blinds. After the meeting, negroes leaving the Hall were assaulted and one was seriously injured.

The next morning a crowd gathered outside the Hall but did nothing worse than shout insults at those who entered. The Mayor, John Swift, was appealed to for protection; he had been zealous a year before in preparing for trouble when a political meeting dealing with the vexed question of banks was to be held in Independence Square. His attitude now was quite different. "It is public opinion that makes mobs," he said to the committee, "and ninety-nine out of a hundred with whom I converse are against you. I shall go there in the evening and make a speech, and if that don't do, I can do nothing more."

The destruction of the Hall could have been prevented, nevertheless. The Sheriff told four members of the Board of Managers that he did not have enough men — he had only three — to protect the Hall and proposed that the Managers should collect men to serve under his direction as special constables. The four Managers replied that if he went to the Hall he could surely get five hundred men to help him; one of them guessed that he could get three times that number. They had just come from the Hall where many had expressed their willingness to assist the proper officers if called upon, but they were not a quorum of the Board and had no authority to act. The Sheriff left, naturally supposing that some hundreds would be ready to help him. However, the Board of Managers hastily met and voted unanimously that they could not undertake to defend the Hall by force. This vote was reported to the President, Daniel Neall, who took it to the Sheriff's office. The Sheriff was not there and Neall left it with a friend to give to him. He received it at the Hall too late to make other plans.[14]

In the evening the crowd increased. The Mayor asked for and received the keys to the Hall, assured the crowd that there would be no meeting, told them, "You are my police," and said that they might go home: "I bid you a hearty farewell for the night." There were cheers, and a crowd of half-grown boys went into an alley and began throwing stones. They were soon joined by one man whom the Sheriff seized but the boys wrenched him away. Then they broke into the building and began ransacking it. A few of them — a man who lived across the street thought not more than twenty — brought scantlings and started a fire. The Sheriff called on the crowd for assistance, without result, made strenuous but useless efforts, and departed. Witnesses believed that twenty or twenty-five men wearing badges could have saved the building. The crowd kept the firemen from doing anything to save the Hall and forced them to give their attention to the surrounding buildings. A group of police enjoying themselves in a nearby tavern treated the affair as a good joke.

While the ransacking of the building was going on, Whittier joined the crowd in disguise and went to his office to get some of the papers there. When he went out, the crowd was clamoring for Whittier and shouting, "Hang him." He joined in the shout and passed safely through the crowd. The next morning he took part in an adjourned business meeting of the Convention held in the street in front of the smoking ruins of the Hall. Garrison had left at midnight and had gone to Bristol, twenty miles from Philadelphia and the mob.[15]

Whittier and Charles G. Burleigh wrote "Address of the Eastern Executive Committee of the State Anti-Slavery Society to the Citizens of Pennsylvania." The most effective part was a reply to criticism of Abolitionists for allowing negroes to sit in the same part of the Hall as whites and for supposedly promoting racial inter-marriage. It pointed out that the seating was in accordance with the sentiment of the Pennsylvania Emancipation Act of 1780. As for amalgamation of the white and negroes races, it was not Abolitionists but slaveholders who promoted that. "Were all the slave children of the South to follow the condition of their fathers, the work of gradual emancipation would be going on more rapidly, and slavery would be in greater danger of speedy annihilation than many at the North imagine."

The May 24 issue of the *Freeman* was prepared by Whittier, but he left Philadelphia before it was printed. He and Joseph Cartland visited the Healys at their country home where he wrote a letter lamenting that Orthodox Quakers, including himself, too often neglected to apply their beliefs to their own conduct.[16] He arrived in New York on the night of May 26 to attend the New York Yearly Meeting of the Society of Friends, and was in Boston May 29 with other delegates who had arrived early for the New England Anti-Slavery Convention beginning May 31.

He was jubilant about the efficient police protection at the dedication of Marlborough Chapel, which had been built by the short-lived First Free Church (Trinitarian Congregational). It contained a hall which seated two thousand and was open to the free discussion of all sorts of reform topics. At the time of its dedication the chief topic was Abolition, and the speakers were vigorous and outspoken. Whittier reported to the *Freeman* that Alvan Stewart said, "The Northern apologist for slavery — whether he be a Governor, a Judge, or an Attorney General — he is the meanest wretch that crawls upon God's earth." The remark was aimed at the Attorney-General of Massachusetts, James T. Austin, who had published a vindication of slavery. Threats were made that the Chapel would be destroyed on the evening of its dedication, and the Mayor ordered three companies of militia to hold themselves in readiness to put down with ball and bayonet any attempts by a mob to injure life and property. Whittier reported this to the *Freeman* with an enthusiasm quite inconsistent with the Quaker doctrine of non-resistance and the resolution that he had presented only a few weeks before at the meeting of the American Anti-Slavery Society. On the evening of the dedication a crowd gathered, a few stones were thrown, and there was some feeble shouting, but the police seized the ringleaders and carried them off to the watchhouse. There was no further trouble.[17]

Whittier attended all of the sessions of the convention except part of one day when he was sick. Before leaving for Philadelphia he crossed the river to Charlestown to look again at the ruins of the Ursaline Convent. The smoke-blackened walls, he believed, were still teaching a lesson to the people of New England, and he suggested that the walls of Pennsylvania Hall be left standing for the same purpose. Financial and legal difficulties later disposed of that suggestion: the remains of the Hall were sold by court order to pay a claim that the Managers had disputed.[18]

Whittier was back at work in Philadelphia June 28 and was sure that his readers would forgive his long absence, William H. Burleigh having done so well in his place. Whittier had not answered a letter which Cushing had sent him in the spring. He now wrote to assure Cushing that Abolitionists would not support Van Buren, and as for Clay, if he wanted the votes of the free states, he must make no further concessions to the South, where his cause had been helped by distribution of copies of the *Freeman* by Clay's friends: Whittier's criticisms of Clay had made Southerners believe that Abolitionists regarded Clay as their enemy.[19]

Whittier was not tied to his desk. He found time to go out into the country and enjoy the scenery. One evening he walked a mile and a half with a group of young people to see the Fairmount Water Works and the fountains gushing up from the rocks on the cliffs overhanging the Schuylkill and spouting through the mouths of marble images. He spent a weekend in Burlington, going with Anna Nicholson, Margaret Wendell, and her mother to visit Ann Wendell, who was boarding there. He and William J. Allinson, whom he had met at the Wendells', walked about the town with the women, and then the young men talked until after eleven on Abolition, Colonization, Peace, Temperance, and Capital Punishment.[20]

In spite of these diversions, he was soon tired of his work. Only five weeks after returning to his editorial duties he wished that he could escape from them for a month or so. The weather had been "hot — hot — without interruption or respite. The thermometer at an average of 90° for the last five weeks — without rain, shower, or storm — a continual glare of sunshine." He was making plans for the volume of his poems to be published by Joseph Healy in the fall,[21] perhaps hoping that he would make enough money to give up editorial work.

He was appointed a delegate to a meeting of the Pennsylvania State Anti-Slavery Society to be held at Coatesville October 30 and urged attendance in the *Freeman* and in a letter to Theodore Weld, whose presence he said would encourage workers contending against tremendous odds.[22] When he left Philadelphia a few days later, the others in the *Freeman* office naturally supposed that he had gone to Coatesville, but he had left for home because of circumstances which he never explained except to say that they had been unforeseen at the time of his appointment. He was in Amesbury October 26, enjoying the company of his friends, the view of the Merrimac River, and the fact that he was on the free soil of an Abolitionised state, where both parties were looking for Abolitionists' support.

From this happy land he wrote encouragement and exhortation to less fortunate Pennsylvania, where the pro-slavery people were rejoicing over the defeat of Governor Ritner for reelection. Truth, Reason, and Humanity would triumph in Pennsylvania, he wrote, as they had in Massachusetts. The letter was read at the Coatesville meeting and described in the *Freeman* November 8 as "full of the vital energy and glow of thought and feeling which are wont to warm almost into life the page that his pen glides over."[23] This enthusiasm by men who were doing his work while he was enjoying a vacation that he had not had the courtesy to announce can be explained only by their liking him so much that they were willing to let him do whatever he pleased.

However, he was not idly enjoying his idyllic surroundings. He was busy in Anti-Slavery work — for which the Amesbury and Salisbury Anti-Slavery Society paid him six dollars in October.[24] He was also working to get Cushing definitely committed to Anti-Slavery. He was at an Anti-Slavery Convention in Salem when a letter from Cushing was read which was a masterpiece of evasion. The next morning Whittier talked with Cushing, who wrote another letter. Both were printed in the *Newburyport Herald* November 10, the second headed "By Request of Mr. Whittier." It concluded: "I did not design it to be understood that I entertained any desire or disposition to change my course, in regard to the subjects embraced in the letter; but on the contrary, being resolved to continue to maintain on all suitable occasions, as I have hitherto done, the principles and the spirit of the resolves of the legislature of Massachusetts appertaining to the right of petition and to slavery and the slave trade in their various relations."[25] Whittier sent it with a letter of his own to one of the leading Abolitionists in Lowell. He said that he considered Cushing's answer satisfactory; Cushing's opponent, Gayton B. Osgood, who had ignored the Abolitionists' questions, was "recreant to humanity and to democracy," and every consistent Abolitionist should vote for Cushing.[26]

As Whittier thought it over the next day, however, he wasn't at all sure that Cushing would not let it leak out that his first letter and not the second expressed his real sentiments. This, Whittier warned him, would not do. Suspicion among the Abolitionists of Essex County that their confidence in him had been misplaced would be a barrier to his future political success. He urged Cushing to speak out (twice underlined) freely against slavery, and to write to some of the prominent Abolitionists, including Orange Scott, then in Lowell. Before sending the letter he reread Cushing's first letter and added a postscript urging him to repudiate it "promptly and efficiently" and warning him not to trust the feeling of Newburyport[27] — which he referred to a few days later as the only pro-slavery corner of Cushing's district.

He wrote this letter in Lynn and started back to Philadelphia the same day. He arrived there tired and unwell but felt better after a few days. He was comfortably situated at the Healys' in a good room in the third story with a cast iron stove in which he burned wood, believing that coal affected his throat.[28]

During his absence his first authorized collection of poems had been published by Healy. About half its contents were poems dealing directly or indirectly with Abolition. The other half were "miscellaneous poems," published, Whittier's introductory note said, "as a matter of self-defense" because they had been mutilated by passing from one newspaper or scrap-book to another until, quoting "Marmion"

The very mother that him bare
Would not have known her child.

There were two poems published for the first time. "The Moral Warfare" was an example of Whittier's new attitude toward his life and work: the forces of evil must be overcome by divine light, truth, and love. "Lines, written in the Common-Place Book of a Young Lady" was "A Lament," written five years earlier, with a new introduction addressed to Margaret Wendell and justifying a sentimentally melancholy poem, hardly suitable for a girl's album, by pointing out that sorrows prepare us for heaven.

The profits on this volume were small, and Whittier continued to be editor of the *Freeman*. In the issue of January 10 he answered the claim of slave-holders that women mill-workers in the North were as degraded as slaves by saying that they were superior to the Southern *ladies* that he had seen at watering places. A week later he published a letter from a Northern worker which he called an "indignant and eloquent answer to the assertion that the Northern laborer was a slave." On the twenty-fourth he attacked the message of the new Governor of Pennsylvania which implied that slavery was a sealed question; "Stanzas for the Times" ("The Response") in the *Freeman* February 28 was an answer to a statement in the same message that it was "a virtual breach of good faith to our brothers of the South" to agitate the slavery question.

In the midst of this turmoil of politics and reform he was not wholly out of touch with contemporary literature; in the same issue he printed, with favorable comments, Richard Monckton Milnes' "The Long Ago" from his recently published *Poems of Many Years*.

Early in February he was in Boston at a meeting of the Massachusetts Anti-Slavery Society, where he found the leading Abolitionists, having nothing else to do, quarreling with each other. As soon as he had arrived he had to listen to Stanton's complaints of Garrison and to Garrison's complaints of Stanton and to the opposing arguments of Maria W. Chapman and Lydia Fuller. He listened to both with "sad civility," convinced that they would never be reconciled unless they had a hall burned and were otherwise violently opposed, as the Pennsylvania Abolitionists had been. However, he did not admit this publicly; his letter to the *Freeman*, written at Boston February 4, called these "trifling dissensions," the inevitable friction of a great move-ment, and he believed the course of Abolition in Massachusetts as safe as Christianity when the Apostles "contended sharply" with each other.[29]

One of the meetings was in Faneuil Hall, where there were no seats and no heat. The outside temperature was seven below zero, and it is not sur-prising that Whittier was unwell a few days later. His Amesbury physician told him that he should not think of returning to his editorial work in Philadelphia for three or four weeks. He remained in Amesbury until early April.[30] During these months the editorials were written by William H. Burleigh and Thomas Earle, while Whittier sent letters to be published.

In his letter February 4, concerned mainly with the meeting of the Massachusetts Anti-Slavery Society, he made some remarks about Harriet Martineau's *Martyr Age in the United States* which gave a very different impression of Congregational ministers from "The Pastoral Letter." Some of them he said, were the best and earliest friends of the cause, had made great sacrifices, and had given the strongest proofs of the sincerity of their profession.

A letter to the *Freeman* February 12, printed February 21 under the title "The Impartiality of Slavery," showed that whites as well as blacks could be enslaved. In the East Indies there were white laborers who had been enticed there from Madeira and Fayal to serve seven-year apprenticeships. They were treated like slaves and driven to work in the canefields in tropical heat, where even the blacks shed tears of pity for them; two thirds of them died within ten months. If slavery in America could do so, it would "as readily lay its hand on the Pennsylvania waggoner and the Jersey gardener as upon the descendants of Africa."

His letter in the *Freeman* February 28 had been printed in the *Amesbury Morning Courier*. A petition had been sent to the Massachusetts Legislature for the repeal of all laws which made a distinction between citizens on the basis of color, including the law forbidding mixed marriages. Whittier's letter was written with a light touch; he was evidently refreshed by his leisurely days at home and by freedom from regular work: "It would seem as if people feared that in case the legislature listened to its prayer, they would be compelled to marry the proscribed class, willing or unwilling. Unmarried gentlemen imagine that they shall be persecuted and beset by the 'ladies of color,' as the venerable Mr. Weller, Senior, in the Pickwick Papers, was by the 'widders' and 'young women of forty' after the demise of his helpmate. Ladies in a state of single blessedness seem to anticipate a visitation from colored gentlemen, as irresistible and furious as that of the Romans on the Sabine Women."

Whatever his illness had been, he was now well enough to write two long letters in one day. The letter in the *Freeman* March 7 occupied nearly two columns and was an attack on Henry Clay and his speech in the Senate on the presentation of a memorial against Abolitionists; Whittier had expected the "unblushing defense of the vilest oppression" but not the "maudlin pathos, the overstrained affectation of patriotism, and shallow sophistries." The letter then drifted to the topic of Quakers: had they perhaps given politicians reason to doubt their sincerity? However, there had been recent evidence that their opposition to slavery was reviving and that they were no longer deluded by Colonization. One thousand copies of this issue of the *Freeman* were bought and circulated by Dr. Wirtar of Philadelphia.[31]

A letter to Elizabeth Neall on the same day lamented the dissension in the Massachusetts Anti-Slavery Society which made Abolitionists laughed at instead of dreaded as they had been, but even in this letter there was a light touch: he had told Garrison he had rather see him and Phelps "have a regular set to at fisticuffs than this everlasting newspaper skirmishing." As for women speakers on Abolition, he quoted the prophet Joel, "Let the daughters prophesy" and then another prophecy would be fulfilled: "The young men shall see visions." But he added contritely that it was a besetting sin of his to joke about matters in which he felt a real and sober interest.[32]

By this time his long absence from his editorial duties was causing concern to the Executive Committee of the Pennsylvania Anti-Slavery Society. He wrote to the *Freeman* that he was not well enough to go back to work, and asserted: "I am anxious to be once more by the side of my Pennsylvania brethren, to whose faithful devotion to the cause of the slave I can cheerfully bear testimony."[33]

He was back in Philadelphia early in April — and homesick. He "would rather see the sunset light streaming through the valley of the Merrimack than to look out for many months upon brick walls and Sam Weller's 'werry beautiful landscape of chimney pots,' " he wrote to Cushing.[34] Pressure of business had, he said, kept him from answering Cushing's letter earlier. He does not appear to have done much during the winter months except write letters, and one may suspect that part of the "business" was reading contemporary fiction, including *Pickwick Papers*. He had, however, kept informed on politics. The Whigs, he thought, were ruined; Van Buren had the South, and it would be hard to swing Vermont, Massachusetts, Rhode Island, and Connecticut to Clay.

Dissension in the Anti-Slavery ranks in Massachusetts continued. "Our folks at the East are amusing themselves, like a parcel of Irish Donnybrookers, breaking one another's heads by way of diversion," he wrote to Weld.[35] These controversies gave him an editorial problem that he dealt with skillfully and firmly in the *Freeman* April 11. He announced that he must reject articles and resolves sent by his Massachusetts friends dealing with these controversies, which he would not please his enemies by extending into Pennsylvania. Some of the combatants were the earliest champions of Abolition and they were all his personal friends, but the issues were irrelevant to the purposes for which the *Freeman* was established, and he had no right to promote causes other than Anti-Slavery.

In spite of this repeated pledge not to use the *Freeman* for anything except the cause for which it existed, Whittier again called attention in the April 18 issue to the plight of the Indian and the consequent threat to the whites.

He had read in *Townsend's Narrative* (an account of a tour to the Columbia River) that great numbers of buffalo were being slaughtered, sometimes merely for rifle practice. Indians depended upon the buffalo for food. With their supply cut off, wouldn't the starving Indians join the slaves in the South to bring vengeance upon their common oppressors?

He filled six columns of the next *Freeman* with "Daniel O'Connell" in answer to a recent speech by Henry Clay. Except a few introductory paragraphs, the article was the same as in the *Iris* five years earlier.

Whittier was absent from his desk several weeks in May attending a meeting in New York.[36] On June 10 he reported to his family that he had been quite ill but was now somewhat better, although suffering from pains in the back and chest. He had been well enough to act as one of the groomsmen at Samuel Allinson's wedding at Arch Street Meeting, but he had decided to restore his health by taking a vacation from the *Freeman* and travelling in western New York.[37]

Two weeks later he announced that because of "protracted indisposition" he was handing over part of his editorial duties to a friend but would still be a contributor, and a week later announced that the friend was Moses A. Cartland. Whittier edited the July 4 issue, to which he contributed his first poem since February, now called "The Relic," written when someone gave him a cane made from the wood-work of Pennsylvania Hall. It was written with evident sincerity but could have said all that it had to say in rather less than fourteen six-line stanzas.

The trip to restore his health was to Western Pennsylvania and not to Western New York. It was for the purpose, Moses Cartland kindly said, of "restoring the tone of his worn and wasted energies: exhausted, as they have been, by unremitting toil in that cause which lies deepest in his affections — the cause of freedom and humanity" — a statement which hardly seems justified by the facts. Whittier had been at work only three months after a vacation of nearly that length.

If his health was as bad as he thought, it is surprising that he was able to go on after the first day. He and Henry B. Stanton planned to have breakfast at David Neall's but got up too late and had barely time to get to the train. After two hours the train stopped at a station where the passengers could have breakfast at a dirty Dutch tavern. Whittier described the meal as "an execrable cup of tea, which would have poisoned a Chinese mandarin, ham tough and solid as sheet iron, which had probably been smoked and salted annually for the last twenty years, and some hot cakes saturated with bad butter, greasy and heavy and anti-Grahamish." He evidently suffered no ill effects. He was able to eat dinner at one and to enjoy the view from the train window of a beautiful countryside which showed the effects of free labor, with farmers swinging their scythes through heavy meadow grasses.

Whittier and Stanton stayed at Harrisburg until the afternoon of July 8, when they went by train to Carlisle and stayed at J. Miller McKim's. The next day they rode to Ex-Governor Ritner's farm about nine miles from Carlisle and left in the late afternoon for Chambersburg and Gettysburg where they hoped to recruit Anti-Slavery lecturers. They continued to Bedford and over the Alleghany mountains, crossing one ridge late at night and going down at terrifying speed, the driver galloping his horses along the edge of a precipice several hundred feet deep.

Whittier returned to Philadelphia a few days later, undecided whether the trip had been good for his health. He stayed a little over a week and then left for a National Anti-Slavery convention in Albany. Abolitionists were moving toward the formation of a political party. It was voted that when neither party nominated a candidate favorable to Abolition, an Anti-Slavery candidate should be nominated if the Abolitionists in that district thought it best to do so.

The convention closed peacefully in spite of a speech by Garrison against Abolitionists voting, and Whittier left immediately by train with Stanton and Amasa Walker for a meeting of the Saratoga County Anti-Slavery Society at Saratoga Springs. On the train he had a lively but pleasant discussion with a Mississippi slaveholder who became convinced that Abolitionists had been libeled and were really the true friends of the South — another evidence that Whittier was, as has been said, "the least irritating of reformers."

He found Saratoga Springs the centre of the fashionable world, and he explained Anti-Slavery to some of the wealthy Southerners, not, he trusted, "without producing a favorable impression."[38] He was also having a delightful time. His health was good — not from drinking "the rascally drugged waters" but from travel, exercise, and open air. It is somewhat remarkable that anyone's health could be improved by the rugged travel conditions of the time, and it is more likely that Whittier simply felt better when he was enjoying himself, was seeing new sights and meeting people, and was not tied down to regular work.

Whittier had a novelist's delight in observing human nature and a humorist's delight in the ridiculous. He found both at Saratoga Springs — "the manifestations of pride, vanity, and jealousy, ... the early developments of love, the agony of disappointment, of baffled aims, of wasted affections, of unshared sympathies, Hope and Despair, Love and Hatred, chastened Desire and unbridled Passion — all crowded to-gether."

From Saratoga Springs he went to Newport. On the boat from New York he got a berth "by dint of pushing and scolding" but when he went to take possession of it he found a six-footer snoring in it. Whittier gave him a punch in the ribs and he "growled like a bear disturbed in his hollow log." The captain was called, and when it was found that he had assigned two passengers to the same berth he pointed to the nearest vacant one and told Whittier to use that. Whittier took possession, but a Frenchman soon came to claim it. Whittier's headache and weariness, he confessed, made him selfish and he kept possession while the Frenchman walked sadly away saying, "Diable! vat vil I do for my sleep?"[39]

He spent a few days at Newport with the Wendells and then proceeded to Amesbury, where he wrote to the *Freeman* urging that Abolitionists continue to send petitions to Congress and appealing for unity within the ranks, which had weakened as their cause had grown more popular and persecution had either ceased or become familiar.[40]

He still regarded himself as unwell and was sorry that certain men in Pennsylvania had attacked him when the state of his health kept him from defending himself, but it did not keep him from going to a party in Haverhill or from strolling along the banks of the Merrimac — probably with Lucy Hooper. She was visiting in Newburyport and, like most girls, found it fun to win the affections of a man who had not yet succumbed to any other girl's charms. She was amusing herself and her friends trying to melt the Ice Cream, as she called Whittier. He dropped in just before one o'clock on August 19, soon after another man calling on her had left, and explained his recent neglect of her by saying that he had been sick at Saratoga and at Newport. She accepted the excuse and they drove to Chain Bridge and walked around Deer Island. She promised to go to the "Rocks" with him the next day, but her mind was not on Whittier only: the man who had left just before Whittier's arrival came again in the evening and stayed until eleven.[41] The trip to the "Rocks" the next day is unrecorded, but may well have included a stroll along the river.

There were ten days when the temperature was ninety, but Whittier kept cool at the seashore. As usual, he was ready to travel and suggested to Caleb Cushing that they take a trip by steamer or packet (sailing ship) along the coast of Maine, but Cushing had too many speaking engagements.[42]

Early in September, Cartland, whose pay was in arrears, decided to return to teaching and announced that Whittier would resume his duties in two or three weeks. Whittier, accompanied by Elizabeth, was in Philadelphia in time to write for the October 10 *Freeman*.[43] His pay was nominally five hundred dollars a year, but he had actually received little more than his board. At a meeting October 30 eight hundred dollars was contributed to keep the paper alive, and Cartland was offered this amount if he would serve as editor and also take charge of the Anti-Slavery office. He declined, and Whittier continued as editor for nearly four months. He still opposed nomination of political candidates by Anti-Slavery societies, but conceded in the issue of November 21 that individuals might nominate Anti-Slavery candidates.[44]

In the December 19 *Freeman* was the announcement of a little gift book, *The North Star: The Poetry of Freedom, by her friends*, printed for a fair of the Female Anti-Slavery Society of Philadelphia. Whittier edited it and helped to get contributions. His own contributions were "The World's Convention" and "The Exiles."[45]

"The World's Convention" expressed high hopes for the anti-slavery convention to be held in London which Whittier had been hoping since summer to attend. Whatever may be said for it as poetry, it showed a thorough knowledge of world history, geography, and literature. Every country in the long list from which Whittier hoped that delegates would come to the convention had a few descriptive lines and something about its connection with the cause of human freedom.[46]

"The Exiles" was a highly fictionalized account of Thomas Macy's departure from Amesbury to Nantucket. Whittier said many years later that it was substantially true, but he must have known better at the time. The story was given him by Joshua Coffin, who quoted the poem six years later in his History of Newbury so that his readers might "have an opportunity of comparing and contrasting the facts of the historian with the beautiful embellishments of the poet."[47] The facts are that Macy did not leave Amesbury immediately after the two Quakers stopped briefly at his house, he wrote a humble letter of apology to the court, and he had arranged for the purchase of land in Nantucket before the incident occurred. He was not living at the time in the house in Amesbury which he had briefly owned and which is still standing, excellently preserved and open to visitors, under the name of Macy-Colby house. But the story was a lively if somewhat improbable narrative and showed that Whittier had not forgotten the possibilities in New England history and legends.

Whittier continued as editor through the first two months of 1840. He denied in the January 16 issue that William Henry Harrison was, as the *Washington Globe* had said, the "candidate of the fanatical abolitionists," quoting what Harrison had said on the subject in 1835: that bloodshed and massacre would result from abolition agitation, that abolitionists were "weak and presumptuous," and that citizens of one state had no right to use their freedom of speech to deprive citizens in another state of their property.

In the January 23 issue he reported the loss of the Steamer Lexington, which burned on Long Island Sound. One of the passengers lost was Charles Follen. Whittier printed a summary of his life, but it is evidence of his lack of interest in poetry that he did not write any poem about Follen for two years; in 1842 he was reminded of Follen by reading an essay of his and wrote "Follen" for the *United States Magazine and Democratic Review*.

A few days later he was in Washington. He was in the gallery of the House of Representatives January 28 when it was voted that any memorial or petition for the abolition of slavery or the slave trade should be laid on the table without debate or further action. The excitement of the occasion had no bad effect upon his health; in fact, he felt better than when he left Philadelphia.[48]

At this time a poem was going the rounds of the press as Whittier's. It was "The Lyre and the Sword" by George Lunt, which Whittier described in the February 13 *Freeman* as "spirited Kornerlike stanzas." "They are not ours," he explained. "and we utterly repudiate their unchristian sentiment." They were still being credited to him a year later when Rufus Griswold planned to include them as Whittier's in *The Poets and Poetry and America*.[49]

The issue of the next week contained the final announcement that Whittier's connection with the paper ceased with that number. His name continued to appear as Editor until March 5, probably because no one got around to removing it. He was owed two hundred dollars, which was still unpaid three weeks later.

These busy months had contributed nothing directly to Whittier's development as a poet. There had been no searching of the depths of human thought and emotion, no sharpening of the tools by which images are moulded, no clearer focussing of his vision. But he had been a fellow-worker and a playmate of men and women who were not of rural New England and were not, with a few exceptions, poets or trying to be. He had seen places which New England village rhymesters never saw and had experiences not in their world; he would never become one of them. His would be a nation-wide audience of people who found that he said better than they could what they wanted to say — or at least thought that they wanted to say — and felt what at their best they liked to think that they felt.

120

Profile Portrait in Miniature of Whittier by I.H. Gillespie, 1839, painted in Philadelphia. It was used for the engraving by John Collins. (Courtesy of Whittier Home, Amesbury)

Elizabeth Lloyd (1811-1896).

The Burning of Pennsylvania Hall.

IX
1840

Whittier and his sister left immediately after his duties on the *Freeman* ended. He was rather sentimental about leaving but, once away from Philadelphia with its good friends and not so good editorial duties, he began to enjoy himself. The trip to New York was pleasant, and they spent three days there, staying most of the time at Isaac Pierce's.[1]

From New York they went by steamer to Stonington and had a fine passage through Long Island Sound. Release from regular work had produced a mood of ebullient gayety and he tried to tease Elizabeth by showing her the life-boats, ropes, fire engines, and buckets and suggesting that they had better stay on deck all night wearing life preservers and holding a bucket of water in each hand ready for fire or explosion — rather questionable humor only a month after the loss of the steamer Lexington. Elizabeth, with Quaker calm, was undisturbed and slept as soundly as if she had been on land. They arrived in Boston at eleven the next morning, and before going to Amesbury Whittier gave Maria Weston Chapman what he called a "regular lecture" — and had to listen to one by her.

The spring and summer months were a time of disappointment and vexation. Everything went wrong. He made various plans for going to the World's Anti-Slavery Convention in London, but each plan ended in his deciding that he was too unwell to go. He first thought of going with Moses Cartland, and then, after being appointed a delegate from the Pennsylvania Anti-Slavery Society, of sailing on a packet with some Pennsylvania friends: "How delightful to be all together, apart from the rest of the world upon the illimitable deep." However, when, late in April, he went to New York and from there to Philadelphia, he found the ride from New York to Philadelphia very fatiguing, he was unwell, and he told the Committee of the Anti-Slavery Society to appoint another delegate in his place. Sarah Lewis, who saw him in Philadelphia, thought that he looked "very ill — and seemed oh so unlike himself." He was greatly disappointed and found it impossible to be wholly resigned to the "allotments of all-wise Providence."[2]

Abolitionists were now nominating national party candidates, a course which Whittier still thought unwise. He feared that prominent men would not accept nominations, there would be opposition from Abolitionists in some parts of the country, there was not enough time to present the claims of the candidates, and it would be better to work toward the promotion of harmony in Anti-Slavery ranks.

A few days after the new party had taken the name "Liberty Party" and had nominated candidates, Elizur Wright suggested that Whittier write to Thomas Earle and urge him to accept the Vice Presidential nomination. He took the opposite course. He advised James G. Birney to decline the Presidential nomination. There was a small attendance at the Convention, he pointed out, and the nominations were made by slight majorities. Friends in various parts of the country had written to him that they opposed nominations at this time. Even in Massachusetts the friends of the New Organization which had resulted from a split in the Anti-Slavery ranks would vote with their political parties, and he did not believe that the men nominated at Albany would get five hundred votes in Massachusetts — he did not know of one Abolitionist in that state who would vote for the Liberty Party ticket.

However, after the nominations were actually made he gave his support to the Party. He thought that he did not have long to live: "This may be the last vote I shall ever have an opportunity of giving for a Presidential incumbent, and I cannot — I dare not, withhold it from the Anti-Slavery candidate."[3] A campaign song in the *Pennsylvania Freeman* July 30 was evidently his.

Within the American Anti-Slavery Society affairs progressed just as Whittier had feared and had tried to prevent. He found the quarreling within the ranks especially distressing because his feelings pulled him one way and his judgment another. Some who were behaving badly had been his fellow-workers in the early Anti-Slavery days; he had not lost his faith in them, and he could not quarrel with anyone who was interested in the Anti-Slavery cause. But he could not agree with Garrison and Maria Weston Chapman, who were unfair to whoever disagreed with them and were dictatorial, censorious, and intolerant.[4]

The split in the organization came in May at the seventh annual meeting — and it was inevitable, whatever the immediate causes, which included non-resistance, women's rights, attitude toward the clergy, sectarian loyalties and prejudices, differing opinions on political action, and, as in all reform movements, personal ambitions. About three hundred members seceded and formed the American and Foreign Anti-Slavery Society, so called because it intended to work with the British and Foreign Anti-Slavery Society against the slave trade. Whittier was glad that he had not gone to the meeting. It was bad enough to hear about it, and he was sick of the folly of both parties. But in his usual practical way he hoped that both Societies would go steadily forward, each in its own way and without attacking each other, to promote their cause.

The American and Foreign Anti-Slavery Society — the "New Organization" — was formed May 15 at a convention in the Fourth Presbyterian Church in New York. It was assumed that Whittier would join it, and he was appointed to the executive committee. He declined to serve, and told

Moses Cartland that while his abolitionism grew stronger daily and his faith in its principles deepened, his faith in the organizations was "not of a saving kind."[5]

Whittier's supposed sympathy with the New Organization was regarded with sorrow or anger by many of his friends and fellow-workers. Lucretia Mott wished that he could have his eyes opened. To Nathaniel P. Rogers he was a lost leader. Lydia Maria Child exclaimed, "Why should I marvel at John G. Whittier, when I recollect that Barnabas himself was 'led away by their dissimulations'?" Even Elizabeth Neall wrote to Elizabeth Whittier, "Thee cannot conceive my dear Lizzie how sorry I am to find you so thoroughly 'new-organized.' "[6] Henry G. Wright accused Whittier in the *Non-Resistant* of being a member of the New Organization, evidently regarding the charge as a serious one, and Charles Burleigh, then editing the *Pennsylvania Freeman*, thought that Whittier had shown a strong sympathy with the New Organization.

Whittier explained his position in a letter to Burleigh printed in the *Freeman* July 30. He was strongly in sympathy with all who were willing to work for the welfare of the oppressed and with the faithful Abolitionists who had formed the American and Foreign Anti-Slavery Society, but he was not a member of that Society and his health was not good enough to let him take an active part in any group. His name was on the Constitution of the old society, and he hoped that its course would be such that he could allow it to remain there. But he did not agree with its officers that abolishing civil and church government was the best way to abolish slavery. He did not intend to wage a war of extermination with religious sects who opposed abolition; he had a strong attachment to the Society of Friends, and while regretting that some of its members were indifferent to the woes of slavery, he could not call it a "pro-slavery" sect. He intended to co-operate with both Societies in so far as they kept to the practices and purpose of the Anti-Slavery Society as first organized, and he would not enter into a controversy with either.

Within the Society of Friends there was also turmoil — as often. Internal dissensions are likely in a religious group that governs itself democratically and whose members are guided by the Inner Light. The Hicksite division, which resulted in two separate organizations and sometimes rival meetinghouses side by side, had occurred only thirteen years earlier. When Whittier was visiting Joseph Healy he observed that the Hicksites in that vicinity had got possession of the Orthodox meetinghouses. The Orthodox, however, had two meetinghouses a few miles from Healy's; one of them was a large new stone building in the midst of a fine grove of forest trees — within sight of the Hicksite meetinghouse.

There were now difficulties in the Society of Friends at Lynn and elsewhere, arising from the current questions of non-resistance and church government.

Whittier was tolerant of opinions that he did not share; he did not approve of William Bassett's course in regard to non-resistance but he thought that Bassett was honest and he did not like the attitude of those who were trying to make trouble for him. Whittier supposed that his friends took his disapproval of Bassett's course and his acceptance of the Yearly Meeting's views on government as an indication that he was no longer devoted to Anti-Slavery. He wished it understood that he had not given up his faith that "a man is a man, and not a mere thing!" He had spoken openly in Quaker meetings in Newport, Philadelphia, and Lynn of his disapproval of the lukewarm attitude of Friends toward Abolition, but he had no intention of leaving the Society of Friends — as William Bassett had done — and joining the "antisectarian sect" about Boston.[7]

Whittier was also unhappy about his relations with William Lloyd Garrison, who called him a compromiser, like Henry Clay, who wanted peace at any price. Whittier replied that some of the "ghosts of treason" that Garrison saw were really faithful Abolitionists. He had no intention, furthermore, of quarreling with a friend of twenty years' standing whom he had known and loved in prosperity and adversity. After Whittier's announcement in the *Freeman* June 27, 1839, that he was handing over part of his editorial duties to a friend, Garrison's comment had been "Had his advice, (honestly expressed) been followed, mischievous consequences would have ensued. Especially at the present crisis does he 'stumble in noonday as in the night' — and through his blindness, others are led astray." In the spring of 1840 Whittier had not forgotten Garrison's attitude. "Garrison, it seems, is 'reconciled' to my leaving the *Freeman*," he wrote to Elizur Wright. "This is consolatory. The great efforts made to render the abolitionists of Pennsylvania disaffected with me, having totally failed and evidently recoiled on their own heads the next best thing is to have me quit the ground, whether by sickness or otherwise."

A minor but real cause of vexation was the excitement in Amesbury and South Hampton over three or four negroes lurking in Great Swamp, on the outskirts of Amesbury, near South Hampton. They were thought to be fugitive slaves who had been left on the coast by some vessel. Pro-slavery people in the two towns were badly frightened — or pretended to be — as if, Whittier said, "the days of the 'Indian war' had come back and a host of savages were lying in wait for their scalps." Boston and New York papers reported that Amesbury had been invaded by a score of runaway negroes who had committed extensive depredations upon the citizens. The "depredations" were no more than the purloining of some coarse food and the occasional milking of cows near the swamp. One of the negroes, a boy, was caught in South Hampton but was quite terrified when visited by Whittier and other Abolitionists and refused to tell where he had come from. He soon escaped — or probably was allowed to escape — and rejoined his companions.[8]

As a result of these irritations, Whittier was receptive to a powerful steadying influence, a new awareness of the strength of a religion that was felt rather than reasoned, and it came about through the sympathetic understanding of a Friend. When Whittier was at the Yearly Meeting in Newport in June he called on Richard Mott and talked about Abolition with John Joseph Gurney. When he left, Mott followed him to the door and said that he wanted to walk with him to his lodgings, feeling what Quakers called a "concern" to speak about Whittier's religious life. By some "exercise of sympathy" he had become aware of the troubled state of Whittier's mind and felt this awareness so strongly that he could not rest without speaking about it, although he had seen or heard nothing to indicate it. He encouraged Whittier to "put aside every weight that encumbers" and to look to God who could "deliver him from every trial". This was familiar Quaker doctrine, but its application to Whittier "in a manner so utterly inexplicable by merely human reasoning" frightened and awed him, and he prayed that it might have more than a passing effect.[9]

This religious impulse was strengthened by a solemn meeting at the Yearly Meeting of Friends at Newport after the news came of the death of Daniel Wheeler, whom Whittier had become acquainted with in Philadelphia. Wheeler became a Quaker in 1796 at the age of twenty-seven after serving in both the British Army and Navy. In 1816 he became a minister and traveled widely. At the Newport meeting John Joseph Gurney spoke of the "lips, now cold, which had been touched by a coal from the Lord's altar — of the kind and generous and benevolent heart which had ceased — of the eye of sympathy and love closed up forever." Whittier had never seen or felt a more solemn meeting. A letter from Ann Wendell confirmed his feeling that he should write some lines about Wheeler.[10]

"Daniel Wheeler" was first printed as a leaflet, and copies were sent to Whittier's friends and probably to others.[11] Whittier had no interest in it as a poem: "It was the idea and sentiment rather than the harmony of versification and originality of language, which I was solicitous about."[12] The result was what one might expect: there is hardly a line in the poem that touches the reader. It has none of the power of his later religious poems that reached people who were groping for simple truth and faith, and none of the "small but permanent portion of beauty" that Howard Mumford Jones once pointed out is found in those poems "in which (alas, too rarely) he presents character."[13] But it is interesting that Whittier turned to poetry when he had thoughts that he wished to transmit to others. The thoughts in "Daniel Wheeler" were partly from Gurney's closing appeal to young Friends to carry on Wheeler's work and partly from his own observation of Wheeler and knowledge of his work.

Whittier's religious thought was now approaching the position that it maintained throughout his life and which found expression in some of his best-loved poems. When he visited his brother and his wife in Portland he found them happy in the Baptist church and felt no urge to bother them with his Quaker attitude toward baptism and other ceremonials, but his own beliefs were firm. "To me . . . . . these *outward* things seem more and more vain and ineffective — while the inward spiritual worship, the silence of the heart before God, the ceasing from outward endeavor, the soul divested of the cherished garments of its works and in nakedness and poverty waiting for the clothing of the Divine Mercy, seems to acquire new beauty and fitness."[14]

After the close of the Yearly Meeting June 19 Whittier went to Amesbury and from there to Boston July 13 and, according to his sister Elizabeth, would leave in the *Brittania* for Halifax "perhaps." Her uncertainty was justified: he was unwell and did not go to Halifax. But he went again to Portland July 24. There he enjoyed the company of Henry Wadsworth Longfellow, whose "Psalm of Life" he found beautiful and instructive. Also in Portland was John Neal, whom he described as "a singular and erratic genius — but in his home and dispensing his elegant hospitalities and enlivening with his good natural wit all around him he is unrivalled."[15]

During the five months that had passed since the Whittiers left Philadelphia there had been frequent and lengthy letters between them and their friends in that city. One of these opened the way, perhaps by intention, for an answer to a question that it was time that Whittier should answer: was he thinking of marrying Elizabeth Lloyd? Ann Wendell wrote that she feared that she had said too much about her. Whittier replied that he did not think so; he thought Elizabeth Lloyd worthy of Ann Wendell's praise and he respected her — too highly to think of marrying her. He could appreciate and admire her and at the same time know that such excellence and loveliness were not for him: "With deep and strong feelings and a capacity of seeing and comprehending worth and excellence, I am nevertheless compelled to forego the idea of appropriating them to myself."

When he said many years later that Elizabeth Lloyd was the only woman he ever loved, he gave poverty and the care of his mother and sister as his reasons for not marrying her. These were not the reasons that he gave Ann Wendell, and they loomed larger in his mind as he looked back on his years of caring for his mother and sister than they had in 1840. He was quite aware that he was poor and, he wrote to Elizabeth Lloyd a month later, must "labor with head, or hands if necessary, for the maintenance of that pecuniary independence which every honorable mind must seek for." But, as would be evident before many months, he could neglect the need of "pecuniary independence" and his obligations as a son and a brother when there was something else that he really wanted to do.

When he answered Ann Wendell's letter he was thinking about himself and the woman that he loved. It was his misfortune that the maturity which made it possible at last for him to love also forced him to use sound judgment and discretion. The reasons which he gave Ann Wendell, which she would of course hand along to Elizabeth Lloyd, came from an accurate analysis of his character and hers. He could not expect her to overlook his "eccentric imagination," lively sense of the ludicrous, and his tendency to caricature and sarcasm. Nor could he expect her to accept his religious liberalism; she had been brought up in a "narrow and exclusive spirit of sectarianism" and as a result had a "fixed habit of thought and "established ideas of propriety."[16]

There is no indication that either Whittier or Elizabeth Lloyd spent any time lamenting that they were not to marry. They were too busy for that, nor did they wish to give up the pleasure of writing to each other. They were hoping that a poem could be written about early Quakers. At first each assumed that the other would write it. She thought that his "peculiar touches of strength and beauty" would "expand our inherent tendencies toward *mere* truth and soberness into a stronger love (that will produce good works) of the self forgetting *nobleness* of primitive Quakerism." This idea wanted only "the setting of J. G. Whittier's poetry to make it the richest jewel and his crown of fame." He replied that she was the one to do it, but he and his sister Elizabeth could do some of the sketches; she could find material suitable for poetry by skimming through Sewel's History — the "painful tome" mentioned in "Snow-Bound" as part of his childhood's reading. A month later he wrote that he was disappointed by her definite refusal; he had thought of the plan only in reference to her — he had had no idea of writing any part of the volume. Poetry had become task-work. For eight years he had been devoted to the cause of Anti-Slavery; now he must do something to earn his living. Moreover, he felt that he was not, as she had implied, spiritually fitted to write such a volume; his heart was not fixed and his faith was weak. She would have to do it all by herself, since his sister had declined to have any part in it.[17] She conceded in her final letter on the topic that the plan would have to be "laid on the table"; she would be satisfied with "nothing short of such a work as no woman ever produced."

However, she did induce him to write one poem, "The Funeral Tree of the Sokokis." Elizabeth Nicholson was making a second copy-book of Whittier's writings, and Elizabeth Lloyd had an embossed sheet of Bristol Board on which to paint a frontispiece: could Whittier not write a poem for which she could make a picture — "some cherished spot of New England scenery yet unsung — something grand — bold — and characteristic?" The poem was printed in *The Knickerbocker* for March 1841, and later in the year Whittier recommended it to Rufus W. Griswold for inclusion in *The Poets and Poetry of America*.[18] The fact that Whittier liked it showed that he was moving toward the kind of poetry that brought him closest to the largest number of readers. It had a long description of a New England country scene with accurate, specific details, and it led to the brotherhood of man and to the truth freed from form and creed.

In October Whittier went with his mother and sister to the Quarterly Meeting at Weare, where he enjoyed the cool, clear weather and the landscape, its gorgeous colors softened by the autumn haze. The young Quakers, twenty-five of whom had tea at Moses Cartland's, were delighted to make Whittier's acquaintance, and one of the girls, Anna Chase, wrote a note to Cartland which perhaps she hoped he would quote to Whittier — as he did — calling Whittier "the Webster of poets — and moreoever, what is much in woman's eye, he is handsome, certainly" and added, "He is a star of fire in the constellation of poets." "Poor John!" was Cartland's comment. "How he is talked about by the 'better half of creation.' "[19]

In one respect Whittier was now finding Amesbury not wholly satisfactory. His increased interest in religion and his association with some of the leading Quakers made him critical of Amesbury Friends Meeting. As he sat in the meeting he felt a lack of life and of the renewing baptism of the spirit, and he sighed for the presence and the words of the distinguished Quakers that he had known. He was aware that this craving to see and to hear was wrong, but thought it was only natural in spiritual weakness to long for the support of an earthly arm.[20] Whittier may have been sentimentally exaggerating his spiritual cravings, as he had once exaggerated his romantic love and broken heart, but it is unlikely that he could find in Amesbury Friends Meeting many people who could talk and think about religion with the depth that he had now reached. He had not yet come to the appreciation of the sturdy simplicity of faith and character that he admired in his later years.

After his return from Weare he did not leave Amesbury for five months except for short trips. He went to a meeting in Boston at Chardon Street Chapel called to discuss the Sabbath, ministry, church organizations, and some twenty other collateral subjects. To his amusement, half of the first forenoon was spent in debating whether a president and a secretary should be elected or whether each member should do and say what seemed right in his own eyes. Then there was a discussion of the Sabbath in which Garrison and others argued that it was not rest from labor but from sin that was wanted, while the conservatives argued for the Calvinistic view of the subject. There were many distinguished men present, but as often happens they took no part in the discussion.[21]

During the fall Whittier sent three letters to the *Freeman*. The first one, written September 24 but not printed until November 12,[22] was mainly about the World's Convention, which had been the scene of a women's rights controversy. Garrison and Nathaniel P. Rogers, among others, had refused to take part in the meetings because women delegates, including a seventeen-year-old girl, were not admitted with full privileges.[23] Whittier was, privately, both disgusted and amused. But the disputes might have a bad effect on Abolition. Opponents were using them to discredit the Convention. In his letter to the *Freeman* Whittier wrote that the Convention had fully realized his most sanguine expectations by awakening new hopes and a livelier faith, and he urged that Anti-Slavery papers should not print anything that would support the claim of the pro-slavery papers that it was a failure. The exclusion of women delegates was no excuse for condemning the Convention if it was an act of conscience but he wondered how Garrison would have acted if women had been admitted — contrary to the intention of those who called the Convention and to the custom of European Abolitionists — and if Birney and others had withdrawn: would Garrison have treated their consciences with the respect that he had claimed for his own? By this time the charge had been made that Lucretia Mott was excluded not because she was a woman but because she was a Hicksite. Whittier refuted this charge by saying that the Orthodox Friends in England had associated with all classes and sects in the United Kingdom and had welcomed Lucretia Mott not as a Hicksite Quakeress but as a friend of the slave.[24] As for Nathaniel P. Rogers' criticisms of the British Abolitionists, he believed that Rogers had little sympathy with anything "staid, sober-paced, formula-fettered," his own Abolitionism being "fervid, imaginative, electric, and sparkling."

Two months at home had given Whittier time to think and to form definite opinions on what the Abolition movement was and what it ought to be. "The Cause," written October 8 and printed in the *Freeman* October 22, summed up the gains and losses of the past seven years. The wrongs suffered by slaves had been made known, the attempt to annex Texas had been defeated, and fugitive slaves had been helped on their way to Canada. But a new slave state had been admitted to the Union, the slave population had increased half a million, there were eight more representatives of slave property in Congress, and Congress no longer received petitions about slavery.

With Abolitionists as numerous as slave holders, why, Whittier asked, did Methodist, Baptist, and Presbyterian churches violate their principles and treat petitions of Abolitionists with contempt? Why did the Bible Society not send Bibles into slave territory? Why did government officials take orders from slave-holders and why did candidates for public office pledge themselves to support slavery? He thought that there were two answers: the slaveholder would not vote for a candidate who did not promise to support slavery; the Abolitionist put political party above principle. He proceeded to some definite suggestions. Abolitionists should rid themselves of the bitterness caused by the dissensions of the past two years which their enemies said proved them to be selfish, ambitious, and hypocritical; they should have no fellowship with slave-holding church members and should not recognize slaveholders as Christian ministers; they should help fugitive slaves, and while not encouraging slave insurrection, they should refuse to assist in suppressing it; they should refuse to vote for any candidate who did not favor immediate abolition; they should influence legislatures to remove legal distinctions based on color; and they should not buy, sell, or use cotton from slave states or do business with slave dealers. His final suggestion could not have made him popular with the leaders of either of the national Anti-Slavery Societies: instead of a Society there could be an Annual Convention, with a Committee of Correspondence to act on interim business between meetings. He believed that this would have the advantage of combining action with more freedom than had been possible in a Society which required strict constitutional uniformity and which necessarily condemned as heresy and disorganization any deviation, however well intentioned, from its established ways.

Three poems written in the winter of 1840-41 were about New England and its history. Away from the bustle of editorial work and Anti-Slavery business, Whittier could say in "The Norsemen:"

My thoughts were with the Past alone!

as he thought about a fragment of a statue found in Bradford, across the river from Haverhill, and reported in the *Essex Gazette* ten years earlier.[25] He pictured Norse ships sailing up the Merrimac with their "iron-armed and stalwart crew." Then, when the present scene returned, he gave thanks that God so fashioned the human mind that a simple object can bring back the past and thus suggest that mind is immortal.

In "The Merrimac" Whittier described the lower Merrimac valley as it was seen in a gush of sunset light. The details gave a true picture of the scene, with the Powow River encircling the hill in a belt of gold, rocks not yet covered by the incoming tide, green islands, boats, farmhouses with maple trees or Lombardy poplars. Fifteen years earlier, in "The Vale of the Merrimac," the description might equally well have referred to other rivers: fireflies, moonbeams, the "dull bird of night," the whippoorwill. As first printed "The Merrimac" did not contain the five lines in later printings beginning "Bathed still in childhood's morning dew," which added to the clarity but were not really needed and slowed down the effective sweep of thought toward the conclusion; their addition was an example of Whittier's dutiful feeling that grew upon him that he *must* make everything clear.

"St. John," an episode in the early history of Acadia, had New England background; Charles de la Tour received aid from Puritan Massachusetts. Like "The Norsemen" and "The Merrimac," it was printed in *The Knickerbocker,* but unlike them it seems written for popular taste.

Also printed in *The Knickerbocker* was "The Cypress Tree of Ceylon," which he had sent to Elizabeth Nicholson to fill a page in her copybook, with the request that she keep it out of the hands of printers and publishers. Writing of any kind, he told her, was fast becoming irksome and unpleasant and the pile of unanswered letters was rising high, but his letter to her was lengthy and explained the origin of the poem. It was the versification of a passage that impressed him as he was reading an old account of Ibn Batuta's travels in the East. Its central thought was repeated in the letter: "Happy is the person who can give everything its relative importance and be at once actively engaged in reforming others and watchful over his own spirit."[26]

The winter of 1840-41 was an unhappy one in the Whittier household. Whittier's health was really bad, beginning with an ill turn which kept him for several weeks from the pleasure of writing long letters to his friends and proceeding to an attack of what was later called the grippe and which he remembered for forty years. He approved of a plan of Moses Cartland for a bi-monthly magazine — not a "Quaker paper" but with a "Quaker bearing" — and had some good ideas about its editorial policy and management, but did not trust his health for any vigorous exertion. He was too unwell even to visit his old friends in Haverhill. As the long winter dragged on, he became fretful and impatient. He and Elizabeth went to Salem Quarterly meeting; she stayed at Salem a month or so, but when she returned to Amesbury she became as unhappy as her brother. They evidently didn't have enough to do or to think about. "We help each other to be uncomfortable," was his description of their situation. "We've talked over everything and about everybody, and in short used all our material. We have done talking. We are as incommunicative as two Chinese Bonzis studying Confucius — or two monks of the Chartreuse with the vows of silence upon them."[27]

He was not too ill to give political advice, but nothing came about as he wished. Early in January he wrote a rather emotional letter to Cushing urging him to be a candidate for United States Senator at the election by the Legislature. Cushing ignored his advice. Later in the month it was known that there would be another vacancy in the Senate when Daniel Webster became Secretary of State in Harrison's cabinet, and Whittier wrote again to Cushing. He was disturbed by the rumors that Rufus Choate would surely be elected and urged that if Cushing found that he could not be elected himself he should give his support to John Quincy Adams. He saw no reason for the election of Choate. "What has he done for the party? What for Massachusetts?" he asked. "He has been acting upon the advice of honest Iago, 'put money in thy purse'; and left thyself and others to peril health, property, and reputation in the long and stern struggle which preceded the late Revolution." Choate was elected, and Whittier commented in a somewhat changed tone that Choate was a man of talents and good character but had not given any particular service to the Whig Party. With some inconsistency he hoped in the same letter that the postmaster in Amesbury, who had surely done nothing for the Whig Party, having voted for Van Buren, should not be removed.[28]

Whittier continued to lament that irrelevant issues had been brought into the Anti-Slavery cause. In a long letter to Abby Kelly he explained a misunderstanding about what he had said in a conversation on the rights of women, especially their part in Anti-Slavery business meetings. He regretted that the platform of the American Anti-Slavery Society had been made an arena for a contest about woman's rights, and at the same time he did not approve of the language and sensitiveness of some of the opponents of woman's rights. He was sick of quarreling with friends that he had once loved and he looked back with mournful regret to earlier Anti-Slavery meetings "when Peace sat hand in hand with Freedom."[29]

In the middle of the winter Whittier was given one hundred acres of land in Pennsylvania as a tribute to his devotion to Anti-Slavery. It was from Samuel Webb, who said that the soil was good and could be cultivated profitably when the district became settled. The possibility of the Whittiers' moving from Amesbury, where Elizabeth was still homesick for the Haverhill farm, had been mentioned in the fall of 1840 by Sarah Lewis and Ann Wendell. When Elizabeth was in Philadelphia in 1839 she wrote enthusiastically about the life of Pennsylvania farmers. There is no evidence that Whittier went further than to concede that the life of a Pennsylvania farmer was perfect comfort "as to the outward." Elizabeth did not give up the idea easily; in a letter to their brother a few months later she wrote that it would be nice if he and Greenleaf could have a farm together in Pennsylvania. Whittier never took possession of the land, which was in a remote part of the state, and it was finally sold for unpaid taxes.

Luckily for Whittier's state of mind, a letter came with an offer of just the sort of thing that he liked best — travel, meeting people, and, fortunately in the light of lack of money in the Whittier household, all expenses paid. The letter was from Joseph Sturge, the wealthy English Quaker and philanthropist, founder of the British and Foreign Anti-Slavery Society, who wanted Whittier to be his companion on a visit to the United States. He intended to look into the possibility of further cooperation between the British and Foreign and the American and Foreign Anti-Slavery Societies, of more active participation by American Quakers in Anti-Slavery work, and of a conference of nations to establish permanent world peace. He did not wish his plan made public, and Whittier did not even mention it to Harriet Minot the next month. He said only that he was thinking of going to New York and Philadelphia "among other things to escape our East Winds which I dread."

In spite of the fact that he thought that his health was uncertain and in spite of his heroic statement to Elizabeth Lloyd that he must labor "with head, or hands if necessary, for the maintenance of that pecuniary independence which every honorable mind must seek after" he met Joseph Sturge at the Carleton Hotel in New York April 4, leaving Elizabeth to support the household by school teaching.[30]

X

1841 - 42

Joseph Sturge was busy meeting Anti-Slavery people, but found time to spend two or three hours with Whittier, who he decided would be a perfect companion. On April 10 they went to Burlington by train and stayed at Stephen Grellet's. On the fifteenth they returned to New York with Dr. Benjamin Fussell, who had been active in liberating negroes illegally held as slaves. Sturge met with the Executive Committee of the American and Foreign Anti-Slavery Society, and then he and Whittier left for Philadelphia, where they attended the Philadelphia Yearly Meeting of Friends; Elizabeth Lloyd was favorably impressed by Sturge, whom she found candid, courageous, and decided in his opinions, but so kind and good natured that no one was offended by what he said. [1]

They arrived in Baltimore on the twenty-eighth, where Sturge discovered that church people, except Friends, were implicated in slavery. He tried to call on a Catholic bishop to ask if it was true that some Catholics in Maryland had sold negro members of their church and had used the proceeds toward a new building. Later he told a priest in Philadelphia that he would like to be able to contradict the report, but the priest never sent him any information about it. Sturge remarked, however, that Catholics were generally less implicated in slavery than other church bodies — especially, he soon discovered, the Baptists. He and Whittier attended the Triennial Convention of Baptists of the United States, where he observed that slave-holding ministers succeeded in keeping Abolitionists off the Missionary Board.

They were courteously received at Hope H. Slaughter's slave trading establishment in a large new building on a principal street. Sturge was pained to see bolts and bars on the windows, but he found everything clean and orderly, and the slaves seemed to be well fed. There were only five or six in stock, a cargo having been shipped a few days before to New Orleans, where the highest prices were paid. They were introduced to the proprietor by a man who had been active in preventing illegal enslavement of negroes; the proprietor approved of his efforts and sent questionable cases to him for investigation. The proprietor claimed that he never parted families, and he succeeded in convincing Sturge that slave dealing was no worse than slave holding. Sturge soon found, however, that people who believed in slavery had a poor opinion of slave trading; this trader was not received in good society, and his wife was avoided by her former friends.

On May 1 they were in Wilmington, where they were guests of Samuel Hilles. The "silk fever" had reached Wilmington, and Sturge, a good business man, was interested to hear that people had lost money by raising so many mulberry trees that the market was glutted. When Sturge left Wilmington May 3, Whittier was sick and remained there for a week, later sending a letter and sonnet as thanks for a week's nursing. He was in Philadelphia May 12 and wrote a cheerful letter to Moses Cartland, reporting that he and Sturge had found much to encourage them in their efforts to arouse new interest in Abolition. He stayed in Philadelphia until Sturge joined him, and on June 6 they went to Wilmington and Baltimore, part of the way with Samuel E. Sewall.[2] From Baltimore they went by train to Washington, a two-hour trip which led Sturge to comment that American railroads were very narrow and the train passed so close to the piers of bridges and viaducts that notices were posted in the cars warning passengers not to put their arms, heads, or legs out of the window.

Sturge and Whittier evidently kept all portions of their persons inside the car and arrived safely in Washington. They went to the Capitol and had seats behind the Speaker's chair in the House during a discussion of the re-enactment of the "gag rule" to the effect that all petitions for the abolition of slavery in the District of Columbia should be considered as objected to and laid on the table. They then visited the Senate where they met Henry Clay, whom Whittier had once admired with boyish enthusiasm and who now, with his fascinating smile and winning voice, playfully reproached Whittier for deserting an old friend.[3] Clay complained that Abolitionists improperly interfered with the affairs of the South but made an exception of the Society of Friends, and Whittier's zeal for Abolition led Clay to ask if he was a Friend in regular standing. They called on John Quincy Adams and found that he had no hope for the success of his motion to repeal the "gag rule."

Sturge found that the District of Columbia was the chief slave-trading center in America. Plantations in nearby states where the soil had been exhausted were now profitable slave-breeding establishments from which slaves were sent to the District of Columbia to be sold and sent to states where their labor was still profitable, overland in chained coffles or by sea in coastwise vessels. Sturge and Whittier visited slave-trading establishments in Washington and across the Potomac River in Alexandria. The slave market in Washington was within sight of the Capitol, and some slave dealers kept their slaves in the city prison for thirty-four cents a day, the prison in which Dr. Reuben Crandall had been confined for lending Whittier's *Justice and Expediency* to another physician. There were rows of small cells, each with five or six prisoners although hardly large enough for one. The heat was like the tropics, and the keeper told them that there was no fire there in the winter.[4] In the Alexandria market they saw some of the younger slaves dancing to a fiddle, but others were not so gay; one woman and her nine children had been sold away from her husband and would probably be sent to New

Orleans where they would be resold and separated. From this market between fifteen hundred and two thousand slaves were sent annually to the South.

What he saw made Whittier feel that all that he had done for Emancipation was trifling, and he thought of Jonathan Edwards' remark: "If these things be enthusiasms and the fruit of distempered brains, let me evermore be hallowed by their happy distemper." It seemed to him that anyone who could visit the slave markets without being stirred by sorrow and indignation must be either more or less than human.

From Washington, Sturge and Whittier went to Philadelphia and New York where they wrote a joint letter to Lewis Tappan urging him not to resign as treasurer and member of the Executive Committee of the American and Foreign Anti-Slavery Society.[5] They then went by steamer to Newport and the New England Yearly Meeting of Friends. Whittier joined a group of young Friends who promenaded the deck. Sturge was friendly and informal, and after the young people were tired of walking he sat with them in a circle at one end of the boat.[6] They arrived at Newport at seven in the morning, and Sturge was pleased to discover that the climate of Rhode Island was almost as temperate as summer weather in England; elsewhere in their journey the temperature had been between ninety-four and ninety-six in the shade. Sturge asked permission to use the Friends meetinghouse with John Candler for an anti-slavery meeting and was refused, but about two hundred people met at his hotel. Sturge and Whittier called on William Ellery Channing at his summer home near Newport; it was the last time Whittier saw him, and he described the visit in the poem "Channing" three years later.

On June 29 Sturge and Whittier left for Providence and New Bedford. In Providence they called at Thomas W. Dorr's in the evening and again the next morning, and not finding him at home wrote to invite him to dinner.[7] Dorr was in the midst of his efforts to get a new constitution for Rhode Island to replace the one inherited from Colonial times which had resulted in the disenfranchisement of over half the adult male voters, but he had not yet resorted to what Whittier later called "violent means."

They were in Boston June 21. Sturge was impressed by the number and size of the hotels and was pleased that at the Marlboro House, as at several other first-rate hotels in New England, no liquor was sold. Sturge talked with Garrison in an attempt to unite the two Anti-Slavery Societies, but Garrison was so insistent upon the question of women's rights that no progress was made. The next day they were in Lynn, where Sturge found that many former Friends had joined non-resistance and non-government groups. In the evening they arrived at Whittier's house in Amesbury, where the entertainment of a guest in such a small house must have been somewhat of a problem. They remained over Sunday, and Sturge attended the Friends Meeting; a neighbor remembered many years later the sense of expectancy in the groups which gathered before the meeting near the long row of carriage sheds.[8] Sturge visited one of the large mills and was favorably impressed. It was clean, and the workers appeared to be comfortable and prosperous. Many of them were young women, none under sixteen. Temperance was enforced: "Any person given to intoxication would be instantly discharged."

During their few days in Amesbury Whittier found time to write to Frederick Palmer Tracy, a Methodist minister active in the Liberty Party in New Hampshire. Whittier had now come to approve of an independent political party definitely committed to Abolition, and he liked the nominations that the party had made in New Hampshire. In his usual practical way he urged that the Liberty Party should try to get the support of the "Old Organization" people and should not waste time quarreling with them and that Moses Cartland be nominated if any of the nominees declined. Cartland's name, he believed, would lead many Quakers to vote the Liberty Party ticket. After Whittier had left with Sturge for New York and returned unwell to Amesbury, he wrote to Elizur Wright suggesting that John Pierpont, then pastor of the Hollis Street Church in Boston, be given the nomination for governor. The Party would then get the Temperance vote, and Whittier was sure that there were thousands who, like himself, would be glad of a chance to honor Pierpont. In the same letter he said that he would be in Boston in a few days if his health was good enough. It evidently was, as he and Wright met with Sturge and others in New York to discuss the best time to hold a second World's Anti-Slavery Convention. He planned to call at the Hoopers' before leaving New York, but was tired and unwell and spent the afternoon and evening in his room suffering what he called "severe pain."[9] He and Sturge left for Boston by steamer July 24.

Sturge, Whittier, and C. Stewart Renshaw visited Lowell, where Sturge and Renshaw were impressed by the high moral and intellectual character of the workers in the textile mills and their contrast to the degraded and oppressed working women of England and the slave women of the South.[10] They noticed that the girls were quiet and orderly even when leaving for dinner. The superintendent told Sturge that in his two and a half years at the mills where about nine hundred fifty girls were employed there had been only one case of illegitimate birth — and the girl was an Irish immigrant. He made another unpleasant remark about the Irish: many of the girls who could not write and had to sign their names with a mark (about five per cent of the number employed) were Irish.

Sturge's visit to Amesbury must have made him aware of the lack of money in the Whittier household. He must also have realized that Whittier had had no chance to earn money since early April. On July 30, two days before sailing to England, he sent one thousand dollars to Lewis Tappan for Whittier's use during the next twelve months with a note that it was "for his personal and other current expenses of housekeeping, traveling, etc., or a visit to a tropical climate for the sake of his health and if he should not need the whole for this purpose he will please apply the remainder to any traveling or other expense connected with his labor with the 'Reporter' or any other anti-slavery object.''[11] Sturge also left one thousand dollars with Tappan for Anti-Slavery purposes.[12] There is no way of knowing what use Whittier made of the money, but his income during the next twelve months was so small that most of it may have been needed for household expenses.

On August 1 Whittier saw Sturge on board the *Caledonia*, a steamer from Boston to Liverpool, and within twenty-four hours was deep in Liberty Party politics. At an Essex County organization meeting August 2 he was nominated for the State Senate and accepted rather than cause embarrassment to those who believed, as he now did, that Abolitionists must have their own party, having nothing to hope for from either Whigs or Democrats. With organization had come a new sense of strength, and he wrote a vigorous letter to Cushing a few days later. He conceded that for the present it would be to Cushing's advantage to go along with the South, but it would be a different story ten years later. In spite of their friendship, he himself could not vote for Cushing if he became convinced that it would be against his Anti-Slavery principles to do so. The letter closed with the graceful personal touch that Whittier was increasingly able to use in letters on a wide variety of topics: he would like to talk the matter over with Cushing and assured him that sincere friendship was the cause of his abruptness and frankness.[13]

In spite of his confidence in the future of the Liberty Party he was quite aware of its present weakness, and two days after his letter to Cushing he wrote a hurried note to Samuel E. Sewall just as the mail stage was leaving, urging that the Liberty Party Committee should issue a call for a state convention. On the same day he sent a petition on the same topic to the Chairman of the Liberty Party Committee, pointing out that a Convention would arouse a stronger and deeper feeling in regard to voting for the Liberty Party.[14] His advice was not immediately followed: the convention was held nearly two months later, October 7.

Whittier had been too busy to do any writing since early spring, but now leisure and a piece of sad news resulted in a poem. On August 6 he saw a newspaper notice of the death of Lucy Hooper and immediately wrote a letter of condolence to her sisters.[15] He had had few friends so dear to him and he wanted to know all about the death-bed scene. But more important, he was sure that she still lived, a conviction that he repeated fully and clearly when he wrote "Lucy Hooper" a few days later. The immortality that he now believed in and that gave him peace and security in his later years — and by which he gave peace and security to countless thousands — was clear and definite. He was sure that his friends in the spirit land were themselves;

Lucy Hooper was living in
> . . . . . Holier beauty now,
> Baptized in immortality.

It would have been well if the situation had ended on this lofty plane. However, a few days after writing the poem he received a letter from Lucy's sister Amelia, complaining that he had given Lucy the impression that he loved her and then had hurt her with his coldness. There had been nothing in Lucy's letters that would suggest this, and Whittier may well have thought that it was a product of Amelia's imagination, but he replied in the only way a gentleman could: he admired and loved Lucy and was compelled to repress his feelings for good and honorable reasons — poverty, illness, difference of religious beliefs, his dedication to Anti-Slavery. As for the coldness by which he had hurt Lucy's feelings, he explained that as something that his friends complained about: he was at one time all warmth and feeling and at another cold and remote. One may wonder how fully Lucy's sisters accepted all this when he declined to edit her poems and, knowing that a poetic expression of his feelings would be expected, economically reminded them of lines which he had sent to them in 1837. He might send them a poem that he had been writing about Lucy's death and which he might not publish — but which he did publish a few weeks later.[16]

While Whittier's sense of loss was probably genuine, it was not overwhelming. On the day when he wrote "Lucy Hooper" he also wrote two letters, one to Harriet Winslow and one to Moses Cartland. Sickness and perplexities made him crave companionship, and he wanted Cartland to come to Amesbury if only to say to him, "Let us all be unhappy together" — but it was not to be a mere sharing of melancholy. They would go to the Liberty Convention at Ipswich on August 24. Perhaps there is some evidence of emotional strain, however, in the mistakes in the letter: he wrote that the "American and National A.S. Society," which must mean the "American and Foreign," had invited a number of Anti-Slavery men including Cartland to write to the "U.S. Reporter," evidently the "American and Foreign Anti-Slavery Reporter."[17]

News that he was to send articles to the *Reporter* had displeased some of his Philadelphia friends who took it to mean that he would war against the Old Organization (The American Anti-Slavery Society). He defended himself in a letter to Elizabeth Neall. He didn't intend to quarrel, any more than he had in the past, with any sincere Abolitionists. After its first number the *Reporter* had said nothing about the quarrels between Abolitionists — and that was one reason he was willing to write for it. But he had no intention of moving to New York, where the office of the *Reporter* was, or doing anything except write editorials when he was well enough. He had been elected to the position in May but did not have time to do any writing until Sturge had left for England. The position lasted only two months, when the paper came to an end from lack of funds. Whittier had to wait six years for his pay.[18]

He also wrote at this time a prose article, "Light Out of Obscurity," printed in the September 4 issue of *The Friend*.[19] He had read a description of two temples in India, one of which was said to be dedicated to the "Creator of the World" and had no images or symbols, and the other was dedicated to "The Invisible." This led him to think that a simple-hearted people had used these temples for a spiritual worship before the "huge structure of emblematic worship" had been erected by the priests. This is such good fundamental Quaker doctrine that one may suspect that it was written to please the editors and readers of *The Friend*. He must also have expected some income at this time from an English edition of his poems that Jonathan Candler had undertaken to have published,[20] but nothing came of it, and the first English edition was three years later.

Whittier now settled down for a few months of comparatively quiet life in Amesbury. He did no campaigning for the State Senate. At the election he received about eight hundred votes; the Whig candidate was elected with about seven thousand.[21]

On election day Whittier could not have given much thought to the number of votes he would get. He was writing a poem. "Democracy" is a sincere statement of his political faith; democracy had been the ideal of his boyhood and he still believed in it because it saw the man beneath all sorts of disguises. The theme is the same as "The Poor Voter on Election Day" written nine years later but the expression is less vigorous and convincing. It was printed in the *United States Magazine and Democratic Review*, which would print fifteen other Whittier poems during the next five years, making it the chief medium by which Whittier reached the public until he became Corresponding Editor of the *National Era* in 1847. The *Review*, established in 1836, was partly political and partly literary and had the distinction of printing more of Hawthorne's short stories than any other magazine. It was the best medium thus far for Whittier's verse, but the profit was in reputation rather than in cash. The editor, John L. O'Sullivan, wrote to Whittier in the spring of 1843 that he was "rather loose in accounts" and did not really know how much he owed. He enclosed an amount which he hoped would be acceptable, but since he said that he had been "considerably embarrassed lately," it was probably not large.[22]

Whittier's popularity as a poet was still rising. An editorial in the *Newburyport Herald* commented favorably on his poems in *Cheever's Commonplace Book of Poetry* and, among scores of others, is proof that Edgar Allan Poe was right when he wrote that Whittier was placed "by his particular admirers in the very first rank of American poets." But Poe was not one of Whittier's admirers. Whittier was a "fine versifier," he thought, as far as strength without modulation was concerned, but he did not like

Whittier's themes, which were chosen with the purpose of giving free scope to a certain *vivida vis* of expression; Whittier was deficient in taste and imagination.[23]

If Whittier saw this comment, it is unlikely that he was greatly concerned. He was thinking more about Anti-Slavery and the Society of Friends than about poetry. It weighed upon his conscience that he had not spoken more openly about Anti-Slavery in Quaker Meetings. He and others who might have spoken were young and found it hard to oppose the ministers and elders; when a few of them did speak against the decision of the Yearly Meeting to forbid Anti-Slavery speakers to use Quaker meetinghouses, they were accused of insubordination.

Sturge was preparing his *Visit to the United States in 1841* and Whittier contributed "The Old School of Abolitionists" and "The Present State of the Anti-Slavery Cause." He was also busy writing for papers and getting up petitions. One of the papers was the *Emancipator*, on which he substituted occasionally for Joshua Leavitt after it was moved from New York to Boston late in 1841.

He was in Boston frequently during the winter of 1841-42. Maria W. Chapman saw him in the Anti-Slavery office lamenting to Garrison that the Society had been divided and asking why they could not all work together. Garrison could see no reason why Whittier and the others could not work with the American Anti-Slavery Society. Whittier replied that it was not what it had once been: "It has the hat and coat and the waistcoat of the old Society, but the life has gone out of it."[24]

He was again seriously worried about his health and was resolved that whether there was a long or short period ahead of him, he would try to use it for human welfare. But his health was better in January when he wrote to Sturge about the excitement caused by a petition to Congress for a peaceful dissolution of the Union which was taking the "blustering Southerners" at their word. This was the so-called Haverhill Petition, which resulted from the determination of a group of Abolitionists in Haverhill to show that the North was not to be intimidated by Southern threats to dissolve the Union. It was written by Benjamin Emerson and was signed by many members of the Union Evangelical Church and by others the next day, a total of forty-six; two withdrew their signatures, one under pressure of his employer. It was presented in the House by John Quincy Adams January 14. A motion to censure Adams was followed by long and bitter debate and threats of assassination. Adams enjoyed the excitement, and petitions poured in against the attempt to censure, which had become a cause of constitutional rights. The matter was finally laid on the table February 7.[25]

Neither the petitioners nor Whittier seriously intended to try to dissolve the Union, even though Whittier wrote in a letter to Samuel E. Sewall that if Texas was to be added to the Union let us say "Disunion before Texas!" That was an impatient exclamation when everything seemed to be going wrong, including a pamphlet by Lewis Cass, then Minister to France, on the Right of Search, which Whittier took to be an effort for the protection of the foreign slave trade.[26] His considered opinion was expressed a few years later when he said that the moral and political power needed to dissolve the Union could more easily abolish slavery. Whittier had nothing to do with the writing of the Haverhill Petition, and if he had been asked to sign it would have refused. However, he came to the defense of Abolitionists when the petition was used as a reason for accusing them of disregarding the welfare of the country and of being determined to get what they wanted by any available means. In a letter in the *Newburyport Herald* February 4 and in the *Emancipator* February 25 he pointed out that the benefits and privileges of the Union were denied to Abolitionists as effectually as if there were not any Union. Petitions for the abolition of slavery in the District of Columbia had been refused consideration and were now absolutely rejected. In some parts of the country men were in danger unless they were silent on the question of Liberty. Whittier himself had been warned that by giving a book about slavery to personal friends in Baltimore he had run the risk of imprisonment for ten years. Torrey had been tried on this charge in Baltimore, and Amos Dresser had been scourged in Nashville.[27] Lynch committees had been formed throughout the South, and free negroes were illegally jailed. No Abolitionist was safe in the District of Columbia, as Dr. Crandall's nine-month imprisonment showed. Abolition publications were excluded from the mails in parts of the country. The Slave Power controlled Congress, where nearly one fourth of the representatives from slave states were representatives of slaves but elected by the owners. This Power had kept slavery in the District of Columbia, injured free labor, distributed surplus revenue to benefit slave holders, spent forty million dollars on a war in Florida to recover five hundred fugitive slaves — and now that it met opposition it threatened to dissolve the Union. If the Union must perish, the responsibility must rest upon slaveholders.

Whittier was still trying to get John Pierpont to be a Liberty Party candidate, this time for Congress. Everyone to whom Whittier mentioned Pierpont was enthusiastic about him, and there seemed to be a good chance that he might be elected. When Whittier wrote to him he seemed favorably inclined but thought that he should consult leading members of his church. Pierpont received the nomination but declined, evidently under pressure from his church members. He wrote to Whittier that he must wait until ministers became free men and the pulpit was no longer controlled by the pews. This freedom he thought should come before the freeing of the slaves.

Anti-Slavery and politics had not crowded out Whittier's other interests. He read some pamphlets written by clergymen opposing the abolition of capital punishment and wrote the lines later entitled "The Gallows" in which he said that the clergy, like Christ's disciples, had misunderstood his teachings, had, in an effective line,

Wet the war-banner with their sacred wine

and, in the torture of heretics, had committed Earth's most hateful crimes in Christ's name. He was thankful to be living in a time when men were beginning to see that revenge is crime and human life more sacred than creed. "Who shall arrest this tendency?" he asked in a most unpoetic line, and answered that if the clergy tried to do it the public would reject them and class them with the pagan priesthood of the past.

In spite of the fact that he was doing little writing — no new poems appeared in 1842 until September — he was still part of the literary world. He was invited to meet Dickens at the dinner in Boston. He did not go, and while he admired Dickens' genius he found some things that he did not approve; still, he thought that Dickens was doing good, especially in his finding good in the lowest and most sinful people and in his recognizing the universal brotherhood of mankind. Later in the year he read Dickens' *American Notes* with infinite satisfaction, delighting in his "good nature, outgushing philanthropy, quaint, calm humour, and marvellous skill of description." He liked especially the "scorching chapter on slavery."[28]

Whittier felt guilty after reading Bulwer's *Zanoni,* which he read because his "organ of marvelousness" was excited by hearing about it. It was written in Bulwer's usual ponderous style and dealt with reincarnation, the Rosicrucians, the secret of living forever, and magnetism, all tinctured with quite sweet romantic love. Whittier's feeling of guilt came from his belief that such topics should be taken seriously. He did not approve of public lectures on magnetism, which seemed to him to have direct bearing on the duality of being, and he was inclined to doubt clairvoyance; yet, having admitted the fact that unnatural sleep could be produced by mesmerism, he wondered if he wasn't bound to accept a great deal more upon reasonable evidence.[29]

He was thinking a good deal about religion. He read Follen's essay about immortality and wrote "Follen," repeating the belief in the survival of personality that he had stated in "Lucy Hooper." He was curious about the details of the future life: were there scenes of natural beauty in Heaven like those on earth? However, he concluded that these were not things that mortals should know. They should trustfully leave Follen with God

While with thy childlike faith we lean

On Him whose dearest name is Love!

The thought in these closing lines controlled Whittier's religious life as long as he lived and is best known through the final stanza of "The Eternal Goodness," written twenty-three years later:

And Thou, O Lord! by whom are seen

Thy creatures as they be.

Forgive me if too close I lean
    My human heart on thee!

In this mood he wrote to Ann Wendell, whose patience and faith during physical suffering he had long admired, that the calm faith that breathed through her letters to him rebuked his restless and inquiring spirit and through them he learned to admire the philosophy which did not look for all the answers but bowed to the will of God.

He also found himself in sympathy with John Woolman and wanted to share him with his friends. It would be twenty-nine years before he would write an introduction for a new edition of Woolman's *Journal*, but he sent copies of an edition published two years earlier to some of his friends. One was sent to a retired Unitarian minister in Newburyport; for a number of years Whittier and his sister Elizabeth enjoyed the friendship of Thomas Tracy and his wife, and Whittier found in him something that he did not quite find in anyone else. Tracy was sixty-one at the time. He was a graduate of Harvard and, having independent means, had retired from the ministry in 1828 and come to Newburyport, where he lived in a house on Brown Square until his death at the age of ninety-one. He was a student of European languages and translated a number of German tales including Fouque's *Undine*. In May, Whittier read Harriet Winslow's poem "Undine" to the Tracys, and Tracy gave him a volume of his translations and *Follen's Memoirs*. Whittier belatedly acknowldged these in June and sent a copy of Woolman's *Journal* along with an address of the Liberty Party to the citizens of Massachusetts, not to force his opinions upon Tracy but simply because it was something that he had written himself. Tracy's reply compared Woolman and Follen and concluded with a statement of faith in immortality like Whittier's own: Follen and Woolman might "have already met and embraced with a joyful reality of union which we are not able to apprehend."[30]

Whittier wrote to Ann Wendell in July that he would defer a visit to Philadelphia until her sister Margaret invited him and Elizabeth to her wedding. The invitation came, with the request that Whittier be groomsman and Elizabeth bridesmaid. Whittier replied rather doubtfully, and Joseph Cartland wrote to urge them; the wedding had been postponed a week in the hope that they would come. Ann Wendell urged Elizabeth not to let worry about clothes keep her from coming. She could just take a white dress of silk or merino for the wedding, and as for the other clothes, she could put them in a trunk, step on them to crowd them down as men do, and just come; if her clothes were wrinkled Ann would have a hot iron ready to smooth them. In spite of these encouragements the Whittiers did not attend the wedding. If Whittier had accepted the invitation, his fashionable cousins would not have been ashamed of his appearance. In spite of his limited means and the time and attention that he was giving to politics, Anti-Slavery, and religion, he dressed well. According to Allen W. Dodge, who saw him in

February of that year, Whittier was "quite a dandy as to dress, which is in the neatest and prinkest Quaker style."[31]

Joseph Sturge (1793-1859).

John Quincy Adams (1767-1848).

Caleb Cushing (1800-1879). Portrait c.1830.
(Courtesy of Historical Society of Old
Newbury)

John P. Hale (1806-1873).

XI
1842 - 43

At a Liberty Convention in Haverhill October 16, 1842, Whittier was nominated for Representative to Congress from the Third District. It was known before the convention that he would accept; he had said that as long as Abolition was an unpopular cause, with church and state united against it, he was willing to serve wherever his friends assigned him, but he would support some other candidate when the Liberty Party was likely to win an election.

There was no chance that Whittier would be elected, but his candidacy could not be ignored. As the election law then stood, the winner must receive a majority of the votes cast, and Whittier's and other scattering votes were enough to prevent an election for over a year. Whittier promised that the campaign would be on a high level, but he did little or no campaigning. His opponents were more vigorous and not so high-minded, and before the campaign was over Whittier was accused of ill-treating his wife. There was objection to him because he was a Quaker and not enough of a democrat, which was answered, with some irrelevance, by a quotation from the *United States Magazine and Democratic Review* referring to him as "The Howard and Clarkson of America."[1]

As far as his own candidacy was concerned, Whittier kept calm. He was no longer disturbed by the ambitions and what he called the selfish hopes of his earlier years. His enthusiasm had been "tamed down by that cross-grained schoolmistress, Experience,"[2] and it was not strong enough to dominate his thoughts and feelings. Late one afternoon he called at Thomas Tracy's when the sunset light was on a picture of Raphael as a boy[3]. As he looked at it, rather sentimentally, the walls of the room seemed to disappear and he saw Raphael's paintings — of which he knew more than might have been expected. The vision taught him a lesson — which to him would justify the poem "Raphael" while to a later generation it would have the opposite effect: We are making our future life by our deeds in the present one — "Man's works shall follow him."

"Raphael" pleased James Russell Lowell. He had written to Whittier in October asking for a contribution to the *Pioneer*, a new magazine of which he was to be one of the editors and which was to "run before" the age and, incidentally, pay authors higher than any other magazine in the United States. Lowell had not received a reply when he wrote again December 16 hoping that Whittier would give him something or at least send word in time for him to plan his second (February) number. "I like your poem 'Raphael' very much indeed,'' the letter continued, ''perhaps better in some ways than any poem of yours. I do not mean that it is better of its kind — but that its kind is pleasanter to me. But I like the others better after all, for the noble causes they have always espoused.'' In the same mood Lowell described Whittier in an article in the *Pioneer* on Longfellow's *Poems on Slavery*: ''the fiery Koerner of this spiritual warfare, who, Scaevola-like, has sacrificed on the altar of duty that right hand which might have made him acknowledged as the most passionate lyrist of his time.''[4]

Whittier sent a poem in time for the February *Pioneer*. It was ''Lines written in the Book of a Friend,'' which, with the addition of sixteen stanzas and the omission of one, reappeared a few months later in *Lays of My Home and Other Poems* and is in the Riverside Edition with the title ''Ego.'' Lowell may have regarded it as a passionate lyric; it was rather a piece of self-centered, plaintive melancholy of the kind often found in autograph albums. He had, it said, spoken out against slavery and in so doing had turned away from love and from poetry about love with consequent loss of fame. It would be pleasant to believe that this self-pity was the mood of a moment and merely the way he happened to feel when the lady handed him her album and asked him to write in it. However, the thought evidently pleased him and he developed it further in the stanzas added for publication in *Lays of My Home and Other Poems*.

A similar thought appeared a few months later in ''To J. P.,'' addressed to John Pierpont, whose ''Airs of Palestine'' he had enjoyed in his boyhood. He wrote that Pierpont, like himself, had found life too earnest and too short
> For dreamy ease and Fancy's graceful sport.

As far as Whittier was concerned, this was of course an over-simplification. He had done some unselfish and efficient work for good causes, but his life had not been a self-denying dedication to any of them.

In contrast to his slight interest in his own candidacy, he could get excited and angry when other Liberty Party candidates were badly treated. He wrote an indignant letter to the *Newburyport Herald*, which had quoted a paragraph from the *Lowell Courier* stating that Samuel E. Sewall, Liberty Party candidate for governor, had voted for Marcus Morton and the whole Democratic ticket. No one who knew the ''stern, habitual integrity'' of Sewall would believe this, Whittier wrote. Sewall had made freedom his great object for the past ten years, and Whittier asked the privilege of pronouncing the *Courier's* statement an ''unmitigated and malicious lie.'' He was happy when Sewall's vote was large enough to frighten the Legislature into doing what Abolitionists wished.[5]

He could also become excited and bitter when other advocates of Anti-Slavery were badly treated. In the autumn he wrote ''Leggett's Monument,'' which he sent to Fields the next spring for inclusion in *Lays of My Home and Other Poems*, calling it ''a bitter sonnet — if it be one and it is the only one I ever attempted to write — which grew out of the hyprocrisy of the N. Y. Locos getting up a subscription to Leggett's monument."[6] Whittier's bitterness and anger were doubtless justified and the quotation at the head of the poem — "Ye build the tombs of the prophets" — applicable to the situation, but excitement does not always result in good poetry:

> And planted in the pathway of his life
> The ploughshares of your hatred hot from hell

is a hopelessly confusing metaphor. He was quite right in doubting that the fourteen lines were properly a sonnet. The first four lines had the rhyme scheme of the Petrarchan quatrain, but the remaining lines rhymed in a rather haphazard fashion and there was no sestet, lines 9 and 10 being the last two of a quatrain.

Bitterness also tortured some of the stanzas in "The Christian Slave." Whittier had read an account of a slave auction in New Orleans where a woman on sale had been described as a good Christian. Again Whittier's bitterness and despair made it impossible for him to write well; hence prosaic lines and poor phrasing and even lack of clarity —

> But her low, broken prayer and nightly tears,
>   Ye neither heed nor feel.

There was less bitterness, more vigor, and better poetry in "Massachusetts to Virginia" because it dealt with a situation that something could be done about. On October 21, 1842, eight years before the Fugitive Slave Law, a negro named George Latimer was seized in Boston without a warrant at the request of a man who claimed to be his owner and was taken to Leverett Street Jail. Whittier shared in the excitement. He wrote to Henry I. Bowditch, who had a leading part in a meeting at Faneuil Hall, "May the God of the poor and oppressed guide, direct, and strengthen you in your effort for Latimer's deliverance — There is but one feeling here with regard to Latimer — that he *must not* be given up." In his usual practical way, he helped in a movement to use the excitement to get the Legislature to pass laws forbidding citizens or state or municipal officers to help restore slaves to their owners.[7] A few weeks later, January 2, he was on the Business Committee of a Latimer Convention in Ipswich, and "Massachusetts to Virginia" was written to be read there. One of the seventy-five people present later recalled that the Convention met in the "gloomy, barn-like Congregational vestry" and that the poem was read by James Boyd of Ohio.[8] It was immediately popular and has so remained. Whittier's emotion this time did not prevent artistic expression, and the reader, even to-day, feels what Whittier felt. The poem has some good imagery and phrasing, as

> . . . . . We fling no torch within
> The fire-damps of your quaking mine beneath your
>   soil of sin.

But Whittier's sense of sound was still imperfect: he rhymed "pen" and "been," as he did twenty-one years later in "Maud Muller". His fondness for geographical lists led him to enumerate eleven of the fourteen counties in Massachusetts.[9]

Thomas Wentworth Higginson, nineteen years old, saw Whittier in a restaurant in Boston and remembered him later as "tall, slender, with olive complexion, black hair, straight black eyebrows, brilliant eyes, and an Oriental, Semitic cast of countenance." Higginson went up to him as he arose from the table and said, "I should like to shake hands with the author of 'Massachusetts to Virginia' " and felt when they shook hands that he was touching a hero's shield. Then there is a pleasant story of a Southern student at Harvard who was challenged to recite "Massachusetts to Virginia," found his own sentiments giving way to those of the author, and became a Northern sympathizer.[10]

If Whittier needed more facts to justify what he had frequently said about the church and slavery, he found them in a pamphlet entitled "Evangelicus" which he reviewed in the *Emancipator*.[11] The pamphlet seemed to him to be an effort to reconcile Christ and Belial. The author thought it unnecessary to inquire whether the New Testament tolerated slavery as a permanent institution. The question, Whittier insisted, must be answered: if Christianity does sanction the vile wrong of slavery, let it perish. But to say that Christ tolerated the "horrible atrocities of human slavery" was blasphemy — and the Christian church in the North must break its connections with blasphemers and slave-holders or perish with them.

He was doing his share of Liberty Party and Anti-Slavery work. He served as chairman of the County Committee of the Essex County Liberty Party. He called a convention September 26, 1843, at the Methodist Church in Newbury to nominate State Senators. He was on the Business Committee of this convention with Frederick P. Tracy and George J. L. Colby, then editor of the *Essex Transcript* and later for many years editor of the *Newburyport Herald*. He called a convention at Lynn October 5 and one at the South Meeting House in Georgetown December 26 for the purpose of opposing the annexation of Texas.[12]

He was also chairman of the County Committee of the Essex County Anti-Slavery Society. One of his pleasant duties was to call a meeting at Ipswich August 1, 1843, to celebrate the emancipation of slaves in the West Indies and to take measures to promote the cause of Freedom in the United States. Whittier's announcement ended on a lofty note: "Let there be a full and glorious meeting of the Abolitionists of Essex County and of all who, to any extent, sympathize with them in their efforts to hasten the day when Liberty shall be proclaimed *throughout the land, unto all the inhabitants thereof.*"[13] Someone added to the notice in the *Newburyport Herald* a detail of lower order with perhaps more drawing power: there would be a "clam chowder served up in the best Ipswich fashion." Whittier was a leading figure at the meeting, calling it to order and serving on the Nominating Committee and as chairman of the Business Committee, and was appointed a delegate to the National Convention. In October he helped to arrange an Anti-Slavery meeting in Haverhill and asked James Russell Lowell to be present, "and if thee could 'open thy mouth for the dumb,' so much the better." He helped to raise money in Amesbury for a negro who wanted to buy the freedom of his four youngest children.[14]

He continued to be interested in other causes. During the winter he worked for the abolition of capital punishment in Massachusetts, arranging petitions and lobbying in Boston, but without much hope of success. He found that the Orthodox clergy and laity and their church newspapers opposed it, calling it a scheme of Quakers, Unitarians, Universalists, and Deists. He then appealed to the public by a poem in the May *United States Magazine and Democratic Review*. "The Human Sacrifice" was more effective than "The Gallows," written a few months earlier. Whittier had read of a clergyman whose belief in the death penalty was confirmed by the anguish of a murderer who died without hope of salvation, and the poem described him somewhat melodramatically as he awoke from a beautiful — and improbable — dream of his country boyhood, with details obviously from Whittier's memories of his own boyhood, to the horror of his approaching death.

Whittier was in sympathy with Thomas Wilson Dorr's cause although not with the violent means to which he believed, erroneously, that Dorr had resorted. He had enjoyed a friendly acquaintance with Dorr and thought it only an act of justice to correct the public impression of his character. Dorr believed in Abolition and in free suffrage and had obtained the repeal of a law which gave banks in Rhode Island certain powers in the collection of debts. Whittier hoped that if Dorr became governor he would believe, as did Daniel O'Connell, that "no revolution was ever worth the price of one drop of human blood."[15]

At the same time Whittier was pleased to see the progress toward universal suffrage in Great Britain, which he thought had not received proper attention in the United States. The National Complete Suffrage Association, led by Joseph Sturge and pledged to universal suffrage and annual Parliaments, had united the middle and working classes on this issue and had the support of a number of distinguished men including Lord Brougham and Daniel O'Connell.[16] Whittier gave them his blessing in "To the Reformers of England"; their weapons were Light, Truth and Love, and he was confident that their peaceful zeal would find

The good which bloodshed could not gain.

He was also confident that love would replace creed and ritual in religion. The Pusey controversy led him to think that the Church of England was ready to go over to Popery and that there was a general tendency toward the old "ghostly mummery and machinery" which would engulf everything except old-fashioned Quakerism. But this, he believed, was merely the forerunner of a complete change in the Christian world when love would take the place of "fast, penance, long prayers, and heathenish sacrifices" and the human heart would be the holy of holies where worship would go on daily and hourly.[17]

This was good Quakerism, but within the Society of Friends love was not the most conspicuous force at the moment. The controversy over John Wilbur's opposition to Joseph John Gurney's evangelical views was at its height, and although the committee of the New England Yearly Meeting which was called in to handle the case had been appointed for the "preservation of love and unity," its methods were more likely to have the opposite effect. When the South Kingston, Rhode Island, Monthly Meeting refused to disown John Wilbur, the Yearly Meeting Committee reported to Rhode Island Quarterly Meeting that the South Kingston Meeting was insubordinate and should be dissolved and its members merged into Greenwich Monthly Meeting. This was done, and John Wilbur was disowned. Whittier wrote to Joseph Sturge that unless great charity and wisdom were used there might be a division in the Society like the Hicksite separation. It is an example of his sense of proportion that he saw that the whole matter was not of major importance. "If J. J. G. does hold some notions of the First Day of the week made in reference to the Scriptures," he wrote, "which are hardly consistent with those of George Fox and William Penn, I can nevertheless believe that he may be a good man still."[18]

Gurney's evangelical approach to religion gained wide acceptance among Friends, and the Amesbury Meeting later came to be considered Gurneyite. Whittier accepted without open protest but occasionally admitted to his friends that he was not pleased.

Within his own Monthly Meeting he found that his views on slavery, temperance, and education were not those of some of the elderly members, and he declined to go to the Quarterly Meeting, feeling that he could not properly represent the Monthly Meeting. He also decided that he could not see his way clear to go to the Yearly Meeting. He had, in fact, virtually reached the conclusion that his place in the Society should be that of a simple member. He later modified this to the extent of being a representative from his Monthly Meeting to Salem Quarterly Meeting, but he was never a representative to New England Yearly Meeting.[19]

From his disappointment with Quakers of his own time he turned to the earlier, heroic days of their persecution. In Sewel's *History of the People Called Quakers*, which Whittier had been familiar with since childhood, there is a brief account of Daniel and Provided Southwick, son and daughter of Lawrence and Cassandra Southwick of Salem, who were ordered by the court to be sold into slavery in Virginia or Barbados when they were unable to pay a fine for non-attendance at church. The order was not popular, and no ship captain was willing to take them. One captain gave as an excuse "that they would spoil all the ship's company." When told that they were "poor harmless creatures and would not hurt anybody," he replied, "And will you offer to make slaves of such harmless creatures?"[20] No further attempt was made to enforce the court order, and the Southwicks were allowed to return to their home. Whittier used his imagination freely. He omitted the brother from the story and gave the girl her mother's name. "Cassandra Southwick" had a long account of the girl's thoughts and a lively and of course wholly apocryphal description of the scene when the ship captain refused, less laconically than in Sewel, to take the girl on his ship. The crowd sided with the captain — a point not mentioned in Sewel and which Whittier explained in the introductory note in the *United States Magazine and Democratic Review* as "that sympathy with the oppressed, which the 'common people,' when not directly under the control of spiritual despotism, have ever evinced." Honesty and fairness to the persecuting Puritan clergy and magistrates compelled him to add that he was not "blind to the extravagance of language and action which characterized some of the pioneers of Quakerism in New England and which furnished persecution with its solitary but most inadequate excuse."

Three prose essays were also an escape to the legendary past and were written with a light touch which showed that Whittier enjoyed writing them. They were printed in successive numbers of the *United States Magazine and Democratic Review* and reappeared in *The Supernaturalism of New England* in 1847, and in 1854, enlarged and revised as "Charms and Fairy Faith," "Magicians and Witch Folk," and "The Agency of Evil," in *Literary Recreations and Miscellanies*.

One day in early summer Whittier found relief from his worries by losing himself in the world of nature, as told in the poem "Hampton Beach." The slow approach to the Beach was part of the experience: the luminous belt of the sea miles away with rocks, hills, and trees clearly seen against it; the horse plodding slowly along a country lane bordered by wild roses and arched over by flowering locust trees; then the cool breeze from the sea. At the Beach he said good-by to Pain and Care and felt as free as the waves, the sea birds, and the far-off sails. But like Wordsworth, he looked for religious significance in nature, and he found it in the thought that after death the soul may rise and join with the vastness of eternity, and the new light of heaven will dawn serene and mild. The poem was written with a delicacy of phrase that suggests the later and more famous "Telling the Bees." Whittier's aesthetic and emotional sensitiveness was not inundated, as it would have been ten years earlier, by youthful exuberance.

The road from Amesbury to Hampton Beach passed the General Moulton House in Hampton,[21] the scene of a New England legend which Whittier had heard in his childhood and which he now told in "The New Wife and the Old." It was written in emphatic trochaic tetrameter lines suggesting the rhythm of Tennyson's "The Lady of Shalott," which had recently appeared in revised form. The story was well told, and those who read it in Whittier's time doubtless liked the concluding lines about the future life: that the weak and innocent triumph unwittingly when they appear in spirit before their less innocent survivors.

Whittier's need of escape from his present cares and worries also found expression in another poem, a revision and enlargement of verses written five years earlier. The present introductory note explains that when he was in Philadelphia in 1838 he often left the heat and bustle of the city to enjoy the quiet and beauty of the scenery near Chalkley Hall, where Thomas Chalkley had lived. The poem was first printed three years after it was written, with the title "Chalkley Hall. Lines written in viewing, for the first time, the scenery around Chalkley Hall, near Frankford, the residence of Thomas Chalkley."[22] Four new introductory stanzas were about escape from the city to the country and were doubtless added for clarity and emphasis, but they may have also been the result of Whittier's recent months in Boston lobbying for the abolition of capital punishment. The larger part of the poem was about Thomas Chalkley and not rural scenes, and, as in "Cassandra Southwick," Whittier enjoyed thinking about the early days of Quakerism, which in this poem were associated with boyhood memories.

In the spring of 1843 Whittier had another worry, one that he ought to have had earlier. He was at last taking his family responsibilities seriously. He wrote two letters on March 30. One was to Amos A. Phelps, telling him that he could not dream of going to the World's Anti-Slavery Convention where he could earn nothing by writing; at home he could earn a little, and his responsibilities as guardian and "in some degree" the supporter of his mother, aunt, and sister required all the exertion that his poor health permitted. The other letter was to James T. Fields about publishing a small volume of his poems. Fields had not been eager to do it when Whittier had written to him over a year earlier and suggested it for the purpose of preserving "a few floating pieces" and "to favor some personal friends," one of whom was Elizabeth Lloyd, who had written, "What a good thing it would be, Greenleaf, if all thy Indian and traditionary poetry could be got together and published in a volume. It would be as eagerly sought after by the lovers of Poetry, as was ever 'Druid mark' or 'Runic sign' by the Antiquary." His letter now was more business-like. He believed that this book would be well received by the public. It would be bought by Anti-Slavery people, although it would not contain Anti-Slavery poems except a few incidental allusions. Fields evidently replied quickly and favorably; a week later Whittier wrote that he knew little or nothing about publication: "I shall leave it altogether to you, trusting that if the work meets with a ready sale, you will do me justice, as I should, I am free to confess, like to realize something from it."

In the same letter he suggested the title: "Lays of My Home and Other Poems."[23]

A favorable review by William Cullen Bryant appeared in the *Evening Post* June 2. "Whittier's verses, we think, grow better and better. With no abatement of poetic enthusiasm, his style becomes more manly, and his vein of thought richer and richer." But the book was not a success as far as money was concerned. Seven years later Whittier wrote that all that he received from it was books valued at $8.20; he had forgotten that he received fifty dollars for the copyright. Fifty dollars was not enough to make any real improvement in his affairs, and later in the year he was forced to confess to J. Miller McKim that he could not afford to go to the tenth anniversary meeting of the American Anti-Slavery Society. In his state of health, he explained, he could do little in the money-making line and was "under the necessity of *calculating* with all the proverbial miserliness of a true Yankee." He did not like this way of living and found it belittling, but there was no way out: "I for one know of no way of realizing Brownson's theory of the 'supremacy of man over his accidents.' Talk as you will of the mind's higher element — of intellectual banquets etc. — the bread and cheese, the pork and greens are also essential."[24]

In spite of his worries about public affairs and his personal responsibilities he could enjoy fun along with other young and not-quite-so-young people. Some of them were in Lee, New Hampshire, in the summer, and just across the town line in Epping was a young school teacher named Rowena Thyng living with an uncle and aunt. Whittier wrote some pleasant verses about her, imagining them to be written by a young farmer who envied the oak tree that she sat under. Rowena was evidently pleased to be written about, although it was clear enough that Whittier was not referring to himself in the poem. For the moment she found it pleasant to imagine him and not a young farmer in love with her. He was thirty-five, sixteen years older than she, but quite likely to stir a young woman's imagination: good-looking, well-dressed, and famous. She cut her initials and his and two enmeshed hearts on the oak tree and in a wall-closet in her uncle's house. There is no reason to suppose that Whittier knew about her brief flight of fancy or the initials and hearts.[25]

During these months the Third District had been unable to elect a Representative to Congress. The Whig candidate at first was John F. Robinson of Lowell, whom James Russell Lowell ridiculed a few years later in "What Mr. Robinson Thinks." The Democratic candidate was Joseph Mansur. At the first attempt at an election there were 1225 votes for Whittier and others who were not regular party candidates, including Caleb Cushing, who stated publicly before the second attempt on February 13, 1843, that he was not a candidate. Amos Abbott of Andover had now replaced Robinson as Whig candidate. Whittier's supporters believed that some who had voted for

Whittier in November voted for Abbott in February because he was thought to have a moderate but not troublesome inclination towards abolition. Early in March it was reported in the *Haverhill Gazette* and denied in the *Essex Transcript* that Whittier had withdrawn. On March 15 a Liberty Party Convention in Haverhill endorsed Whittier and urged house-to-house canvassing. Whittier expected that the Liberty vote in the election April 3 would show a considerable increase, and his vote was higher by three hundred three than in February, but he still received only fourteen per cent of the total vote. There was an enthusiastic letter about him in the *Essex Transcript* June 2, but his vote rose only to fifteen per cent in the election June 6. In September the *Essex Transcript* was advising a vote for Whittier as the only man who could be elected, and then, somewhat inconsistently, warning that if Abbott *was* elected and if the next Presidential election should go to the House of Representatives, he would vote for Clay, the "duelling slavite." In November the *Essex Transcript* appealed to three groups: to working men it said that the issue was between free and slave labor; to Temperance men, that Liberty Party candidates were Washingtonians while nominees of other parties were notorious for wine-bibbing and even drunkenness; and to Abolitionists, that they should forget all minor differences. At the election November 13 Whittier received twelve per cent of the total vote; Samuel E. Sewall, Liberty Party candidate for Governor, received seven per cent. Again no candidate had a majority, and another election was scheduled for January 1, 1844. An editorial in the *Essex Transcript* December 15 described Whittier as a working man and a scholar; he knew "equally well how to turn a furrow or a period."

On January 1 Whittier received fourteen per cent of the total vote, but Abbott's vote was only two hundred three below the number needed for election. On the same day Whittier wrote a letter to the *Essex Transcript* withdrawing from the contest. He had accepted the nomination, he said, when the Liberty Party could count only three or four hundred votes in the district; in the Nomember election he had received nearly thirteen hundred (the exact number was 1282). The Liberty Party had risen slowly, upon the principle of impartial democracy, and a change of candidate at this time could not retard its onward progress. He had wished to withdraw earlier but had been persuaded not to. The letter concluded: "As a candidate, for the last fifteen months, my hands have been in a great measure tied. I have been obliged to stand an almost idle spectator of the contest in which my friends have been engaged, giving to the cause of freedom only the poor benefit of a name, when I longed to dedicate to its service my head, hands, and heart."[26]

XII
1844 - 45

The year 1844 began pleasantly, with a review in the January *North American Review* of Rufus W. Griswold's *The Poets and Poetry of America* by Edwin P. Whipple commenting favorably on Whittier's poems. Whittier had already received plenty of favorable reviews, but he felt a life-long gratitude for this one. In 1883 he dedicated *The Bay of Seven Islands* to Whipple and once said to him, "I have always been grateful to thee, Edwin, for from thee I first won recognition; and although I was partly conscious of what in me lay, thy assurance gave me courage to go on with my work." He had evidently forgotten earlier encouragement and remembered Whipple's review for a reason that also explains why it seemed so important to him at the time: he had a high opinion of Whipple, whom he regarded as the ablest critical essayist of his time with the possible exception of James Russell Lowell and Matthew Arnold.[1]

By the time Whittier read Whipple's review he was looking forward to the printing of a volume of his poems in England. But all this increasing importance did not make him less interested in his own neighborhood. He was elected to the Town School Committee, which had among its duties the choosing of books to be used in the schools. None had been added since 1836, and the new Committee added *Smith's Geography, The Village Reader, Greenleaf's Arithmetic, Worcester's Dictionary,* and *Child's Guide.*[2]

His most time-consuming activity was still Anti-Slavery and the Liberty Party. He could not attend the Party's District Convention in Haverhill to nominate someone to take his place on the ballot — he had to be in another part of the County on Party business — but he wrote a long and forceful letter. The Liberty Party, he wrote, had accomplished a great deal in the state and in the nation. In Massachusetts the law forbidding the marriage of whites and negroes had been repealed, and a resolve had been adopted asking for a change in that clause in the Constitution which allowed the South to send twenty representatives to Congress on the basis of slave population. Newly elected members of Congress, frightened by the increasing vote of the Liberty Party, were willing to consider Anti-Slavery petitions. Leading politicians and editors were now claiming that they believed in Abolition — at least in the abstract — and these politicians, the same men that had mobbed Abolitionists before the formation of the Liberty Party, were now calling themselves Whig Abolitionists and Democratic Abolitionists. While they now took the stand that it was all right to talk about slavery and to pray against it, they still turned their wrath toward those who voted against it. But they would soon change on that point also: "Ears deaf to our prayers and entreaties are open to the 'terse rhetoric of the Ballot-box'."[3]

Along with his shrewd practicality in political business, Whittier had kept the idealism of the reformer. This letter continued on a note of fervor suggestive of the early days of Anti-Slavery. Let there be no leaders in the Liberty Party, no worship of Whig or Democratic idols, no rewards offered for labor in a cause which was itself a reward. If there are those in the Liberty Party who do not feel that way about it, let them leave: their numbers would be less, but those left could feel true hearts beating beside them.

The final paragraph was a paean to Liberty which spoke the conviction of the idealistic first half of the nineteenth century as well as Whittier's own:

"Liberty — the great interest of humanity — Universal Freedom! — Who does not feel his heart glow within him at the thought of laboring in such a cause? — Does it not enlarge our souls and expand our sympathies? — Does it not bring us nearer to the great and good of past ages? — From the damp depths of dungeons — from the stake and the scaffold — wherever the confessors and martyrs of Liberty have sealed their testimony, solemn and awful voices call upon us to persevere and press onward. We are surrounded by a cloud of living witnesses. In France, Ireland, England, Italy, and Germany, wherever the long-oppressed millions are rising up from their debasement and struggling into freedom, every true and liberal heart beats warmly with ours. Freedom throughout the world is interested in our struggle. Pure and undefiled Christianity everywhere rejoices in our progress. For, to use the language of Robert Hall in his glorious defense of Christianity as the inseparable friend of Freedom, 'he who breaks the fetters of Slavery and delivers a nation from thralldom, forms the noblest comment on the great Law of Love.' "

Whittier's withdrawal as a candidate had not weakened his position in the Party. Henry B. Stanton wrote to him February 3 that he would be expected to draft the resolutions at the Liberty Party State Convention February 24. At this Convention Whittier was nominated for Presidential Elector.[4]

The main purpose of Stanton's letter was to urge Whittier to tell the readers of the *Essex Transcript* about the Convention — to "blow the trumpet loud and long." A great Convention was needed to make plans and arrange for an agent to make more plans, to lecture, to get up Conventions, and to "set the Commonwealth on fire." There was to be "choice singing" and "a splendid teaparty."

Stanton evidently thought that Whittier was in charge of the *Essex Transcript*; he wrote "the Essex Transcript (you?)." At this time, however, George J. L. Colby was editor and the publishers were Pettengill and Colby, but plans may already have been made for Whittier to take charge when Colby left. In the February 16 issue J. M. Pettengill was "Publisher and Proprietor" and no editor was named.[5] In a letter to James Russell Lowell April 17,

Whittier said that he had "the principal charge of our weekly paper here (*weakly* would be the better word)."[6] He probably continued to have some connection with the paper and to write some of its editorials for several years, although they were unsigned and his name never appeared as editor.[7] When he was out of town or ill, editorials were written by Abner L. Bayley or George G. Strickland. He would sometimes read the newspapers in the *Transcript* office and if he found anything of importance would immediately write something for the *Transcript*, writing rapidly but legibly and seldom making additions or corrections.[8] Whittier evidently did not always closely supervise the contents of the *Transcript*. In the June 21 issue Nathaniel P. Willis' "Chamber Scene" was printed as Whittier's with the title "The Maiden's Prayer."

It is impossible to do more than guess which editorials are Whittier's. He probably wrote "Trial of O'Connell" in the February 23 issue, which pointed out that O'Connell was being tried before a jury of Tory Protestants, four of whom were wine merchants and doubtless regarded Father Matthew's temperance movement under O'Connell's patronage as dangerous to the public welfare. He also probably wrote two editorials entitled "The Indians" in the March 8 and 15 issues. They show a thorough knowledge of the topic and concluded with a quotation from the *United States Magazine and Democratic Review*.

An event that aroused indignation and disgust throughout Europe and America stirred Whittier to write a poem for the *Essex Transcript* of March 22.[9] A young white man named John L. Brown had been sentenced to death for helping a slave girl, whom he had married, to escape from slavery. The judge added to the sentence a long, pious exhortation to Brown to repent and to call upon Jesus Christ the Lamb of God who taketh away the sins of the world and through whom mercy might crown him as a saint in an everlasting world forever and ever. The poem was introduced by an editorial which gave the facts with one significant exception: It did not mention that Brown had married the girl. The writer of the editorial doubtless remembered the charge against Abolitionists in 1838 that they favored racial amalgamation. The poem, as always when Whittier saw the situation as a spur to action with hope of success, was clear and vigorous, and the irony was effective: the clergy who defended slavery on religious grounds — three of them were listed in a footnote — were told to pray to God that bright-winged cherubim should guard, bless, and sanctify the scaffold. But irony, the poem continued, is cold and out-of-place in dealing with a deed like this one. Men should speak out — and the speaking should be in acts (in a curiously un-Quakerly metaphor

> In vain against the clang of swords
> The wailing pipe is blown.)

Slavery should be ended; tongue, pen, vote, and prayer should be used against it.

The changing of Brown's sentence a few weeks later to scourging and banishment was, Whittier believed, at least partly the result of protests which came even from pro-slavery editors and ministers who were shocked by the "devilishly religious" tone of the sentence.[10]

Another poem in the same month was also written in excitement. Since 1836 the question of the annexation of Texas had been agitating politicians and Abolitionists. On the ship returning from America in 1841 Joseph Sturge was told by a fellow-passenger who had been in Texas that the state of society there was as bad as it well could be and continue to exist. Planters had come to Texas with their slaves to escape their creditors, and the white inhabitants were living in as much fear of each other as of hostile Indians. Before writing his *Visit to the United States in 1841* Sturge received a letter from a friend in America — probably Whittier. [11] At the last Presidential election in Texas, the letter said, the successful candidate, General Houston, was "a man notorious for his open contempt of all the decencies of civilized society — brutal, brawling, profane, and licentious." Gangs of organized desperadoes were roaming about committing brutal outrages. It quoted an article in the *Houston Telegraph*: "While we deeply commiserate the situation of our sister republic, in regard to the political scourge of abolitionism, it is pleasing to reflect that our country enjoys a complete immunity from its effects." Southern planters would "look to Texas, as the Hebrews did to the promised land, for a refuge and a home." It was at this time that Whittier exclaimed in a letter to Samuel E. Sewall, "And if Texas is to be added to us, as there are no doubtful indications, let us say 'Dis-union before Texas.' "[12]

Now, in 1844, James Russell Lowell's "Rallying Cry for New England against the Annexation of Texas" appeared anonymously in the *Courier* March 19, and two days later Lowell wrote to Whittier urging him to write a poem on the same topic. A week later Whittier sent his hurriedly written "Texas, Voice of New England." When he had not heard from Lowell April 14 he wrote that if it had not already been published in the *Courier* it might better be sent to the *Morning Chronicle*. He found that he had omitted two stanzas but had forgotten so much of the poem that he could not be sure where they belonged. Three days later he received the *Courier* with his poem and a laudatory introduction by Lowell.[13]

Whittier immediately made many changes in the poem, and when it was printed in the *Essex Transcript* April 26, it was the same as the present version except that it did not have the fifteenth stanza, and the eleventh and fourteenth were differently worded.

The editor of the *Courier*, Buckingham, thought it wise to add a note of apology for the fiery tone of the poem. "If any of our Southern readers think Mr. Whittier's poem a little fierce, they will please to recollect Mr. Hayne's apology for South Carolina nullification, — 'Something must be pardoned to the spirit of liberty!' "[14] The fierceness was in the phrasing and not in the thought: "Like a lion growling low," "On your own free threshholds die," "Fling to heaven your signal fires." The message to the South was that of the Quaker non-combatant: Break up the Union with your impossible demands and you will soon be sorry; leave the North with its freedom and honest labor and you will look at it as the damned [softened to "lost"] look at Paradise. Whittier would take a similar attitude at the beginning of the Civil War.

It may have been his awareness that the annexation of Texas was inevitable that led him to write "Ezekiel." However optimistic his letter to the District Convention of the Liberty Party in January, he must already have seen that the annexation would be a tremendous help to slavery and might prolong its existence for a generation. He was thinking of himself and other Anti-Slavery workers when he wrote "Ezekiel," and his familiarity with the Bible led him to a passage that applied to their situation. The prophet Ezekiel spoke to people who heard his words but paid no attention to them, as did prophets in all ages, including Christ. But the prophet should not shrink from his task; the future would reveal the truth of what he had said.

Whittier was not thinking about public affairs all of the time. In the spring he was complaining that the east winds kept him from enjoying the release from the long cold winter. Amesbury is near enough to the coast so that a "sea-turn" — a sudden rush of wind from the ocean — can cause a temperature drop of twenty degrees in as many minutes. It was a good time to stay in the house and read. Whittier and his sister Elizabeth were enjoying some books that Thomas Tracy had lent them. They were especially interested in Allston's Romances, and Whittier found much to love in the sermons of Henry Ware, "apart from some of their peculiar doctrines".[15]

He wrote an indignant communication to the *Essex Transcript* in May about the use of one of his poems by supporters of Henry Clay and slavery.[16] The Geneva, New York, *Courier*, had as its standing motto a eulogy of Clay by Whittier. The "effusion," he explained, did not of course express his mature opinions.[17] As he wrote, his indignation increased. "Men who have assailed me with all opprobrious epithets, and marked me out as a fitting object for the exercise of mob-conservatism and a candidate for the honors of Lynch law have placed my name in their newspapers as the endorser of their Presidential candidate, and quoted my ill-considered rhymes as his most fitting eulogy!" The song had been sung at slave-holders' barbecues, had served as the motto on banners at Whig gatherings, had been used in printings of Clay's speeches, and had been recited when Clay was welcomed to Vicksburg "in behalf of its community of gamblers, duellists, street fighters, and negro-traders.'' Whittier had admired Clay when he spoke in the Senate as the champion of freedom in South America and Greece, and Clay might have been the O'Connell of the Western Hemisphere; instead, he was a slave holder and slave breeder who had opposed the abolition of slavery in the District of Columbia, had favored slavery in Florida and the internal slave trade, and had prevented the calling of a convention to abolish slavery in Kentucky. The communication concluded more in sorrow than in anger — and, in Whittier's usual way of focusing on essentials, with an attack on slavery from a new angle: "When I see such a man debasing his noble intellect to the services of slavery, I am more than ever disposed to do battle with the infamous system, which has thus perverted a spirit which might otherwise have been a blessing to humanity.''

Doing battle with the infamous system meant Liberty Party and Anti-Slavery business. At a Liberty Convention at Danvers in June Whittier urged the need of immediate preparations for the fall election, especially neighborhood meetings in school districts to discuss Liberty Party principles and measures.[18] He wrote a song, part of which later became "Seed-Time and Harvest,'' for a Liberty Party meeting at Prospect Hill in Somerville on the Fourth of July.[19] He also asked James Russell Lowell to write one for an Anti-Slavery meeting in Salem in August to commemorate Emancipation in the British West Indies.[20]

By July Whittier was probably working on "The Bridal of Pennacook'' and was therefore not moved to write a poem about the arrest of Charles T. Torrey in Baltimore on the charge of helping slaves to escape. Torrey was a Congregational minister and had been pastor of a church in Salem before entering anti-slavery work. An appeal for contributions to a fund for Torrey appeared in the *Essex Transcript* July 12, and Whittier wrote to Thomas Clarkson, one of the first anti-slavery agitators in England and friend of Charles Lamb, asking that Torrey have the prayers and sympathies of the friends of Freedom throughout the world.[21]

Most of "The Bridal of Pennacook'' was probably written before Whittier began his work on the *Middlesex Standard*, his last editorial work away from home. The first portion was printed in the September *United States Magazine and Democratic Review* and the entire poem in the June 1845 *Review*, the second part having been delayed nine months in the mail. The poem, as explained in the introductory blank verse, was an attempt to bring back part of the New England of earlier days, the same thing that he had done with only partial success in *Legends of New England* and had hoped that others would carry on further, and that he had also done with less than complete success in "Mogg Megone.''

"The Bridal of Pennacook'' was better than the earlier legendary poems. There was none of the boyish sentimentality of the *Legends* or the crude blood and vengeance of "Mogg Megone.'' It was based mainly on published histories, with which Whittier was thoroughly acquainted, but a few details were from local traditions and Whittier's own observations. The stanzas describing the bleak winter landscape near what is now Lynn had the same accuracy and graphic detail that are found in Whittier's later and better-known poems of Essex County. These and the descriptions of the country surrounding the heroine's childhood home were, however, merely decorative pictures with only the slightest connection with character and incident, not, as in Whittier's later poems, an integral part of the narrative.

The blank verse introduction was a little like the framework of the *Decameron*, as Whittier reminded the reader. A group of White Mountain tourists, delayed at an inn by the illness of one of them, wrote the poem for her amusement. The situation was obviously fiction, like the framework of "The Tent on the Beach," but unlike that and the *Decameron*, there was no reference to the supposed narrators after the introduction, and the poem proceeded without interruption. The characters in the introduction may have been real persons, as were the story-tellers in *The Tent on the Beach*, but if they were, Whittier was not interested to name them. When Horace E. Scudder was helping Whittier prepare the 1888 Riverside Edition of his works, he suggested changes in the introductory note including an explanation of "we"; Whittier replied, "I prefer to let the note stand as it is."

In July Whittier became editor of the *Middlesex Standard*, a new Anti-Slavery and Liberty Party weekly published in Lowell. He did not stay in Lowell all of the time and probably continued his unofficial connection with the *Essex Transcript* . He wrote only three poems during his eight months as editor and only one of them was printed in the *Standard*. He instructed Ann Wendell to tell Elizabeth Lloyd that even her "fine phrenzy" would suffer in such a place as Lowell and that living there amidst the din of the shuttles would drive poetry out of her head as it had out of his.[22] However, even before he went to Lowell the year had not been a productive one in poetry: he had written only three poems before "The Bridal of Pennacook."

Lowell was perhaps not the kind of city to inspire poetry, but it was not an unpleasant place in which to live and work. None of the hideous aspects of the Industrial Revolution had appeared in it. The thirty-two big brick textile mills were new and clean; the site had been woods and farmland in 1813. There was none of the blackness from soft coal smoke that had stained British manufacturing towns or of the air pollution by oil of a later day: machinery in the mills was operated by water power, and heating was by wood or anthracite coal. To Charles Dickens, one of the many visitors to the new city, it seemed as if the river acquired a new character from the fresh buildings of bright-red brick and painted wood, and the golden pestles and mortars serving as signs outside drug stores appeared to have been just issued by the United States mint.

As in most New England mill towns, the women workers, who outnumbered the men nearly three to one, did not constitute a distinct working class. Most of them came from country towns or farms in New Hampshire or Vermont. They were attracted to Lowell because they could earn money there for clothes or wedding expenses or a brother's college expenses or the payment of the mortgage on the farm. In 1840 nine hundred seventy-eight girls had deposits totalling about one hundred thousand dollars in the Lowell Institution for Savings. Some worked only half a year and went to private schools the other half, and some taught school during part of the year. They found life pleasant in Lowell, which was a city of young people, more than half its population being between fifteen and thirty. Most of the girls lived in boarding houses, some privately owned and some owned by the corporations, all of them carefully supervised by the mill owners with the full approval of the girls themselves. Lucy Larcom, who worked in one of the mills and whose mother ran a boarding house, remarked that Lowell had a high reputation for "good order, morality, piety, and all that was dear to the old-fashioned New Englander's heart." A visitor from England who expected to find the "moral condition of females about as elsewhere" found the character of girls and their moral condition unusually high and remarked on the "self-consideration and regard for moral character of the female operatives." He observed that they were well dressed and, as Joseph Sturge had remarked, were quiet and well-mannered: There was a "becoming propriety and respectability of manner approaching with some to genteel." Some even carried parasols. Their composite photograph, Lucy Larcom said, would have been the representative New England girlhood of those days; most of her mother's boarders were from New Hampshire and Vermont, and there was a "fresh, breezy sociability about them." There was plenty of religious life with twenty-two churches of ten denominations, not separated by social levels; while still a mill worker, Lucy Larcom taught a Sunday School class in which one of her pupils was the daughter of her mill superintendent. There was also plenty of the intellectual life that was sought so eagerly by Americans in the first half of the nineteenth century. There were lectures on phrenology when that was a popular craze, and later on mesmerism. Lyceum programs were more popular than entertainments, and some of the best-known lecturers in America spoke at the Lowell Lyceum: John Quincy Adams, Edward Everett, John Pierpont, and Ralph Waldo Emerson. In spite of a long working day some of the girls found time to meet and to produce literary magazines.

There was not much child labor; a Massachusetts law required all children to attend school three months in the year. The few little girls who worked in the mills found it fun. Lucy Larcom went to work when she was eleven, and her account gives a very different impression from the traditional one of child labor in Elizabeth Barrett Browning's "The Cry of the Children." Lucy and half a dozen other girls changed bobbins every three quarters of an hour and had more than half their time for play. They frolicked among the spinning frames, played games, told stories, explored the various rooms, and were sometimes allowed to go down to the river level and watch the big water wheel. They were forbidden to bring books to read and even Bibles were confiscated, but they were allowed to paste newspaper clippings on the sides of the window seats. They could raise house plants, as many of the grown-up women did. But still, there must have been many hours when children and adults wished the working day would end; it was between twelve and thirteen hours long, and the noise of the machines was not pleasant.

The mills in Lowell were much like those in Amesbury and Salisbury Mills Village, and Whittier would not feel in wholly strange surroundings. The people that he would try to reach through the *Middlesex Standard* were not different from those in his own neighborhood. There were the male mill workers — "mechanics" — and while there were only one third as many of them as of female workers, they numbered 2345, and they were old enough to vote or soon would be. On the outskirts of Lowell, as of Amesbury, there were the farms that fed the twenty-five thousand population, and in the center were many stores which did a good business with the mill workers, especially the girls.

While the executives in mills producing over seventy-four million yards of cotton cloth annually were not likely to look with favor on any movement that opposed slavery, the large proportion of young people might make the district fertile ground for the Liberty Party. Whittier meant to double the Liberty Party vote.[23]

There was nothing in Whittier's manner or appearance to make him a misfit in a city of young people. He showed no effects of his periods of poor health, real or imagined. "Well made, with black hair and large clear black eyes — and his walk is graceful and energetic like his verse," was one observer's comment.[24]

He began his editorial work on the *Middlesex Standard* with vigor and sincerity. In the first issue, July 25, he announced that the paper would support the Liberty Party and made a forceful attack on Henry Clay. The Whigs, who at least in Massachusetts had professed friendship to the Anti-Slavery cause and opposition to the annexation of Texas, had nominated as their Presidential candidate a slave holder who had done more than anyone else to extend and perpetuate slavery, who still gloried in his Missouri Compromise, and who was openly hostile to abolition. Two weeks later Whittier condemned Clay as "a deliberate robber of the poor." In the August 1 issue he announced that he would have no ill feeling toward honorable opponents and would have the courtesy that an editor ought to have; if in his earnestness and enthusiasm he forgot the Christian rule of action, he would be ready to acknowledge his error.

The first error that he had to acknowledge was not the result of his earnestness and enthusiasm. He had copied with indignant comments an article from the Ithaca, New York, *Chronicle* containing a purported extract from the journal of a traveller in the United States which charged that James K. Polk, Democratic candidate for President, had branded his slaves with his initials. When he learned that the story was a fraudulent addition to the journal, he wrote to the Lowell *Advertiser* to correct the error and printed his letter in the *Standard*; as a Liberty Party man he could have no motive to misrepresent either Polk or Clay; they were alike in being slaveholders and hostile to emancipation and had no claim to the support of Abolitionists.[25]

In the August 15 issue he made an indignant comment on an occurrence of race prejudice in Lowell. Some negro children were refused admission to an exhibition of "Chemical Paintings." Whittier said that if Raphael's paintings were exhibited in Lowell with such restrictions he would not go to see them and he urged Abolitionists not to patronize the exhibit.[26]

Whittier's editorial duties did not keep him from political activities. Knowing that a new party needs candidates who have no political stigma and who are well known and respected in their own fields, he wrote to David P. Page, principal of Newburyport High School, to ask him to accept the Liberty nomination for Congress. He was sure that Page would be a good vote-getter. The Liberty Party was now well organized, and with two Liberty papers in the district, the only need to assure success was a candidate like Page.[27] Page replied in a school teacher's tone of superiority: he considered his profession the highest in which he could engage and his mind "must never be distracted by the strife of a political canvass." He may already have known that he was soon going to a better position in another state; before the end of the year he became headmaster of the Normal School at Albany, New York.

Whittier wrote a similar letter to Henry Wadsworth Longfellow, who declined with more humility than Page. He was not qualified for the duties, he said, and although a strong anti-slavery man was not a member of the Liberty Party. Partisan warfare would be too violent and vindictive for his taste, and he would be a "weak and unworthy champion in public debate."[28]

Editorial work and politics did not keep Whittier from looking at his surroundings with a still youthful and lively interest. In the second issue of the *Standard* he began a series of essays entitled "The Stranger in Lowell"; a title for each essay was added when the series was published in a volume the next summer and with a few exceptions these titles were used in the Riverside Edition. The first essay, now part of "The City of a Day," presented Lowell as a modern miracle and work as its patron saint; it accepted without question Carlyle's definition: "Divine labor, noble, ever fruitful — the grand, sole miracle of man." One passage in the present form of the essay is a later addition and wholly out of tune with the rest. It questions the gospel of work which would redeem mankind and says that every web from the factory looms has a history connected with sin and suffering, beginning with slavery and ending with overwork and premature death. When it was added, Whittier had become disillusioned with Carlyle and his theories, and the passage replaced the second quotation from Carlyle.[29] The series continued in the third issue of the *Standard* with an essay entitled "The Heart of the City" in *The Stranger in Lowell* and now also part of "The City of a Day." The population of Lowell included people from almost every part of the civilized world, and there was a long passage, later eliminated, expressing Whittier's belief in human brotherhood. A rather poetic passage about the Irish immigrant was taken from Whittier's introduction to "Lament of the Irish Immigrant" in the *Pennsylvania Freeman* of February 13, 1840.

Soon after arriving in Lowell, Whittier received the current number of the *Lowell Offering*, edited by Harriet Farley, containing prose and poetry by the mill girls who belonged to the Improvement Circle. His comments on it were favorable, and a few days later he attended a meeting of the Circle and listened to the reading of several articles. His comment was, "We know half a dozen Congressmen who, if they were promised as a reward the New York Custom House or the office of Minister to the Court of St. James could not write with so much point, beauty or good taste as these 'Factory Girls'."[30] He commended a poem entitled "Pentucket" but did not seem interested in Lucy Larcom's "Sabbath Bells" — perhaps, she thought, because Quakers did not approve of church spires and bells. After the readings Whittier sought her out and talked with her, beginning a friendship which included his sister Elizabeth and lasted a lifetime. She was too overawed to say much but must have made more of an impression than she supposed; he referred to their meeting in the *National Era* four years later.[31]

This visit to the Improvement Circle led to his writing the third essay in the series, entitled "The Factory Girls" in *The Stranger in Lowell* and not included in the *Works*. It began with a rhapsody: "Acres of girlhood — beauty reckoned by the square rod or miles by long measure! The young, the graceful, the gay — flowers gathered from a thousand hillsides and green valleys of New England!" But the tone quickly changed. The girls were Sisters of Thrift and Sisters of Charity, dispensing comfort and happiness to the people that they had left in their country homes. Their work was noble and ennobling; it brought dignity to woman, who thus became a helpmate and blessing to man instead of a beautiful but expensive burden. Whittier had written earlier about the dignity of labor in his editorials addressed to the "mechanics" of New England, within a year would begin his "Songs of Labor," and only two weeks earlier had quoted Carlyle's ecstatic definition of "divine labor." But he had no patience with the rich woman who, looking from her cool verandah on woods and streams, surrounded by music, poetry, and romance and waited on by servants, sentimentalized over the "working classes" and quoted Carlyle and Goethe about the romance and beauty of work — in the abstract. Many foolish essays had been written on the beauty and divinity of labor by those who had never worked at the bench or loom. As a general rule, mind and body were too tired after twelve or more hours of work for intellectual effort; the writings in *Mind Among the Spindles* were an exception. It may be suspected that Whittier referred to this book containing selections from mill girls' writings rather than to the *Lowell Offering* because the title gave him an opening for a further remark: "The mind of the humblest worker in these mills is of infinitely more consequence in the sight of Him who looks on the realities of His universe than all the iron-armed and steam-breathed engines of mechanism."

Whittier still had a youthful curiosity about anything new, and when he heard a loud voice holding forth in the second story of a building on Merrimack Street he climbed the stairs to a long, narrow room where he found between fifty and a hundred people listening to a Mormon preacher. Whittier's next essay, August 22, was about the preacher and the Mormon faith. The preacher was evidently unlearned and innocent of any dealings with such "abominable matters as a verb or a noun, which no Christian ever can endure," but he spoke with a force and sincerity that disarmed Whittier's criticism. He talked of the power of faith and gave examples from the Bible, including Enoch, who overcame death itself and "instead of dying, God suspended the law of gravitation and took him right up bodily." Whittier thought that the success of the Latter Day Saints in making converts came from this emphasis on faith which led men who had been struggling with unbelief to grasp at the Mormon delusion. But he hastened to add that his use of the word "delusion" applied only to the apocryphal *Book of Mormon*. He believed that the great majority of the Mormons were honest and sincere fanatics, who had made great sacrifices and endured persecution for their faith, and he did not believe the charges made against them by those who had persecuted them. As for Joseph Smith, Whittier had read an account of the scene when he left his holy city to surrender to the authorities; there were two thousand armed fanatics ready for action, but Smith told them to obey the laws of the state and to give their enemies no excuse for persecution.

A walk to Patucket Falls prompted the next essay, later entitled "Patucket Falls." He found that the wild river had been tamed by the canal which drained it above the falls and brought the water to the mills, and he wondered how the falls looked to the Puritans who first saw them in 1652, surmising that they would not have been interested in the beauty of the landscape. Some of his unflattering remarks about them were later cut out of the essay: that the Puritans were "sour-featured and grim. . . . . a most prosaic, earthward-tending people." He also cut out later an incident which he thought showed that much of the old Puritan feeling still remained, the disposition to shut the eye to Nature's beauty and the ear against her harmonies. A friend of his who had recently been a student at Andover Theological Seminary, then in Andover, Massachusetts, told of a "long, pale, solemn looking" candidate for the ministry who was induced one autumn Sunday to walk a few rods from his lodging, and when his attention was called to the beauty of the foliage on the distant hills, turned away from it with a groan and ejaculated, "Lord, turn off my eyes from beholding vanity." But Whittier was enough of a Yankee not to write a sonnet against the mills as Wordsworth had attempted to exorcise the railroads in the Lake country, for after all, in a region that had seven months of cold weather, weren't shirts and coats better than scenery?

The next four essays, all of them included in the *Works*, dealt with aspects of religion, which had now become a vital part of Whittier's life and thought. "Hamlet Among the Graves" affirmed the assurance which he never lost and which through his later religious poems confirmed the faith of hundreds of thousands: God has not left us without an answer to the deep mystery of death, and while we do not know the conditions of the future life, we need not be afraid to follow where Christ has led and where God will take care of us — the thought which had already appeared in "Hampton Beach" and which appeared later in the much-quoted stanza in "The Eternal Goodness:"

> I know not where his islands lift
>> Their fronded palms in air.
> I only know I cannot drift
>> Beyond his love and care.

This same question of life after death led in the next essay, "Swedenborg," to an account of the various churches in Lowell and Whittier's visit to a meeting of Swedenborgians. Whittier's interest was mainly in the earthly human quality of Swedenborg's revelations and he wisely did not attempt an analysis of his teachings.

His lively interest in everything new led him to board a stage one day whose driver was announcing, "Seventy-five cents to the Second Advent campground." The resulting essay was "Father Miller," in the *Works* "The World's End." It showed considerable knowledge of earlier prophecies, but Whittier seemed fully as interested in the ludicrous aspects of the movement and the picturesque effects of a similar outdoor meeting that he had attended in East Kingston a few years earlier. For his own interpretation of the Second Coming he quoted from a rational statement of William Ellery Channing concluding "Christ comes in the conversion, the regeneration, the emancipation of the world."

Whittier's attitude toward Sabbath observance was liberal, as he described it in "Sabbath in Lowell" (in *Works*, "First Day in Lowell"), although it did not suggest anything like the hectic carousel of Sunday a century later. In the 1840's a day of rest was welcome, and young people were happy to walk quietly along the streets, dressed in their best clothes. Whittier saw nothing wrong in this, and he noted one of the strange contradictions in conventional morality. Strict Sabbatarians did not object to canals being repaired on Sunday: "Church indulgences are not, after all, confined to Rome."

The wide range of Whittier's interests did not make him lose interest in Anti-Slavery. There had recently been one occurrence which he joyfully reported in the *Standard* — and one which he lamented and did not report. He was happy when he read the pamphlet containing Emerson's August 1 speech on emancipation, which he reviewed favorably September 12, rejoicing that Emerson was no longer calmly remote from the Anti-Slavery struggle: "We had previously, we confess, felt half indignant that, while we were struggling against the popular current, mobbed, hunted, denounced from the legislative forum, cursed from the pulpit, sneered at by wealth and fashion and the world's shallow aristocracy, such a man as Ralph Waldo Emerson should be brooding over his pleasant philosophies, writing his quaint and beautiful essays in his retirement on the banks of the Concord, unconcerned and 'calm as a summer's morning.' "

Whittier had persistently tried not to quarrel with Garrison, and he was not happy when he read Garrison's charge in the *Liberator* that Liberty Party papers were trying to help Polk and the annexation of Texas. Garrison could have learned that this charge was untrue by reading the *Standard*. "I ask no favor in the matter," he wrote to Garrison. "I simply claim justice. And unless William Lloyd Garrison has totally changed from what he was when we stood shoulder to shoulder in the old struggles of abolition I shall not claim it in vain."[32]

He was still writing letters to promote Anti-Slavery meetings. He asked Emerson and Lowell to come to the Middlesex County Convention in Lowell, or if they could not come, to send letters to be read.[33] Instead of a letter about Anti-Slavery, Lowell sent Whittier a poem for the *Standard*, "Hunger and Cold," which was printed September 19. In an introduction Whittier said that the poem, which reminded him of Shelley at his best and which Lowell had said in a note was suggested by England rather than New England, had arrived just as he finished reading a letter from Joseph Sturge, who, trying to secure the rights of citizenship for the laboring poor, was "assailed on all hands by aristocracy and priestcraft, feebly supported by the middle classes, constantly shocked by the sight of misery which he cannot relieve."

For several weeks Whittier was unwell. A few years earlier he would have resigned his editorial position or would have left others to do his work while he travelled and attended conventions. He was now mature enough to keep at his task, although he knew that he was not doing his best work. However unwell he was, he was now able to think of someone beside himself, and he wrote an entertaining letter to Ann Wendell. A large square bundle had arrived by express. It was carefully wrapped, the inner wrapping being a valuable cashmere shawl. When he unfolded this he found a "splendid old painting — Carlo Dolce's Magdalen, exquisitely beautiful." It was now hanging in his room, "with its holy look of repentance for sin forgiven." But what should he do with the shawl? A friend had suggested that he cut a hole in it and wear it like a Mexican blanket.[34]

Illness kept him from going to Boston October 10 to attend a meeting of the Governor's Council which was considering a pardon case in which he was interested,[35] but it did not interfere with his editorial and political work. He continued to write vigorous political editorials in the *Standard*. "Unprecedented Falsehood! The Last Resort of a Desperate Party" was the headline October 17. A statement in a Detroit paper that Birney had been nominated for the Michigan legislature by the Democrats of Saginaw County had been seized upon by Whig papers as proving a coalition between Polk Democrats and Liberty Party men. Birney, according to Whittier, had been given no official notice of the nomination, and if it was true that he had been nominated, it simply meant that the Democrats had chosen to support a Liberty Party man, as had happened in other instances. The Whigs who had brought this charge were the men who had mobbed Abolitionists eight years earlier, who had invoked legislative enactments against them, and who had applauded Harrison Gray Otis when he had eulogized slavery and slaveholders in Faneuil Hall.

All three of the "Stranger in Lowell" essays published in October started with a local scene or incident leading to a topic that Whittier was interested in.

In "Modern Magic" he asked who could have guessed the purpose of two men who had driven a wagon slowly along Central Street a fortnight ago. It was part of an apparent instance of psychic phenomena, a topic which Whittier never lost interest in. A six-year-old boy in a town near the mouth of the Merrimac had disappeared. Three clairvoyants had independently given similar information. This, according to some of Whittier's friends who were interested in mesmerism, was explained by the fact that the boy's father, a ship captain, had had trouble with one of his sailors who was suspected of decoying the boy away from his home; this fact had been transmitted by thought transference to the clairvoyants from those who were questioning them. Whittier was convinced that mesmerism was not wholly charlatanry and was unwilling to reject everything not consistent with a materialistic outlook on life; who, he said, can determine the exact workings of the mysterious connection between mind and body?

Illuminating gas was coming into use, and Whittier walked across the bridge just after sunset September 20 to see the lighting of the mills for the first time. In "The Lighting Up" he approved of the aesthetic effect but not of the twelve-and-a-half-hour working day. He was sure that a ten-hour day would be better, but he knew human nature well enough to be quite aware that the workers would object to it as strongly as the stockholders. They had come to Lowell to earn big pay, and health was a secondary consideration.

Whittier's chief thought was of the women workers, and he had especial respect for the unmarried women, who preferred to work rather than ask their friends for sympathy and support. It pleased him, furthermore, that in these mills, more than in other factories, women were on an equality with men. This led him to make some unfavorable comments on men's ill-bred surprise that factory girls could write essays. In a passage later omitted he told of his amusement when he read a speech made at a political meeting in Delaware. The orator had expressed his surprise at seeing the daughter of an Episcopal clergyman and niece of a bishop working in a textile factory, and his greater surprise that "the fair Gertrude — and fair she was — her brow as Parian marble — her eye dark and bright, and full like the gazelle's" felt no embarrassment in so doing. Stranger still to the orator was the fact that a respectable man thought as she did and so "transplanted this factory rose-bud to a neat cottage somewhere in the Land of Steady Habits, which has shrubbery about it, and which is already filled with 'little rose-buds.' " "Truth," Whittier continued, "is stranger than fiction. One can imagine with what open-mouthed wonder the ague-shaken and shabby 'chivalry' of Lower Delaware listened to this marvellous narrative of what the orator had seen with his own eyes."

One beautiful morning in what he called the loveliest season of the year, the interval between the equinoctial storms and the dark days of late fall, Whittier took a walk along the river. He sat down to rest on a slope where there was a view of the Dracut woods. His reverie was interrupted by a grunting sound from some bushes near him, a sound "like that of a dyspeptic porker" (later softened to "half bestial, half human"). A man was lying drunk, face down upon the ground, and a little boy was looking at him. When the boy asked him why he was lying there, the man tried to get to his feet, lost his balance, and fell again face down, muttering "I'm taking comfort." "It was a case," said Whittier in a passage later omitted, "for the deep and tender sympathy of our excellent Washingtonian, Kimball, or the scorching and vehement rebuke of my friend Cartland, of 'The White Mountain Torrent' — a rebuke, not of the drunkard, but of the mercenary wretches who have made him so." The essay, later entitled "Taking Comfort," concluded with Whittier's blessing on the Washingtonian (later changed to "temperance") movement. The next to the last paragraph, which was suggested by and included a quotation from Emerson's "Nature" in his *Essays Second Series*, is a later addition. Emerson had sent a copy of this volume to Whittier, who marked many passages in it.[36]

Whittier was in Amesbury November 1, and away from the disturbances and distractions in Lowell was able to write a memorial poem about a young Amesbury woman, Harriet Nelson Greeley, who had died of typhus fever October 25. It had seven stanzas, these being, with variations, stanzas 1, 2, 7, 12, 13, 14, 15 of "Gone", which was printed in the *United States Magazine and Democratic Review* for March 1845. Harriet Nelson Greeley attended Bradford Academy, became a teacher, and did some writing, drawing, and painting.[37] The references to her character and personality do not necessarily prove that she was an intimate friend of the Whittiers; they might have been derived from the obituary in the *Essex Transcript*.

Early in November Whittier was nominated as Liberty Party candidate for Representative from Amesbury to the State Legislature. This was not another instance of letting his name be used to help the cause. He was eager to be elected. He was not yet convinced, as has often been assumed, that poor health would keep him from active public life. He must have known that his position on the *Standard* was not likely to last much longer, and he had a mother, sister, and aunt to support. He proved to be a good vote-getter and ran far ahead of the ticket in Amesbury. A majority of the votes cast was still needed for election, and when the meeting dissolved after the fourth ballot, thereby deciding that the town would not send a Representative that year, Whittier lacked only four of the necessary votes.[38]

Whittier's work as editor of the *Standard* was well done, but the paper did not have the effect on the vote in Middlesex County that he had hoped. The Liberty vote in Massachusetts had increased nearly two thousand over 1843, comparing Birney's vote for President with Sewall's vote for governor in 1843. However, in Middlesex County Birney had only forty-two more votes than Sewall had received.[39]

With the election over, there was the question of what should be done with the *Standard*. It was decided to make it a family newspaper and at the same time to keep it an Abolition journal. Chauncey L. Knapp had become a partner of the publisher J. S. Pillsbury, forming the firm of Pillsbury and Knapp. Whittier and Knapp were both listed as editors. Knapp had considerable editorial experience and was well known as an Abolitionist. He was later editor of the *Lowell Citizen*.[40]

There is no way of knowing which editorials were Whittier's. "Clay in Defeat" in the November 28 issue seems to have been his; it referred to the writer's boyish enthusiasm and admiration for Clay's talents, republicanism, and eloquence. He would not rob Clay of his just fame as a statesman and man of genius but could not advocate him for the Presidency in the light of his attitude toward Freedom.[41] Whittier contributed only four more essays: the two parts of "The Scottish Political Martyrs" November 21 and 28, "The Beautiful" December 19, and "The Black Man" January 13, which included a translated poem, "The Prayer of Placido."

Most of "The Scottish Political Martyrs" is now included in "The Scottish Reformers." It began with an incident which was later omitted. Whittier had just talked with an old man who had been in Edinburgh in 1793 when the leaders of a reform group known as "Friends of the People" were tried, convicted, and sent to the convict colony of Botany Bay, and who called his attention to recent newspaper accounts of the laying of the corner-stone of a monument in their honor. Also later omitted was a description of the treatment of convicts based on accounts given by some who had returned. The belated tribute to the Friends of the People led Whittier into a consideration of the life of a reformer, including a warning that he must be sure that his own heart is free from ambition, impatience, and pride of opinion; he must guard himself against the knight-errantry of championing every new scheme of reform; he must remember that the public may be right and he may be wrong, and that "folly has its martyrs as well as wisdom."

"The Beautiful" had a livelier introduction than in its present form. There was the same quotation from the book that Emerson had just given him, and the first sentence was the same, and then —

"I felt my arm suddenly pressed. 'Did you see that lady who has just passed us?' he inquired. I turned and threw back a glance. 'I see her,' I replied; 'a good figure, and quite a graceful step — what of her?' 'Why, she is almost beautiful — in fact very nearly perfect,' said my friend. 'I have seen her several times before, and were it not for a chin slightly out of proportion, I should be inclined to confess that there is at least one handsome woman in the city.' 'And *but* one, I suppose,' said I laughingly. 'That I am sure of' said he. 'I have been to all the churches, from the Catholic to the Mormon, and on all the Corporations, and there is not a handsome woman here, although she whom we have just passed comes nearer the standard than any other.'

"Just as if there were any standard of beauty — a fixed, absolute model of form and feature and color!"

Whittier's advice to women, which followed, was conventional: they should not think of what they see in the mirror but of their picture "on the retina of human sympathy."

In "The Black Man" Whittier told of receiving a letter from a free negro who had succeeded in collecting enough money to buy his wife and children out of slavery. He had made a good impression on Whittier when he visited Lowell, where he had received generous contributions. After telling of his experiences and sufferings, Whittier proceeded to an account of another negro, Juan Placido, who had been executed in Havana for his part in a slave uprising. This portion of the essay is now entitled "Placido, the Slave Poet." Placido was a former slave and had written poems in Spanish which Whittier, who knew them only in translation, praised with more generosity than critical acumen. The poem which Whittier put into English verse after a friend had translated it for him was a prayer written when Placido was in the Chapel of the Doomed and recited as he was being led to his execution.

Late in the year a call was issued for a meeting in Faneuil Hall of citizens opposed to the annexation of Texas and the further extension of slavery. Whittier printed the first of his two poems written for the *Standard* in the January 2 issue, "To Faneuil Hall." It justified Whittier's earlier statement that the atmosphere of Lowell was not conducive to poetry. Every stanza ends with "hall," a device requiring a certain adroitness but unlikely to result in good verse. The meeting was held January 29, and Whittier was one of the four secretaries. It denounced the annexation of Texas as a violation of the Constitution, since the Constitution does not mention the power to annex a foreign state, and as calculated to uphold the interests of slavery, extend its influence, and make it permanent.[42]

By the middle of February it was evident that Whittier would soon be out of work. Negotiations were going on for the sale of the *Standard* to R. E. Hubbard of Worcester. Whittier was in Amesbury February 18 doing his editorial work by correspondence when his fellow-editor and publisher, Chauncey L. Knapp, wrote to him that Hubbard had at last made a definite offer to take over the *Standard's* subscription list, sending a joint paper made up of the *Standard* and his Worcester paper to subscribers and leaving the publishers to collect debts through March 6, when the "annexation" would take place. Knapp thought that Hubbard might improve this offer a little but not much — and Hubbard had said nothing about Whittier.[43] This plan was carried out, and on March 13 it was announced that the paper would be published simultaneously in Worcester and Lowell and would be known as the *Worcester and Middlesex Gazette*, with Hubbard and Knapp as editors.

Whittier continued to perform his duties faithfully to the end. His editorial February 27, "The Whig Party," took the same position as his editorial in the first issue of the *Standard*, July 25.[44] The Whigs had passed good resolutions on a number of topics, including the annexation of Texas, but their policy remained doubtful and they had lost credit for sincerity when they nominated a slave-holder for the Presidency. The Liberty Party was stern and inflexible against slavery, "offering a rallying point to the Democracy of all parties; uttering at every election its indignant protest against pro-slavery legislation, and demanding the eternal separation of Republicanism and Slavery, which God has *not* joined together."

Lucy Larcom (1824-1893).

Lydia Maria Child (1802-1880).

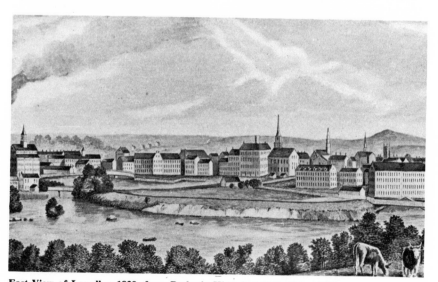

East View of Lowell, c.1839, from Barber's *Historical Collections*, 1839.

Daguerreotype of Whittier, c.1845. (Courtesy of Whittier Birthplace, Haverhill)

Ambrotype of Whittier, 1857.

Engraving of Whittier by A.C. Warren, 1848-49, after A.G. Hoit's portrait of 1846.

Crayon drawing of Whittier by Charles A. Barry, 1858.

XIII
1845 - 46

While still editor of the *Middlesex Standard* Whittier added eight stanzas to the memorial poem about Harriet Nelson Greeley and made a few revisions in the original seven. The poem was printed in the *United States Magazine and Democratic Review* for March, with an introductory quotation from Charles Lamb's "Hester," from which the title "Gone" was taken. Some of the added stanzas had the popular sentimental melancholy of the day. One stanza, however, suggests the moving simplicity of Wordsworth's poems of nature and death:

> The light of her young life went down,
>   As sinks behind the hill
> The glory of a setting star,
>   Clear, suddenly, and still.

But for several months poetry was only a minor interest. Whittier was on the Prudential Committee for Amesbury's School District Number 2, conscientiously attending to the details of administration, which included disbursing the money assigned to the District. He bought four dippers for thirty-three cents, paid twelve dollars for firewood and twenty cents for sawing it, and, with a regard for aesthetic effect somewhat in advance of his time, boldly spent one dollar and sixty cents for ten trees for the schoolhouse yard and fifty cents to set them out. The principle of equal pay for women, which he had approved in Lowell, did not apply to Amesbury teachers; the male teacher in District Number 2 received thirty-one dollars a month and each of the women received ten dollars and fifty cents. His duties ended August 23, when he handed a balance of six dollars and nine cents to his successor.[1]

While he was doing these chores with no thought that they were beneath him, he was an important enough person for his affairs to be of public interest. One of the Boston papers published a report, which seems to have been without foundation, that he was going to live in the West.[2] He was still finding Amesbury a pleasant place to live in. An editorial in the *Essex Transcript* was probably his. The writer did not know any factory village that offered so much to workers. They were given ample time for meals, which workers did not have in the larger manufacturing centers — as Whittier had pointed out in Lowell — and their average working day was shorter than in Lowell. There were churches to meet all religious tastes. There was an excellent academy. The beaches were not far away, game was plentiful, and there were excursions to Black Rocks and the Isles of Shoals. The point most emphasized was the almost entire absence of "that pitiful aristocracy which regards 'Factory folks' as out of the pale of good society."[3] The workers in the Amesbury and Salisbury mills were either local or, as in Lowell, young people from New Hampshire or Vermont small towns and farms. All this would change in a few years, but no one could have foreseen it in 1845.

For a few weeks there was little political activity, and Whittier had time and energy for other interests. He wrote an editorial for the March 28 *Essex Transcript* about Theodore Parker, whom conservatives among the Unitarians had accused of heresy — the very thing that they had accused Orthodox Congregationalists of doing to them. Whittier was scornful of their inconsistency in trying to shut Parker out of their pulpits while they would admit a slaveholder to their pulpits and their pews.

He was still interested in temperance and, as he had indicated in "Taking Comfort," in the Washingtonian Total Abstinence Society. He was at the annual meeting of the Essex County society April 9, where he served as secretary pro tem, made a motion that a committee of five be appointed to work with the Committee to make the Fourth of July meeting a large and successful one, and was made a member of this committee.[4]

However interesting these activities were and however satisfying to his social conscience, they did not bring him any money. He had found that volumes of poetry were not money-makers, and so he thought that he would try a volume of essays. Those that he had written in Lowell had had only a limited circulation, and plans for their publication in a small volume were being made in April. The introductory note to *The Stranger in Lowell* explained that his position as editor before an exciting election had brought him into conflict with both of the major political parties, and he had felt it a duty to keep himself open to the kindliest influences of nature and society, the essays being "impressions made upon his mind by the common influences of daily life." The volume was ready in late June. It included three essays that had not been used in the *Middlesex Standard*, although internal evidence indicates that they were written in Lowell.[5]

"Yankee Zincali" is now part of "Yankee Gypsies" (*Works* V) but did not have the section from pp. 333-337, nor the second half of the first paragraph on page 342, which includes a pleasant reference to Mary Russell Mitford. There were good passages of description in the nineteenth century manner, a piling up of concrete details to give a clear and forceful effect without any attempt at significance hidden in the subconscious, and lively characterizations of individuals which show that Whittier had at least some of the qualities that brought success to nineteenth century novelists.

"The Farmer Poet of Windham" is now pp. 240-260 of "Robert Dinsmore" (*Works* VI). Whittier was reminded of his youthful enjoyment of Dinsmore's verses when he saw some of them in a paper that had come to his office as an exchange. His comments on Dinsmore's homely verse were pleasant and humorous. It is rather surprising, however, that in spite of his acquaintance with Burns' poetry, he said of Dinsmore's "The Sparrow" only that it had "something of the simple tenderness of Burns." In thought, form, and detail it was an imitation of Burns' "To a Mouse. On Turning Up Her Nest with the Plough, November, 1785." Dinsmore crushed a bird's nest while ploughing.

"The Training" was evidently written at the time of the September training days of the militia, and its publication during a political campaign would have been unwise. The *Middlesex Standard* was in business to get votes for the Liberty Party, and some Anti-Slavery sympathizers would not have agreed with Whittier's opinion of the militia and its semi-annual training days nor would they have accepted his characterization of the Battle of Waterloo as a gladiatorial murder game.

The final paragraphs of "The Training" were about Milton in his blindness, who was close to Whittier's mature conception of a true hero and who proved the truth of the lines in "Samson Agonistes:"

But patience is more oft the exercise
Of saints, the trial of their fortitude,
Making them each his own deliverer,
And victor over all
That tyranny or fortune can inflict.

He did not go to the trouble of looking up the lines to quote them correctly, but thinking about Samson led him to write the last of his poems based directly on an incident in the Bible. In "The Wife of Manoah to Her Husband" Whittier treated the theme with considerable freedom and with more success than in his earlier Bible poems. Some of the stanzas had the monotonous rhythm and simple explanatory tone, as if they were written for children, that grew upon Whittier through the years, but others had good sense impressions:

I slept not, though the wild bees made
A dreamlike murmuring in the shade,
And on me the warm-fingered hours
Pressed with the drowsy smell of flowers.

During the summer and autumn Whittier was busy with two Anti-Slavery projects: opposing the admission of a new Slave state and increasing the Liberty Party vote in the Presidential election.

Congress had passed a resolution in March for the annexation of Texas. Privately, Whittier admitted defeat: "So we must have Texas! God help us!" he wrote to Dr. Bowditch. "The North is dumb: she cares for nothing as long as trade flourishes." But in a letter in the *Essex Transcript* addressed "To the Friends of Freedom in Essex County," he urged them to show that their zeal was undiminished. They should not be discouraged by the probability of the annexation of Texas but should meet the crisis like Benjamin

Lundy, who alone in 1820 retained his faith in spite of the paralyzing effect of the Missouri Compromise on Anti-Slavery feelings. Every Liberty man should talk to his neighbors, circulate Anti-Slavery papers and books, and arrange for lectures on Anti-Slavery.[6]

It was more important than ever to keep the sins of the pro-slavery South in public view. A good opportunity came early in August when a Federal court in Florida made a martyr of Jonathan Walker, a conductor on the Underground Railroad. In 1814 four slaves asked him to help them escape. They were joined by three others, and on June 23 Walker left with them in an open boat to try to get to Nassau. Walker became ill, perhaps from sunstroke, and he and the slaves were picked up by a Revenue Cutter July 8 and taken to Key West. From there he was taken, in heavy irons, in the hold of an American steamer to Pensacola, where he was kept for a year fastened to a large ring bolt by a chain of half-inch iron with a five-pound shackle around his ankle. The court convicted him, fined him one hundred fifty dollars, and sentenced him to stand in the pillory for one hour, to serve fifteen days in prison, and to be branded S S (Slave Stealer) on the right hand.[7]

Whittier made good use of the event in "The Branded Hand," which was printed at least four times during the year and again in April 1846. One of the printings was in tract form, and ten thousand copies were printed to be given away. The poem was well written to arouse sympathy and admiration for Walker and scorn for his persecutors: Walker had learned the truth that Man is the only sacred thing on earth, and should display his hand with the S S prophesying "Salvation to the Slave."

Whittier busied himself in the affairs of the Liberty Party with a mixture of confidence and irritation. The superior numbers in the Whig and Democratic parties did not seem to him to be alarming. After all, Whigs and Democrats were human, men with warm hearts and consciences and moral perceptions, interested in the honor and welfare of the country, and Whittier was confident that the best among them would join the Liberty Party with the zeal of fresh converts. But he was impatient at the delay in calling a County Convention which had been scheduled for August 1 and asked that he be notified in a day or two at the latest so that he could write the call and publish it in the *Essex Transcript* and the *Emancipator*.[8] It was decided, however, to postpone the Convention until it was time to make the party nominations.

The growing opposition to the annexation of Texas had spread beyond Anti-Slavery societies and the Liberty Party. When Whittier received a notice of a meeting at Concord, called by Henry Wilson, he sent a forceful letter to Ralph Waldo Emerson to be read there. He was glad that the call had been issued, but addresses and resolutions were useless unless followed by action. "An angel speaking down the blue spaces might do his whole duty in the simple utterance of his rebuke of wrong and commendation of right.

By a law of his high nature he could be to us only a voice. But man, if he would benefit his race, must *act out* that which he *speaks.*" What should be done? Not dissolve the Union: The moral and political power requisite for doing it could far more easily abolish every vestige of slavery. There was one thing that the Northern opponent of slavery could do: he could vote against slaveholders and refuse to support pro-slavery clergy. At this point Whittier recognized that he would be said to be looking for recruits for the Liberty Party. He admitted that he was convinced of the impossibility of acting against slavery except on the principle of that Party, but its members would be happy to give place to men of wider influence and greater capacity. If the Whigs and Democrats would work against slavery, the Liberty Party would no longer be needed.[9]

This meeting, which came to be known as the Middlesex Convention, was adjourned to October 21. In the meantime the County Convention of the Liberty Party was held at Ipswich September 24. The Party had evidently achieved respectability or at least a moderate amount of political importance; the County Commissioners gave the use of the Court House. The day was stormy and Whittier did not go but sent a letter of practical suggestions urging activity of the grassroots sort. Every town in the County should be visited by some active, energetic Abolitionists. The Convention should divide the County into districts and assign one or two workers to each.[10]

Six days later he was at the State Liberty Convention in Tremont Temple, Boston, and in spite of his doubts about the value of resolutions was on a committee to prepare resolutions and an address to the voters. The address was printed in the *Essex Transcript* October 17, along with an address "To the Liberty Men of Essex County" signed "In behalf of the County Liberty Committee, John G. Whittier Sec'y." It contained suggestions similar to those in his letter to the County Convention.[11]

Whittier was again irritated by the incompetence and confusion at Liberty Party headquarters, typical of politically inexperienced idealists who lacked Whittier's practical ability and sagacity. In the October 16 issue of the *Emancipator* there had been an announcement that Brewster had been nominated for Lieutenant-Governor and in the same issue a call for a meeting of the State Liberty Committee to nominate someone in Brewster's place. "Is that your way of doing business? For heaven's sake, let me know here what you have concluded upon. The Transcript here had Burritt week before last, last week it had Brewster, and this week nobody! All this looks like child's play — or rather that for want of due energy at headquarters, our election is going by default."[12]

As the date of the Middlesex Convention approached, Whittier was not hopeful about its accomplishments. It must emphasize that slavery was the reason for opposing the annexation of Texas; the Anglo-Saxon races liked to acquire territory, and trying to stem the tide of this feeling would be attempting the impossible. He prophesied that the labor, responsibility, and expense of the movement would fall as usual on the poor despised Abolitionists. If Phillips, Hoar, and Child would do one twentieth as much as poor men like Elizur Wright and himself, it would be more help than a ton of speeches. One thousand dollars was needed to do the work properly. Men and women should go from house to house getting signatures on a remonstrance. A committee should be chosen to correspond with anti-Texas men in other states and another committee to raise money to carry on the work and secretly to help defeat candidates of the pro-Texas party in New Hampshire.

Two of Whittier's suggestions were followed. The Convention appointed a committee which published a pamphlet with a remonstrance and space for signatures, giving slavery in Texas as the reason for opposing its admission as a state. Whittier was a member of this committee, called the Massachusetts State Texas Committee, and was appointed with Henry Wilson to present the remonstrance to the Congress.[13]

Getting signatures for the remonstrance was delayed by the approach of the election. Whittier's devotion to the cause led him even to attempt public speaking, which he did not enjoy and which he knew he did not do well. At a Liberty meeting in Haverhill, when it came his turn to speak, he began, according to his own account, with as much vehemence as Mr. Pickwick did in the sedan chair at Ipswich but gradually subsided into a melancholy monotone which under other circumstances might have been effective, but he was not sanguine of its effect on the audience. But if he was not successful as a speaker, he seems to have done as well as anyone could have in keeping peace between hostile factions. After the Liberty meeting he went to Bradford where he called on Gardner Perry, listened patiently to his complaints against some dissidents, went to them and listened with equal patience to their complaints against Perry, and urged both parties to stop quarreling and to emulate each other in the good cause of Liberty.[14]

As election day approached, Whittier did not let the readers of the *Essex Transcript* forget the crimes of slavery. A friend in Baltimore had written of his distress when he saw the two children of a poor negro woman sold at a public auction. "Think of this, mothers of New England," Whittier wrote. The *Washington Union*, the organ of the Polk administration, carried an advertisement of the sale of a man at the jail of Washington County in District of Columbia. "Democrats, how does this look? Have you not a beautiful organ of your party at headquarters? Is this selling *men* like cattle a 'democratic' measure?"

A week later the *Essex Transcript* printed a poem by Charles Torrey, with an introductory note by Whittier: "It is greatly to be feared that he will finish his days in prison. He is said to be emaciated, pale and broken down in health. Let us remember him as he would ask to be remembered, by emulating his zeal and faithfulness in the cause of freedom, and avenge him as he would wish to be avenged, by redoubling exertions to overthrow the hateful system of Slavery."[15]

Whittier was taking an active part in the campaign. At a meeting of Friends of Freedom in Amesbury and Salisbury to get support for the Liberty Party candidates, there was lively discussion of resolutions which he read, expressing confidence in the Liberty Party and in the cause of Liberty. He wrote a communication for the *Essex Transcript*, "Samuel E. Sewall, the Liberty Candidate for Governor," in reply to an editorial in the *Northhampton Gazette* advising Liberty men to vote for Briggs instead of Sewall because Briggs had more political experience and was a Temperance man. Whittier conceded that Briggs was in many respects estimable, but he and his Council had appointed a favorite of the "rum-party" who was a Whig in preference to a Temperance Liberty man. Sewall was well-read and understood constitutional law and legal and political history. Cushing had once written to Whittier, "There is not a sounder lawyer or a better man among us."[16]

All this work had little result. The weather on election day was bad, and there was a decline in the Whig and Democratic vote while the Liberty vote was only slightly larger than the previous year, one in twelve instead of one in fourteen.[17] This was far below the gain that Whittier had hoped for — or said he hoped for — and perhaps for that reason he wrote a poem about an event that he could be jubilant about. In January 1844 John P. Hale, Democratic Representative in Congress from New Hampshire, had written a letter to his constituents which was printed in the *Exeter News Letter* denouncing the annexation of Texas as promoting the interests of slavery and "eminently calculated to provoke the scorn of earth and the judgment of heaven." Whittier wrote to Hale to say that he had rather be the author of that letter than President of the United States and urged Hale to make no retreat or concession. Living on the border of New Hampshire, Whittier had found that the better Democrats believed Hale to be right. Nevertheless Hale was promptly read out of the Democratic party at a special convention February 12, and his victory, which Whittier said forty-seven years later in one of his last letters "culminated in the abolition of human slavery and the establishment of the Union on an immovable basis," did not come until Hale was elected to the United States Senate in 1846.[18] Whittier's poem "New Hampshire", printed in the "Free State Rally and Texas Chain-Breaker" December 6, 1845, was inspired by Hale's letter and answered the question he had asked eight years earlier of John Farmer of the New Hamsphire Anti-Slavery Society: "Where is the voice of New Hampshire?".[19]

Now that the election was over, an effort could be made to get an impressive number of signatures on the remonstrance that Whittier and Henry Wilson were to present to the Congress. Whittier wrote a letter to the *Essex Transcript* urging that Whigs, Democrats, and Liberty Party men in the Free

States who had a common interest in the welfare of their country should advise their Representatives in Congress to say: "Welcome to Texas as a Free State; eternal hostility to her as a land of chains and slaves." This was followed by the form of remonstrance.[20]

The time and attention given to Anti-Slavery and the Liberty Party did not keep Whittier from being interested in other matters. He read one of the first issues of *Harbinger*, published by the Transcendentalists and reformers at Brook Farm, and wrote to Charles A. Dana that he liked it. Dana replied with a request for an occasional contribution of verse or prose. The poetical department, he said, was not an easy one to fill; the New Spirit had hardly made its way among the gentler muses, though when the Poet had once comprehended the Destiny of Man, such strains would burst from his lips as the world had never echoed with.[21] Whittier's response hardly rose to that height; it was "To My Friend on the Death of His Sister." It was written to Joseph Sturge after his sister Sophia's death in June, and its real sympathy and sincerity may have come from Whittier's feelings about his sister Elizabeth's illness. It contributed nothing to the philosophy that Dana had outlined in his letter.

The first three of the six "Songs of Labor" were written and published in 1845, "The Shoemakers," "The Fishermen," "The Lumbermen." Whittier intended to write a longer series, for the "*working, acting,* rather than thinking people" and "to invest labor with some degree of beauty."[22] He had not yet arrived at the attitude toward labor in the paragraph that he added to "The City of a Day" for publication in *Literary Recreations and Miscellanies* in 1854: "Labor, graduated to man's simple wants, necessities, and unperverted tastes, is doubtless well; but all beyond this is weariness to flesh and spirit." There is no suggestion of either kind of weariness in these songs; work is good, jolly, vigorous fun, an attitude that Whittier did not have in his brief experience in shoemaking — and he had never gone on a fishing schooner to Labrador or cut down trees in the Maine forests. All three poems are clear and specific and show Whittier's ability to amass and make use of a great number of scenic and factual details, many of them from reading; a note on "Meccatina" with the first printing of "The Fishermen" quoted Audubon's *Voyage to Labrador*.

When he returned some German books which Thomas Tracy had lent him, he sent Philip James Bailey's *Festus* in which he thought that Tracy would find some powerful passages.[23] *Festus* is a long, moralized version of *Faust*, which may have led Whittier to the soul-searching revealed in "My Soul and I." The assurance that he gave to his soul was deeper and more thoughtful than the simple confidence of most of his religious poems and had echoes of Swedenborg.

The months since Whittier lost his position on the *Middlesex Standard* had been busy but not productive of income. In November a letter from Joseph

Sturge brought good news. Sturge had learned from Lewis Tappan that Whittier needed money and asked that he might have the privilege of helping.[24]

One cannot help thinking that Whittier was rather too willing to accept charity and even to ask for it. Lewis Tappan could not have known of his poverty if Whittier had not told him about it or had not told his troubles to others who would be likely to tell him. It is hard to see why he did not try to get work in New York. He knew Horace Greeley well enough to write to him about Frederick Palmer Tracy, the Methodist minister who had been active in Abolition, and he seemed certain that Greeley would introduce Tracy to his editorial friends and perhaps employ him himself.[25] The poor health which he felt as a handicap had not kept him from editing the *Middlesex Standard* and travelling by stagecoach from Amesbury to Lowell every few days and would not keep him from going to Washington a month later. He was deep in Anti-Slavery work and other worthy causes, but his Anti-Slavery writing would surely not have been restricted by Horace Greeley, and through the *Tribune* he might have done a great deal more for the cause than he could do as an unemployed free-lance writer and party worker in Essex County. He would have no difficulty in meeting and working with important men. He always made a good impression; Ralph Waldo Emerson, for example, was greatly pleased with his "handsome person and beautiful manners." The best answer is that Whittier had become settled in a way of life which a bachelor in his thirty-ninth year would find hard to change. Horace Greeley had remarked to Moses Cartland four years earlier that Whittier was getting into some of the whims of the bachelor.[26]

The Texas question was to be settled in December. Whittier hesitated about going to Washington, thinking that he was not well enough to do everything that ought to be done in a final effort against annexation. However, if no one else could be found, he would go if his health improved. As might be expected, he went, and arrived in Washington tired and unwell but still able to do some lobbying. He talked with Northern Democrats, who agreed that it was a bad thing to have Texas come in as a slave state and cursed "between their teeth as it were the whole Southern wing of their party" but with one exception would not promise to vote against it. They had evidently not come to any understanding with each other, and each seemed afraid of his neighbor and all were afraid of the South. The Whigs, with a few exceptions, were without heart and feeling about slavery; Henry Wilson had been talking with them without much success. Thousands of remonstrances however, were pouring in, many of them from Massachusetts, and Whittier believed that if other free states had done as well, annexation would have been defeated.

The annexation bill passed the House of Representatives December 16, and Texas was admitted as a slave state. Whittier had expected this, but he was still bitter and thought that he had seen human nature at its worst, Northern men protesting against the annexation in the name of Heaven and Earth "and a worse place than the latter" and then voting for it an hour later, evidence that the slave power ruled Congress absolutely. He left Washington for Philadelphia, where he arrived in such a state of nervous excitement and looking so unwell when he called at the Pennocks' that one of them thought that they would not see him again.[27]

It was now twelve years since Whittier had helped to form the American Anti-Slavery Society and had printed *Justice and Expediency* at his own expense. Despair and acceptance of defeat might have been expected, but Whittier was not that type. He used his bitterness to give force to the first stanzas of "At Washington," and then his courage and faith reasserted themselves. Human feeling was not dead; there would be Southerners who would do more for freedom than the North had done. He could only wish that his fellow-Abolitionists had got the message that he had and would bury their feuds and do the work that lay before them.

An attempt was being made to do this by forming an Anti-Slavery League. Whittier was in sympathy and thought that it would not injure the Liberty Party.[28] The *Essex Transcript* was not letting its readers forget the horrors of slavery. It quoted an advertisement January 22 from a paper in Livingston, Alabama:

Negro Dogs
The undersigned having bought the entire pack of Negro Dogs
(of the Hays and Allen stock), he now proposes to catch
runaway Negroes. His charges will be Three Dollars per day
for hunting, and Fifteen Dollars for catching a runaway.

The winter lull in Liberty Party business gave Whittier more time to think about other things. He served as secretary at a local meeting of Friends of Temperance. His interest in the Liberal movement in the Catholic Church in Germany led him to address a poem to Johannes Ronge which he sent to the *United States Magazine and Democratic Review* for its March number, encouraging him and warning him to avoid Luther's mistake of entanglement in creeds.[29] A similar emphasis on religion as the torch of truth and freedom appeared in "Lines. From a letter to a young Clerical Friend," printed later in the year in *Voices of Freedom*. One situation that did not occur to him as needing attention was the pay of mill workers in Amesbury. Their lot was perhaps better than that of workers in most mill towns, but their pay could have been increased without hardship to the stockholders, who had just received a ten per cent semi-annual dividend.

He was finding time to do some reading and study. He had read Carlyle's *Letters and Speeches of Oliver Cromwell* when he wrote the prose essay "James Nayler" for the March *United States Magazine and Democratic Review*. It seemed to him that Carlyle's "Hero Worship" was at times nothing less than devil worship and that Carlyle gave distorted pictures of Cromwell's contemporaries and tried to justify the persecution of Quakers during the Protectorate by describing the harmless fanaticism of a few of them, one of whom was James Nayler. Whittier's essay showed considerable study of sources and was written with sympathy for Nayler in his "craziness and folly," as he termed it in "John Roberts," and with admiration for Nayler's later beautiful and blameless life.

Politics started up again in late February. At a meeting of the Liberty Party in Marlboro Chapel, Boston, Whittier was elected a member of the State Central Committee for Essex County, which had the duty of seeing that the State was organized, of employing men for this purpose, and of producing documents to be sold or given away.[30] One of these, signed by Whittier and other members of the committee, was *Address of the Liberty State Convention*. The party opposed the Mexican War, which was unconstitutional, and Governor Briggs' call for volunteers, which was unnecessary because the country was in no danger.

Whittier's delight over the March elections in New Hampshire led to his writing the lively and triumphant "A letter supposed to be written by the chairman of the 'Central Clique' at Concord, N.H. to the Hon. M. N. at Washington giving the result of the election." The chairman of the "Central Clique" was Franklin Pierce and the Hon. M. N. was Moses Norris. It did not contain all the stanzas in the present version and there were some variations in others. There were notes explaining any references that might not have been clear to readers less versed than Whittier in contemporary affairs.[31]

John P. Hale's election to the Senate in June also gave delight to Whittier and the Anti-Slavery group, who must have reasoned that the end justified the means; it was brought about by a political deal that clearly thwarted the will of the people. In the popular vote for Governor of New Hampshire, the Democratic candidate, Jared W. Williams, led with 26,740, only 858 below the number needed for election. The Liberty candidate, Nathan S. Berry, had 18,379, and the Whig candidate, Anthony Colby, had only 17,707. The election was then thrown into the House of Representatives, where the Independent Democrats said to the Whigs, "We will put your man, Anthony Colby, into office as Governor of the State, if you will elect John P. Hale to the Senate." This was done; Colby was elected Governor June 3 and Hale elected to a six-year term in the Senate. Whittier wished that a similar deal might be worked in Massachusetts. Couldn't Massachusetts be "New Hampshirized"? Weren't there any honest Democrats in Massachusetts who would unite with Anti-Slavery Whigs and Liberty Party men? If twenty such men could be elected to the Legislature, Sewall could be elected Governor.[32]

Whittier continued to attack churches which did not take firm Anti-Slavery stand or were even pro-slavery. He had supposed, he wrote in an article in the *Essex Transcript*, that the division in the Methodist Church meant that the Northern section would be at least nominally Anti-Slavery, but the Baltimore Conference, part of the Methodist Church North, had voted not to have any connection with any ecclesiastical body that made slaveholding a bar to membership, and this resolution had been endorsed by the Methodist *Zion's Herald*. A few weeks later he asked some questions of all the clergy. If slavery is inconsistent with the purpose of the Gospel to make men happier and to overthrow all wrong and oppression, should not Gospel ministers speak against it? If the Bible sanctions slavery, is it really the word of God? If a Christian may keep slaves, with cruelty and abuse, and still be a preacher or church member, is Christianity any better than paganism? He commended and quoted from a speech by George S. Hillard before the American Unitarian Association, "Christianity in Politics," which argued that the course of the United States toward Mexico was far below Christian standard and that the country needed leaders who would "hate the cowardice of doing wrong." He then proceeded as usual to a practical political conclusion: he wished that Hillard, Sumner, Stephen C. Phillips, Charles Allen, and Charles Francis Adams would cease to support the political party which had "just manifested the guilty cowardice of voting in Congress on the side of oppression and atrocious wrong and of sustaining the unconstitutional usurpations of a political enemy, because the Slave Power demands it."[33]

Whittier had not forgotten that emotion is more powerful than reason. He wrote "The Slave Pauline" for the May 7 *Essex Transcript*, with an appeal to mothers to teach their children to hate slavery and to pity its victims. The story was of a beautiful slave girl in New Orleans who was loved by her master and struck her mistress in the ensuing quarrel. She was sentenced to death but was returned to prison, and the execution was postponed until her child should be born. "And the bells there called to mass and prayer-meeting, and Methodists sang, and Baptists immersed, and Presbyterians sprinkled — and young mothers smiled through tears upon their newborn children; and young maidens and matrons of that great city sat in their cool verandahs and talked of love and household joys and domestic happiness — while all that dreary time the poor slave-girl lay on the scanty straw of her dungeon, waiting with what agony the dear and pitying God of the white and the black only knows, for the birth of the child of her adulterous violator!"[34]

The death of Charles T. Torrey May 9 was played for all it was worth to arouse Anti-Slavery emotion. Not all Abolitionists were admirers of Torrey; Theodore Weld called him "an exceedingly vain, trifling man, with no wisdom or stability," but no one objected to treating him as a martyr. The *Essex Transcript* of May 14 had heavy black borders on the columns of the middle pages and an editorial by Whittier, "The Prisoner is Free." Whittier did not miss this chance to attack the Mexican War: the people of the United States were lavishing blood and treasure on the banks of the Rio Grande to sustain slavery. He would write on the life and labors of Torrey in a later issue — he was too indignant to do it now.

Whittier was at Torrey's funeral in Tremont Temple, Boston, May 18 and at a meeting in Faneuil Hall in the evening where he acted as secretary, and reported the funeral in the *Essex Transcript* May 21. Torrey, he said, had helped between three and four hundred slaves to escape to freedom but had had no hand in planning the escape that was the cause of his arrest and imprisonment in Maryland. It had been arranged by a most respectable lady of Baltimore, and Torrey's only part had been to drive the carriage when no other driver could be found. Whittier's opinion of Torrey was quite different from Weld's: "He had fine talents, improved by learning and observation, a clear, intensely active intellect, and a heart full of sympathy and genial humanity." When Whittier looked at Torrey in his coffin he felt for a moment like grasping God's "dread prerogative of vengeance."[35] But his emotion did not lead him to any sentimental lavishing of money on Torrey's widow. He specified that the nine dollars that he sent to Dr. Bowditch was for Torrey's monument and funeral expenses only. Mrs. Torrey's father, Rev. Jacob Ide, had a larger income than the Abolitionists in Whittier's neighborhood and ought not to throw his daughter on the charity of strangers.[36]

Although it might seem that Whittier was merely using the Mexican War as a means of getting votes for the Liberty Party, he was really, as he wrote to Henry I. Bowditch, heart-sick over it. Massachusetts, after being "kicked and cuffed and spit upon by slavery," was being asked to raise three regiments to conquer more territory for the new slave states. A letter to the North Western Liberty Convention at Chicago emphasized that the War was gaining new territory for Slavery. The armies were pushing forward into the heart of Mexico. "The land before them is consecrated to personal freedom; behind them they leave slavery; the clank of chains mingles with the music of their march."[37] The same thought reappeared a few days later in an unsigned poem "Palo Alto" in the *Boston Chronotype*, presented as a translation from a Mexican poet:

> Hearken! up the Rio Bravo
> > Comes the negro-catcher's shout:
> Listen! 'Tis the Yankee hammer
> > Forging human fetters out![38]

When the Essex County Liberty Convention was held in Amesbury July 4, Whittier was on the committee to present resolutions, one of which referred to the Mexican War as disgraceful and deeply regretted the willingness of the Governor to call for volunteers.[39]

Whittier, however, now had one cause for rejoicing. The dispute between the United States and Great Britain over the Oregon territory, which had threatened to lead to war, had been settled peacefully. Joseph Sturge had written to John Quincy Adams, whom he had met on his visit to Washington with Whittier in 1841, that he and most Englishmen were grieved over Adams' inflammatory remarks in the House of Representatives and he had urged Adams to use his influence on the side of peace. On June 12 the Senate voted to advise President Polk to accept the treaty offered by the British Government placing the boundary at 49°. Whittier heard the good news three days later and wrote to Sturge to congratulate him and all peace-loving Englishmen on the happy ending; his heart was full of thankfulness — although his joy was subdued and chastened by the Mexican War, which was a "war for Slavery and plunder."[40]

In the spring of 1846 Whittier and his mother and sister Elizabeth had colds and were tired from taking care of Aunt Mercy, whose death from "inflammation of the lungs" occurred April 11. They did not feel well enough to go to Moses Cartland's wedding. "God bless you both!" Whittier wrote to Cartland. "You have done right, and His blessing is always with the right. I see I shall be left alone in my old bachelorship. I wish it could be otherwise; but as it is, I make the best of it."[41] Perhaps he thought that he meant it.

He wrote a few poems in the spring, the most important of which was another Song of Labor, "The Shipbuilders," which appeared in the *United States Magazine and Democratic Review*. It revealed accurate knowledge of the details of shipbuilding but had more romantic concepts in the last four stanzas than workmen in a shipyard would have been likely to have. One can hardly imagine them saying or thinking

> Look! how she moves adown the grooves,
>   In graceful beauty now!
> How lovely on the breast she loves
>   Sinks down her virgin prow!

Launching a ship was a dangerous business, with good chance of injury or death if something went wrong when the blocks were struck away "to set the good ship free."

"The Freed Islands" was evidently planned and perhaps written in the spring, to be used August 1 at an anniversary celebration in Milton of the freeing of slaves in the British West Indies. Elizabeth's friend Ida Russell was making the arrangements and could not decide whom to get to do the reading. Dr. Channing, she thought, had a "dainty gingerly way of reading that does well enough when he reads Lowell's poems but I believe I should fairly stamp with impatience to hear him read anything of John's in that 'super-fine' style."[42] "The Freed Islands" was well suited to its purpose, as were all of Whittier's poems for occasions; he knew human nature well enough to write something not too long that could be easily read and that could be understood by a listening audience who could carry away a definite impression.

In the summer Whittier was anxiously awaiting the proof sheets of *The Supernaturalism of New England*. His *Voices of Freedom* went on sale in August for seventy-five cents.[43] It contained only three previously unpublished poems, but there were changes in others; the changed forms became the permanent ones.

Early in September plans were made for a mass meeting at Newmarket, New Hampshire, of the united parties in Rockingham County, the Liberty and Independent Democratic Parties which had elected Hale to the Senate. Whittier urged Charles Sumner to be there — "Thou couldst do well to step into the cars and join us." (The "cars" were of course the railroad train, which had made travel miraculously swift and easy.) If Sumner was there he was not one of the speakers. Among those making brief remarks was Moses Cartland, whom Whittier ecstatically described as having a "fine intellectual face, glowing with the fire and enthusiasm of genius, as if, to use Carlyle's description of the face of Camille Desmoulins, a naphtha lamp burnt within it." Resolutions were passed that Liberty men and Independent Democrats were in agreement with Hale.[44] A few days after the meeting Whittier wrote to Hale, who was to lecture in Faneuil Hall on September 14. Could some common ground be found for all opponents of slavery to unite on and form a great League of Freedom, making Abolition the paramount political question and agreeing not to vote for slaveholders or men who had political connections with them? There were eighty thousand Liberty voters, and a majority of the old parties were almost ready to join such a movement.[45]

This dream did not keep him from present political activities. He was one of a committee of three to call a Liberty Convention at Haverhill September 17 to nominate a candidate for Congress and he evidently wrote the notice. Reform, it said, was needed in Congress; humanity had its claims, and the rights of persons should be held as sacred as those of property. "And where should the needed reform in our national representation commence, if not in Massachusetts, whose hill-tops are crowned with church spires, whose whole surface is dotted with school-houses, whose sons are descendants of those Christian republicans of the seventeenth century, who in Parliament and General Court were not ashamed to acknowledge their allegiance to the paramount Law of God!" Whittier called the meeting to order, served as Chairman of the Business Committee, and moved to make unanimous the nomination of Chauncey L. Knapp, who had been his fellow-editor on the *Middlesex Standard*.[46]

On September 23 there was a Whig Convention in Boston. Stephen C. Phillips offered an Anti-Slavery resolution which was supported by Charles Sumner but rejected by the Convention — "an evidence," Whittier wrote to Sumner, "that the end and aim of the managers of the convention was to go just far enough to scare the party, and no further." As for Daniel Webster, who had been lauded in one of the resolutions, "He is I fear no better on this question than a colossal coward."[47] With the letter he enclosed his poem "The Pine Tree" calling for another "strong-voiced Adams" who could summon Massachusetts to noble deeds like those of the past. The second stanza had the same thought as a paragraph in the call for the Convention at Haverhill: man is more important than property.

The State election was a victory for the Whigs. Many Democrats had gone over to the Whigs or did not vote. The Liberty vote increased slightly, between one and two thousand. In the national election the Liberty gain was between fifteen and twenty thousand.[48]

A pleasant incident in the fall took Whittier's mind briefly away from the sadness and strain of the year's events. Rebecca Davis, a young woman who lived across the street, gave him a pumpkin pie. Whittier found her good company and would drop in to play euchre with her before she had washed the breakfast dishes, and he loved pumpkin pie. He expressed his pleasure and gratitude in "Song of the Pumpkin," the first non-satirical humorous verse that he had written for many years.[49] The tone was light and there was a happy reminiscence of his boyhood.

Whittier had a narrow escape from death during the same harvest season. He was picking grapes in an arbor in his garden when a bullet struck his cheek, glancing along the bone without penetrating it. It had been fired by a boy in the next yard, who missed his aim at a target, and the bullet came through the fence. Whittier went to his physician, Dr. Sparhawk, a short distance around the corner on School Street, and had the wound dressed before telling his mother and sister. He listened kindly to the tearful confession of the boy, Philip Butler, who after he had become an artist painted at least two pictures of the Whittier homestead at Haverhill. Whittier tried unsuccessfully to keep the story out of the newspapers, and an exaggerated account reached Joseph Sturge, who wrote that he hoped that Whittier would let him pay the expenses of his fearful accident or for anything that could add to his comfort so that mental anxiety would not be added to his sufferings.[50]

Two poems were written for annuals to be published in 1847. Henry Peterstone wrote to Whittier in May that a friend of his was preparing a Temperance Annual and would like to have Whittier write a poem for it on Temperance or any general subject. Peterstone had said that Whittier would ask about twenty dollars.[51] The poem that Whittier wrote was "The Reformer," in which only one stanza referred to Temperance. The theme was that the Reformer builds as well as destroys, and the last stanza had a note of confidence that was a sincere expression of Whittier's own faith:

> God works in all things; all obey
>> His first propulsion from the night:
> Wake thou and watch! The world is gray
>> With morning light!

"Worship," written for the 1847 *Opal*, is one of Whittier's several poems with stanzas so close to a universal religious sentiment that they have been used as hymns by denominations far from the Friends in thought and practice. These hymns, however, do not, needless to say, include this stanza:

> As if the pomp of rituals, and the savor
>> Of gums and spices could the Unseen One please;
> As if His ear could bend, with childish favor,
>> To the poor flattery of the organ keys!

The time was at hand when Whittier would not be in such pressing need of help from Joseph Sturge, although he would have to live frugally for the next twenty years, and gifts from Sturge were still welcome. Plans were being made by the American and Foreign Anti-Slavery Society to publish a weekly paper at Washington called *The National Era*. Gamaliel Bailey would be the "principal editor" and Whittier and Amos Phelps would be "regular contributors" — a better term than the misleading "corresponding editors" which was used in the paper itself. Whittier had nothing to do with editorial policy and no specific assignments but could send anything that he wished, either prose or poetry. With a few exceptions everything that he wrote for the next ten years was printed in the *Era*.

He helped to get a good reception for the paper, writing to well-known men asking for their endorsement by a letter to be printed in the first issue and offering to take subscriptions in Amesbury and adjoining towns at two dollars a year "always in advance." He explained that it was not the purpose of the *Era* to draw support away from other Anti-Slavery publications, all of which deserved support, but it was hoped that the *Era* would cause an increase in interest in the older papers.[52]

XIV

1847 - 48

The Supernaturalism of New England was published in January 1847. It could not have been highly profitable — it sold for twenty-five cents — and the larger part of its contents had appeared in the *United States Magazine and Democratic Review* four years earlier. Hawthorne reviewed it in *The Literary World*, admitting that he liked it in spite of some serious defects: Whittier had been unable to free himself from his sense of duty, which forced him to say that he did not believe his ghost stories even while he was telling them; his style sparkled too much; and he made too much use of his learning and quoted a needless array of authorities.

Whittier had no desire to escape from his sense of duty, even for the sake of poetry and romance — "that stern duty which the true man owes to his generation to expose error, wherever and whenever he finds it," as he explained in the Introduction. The volume would show the hold that superstition still had on the common mind; men were too prone to forget their own follies while thinking about those of earlier times.

"Dedication," later entitled "To My Sister," was the only new poem in the volume. The sister was of course Elizabeth, and the poem showed the growing sympathy of thought and feeling between the brother and sister; Whittier knew that she would share his enjoyment of youthful memories and recollections of legends which they had heard when they were young. It also looks forward to "Snow-Bound," written nearly twenty years later, in its pictures of children listening to stories in front of the fire and in its nostalgic turning to childhood memories after a time of work and conflict.

The January thaw that is a feature of the New England winter came early that year, and Whittier wrote "A Dream of Summer" January 4. At noon the day seemed as warm as summer, the ground was bare, and ice had melted in the streams. The description filled two stanzas, and the remaining two were a list of analogies: there will be cheerful days in times dominated by sad memories, Hope and Faith revive and show that seeds of happiness are still in the soul, and the stars shine behind the clouds, for God has given Hope to all mankind. Everything was fully explained; nothing was entrusted to the reader's interpretive powers — just as Whittier thought that it ought to be and just as his readers liked it.

Whittier was too unwell in January and February to go to Washington, as he had planned.[1] However, he was able to be at a Massachusetts State Liberty Convention in Faneuil Hall, Boston, January 20 and to take an active part in it. He was on the Business Committee and on the State Central Committee for Essex County, and was one of the three secretaries who wrote a set of resolutions approved by the Convention. These included resolutions against the Mexican War, calling the War unjust, unnecessary, and inhuman, and claiming that it was a citizen's duty to withhold all aid from the prosecution of the War and to discourage and discountenance it to the best of his ability. Shedding of blood in such a war was murder, and Congress should refuse to vote supplies and should force the President to withdraw the troops and to offer peace, leaving the boundary dispute to be settled by negotiation and arbitration.

Although Abolitionists were not the only outspoken opponents, there was also plenty of enthusiasm for the War. Henry Clay, aged seventy, regretted that he could not join the army in Mexico. At the evening session of the Convention some Mexican War volunteers interrupted the speaker but were quieted by the police.[2] Whittier missed this excitement; he had not felt well enough to stay through the evening.

His poor health kept him from writing as much as he wished for the *Era*. What he wrote he described as a sick man's task work, and he was unable to do any revising or correcting. Whatever he sent was printed directly from the manuscript and there were consequently numerous errors, for which he took the blame, conceding that his writing was, as he had been told, scarcely less difficult to decipher than the plates of the Mormon Bible. The editor of the *Era*, Gamaliel Bailey, allowed Whittier complete latitude in the number and length of his contributions.[3] Some of the prose items were brief, while others used several columns and ran through several issues. The longest during the winter of 1847 was "Thomas Ellwood," the first of what Whittier intended to be a series of "Old Autobiographies." Whittier knew the art of biography. The essay had clear and lively pictures of Ellwood against the background of his time and his contemporaries, especially John Milton — Ellwood was the first reader of "Paradise Lost."

The only other in the series was "John Bunyan," in the *Era* in April. It was one of Whittier's best prose essays. Whittier's deepening trend toward introspection and his reformer's interest in the Seventeenth Century, which he called the golden age of England, made him quite at home with Bunyan's *Grace Abounding to the Chief of Sinners*, which he had just read with delight.

In January and February there was a series of five "Letters from the East" containing a variety of news and comments on recent events, including Caleb Cushing's appointment as colonel of a regiment of Mexican War volunteers: "Of his peculiar qualifications for such a post, no one can doubt. During his late Oriental embassy, he had ample opportunity to study the military tactics of the Chinese, and will doubtless be prepared to oppose Santa Anna, after the manner of that redoubtable people, by turning upon him the muzzles of pickle jars and gallipots, setting up scarecrows, and issuing high sounding proclamations."

"The Heroism of Philanthropy" in the January 14 *Era* told about James Richardson, who had followed the route of slave caravans toward Central Africa. Passages from his Journal had been printed in the *British and Foreign Anti-Slavery Reporter*. It was from one of these that Whittier got the suggestion for "Song of Slaves in the Desert," of which the first version, containing three stanzas, was printed in the *Era* a week later.

Whittier, like most of the civilized world, was aroused by accounts of the famine in Ireland. Cannot something be done? he inquired in the *Era* January 28. Three centuries of oppression had made the Irish peasant what he was, dependent for his existence on a favorable season for his potato patch. In the March 4 issue he noted that accounts from Ireland were even more afflicting and, briefly, a nation was starving. But his faith in human nature was restored by the public response to appeals for help. He was convinced that there was good in all and that the hardest heart was not wholly stone. This led him to an attitude toward himself and toward his criticisms of others that became confirmed as he grew older. He was growing more charitable and shuddered at his fierce rebukes of the wrong-doing of others when he considered his weakness and sins of omission and commission.[4]

In this mood he submitted meekly to an attack in the Brook Farm *Harbinger*. Whittier had alluded to a remark of Leigh Richmond's about Robert Owen's establishment in a way which the *Harbinger* called "cant" and "faded and tattered remnants of a strong and rigid old fanaticism." Whittier's reply was, "Honoring as I do their devotion, self-sacrifice, and warm sympathy with suffering humanity, I shall not take offense at their criticism."[5]

This same feeling of patience and forgiveness was the theme of "Barclay of Ury," in the *Era* March 4. After a career as a soldier under Gustavus Adolphus, Barclay of Ury became a Quaker and bore patiently the insults of the crowd in the Aberdeen streets. The poem was longer than it needed to be and had four quite unnecessary stanzas pointing out the lesson to be learned from the story.

All these contributions not directly connected with Abolition helped to make the *Era* interesting. Other articles promoted the cause for which the paper existed. In writing about Alexander Pushkin, Whittier lamented the injustice of the prejudice against negroes in the United States. Pushkin, the favorite of the Russian emperor and people, was not ashamed of the fact that his maternal grandfather was a negro.[6]

He told the story of the end of slavery within the Society of Friends in the *Era* April 8, 15, and 22. The larger part of this article was later used in the Introduction to his edition of *John Woolman's Journal* and is included under that title in Volume VII of the *Works*. It concluded with the remark that Friends of the present day should ask themselves if they were maintaining the lofty standard of the old Quaker worthies. It seemed to Whittier that their increased zeal for verbal orthodoxy and distinctions of creed had led to a decline in practical, active testimony against evil customs, unrighteous laws, and popular sins.

"To Delaware" in the *Era* March 18, was written to welcome that state to the group of Free States in the North and West when it should achieve the abolition of slavery by a bill then in the Legislature; the news would come by a new invention, the telegraph, which would

— Tremble northward with its words of fire.

"Yorktown" in the *Era* April 15, gave two contrasting pictures: the rejoicing in the Colonies at the surrender of Cornwallis, and the slaves at Yorktown who were classed with household goods and animals. And the flag of that war for freedom was now a symbol of slavery in conquered Mexico.[7] A similar contrast was the theme of "The Two Processions," a prose sketch in the *Era* June 24. There was great public rejoicing in Washington over the July Revolution in Paris in 1830, and a procession, including the President, moved majestically toward the Capitol, its effect somewhat marred by a gang of handcuffed slaves moving in the other direction.[8]

A letter with welcome news arrived late in April. Whittier had written to Lewis Tappan April 16 telling of his poor health and poor pay. Tappan replied promptly that he would ask the Executive Committee of the American and Foreign Anti-Slavery Society to increase the compensation for Whittier's contributions to the *Era* and wished that Whittier could be paid according to the real value of his writings and not by their length. He enclosed a check for one hundred dollars and reported that Joseph Sturge had authorized him to give Whittier one thousand dollars to invest in real estate.[9]

Whittier accepted the money but used it to enlarge his own house. A second story and attic were added at the east end with a guest room at the front and a bedroom for Elizabeth looking out on the garden. This room was over the study, called the Garden Room, which was an enlargement of the room added for Aunt Mercy in 1836. A one-story ell containing a kitchen and woodshed was added at the other end of the house. The old kitchen in the middle of the house now became the dining room. Whittier and his mother still had bedrooms on the first floor, leading from this room. No further structural changes were made until 1884, and some of the visitors who came in great numbers, especially after the success of "Snow-Bound" in 1866, were surprised to find Whittier living in a house so inferior to the homes of Lowell, Longfellow, and Emerson.

From now on, Whittier did most of his writing in the Garden Room. It was the room where he talked with his friends and the favored visitors whom he led there from the parlor; as he grew older, less favored visitors were left to talk with others in the parlor or to take the hint and depart, while he escaped to the Garden Room.

The fact that Whittier spent so much money on his house instead of buying real estate from which he could receive an income suggests that he was not as poor as his friends had been led to believe. It also indicates that he liked Amesbury well enough to plan to stay there for some time. Amesbury was still a pleasant place to live. The textile mills were in full operation and making money. The Eastern Railroad was building a passenger station for a branch line from East Salisbury to Amesbury; Whittier would soon be able to board a train at this station only five minutes' walk from his house, which would take him to Boston or would connect with a train to northern New England. The Friends Meeting in Amesbury was flourishing and would soon find it necessary to build a larger meetinghouse. Abolition meetings were still held without disorder in Amesbury, while no further away than across the river in Newburyport an Anti-Slavery meeting ended in rioting.[10]

During the spring and summer Whittier continued to send an assortment of items to the *Era*. The clergy were objecting to the operation of railway trains and the moving of mail on Sunday; they had better turn their attention to the Mexican War, where military and naval action did not stop on the Sabbath. General Scott, "after raining down fire upon Vera Cruz for four days and nights, burying one thousand women and children under the ruins of their dwellings, blowing up crowded hospitals, dropping ninety-pound shells through the roofs of churches, and sprinkling altars with the blood of kneeling worshippers" had been seen in a cathedral "very calmly holding a long wax candle." A negro had been hanged by the Army for doing what he had seen his "betters" do, forgetting that white gentlemen may, like the privileged saints of *Hudibras*, do with inpunity

What other folks are damned for doing —

in this instance appropriating the wives and daughters of the enemy.[11]

He wrote "The Angels of Buena Vista" after reading a letter from Mexico telling of Mexican women near the battlefield impartially helping wounded Americans and Mexicans. In the poem he added to the dramatic effect by imagining that a Mexican woman whose husband had died with his head in her lap turned immediately to care for a young American who murmured "Mother" as he died.

It was not too early to be thinking about the 1848 Presidential election. Whittier feared that both Whig and Democratic candidates would be slaveholders and that the Liberty Party would be left alone as the rallying point for lovers of freedom and democracy. This party could command ten times the votes that it had when he joined it in 1846, and while he could not hope that it would win this election, he was confident that its influence would continue.[12]

Whittier's first choice for the Presidential nomination was John P. Hale, and he wrote Hale a letter with his usual political acumen. The nomination, he said, would strengthen Hale's position in the Senate and put an end to any suspicion that he was playing into the hands of the Whigs. He suggested that Hale should affirm his Democratic faith in the doctrines of Jefferson, Leggett, and Sedgwick and let it be known that the Anti-Slavery resolutions of the Newmarket Convention of the previous year expressed his sentiments.[13] At the same time Whittier wished it understood that he was more concerned with party unity than with anyone's candidacy. As far as he was concerned, he did not care who the candidate was if he was good and upright and sound in principle.

He was not ignoring candidates of other parties. He thought that the Southern President-makers might nominate Levi Woodbury if Taylor or some other slaveholder was not available. Woodbury, who he conceded had good qualities in private life, was a Northern man with Southern principles, "the great model Doughface," and he added, with more comic effect than good taste, that Woodbury attended to the wants, humors, and necessities of slavery as an apostate from Christianity in a caravan of Mecca pilgrims follows "with brush and pitcher the camel who bears the Koran, in devout attendance upon the rear of the holy brute."[14]

When the Whig Party in Massachusetts named Daniel Webster in September as a suitable candidate, Whittier acknowledged Webster's great intellectual powers but was sure that he would not be accepted by friends of freedom. In his instructions to the United States Minister at the Court of St. James, Webster had exhausted his legal subtlety and constitutional lore in an effort to extend the law of slavery over the world. He had done everything possible to vindicate the double-dealing and perfidy of the United States government in its dealings with Texas and Mexico.

A Liberty Party convention at Worcester in September announced that Massachusetts Liberty voters would support Hale, John Jay, Samuel Fessenden, or Francis J. Lemoyne, and voted a resolution approving Hale's course. Hale was nominated at the General Liberty Convention in Buffalo September 21, and Whittier, confined to his house by illness, wrote Hale a hasty and incoherent letter, urging him to take a bold Anti-Slavery stand; if, after thinking it over, Hale could not do this, Whittier would not wish him to accept the nomination, nor would he ask it if Hale thought that he had better enter the Senate without any party connections. A few days later he wrote again, and this time without any reservation urged Hale to accept the nomination.[15]

Two historical articles in the *Era* had contemporary relevance. "Samuel Hopkins" was a sketch of the Newport minister who attacked slavery in his pulpit although many of his church members owned slaves and derived their income from the slave trade. "Black Men in the Revolution and the War of 1812" was a revision of "Black Soldiers of the Revolution," written six years earlier. Whittier was careful to explain that he did not wish to eulogize any shedders of blood even in a righteous cause, but when he saw Fourth of July celebrations ignoring the negro soldiers in the two wars, he could not help calling attention to historical facts. Negro soldiers and sailors served loyally and heroically in both wars, and "if pulpits must be desecrated by eulogies of the patriotism of bloodshed, we see no reason why black defenders of their country in the war for liberty should not receive honorable mention as well as white invaders of a neighboring republic who have volunteered in a war for plunder and slavery extension."

"The Poetry of the North" was a rather discursive introduction to "The Norseman's Ride," which was copied from the *United States Magazine and Democratic Review*, where it had appeared without the author's name. Whittier liked its boldness of tone and vigor of language. A few weeks later he received a grateful letter from its author, a young man of twenty-two named Bayard Taylor.[16] Thus began a friendship which gave a great deal of pleasure to the Whittier household and lasted until Taylor's death in 1878.

Through the fall Whittier continued to send miscellaneous items to the *Era*. Slavery had been abolished in Tunis; it was a mortifying reflection that the Republican and Christian government of the United States had been strengthening and protecting the slave market: "Shall the Bible enslave the world?" He read "The Clergy and Reform" by Thomas Wentworth Higginson in the *Christian World* in which Higginson said that the clergy had deserved the censure they had received from the friends of Liberty and Peace and were unworthy of their vocation and unequal to the need of the times. Whittier's comment was that he had long believed that the clergy must abate their pretensions or be what those pretensions required. He would be happy to see realized in them the wish of Gregory VII: "Every Pope should be a saint."[17]

The publication of *A Collection from the Newspaper Writings of N.P. Rogers* led Whittier to write "Nathaniel P. Rogers," which was printed in the *Era* of October 21. Most of the long quoted passages in Volume VII of the *Works* were added three years later when the essay was printed in *Old Portraits and Modern Sketches*. The tone was enthusiastic throughout, and when Whittier commented on Rogers' power of indignation which launched wit and sarcasm like bolts from heaven, he generously refrained from saying that he had been the victim of it in 1840 when Rogers had said that "New Organization" had tamed Whittier's ethereal spirit and fettered his free limbs in its narrow harness.

The nineteenth century gave a great deal of thought to life after death and was ready to read endless discussions of the topic. Whittier's little half-sermon essay "The Better Land" in the *Era* of November 11 was doubtless welcome to its readers. It pointed out that we expect to find in Heaven the things that we love and reverence on earth, such as Catholic rites and Methodist camp-meetings.

The publication of Longfellow's *Evangeline* caused Whittier to exclaim, "Eureka! Here, then, we have it at last." He had lamented in the *Era* of

November 9 that American literature contained no pastorals and that its poetry was abstract and imitative. "Evangeline" was an American poem, with "exquisite pictures of the striking and peculiar features of life and nature in the New World." Whittier gave one opinion that most readers would not share, that "Evangeline" would have been as acceptable to the public taste if it had been written in the "poetic prose" of Longfellow's "Hyperion." This brief review appeared November 25; the larger part of the essay as it is printed in the *Works* was a follow-up in the *Era* of January 27, 1848, entitled "Evangeline — The Puritans."[18] Another follow-up appeared in the *Era* a year later (February 8, 1849). The interest aroused by "Evangeline" in the sufferings of the Acadians in exile warranted, Whittier thought, an account of one chapter in their history. Five hundred of them were taken to Philadelphia, where Anthony Benezet found them quartered in military barracks, destitute and suffering. He administered relief to the sick and dying, raised money to build houses, found ways for those able to work to earn a living, and personally paid annuities to some of the oldest and the most helpless.

The final poems in the "Songs of Labor" series appeared in November and December.

The first and last stanzas of "The Drovers" were better than in the present form. They did not have the awkwardly inserted and irrelevant moral:

There's life alone in duty done,
And rest alone in striving.

These lines are ridiculously out of character; they surely would not have been thought, much less spoken, by the kind of man that was hired to drive cattle over the road. There were good descriptive details, as always when Whittier dealt with New England rural scenes, and one specific line later softened and weakened.

And cows with dust-dry udders

became

And cows too lean for shadows.

One fortunate change was made: at James T. Fields' suggestion the rhyme of "winter" and "shorter" in the last stanza was eliminated.

"The Huskers" was closest to Whittier's own experience and was therefore the least sentimentalized of the Songs. The descriptive details were true, and there was no attempt to put literary language in the mouths of country people. The "Corn Song", which formed part of "The Huskers," without separate title, was sung by the schoolmaster and its diction was thereby justified. Whittier good-naturedly changed one phrase at the suggestion of James T. Fields. "Corn-fed girls" became "farmer girls" — "notwithstanding Allan Ramsay or somebody else talks of "kail-fed lassies!""[19]

Whittier's health improved early in January and he was able to do more writing. "The Slaves of Martinique" in the *Era* of January 13 had seventy-two octameter lines. The story was imaginary, suggested by a picture of two negro figures, and the theme was the power of love, the only source of happiness in this woeful and sinful world.

"To a Southern Statesman," entitled "To John C. Calhoun" in the *Era* of January 27, was quite different in conclusion and explanatory note from the later version. It was not prompted by Calhoun's opposition to the acquisition of Oregon but by his speech against the proposed annexation of Mexico, which he feared would take from slavery the advantages gained by the Mexican War, as the states formed from Mexican territory would surely be free states. In place of the last three lines of the present form, which are quite unrelated to their context, there were four lines directly connected with those preceding:

A myriad-headed Aztec host may pour,
And swarthy South with pallid North combine,
Back on thyself to turn thy dark design
And heave the engineer of Evil with his mine.

In a letter to Bailey in December Whittier had said that he would go to Washington in the winter if his health improved. He was in Washington February 10, visiting the Senate with Henry B. Stanton. He talked with John Quincy Adams a few days before Adams' final illness, and Adams seemed reanimated with his old vigor when he spoke of slavery.[20] Bailey arranged a reception for Whittier at his home. One of the less important guests, Mrs. E.D.E.N. Southworth, later gave a pleasant account of Whittier's kindness to her. He was standing in the rear of the back drawing-room receiving with quiet courtesy the homage of distinguished guests. When she was presented, he greeted her, a poor, obscure young public school teacher, as courteously as if she had been somebody. As was true all of his life, he did not look like an invalid. Mrs. Southworth remembered him as a "tall, muscular, dark complexioned man with short black hair and whiskers framing a strong, fine face."[21]

After staying two weeks with the Baileys, Whittier started for home. In New York he visited the store of Hoag and Wood, who stocked only products of free labor. A few weeks later he called attention to their advertisement in the *Era* and argued that if all friends of Freedom refused to buy or sell slave-produced articles, the market price of such articles would go down; the refusal of Quakers and others in Great Britain to consume slave-grown sugar had hastened the abolition of slavery in the British colonies. Before reaching Amesbury he was taken ill and was unable to call on Longfellow at Cambridge. No contributions appeared in the *Era* from February 24 to March 30, when Bailey announced that Whittier had been unable to use his pen. This was not literally true; Whittier wrote to Longfellow March 8 to ask for some prose or poetry for the *Era*, which now had twelve thousand subscribers. It had become the property of Bailey January 1 and had to be self-supporting.[22]

Whittier had three contributions in the *Era* of March 30, one of which was the poem "The Crisis." "I have done my best to say the needed word in this piece," he wrote to Bailey; "at all events I have thrown my heart and soul into it. Would to God I could present the Crisis to my countrymen as it appears to me."[23] The crisis was the fate of the territory ceded by Mexico. The nation must decide whether it would be free or slave territory.

He had rejoiced over the election of John P. Hale to the Senate, but now the trick by which it had been done backfired. A Democratic governor had been elected in New Hampshire as a result of the support given by Liberty men and Independent Democrats to Governor Colby. Whittier did not say, although he must have known, that this was the only way Hale could have been elected. The unfortunate result that he did mention was that the support of confirmed Whigs by Liberty men made the contest seem to be between Federalism and Democracy, and the Whigs had claimed the election of Hale as a victory for their party.[24]

Whittier was still as enthusiastic about the republican government in France as Wordsworth had been about the first French Revolution. Like Wordsworth, he wanted to go to France, but unlike Wordsworth, he would not go unless he could do something more than gratify his own feelings. The position of the leaders of the Republic was sublime, he thought, but carried with it terrible responsibilities. He was in sympathy with their motives, although his practical common sense made him uncertain whether their plans would succeed. He pointed out that they were not Agrarians or levellers; they were trying to make the interests of capital and labor identical and thus elevate the down-trodden classes by more equal distribution of the rewards of labor. He was careful to say that he would not advocate violent measures and compulsory distribution of wealth, but in France the old order had already passed and there was reconstruction to be done. Here was a precious opportunity for realizing the ideal of a Christian Commonwealth. While some of the popular demands might be unreasonable and impracticable, he could still see in their aims and purposes "the influence of that Divine Spirit which, in all ages, has promoted the reformation of abuses in human society." And if the French Republic worked well, it would make all the thrones of Europe totter.[25]

The French Republican leader who most aroused Whittier's interest and admiration was Lamartine. In a long introductory note to "The Holy Land" in the *Era* of April 6 Whittier remarked that a few months earlier Lamartine had been in his study writing the history of the first French Revolution; now as Minister of Foreign Affairs in the Provisional Government he was taking an active part in the history of the third. His poems were little known to

English readers, and so Whittier had written a paraphrase of one of them which he thought breathed "the true spirit of religious reverence — the poetry of Christianity."

Two of his contributions to the *Era* in May had direct application to the time. In "The Curse of the Charter-Breakers" he assumed that the thirteenth century bishops who pronounced excommunication against any who violated the principles of the Magna Charta were acting in behalf of the poor. Either Whittier's knowledge of history was at fault or he altered the facts to serve his purpose, which was to lament that the clergy now were too often subservient to the state and gave their approval to fraud and slavery.

All of the essay "Andrew Marvell" except "An Horation Ode upon Cromwell's Return from Ireland" was based on an article in the *Retrospective Review* Volumes 10 and 11, London 1824-25, which Whittier got Sumner to send to him. Whittier made one curious error; he said that Marvell was Latin Secretary of the Commonweath, a position which Milton held. Marvell was Assistant Secretary, as was correctly stated in the *Retrospective Review*. Whittier thought that Marvell's boldness, integrity, and consistency set an example which should be followed by members of Congress.

Whittier would be deeply concerned with politics for the next five months, and was now worried about an attempt being made to get Anti-Slavery support for Henry Clay. He had written to Sumner that he would be as willing to vote for Zachary Taylor as for Clay,[26] and in the *Era* of May 5 he gave a long account of Clay's record: ". . . . . The friends of Liberty have seen no reason for abandoning their resolutions to vote for no man who is a slaveholder or an apologist for slavery." But Whittier's writings and other activities would as usual cover a wide range of interests.

His closest approach to a novel began in the *Era* of June 1, 1848, and continued intermittently until the final installment November 9. The title in the *Era* was "Stray Leaves from Margaret Smith's Diary in the Colony of Massachusetts"; when the story was printed in a separate volume a year later, the title became *Leaves from Margaret Smith's Journal in the Province of Massachusetts Bay*. The story is on the whole well told and arouses the reader's interest and sympathy: will Rebecca Rawson marry the honorable but unpolished Robert Pike or the charming and fashionable young Englishman, who turns out to be an imposter? But there is one weakness which keeps the narrative from being wholly convincing. Whittier was too obviously determined to prove that seventeenth century Quakers were always virtuous, honorable, and lovable.

Whittier was well acquainted with Colonial history, and when he altered historical facts he did it for the purposes of the narrative, as, for example, his reference to Eunice Cole locked fast in Ipswich jail: there is no record that she was ever confined there. He had his saintly Quaker heroine, Margaret Brewster, enter the meetinghouse in Newbury barefooted and wearing a coarse canvas frock. The real Margaret Brewster had entered the South Church in Boston with four other Quakers, as told in Whittier's poem "In the 'Old South.' " The Quaker who entered the meetinghouse in Newbury, naked — or according to the constable, "part naked" — was Lydia Wardell of Hampton. When Whittier's heroine was spoken to kindly, she wept and said that it had been a sorrowful cross to her to do as she had done, but that it had been a long time in her mind and now she felt relieved that she had found strength for obedience. She aroused the sympathy even of the minister, John Richardson — who was not the minister in Newbury in Lydia Wardell's time — and three of the men of the church paid her fine. Neither the real Margaret Brewster nor Lydia Wardell showed such emotion or touched men's hearts; they were both whipped, and Lydia Wardell was also fined. The little that is known about John Richardson suggests that he was rather different from Whittier's picture of him. A man who would say "God works now by men and means, not by miracles. Neither can it be said that the walls of Rome as the walls of Jericho shall fall with the sound of a Ram's horn" would seem unlikely to be as readily credulous in a witchcraft case as Whittier showed Richardson to be.[27]

In spite of all the evidence against it, the belief persisted that the Diary was a real one. The *Newburyport Herald* announced July 15 that the *National Era* had recently published a series of interesting extracts from the diary of Margaret Smith, written during a visit to the colony of Massachusetts. Whittier's note with the concluding installment should have aroused suspicion: "In the course of the publication of these passages from the Diary of Margaret Smith, I have noticed several slight inaccuracies in relation to persons, places, and dates." The volume published the next year was more specific: "That there are passages indicative of a comparatively recent origin and calculated to cast a shadow of doubt over the entire narrative, the Editor would be the last to deny, notwithstanding its general accordance with historical verities and probabilities." Nevertheless, thirty years later James Pike, who had just completed his *The New Puritan,* a life of Robert Pike, wrote to Whittier that he had read the Journal of Margaret Smith, which had some interesting matters relative to Pike. "As I learn that you had some hand in the discovery and publication of this journal, I make bold to inquire of you as to its authenticity. When I first read it, I innocently supposed it to be a true story, and I see that the author of the Rawson genealogy in his large book on that family, goes upon the same supposition. But on perusing the preface and taking note of some little historical inaccuracy in the book, I conclude there is room for doubt on this subject."[28]

Whittier was vexed to read in the papers that *Margaret Smith's Journal* was probably suggested by the *Diary of Lady Willoughby.* "I never read half a page of the latter," he wrote to Fields, "and only saw the book twice, once at a periodical store in State Street, and the second time in your own store, when I showed thee a copy of Margaret Smith.'' The report persisted and was mentioned in *The North American Review*, July 1854.[29]

In the same issue of the *Era* as the first installment of ''Stray Leaves from Margaret Smith's Diary'' was ''The Horrors of Fanaticism,'' an account of the murder of a mother and four children with an axe and the suicide of the father by cutting his throat. The father had been brooding over religious matters, and the tragedy seemed to Whittier a warning to man not to attempt to pry into the mysteries of the future life or to confuse himself with Oriental imagery and obscure Hebrew passages. Simple, cheerful faith in God the Father and love of men as our brethren was best for the world. (Three weeks later he quoted what he called a ''beautiful little poem'' from the *Pennsylvania Freeman* beginning ''I thank thee, Father, that I live!'' and breathing, he thought, ''the gentle and generous spirit'' and ''lighted up with the cheerful faith and hope of Christianity.''[30]) If one with excitable temperament is led astray, Whittier continued, by the notion that mental agony and bodily torture are pleasing to God, he will be led into horrible excesses. Such was the fate of the hero of Charles Brockden Brown's *Wieland* which Whittier said resembled the recently published *Wuthering Heights* in having great strength and power but no beauty, but differed from it in being useful.

Whittier reported another tragedy in the next week's issue. Two slave parents were to be sold away from their child. The mother cut the child's throat, the father seized the knife and killed the mother and tried to kill himself; he was found alive but was not expected to recover. Their blood, said Whittier, with a concept of social responsibility in advance of his time, rested upon the entire nation and the church, for Congress had the power to prevent such tragedies by prohibiting the interstate slave trade.[31]

These tragic events were not reflected in the tone of daily living in the Whittier household, where there was nothing morbid or unhealthy or dull. The Whittiers were hospitable, like most New Englanders with farm background, and enjoyed visitors. Grace Greenwood (Sarah J. Clarke) came early in August and carried away an invitation to Bayard Taylor. In the same month Lewis Tappan made a brief visit.[32] The vigorous and radical Thomas Wentworth Higginson, then minister at the Unitarian Church in Newburyport, enjoyed his calls at the Whittiers'. He would walk or drive to Amesbury, or sail or row up the river. He would be invited to dinner. Whittier and his mother said little and Elizabeth said a great deal, with much gay raillery which Whittier thoroughly enjoyed.

Elizabeth had evidently not been saddened by a brief romance that had come to nothing seven years earlier. A young Quaker, Philip Jones, had become worldly to the extent of driving a gay tasseled sleigh with a pair of grays — and he drove ''gloriously.'' ''There were such rides,'' she wrote to one of her friends, ''dashing in the tasseled sleigh.'' But except for his equipage he remained conservative, bound by family ties and Quaker traditions, while Elizabeth was ardent and artistic and shared many interests of the "world's people." The romance ended amicably and they remained permanent friends.[33]

Elizabeth was not as good looking as her brother. She had a sallow complexion and a large nose. "How does thee like Quaker noses?" she once said to a little girl who was staring at it in fascination but she turned quickly away and talked about something else so that the girl would not suffer too much embarrassment.[34] Higginson noticed her "great luminous eyes, always flashing with fun or soft with emotion. . . and she has odd motions of the head, so that her glances seemed shot at you, like sudden javelins, from each side of a prominent outwork."[35]

During these months Whittier was watching, with high hopes and strong feelings, the formation of the Free Soil party. It was made up of "Conscience Whigs," who had not accepted the nominations of Zachary Taylor, Independent Democrats, and Liberty Party men, "odds and ends of all parties and sects," its enemies said, "and the representatives of all species of isms."[36] Whittier hoped that it would be a great party of Christian Democracy and progress that would prostrate the slave power in the dust. The leader must be a new and bold man, ready to discard all old notions and practices on the subject of slavery. Whittier's first choice would be John P. Hale, and if he declined, John Van Buren. The nomination of Martin Van Buren, who had vetoed a bill for the abolition of slavery in the District of Columbia in 1836, would put the new party in a riduculous position.[37]

The practical politicians at the Free Soil convention ignored Whittier's advice, and Martin Van Buren was nominated. Liberty Party men generally were displeased. They thought that Hale had been badly treated and that Stanton had betrayed Hale and the Liberty cause. But Whittier, with his usual sound judgment, saw no better way to serve the cause of Liberty than to give enthusiastic endorsement to the Convention and an ingenious defense of Van Buren. "Paean," in the *Era* of September 7, sounded a note of exultation: the dreary night had passed, and in the dawn the "frowning foemen of the night" had joined the time-worn ranks of the faithful. " 'Bygones' — Martin Van Buren in 1837" was in the same *Era*. It explained that Whittier had opposed Van Buren in 1837 because he had occupied a wrong position regarding slavery, in accord with public opinion at that time. Van Buren had now set himself right before the country and the world and had rescued the honored name of Democracy from the reproach of an alliance with slavery. In another item he ridiculed Quakers who were planning to vote for Taylor, quoting a friend just returned from England who had seen a portly Quaker with a truncheon in his hand in the ranks of the citizen soldiery in London during the Chartist movement; since his return he had seen something stranger still: a Quaker elder quieting the scruples of two Methodist ministers who thought that they could not conscientiously vote for Taylor, a professional soldier and a slaveholder.

A month later further defense of Van Buren was needed. The Whigs were asking Abolitionists to vote for Taylor and were questioning the soundness of Van Buren on the slavery question. But 1848, Whittier pointed out, was very different from 1840, when Van Buren was ready to veto the abolition of slavery in the District of Columbia and was the candidate of a party allied with slavery. Now he was ready to sign a bill for abolition in the District of Columbia, and was being denounced by slaveholders. In fact, he now stood where the Liberty men had stood eight years earlier. Taylor was a hard, stern proprietor of a Louisiana plantation with two hundred slaves, and there was, Whittier believed, a boldness of assurance on the part of Northern advocates of Taylor which did more credit to their courage and hardihood than to their discretion.[38]

There was an evangelistic fervor on the part of Liberty men that expressed itself in song. Whittier's contribution was "A Song for the Time," which was popular enough to be revived eight years later during the Fremont campaign and printed in George W. Clark's *The Harp of Freedom*, to be sung to the tune of "The Campbells Are Coming." It was written in the same meter, anapestic tetrameter, that Whittier used in other campaign songs. The final stanza had an echo of the second stanza of Byron's "The Destruction of Sennacherib:"

> Like leaves of the summer once numbered the foe,
> But the hoar-frost is falling, the northern winds blow;
> Like leaves of November erelong shall they fall,
> For earth wearies of them, and God's over all![39]

As usual, Whittier was active in the business of the campaign. At a Free Soil Convention in Boston September 6 and 7 where Stephen C. Phillips was nominated for governor and John Mills for lieutenant-governor, Whittier was appointed chairman of the State Central Committee for Essex County and called a County Convention to meet at Ipswich to nominate candidates for the State Senate. He wrote to *The Beacon of Liberty* giving the qualifications of Chauncey L. Knapp, who had been nominated as a Free Soil candidate for Congress: he was "a man of intellect and refinement cheerfully earning his daily bread by the sweat of his brow."[40]

Whittier made a shrewd guess about the election, that the Free Soil vote would be more than four times the Liberty vote of the previous year. His prophecy was right if he meant it to refer to the 1844 Presidential election, when Birney's vote had been 62,263; the vote for Van Buren and Adams was 291,342. He was optimistic about the next Presidential election: "The prophecy of John C. Calhoun bids fair to become history in 1852 by the election of the candidate of the Free Democracy to the Presidency."[41]

He was also optimistic on the topic of world peace. In "The Peace Convention of Brussels" he was confident that, in spite of wars in progress that made the skeptic say that the Convention was mere folly and in spite of the fact that Heroworship (an obvious reference to Carlyle) would still kneel before the Strong, the "great hope resting on the truth of God" still lived:

Evil shall cease and violence pass away
And the tired world breathe free through a long Sabbath day.

During the weeks of the campaign, Whittier's reading, if one may judge by his references in the *Era*, was limited mainly to the writings of people in whom he had special interest: Lucy Larcom, Lucy Hooper, Bayard Taylor, Grace Greenwood, James Russell Lowell, Sydney Smith, Frederick Douglass. He found exquisite beauty in some of the passages in Henry Beck Hirst's *Endymion* but disapproved of the hero, whose beauty was feminine with nothing manly about it, so that one must wonder at the bad taste of the goddess in "tendering to such a delicate and unsexed libel upon manhood the immortality of her celestial favors."[42]

At the close of the campaign Whittier was suffering from a nervous reaction to its strain and excitement, which appeared in "The Wish of Today." When Sumner read it in the *Era* of November 30 he wrote to Whittier in some concern. "Are you well? I fear that you are not."[43] The first two stanzas were an echo of Emily Bronte's "The Old Stoic." Whittier did not ask for wealth, fame, or love. But the wish in her poem was more vigorous and masculine than the one in his. She asked for liberty and courage, while Whittier, like a tired old man, asked only a spirit of resignation and peace and rest.

Whittier must have found some solace at this time in another gift from Joseph Sturge of a thousand dollars to be invested in bank stock or any other stock that Whittier chose; for the present, Lewis Tappan, who acted as agent for Sturge, was paying Whittier six per cent interest.[44]

In December a new edition of Whittier's poems was published in Boston by Benjamin B. Mussey and Company. It was an attractive volume, with illustrations by Hammatt Billings, an artist and architect who designed the Pilgrim monument at Plymouth and did the illustrations for Hawthorne's *Wonder Book*. A year later Whittier was paid $230.22, this being two and a half per cent on the sales,[45] and there were also later printings. The only new poem in the volume was "Proem," which was later used in a number of other editions and is often quoted as Whittier's analysis of his own limitations as a poet. The third stanza said that his poems were

The jarring words of one whose rhyme
Beat often Labor's hurried time,
Or Duty's rugged march through storm and strife.

At about the same time he wrote to James T. Fields: "As Burns' Macpherson says, 'I've led a life of sturt and strife' and have had no leisure when in tolerable health for any polishing of my rhymes."[46] The fifth stanza was significant in its acknowledgement that he could not explore the depths of the subconscious; he lacked the power

> To drop the plummet line below
> Our common world of joy and woe,
> A more intense despair or brighter hope to find.

What "Proem" failed to say was that Whittier saw the common world of joy and woe clearly and appreciatively and could help others to enrich and strengthen their lives by seeing it through his eyes.

Plans were now being made for publishing *Leaves from Margaret Smith's Journal* in book form by Ticknor, Reed, and Fields. Whittier's chief concern was to have it published as soon as possible. It read better in proof than he had feared and he was sure it would sell if it could be got out in season. Additions included the ballad "Kathleen," to which he added three stanzas in a letter to Fields, although he thought — correctly — that the poem was already too long.

Whittier received ten per cent of the sale price, which was fifty cents for the paper-back and seventy-five cents for the cloth-bound volume. Two thousand copies were printed, and in August seven hundred ninety-eight paper and eleven hundred two cloth volumes had been sold, giving him $122.55.[47]

He now had plenty of time for reading and for telling the readers of the *Era* about it. Some of his comments were on books and pamphlets now forgotten, but other books that he read and reviewed became a permanent part of literature. Oliver Wendell Holmes' poems brought out a lively review entitled "Mirth and Medicine" and now included, with a few minor changes, in the *Works*. Whittier found Lowell's *A Fable for Critics* "brilliant and good-natured satire and discriminating criticism." He modestly did not refer to the lines about himself but quoted the passage about Lydia Maria Child.[48]

He reviewed the first two volumes of Macaulay's *History of England from the Accession of James II*.[49] Macaulay's style he found brilliant, epigrammatic, and vigorous, but not the "safest medium of truth to the simple-minded inquirer." As might be expected, he disliked Macaulay's treatment of William Penn. "Humanity is not so rich in models of purity and goodness as to be able to sacrifice such a reputation as that of William Penn to the point of an antithesis or the effect of a paradox."

Lewis Tappan had recently written to Whittier that the members of the American and Foreign Anti-Slavery Society had been kept from giving attention to the moral and religious aspects of Anti-Slavery by their political activities in the Liberty Party.[50] With this in mind, Whittier wrote a long article entitled "Cuba" for the *Era* of February 15. The result of recent investments of American capital in Cuba, he pointed out, was that the American system of slavery was being introduced there. Slavery under the Spanish government had not been as bad as slavery in the United States. Americans now in Cuba were regarded as the hardest slave drivers on the island.

Interested in anything that promoted human welfare, he was impressed by an account of a meeting of a large group of professional thieves in London with Lord Ashley and other philanthropists who were interested in emigration as a means of relief and reformation to the criminal poor. All the thieves declared that they were ready to follow Lord Ashley's advice. Whittier's comments were in line with the tenet of the Salvation Army a generation later that a man may be down but he's never out: "No one is to be despaired of. We have no warrant to pass by any of our fellow-creatures as beyond the reach of God's grace and mercy; for, beneath the most repulsive and hateful outward manifestations, there is always a consciousness of the beauty of goodness and purity and of the loathsomeness of sin." Thus far "Lord Ashley and the Thieves" was printed in the *Era* as it appears in the *Works*. But there was a concluding paragraph not in the *Works*. Lord Ashley was said to have recommended that some of the London criminals be emigrated to the United States. Whittier either thought that the influences of American life were as bad as those of London or he simply did not want criminals, even with a consciousness of the beauty of goodness, in his vicinity. Lord Ashley, he said, with the best of motives would undo his work by letting his protegés be sent to places where the temptation to return to their old habits would prove too strong for their newly formed resolutions. The essay concluded with a criticism of Lord Ashley as a reformer that has a modern note. As a Tory, Lord Ashley was willing to work to correct evils but not to make those changes in the social and political structure of Great Britain which would remove the causes of crime, to be found in evils originating in the aristocracy of Church and State.[51]

There was no such aristocracy in the United States, and Whittier was not so ready to suggest that crime here was caused by social and political evils. He approved without reservation the new reform school for young criminals about to be opened in Worcester. The boys were to be instructed in piety and morality and were to learn a trade. It pleased him to think of the gain in humane treatment of criminals in the past hundred years.[52]

With his mind still on humanitarian efforts, he wrote "The Christian Tourists," a poem about the journey of two Quakers, William Allen and Stephen Grellet, through Europe in 1818 and 1819, based on Allen's account. Allen had been especially concerned with popular education and the distribution of Bibles, and Grellet with preaching and with the improvement of prison conditions, but they travelled and worked together harmoniously until Allen's illness forced him to return to England. The poem had one of the ornamented geographical lists that Whittier was so fond of but had one good observation: Grellet and Allen were not prevented by their love of mankind from seeing the beauty surrounding them, and this led to one of those simple and clear statements of a religious truth that helped to show the meaning of life to Whittier's readers:

Sure stands the promise — ever to the meek
A heritage is given;
Nor lose they earth who, single-hearted, seek
The righteousness of Heaven!

Whittier never got over his fondness for writing sentimental missives to attractive women. He wrote a valentine to a neighbor, Mary Esther Carter.

Long have I sought and vainly have I yearned
To meet some spirit that could answer mine.
Then chide me not that I so soon have learned
To talk with thine.

Oh thou wilt cherish what some hearts would spurn,
So gentle and so full of soul thou art,
And shrine my feelings in that holy urn —
Thine own true heart.

Mary Esther Carter was thirty-two, good-looking and gracious in manner, and of independent means. She had moved from her native town of Newbury to be near the Whittiers and lived around the corner from them in half of a house on School Street. She was the leader of a group of Spiritualists that met in the other half of the house; the Whittiers sometimes attended their meetings.

A woman of thirty-two receiving a valentine of this sort from a man of forty-one would not be likely to take it as a joke or a bit of light boy-girl sentiment. Mary Esther Carter took it seriously, but as usual Whittier's good luck or skill prevented any hard feelings. She was evidently happy in the belief that he loved her and would have married her if he had not thought that it would be wrong for him to marry anybody. That was her relatives' opinion, and it was confirmed in her niece's mind when Whittier told her many years later that he was glad that he had never married. "Matrimony doesn't seem to have agreed with any of my family," he said. "I should be sorry for the woman who should marry me."

Her friendship with Whittier continued as long as he lived. He took her out driving with a neighbor's horse — and once when they were picking ferns and flowers the horse walked home, leaving them to do the same.[53] They played authors, using cards that he had made himself. After she had moved to a house on Friend Street near the Friends Meeting House she gave garden parties, her garden decorated with Chinese lanterns; ices were served by small boys and girls in Oriental costume. He stopped at this house one day on the way home from Friends Meeting and recited the first stanza of "Laus Deo." She was one of the group of women that went with him to the mountains and seashore. Soon after the death of his mother she wrote to him that she had received a spirit communication from her and his Aunt Mercy, and after his death she would go into the Garden Room alone and commune with him in spirit.[54]

Whittier had done a great deal of writing during the winter, which may have been the cause of his feeling mentally tired in the spring, although he attributed it to his years of Anti-Slavery activity. A letter from Charles Sumner brought relief. It contained a passage that Sumner had copied from Mrs. Jameson's *Poetry of Sacred and Legendary Art* with the suggestion that it was a fit subject for a poem. It is an indication of what Whittier's readers expected of him that Sumner added, "Under your hands it may become a lesson to our people."[55] Whittier stopped looking out the window at the late spring storm which was leaving snow where there should have been lilac buds and wrote "The Legend of St. Mark," with its assurance that God is all-powerful and will send his angel to break the chain of slavery.

He was not too tired to enjoy writing the essay "John Roberts," which appeared in the *Era* May 24, with the sub-title "A Yeoman of the Seventeenth Century." He was unwell for the next two months and sent no prose contributions to the *Era* and only two poems, "The Men of Old" and "The Lakeside." His poor health, as in his earlier years, did not keep him from travelling, and he spent several weeks in northern New Hampshire. He was in Center Harbor when he wrote "The Lakeside," the tone of which indicates that the mountain scenery was giving him the peace of mind that he needed, and he found the love of God, as he believed the Indian did, in the hills, lakes, and woodlands. He visited the family of Nathaniel Rogers in Plymouth, and by July 14 was back in Amesbury where a letter from Lewis Tappan was waiting for him. Joseph Sturge had offered to pay Whittier's expenses if he would visit England. Whittier declined, believing that his poor health would keep him from being of any use there, and he was incapable of visiting as a mere looker-on.[56]

Whittier Home, Amesbury, as it appeared from 1847 to 1884.

The Garden Room at the Amesbury Home.

Elizabeth Hussey Whittier (1815-1864) from a crayon portrait by Helen Reed. Lucy Larcom had it made and presented it to Whittier shortly after Elizabeth's death in 1864. (Courtesy of Whittier Home, Amesbury)

XV
1849 - 51

Whittier returned from his New Hampshire vacation refreshed in spirit and ready to plunge into his usual activities. In the *Era* of August 2 there was a prose article "Benton and Clay," in which Whittier happily announced that these two men were changing with the times. Thomas H. Benton, although a slaveholder and a representative of a slaveholding state, had taken his stand in a recent speech with the friends of free territory and the enemies of slavery. As for Clay, a recent letter of his committed him to the cause of emancipation in Kentucky.

In the next issue he gave his readers a rest from politics and causes by an amusing account of an episode at the beginning of the American Revolution. In "The Great Ipswich Fright" he described a false alarm which terrorized the people of Ipswich and towns north to the New Hampshire border April 21, 1775. Whittier's grandfather had been one of the few who refused to panic; when a half-dressed horseman dashed past the Whittier farm shouting that the British were landing on Plum Island, he calmly replied that he was glad to hear it and wished that they might be obliged to stay there.

A poem in the *Era* of August 16 showed that Whittier's strongest feelings were not confined to Anti-Slavery. "To Pius IX" is one of two bitter invectives against Pope Pius IX, who had asked and received military aid from France. Whittier read in the *Boston Daily Evening Traveller* July 23 an extract from a letter by an Italian priest, Ventura di Raulica, who had advocated the separation of ecclesiastical and temporal authority and had recognized the Roman Republic and opposed French intervention. French troops had fought their way into Rome, and Father Ventura's letter was as bitter as Whittier's poem: "What a fine victory this will be for France! What a great restoration of the Pope!" The lesson of history was that "Thrones raised upon dead bodies in blood are certain to be soon overthrown." More grievous to Catholics was that each cannon ball that ruined the walls of Rome would destroy the religious faith of the Romans. The poor, whose homes had been destroyed by French shells, were cursing the Pope and the clergy.

Father Ventura made one point that Whittier overlooked in his excitement — or in his awareness that the effect would be weakened if the attack were not concentrated upon one person. It was Father Ventura's belief that the Pope neither desired nor even knew about the suffering that was being caused; if the Pope had been left to himself, he would not have gone from Rome or at least from the Roman states and would have said, "Let me stay in exile rather than appeal to arms which would perhaps subdue but would cause the loss of the hearts of my people." Whittier's invective was against Pius IX himself, whom he called the Nero of the time, the Scandal of the World, a poor mean idol despised by its own worshippers. Whittier was not in the mood of utter despair which would have inhibited the force of his writing; the poem concluded that Earth and Heaven were tired of kings and priests who were false to Liberty and to God, and the Romans had not bled in vain if the world was aroused to tread down those twin-born vampires. A quarter of a century later he did not regret writing this poem or its companion piece four years later, "The Dream of Pio Nono." "As a Quaker loving peace and a republican," he wrote, "I could say no less, and have nothing to retract."[1]

Whittier was writing as usual on varied topics. There was a brief article in the *Era* of August 23, "Bissette of Martinique," about a young negro who after being tried and convicted of a conspiracy against the French Colonial Government had been released and had been agitating for emancipation in the French colonies. There was a review September 20 of Mrs. E.D.E.N. Southworth's *Retribution: or The Vale of the Shadows: A Tale of Passion*. The story reminded Whittier of *Jane Eyre* and the "later productions of that school," with their strength and sustained intensity but with the addition of a moral lesson. In the same issue was "Calef of Boston," a poem about Robert Calef, a Boston merchant who wrote an answer to Cotton Mather attacking the proceedings of the Salem court.

A letter from Elizabeth Lloyd early in September thanking Whittier for a copy of *Margaret Smith's Journal* mentioned Baxter's *Saints' Rest*.[2] Whittier's "Richard Baxter" appeared in the *Era* October 4 and 11. It was much shorter than the form in the *Works*. Both forms are good reading and make one wish that Whittier had tried his hand at a full length biography. He corrected the popular impression that Baxter was a champion of civil and religious freedom; although Baxter had more liberty in preaching the Gospel under Cromwell's Protectorate than he would have had under the King, he continued to favor the ancient monarchy and the unity of the church and to say so even to Cromwell himself. But Whittier admired him as an honest man with high motives.

The politics of Anti-Slavery was never long absent from Whittier's thoughts. He remarked in the *Era* of September 13 that the Slave Power appeared to be about to support the Democrats. It had long been alternating between the great parties, he pointed out, tearing down and building up to serve its own purposes. It had kept the Whigs from becoming Abolitionists in 1839 by electing their candidate for President. It had offered to help the Democrats in 1843 if they nominated a slaveholder. In the election of 1848 it had controlled the Whig convention at Philadelphia and had helped to elect the slaveholding candidate nominated there. It said to the Whig or Democrat who asked for its votes what Jack Cade had told Stafford to say to the King:

"I am content he shall reign, but I'll be protector over him."[3]

He was still willing to take active part in politics, to be a candidate, and to serve in public office. Early in November he was nominated by a Free Soil and Democratic coalition as one of the five Essex County candidates for the State Senate. None were elected, although the election was close. Whittier was second highest.[4]

Whittier had long since learned to take a candidacy calmly. The election did not drive other matters out of his mind, and he wrote "Our State" for the dedication of Newbury High School. The town of Newbury now had the population which by Massachusetts law required a town to have a high school, and one was opened in the Town House. A few months later Leonard Withington, minister of the First Church in Newbury and a friend of Whittier, gave the land for a high school. A schoolhouse was built and was dedicated November 2, 1849, with plenty of praying, reading, and speaking, including an address by Caleb Cushing.[5] Whittier's poem, entitled "Original Hymn," was printed in the Order of Exercises; it had been printed the day before in the *Era*, entitled "Dedication of a Schoolhouse." It was well suited to its purpose and is another example of Whittier's skill in writing occasional verse of dignity and simplicity, not too long or involved for public reading or singing. The central thought and some of the phrasing were evidently suggested by Horace Mann's annual report as Secretary of the Board of Education in Massachusetts, quoted by Whittier in the *Era* of September 30, 1847. Both said that the prosperity of the state came from education and not from natural resources.

In the *Era* of December 13 he reviewed Sarah J. Clarke's *Greenwood Leaves: A Collection of Sketches and Letters. By Grace Greenwood*. The Whittiers and Sarah J. Clarke were personal friends. She had sent Whittier an eagle quill the previous winter and Whittier had replied with the twenty-stanza "Impromptu. On Receiving an Eagle's Quill from Lake Superior." The eagle's quill had interrupted his gloomy thoughts and had stirred his imagination. He had seen in his mind's eye Lake Superior and the Westward migration of the Yankee, who had taken his characteristics with him —

>He's leaving on the Pictured Rocks
>His fresh tobacco-stain —

lines later refined into

>He's measuring o'er the Pictured Rocks
>With eager eyes of gain.

In August Elizabeth sent an invitation to her to visit them and repeated it by a message in a letter from Whittier to James T. Fields.[6] But Whittier did not let friendship influence him to write a wholly favorable review. He thought that the letters were the best part of the volume, with keen perception of the ludicrous and with quick and earnest sympathies, but the stories, although witty and amusing, lacked simplicity and had too many foreign phrases and too much love making, and the heroes and heroines were not true to life.

Whittier had been interested in Fredrika Bremer since 1843 when she had said in an interview that she admired America but condemned the frightful anomaly of its slavery.[7] When she came to the United States for a tour in 1849, Whittier and his sister wrote a joint poem of welcome, "To Fredrika Bremer," which was printed in the *Era* of November 15.[8] She replied, "Thou art a noble Poet, thou art a Friend, thou art my Friend! Thou hast warmed my heart and made it expand in delightful emotions of love and gratitude." He made a good impression on her, as he did on everyone. She observed that he had a "pleasing exterior," tall and slender, with a beautiful head and refined features, black eyes full of fire, dark complexion, a fine smile, and a lively but nervous manner. She believed that he would have advanced with firmness and joy to martyrdom in a good cause but was not comfortable in society and looked occasionally as if he would like to run out the door.[9]

Whittier's *Old Portraits and Modern Sketches* was issued by Ticknor, Reed and Fields in January 1850. It had been suggested by James T. Fields in the summer but Whittier had been uncertain; he had a mass of material but it was "like chaos, without form, and what is worse, oftentimes *void*." The volume contained ten essays, all of which had been previously printed, and was dedicated to Gamaliel Bailey. Fifteen hundred copies were printed and evidently fourteen hundred were sold; Whittier received a total of one hundred five dollars.[10]

Another volume of poems by Longfellow had appeared, *The Seaside and the Fireside*, which Whittier briefly reviewed in the *Era* of January 3. Longfellow, he thought, was one of the sweetest poets of the time, and the pieces in this volume had "the careful moulding and patient polish by which Art attains the graceful ease and chaste simplicity of nature." Whittier had not acquired a taste for Browning: "All those whose ears have been tortured by Browning's burlesque of rhythm should resort at once to the healing influences of the 'The Seaside and the Fireside' melodies of Longfellow."

Two weeks later he announced a two-volume edition of Lowell's poems. Whittier's obsession with clarity made him happy that Lowell had overcome a slight tendency to mysticism and metaphysics and was "no longer afraid of the sharp outlines of reality." If his thought was fully and forcefully expressed he seemed "careless of the niceties of diction and metaphor."

The *Era* of January 10 had two contributions showing Whittier's interest in the underprivileged. He had just heard of the death of Ebenezer Elliott, whose *Corn-Law Rhymes* had helped to turn attention to the poor in Great Britain. Whittier's poem "Elliott" was a vigorous insistence that Elliott should be buried without pomp and ceremony and without the help of any "tithe-fat plunderer" or "trick of priest-craft," in "green and daisied ground" near the Sheaf river, with laborers as mourners. Whittier had evidently read Elliott's "A Poet's Prayer:"

Let him be buried where the grass is green,
Where daisies, blooming earliest, linger late.

Elliott's will, which Whittier evidently had not seen, was in the same spirit but with different details.[11] In the best stanza in the poem Whittier said in an effective metaphor that the submerged feelings of the English people caught a spendor from Elliott's verse like the steel from his forge, and a shower of sparks came from his anvil: the curse of God, Human wrong, and the wrath of Hunger.

Nearer home, racial segregation was being challenged. Charles Sumner was arguing before the Supreme Court of Massachusetts that separate schools for negro children in Boston were unconstitutional. The case was of a negro girl in whose behalf the city was being sued for excluding her from a public school. In "Caste in Massachusetts" Whittier said that these schools were one of the last vestiges of caste in the state, where there were now negro dentists, doctors, lawyers, and judges, and the Governor of the state could be seen riding on the same seat as a black man in a railroad car or stagecoach, engaged in familiar conversation with him.

On March 7, before an audience which crowded the floor, the galleries, and the antechambers of the Senate, Daniel Webster delivered his speech aimed at reconciliation of the North and the South, "The Constitution and the Union." The telegraph brought news quickly to New England, and two days later Longfellow recorded in his Journal that when he went to town he found everybody condemning Webster. " 'Fallen, fallen, fallen from his high estate!' is the universal cry, in various phraseology."[12]

Whittier told an enquirer many years later that he had written "Ichabod" just after Webster's speech in support of the Fugitive Slave Bill,[13] but this statement is not quite accurate: support of a Fugitive Slave Law was only one of several items in the Seventh of March Speech, and Webster's speech on a specific Fugitive Slave Bill was on June 3, a month after the printing of "Ichabod."

Whittier's reaction was slow. Nearly two months passed without any reference in the *Era* to Webster's speech. Belatedly, "Ichabod," one of the most quoted and anthologized poems in America, appeared inconspicuously on an inside page of the *Era* of May 2, without introduction and without footnote. Doubtless most readers knew whom it referred to, and there was then such wide knowledge of the Bible that they probably also knew the meaning of the title and the story of Noah's two respectful sons referred to in the last stanza. The poem was terse and forceful, tightly knit and perfectly proportioned. There was neither wearisome geographical list nor needless didactic conclusion. The opening phrase, "So fallen," evidently came from the comment of the public as Longfellow heard it in Cambridge and as Whittier doubtless heard it. The title may have come from a sentence in an article by James Russell Lowell in the *National Anti-Slavery Standard* four years earlier: "Shall not the Recording Angel write Ichabod after the name of this man in the great book of Doom?"[14]

The Whittiers lived quietly during the spring months, having few visitors. Whittier and his sister were quite unwell,[15] but he did not spend his time thinking about himself. The statement had been made — and it is still heard occasionally to-day — that New England mill workers were worse treated than Georgia slaves. In preparing a reply, Harriet Farley wrote to Joshua Aubin, agent of the Amesbury Flannel Manufacturing Company, for information, and he handed some statistics to Whittier with the request that he send them to her. Whittier sent a letter with the statistics, and both were printed in *Operatives' Reply to Hon. Jere Clemens.*[16] He thought that Amesbury was "the pattern manufacturing village in New England" and that there was perfect harmony between Aubin and the employees, a feeling of esteem on their part and almost paternal care on his. The company had opened an evening school for girls between fourteen and eighteen, and a library was soon to be opened with books given by the company. (Actually, the books were given by Aubin personally, and six years later were given to the new Amesbury Public Library.)

Louis Godey's treatment of Sarah J. Clarke (Grace Greenwood) provoked one of Whittier's liveliest satires. On the complaint of Southern subscribers, Godey had removed her name from the list of contributors to his *Lady's Book* because she had written against slavery in letters to the *Era*. Whittier's "On the Portrait of a Celebrated Magazine Publisher, Who Has Lately Saved the Union and Lost a Contributor" appeared in the *Era* of April 4. Godey had recently published his own portrait, and Whittier showed more fertility of imagination than good taste in his ridicule of both the portrait and the publisher.

Plans were being made for the publication of *Songs of Labor and Other Poems*. Whittier wished to keep the copyright and asked Fields what arrangement the firm had made with Longfellow, Lowell, and Holmes, but he was not so absorbed in business matters as to forget to congratulate Fields on his marriage and to add, "Were I autocrat I would see to it that every young man over twenty-five and every young woman over twenty was married without delay. Perhaps, on second thought, it might be well to keep one old maid and one old bachelor in each town, by way of warning, just as the Spartans did their drunken Helots."[17]

In the same issue of the *Era* as "Ichabod," Whittier attacked Thomas Carlyle's "Occasional Discourse on the Nigger Question" which he had read in the December 1849 *Fraser's Magazine*. It was based on the reported unwillingness of emancipated negroes to work in the cane fields for the wages offered when they could live comfortably on the crops that they raised. Whittier quoted from a report of one of the colonial governors that negroes, if properly paid and treated, were good workers, and furthermore, the slavery system was working so badly in Dutch Surinam that emancipation of the slaves was being advocated there. But Whittier must have read the "Occasional Discourse" hurriedly. He missed a number of points that he might have used effectively. He cleared the title of its bad manners by changing "Nigger" to "Negro," and he did not mention another piece of bad manners, Carlyle's references to negroes' looks: "those excellent horse-jaws of theirs," "their beautiful muzzles."[18]

Many people whose feelings against slavery needed to be aroused or strengthened would not be deeply moved by attacks on either Webster or Carlyle. There was more popular emotional appeal in "A Sabbath Scene" in the *Era* of June 27, which described a fugitive slave girl, barefooted and thin, running into a church to be protected from the slave hunter following her, whip in hand. She was caught, with the help of the minister, who explained to his congregation the Scriptural justification of slavery. Just as Whittier imagined that he was protesting in language which caused the minister to exclaim "Infidel" and a lawyer "Treason", he awoke and found that it was a dream caused, as he explained in a stanza later omitted, by some reading that he had been doing:

> I woke, and lo! the fitting cause
> Of all my dream's vagaries —
> Two bulky pamphlets, Webster's text
> With Stuart's Commentaries.

Work continued on *Songs of Labor and Other Poems*. Proof and letters were going back and forth between Whittier and Fields with changes in rhymes. Recent poems were added, but Whittier found that he could not write more "Songs of Labor" — he could not get the spirit of the early ones. Finally he wrote, "Pray get out the book as soon as possible, for your own sake; I have a terrible propensity, always after it is too late, to see something which I ought to have seen before."[19] Two months passed, however, before the book was published.

Whittier was still sending prose articles on varied topics to the *Era*. "Instruction of Idiots," now included in "Peculiar Institutions of Massachusetts," was an account of an experiment in teaching ten feeble-minded children at the Asylum for the Blind under the direction of Samuel G. Howe. One detail of interest to present-day teachers of reading is that the children could not learn to read by what is now called the phonic method but could learn the meaning of complete words without knowing the letters or the sounds that they represented. Whittier was especially interested in this experiment because one of the children was the son of a neighbor, Jacob Rowell, who lived in the brick house on the corner of Friend and Pond Streets.

A few months later Whittier wrote to the Amesbury *Villager* that he could testify to the wonderful improvement in George Rowell. "The change is almost like a resurrection of a mind from death — or, rather, a new creation."[20] George Rowell never became mentally normal and was cared for by his mother until his death at the age of sixty-one.

Three articles had some bearing on slavery. "The Black Law of South Carolina," in the *Era* of June 27, told that the London *Anti-Slavery Reporter* had demanded that the British government take measures to prevent South Carolina from imprisoning black seamen that came into Charleston on British ships.

"New Mexico — Its Population" in the *Era* of July 18 refuted the claim that the voters there were unfit to govern themselves and to apply for admission to the Union as a free state. One of his arguments showed a fear of European immigrants which many New Englanders then felt. More immigrants came each year from the old world, he said, poor, ignorant, and vicious, than the entire population of New Mexico. We should not close our ports against them or refuse them asylum. "But who would not prefer to the refuse and squalid over-plus of crowded European cities and the annual disgorgements of their jails and workhouses, the quiet, home-loving, and pastoral people of New Mexico."

"The Mormons and Their City of Refuge" was based on Thomas L. Howe's "Discourse Before the Pennsylvania Historical Society." Mob violence drove the Mormons from Nauvoo in 1846, and when they reached Great Salt Lake they decided that they had reached the Land of Promise. Joseph Smith "could only be characterized as a cross between Sam Slick and Mokanna of Khorassin." The main point was that Utah should not become a slave state. Toleration of slavery would hardly increase the Mormons' chances of being recognized as Saints of the Latter Day, and they should be warned by the divisions of the older sects on the question of slavery and exclude it early as an element of disturbance.

Songs of Labor and Other Poems was published in August. One of the new poems in it was "The Hill-Top," which had been in the *Era* of May 30. The hill was Shepard Hill in Holderness, New Hampshire,[21] and the scene and incident were evidently derived from his vacation in New Hampshire the previous summer. The poem showed Whittier's delight in picturesque scenery, which increased as he grew older. The two latest poems in it were "All's Well," which had been in the *Era* of July 18, and "To A. K. On Receiving a Basket of Sea-Mosses," which was in the *Era* August 22, the day the volume was entered for copyright. The tone of both was the optimism of the mid-nineteenth century. "To A.K." was written to Avis Keene, a Quaker minister whom Whittier later described in "The Meeting." The central thought in "To A.K." was that beauty is everywhere and, of course, teaches a lesson: "God's love and power are one."

"Dedication," which applied only to the "Songs of Labor," expressed what had become Whittier's fixed attitude toward his poetry: it wasn't very good, but it was justified if it helped somebody, in this case the working man, who might be more contented with his lot, for work was no longer a curse but a blessing since Christ was a poor man working with the poor.

The profits of the volume were not enough to make any difference in Whittier's fortunes. Of the first printing of one thousand copies, nine hundred were sold, from which Whittier received forty-five dollars — five cents a copy. A second printing in the fall brought him another twenty-five dollars.[22] But now he was at least above the poverty level. When he learned that Hawthorne had not been paid for "The Great Stone Face," which had been printed in the Era January 24, he immediately sent the twenty-five dollars — which he thought inadequate — although he had no connection with the business affairs of the paper.[23]

The summer of 1850 was a busy and important time in Massachusetts politics and consequently in American history. The Free Soil leaders were considering a coalition with the Democrats to elect a Democratic governor and a Free Soil senator. The former "Conscience Whigs" opposed the plan, which seemed to them like jockeys selling a race, but it was promoted by the more practical politicians, and Whittier may have had a hand in it.[24] At least he had some part in persuading Charles Sumner to be a candidate for the Senate. Whittier believed later that he had been the first to suggest it. However, Sumner may have had it in mind and have been more ready to be persuaded than Whittier was aware when they talked on a moonlight night at Phillips Beach in Swampscott, while they watched the waves break against a rocky wall — symbolic, Whittier later thought, of Sumner's stand against the hosts of Error.[25]

Since the election of a United States Senator was by concurrent vote of the two chambers of the State Legislature, there could be no direct campaigning for Sumner, and as far as Whittier was concerned, there was a lull in politics in the late summer and early fall. He spent some time pleasantly in Lynn. He called on the Longfellows at Nahant and talked to them about Alice and Phoebe Cary. He would have his publishers send Longfellow a copy of Songs of Labor and Other Poems as a poor return for the pleasure he had received from Longfellow's writings.[26]

A new Friends Meeting House was being built in Amesbury and Whittier was chairman of the committee in charge. Some of the conservative members of the Meeting were afraid that he would favor an ornate building but were reassured when he employed a Quaker minister and two elders and left them to follow out their own plans. The building, which was completed in the fall, is still standing, little changed from its original form. Whittier attended this meeting regularly as long as he lived, in spite of his dissatisfaction with some of the later innovations which departed from traditional Quaker worship.

Whittier's only verse contribution to the *Era* in the fall was "Derne", printed October 26 without the present headnote which says that the heroism of Christian self-denial and sacrifice is higher than the courage shown in the feat described in the poem. The truth is that Whittier had not wholly outgrown his boyhood delight in battles, although his interest in the storming of Derne came largely from the rescue of the Christians held in slavery there. The poem concluded with a timely lesson: anyone who praised the military leader for bringing about the deliverance of the slaves in Derne should not attack the heroes of his own time who were sacrificing themselves for Freedom.

In October his Philadelphia friends David and Mary Pennock Sellers called and found him with a toothache and his face tied up.[27] He also had political worries. The opposition of the former "Conscience Whigs" had kept the Free Soil leaders from any formal coalition with the Democrats, but in many districts Free Soilers and Democrats worked together informally. On the morning of October 4 Whittier was surprised to learn that he had been nominated for the State Senate at the Essex County Democratic Convention. He immediately wrote to the editor of the *Bay State* of Lynn declining the nomination and giving as one of his reasons that he was a nullifier as far as the Fugitive Slave Law was concerned, an attitude which he was afraid that his fellow citizens would not approve.

Whittier was closer to public sentiment than he supposed. Long years of being in a minority on the issue of slavery had made him think that he would always be there, but now, at last, he was as close to the feelings of his fellow-citizens on this topic as he always had been and always would be on many others.

The Fugitive Slave Law had become a matter of emotion, and it was useless for its supporters to attempt to defend it logically, as Daniel Webster tried to do in a letter to some of his supporters in Newburyport. State laws, he said, preventing the enforcement of Article IV Section 2 of the Constitution and of an enforcement act approved by Congress, without opposition from Massachusetts, in 1793, had made it necessary that Congress should make further provision for carrying this act into effect. "And now, gentlemen," he concluded, "does not every sober-minded and patriotic man see the necessity and feel the duty of rebuking that spirit of faction and disunion, that spirit of discord and crimination and recrimination, that spirit that loves angry controversy, and loves it most especially when evils are imaginary and dangers unreal, which has been so actively employed in doing mischief and which, it is to be lamented, has received countenance and encouragement in quarters whence better things were hoped for."[28]

All this was good reasoning, but the Law, with its requirement that citizens could be called on to assist in the arrest of a fugitive slave, was arousing opposition as nothing else had during the Abolition agitation. Emerson may have been one of the men that Webster had in mind when he spoke of "quarters whence better things were hoped for." He was making speeches against the Law and quoting Whittier's "Ichabod," and recording in his Journal, "We shall never feel well again until that detestable law is nullified in Massachusetts and until the Government is assured that once for all it cannot and shall not be executed here. All I have and all I can do shall be given and done in opposition to the execution of the Law." Hawthorne wrote to Longfellow, "This Fugitive Slave Law is the only thing that could have blown me into any respectable degree of warmth on this great subject of today [Anti-Slavery]."[29] Respectable organizations such as the American Missionary Association were announcing publicly that they would not obey it.

Whittier's own feeling about the Fugitive Slave Law was again expressed in verse a few weeks later. "Stanzas for the Times" (now "In the Evil Days") was more serious than "A Sabbath Scene." The tone was sorrowful instead of satirical, and the line of conduct toward the Fugitive Slave Law was that the law of God should be obeyed and not the law of man, but the man who accepted the penalty of disobeying man's law was not being untrue to it. This was the attitude of many conscientious people and was the theme of "The Fugitive Slave Law: A Discourse Delivered in the Congregational Church in West Bridgewater, Massachusetts, by J. G. Forman, Minister of the Congregation," reviewed by Whittier in the *Era* of January 2, 1851.

In "Slavery in Massachusetts" (now "A Chapter of History,") in the *Era* of November 11, Whittier showed that it was unlikely that the people of Massachusetts would help to arrest fugitive slaves; they could not be expected to adjust themselves to "constitutional duties which in South Carolina and Georgia are reserved for trained bloodhounds." He went about Amesbury getting signatures on a petition to the Massachusetts Legislature for an Act making any person who assisted in enforcing the Fugitive Slave Law incapable of holding public office.[30]

Just before the election Whittier reminded the readers of the *Era* that the Massachusetts Legislature about to be elected would choose the United States Senator to take the place of Daniel Webster, now Secretary of State. The Whig Party was largely controlled by Boston capitalists and manufacturers and was too confident of success to make concession to the Free Soil Party. The Democrats, however, were inclined to cooperate with the Free Soilers, and if a majority of Democrats and Free Soilers were elected to the Legislature, a friend of human freedom would be elected to the Senate.[31]

The results of the election were as Whittier had hoped: enough Democrats and Free Soilers were elected so that if they combined they could control the Legislature and elect not only a United States Senator but also a governor and lieutenant-governor, as no candidate had received a majority of the popular vote. Publicly Whittier said that he was now confident that Webster's place would be filled by someone who would represent the sentiments of Massachusetts and work for the repeal of the Fugitive Slave Law and against the extension of slavery. Privately he was not so sure. With his usual political prescience he foresaw that Cushing and other conservative Democrats would not go along with the unwritten agreement that the Democrats would vote for the Free Soil candidate for the Senate if the Free Soilers would vote for the Democratic candidate for Governor, George S. Boutwell. If he were in the Legislature he would not vote for Boutwell unless the Democrats signed a pledge that they would vote for the Free Soil candidate for Senator.[32] Events occurred just as Whittier foresaw, and it took four months to elect Charles Sumner.

"Stanzas for the Times" was his only poem in the *Era* in December and there was none in January and February, but he sent a good amount of prose to be used in the January 2 issue. His "Pope Night" was the last prose in the *Era* which he considered worthy of inclusion three years later in *Literary Recreations and Miscellanies* and the last, except for the later chapters of "My Summer with Dr. Singletary," to be used in the *Works*. "Pope Night" commented on the recent revival in England of Guy Fawkes Night and its observance in New England, where it had died out everywhere except in Amesbury, where bonfires were built and enjoyed by both Catholic and Protestant children who had never heard of Guy Fawkes and the Gunpowder Plot of 1605. The essay concluded with an appeal for a universal church in which Cowper, Augustine, Channing, Thomas à Kempis, Woolman, and Bossuet would be "lights for a common altar" — a radical concept in Whittier's times.

The *Era* of January 2 also contained the first chapter of "My Summer with Dr. Singletary," which Whittier evidently intended to be longer than the present six chapters; it did not have the present sub-title "A Fragment." It is hard for the present-day reader to see anything in this chapter to cause the editor to write to Whittier, "If you can possibly make your 'Singletary' every week, I hope you will do it."[33] It was a sentimental treatment of Dr. Singletary's death and of the changes made by an herb doctor who took his place and a description of a New England river town and its cemetery. But this was the sort of sentimentality that was popular in mid-nineteenth century America, partly as a reaction against the Calvinism that middle-aged people had known in their childhood. Americans also liked rural settings, as would be clearly demonstrated fifteen years later in the popularity of "Snow-Bound." The second chapter, which appeared two weeks later, had more detailed description of a New England village and introduced Doctor Singletary, with his love of nature and his philosophy that "an earnest life, rich and beautiful with love and hope, or dark with hatred and sorrow and remorse" can be found beneath the surface of everyday common people. The third chapter contained the first bit of narrative, "The Doctor's Match-Making." It was a piece of typical mid-nineteenth century sentimentality: the poor girl with a cruel stepmother, the virtuous country boy, the fashionable and rascally villain, the girl's remorse, the shipwreck, the rescue of the country boy turned sailor, their marriage in spite of public opinion, their darling little daughter.

No more of "My Summer with Dr. Singletary" appeared until the next year. "Pray, what has become of Dr. Singletary?" a subscriber wrote to the editor in August. The answer was that Whittier's health had been such as to prevent his continuing the series.[34] In fact, he was sick a good part of the year. He was unable to go to Boston to talk with Sumner when the political situation developed exactly as he had foreseen. The Free Soil members of the Legislature had joined with the Democrats to elect George S. Boutwell as governor, but a group of about thirty Democrats, following the orders of Caleb Cushing, refused to vote for Sumner, who had been nominated at a Free Soil caucus January 7 for the six-year term as United States Senator. Balloting in the House began January 14, and there were four ballots in two days, with Sumner failing to get a majority. Whittier watched the situation with intense anxiety and saw no hope of Sumner's election. He wrote a hurried and excited letter to Sumner on the sixteenth, advising him to decline the nomination and asserting that the three Free Soil members of the Governor's Council, who had been elected as part of the coalition agreement, should resign. If Whittier were in the Legislature he would vote for George W. Briggs, the retiring governor, for the term of the Senate; he was anti-Webster and anti-Fugitive Slave Law.

Sumner, in Whittier's opinion, was acting honorably, and even his enemies agreed. He was willing to withdraw, but the majority of the Free Soilers thought that no one else would have as good a chance of success. He was elected by the Senate January 22, but failed to get a majority in five ballotings in the House within the next two days. After he failed by two votes on February 7 and nine on February 14, he wrote to Henry Wilson urging that his support be transferred to some other candidate, but at a Free Soil caucus March 17 it was determined to present no other candidate than Sumner.

Two weeks later Sumner wrote to Whittier asking him to come to Boston to talk over the situation.[35] Whittier had been well enough to take part in local activities against the Fugitive Slave Law, but he was not sure that he would feel able to go to Boston, and if he did, he could hardly venture to offer advice. He feared that if Sumner withdrew, no Anti-Slavery man could be elected, since the Democrats would feel no obligation to vote with the Free Soilers. On the other hand, if no one was elected that year the election by a new Legislature would be controlled by the Whigs. He invited Sumner to spend Sunday in Amesbury. Sumner came, but there is no record of the conversation.

Finally, on April 24, Sumner was elected by a majority of one. There was great excitement, both jubilant and otherwise. Men and boys of the opposition in Boston wore black crepe on their arms; Whittier, lying in bed with what he called a "sudden and severe attack of illness," rejoiced, in spite of being a Quaker, to hear the guns fired in celebration. He devoutly believed that Sumner's election was the work of God and that it would soon bring the "certain doom of the wicked slave law." (Here, of course, he guessed wrong; the Fugitive Slave Law lasted until 1864.[36])

Sumner's election was especially pleasing to Whittier because of an event in Boston a few days earlier. A fugitive slave, Thomas Sims, was taken from Boston in the darkness just before dawn by a Federal marshall aided by Boston police evading the State officers who could have prevented his removal under Massachusetts law. Whittier was unhappy to read in a report given in the Massachusetts Senate that fifteen hundred respectable citizens, including merchants and bankers, had offered to help the Federal marshall. But soon there would be a change for the better, he announced in two poems about the Sims case. "Moloch in State Street" was sent to the *Era* early in May and was printed May 22, and what he called "a bit of doggerel" was written to be read at an evening party. The last two stanzas in "Moloch in State Street" referred to Sumner's election. In the "bit of doggerel" entitled "What State Street Said to South Carolina and What South Carolina Said to State Street," State Street (Boston business interests) assured South Carolina that they had turned from the ways of their fathers and had sent a negro back to slavery, but South Carolina replied

. . . Just wait till December
Shall see your new Senator stalk through the Chamber,
And Puritan heresy prove neither dumb nor
Blind in that pestilent Anakim, Sumner!

Whittier's illness, whatever it was, was the worst that he had had for years, and for a time he thought that it might be fatal. When in the middle of May he was able to go out and enjoy the spring scenery and the warm, sunny weather, the world seemed especially beautiful to him and he felt "terribly rooted" to it.[37]

Two religious poems written during these weeks of illness and inactivity had to do with the individual soul. "The Hermit's Chapel" in the *Era* of March 6 was less than half the length of its revised form "The Chapel of the Hermits" and did not have the introductory and concluding framework. As in the later form, there was a lesson: the saving truth is within the man himself who can live as the saints lived. Whittier had thought his way to this conclusion because he needed a path to guide him in his own disillusion with the world around him. "Invocation" appeared in the *Era* of April 10, introduced by a quotation from Thomas à Kempis which is the theme of the poem: "Send forth thy light and thy truth, that they may shine upon the Earth; for I am an earth that is empty and void until thou enlightenest it."

No prose articles by Whittier appeared in the *Era* during the summer and early fall. There were three poems, all showing his increasing love of nature.

They were not written primarily for publication but were sent to the *Era*, as was now Whittier's custom with nearly everything that he wrote.

"Wordsworth" was written on a blank leaf in the first volume of *Memoirs of William Wordsworth, Poet-Laureate, D.C.L.* by Christopher Wordsworth. The lines were headed "To Thomas and Ann Tracy from their friends J. G. and Elizabeth Whittier" and were dated "Amesbury 2nd 6th mo. 1851."[38] They were printed in the *Era* ten days later. Whittier's reason for writing them and for sending the volumes was his belief that the Tracys resembled Wordsworth in finding beauty in the simple things of nature.

"In Peace" was in the *Era* of July 3 entitled "In Pace." The central thought of the poem was rather improbable: that the dead person whom it was written about would be remembered by details of natural scenery. The tone, however, was good and continued the quiet opening which has been commended as one of the lovely passages in Whittier that show "how good and simple and direct the nineteenth century at its best could be:"

> A track of moonlight on a quiet lake,
> Whose small waves on a silver-sanded shore
> Whisper of peace.[39]

Under the influence of this tone the reader hardly notices the forced metaphor of lilies as angels swaying on invisible stems, swaying being a form of motion not likely to be associated with angels. The absence of "sob of grief" and "wild lament" was an attitude that needed to be impressed upon the nineteenth century, which loved sentimental and theatrical mourning. Tennyson gave the same advice in a more famous poem, "Crossing the Bar," nearly forty years later.

When a subscriber asked what had become of Dr. Singletary, the editor of the *Era* replied August 8 that Whittier's health had been such as to prevent his continuing the series or contributing as much to the paper as formerly. His health, however, was not bad enough to confine him to his house or to keep him from enjoying himself when he wished. One Monday morning he hired a horse and carriage and drove toward Newburyport across Chain Bridge. He then discovered that he did not have any money to pay the toll when he returned. He drove to the Cursons' house at Curson's Mill, where the Artichoke River flows into the Merrimac. Mrs. Curson's daughters, Mary and Margaret, were pinning sheets on the clothes line. They welcomed him good-naturedly, lent him money for return across the toll bridge, and took him out in their rowboat on the Artichoke; they did the rowing — they were among the few women of that time who could row or would admit that they could. When Whittier returned the money a few days later, he sent a poem with it, "To —. Lines Written After a Summer Day's Excursion." All of the poem except the first stanza, which mentioned the money that he was returning and the fair nymphs surprised on a washing day, appeared in the *Era* July 24.[40]

The editor of the *Era* told his readers that Whittier's health was improving and that they could expect to hear from him again soon. However, nothing appeared in the *Era* in August or September, and in late August his health was worse. He was confined for a time to his house and did not feel well enough August 20 to go to Boston to hear Sumner's speech at a meeting called to express sympathy for Hungary, which was fighting a war for independence against Austrian troops aided by a Russian army. Whittier was practical enough to see that Hungary was doomed to defeat and that the sympathies and congratulations of friends of freedom in other countries would be "like delicates poured upon a mouth shut up or as meats set upon a grave."41

The Lyceum movement had reached Amesbury, which welcomed it enthusiastically and listened to an impressive list of speakers. Whittier gave a good deal of time to its affairs. He was on the committee that drew up its constitution and presented a slate of officers, and he was one of the curators elected September 8. During the fall and winter he secured two lecturers, Charles Sumner, who spoke November 17 on "The Improvement of Time," and Ralph Waldo Emerson, who spoke February 27 on "Power." He was careful to make convenient arrangements for the speakers, telling them what train to take from Boston and inviting them to have supper at his house and to stay over night.42

He now became convinced at the age of forty-four that his days of active work were over. He regarded himself as a tired onlooker through the day's decline and must leave the gleaning of the field to other hands. But he would neither repine nor boast of the "easy self-denial" that had been part of his work for freedom; in the broadening of his sympathies he had gained more than he had lost, and he could still enjoy the beauty of nature and friends whose love was warm, soft, and golden like the autumn day. He prayed that he might not indulge in "the bitter longings of a vain regret" but might think of others, as he had been doing on the day when he wrote "The Prisoners of Naples." It was dated October 1 and resulted from his reading of Gladstone's Letter to Lord Aberdeen, published as a pamphlet when Lord Aberdeen was slow in trying to bring about an improvement in the prisons of Naples, where twenty thousand political prisoners were kept in indescribable conditions of filth and cruelty. Gladstone had visited one of the prisons and had returned to London in a state of indignation that was soon shared by thoughtful people everywhere: "Look at Popery taking off the mask in Naples!" Charlotte Bronte exclaimed.43

Thinking about Naples and about freedom evidently brought Shelley into Whittier's mind. There is an echo of the last lines of "Ode to the West Wind" in

> Since all who suffer for thy truth send forth,
> Electrical, with every throb of pain,
> Unquenchable sparks, thy own baptismal rain

Of fire and spirit over all the earth,
Making the dead in slavery live again.

Whittier's hope that the prisoners would be able to bear years of unutterable torment like "the chained Titan victor through his will" is reminiscent of "Prometheus Unbound."

In the same issue of the *Era* was "Benedicite," with the headnote "From an Unpublished Poem." Whatever the longer poem was from which this was taken, it was never published and probably never completed. The suggestion has been made that it was addressed to Elizabeth Lloyd,[44] but there is nothing in it that definitely refers to his friendship with her.

Immediately after he wrote these poems his health became worse, and when Rufus W. Griswold asked him to write a preface for a volume of stories by Alice Cary, he replied that he was forbidden to write. He did not approve of prefaces, he added, which the public regarded as an attempt to "pass off by aid of a known name, what otherwise would not pass current," and Alice Cary did not need this sort of support; she could stand on her own merits. He offered to write notices of the volume[45] — evidently he hoped to resume writing before long — and a pre-publication notice of *Recollections of Our Neighborhood in Ohio* appeared in the *Era* of October 30. Whittier had learned not to praise his friends' books without qualifications, and while he said that these stories bore the true stamp of genius, he added that they occasionally had too sad an outlook on life, although the sober-hued background was often relieved by a vivid perception of the ludicrous and humorous.

He did not feel well enough to bear the fatigue and excitement of a political convention in Worcester and was doubtful of the wisdom of a coalition of Liberty Party and Independent Democrats; he found what he called his "old Liberty Party impracticability" hard to overcome. Still, the proceedings of a recent Whig convention had done much to reconcile him to the attitude taken by Sumner, who had written a few days before that he distrusted himself when he differed from Whittier but believed that a coalition in the fall elections was the only way to keep the balance of power in the Legislature on the side of freedom. Sumner wrote again October 7 that he felt that Liberty men should not neglect the opportunity offered by an "alliance — not fusion" with the Democrats, but Whittier, while he would not put any obstacle in the way, could not vote for an open defender of the Fugitive Slave Law.[46]

He was keeping up his reading of recent publications, and felt an honest pride in Bayard Taylor's *Book of Romances, Lyrics, and Songs*, which he thought had more than redeemed the promise which his most sanguine friends had made about him when his first book appeared. In the same issue of the *Era*, November 6, he commented favorably on Richard H. Stoddard's *Poems*; one of the seaside poems, he thought, was worthy of Tennyson — which was the highest praise that could be given to any poem at that time.

It must be admitted that Whittier was often over-enthusiastic in his judgment of writers, but so were most critics then. A poem by Elizabeth Lloyd was included in an edition of Milton's works, was copied in the *Era*, and was described there as a "sublime and affecting production." In the *Era* of December 25 Whittier reported that the poem was by Elizabeth Lloyd and commented that the fact that competent judges attributed the lines to Milton was a compliment to the author. Today it would be said that judges who thought that the poem was by Milton were wholly incompetent. It is hard to see how anyone with any critical ability could suppose that Milton wrote:

I am old and blind!
Men point to me as smitten by God's frown;
Afflicted and deserted of my kind;
Yet I am not cast down.

Whittier joined in the welcome given to Louis Kossuth by writing a poem for the *Era* of December 4. Kossuth made a great sensation in Washington. He did not conceal the fact that he was a military man: he wore a military uniform and a sword, and the guards at his hotel quarters were armed with muskets and bayonets.[47] Whittier added a footnote to "Kossuth" explaining that there were parts of Kossuth's history and character worthy of the admiration "of even those who question the expediency and rightfulness of an appeal to the sword for the redress of political wrongs." In the poem Whittier wondered who of the officials in Washington could properly welcome a man who had freed the serfs in his own land — surely not Daniel Webster.

In April of the next year he wrote to Samuel Gridley Howe, "On this wide earth there is but one Kossuth — the true hero of his time," and regretted that he was not well enough to accept Howe's invitation to meet Kossuth at his house. He was wise enough not to try to get Kossuth involved in Anti-Slavery activities in this country. He was concerned when he read a speech of Kossuth's which showed that he had been listening to men who thought — or said they thought — that the slavery question might lead to the dissolution of the Union, and he wished that Kossuth could be assured that the solicitude of the "Union Savers" was for political effect. "I do not wish him to be mixed up in *any way* with our domestic matters," he wrote to Sumner. "He has his mission; we ours."[48]

Uncle Tom's Cabin had been appearing serially in the *Era* since June 5, and one would suppose that Whittier's popularity would have been quite overshadowed, at least for the moment, by Mrs. Stowe's. However, a correspondent wrote to the editor of the *Era* asking him to induce Whittier to publish a cheap edition of his poems: "In the name of friends of humanity and lovers of good poetry among the poor, I demand a cheap edition of Whittier,"[49] and in the last issue of 1851 the editor informed his readers that another chapter of "My Summer with Dr. Singletary" had arrived and would appear in the next issue.

Daniel Webster (1782-1852). Oil painting by Joseph A. Ames. (Courtesy of Haverhill Public Library)

Charles Sumner (1811-1874).

Friends Meetinghouse, Amesbury.

XVI
1852 - 1853

Unwell, confined to the house, and unable to write except at rare intervals, Whittier was thinking a good deal about religion. The long-awaited fourth and fifth chapters of "My Summer with Dr. Singletary," in the *Era* January 1 and 8, were conversations about immortality leading to conclusions which became part of Whittier's sincere convictions and which were devoutly believed by the average American of the nineteenth century. Dr. Singletary pitied Horace because he had no hope of a future life, as Whittier later in "Snow-Bound" pitied the man who did not see the stars shining through the cypress trees. Although Dr. Singletary liked to think that memory would remain and that earthly scenes would live in eternal reproduction, he and Elder Staples decided that it was best that men should not have a clear picture of the future life — as Whittier later said in "The Eternal Goodness."

But he was doing too much reading and thinking to remain in placid security. A late spring delayed the confidence in the goodness of life and love which he would find in the first warm days and the early flowers. There was still snow on the ground in April, and the buds on the ground-laurel which should have been opening were buried under drifts. Day after day the raw northeast wind wailed and shrieked up the Merrimac valley, and in the poem "April" he asked why the south wind, the soul of the spring-time, delayed so long in renewing the great miracle of resurrection, which made faith revive as it saw symbolism in the blooming flowers and the budding trees. When Whittier used symbolism he was careful to explain it; the life of the springtime represented the life of the whole, and love came to the soul as the sun came to the sleeping earth.

The bad weather gave him plenty of time to do some thinking which led to fundamental queries in "Questions of Life" in the *Era* May 6. He assured the reader that he did not wish to shake anyone's already weak faith or to remove an error which might be someone's protection against doubt — a statement which nineteenth century readers would wholly approve. But he could not help asking questions, although he knew that he ought simply to trust. When nature did not answer, he turned to the old bards and prophets and then to books; he found divine light in all of them, Socrates, Plato and Kreeshna — he had evidently been reading the copy of the *BhagavadGita* that Emerson had lent him, which greatly excited his curiosity to know more of the religious literature of the East [1] — but of course he found more light in the Bible. Still, trying to find an answer was like tracing blindly the stone serpent on an Aztec ruin, symbol of the endless and unknown, and coming back to where one started. Then, his Quaker training coming to his rescue, he asked:

Why idly seek from outward things
The answer inward silence brings?

Spring weather had come by early May when he wrote the first of the two companion pieces entitled "Pictures"; the sights and sounds of spring were attendant angels to the house of prayer, and he shared with them what he had longed for a few weeks earlier, a resurrection morning as beautiful as when Christ rose from the dead. Four months later when he wrote the second of the pictures his thought about religion had become didactic — he must explain clearly and must leave nothing for the reader to find out for himself. The poem had good description of a hot August day in lines that were free from the monotonous rhythm that too often marred his verse. Then he could feel the western wind which told of meadows and streams and cool mountains; in just this way the pilgrim along life's summer waste is fanned by the airs from "the blessed Heaven for which we pray."

By the end of the year he had had enough of asking questions and had arrived at a position which he never left, however much he enriched it with fragments of other religions and however much he reached out from it into new applications. In "First-Day Thoughts" he was once again in the calm silence of a Quaker meeting where he could hear the still small voice, restrain his restless thoughts, and see clearly the path of duty which he would cheerfully follow. In "Trust" the old baffling questions could not be answered; he could only say what his mother had taught him, that everything in the present and future is of God and God is good, and so rest in childlike trust upon God's will.

Thinking about religion had not made him forget Anti-Slavery. When he read the proof-sheets of a memoir of Richard Dillingham, who had died while serving a prison term in Nashville for aiding the escape of fugitive slaves, he wrote "The Cross" and sent it to the *Era* for the February 26 issue. The first two lines were an enlargement of Thomas à Kempis: "Si crucem libenter portes, te portabit." The last two stanzas were an echo of Whittier's earlier "Seed-Time and Harvest." He approved of Samuel Allinson Jr.'s *Jamaica — Its Advantages as a Home for Colored Emigrants* but made clear that its purpose was to help free negroes who might wish to settle there and that the author had "no sympathy with the unchristian prejudice which strives to drive from our country those who, next to the Indians, have the best right to it."[2]

Nor had he forgotten what was going on in other parts of the world. In "The Peace of Europe" he found a bitter irony in the announcements of kings and priests that order reigned from the Tiber to the Danube, when everywhere could be heard marching men, night alarms, the call of sentries, and the dying groans of exiles. But his bitterness did not result in a fixed mood of despair. Later in the year some lines from Ben Jonson suggested "Astraea," a prophecy of a perfect world described in an amalgam of pagan and Christian beliefs, a Saturnian Golden Age of freedom, justice, and brotherhood, with the money changers driven out and God's will done on earth as in heaven.

Along with Whittier's enthusiasm for the writings of others was a complete lack of jealousy of their success. *Uncle Tom's Cabin* was already a best seller; by May 20, according to a jubilant announcement in the *Era*, fifty thousand copies had been sold. Whittier had not had that kind of success and had no reason to suppose that he ever would, but there is no trace of envy in his letter to Mrs. Stowe beginning "Ten thousand thanks for thy immortal book" and reporting that a friend of his had been reading it to a group of young women, daughters of Louisiana slaveholders, who lived near the scenes described in it and who said that it was true.[3]

Unfortunately in his enthusiasm for *Uncle Tom's Cabin* there was a sentimentality that led him into writing his worst poem since boyhood. As usual, his feelings were those of his contemporaries; his "Eva" was one of six songs based on *Uncle Tom's Cabin* advertised for sale in August, and the death of Eva was one of the high points in the productions of *Uncle Tom's Cabin* by travelling companies which lasted into the second decade of the present century. But that is no excuse for stanzas crammed with pious clichés and rhyming "Eva" with "leave her," "give her," "receive her," "never," "grieve her," "believer," and "river."

Whittier's fame had now reached the point where people were interested in his personal life. The first of the long list of visitors who published accounts of their visits was George W. Bungay, who reported that Whittier himself answered his knock at the door, led him into the Garden Room, introduced him to his mother, and invited him to tea. Bungay found him unassuming, accessible, frank, and well acquainted with public affairs.[4]

Although not well enough to take an active part in the political campaigns of 1852, Whittier was interested in what was going on. He was unable to go to the Independent Democratic convention of the Third Massachusetts district in July but wrote that he was in hearty sympathy with its objects. The Whig and Democratic parties had surrendered without qualification to the Slave Power and could not ask the votes of the Free Soilers. Of the two candidates, one (Franklin Pierce) was "worthy of their common platforms," and the other (Winfield Scott) had "adjusted himself to it with military promptness and precision." He thought that there was strong popular feeling for John P. Hale, who might do much to defeat "Hunkerism in the disguise of Democracy."[5] Hale was nominated but received no electoral votes. Whittier was listed as a Free Soil Presidential Elector on a broadside headed "Free Democratic Ticket."

Whittier's thought about the election led to one of his popular poems, "The

Poor Voter on Election Day,'' which appeared in the *Era* of December 13. It was doggerel but it said some things that readers liked to think were true: that the poor would use their votes to bring justice, to place human values above money, and to right wrongs.

The need of reform leading in this direction had been made evident by events in Amesbury during the past few months.

In the spring a new agent was appointed to take charge of the Salisbury Manufacturing Company, which had absorbed the Amesbury Flannel Manufacturing Company. The retiring Agent of the Salisbury Company was James Horton, who had grown up with many of the workers. They regarded him as their friend, and he had helped many of them to own their homes. Joshua Aubin, who had been Agent of the Amesbury Company, had also been on the best of terms with his employees. He gave every worker a turkey at Thanksgiving, which he often delivered personally, and he bought seven hundred fifty books for a library for the employees.

The new Agent, John Derby, did not know the type of community or workers that he was dealing with. He later said that he had not expected to find so much intelligence in the town, and he found it hard to distinguish between the different social classes. A few weeks after he took over the management he posted notices abolishing the "luncheon privilege," a mid-morning break of fifteen or twenty minutes at ten o'clock; the hours in the mills were 5:00 a.m. to 7:00 p.m. with a half hour for breakfast and three quarters of an hour for dinner. The "luncheon privilege" applied to the men only. Some used it to buy household supplies in the open-air market while others used it for eating and drinking — not always non-intoxicants. The order might have been defended as a safety precaution for men working around power-driven machines, but no explanation was given, and when the first notice was ignored a second one was posted with a warning that anyone leaving between opening and closing hours would be discharged. On the day when the notice went into effect the spinners, block printers, mechanics, and other male employees left in a body at the usual time. When they returned they were discharged. On the following day they found a temperance banner reading "Come with us and we will do you good," which they displayed at the gate of the mill yard at luncheon time, whereupon the women left the mill and joined them. A procession was formed, with a band, which marched to James Horton's house and gave three cheers and then to the house of the new agent, whom they saluted with hisses. Excitement ran high. More banners were displayed, one reading "Down with Factory Tyranny." The band played, boys threw sand in Derby's face as he rode in an open carriage, and his effigy was hung on the Liberty Pole. A committee of citizens met with Derby and four of the company directors, who spoke in the tone of parents admonishing a disorderly child: they were sorry to learn of such a spirit among the operatives who had seen fit to violate the rules laid down by Mr. Derby;

the hissing and shouting at Mr. Derby and the hoisting of flags with mottoes inscribed thereon they considered very wrong. They announced that they would sustain Derby.[6]

Whittier was asked to draw up a set of resolutions which were adopted at a meeting of citizens June 5. One of them acknowledged that some individuals might have abused the luncheon privilege and should have been discharged, but in general the character and conduct of the workers made the new rule unnecessary. The employees had been faithful in the performance of their duties, most of them were permanent residents, the town was law-abiding and orderly. It would be a matter of serious regret if "a proportion of those whose industry and good conduct have enlarged the dividends and established the honorable reputation of the Salisbury Company are driven elsewhere for labor and their places supplied by a vagrant and unsettled class." Whittier was a member of a committee of the Town of Amesbury which joined with the Town of Salisbury to issue a circular two weeks later; his name appeared first in the list of signers, and the circular showed a clarity of vision and a knowledge of legal and legislative developments that Whittier would have been more likely to have than other members of the committee. It said nothing about the luncheon privilege or the strike, which was already a lost cause. It appealed for support of a bill submitted to the Legislature to provide for a gradual reduction of the hours of labor to ten hours a day by July 4, 1853.

Whittier believed that the Ten Hour bill had a good chance of success at the next election.[7] His guess was wrong; the Ten Hour Law was not enacted until 1865. But the strike gave impetus to the movement, and one of the signers of the circular, Jonathan Nayson, a Democrat, was elected to the Legislature.

Whittier was right when he prophesied that a new working class would come into the towns. The Salisbury Manufacturing Company brought in recent Irish immigrants as strike-breakers, and many more came and remained as permanent residents. The majority of them were not the vagrant, dependent and irresponsible class that Whittier feared, but for many years they remained socially and culturally apart from the native population and the recent English immigrants. Their presence gave local impetus to the Know-Nothing movement in politics — which Whittier opposed.[8]

As early as April of 1852 Whittier had been thinking about a new volume of his poems, especially those that had been printed in the *Era*. The printing of *The Chapel of the Hermits and Other Poems* was completed by September, but the copies were not ready in time for the Christmas trade, and Fields thought it best to delay publication until the New Year's excitement was over. Publication finally came on February 9. Advance copies had been sent to Whittier, and he sent one to Harriet Beecher Stowe with the request that she notice it in the *Independent*, to which she was regularly contributing.

He was painfully aware of faults in the volume, he told her, but had been too ill to correct them. Nevertheless he was already preparing what he thought would be two volumes of prose stories, essays, and sketches which he regarded as better than anything that he had yet published and which would be entitled "Literary Recreations and Miscellanies." He did not tell Fields that everything that he intended to use had already been printed in one form or another. Fields was enthusiastic, but he might not have been if he had foreseen that *The Chapel of the Hermits* would not be a success. Not as many copies were sold as had been expected. The two editions published by Ticknor, Reed, and Fields totalled fourteen hundred copies and gave Whittier a profit of only seventy dollars. There was an English edition, but this was before the day of international copyrights and Whittier probably received nothing from it.[9]

One of the previously unpublished poems in *The Chapel of the Hermits* was "To My Old Schoolmaster." It was written on pages torn from a ledger, on one of which is the name "Sally Weld." They were evidently from Dr. Weld's ledger, had been given to her to play with, and had been left at the farm when she was playing with the Whittier children. Finding them perhaps reminded Whittier of his boyhood and one of the teachers, Joshua Coffin, who was now living in Newbury, where he was Town Clerk and Justice of the Peace and had written the *History of Newbury*. In spite of its light touch and the note of sentimentality and playful condescension typical of the public attitude toward schoolteachers, it was not hurriedly or carelessly written. The manuscript has many corrections and experimental lines.[10]

Whittier did little writing this winter. He told Gamaliel Bailey that he could not write except at long intervals without suffering so intensely that he lacked the courage to continue. The Hutchinson Family Singers gave a concert in Amesbury in January and called on Whittier, but he was not well enough to go to their concert. His health may have suffered from a disagreeable duty that he had to perform during the winter, administering the estate of his brother-in-law Jacob Caldwell, who had hanged himself in his barn.[11]

In March Whittier was still unable to write without a great deal of suffering, but he was stronger and was able to go to a temperance meeting in Boston, where Henry Ward Beecher was the chief speaker. He was also able to be active in local affairs. He arranged another Lyceum lecture for Emerson and planned the details with his usual care. Emerson would have time for tea at Whittier's before the lecture at 7:30.[12]

At the spring Town Meeting Whittier was elected to the Amesbury School Committee, to serve until March 1, 1854. School committees were in effect administrators, and Whittier was paid $24.25 for the year. The school committee of the town had the duty of certifying teachers, who were elected and paid by the committees in the different districts. It also determined questions of policy, and Whittier gave serious thought to one problem that came before the Committee later in the year. A Catholic boy objected to reading the Bible, which was part of the course of study. It was Whittier's opinion that it would be well if all children could be induced to read the Bible, but forcing a child to read it, especially if his parents had conscientious objections, would be a form of persecution.[13]

He was keeping himself informed on current issues, especially those involving slavery. In New Mexico the United States government had failed to keep its promise to protect persons and property. Conditions, he thought, were like those in the Scottish lowlands; the depredators were, like the Frasers and the Rob Roys, not wantonly cruel, and in fact might make respectable citizens if they were instructed in the arts and introduced to the comforts of civilization that would come as the reward of industry. With due care and protection, New Mexico would become a valuable member of the Union. One reason for its present disparagement was the belief that negro slavery was not adapted to its industrial needs or the feelings and habits of its people.[14]

A remark by Stephen A. Douglas that Great Britain was using *Uncle Tom's Cabin* to libel American institutions led Whittier to say that it was a hopeful sign of the times when men were aggrieved by the exposure of a system which they cherished as peculiarly democratic and American. They evidently expected that Great Britain and the entire civilized world would shut their eyes to the existence of slavery — or at least would forget it and not venture, like Captain Cuttle (in *Dombey and Son*) " to make a note of it." Furthermore, the plea could no longer be made that the story was libel and exaggeration. William Goodell's *The American Slave Code*, recently published by the American and Foreign Anti-Slavery Society, showed that American legislators had united the extremes of liberty and tyranny in the same statute book.[15]

When he read a state paper in which divine law was invoked to defend slavery, he wrote "Official Piety" (then entitled "Lines") which appeared in the *Era* of March 24. Crime, the poem concluded, never lacked spiritual cheer and pious gratitude. Satan modestly gave God the credit for his evil offspring, and we need not marvel to see official piety locking the door of hope against three million souls and

Whining a prayer for help to hide the key.[16]

"Tauler" was in the *Era* a few weeks later. Its central thought was the same as the simple answer to baffling questions that he learned from his mother and had quoted in "Trust" a few months earlier. In "Tauler" the famous preacher heard it from a poor old stranger. This poem was one of those that brought assurance and steadiness to people who were bewildered and frightened as Calvinism collapsed into dust like Holmes' "Wonderful One-Horse Shay." One of them wrote to Whittier that "Tauler" helped to quiet her mind on the essentials of religion, when the old theories were breaking up. She and her husband had tried to reconcile the first chapter of Genesis with the science of geology and had received no help from their pastor, who told them to leave all questionings of that kind and not to allow themselves "to be drawn away from the Sacred Word." They then knew that they must leave the church — that they must "step out" but "what to step *upon* was the question." They found the answer in "Tauler," especially the section beginning "What Hell may be I know not; this I know."[17]

Whittier's imagination could still be stirred by a heroic deed. "The Hero" is an account, with considerable decoration, of an adventure of Samuel Gridley Howe in the Greek War of Independence. Whittier heard the story from Charles Sumner, who had, according to Dr. Howe, "wormed it out of him," and, he modestly said, Whittier made quite a scene out of very ordinary material, transforming the sorry beast that he rode into a gallant barb. Whittier did not use Dr. Howe's name in the poem, and the present headnote was added later, but the reference to

> The Cadmus of the blind
> Giving the dumb lip language
> The idiot-clay a mind

must have identified Dr. Howe to most readers.[18]

However much he rejoiced at the success of *Uncle Tom's Cabin*, Whittier was now astute enough to know that slavery could not be destroyed as easily as he had thought when he wrote *Justice and Expediency* twenty years earlier. In declining an invitation to a festival in Boston in honor of John P. Hale he made a statement that proved to be prophetic: "The signs of the times, although not without encouragement, admonish us that all we have done heretofore is but the preparation for the great and final conflict between Democracy and Slavery."[19]

A few weeks later he saw where the first part of that conflict would occur. "The Mauvais Terres of Nebraska," in the *Era* of June 30, began with a description of a valley in Nebraska three hundred feet below the surrounding country, rich in remains of animals long extinct and in grim secrets of an early world where monsters roamed in a period so remote that the mind staggered under the effort of computation, when the inland mountain chains were the seaboard of the Atlantic. However simple Whittier's religious faith, it obviously did not include belief in the literal interpretation of the Bible, and it may safely be said that he was better read than the average person of the time in prehistoric geology and zoology. But the chief purpose of the article was to say that the reason for the delay by the Senate in organizing Nebraska as a territory was to allow slaveholders to get a foothold there. The restrictions of the old Missouri Compromise were being disregarded, and nothing but a revival of Anti-Slavery feeling in the Free States could prevent the spread of slavery north of thirty-six degrees thirty minutes.

Whittier's tribute to Robert Rantoul, whose opposition to the Fugitive Slave

Law had placed him definitely in the Anti-Slavery ranks, was rather belated in publication. Rantoul died August 7, 1852, and the poem did not appear in the *Era* until July 14, 1853, although at least part of it seems to have been written in the winter. Whittier had come to regard Rantoul as the potential leader of the Anti-Slavery forces and said in the poem, as he had said in an editorial in the *Era* January 27, "Our Prospects and Our Duties," that there was no one in sight to take his place. But the poem was not wholly unqualified praise of Rantoul:

We saw his great powers misapplied
To poor ambitions

and his power

Was lent to Party over-long.

Before leaving for his summer vacation he sent "The Pope and Saint Peter" (now "The Dream of Pio Nono") to the *Era*. Time had not softened his attitude toward Pius IX, and his description of the slaughter in the streets of Rome was vigorous and incisive. Ten years later he could have found horrible scenes in the Civil War to write about, but there was no such emotion to prompt him to do it. "The Dream of Pio Nono" wasted no words and had no sentimental or moralizing conclusion. Whittier for once wrote what he felt without thinking of the good that the poem might or might not do.

On August 21 he left for a Free Democratic Convention at Wolfeboro and a vacation in the White Mountains. The convention met August 24 in a pine grove. Steamers and carriages had brought three thousand people, who cheered when Moses A. Cartland denounced the Fugitive Slave Law and greeted John P. Hale with cheer after cheer and waving of handkerchiefs. Whittier was optimistic about the coming election for quite practical reasons: the old Democratic Party was not united, and Franklin Pierce had failed to satisfy all the applicants for public office. From Wolfboro he went by steamer to Centre Harbor, where he was a frequent summer visitor for the rest of his life. It was then a quaint, old-fashioned village, a "quiet, slumberous, comfort-promising spot," an inviting retreat from "the noisome city and the feverish unrest of money-getting." The recent occurrences in the mills in Amesbury had cured him of his belief in manufacturing plants as blessings to New England villages, and he noted that Centre Harbor had "no unsightly manufactory, no over-worked spinners and weavers, no self-important corporation agent."[20]

He spent a week with some of the Rogers family, and Nathaniel F. Rogers' daughters found him a delightful companion. They sang to him, and he especially liked the negro melodies. One evening he wrapped a white shawl around Ellen, put a Quaker bonnet on her head, and made her sing through the long twilight; it was a pleasant event to remember in the winter, and he wrote and sent her "A Memory" — and also sent it to the *Era* for publication January 28.[21]

His health was better after his weeks in New Hampshire and he was able to do more writing for the *Era*. His vacation also resulted in two poems, "Noon" and "Evening," companion pieces in "Summer by the Lakeside," which he called a "specimen of the quieter mood of a rough reformer and controversialist."[22] In "Noon" he found himself one with the mountain scenery and consequently at peace, assured that God would do what was best for him and for the pine trees. There was better description in "Evening," with Whittier's own sincere impressions:

> How start to light the clustering isles,
> Each silver-hemmed! How sharply show
> The shadows of their rocky piles,
> And tree-tops in the wave below!

He did not feel able to go to a Free Democracy meeting in New York September 29 and wrote that he had no skill in solving the riddle of New York politics, but he was sure that no one supported the Fugitive Slave Law from love of it except the lowest class of official kidnappers. Recent attempts to enforce it were "dastard cruelty and low brutality which would drive a Bedouin Arab in disgrace from his caravan and put a Feejee Islander in taboo as unfit for the society of respectable cannibals." He did not go to the meeting in Philadelphia on the twentieth anniversary of the American Anti-Slavery Society but wrote that he did not regret signing the Declaration and did not wish to be released from its obligations. It had cost him nothing for which he had not been more than compensated. The Anti-Slavery forces had compelled the church to see Slavery as it was and had hastened the long foreseen crisis. "The result is in God's hands, and we need not fear for it. Divine attributes are pledged to the side of righteousness and truth."[23] This thought was more fully developed a few weeks later in "The Voices," which appeared in the *Era* January 3.

Among the visitors in November were John Wilde and Ralph Waldo Emerson. Wilde, with a letter of introduction from William S. Robinson, came to Amesbury on business connected with the proposed ten-hour law. Emerson came to lecture again at the Lyceum October 28, this time on "England and the English." As usual, Whittier made the arrangements, and his letter to Emerson contained some sentiments with which Emerson must have been in sympathy. "Amidst the autumnal opulence of the last two weeks I have lived more than regally. How poor and mean in comparison seem all the pomps and shows of kings and priests! And what folly to run abroad over the old world when all that is beautiful may be seen from our own door-stone! Munich, the Louvre and the Vatican are doubtless well worth seeing, but I fancy I see all and much more in my own painted woodlands."[24]

Oliver Wendell Holmes came to Haverhill to lecture at the Haverhill Atheneum, and Whittier met him there for the first time. Holmes' lecture was "witty and genial," and Whittier wrote to James T. Fields, "There is rare humor in him, and I suspect he knows it. But I like him."[25] Their friendship continued as long as they lived, reaching its height in their old age when they were the last survivors of the group that had made the literary fame of New England.

Another friendship that lasted through the years was between the Whittiers and Lucy Larcom. Whittier tried to find a publisher for her "Similitudes, from the Sea-Side and the Prairie." He sent the manuscript to Fields, assuring him that the author had no ambition to appear in print and that the "little prose poems" were unique in American literature and reminded one of Lessing. Fields was not convinced, and Whittier soon wrote to Lucy Larcom that Jewett would publish it.[26] In the *Era* of September 29 he announced that the book was in press and that its prose poems evinced "delicate fancy and great beauty of thought and expression," and he had another enthusiastic notice in the *Era* of December 22.

In September Caleb Cushing sent a letter for publication in the *Boston Post* ordering Massachusetts Democrats to give no further support to the coalition of Associated Democrats and Free Soilers. To do so would be to give countenance and power to Anti-Slavery agitators and would therefore be in the highest degree hostile to the Administration. President Pierce, the letter said, had immovable convictions on that point, and all his followers should help him to crush Abolitionism, in whatever guise or form it might appear.[27]

This "Ukase," as it came to be called — Whittier called it "the Vermilion Edict of the late Ambassador to China, peremptory and dictatorial as those of Grand Commissioner Lin" — resulted in the defeat of several amendments to the Massachusetts Constitution which would have been helpful to reform movements and especially to Anti-Slavery. Whittier was resolved to have nothing further to do with coalitions except on Anti-Slavery grounds. Free Soilers should stand on their old platform with inexorable firmness and invite all who were sick of the rule of the slave power to join them in open and manly opposition to it.[28] The break-up of the coalition was regrettable, he wrote in the *Era* of December 22, as involving the loss of the Reformed Constitution but was not permanently detrimental to the cause of Liberty and Progress. Attention could now be given to vital matters and need not be distracted by local and side issues. The advocates of constitutional freedom would have ample exercise for all their powers of thought and action.

XVII
1854 - 1855

The Kansas-Nebraska Bill was reported from Stephen A. Douglas' committee early in January 1854, and the crisis in national affairs which Whittier had foreseen was approaching. But he was not wholly absorbed in politics and Anti-Slavery. Julia Ward Howe had sent him her *Passion Flowers*, a volume of poems, some of which had resulted from a winter in Rome. He told the readers of the *Era* that the author had a deep and passionate appreciation of Rome but did not overlook the grim background of political evils, "a government of spies and priests, propped by foreign bayonets, and resting on the dungeons of thirty thousand political prisoners dying by inches in their living tombs."[1] He was also pleased that Sarah Jane Clarke Lippincott ("Grace Greenwood") had not been seduced by life at Rome and had retained her Protestantism and Democracy. In a review of her *Haps and Mishaps of a Tour in Europe* in the *Era* of February 13, he found her "representations of religious theatricals and the way in which Christianity is caricatured and common sense outraged thereby" to be spirited and effective.

He had resumed work on "My Summer with Dr. Singletary" and published Chapter VI, two years after Chapter V, in the *Era* of January 3. It was a pleasant little love story about a Dartmouth student who lost his health by too much study and went on a fishing schooner to Labrador where he met a pretty French girl, married her, and went into business with her father. The story was well told, with lively and humorous conversation, but it had some needless moralizing toward the conclusion, without, however, the present final paragraph with its irrelevant comment on Calvinism. Whittier evidently intended to write more chapters. Chapter VI is headed "From 'My Summer with Dr. Singletary,'" as was "Martha Mason, A Song of the Old French Wars"[2] in the *Era* of May 25, and he wrote to Fields: "My 'Singletary Papers' still drag their slow length along."[3]

The only poem in the winter of 1853-54 having to do with slavery was "The Haschish" in the *Era* of January 13. It had a number of variations from the present form, including two vigorous stanzas later omitted:

> It makes the merchant class, with ware
> And stock in trade, his fellow sinners;
> And factory lords, with equal care,
> Regard their spindles and their spinners.

For seraph songs he [the preacher] takes the bark
    And bay of bloodhounds northward setting:
The planter for a patriarch,
    With servants of his own begetting.

It had a long introductory note explaining that haschish had narcotic and intoxicating qualities which produced an agreeable hallucination or fantasia, disposing the eater to all kinds of exaggeration and extravagance, and the cotton plant had similar mental, moral, religious, and political effects upon the people of the United States.

With his usual belief in the importance of local action on national issues, Whittier was one of the signers of a call for a meeting February 27 of citizens of Amesbury and Salisbury for the purpose of remonstrance against the Kansas-Nebraska Bill. Many such protest meetings were being held, and they were in effect the beginning of the Republican Party. A set of resolutions which he prepared for this meeting was unanimously adopted. One of them argued that if the South persisted in breaking faith with the North on the plea that the Government had no right to concern itself with slavery, the principle should be carried out consistently, and, in the next resolution, the South could have no pretext of complaint if the Fugitive Slave Law was abolished. Another resolution was a shrewd appeal to a motive that had more effect than Abolitionist sentiment in arousing the North and East: the Bill interfered with their industrial and commercial interests; Free Labor would be shut out from the "Great Central Garden" of the continent.[4]

The Kansas-Nebraska Bill passed the Senate March 3. Whittier thought that if Daniel Webster were now living he would "make a 'North' " and, a shorn and blinded prisoner of the South, would make sport for the slaveholders as Samson did for the Philistines when he pulled down the temple on their heads. Whittier had already started a movement to have the Massachusetts Legislature pass a law granting jury trials in Fugitive Slave cases, which would have the effect of nullifying the Fugitive Slave Law.[5]

This plan appeared as one of the items in an article in the *Era* of March 30, "The Occasion and Its Duties." When he wrote this article he was resigned to the fact that the Kansas-Nebraska Bill would become law, in spite of Sumner's belief that the Bill might be defeated in the House; the moneybags of the Treasury had been turned into the scale, and the President had the needed number of Congressional traitors. Worst of all, even if slavery did not get a foothold in Kansas and Nebraska, the repeal of the Missouri Compromise and the establishment of the principle that Congress could not interfere with slavery in territories would leave the way open for slavery in Cuba, Haiti, Mexico, and Central America, for young America was grasping for territory and a scheme of conquest and annexation was already in progress. He quoted Emerson: "The Fugitive Slave Law partially unglued the eyes of the North, and now the Nebraska Bill leaves us staring.'' A League of Freedom should be formed — and here Whittier was following a suggestion of Sumner. The influence of the Free Soil party was weakened by helping the Whigs in one State and the Democrats in another, Sumner pointed out, and he would support any plan of union of all the opponents of slavery if it was based on a broad, liberal, and comprehensive principle.[6]

The Kansas-Nebraska Bill had been planned as a peace measure but it obviously had not been a success, and Whittier saw a chance for a bit of satire. Stephen A. Douglas, he said in the *Era* of April 15, needed some novel expedient to save him from the consequences of a blunder, which in the scale of political morality was worse than a crime. Two other men in awkward situations had made convenient use of miracles. A Papal Envoy to the United States, Monsignor Bedini, who had encountered popular demonstrations caused by reports of his approval of atrocious crimes and barbarous treatment of patriots in Bologna when he was governor there, wrote that Heaven had shown its approval of his administration by causing the image of the Blessed Virgin of Rimini to roll up its wooden eyes. Nicholas I of Russia was robbing the Turks of territory; in a battle between Russians and Turks, the Turks fled when the Holy Mother of God descended from Heaven accompanied by two warriors. Douglas might use similar tactics and get a clerical friend to say that while Douglas was speaking he saw a vision of the Apostle of the Gentiles carrying into execution the old Roman Fugitive Slave Law and tying Onesimus hand and foot to give him over to his master Philemon.[7]

The Kansas-Nebraska Bill passed the House May 22, and since it had been forced through a reluctant Congress by White House pressure, there was no doubt that it would be signed by the President.

Four days later, while feeling was still running high in Massachusetts, a meeting was called in Faneuil Hall by the Boston Vigilance Committee. Anthony Burns, a Negro working in a clothing store in Boston, had been claimed by his Southern owner as a fugitive slave. The meeting in Faneuil Hall broke up abruptly when it was announced that some Negroes were trying to rescue him. There was a rush to the court house where an attempt was made to enter by breaking windows and doors. A few men, including Thomas Wentworth Higginson, forced their way in but were driven out by the marshall and his aids, who beat them on the head with clubs. The beating must have been relatively gentle; Higginson was surprised to find that clubbing was not as bad as he expected.[8]

Earlier in the day, just as the mail was closing, Whittier had written a hurried and excited letter to Henry I. Bowditch: ''That man *must* not be sent out of Boston as a slave. Anything but that! The whole people must be called out, the country must precipitate itself upon the city — an avalanche of freemen! Where are your circulars and your expresses? In the name of

God, let the people be summoned! Send out the fiery cross without further delay! Tell us what you want and what we can do!''

As Whittier would have foreseen if he had written in a calmer moment, this letter was interpreted as urging violence if the Court ordered Burns' return to slavery. It was read at a meeting of Negroes in Boston where extreme measures were proposed. In haste and alarm Whittier wrote three letters on May 29. "I am sorry to see such a spirit of violence manifested, as it is useless and wrong in itself," he wrote to Dr. Bowditch. "I wish the demonstration of feeling to be deep and serious, but earnestly pray that there may be no resort to force. . . . I regret the use of my letter to thee at a meeting of our colored friends. Surely no one who knows me could suppose that I wish to have any violent measures adopted. Pray see to it that no such impression was left in the minds of our colored friends. Oh! let them beware of violence!'' If he were not seriously ill he would come to Boston to use his influence on the side of freedom and peace. Letters to Samuel E. Sewall and to the *Boston Times* made the same appeal, but had little, if any, effect.[9] When Burns was sent back to slavery June 2, there were such threatening crowds in the streets that martial law was proclaimed. He was taken down State Street to a steamer chartered by the Government, guarded by United States troops, Massachusetts militia, and Boston police. Dr. Bowditch was in the crowd and twice saw troops charge with bayonets and the cavalry charge with drawn swords — "in Parisian style," as he described it.

When Whittier heard what had happened he wrote "The Rendition" (then entitled "Ichabod"). It was printed in the *Era* July 29 without the present introductory note, but the case had attracted so much attention that readers doubtless knew what Whittier was referring to in

. . . . . Liberty
Marched handcuffed down that sworded street.
The final stanza appealed to Massachusetts to rise awful in her strength —
Ah me! I spoke but to the dead;
I stood upon her grave!

A few days after the attack on the court house Whittier was worried about what might happen to Higginson. He thought that Higginson's injuries could not be severe, as he had said nothing about them; actually he had received a bad cut on the chin, and the scar remained with him for life. But there might be serious legal consequences, and Whittier hoped that Higginson would be careful "to avoid the Philistines who would be glad to make an example of him."[10] Higginson was anything but cautious. He scolded Whittier for counselling non-resistance, and on June 4 he preached a sermon in his church in Worcester, "Massachusetts in Mourning," which was immediately printed.

Six months later, Higginson and others were tried in the United States Circuit Court in Boston. Whittier wrote "For Righteousness' Sake" (then called "Lines. Inscribed to friends under arrest for treason against the Slave Power"). It contained some frequently quoted lines expressing Whittier's confidence in the final triumph of right:

> God's ways seem dark, but, soon or late,
> They touch the shining hills of day;
> The evil cannot brook delay,
> The good can well afford to wait.

Theodore Parker was the only one of the defendants who regularly attended the trial, and he prepared a long and elaborate defense which he did not have a chance to use. The indictment was quashed as imperfect and, as Higginson said, they "all got out of the affair, as it were, by the side door."

Whittier was not really as hopeless about Massachusetts as the final lines of "The Rendition" would indicate. Although he did not approve of the violence attempted by some members of the Boston Vigilance Committee, he sent a contribution from himself and one from Amesbury Friends Meeting.[11]

As usual, Whittier was making the best possible use of an unhappy situation. He was skillfully maneuvering toward the formation of a new political party, which would later take the name of Republican. Robert C. Winthrop seemed to him to be the best leader of such a party, which would save the country from the horrors of a bloody revolution certain to result from the next attempt to execute the Fugitive Slave Law in New England. He thought that the new party might well begin in Massachusetts, and he wrote to Winthrop that Free Soilers were ready to support Whigs and Democrats in a new party.[12]

He encouraged the groups migrating to Kansas to make it a free territory by writing a song for them although he was not sure that Kansas would be Anti-Slavery in national politics. He sent "The Kansas Emigrants" to the first party to leave Boston, and they sang it to the tune of "Auld Lang Syne" on their departure, along the way, and in their new home. This may seem unbelievable until one remembers the vogue of the singing school in New England, when group singing was taken for granted.[13]

As usual, Whittier kept his life in balance by varied interests. He reviewed three recent books in the June 28 *Era*: Phoebe Cary's *Poems and Parodies*, Mary R. Mitford's *Atherton and Other Tales*, and Edmund Quincy's *Wensley. A Story Without a Moral*, which he thought the most readable book of its kind since Hawthorne's *Blithedale Romance*. He did not mention *Walden*, which was published August 10, but he read it promptly and commented to Fields four days after its publication that it was "capital reading, but very wicked and heathenish. The practical moral of it seems to be that if a man is willing to sink himself into a woodchuck he can live as cheaply as that quadruped; but after all, for me I prefer walking on two legs." This was not Whittier's final opinion of Thoreau; he read everything that Thoreau wrote and was a warm appreciator of his work. After he had reread *Letters to Various Persons* he wrote to Thoreau's friend Daniel Ricketson, "What a rare genius he [Thoreau] was! To take up his book is like a stroll in the woods or a sail on the lake — the leaves rustle and the water ripples along his pages."[14]

Whittier's prose contributions to the *Era* were tapering off, but poems were appearing about once a month. "William Forster" showed Whittier's sincere admiration for Forster's "tranquil strength" and his activity in various causes for human welfare. "The Hermit of the Thebaid" doubtless gave pleasure to many Protestants who looked upon monasticism with suspicion and contempt and to sentimental readers who loved a happy ending. "The Fruit-Gift," written when someone brought him a basket of fruit one evening, had a clever suggestion of the vine's origin in Eden which must have been better appreciated in Whittier's time than today; most people then knew the Book of Genesis. "To Charles Sumner" had facile and informed use of mythology. "Letter from a Missionary of the Methodist Episcopal Church South, in Kansas, to a Distinguished Politician" appeared unsigned. Whittier may have been, quite needlessly, ashamed of it, or at least aware that it was not what his public expected of him. It was lively and amusing, with clever use of the sanctimonious, self-righteous tone of a pro-slavery preacher. The blank verse was well handled, with varied cadences and arrangement of thought and lines. Whittier called it a "jingle" and "one of those pieces that make themselves, and come to you uncalled for."[15]

Two of the poems written during the fall came to be among Whittier's most popular and most quoted verses. After "Maud Muller" was printed in the *Era*, copies were in demand, and it was printed on single sheets to be sold in stores. Whittier himself did not have a high opinion of it. He once called it an idle poem, and he replied to one of the many correspondents who plagued him with questions about it that he did not think it was worth analysis.[16] He told inquirers that he pronounced the name with a Yankee "u" but was willing that any reader should pronounce it as he wished — and in fact, it would have been better to call the girl "Maud Miller."

"Maud Muller" is certainly not Whittier at his best. The rhyme in the much quoted couplet

> For of all sad words of tongue or pen,
> The saddest are these: "It might have been"

leaves the critic in despair over Whittier's defective sense of vowel sounds. The narrative thoroughly deserved the parodies of Phoebe Cary and Bret Harte; the latter demolished the romance in one couplet:

> For there be women fair as she
> Whose verbs and nouns do more agree.

But its popularity was neither short-lived nor limited to one class of people. When George Templeton Strong read it he wrote in his diary that he must learn more about Whittier. "Maud Muller," he wrote, "hits me very hard. It's a sign of real power to make familiar and rather commonplace names and associations effective. It's a good sign that a man who can write with vigor and depth of true feeling ventures to deal with matters of A.D. 1855 and tries to idealize the realities of our daily life." Curtis Guild wrote that it was his favorite poem and invited Whittier to dinner and to see a picture of Maud by a Miss Gardiner.[17]

The reason for its popularity was that it dealt so simply and directly with a universal human experience that readers overlooked its absurdity. "How many hearts it has spoken to," was Hannah Lloyd Neall's comment in a letter to Whittier; she included her own, since she added that she ought to have had a career but it was now too late to begin.

The poem as first printed did not have the introductory note which explains that the story has no basis in fact but was suggested by an incident when Whittier and Elizabeth were driving along the Maine seacoast. The spring is thought to be the one on the north side of Route 91, between York and South Berwick.

In the October issue of *The Little Pilgrim* Grace Greenwood announced that she had received "The Barefoot Boy," which would appear later in the year. In the December number she announced that it had been crowded out but would appear in January and was now being illustrated. It appeared as promised and occupied most of the first page. There was one illustration by John Andrew, showing a plump little barefoot boy, with trousers rolled half-way up to his knees, in a rather statuesque pose, with one hand on a fence post and the other holding some flowers. It was not as good as the lithograph by Louis Prang, which Whittier commended and then was vexed to see his words applied to an inferior imitation by another publisher.[18]

The poem immediately became popular and, as a pleasant bit of nostalgia, appealed to adults rather more than to children. Cornelius Conway Felton, later president of Harvard, read it in the *Transcript* after teaching Greek on a hot June day. It called up memories as "delicious as a shower in a summer afternoon" and he "revelled again in the days of jacket-hood, torn hat-hood, barefoot-hood." He sighed to think of the boots he would have to wear until wearing anything would be bootless, and quoted from one of his lectures at the Lowell Institute in which he said that of all the enjoyments of childhood and youth in the country in former times, that of the "soft fresh feeling of the genial earth pressed by the unshod sole of the foot" was undoubtedly the most delicious and was a pleasure fast passing away.[19]

Literary Recreations and Miscellanies was published by Ticknor and Fields in September. It contained no new material, but Whittier liked it well enough to send a copy to Mary R. Mitford, whose books he greatly admired.[20] Nathaniel Hawthorne had a different opinion: "Whittier's book is poor stuff! I like the man, but have no high opinion either of his poetry or of his prose."

The public evidently thought better of the book than Hawthorne did but was not wildly enthusiastic. Thirteen hundred fifty of the fifteen hundred printed were sold at one dollar. Whittier received the usual ten per cent, one hundred thirty-five dollars.[21]

There was not much snow in the winter of 1854-55, but the weather was damp and changeable and Whittier was so unwell that he even dreaded the coming of spring. He had to give up his hope of accepting Elizabeth Lloyd's invitation to visit her and her husband. After her marriage to Robert Howell early in 1853, she sent a note to Whittier on a visiting card telling him when she would be at home and explaining that illness had kept her from writing to him before her marriage. This was followed later in the year by a letter inviting him and Elizabeth to visit them in their Philadelphia home. The Whittiers were kept informed of her attempt to retain her membership in the Society of Friends,[22] and Whittier was pleased to hear that she had been successful.

His letter to her on February 4, 1855, was his belated reply to the invitation that she had sent November 21, 1853. He enclosed a copy of his "Letter from a Missionary" and was evidently beginning to be proud of it. President Wayland of Brown University had said in a review that it was worth all the sermons that had been preached on the subject and was the only way to deal with pro-slavery missions.[23]

Whatever the state of Whittier's health during these months, he was able to do a good deal of writing. On the same day that he wrote to Elizabeth Lloyd Howell he also wrote to James Russell Lowell commending his recent lectures on the English poets and giving his opinion that the great poets were Chaucer, Spenser, Shakespeare, Milton ("I had almost said Dryden"), Burns, and Shelley. "Flowers in Winter", acknowledging a painting of flowers on a porte livre sent him by Margaret Curson, and an article about Henry Wilson appeared four days later.[24] Wilson, who was a candiate for the United States Senate to succeed Edward Everett, had been elected by the Massachusetts Senate but not by the House. Whittier explained that the election of Wilson, who had been active in Anti-Slavery for the past ten years, by the only Legislature controlled by the Know-Nothing Party would arouse indignation in the Southern wing of that party, but the fact was that Nativism had less to do with his election than the popular hatred of slavery, which had been kindled to a white heat by the Fugitive Slave Law and the repeal of the Missouri Compromise. Everybody in Massachusetts, he said, knew that the return of Anthony Burns to slavery had more influence upon Wilson's election than the coming in of all foreigners and "outside barbarians" since the Mayflower.

Whittier and his mother had colds and Elizabeth was worried about them, but he was well enough on May 1 to go to the Baptist Meeting House to hear Charles Sumner lecture on "The Necessity, the Practicality,and the

Dignity of the Anti-Slavery Enterprise.'' There were seven hundred present, who heard Sumner recommend Anti-Slavery to young men as a field in which they might labor with profit and success.[25]

He was thinking a good deal about religion. Early in May he was invited to the Third Yearly Meeting of the Society of Progressive Friends, a group in Pennsylvania that had declared its opposition to a long list of evils: slavery, intemperance, war, capital punishment, denial of equal rights to women, oppression in all its forms, ignorance, superstition, priestcraft, and ecclesiastical domination. Whittier's reply contained in brief all of the concepts and convictions which appeared a decade later in his best-loved religious poetry and which were the beliefs of an increasing number of the more thoughtful and intelligent Protestants of various denominations:

"I attach little importance to creeds, forms, professions and outward organizations. But the assembling of ourselves together in reverent recognition of our dependence upon our Heavenly Father for strength and guidance, seems to me at once a solemn duty and a great privilege. Christianity is the ultimate — the highest possible ideal — and all the lines of human progress, however widely apart at the outset, converge upon it. I see nothing, in any school of philosophy to compare with the sublime simplicity of its truth, as adapted to the wants of our nature. Looking over the ages I see nothing higher and holier than its great Teacher. I believe in the divine efficacy of His life and its consummation of sacrifice; and I regard the record of His precepts and example as the true text-book of the reformer. With you, I believe that our faith in Him is best manifested by purity of life and devotion to the welfare of our fellow-men."[26]

With his mind still on religion, he wrote "My Dream," which appeared in the *Era* of May 24. It said rather well what Whittier's contemporaries could not hear too often: that death, which looks so terrifying, really isn't bad at all but is a soothing prelude to a happy meeting with old friends who are now free from pain and sorrow. The allegory was simple and clear, and could not have been misunderstood by a reader of normal intelligence, but Whittier felt under obligation to tell what it meant. The average reader of his time, even if he did not need the explanation, would think that it was proper that Whittier should give it and would like the simple and easy-to-remember lines:

> And this heart-consuming care,
> All our fears of here or there,
> Change and absence, loss and death,
> Prove but simple lack of faith.

Thoughts of eternity did not take Whittier's attention away from the present. He was pleased when Massachusetts passed a law protecting her citizens from the Fugitive Slave Law. The poem that he wrote, "Arisen at Last" (entitled "Massachusetts" in the *Era* of June 7) began with a reminder of what he had said a year ago, that when he called to Massachusetts to rise awful in her strength he had spoken but to the dead: he stood upon her grave. Now Massachusetts had risen, and, in somewhat melodramatic phrases, she was a lioness guarding her young, with a power in her eye to smite the wild wolf backward: here the "fell lycanthrope" found no prey. Whittier liked the poem well enough to ask William Lloyd Garrison to read it when he lectured on Whittier at Newburyport four years later.[27]

He also found cause for rejoicing — and a chance to say a word for the new Republican Party — in political developments in New Hampshire. On June 13 the House of Representatives elected John P. Hale and James Bell to the United States Senate. Bell was a personal friend of Hale and was understood to have Anti-Slavery sympathies. The reelection of Hale, Whittier assured his readers, was not a Know-Nothing victory. He regretted that what he called the obstinacy and blindness of the leaders of the "late" Whig Party of the North had prevented the formation of the Republican Party in 1854 and had driven people into the Know-Nothing movement. But, as usual, "Let bygones be bygones." The liberal Whigs and Democrats, Know-Nothings, and Free Soilers should unite without delay on a platform of No Slave Territory, No New Slave States, Repeal of the Fugitive Slave Law.[28]

Whittier did not do any writing during the fall of 1855 except "The Panorama," written to be read at one of a series of Anti-Slavery lectures in Tremont Temple in Boston. It was long — five hundred seventeen lines of heroic couplets — well planned and carefully written. The last sections had some good invective and satire and some sound advice to youthful zealots who were impatient with the cautious counsels of those who

. . . . . Temper and restrain
The o'erwarm heart that sets on fire the brain.

The poem closed on a personal note. Whittier had not voluntarily turned from the pleasant paths of song to invective and satire; he would have preferred to write legends and pastoral and domestic verses about his native North. (In this he evidently spoke sincerely; during the next year he would write "Mary Garvin" and "The Last Walk in Autumn." He was moving toward "Telling the Bees" and "Snow-Bound.")

"The Panorama" was read by Thomas Starr King on the first night of the Anti-Slavery series, following a lecture by Horace Mann. It took forty minutes and was frequently interrupted by applause.[29]

Whittier received one hundred dollars for the poem. There had been a suggestion that it be read at another Anti-Slavery lecture where Mary Webb, a Negro elocutionist, was to read a dramatized version of *Uncle Tom's Cabin*. Mrs. Stowe evidently objected, and after Whittier received a letter from her, which he was not sure that he understood, he decided that he did not wish to do anything that would interfere with her plans or interests or with Mrs. Webb's; he was half inclined to let the poem die.[30] Its value as a Republican campaign piece had not yet occurred to him.

XVIII
1856 - 57

During 1856 Whittier was so busy with a wide range of interests that, in spite of his lament that his poor health kept him from active part in the Fremont campaign, he seemed once more to have the energy and enthusiasm of youth.

The year began badly. The weather was so cold that, he said, Bayard Taylor could have found Lapland in Amesbury and need not travel over the Lapp mountains. His mother had become feeble, able to get around the house but seldom able to go to Friends Meeting, only a short distance from the Whittiers' house. Elizabeth had not fully recovered from typhoid fever. Word had come of the death of Stephen Grellet; Whittier's response, however, was not a lament but a reaffirmation of his own faith: "He is Stephen Grellet still; and the prayer of my heart is that I may be permitted through infinite mercy, all unworthy as I feel myself to be, to see him once more where there is no death."[1]

Whittier's attitude toward "The Panorama" had changed, and he wished to have it published immediately in book form. Fields pointed out that it would be too late for the holiday season and suggested the fall of 1856. Whittier persisted: "The Panorama" was a poem for the present time, and he would like to have it put through the press with other pieces at once. One of the other pieces was "Mary Garvin," which was then in manuscript and which Whittier liked better than "Maud Muller."[2] "Mary Garvin" did not attain anything like the popularity of "Maud Muller," but it is easy to see why Whittier liked it. It was a relief from the polemical writing that he had been doing, especially the lengthy "Panorama". It began with a contrast between past and present, a theme which Whittier always enjoyed, and it had a pleasant bit of romance proving the original last line of the fourth stanza:

Tradition, snowy bearded, leans on Romance, ever young.

It also gave a chance for another reminder of a truth that Whittier helped nineteenth century America to learn:

Creed and rite perchance may differ, yet our faith and
        hope are one.

The Panorama and Other Poems was published in March. Two thousand copies were printed, of which eighteen hundred were sold at fifty cents, Whittier's royalty being one hundred eighty dollars. Whittier sent a copy to Josiah Quincy, who acknowledged it in a letter written in the formal style of an earlier day. Few, he said, could "compete in the purity of motive and

elevation of purpose, conjoined with the searching keenness of Christian-
ized invective." Later in the year *Songs of Labor and Other Poems* was
reissued in a third edition of five hundred copies for which Whittier received
twenty-five dollars.[3]

In March a poem appeared in the *Era*, rather belatedly, about an event
which had occurred in Kansas in December. Thomas Barber, a free-state set-
tler from Ohio, was shot and killed near Lawrence. In "The Burial of Barber"
Whittier pictured the corpse being carried up the icy hill but did not mention
that the funeral was held in the Free State Hotel.[4] The emphasis in the poem
was on an appeal to patience and trust in God that a better time would come.

Spring opened unhappily. In spite of his improvement in health, Whittier
complained that the winds were cruel. Elizabeth had suffered emotionally
from her long illness, and he had been forced to look on at her sadness and
suffering without being able to cheer her. He was worried about a bill in
the Massachusetts Legislature to repeal the Personal Liberty Law which he
had celebrated in "Arisen at Last" less than a year ago.[5]

His picture, in a group lithograph by Leopold Grozelier entitled
"Freedom's Champions," seemed to him to indicate more health and robust
life than he could boast of. But his mother approved of it and a three-year-
old boy had recognized it, and so he thought that it must be somewhat of
a likeness. Whittier's criticism of the picture seems justified when one com-
pares it with an ambrotype taken only a year later. He hoped that the
publisher would lose nothing by his kindly attempt to gratify public curiosity.

The public was gratifying its curiosity in another way. Visitors came to
the Friends meeting in Amesbury for the sake of looking at him.[6] He was
also paying another price for fame, one which his kindness and sense of
obligation to others kept him paying as long as he lived. He was asked for
help and advice in placing manuscripts. . . . . . "Hoping that the little obscure
maiden struggling in the tide at your feet may not be considered presumptuous
in reaching up for a helping hand to one so secure in his serene and beautiful
elevation," one young authoress wrote to him. But fame brought compensa-
tions. He must have felt some satisfaction when he read a review in the
highly-regarded *Putnam's Monthly* for July: "His place is as determined and
distinctive as any of our acknowledged poets. Many of his abolition poems
are superb specimens of poetic indignation."[7]

His growing importance did not keep him from doing his share of community work. He was active in the newly organized Amesbury and Salisbury
Agricultural Society and in the newly founded Amesbury Public Library.
The Agricultural Society was organized April 14 with Whittier as its Corresponding Secretary.[8] He continued his interest in the society for many years,
entering pears in its annual fairs and writing hymns for its religious services
or getting friends to write them.

The Public Library met a real need. Few people in Amesbury and Salisbury could afford to buy many books, and the Salisbury Manufacturing Company had not continued Joshua Aubin's policy of maintaining a library for its employees, although it offered a room rent-free in one of its buildings. Joshua Aubin had taken his books to his home in Newburyport when he retired, and now offered them to the new Amesbury and Salisbury Library Association. They were accepted and placed under the control of a Board of Trustees which included Whittier. This Board worked harmoniously with the officers of the Library Association, and a joint committee, of which Whittier was chairman, was appointed to buy two hundred dollars' worth of books. The Library was opened early in June with eleven hundred seventy volumes and two hundred twenty-four subscribers. It received no support from public funds in either town and was public only in the sense that anyone in either town might become a subscriber by paying one dollar a year. Whittier remained a Trustee of the Aubin books and later a Trustee of the Library as long as he lived. For many years he chose and bought the books, often getting them at a reduced price through James T. Fields, and he wrote all or part of some of the annual reports. He frequently presented books, some of which are still on the Library shelves.[9]

His acquaintance with new books must have helped him to make good selections. In the *Era* of May 1 he noticed Frederick Law Olmsted's *A Journey Through the Seaboard Slave States* and reported that every phase of Southern life and manners was pictured with minute detail. Mrs. Southworth's *India*, which had appeared in the *Era* under the title of "Mark Sutherland," was an "admirable tale." *Edith Hale* was a "spirited and graphic New England story," and *Wolfsden*, as a picture of New England rural life, had few equals in American literature, but its plot was not particularly ingenious and its style sometimes in bad taste. A new, revised edition of Bayard Taylor's *Poems of Home and Travel* aroused his enthusiasm, and he made a comment which was doubtless as acceptable to his own time as it would be distasteful to the literary world a century later. The poems had the "healthful warmth of a strong, brave, and beautiful life, in which romance and adventure are tempered by an abiding sense of moral obligation, and that charity and kindly sympathy with human life in all its phases, which mark the travelled gentleman and Christian cosmopolitan."

A friend living in Plymouth sent some mayflowers on April 30 with a note: "There is such meaning in the mayflower to all descendants of the Pilgrims and to all lovers of freedom."[10] He replied with the poem "The Mayflowers," which was printed in the *Era* of June 6 with only the first sentence of the present headnote. The last two stanzas developed the thought in the note sent with the flowers: the ship *Mayflower* is symbolic of the struggling cause of Freedom.

The cause of Freedom had an unexpected bonanza May 23. Charles Sumner, seated at his desk in the Senate Chamber, was beaten on the head with a cane by Preston Brooks. The assault may have been prompted, as has been claimed, by Sumner's remarks about a relative of Brooks, the elderly Senator Andrew P. Butler of South Carolina, of whom he said in a speech in the Senate May 19 and 20, "The Senator from South Carolina has read many books of chivalry, and believes himself a chivalrous knight, with sentiments of honor and courage. Of course he has chosen a mistress to whom he has made his vows, and who, though ugly to others, is always lovely to him; though polluted in the sight of the world, is chaste in his sight — I mean the harlot, slavery. For her his tongue is always profuse in words."[11] But the assault aroused Anti-Slavery sentiment as nothing else could have done and made Sumner a martyr whose cause was greatly strengthened. The once conservative *Newburyport Herald*, after asserting that there were no Abolitionists in Newburyport (a false statement: there were a few but they were, in general, unimportant persons) said that the moderates could no longer be moderate. Violence might be met with violence, blood might follow blood, but they would yield no more; they forgot the guilty culprit in their curses upon the institution that made such culprits.

Whittier wrote to Sumner June 13. His heart was full of gratitude and joy that Sumner's life had been spared to his friends and to Freedom. His speech on May 19 and 20 was "a grand and terrible phillipic, worthy of the great occasion." Everything indicated that it had saved the country. If a Free State President was elected it would be solely through the influence of that speech. But he cautioned Sumner not to return to his Senatorial duties during that session and to avoid all excitement; he almost dreaded to have Sumner come North because the feelings of people of all classes were so wrought up that they might retard his recovery by their demonstrations.[12] The same thought occurred to Amos A. Lawrence, whose attitude is a good example of popular sentiment. He was wealthy, a conservative, and not a supporter of Sumner, but he regarded Brooks' assault as a national issue. When Sumner had partially recovered and was on his way to Boston, Lawrence arranged to have him taken from the train at Cottage Farm Station to Lawrence's beautiful home, with its open lawn and oak grove, to rest over Sunday.[13]

In Amesbury, as everywhere else, Sumner sympathy meetings were held. These meetings had no definite purpose, but people wanted to express their feelings and the only way to do it was to have a meeting, which often turned into a Republican organization meeting or at least led in that direction. Whittier meant to have this happen in Amesbury and wrote a letter, one phrase in which, according to the *Villager*, seemed to animate all minds, and which turned the feelings of the gathering into anger against the slave-holding South. The letter said that he sympathized with the object of the meeting, but it was no time for indulgence of emotions. Why had the South dared to treat the North in this way? There was a simple answer: the North was not united for Freedom as the South was for slavery. Couldn't a start be made in this very neighborhood, Whigs, Democrats, Free Soilers, and Americans (as the Know-Nothings now called themselves) joining in defense of freedom? They must — this was the phrase that made the strong impression — "forget, forgive, and unite," not to threaten violent reprisals but simply to vote against slavery.[14]

The Republican national convention met in Philadelphia June 17. Whittier was of course pleased with the nomination of Fremont, which he thought appealed to all that was good and generous in young America and touched the popular heart. But he was not pleased with the Vice Presidential nomination. There had been an informal understanding among the leaders of the convention that the man nominated by the North Americans, a moderate Anti-Slavery group that had seceded from the Americans, should receive second place on the ticket. When the Republican leaders saw the heavy vote for Fremont they decided that compromise with the North Americans was no longer necessary and nominated their own candidate. This, Whittier thought, was a blunder and should be admitted by the Republicans: "We must *not* divide on so small a matter if, as I believe, a frank confession of error can prevent it."[15] However, he did not make this objection known to the public, and he entered whole-heartedly into the Fremont campaign.

Fremont ratification meetings were held everywhere as a way of showing that people approved of the nominations. The meeting in Amesbury was on July 2, and the next day the *Villager* printed a song used there. This song, with the omission of the second and fourth stanzas, was printed in the *Era*, unsigned, on the same day. It was without question written by Whittier; it was in the iambic tetrameter couplets that he used in other campaign songs and was probably the one referred to by Elizabeth in a letter to Moses Cartland July 25. It was no better than campaign poetry usually was, and the various rhymes with "Fremont" showed again Whittier's poor sense of vowel sounds: hunt, confront, upon't, point, bout, disappoint, front.

Whittier was chairman of the committee that presented a set of resolutions. It contained an obvious appeal to the American and North American parties and to Anti-Slavery Democrats: Fremont's administration would "combine the Americanism of Washington with the Democracy of Jefferson," and the friends of freedom in all parties must remember that without union nothing could be done. Then there was an address by Stephen H. Phillips, who had been a delegate to the Republican convention. By this time there had been as much seriousness and dignity as the audience could enjoy, and there was a call for Nahum Osgood, the muscular butcher who had stood at the head of the stairway at Franklin Hall ready to throw anyone downstairs who threatened to disturb Anti-Slavery meetings. He came forward and made what the *Villager* called "one of his eccentric appeals," to which the audience replied with applause and shouts of approval.[16]

Whittier had strong hopes that Fremont would be elected and that his election would be the beginning of national regeneration. In fact, for once everything seemed bright and cheerful. Early in August he and Elizabeth went to a Fremont rally in Exeter, New Hampshire; the weather was beautiful, the rally large and successful, and they "enjoyed it exceedingly." They were also enjoying some maple syrup that the Cartlands had sent them, the nicest and clearest that he had ever seen and which had "the flavor of the free hills of freedom."[17]

To keep clear the picture of Fremont that appealed to the public, especially the young — and on this topic Whittier himself was young at heart — he wrote "The Pass of the Sierra," which appeared in the *Era* of July 17. The summons to Fremont in the last stanza to put on his hunting-shirt once more and lead in Freedom's van would not attract thoughtful voters — an explorer is not necessarily, or even probably, likely to be a good President — but Whittier had learned that not all voters are thoughtful, and as far as Fremont was concerned, Whittier himself was not. A song by Whittier and one by Elizabeth, who was as enthusiastic as her brother about Fremont, were written to be set to music and used in the campaign. Whittier's was "We're Free" and hers was "Fremont's Ride;" they were both printed anonymously in the *Era* of August 14.

Charles A. Dana of the *New York Tribune* had written to Whittier in June telling the importance of songs in the campaign. Whittier's song, later called "A Fremont Campaign Song," written to the music of "Suona La Tromba," was entered in a contest which was won by Charles S. Weyman, whose song was printed in the *Tribune* September 13.[18] Whittier's song was printed in the *Villager* September 11 and in a song sheet with seven other Fremont campaign songs published in Hartford, Connecticut.

A more thoughtful poem than these campaign pieces was the Apocalyptic "What of the Day?" printed without title in the *Era* of September 4, with some variations from the present form. There is no doubt that it expressed Whittier's sincere conviction that a major crisis was at hand and that he wished he could have faith in the ultimate triumph of right. It is an interesting example of Biblical imagery and phrasing, and for once Whittier did not add lines to explain in simple language what he meant. In fact, he once said that he didn't know himself what he meant by it. Years later his friends thought that they knew and suggested it be placed in the appendix of the biography that Francis H. Underwood was preparing; they regarded it as an almost prophetic foreshadowing of the Civil War.[19]

"To Pennsylvania," written September 19, was also serious and thoughtful: God had given Pennsylvania the power to ruin or to save in Freedom's hour of sorest need. It was evidently intended to influence the state election in October, and on the day he wrote it he offered it to George William Curtis to use in one of his speeches. When the state went Democratic by a small margin, Whittier wrote to Richard H. Dana Jr. urging him to visit Pennsylvania before the National election to speak in Philadelphia and perhaps in other places, mainly to the Friends and the cautious conservative class who were repelled by the usual campaign tactics. Dana replied that he was gratified by the compliment and had offered to go to Pennsylvania as soon as he heard of the Republican defeat. He agreed with Whittier that this election was the last chance that they could rely on for the cause of freedom.[20]

Whittier was not too absorbed in the Republican campaign to write an ode, now entitled "A Lay of Old Time," for the Essex Agricultural Fair in Newburyport. The fair was grand and respectable. On the second day, October 2, seven hundred carriages came into Newburyport over Chain Bridge, and a crowded passenger train, the longest ever seen on the railroad from the farming section of Essex County, arrived at 9:30. Among the passengers was George Peabody, who had once worked in a store in Newburyport and was now living in London, fabulously rich and philanthropic. Fourteen hundred persons had a dinner of beef, ham, potatoes, turkey, chicken, roast pig, bread, a variety of pies, and fruit — but no stronger drink than cold water. Then there were speeches, and finally Whittier's ode, sung by a member of H. S. Thompson's Glee Club. Whittier received a vote of thanks. He had already sent the ode to the *Era*, where it appeared the next day.[21]

After the Republican defeat in November, Whittier was not in the mood of despair that would be expected from his earlier attitude that only the election of Fremont could save the country from disaster and disgrace. The result, he wrote to Sumner, was better than he had dared to hope — thus directly contradicting what he had said in the summer. If the party could hold what it had gained, victory would be only delayed four years.[22]

The Republican leaders were equally confident — or at least said that they were — and Whittier's post-election "Song, Inscribed to the Fremont Clubs" sounded a popular note. It had some curiously military and un-Quaker-like metaphors: closing the ranks, sounding the bugles, calling the muster-roll, and

> Another Balaklava
> And the Malakoff is ours!

Perhaps Whittier was trying to reach readers who were familiar with Tennyson's "Charge of the Light Brigade," but one cannot avoid the suspicion that in his enthusiasm and excitement he had reverted to his boyhood love of battles. The final stanza of the Song as it appeared in the *Era* was later omitted. It was probably not looked upon with favor by the leading Republicans at the time, and would have been wholly unacceptable four years later:

> But keep the same old banner,
> For better none can be;

Pass on the same old watchword
Fremont and Victory![23]

Among the blessings that Whittier had believed would come from Fremont's election was law and order in Kansas. He had heard that a Friends school in Kansas had just been broken up, and he thought that the Friends there were deserving of sympathy. "Almost anyone can fight even in a bad cause," he wrote, "but the sublime self-abnegation of martyrdom is rarely found."[24] A few weeks later he quoted in the *Era* a letter in the *Friends Review* from Richard Mendenhall, who had just settled with his two brothers and their families near Osawatomie and who became, strangely enough, an intimate friend of John Brown. The letter described the difficult situation of about twenty Quaker families scattered over the territory. Since the Quakers could not fight even in self-defense, Whittier made the practical suggestion that funds for the relief of sufferers in Kansas might be sent to them by people who wished to be sure that their contributions were not used for military purposes.[25]

As a member of a local committee collecting money for Kansas relief, he wrote a newspaper appeal. There were few people, he said, who could not spare at least a small sum "to save from actual suffering a noble and heroic community, striving to maintain free institutions in the distant prairies of the West."[26] Whittier and the Baptist minister signed the acknowledgements of the committee and published a final report in the *Villager* of December 11; $171.75 had been collected in the Mills District in Amesbury, $156.38 in Salisbury, and sixty dollars had been made by a levee.

On the same day, "The Conquest of Finland" appeared in the *Era*. Whittier had read a letter in the *Friends Review* telling that Joseph Sturge and Thomas Harvey had been visiting the towns and villages of Finland along the shores of the Gulf of Bothnia which had been burned and ravaged by the British fleet during the Crimean War, to make a survey of the needs of the poor sufferers. (Sturge and his brother gave one thousand pounds to a relief fund of nine thousand pounds.) The poem was longer than necessary, but was obviously Whittier's sincere rejoicing that the hatred caused by wanton destruction had been replaced by a feeling of brotherhood, and it made Charles Sumner's pulse beat quick and his eyes moisten with tears.[27]

On a late fall day Whittier walked along the path by the Merrimac River in Pleasant Valley, observing what was about him with his usual keenness and accuracy and thinking about his own place in the scheme of things. There was only the slightest connection between what he saw and what he thought, as is the way of the average man, who does his thinking when he is experiencing something that does not demand his action.

The descriptive stanzas in "The Last Walk in Autumn" have some good lines:

The sea's long level dim with rain

The hoar plume of the golden-rod
and the wild geese
Like a great arrow through the sky,
Two dusky lines converged in one.

The stanzas telling his thoughts have little to interest the critic, but were a good explanation of the sane and balanced adjustment to life of a humanitarian and lover of beauty. Like the Transcendentalists of his day, within his own surroundings Whittier could see the entire world and the universe:

Earth wheels with all her zones, the Kosmos
stands revealed.

He was doubly blessed with the companionship of books and of men. He loved New England and its ways, and as he watched school children from his window he could live his youth over again in theirs. As for his hopes for mankind, he might never see them become facts, but he had faith that they would in due time.

Although Whittier told Fields that "The Last Walk in Autumn" was written for him and other friends and that he did not think that the public would see much in it, he sent it to the *Era*, which printed it January 1. He later said that he felt more satisfaction with it than with any except a few of his poems.[28]

The winter weather had its usual bad effect. For a time he could not leave the house without a great deal of suffering, and he could do little reading or writing. Still, he read some of Ticknor and Fields' new books, including a translation of Faust, which gave him for the first time an adequate idea of Goethe's genius. He liked the two-volume Blue and Gold Edition of Longfellow's poems which the firm had just issued at $1.75, and he thought that he would like to have his own poems published in the same edition. There was one obstacle. The copyright on the poems in the 1849 edition published by Benjamin B. Mussey & Company was owned by Sanborn, Carter, Bazin & Company. Fields reported that he had been trying to buy it, without success, but would continue his efforts. In the same letter he invited Whittier to spend a week or two at his new home at 37 Charles Street.[29] Whittier did not accept the invitation at this time, but he was a frequent visitor at the Fields house for many years, and his friendship with Mrs. Fields gave him a great deal of pleasure as long as he lived.

Fields was happy to report a month later that an arrangement had been made with the owners of the copyright, and Whittier's poems would be published in a Blue and Gold Edition. Fields described the expense of the arrangement as a very large one and said that it might be a long time before the firm got its money back. It would also be a long time before Whittier would get his usual share of the profits; because of the expense to the firm he received only five cents a copy. Three thousand copies of the first issue were printed of which twenty-eight hundred were sold, giving Whittier one hundred forty dollars.

Fields was eager to get the stereotyping done immediately and asked Whittier to send him any changes that he wished and any recent poems, along with a "pleasant daguerreotype" from which an engraving could be made.[30] The daguerreotype that Whittier sent had been taken nine years before, and he also sent an ambrotype taken recently which his friends thought was good except for "a slight grip of the mouth, giving it a little twist by way of variety" — to which he did not object: "Twists are natural to men of one idea." However, the ambrotype had given his hair and complexion a bleached look, whereas his hair was black sprinkled sufficiently with gray to give him "the *external* sign of wisdom." An engraving from the ambrotype was made by S. A. Schoff, who made the hair black and added an overcoat with an un-Quakerly collar giving added breadth to the chest and shoulders.

Whittier made numerous changes in some poems and sent the recent ones as requested. He also marked some for omission, including "Mogg Megone," which he now thought was in poor taste and objectionable from a moral point of view. Fields did not agree, and Whittier conceded that it was poetic justice that Mogg, whom he had no business to make, should haunt him like Frankenstein.[31] He wrote an apologetic introduction for the volumes, which appeared in July. He had been too ill to do the revising and rearranging that he ought to have done, and pieces were included that he would have preferred to let die.

In March his eyes were troubling him, and Elizabeth read to him Blackwood's review of Elizabeth Barrett Browning's "Aurora Leigh." His eyes were evidently better by early May. He was on a committee to write the first annual report of the Public Library and, as would be true for many years, was on the committee to buy new books.[32]

He was raising money for his early schoolmaster, Joshua Coffin, who was in the Worcester Asylum for the Insane, suffering from a physical and mental breakdown brought on, it was thought, by poverty and fear of want. Whittier wrote first to Fields, asking him to get Haskell, the editor of the *Boston Transcript*, to start a subscription and to serve as treasurer of the fund, which would be a testimonial to Coffin's services as a historian and antiquarian. Whittier described Coffin as kind-hearted, quaint, and genial, and resembling Burns' Captain Grose. Fields replied promptly with a contribution of five dollars, a promise to see Haskell, and a parody of Burns' "Written on an Envelope, Enclosing a Letter to Captain Grose."[33] He kept his promise and showed the letter to Haskell, who quoted from it in the *Transcript* of

May 7 and also quoted in full a letter which Whittier had written to the *Newburyport Herald*, which had printed it May 6. Whittier himself sent five dollars to Fields to give to Haskell, with the injunction that Haskell should not use his name again in the *Transcript* and some humorous stanzas suggested by Fields' parody. He asked help from some women in Newburyport, including Mrs. Samuel J. Spalding, wife of the pastor of the new, prosperous, and fashionable Whitefield Church, and from some of his personal friends including Daniel Neall and Samuel E. Sewall.[34] The subscription was a success, Coffin's health improved, and he was able to return to his home.

Whittier's five-dollar contribution to the fund for Coffin was more than could have been expected. His friends regarded him as in need of help himself. He was no longer writing long prose essays for the *Era*, and Elizabeth's illness must have caused some expense. Fields had offered him a loan, with the suggestion that it need not be returned. Some English Quakers heard of his difficulties and sent money which he reluctantly but gratefully accepted. His health continued bad, and he was suffering from rheumatism. Joseph Sturge offered him free passage in one of his ships in the hope that a sea voyage would restore his health. He was well enough in June, however, to go to the New England Yearly Meeting of Friends in Newport, where Augustine Jones saw him for the first time and was impressed by his "remarkable countenance," which awakened "the deepest interest in the stranger."[35]

Two months later he called on Charlotte Forten at the Remonds' home in Salem. She was impressed by his "noble, spiritual face" and "glorious eyes" — and was so overawed that she could not think of anything to say and was tormented by the thought that he would regard her as stupid and foolish. He tactfully made a few brief remarks that put her a little at ease and then talked with Miss Remond until Charlotte completely recovered and was ready to talk with him. The talk drifted to spiritualism, which was then receiving a good deal of attention. Whittier had become interested in it and sometimes went with his mother and Elizabeth to the meetings of a spiritualist circle under the leadership of Mary Esther Carter in a house around the corner on School Street. He never lost interest in the topic but kept the same attitude that he had during this conversation with Charlotte Forten: he could not believe in it but was tolerant of those that did. From this there was a natural transition to the topic of life after death, in which, as he would do again and again for the rest of his life, he expressed his perfect faith.[36]

Whittier was now turning more often and with obvious pleasure to Essex County history and legend. When he read in Mirick's *History of Haverhill* that the sycamore (buttonwood) trees in front of the house now owned by the Haverhill Historical Society had been set out in 1739 by "one Hugh Talent, a wanderer from the green fields of Erin, and who was a famous fiddler," he wrote the first draft of a stanza of "The Sycamores" on the margin of the page. As happened in the writing of other poems, an incident suggested a story which he wrote without trying to find whether the account was correct or whether there were further facts that would enrich the narrative. "The Sycamores" appeared in the *Era* of June 11, where it attracted the attention of Caroline L. Tallant of Nantucket, great-granddaughter of Hugh Tallant, as the name was now spelled, and she wrote Whittier to ask if her ancestor was the Hugh of the poem. Whittier replied that he was almost as much surprised by her letter as if Hugh himself had appeared; in fact, he had thought of the story as a myth. He had now looked up additional facts and wished that he had done so before writing the poem.[37]

Two other poems with origins in Essex County soon appeared in the *Era*. An early form of "Mabel Martin" entitled "The Witch's Daughter" was in the issue of August 20. It consisted of Parts II - VI of "Mabel Martin" with the exception of seventeen stanzas and with two stanzas later omitted. The story was a fictional account of the marriage of Ezekiel Worthen ("Esek Harden") and Hannah ("Mabel") Martin, step-daughter of Susanna Martin of Amesbury. It showed Esek defending Mabel when she was shunned and insulted because her mother had been hanged as a witch and following her to her home to tell her that he would marry her. Actually Ezekiel Worthen married Hannah Martin in 1661, thirty-one years before Susanna's trial and execution. Readers liked the sentimentality and the happy ending, and were not well enough informed about New England witchcraft to notice the improbability; witchcraft was too deadly a topic to be referred to as lightly as the remark of a pert young girl at the husking bee when Esek defended Mabel —

> The little witch is evil eyed!
> Her mother only killed a cow,
> Or witched a churn or dairy-pan;
> But she, forsooth, must charm a man!

There was better and more realistic treatment of legendary material in "The Garrison of Cape Ann," dated October 12, in the *Era* of October 22. The introductory stanzas described Whittier's more mature awareness of the values in New England folklore of the time when life was outwardly coarse and mean but inwardly made grand by awe and reverence. There were good descriptive lines:

> Wood and rock and gleaming sand-drift, jagged capes,
>   with brush and tree
> Leaning inward from the smiting of the wild and gusty sea.
> . . . . . the beach-bird seaward flying with his slant wing to
>   the sun.

The soldiers in front of the fireplace, holding their muskets, eating from a haunch of venison on a rough oak table, and drinking from a pewter tankard handed from one to another were true to their time, superstitious and fearful of the unknown. The poem was far superior to Whittier's "The Spectre Warriors" of 1830, and the concluding stanzas on prayer had at least the merit of telling the effect of prayer on one's own thoughts and not, as many of Whittier's contemporaries would have been willing to accept, on outward forces.

His increasing appreciation of the past did not distract his attention from problems of the present. He was chairman of the business committee at a meeting of the Essex County Temperance Society in Amesbury September 17 and reported a set of resolutions which was not confined to approval of anti-liquor laws. It included the recommendation of homes for alcoholics in all large cities and towns. It recognized that the problem of the young drinker must be met by something more than a negative prohibitory attitude and suggested lyceums, reading rooms and libraries, and social gatherings.[38]

A few weeks later, Elizabeth was reading Browning's *Men and Women* and was telling her brother that it was "great." He dipped into it here and there but did not find it "comfortable" reading. It seemed like a galvanic battery in full play, and its "spasmodic utterances and intense passion" made him feel as if he had been taking a bath among electric eels.[39] A poem which he wrote at the time, however, showed Browning's influence in its metrical form, which approached Browning's "spasmodic utterances" although it had no touch of his intensity of passion. "The Eve of Election," written November 2, was a solemn appeal to voters to make noble and unselfish use of the privilege of the ballot, won for them by the sacrifice of martyrs. The tone of the poem was set by the quiet of an Indian Summer moonlit night, for which the alternating long and short, abrupt lines were hardly suitable and suggest that the rhythm of Browning's "A Lover's Quarrel" and "A Pretty Woman" was in Whittier's mind.

This poem ended Whittier's eleventh year of writing for the *National Era*, the last year in which the larger part of his work was published there. He had now achieved a recognition that was to place him with the leading literary group in America. He had come a long distance from the days on the farm when his sister Mary sent his poems to a little weekly newspaper in Newburyport.

John C. Fremont (1813-1890).

Joshua Coffin (1792-1864).

James T. Fields (1817-1881).

Annie Fields (1834-1915).

XIX
1857 - 58, 59

Nothing could have been better proof of Whittier's acceptance by the literary world than a letter from James Russell Lowell asking him to be a a regular contributor to a new magazine to be published in Boston. Lowell was already sure of Emerson, Longfellow, Holmes, and Hawthorne,[1] and it was evident that the magazine, which would soon be named the *Atlantic Monthly*, would be the leading literary periodical in America.

The first number of the *Atlantic* appeared in November and had Whittier's "Gift of Tritemius," the story — "invented," according to Whittier — of the gift of the altar candlesticks of silver to redeem a poor woman's son from slavery and the miraculous replacement of them by candlesticks of gold. Lowell, who was the real editor while Francis H. Underwood handled business details, disliked the four consecutive rhymes "door, poor, store, more," and meant to ask Whittier to change them in the proof, but neglected to do so and found that no one else seemed to be bothered by them. Everybody liked the poem, he wrote to Whittier, and it was "going the rounds."[2] Whittier's contemporaries evidently found its message convincing. Two years later Thomas Starr King read it to a meeting in San Francisco as the conclusion of an appeal for contributions to an orphan asylum: three hundred dollars was as much as the committee expected, and King was sure that Whittier's poem could be credited with the added four hundred dollars.

The second number contained "Skipper Ireson's Ride." As on other occasions, Whittier saw a chance for a good story and wrote it without verifying the facts. It was suggested by a rhyme which he thought that he had heard repeated by a schoolmate from Marblehead, but he may have remembered it from the *Newburyport Herald* of July 18, 1828, where it was quoted in a letter signed "A Native of Marblehead."[3] Lowell was familiar with it and suggested that the refrain be in dialect, and his opinion was confirmed by Underwood, who consulted Charles W. Storey, a native of Marblehead. Whittier agreed to the change when the lines occurred as a quotation from the song of the Marblehead women.[4]

Lowell liked the poem and wrote to Whittier: "I defy you or anybody else to write anything so good as Skipper Ireson within the twelve-month."[5] He was no more interested than Whittier in verifying the facts, which could have been found in several newspapers published in November 1808, soon after the event occurred. Over twenty years later Samuel Roads told the correct story in his *History of Marblehead*. It was Captain Ireson's crew and not the Captain himself who was responsible for sailing away from a sinking ship. Roads sent a copy of his book to Whittier, who replied in a letter May 18, 1880, printed in the second edition of Roads' *History* and in the headnote to the poem in later editions. He had supposed that the story dated back at least a century, he knew nothing of the particulars, the narrative was "pure fancy," and he was glad that the facts had been given in Roads' book: "I certainly would not knowingly do injustice to anyone, dead or living."

The poem contained an error in a literary reference which evidently neither Lowell nor Underwood noticed. The fourth line:

Or one-eyed Calendar's horse of brass

must have been intended to refer to the third Calendar (or royal mendicant) in the Arabian Nights who was mounted on a magical black horse, not a brass one, which, when struck, expanded a pair of wings, soared to a great height, alighted on a roof of a palace, and struck out his rider's eye with a blow of his tail.

He sent "The Eve of Election" to the *Atlantic* and then decided that it would be better in the *Era*.[6] In its place he sent "The Old Burying Ground," which appeared in the February *Atlantic*. Lowell's first impression was that it would be more effective if it were shorter; he changed his mind a few weeks later and explained that he was too tired to appreciate fully anything in manuscript. The present-day reader would agree with Lowell's first impression. There is good nature description, with the simple, sharp-cut details from accurate observation and clear pictorial memory that Whittier could do especially well, but the reader finds it hard to follow from nature's beauty in the neglected graveyard to the Transcendentalist concept that all things are one. Whittier himself said that the poem was not as good as he had hoped; for some weeks his mother's serious illness kept him from any revision. After his mother's death December 27 he was able to give it some attention, and he sent Lowell a few suggested changes. The poem now had added significance; part of it had been written while he was watching at his mother's sickbed during the three weeks of her final illness.[7]

Bachelors are more affected by the illness and death of parents than married men are, and Whittier was no exception. "We are stunned by the great bereavement," he wrote to Sumner. "The world looks far less than it did when she was with us. Half the motive power of life is lost." He found some satisfaction in the fact that her mind was clear until the end, and she died in "exceeding peace and with an unshaken trust in the boundless mercy of our Lord." He and Elizabeth had Thomas Lawson paint her portrait, at a cost of forty dollars.[8]

The relief by a Scottish regiment of the besieged British in the city of Lucknow during the Sepoy rebellion stirred public imagination, and Whittier was not the only one inspired to write about it. In fact, someone got ahead of him in sending a poem to the *Atlantic*. On January 10 Whittier sent his poem, "The Pipes at Lucknow," and followed it with a letter adding a stanza and assuring Lowell that he had strictly followed the facts. When he had not heard from Lowell by January 20, he wrote to Underwood that he would like to make other changes if the poem was to be used. Underwood called the matter to the attention of Lowell, who wrote an apologetic letter to Whittier, holding out his hand, he said, "for the ferule like a man." He explained that the constant distraction of the printing office had made him neglect to write to Whittier.[9] Before the arrival of Whittier's poem another poem on the same topic had been received and set in type, Robert T.S. Lowell's "The Relief of Lucknow." It was decidedly inferior to Whittier's, which appeared in the *Era* of February 4.

The next poem to be published in the *Atlantic* was "Telling the Bees," which has been generally looked upon with favor even by those who criticize or ridicule Whittier's all-too-frequent faults; it was exactly the right length and told its story with moving simplicity, true but restrained emotion, and delicately outlined pictures. But Whittier had doubts: "What I call simplicity," he wrote to Lowell, "may be only silliness, and my poor bantling only fit to be handed over to Dr. Howe's school for feeble-minded children." He had evidently been amused by a letter that he had recently received asking him to write some verses to be sung by the children in the Pennsylvania School for Feeble-Minded Children as part of an appeal to the public and legislature for funds for a new building. The setting of "Telling the Bees" was the farm at East Haverhill, and the description was accurate, the story fictitious. "Snow-Bound" would have the same setting and the same accuracy of description but would be autobiographical.

A second letter to Lowell about "Telling the Bees" made some changes and told him to send it back if he had any doubts about it, without troubling to give reasons. The letter concluded: "But at any rate let me hear from thee in some way. If thee fail to do this, I shall turn thee out of thy professor's chair, by virtue of my new office of 'Overseer'."[10]

This humorous comment on a very important appointment indicates a surprising sense of values on Whittier's part. He had recently been elected an Overseer of Harvard College and he remained a member of the Board until 1871. In March he was appointed chairman of the examining committee on the modern languages. During these years he was present at only four meetings.[11] Nothing could be better proof of his being, like most Americans of his time, essentially small-town and rural than the fact that he was more interested in Amesbury Public Library than in Harvard College and took his duties there more seriously than those as Overseer of one of the most important institutions of learning in the Western Hemisphere.

In 1858 he was chairman of a committee to examine the books in Amesbury Public Library and prepare an annual report. Later in the year he sent Fields a list of books for the Library, including, along with some recent fiction, Carlyle's *Frederick the Great* and Holmes' *Autocrat of the Breakfast Table*, which had been appearing in the *Atlantic* and which he called "thrice excellent," adding a prophetic comment: "The Chambered Nautilus" was "booked for immortality."[12]

He also continued his interest in the local agricultural association, which in September held the first of a series of annual Agricultural and Horticultural Fairs. Whittier entered some pears and won first prize on his Flemish Beauties and second on his Beurre de Capiaumonts. The Fair included a religious service September 28 at the Congregational Church. Whittier wrote a hymn to be sung there, now called "A Song of Harvest," and was rewarded by a gift of fruit and flowers from the Fair, and a few weeks later by an "elegant fruit basket." The letter of thanks for the fruit basket concluded with a paragraph which was unquestionably sincere and was evidence of his local interest and sentiment:

"I value this testimonial all the more, that, coming from my immediate neighbors, it evinces the fact of mutual good feeling and regard. A token of approbation even from strangers is not unwelcome; but I place a higher estimate on that which assures me of the esteem of my everyday acquaintance, and that I have a place in the kind thought of 'mine own people'."[13]

"Song of Harvest" got more attention than it would a century later, with its didactic moralizing and its conclusion that good deeds will come to fruition in Heaven. It was translated into Portuguese by Rev. James Cooley Fletcher and read by Dom Pedro at a harvest festival in Brazil and into Italian to be sung at peasants' gatherings in Italy.[14] One cannot help wondering what Brazilian or Italian peasants found to respond to in a poem so purely New England-Protestant-rural.

He also continued his interest in temperance and made some suggestions at a meeting in Amesbury in November which enlarged upon those that he had made a year ago. They showed that Whittier was aware of what was happening in fields in which he himself had no especial interest and also of the newly awakened interest in athletic sports — until recently everyone except the rich got all the physical exercise he wanted and more in his daily labor:

"I would throw open, as far as possible, to the young the curious and beautiful in art, science, and literature — the telescopic revelations of astronomy — the wonders of geology — the lithography of the eternal finger on the primal formations. I would open to them new sources of enjoyment in the studies of natural history and botany, and show them the almost magical results of experimental chemistry. I would give them every opportunity to listen to lectures and discourses from variously gifted orators and thinkers. I would encourage reading circles, healthful sports and exercises and excursions amid the serene beauty of nature, so well calculated to exalt the mind towards that which St. Augustine speaks of as 'the Eternal beauty new or old.'

"I would promote libraries and debating clubs, whatever, in short, promises to promote enjoyment with the culture of the mind and heart and the healthful development of a sound mind in a sound body."[15]

George B. Cheever, pastor of the Church of the Puritans in New York, to whom Whittier addressed a poem of four stanzas printed in the *Era* of April 1, was a vigorous controversialist on various issues. He had written "The True History of Deacon Giles' Distillery," an account with fictitious names of a distillery owned by a church deacon. Not all of his ideas would have been acceptable to Whittier: he advocated capital punishment. But Whittier approved his attack on slavery in *God Against Slavery*, published in 1857. "To George B. Cheever" compared Cheever to Amos, Hosea, and Isaiah: he was smiting a guilty nation's ears with truth.

There was nothing in "To George B. Cheever" nor in "Le Marais du Cygne" to support Longfellow's comment after meeting Whittier at Ticknor and Fields': "He grows milder and mellower, as does his poetry." In fact, when writing of the massacre in southern Kansas which was the subject of the poem, first called "The Marsh of the Swan," he felt "a good deal more like a wild berserk than like a carpet minstrel 'with his singing robes about him'." He sent it to Underwood with the question, "Do you publish such incendiary pieces as this?" and the request that it be returned *at once* if it could not be printed in the August *Atlantic*; perhaps it could take the place of "To —. On receiving his 'Few Verses for a Few Friends'," which was already in type for the August number.[16] In spite of Whittier's injunction, the poem was delayed until September, and "To —" (later entitled "To James T. Fields") appeared in August.

"To —" was hastily written, but Elizabeth thought that it was good enough to publish.[17] The stanzas were in the same form as Tennyson's "In Memoriam," which Whittier referred to a year later as "great and deep and earnest and loving." There was an echo of Wordsworth in one stanza:

. . . . . Craves its common food —
Our human nature's daily bread

reminds the reader of the lines in "She Was a Phantom of Delight":

A creature not too bright or good
For human nature's daily food.

The mildness and the mellowness that Longfellow thought he saw in Whittier appeared now and then. In the spring he and Elizabeth drove to Folly Mill Woods in Seabrook, just across the New Hampshire line, and picked mayflowers. Early in the summer Charles A. Barry made a crayon drawing of him,[18] which looks mild and mellow to the point of weakness, and is as sentimental as the poem "The Sisters" which he wrote about a picture by Barry in the Boston Atheneum. It is another bit of evidence of Whittier's being in tune with his time that he could write these lines and allow them to be used in collections of his poems:

So come to me, my little one, —
   My years with thee I share,
And mingle with a sister's love
   A mother's tender care.

"Trinitas" appeared in the *Era* of April 8. It was a rather fanciful and sentimental interpretation of the doctrine of the Trinity and must have been welcomed by many people who were increasingly repelled by the hard logic of Calvinism and by what Whittier called the "creedmongers."

"The Swan Song of Parson Avery" appeared in the July *Atlantic*. Whittier got the title from the account in Mather's *Magnalia* of the wreck of the ship in which Parson Avery and his family were sailing from Newbury to Marblehead.[19] One may doubt that the church at Newbury was especially "stricken" by the news of the drowning of the Avery family. There is no record that he had any official connection with the Newbury church, of which Thomas Parker was the recognized pastor. Possibly he had come to Newbury with the plan of acting as assistant to Parker. He could not have been in Newbury more than a few weeks when he left August 15 to become pastor at Marblehead. The fourteenth stanza in the present form was not in the *Atlantic*, and perhaps Whittier added it after reading Rosetti's "The Blessed Damozel."[20]

In September the *Villager* quoted from the *Newburyport Herald* the regret of the editor that "a well-known gentleman of a neighboring town is not so situated that he can be induced to become a candidate." The reference was to an election to Congress in the Sixth Essex District. The editor of the *Villager* knew that the Newburyport editor referred to Whittier, and that the district would give a unanimous and hearty approval. Whittier does not seem to have been interested, but a few days later was concerned about a suggestion that Charles Sumner should resign. Sumner had been reelected and had returned to the Senate in December, against the advice of a specialist whom he had consulted in Edinburgh. He had found himself unable to perform more than a small part of his duties and had gone to Europe again in May. He was treated by a prominent physician in Paris and was now in Aix, having more treatments. His enemies were accusing him of amusing himself in Europe while pretending to be ill. Whittier wrote an indignant letter to the *Atlas and Daily Bee*; Massachusetts, he said, would allow no one to thrust himself between her and the man who, more than any other, was entitled to her sympathy, her love, and her gratitude.[21]

On August 8 Whittier sent Lowell the poem now entitled "The Cable Hymn" celebrating the completion of the Atlantic cable. The next day he sent two additional stanzas, the present fifth and sixth, and hoped that the poem might be printed in the September number on one of the pages reserved for notices of recent events, since, he thought, the value of such a poem depended upon its timely publication. He was evidently told that this could not be done, and he sent a revision of one stanza August 28.[22] The poem was printed in the October *Atlantic*, with the title "The Telegraph," with some variations from the present form. Whittier was so optimistic as to believe that world peace would come from improved communication, and, with the assurance that was developing in the United States along with national growth and increase in wealth, thought that the intellectual vigor of the North would be conveyed to the exhausted peoples of Asia, Africa, and the Orient.

In December Whittier had the pleasant experience of discovering that nothing succeeds like success. His position as one of the leading writers in the United States and a valued contributor to the *Atlantic*, made his poems desired by other editors and publishers. The first was Theodore Tilton, editor of the *Independent*, who wrote to him December 11 to urge that he write more than the two or three poems that he had offered to write for the *Independent* which, Tilton said, had far more readers than the *Atlantic* and included "the best minds in the country interested in the progress of freedom." Whittier would be listed as a special contributor, along with Harriet Beecher Stowe and Henry Ward Beecher.

Whittier was persuaded, and in the next two years sent more poems to the *Independent* than to the *Atlantic*, in spite of his high regard for the *Atlantic* and its contributors. "The last number of the magazine is excellent well," he had written to Lowell August 28. "Emerson is outdoing himself, and the 'Autocrat' is better and better."[23]

The letter from Tilton mentioned one other significant fact: Whittier would receive one hundred dollars for "The Prophecy of Samuel Sewall," which would appear in the *Independent* of January 6. This was twice what he was paid for poems published in the *Atlantic*. He soon decided to recall two poems that he had sent to the *Atlantic* and send them to the *Independent*, and he wished Lowell to return them immediately. The two were "The Great Awakening" ("The Preacher") and "Voyageur on the Red River" ("The Red River Voyageur"). He sent Lowell at the same time "The Double-Headed Snake of Newbury," which he probably regarded as less important: unlike the two poems that he was recalling, it did not teach anything about religion. It had a pleasant, light touch which makes the reader wish that Whittier had not increasingly restricted himself to serious themes.[24]

Joseph Sturge was still eager to do something for the Whittiers and made another suggestion in a letter written December 23. Since Whittier and his sister felt unequal to a transatlantic voyage, which he thought, along with living for a time in Europe, might do them some good, why not try a winter in the West Indies? He had recently bought an abandoned sugar estate in Antigua to test his theory that sugar could be produced as cheaply by free labor as by slaves. He made his offer of board, room, and travel expenses seem less like charity by saying that he was doing it for the sake of the good that Whittier would do to the people on the estate by merely living among them, and he hoped that Whittier's life-long attachment to the Abolition cause would induce him to accept the offer.[25]

Sturge told Whittier that he was failing fast, although at sixty-five he thought that he had no cause for complaint. His death occurred five months later, May 14, 1859. Whittier's "In Remembrance of Joseph Sturge" appeared in the *Independent* of July 21. The first three stanzas were a satirical account of the official mourning in the court of Queen Victoria for Ferdinand II, "A name that stinks to Heaven" (later softened to "Her foulest gift to Heaven"), while in Naples there was "mute thanksgiving," but the sorrow for Sturge was genuine among working people, the old and the poor, the slave, and foreign lands that he had visited.

The first poem that Whittier sent to the *Independent*, "The Prophecy of Samuel Sewall," was a pleasant but inaccurate treatment of an incident in colonial history. The picture of Samuel Sewall, an old man "propped on his staff of age," looking down from Oldtown Hill on his native town of Newbury, contained two errors which Whittier could have avoided by looking up the facts or by asking Joshua Coffin about them. Sewall was forty-five when he wrote the prophecy in 1697, a date which Whittier knew and placed after the title and which was later omitted. Newbury was not Sewall's native town; he was born in England. But the description of Newbury as seen on an autumn day from a hill in Amesbury was graceful and true, and the tribute to Sewall's Puritan virtue was strong and sincere and gave an opening for Whittier's scorn for the venal judges of his own time who ruled that the will of the strong was always right and that poverty and weakness were wrong and who were as deaf to the pleas of the weak and wronged as "Egypt's gods of leek." Whittier evidently worked over this part of the poem: an early draft does not have some of the most forceful lines.[26]

The descriptive stanzas of "The Red River Voyageur" were an example of Whittier's ability to visualize scenery and to write about it so well that readers thought that he must have seen it.[27] The poem was evidently suggested by a passage in J.W. Bond's *Manitoba and Its Resources*. It concluded with a rather strained analogy which doubtless pleased contemporary readers: our hearts are oarsmen upon the Red River of life, and when they are faint and our eyes dim with watching, happy is the man who hears the bells of Heaven telling that death will release him from his rowing.

" 'The Rock' in El Ghor" also concluded with an application of the scene to the religious life of the present: in the paths of modern life we need the shadow of a rock and the guidance of angelic cloud and fire as much as the ancient Hebrews did.

"The Over-Heart," a more thoughtful religious poem, at points anticipated "Our Master." In Greek philosophy and in Hindu mysticism there was the Transcendental concept of God in everything, the poem began, and guilty man feared the God that was in the earthquake and the storm. But loving hearts turn to Christ, who requires of them no painful rite or bloody sacrifice but only the kindly brotherhood of man, and the law of love alone will remain.

Whittier was unwell late in January and unable to attend the Centennial Festival of the Boston Burns Club at the Parker House on January 25. He sent a note of regret and the poem now entitled "The Memory of Burns." It was read by Emerson, who gave a brief address, and Holmes and Lowell read poems that they had written for the occasion. Whittier's poem "had a rapturous reception, each sentiment being the signal for applause." The chief speaker was William Carruthers of Amesbury, a deacon of the Baptist church and president of the Amesbury and Salisbury Library Association. He was a native of Dumfries, Scotland, and as a boy had marched in the procession from the new kirk to the old to lay the foundation of the Burns mausoleum. He must have seen Whittier's poem when preparing his speech; he used its final concept, the blending of the holly and the pine, in his conclusion.[28]

Over a year earlier Hannah Lloyd Neall had asked Whittier to come to Philadelphia. His visit would do good to his friends there, among them Elizabeth Lloyd Howell. Her sorrow for the death of her husband had wrecked her beauty, people told her sister, but it had made her character softer, and she was "noble, good, and lovely." Whittier now made plans for the trip to Philadelphia. His health was good and his income had increased: his poems were sure of acceptance by the *Era*, the *Atlantic* and the *Independent*. He told Lucy Chase of his coming trip when he met her at a convention in Boston before March 3, and she wrote the good news to his Philadelphia friends.[29]

Daguerreotype of Abigail Hussey Whittier (1779-1857), from which John and Elizabeth had a painting made in 1858 by Thomas B. Lawson. (Courtesy of Whittier Home, Amesbury)

280

Illustration for "Telling the Bees" by S. Eytinge, Jr. which appeared in *Ballads of New England*, 1870.

Illustration for "Skipper Ireson's Ride" by Alfred Fredericks which appeared in *Ballads of New England*, 1870.

XX
1859 - 60

Whittier was in Philadelphia during part of April and May, staying at Hannah Newhall's and calling often on Ann and Margaret Wendell. He was as popular in Philadelphia as he had been twenty years earlier and received so many invitations that he had to decline some of them.[1]

He was seeing a good deal of Elizabeth Lloyd Howell — as much as possible. When he could not see her, he wrote notes. One day he wrote to ask about a portrait of her that was being painted for him. On another day he wrote to say that he enjoyed his visit with her to one of her friends. When he left for home he would carry with him many regrets but also many sweet and precious memories. It seemed to him that he had been happier than he had ever expected to be.[2]

It is evident enough that Whittier's love for her had reawakened and was deeper and stronger than it had been twenty years earlier. They were not too old to be in love; he was fifty-one and she forty-seven, and if her beauty had suffered from her grief over the death of her husband, she had become softened in temperament. Her poor health may have given an added appeal. Whittier was in better health than usual and could have the unusual experience of giving sympathy rather than having to receive it. Obstacles to their marriage twenty years before were now removed: he was earning more money, and had only his sister Elizabeth dependent upon him.

However, he left Philadelphia without anything being said about marriage. He planned to leave on May 9, but the arrival of Ann Wendell at Hannah Newhall's caused him to stay until the next morning. He had a "longing desire" to see Mrs. Howell again, but "knew it would be wrong to attempt it." He left Philadelphia for Burlington and stayed with William J. Allinson, spending one day with Eliza Gurney, who spoke of Mrs. Howell with affection and sympathy. He had been thinking of Mrs. Howell and praying for her. "The sweet memory of our communion during the past three weeks," he wrote to her, "dwells with me — a dear and sacred possession. I am better and happier for it — rich beyond my hopes." There is a suggestion here that he preferred to enjoy a happy memory rather than to plan a happy future, but Mrs. Howell, as later evidence showed, did not analyze closely — or chose not to accept the results of an analysis — and Whittier himself was probably not sure of his own feelings. He promised that he would write to her from New York or Boston; he was evidently not so deeply immersed in love as to find it necessary to write every day.[3] Nor did thoughts of Mrs. Howell keep him from enjoying himself in New York. He had dinner at Elizabeth

Neall Gay's along with George William Curtis, whose *Prue and I* had been widely popular. Henry Ward Beecher drove him around the city at breakneck speed behind a high-spirited span of horses and took him to see Church's painting "The Heart of the Andes," which so impressed him that he thought it would hang in his memory forever.

He left by steamer for Stonington, Connecticut, where he arrived at midnight and boarded a train for Providence. He arrived at half past three and wandered over half the city hunting for the hotel, cold, tired, and vexed with himself for taking this route. He was up at eight o'clock and went to the Friends' Boarding School to see his cousins Joseph and Gertrude Cartland, who were the principals, and his nieces, who were students. He reached home tired and, faced with a basket full of letters to answer, could write only a brief note to Mrs. Howell, promising to write more fully in a day or two.[4]

He kept his promise and wrote a long letter the next day. It was as well written as his early letters to women, but, unlike them, was an expression of real and not imagined feelings. The future was uncertain and he asked no promises and made no demands. "The sweet memory of the past few weeks makes me rich forever. Asking nothing of thee and with the tenderest regard for thy griefs and memories, I have given thee what was thine by right — the love of an honest heart — not as a restraint or burden upon thee, imposing no obligation and calling for no solicitude on thy part as respects myself. Nobody is a loser by loving or being beloved." Mrs. Howell was in a sanitarium in Elmira, New York, having hydrotherapeutic treatment, but it seemed to him that it would have been just as well for her to spend the summer with him and Elizabeth in Amesbury, with its beautiful rural surroundings, its cool and bracing sea air, and its fine drives. There were then no houses across the street, and the windows looked out on the hills on the northwest border of the town.[5]

Mrs. Howell sent him an account of the sanitarium, and he wrote a lively and humorous reply which she must have enjoyed in the midst of her discomforts. He had heard the theory that a water cure washed away the old body and substituted a new one. "If this be true, in what shape will thee emerge from Elmira? How shall we identify the butterfly in bloomers with the chrysalis in skirts? I give thee fair warning. If thee comes out of Dr. Gleason's laboratory transmuted and metamorphosed into anything more or less than the identical Lizzie Lloyd of old times, I, for one, am not going to like thee at all. Red republican as I am, I am terribly conservative in that respect." He thought that she could trust the doctor in charge of her treatment, but supposed that he would, as had been said, have "his cold water *warm*" until she could bear the ice-cold water from the North side of the pump. It was better to take things as comfortably as possible: "If one has to go a pilgrimage with peas in the shoes, it is safer to have them boiled." There was also a serious note. The death of Joseph Sturge was a loss to Friends and the world;

he had lived a life of practical righteousness. "So they pass — one after another — and we are spared a little longer. May God enable us to so live that death may be a glad surprise!"[6]

When he wrote a week later he was half sick; perhaps it was his own sufferings that made him think of hers. He seemed to know that she was suffering a great deal, and suggested that they should think of their many blessings in pain and trial. Three days later he was at Friends Yearly Meeting at Newport, still suffering a pain in his side and unable to sleep. A letter from her had confirmed his suspicion that she was sick — sick and sad, and he could not be with her to cheer her. He wished that she could be with him at Newport; the early summer Sabbath was as beautiful as the one in George Herbert's poem: "The bridal of the earth and sky." The hotel was filled with Friends, and he had never seen a jollier set than these sober-dressed Quakers. From Newport he went to Providence, stayed at the Friends' Boarding School, and met a number of interesting people, including Charles S. Brooks, who had translated Goethe's *Faust*. From Providence he went to Boston, stayed over night, and went the next day to Amesbury.[7]

Whatever Mrs. Howell thought of the possibility of their marriage, she should have known that her growing distaste for Quakers would make it very difficult. Whittier was deeply concerned by what she had said about them. She was a Quaker herself, he reminded her, (she would soon cease to be one, as he may have guessed), those who loved her best had learned to love her as a Quaker, and she owed too much to Quaker training and culture to disown Quakers. In his attempt to convince her, he clearly described his own convictions, which were reasoned and thoughtful in contrast with his youthful acceptance of Quaker doctrines. He reminded her that he was not a sectarian but regarded the philosophy underlying Quakerism as the truest and purest the world had ever known. His reason, his conscience, his taste, his love for the beautiful and harmonious, made him love the Society. He could not understand her feelings; he could only be sorry for them.

Still, he wished that she were with him. He did not feel equal to the journey to visit her at Elmira. After two weeks of rain the weather was "as fresh and bright as Eden before Adam's unlucky bite of the apple," but he missed "*someone* and *somebody*" to enjoy it with him. He would be proud and happy to have her with him the next day at the "Laurels."[8]

The "Laurels" was a natural amphitheater near the Newburyport shore of the Merrimac River where William Ashby and his friends had an annual party when the mountain laurel was in bloom. Ashby was the proprietor of a foundry, an Abolitionist, and one of the first men in the vicinity to take a serious interest in horticulture. Whittier, rather surprisingly, enjoyed the parties, although he usually avoided crowds, especially if he might be expected to speak or read. At first the parties were small and informal; by 1859 they had become much larger, and guests came from as far away as Boston and New Bedford. The company June 30 Whittier described as "a little too fashionable and conventional for the comfortable lapse into savage freedom that a picnic implies, but there were many of the true kind." The day was very hot, but the river, the trees, and the flowers were most inviting. In the evening he visited the Cursons at their home not far away at the junction of the Merrimac and Artichoke rivers, and watched the sun go down through the oaks, making the water look like a river of light. "How I wished for thee!" he wrote to Mrs. Howell. "I would fain have all I enjoy with thee!"[9]

If Mrs. Howell had read between the lines, she would have known that he would also want to share his religious life with her, and she was making this quite impossible. She was becoming an Episcopalian, and he told her he was heart and soul a Quaker and as far as forms, rituals, priests, and churches were concerned, as unsparing an iconoclast as Milton or John Knox; he saw no saving virtue in candles, surplices, altars, or prayer books.[10]

On July 9 he was in Boston, where Thomas Wentworth Higginson met him in a bookstore trying to decide whether to go to a dinner of the Atlantic Club, a short-lived club of contributors to the *Atlantic Monthly*, or go home on the next train. Higginson tried to introduce him to Harriet Prescott; each seemed to want to run away from the other. Higginson thought that Whittier was bashful; it is more likely that he was thinking of Mrs. Howell and found no especial delight in making the acquaintance of an unimportant young authoress.[11] Whittier decided to go to the dinner, which was in honor of Harriet Beecher Stowe. There was discussion of literature, manners, races, national characteristics, and of course religion. Holmes was in his "Autocrat" vein, and Mrs. Stowe talked "wonderfully." Whittier was not silent. One of his reasons for disliking dinners was that when he started talking he said more than he meant — was "extravagant and overstrong" in his assertions. He was afraid this time that he said things that he ought to be sorry for. He left while the more worldly members — Longfellow, Holmes, Quincy, Lowell, and Whipple — were still lingering over their claret and cigars, and went to the Marlboro House too tired to write at length to Mrs. Howell.[12]

He went home within a few days, still too worried and unwell to write to Mrs. Howell. He was suffering from pain in his head and eyes, Elizabeth was weak and depressed, and his brother's affairs were in confusion. Matthew Franklin Whittier and his second wife, Jane Vaughan, were in the process of separation. He was unstable and improvident and changed residence as often as positions; she was a woman of sound Christian character but unyielding in nature. For a time the three children, Charles Franklin, born in 1843, Elizabeth Hussey, born in 1845, and Alice Greenwood, born in 1848, lived with the Whittiers in Amesbury.[13]

Whittier had recently made few contributions to the *National Era*, but news of the death of Gamaliel Bailey aroused him to write an article about him for the *Era* of July 7. Bailey was a "gifted and dear friend. . . . . . He was one of those who mould and shape the age in which they live.'' In spite of this opinion of Bailey, Whittier was not interested in helping his widow, who announced that the *Era* was the only means of support of the family. She wrote to Whittier urging him to resume his active connection with the paper and to Lewis Tappan, asking him to write to Whittier in her behalf. Tappan wrote that he could not urge Whittier to take on additional duties, but he would be pleased if Whittier could do as much as he had formerly done for the paper. Whittier thought that his health was not equal to the exertion, and that he had done much more for the *Era* than the pay that he received justified, and had in fact been unjust to himself in his dealings with Bailey.[14] He continued to send his important poems to the *Atlantic* and the *Independent*, and the only other poem appearing in the *Era* was "For an Autumn Festival."

This poem was written for the exercises at the Congregational Church as part of the annual fair of the Amesbury and Salisbury Agricultural and Horticultural Society. Whittier and his sister were both ill and unable to attend, but even if he had been in the best of health he would hardly have consented to do what the committee in charge wished, which was to march in a procession with the presiding officer, two clergymen, a brass band, and local fire companies. The church was filled to overflowing, and Whittier's poem was sung by the choir. Whittier commented that the piece was not very brilliant but luckily it was written before he was sick or it would have been worse.[15] He made some revisions after sending it to the *Era*. The first two stanzas were better than the present form. They did not have the prosaic lines:

> And woman's grace and household skills
> And manhood's toil are honored yet.

There was an additional stanza after the present third that brought in a similar thought rather more gracefully:

> With manhood's strength and maiden's glance,
>> To lend our Christian holiday
> The beauty of the Persian dance,
>> The vigor of the Grecian play.

Another poem written for an occasion appeared in the *Independent* September 8, "Kenoza Lake," read at the dedication of a park in Haverhill. Rufus Slocum, who had prevented a catastrophe at an Anti-Slavery meeting in 1836, had given a piece of land on the shore of Great Pond to the people of Haverhill and Bradford on condition that it be kept as a free public park. Money was raised to build a clubhouse, and then, somewhat to his amusement, Whittier was asked to find a name for the park. As he hunted through Indian vocabularies he pitied Adam, who had to find names for so many things.[16] He found that an Indian word for "pickerel" was "Kenoza," and the park was christened, the clubhouse dedicated, and his poem read August 31.

Whittier's only poem in the *Atlantic* in 1859 was "My Psalm," in the August issue. It contained stanzas that still appeal to people who need calmness and reassurance. The stanzas beginning

> All as God wills, who wisely heeds
> To give or to withhold

are often used as a hymn. Two much-quoted lines:

> That death seems but a covered way
> Which opens into light

may have been suggested by lines in Longfellow's "A Covered Bridge at Lucerne" in "The Golden Legend":

> The grave itself is but a covered bridge,
> Leading from light to light, through a brief darkness.

"My Psalm," Whittier said, was the way he felt at times and the way he knew that he ought to feel all the time, since he had so much to be thankful for, "but the spirit is willing often when the flesh is weak."[17]

By late July Mrs. Howell evidently thought that it was time to have a definite understanding. She wrote that there was a change in his letters. None is observable. He was writing as frequently as ever, with solicitous questions about her health, and he still signed his letters "affectionately"; perhaps she had hoped for more letters signed like the one dated "31st, 6 mo." "Ever and truly thine." The likelihood is that she chose to imagine a change in tone which she could mention and thus discover just what his feelings and plans were — or force him to make plans. She got an answer which showed Whittier's kindness and soundness of judgment. There had been no change in his feelings toward her, he wrote, but his old self-distrust had come back all the stronger for having been held in abeyance for a time. His way of life was old-fashioned and homely; he could not bear the restraints of fashion and society. She lived in a different world, and her artist-nature could not thrive in the kind of life from which he could not escape without feeling that he had abandoned his post of duty. These considerations and his illness he thought might have affected the tone of his letters. But more than that, he knew that he could never be to her what Robert Howell had been, and if in his happiness in being with her he had seemed to forget this, she surely knew that he would not intentionally thrust himself between her and her loving memories nor intrude upon her sanctities of sorrow.[18]

Whittier was quite right in deciding that he could not live in the world which she had entered. She had gone, her sister reported, "into a social atmosphere so unlike that of her younger days, so imbued with the spirit of everything English, so foreign from Friends" that she must be greatly changed. "The forms of the Episcopal Church," her sister wrote, "are so congenial to her that I wonder how she could ever have been the enthusiastic Quaker she once was, for she seems to have a positive distaste for that sect in which she was brought up."[19] It is clear enough that Mrs. Howell could not return to the Quaker faith; if Whittier had married her he could not, as the rule of the Society of Friends was then, have remained a Quaker. His early acceptance of the principles of the Friends had been unthinking and conventional; his faith was now reasoned, deep, and sincere. To change it would split his life into fragments; to remain a Quaker at heart while joining with his wife in Episcopal worship would be impossible for him, with his serious attitude toward religion; to attend Quaker meetings when no longer a member of the Society of Friends while his wife worshipped at the Episcopal church would cause inner conflicts in both of them that would make happy marriage an impossibility.

It may be argued that Whittier in his later years associated with people of as high social position as Mrs. Howell. He was a frequent guest of the Claflins and the Fieldses; these people were, if not in the highest social rank, at least at the top of the second — but he visited them on his own terms, meeting people that he wished to meet and avoiding the others. If he had married Mrs. Howell there would have been no escape from social obligations; and a man of fifty-one may be wholly in love and yet quite aware of his own limitations.

There was no immediate and unhappy ending to their correspondence or their affection. Whittier was not saddened or embittered. Mary Abigail Dodge ("Gail Hamilton"), who now met him for the first time, found him "irresistible" and "even sweet."[20]

His sweetness did not cause him to soften his attitude on moral issues. Lovers of freedom and humanity everywhere were shocked and sickened by news from Italy. "In what a sad condition Napoleon III has left Italy!" he wrote. "Her last estate is worse than her first. One cannot help but pity the poor exiles and refugees who rallied from all parts of the world for the liberation of their Fatherland; thousands of them are now lying in hospitals, sick, wounded, and despairing. But then good God sees all, and the lie of Priestcraft and Kingcraft cannot live forever. We have this promise, that He will turn and overturn until He whose right it is shall reign."[21] Curiously, it was James Russell Lowell and not Whittier who wrote a poem reiterating that all would come out right in the end, that the Fates would ultimately destroy Pope and Emperor, the "second-hand Napoleon" who had allowed Austria to keep possession of Venice. Whittier's poem, "From Perugia," had no such hopeful prophecies. It was a vigorous description of the cruelties of the soldiers whose slaughter of civilians, according to the quotation from Harriet Beecher Stowe in the headnote, had been approved by Pius IX. It was in anapestic tetrameter couplets and triplets and moved with more swiftness and vigor than the two earlier poems on the sufferings of Italy. It consequently lacked the simple and direct incisiveness of some of the quatrains in "To Pius IX" and the deliberate irony in the blank verse of "The Dream of Pio Nono." But it was straightforward, and no reader could doubt what the author meant. It began with the present fifth stanza, thus getting directly to its attack on Pius IX, of whom the liberals had once had such great hopes, and on Cardinal Antonelli.

There were also events to cause concern not so far away. On October 16 John Brown and his twenty-two companions attacked the United States arsenal at Harper's Ferry, Virginia, as part of an attempt to arouse slaves to insurrection. Two days later he was a prisoner, and his trial October 27-31 ended in his conviction and death sentence; he was hanged December 2.

Whittier was pained and troubled by Harper's Ferry, not merely for itself but for the opportunity it offered to unscrupulous politicians to make capital out of it. A meeting was to be held in Haverhill to raise money for the relief of John Brown's family, and he hoped that nothing would be done in anger or impatience to interfere with the cause of freedom; John Brown was a mistaken but brave man, and Virginia should be magnanimous and brave enough to spare him. Whittier found himself for a time quite incapable of writing anything on the topic, although it seemed to him that nobody had said the right thing and that he could and must say it. Lydia Maria Child also thought that he was the one to write something and asked him to do it for a meeting in Boston on the day of Brown's execution. He did not respond to this appeal, but he wrote an editorial for the December 1 *Villager*. The people of the North deplored Harper's Ferry, he wrote, but admired the noble elements in Brown's character; Southern papers, which were demanding Brown's death, had approved of Brooks' attack on Sumner. He sent the editorial to Sumner and said that he was anxious that the Republican members of Congress should condemn all filibustering, whether for freedom or slavery. A clear distinction should be made between sympathy for Brown and approval of what he had done.[22]

He finally wrote "Brown of Ossawatomie," not without a good deal of difficulty and indecision. He first wrote experimental lines on the back of a letter, among them:

> Let his evil perish with him
> Let the rifle rust
> Never more in these cold mountains
> The Northern rifle sing ["sing" crossed out and replaced by "hear"]

The only lines worded exactly as in the present form were the last two in the fifth stanza (now one line):

> To teach that truth is more than might
> And justice more than mail.[23]

The poem was built around these lines. The name "Ossawatomie" in the title was doubtless understood by every reader at the time. It was the name (properly spelled with one "s") of the town occupied mainly by neighbors and friends of John Brown and defended by him and a small force against a much larger force of pro-slavery border fighters.

After he sent "Brown of Ossawatomie" to the *Independent* he was still dissatisfied with it and thought that it was not what it ought to be. If it was not in type he would like to rewrite it. It appeared in the *Independent* December 22, with lines half their present length and eight lines in each stanza. One line in the third stanza and one in the fifth were somewhat different from the present form.

As usual, he did not think of verifying his facts. He remarked many years later, "In my little trifle, 'John Brown of Osawatomie' I allude to his act of kissing a negro child which I am told is apocryphal, a poetic license."[24]

Nathaniel Hawthorne liked the poem better than he liked John Brown: "I shall not pretend to be an admirer of old John Brown any more than sympathy with Whittier's excellent ballad about him may go."[25] Garrison conceded that the sentiment was gracefully expressed but thought that there was not the "magnanimous recognition of the liberty-loving heroism of John Brown which is found in many of the poet's effusions relating to the war-like struggle of 1776 and 'our revolutionary fathers'." There seemed to him to be an "invidiousness or severity of imputation" in certain phases: "rash and bloody hand," "grisly fighter's hair," "folly that seeks through evil good," and he thought that believers in the doctrines of peace should give John Brown at least as much credit as they gave to Joshua or Gideon, Washington or Warren. Garrison quoted lines in "Our Countrymen in Chains," "The Moral Warfare," "New Hampshire," "Massachusetts to Virginia," and "Yorktown" which seemed to imply Whittier's approval of war — or at least did not imply disapproval.

Whittier wrote a reply two days after Garrison's article appeared in the *Liberator*. In almost every instance the poems quoted by Garrison had "distinct and emphatic declarations of the entirely peaceful character of the Anti-Slavery enterprise and equally emphatic denunciations of war and violence in its behalf." "Yorktown" was "simply a dramatic representation of the capture of Yorktown and the re-enslavement of the fugitive slaves in the abused name of Liberty. No eulogy of war was intended or given — none can be so understood." No one who knew him or had read his writing could be doubtful as to his position: "utter abhorrence of war, and of slavery as in itself a state of war, where the violence is all on one side," and he quoted the last stanza of Garrison's "Universal Emancipation," beginning

Not by the sword shall your deliverance be.[26]

Whittier was also careless about the facts in "The Preacher," which had been sent to the *Independent* a year earlier and was finally printed December 29. The poem gives the impression that the larger part of George Whitefield's preaching was done at Newburyport; the fact is that Newburyport was only one of many towns in which he preached at what would now be called revival services. His special connection with Newburyport is that he happened to die there and was buried under the meetinghouse that had been built a quarter of a century earlier after he had been forbidden to preach in the socially upper-class Third Church. Whittier was also in error about the name of the church; the church on Federal Street in which Whitefield preached and under which he was buried and whose spire Whittier and Lucy Larcom saw gleaming in the sun was the Old South (First Presbyterian) Church. The church named for Whitefield was a Congregational church on State Street, of which Samuel J. Spalding was pastor when "The Preacher" was published. Whittier was well acquainted with the Spaldings, and it is surprising that he was confused about the name of the church.

The main portion of "The Preacher" had been written long before. The introduction was recently added and described a sunset view of Newburyport and the lower Merrimac Valley as Whittier and Lucy Larcom once saw it from Whittier Hill. The vigor of the attack on slavery, the reference to slave ships, and a striking use of onomatopoeia —

> But grates and grinds with friction hard
>
> On granite boulder and flinty shard —

all confirm that the main part of the poem was written many years before it was published. But the paraphrase from the *BhagavadGita* could not have been written before 1852, when Whittier read it for the first time in a copy that Emerson lent him.[27]

The winter of 1859-60 was an unhappy time. Bad weather began early in December, with frequent snowstorms and extreme cold. Whittier and his sister Elizabeth were both ill and neither one could do much to cheer the other, although he said that he occasionally succeeded, like Mark Tapley in *Martin Chuzzlewit,* in being jolly "under creditable circumstances." He described his illness as "a complicated nervous affection" along with the headaches and stomach trouble that he had suffered from since childhood.[28]

The death of William Carruthers on March 6 was a shock to the community as well as to the Whittiers, who had been worried about Carruthers for several weeks before his death. He had broken down under the influence of various troubles including his wife's insanity. He hung himself in the cellar of his store, which was so low that he had to kneel. Whittier described him as a genial, generous, warmhearted man.[29] He and Whittier had a number of common interests: he had been active in Liberty Party affairs; he presided at a meeting in Amesbury on the day of John Brown's execution; he had been active in temperance organizations. A little over a year before his death he had been the chief speaker at the Boston Burns Club's celebration of the birth of Robert Burns, at which Whittier's "The Memory of Burns" was read. At the time of his death he was president of The Amesbury and Salisbury Library Association.

The gloom over Whittier's spirit was not reflected in two of the poems in the first part of 1860. They show rather the effect of his love for Mrs. Howell, which had opened his mind to a new awareness of human affection. In "The Truce of Piscataqua" the love was between an Indian chieftain and a young captive white child who chose, half regretfully, to be returned to her own people. Years later she prayed, after shedding some tears, for Squando, who had given her daughter a silver cross with his sign engraved on it. The story had some historical foundation, as Whittier explained to Horace E. Scudder when the Riverside Edition was in preparation. Squando returned some prisoners after a war caused by the abuse and resulting death of Squando's child by some white ruffians.[30] "The Playmate" (now "My Playmate") told of the love of a bashful farm boy for the girl who left for a life of wealth and luxury in the South. Whittier was uncertain about this "bit of pastoral song," as he called it; he wasn't sure whether it was very simple or very silly and left it to Lowell to decide. Lowell may also have been undecided; the poem was not printed for four months, and several changes were made, one at least at Lowell's suggestion. "Bugsmouth hill" in the first line was changed to "Ramoth hill"; it is another evidence of Whittier's blindness toward the best and the worst in his own writing that it did not occur to him that the name "Bugsmouth" would not blend with the rather sweetly sentimental tone of the poem. To make the poem still specifically local after removing "Bugsmouth," the name of a hill in South Hampton, he added the reference to Folly Mill Woods, where he and his sister Elizabeth picked mayflowers. The poem has always been popular: Tennyson thought that it was a perfect poem.[31]

Both of these poems were in the *Atlantic*. Two poems dealing with religion were published in the *Independent*. "The Shadow and the Light" asked the old question about the origin of evil and suffering and was introduced by a passage from Augustine's *Soliloquies*. The poem added little to the endless discussion of the question, which was old when someone tried his hand at it in the Book of Job, but gave a simple answer which could be helpful to ordinary people if not to philosophers: God is good, whatever happens is best, love is stronger than death or sin. Whittier had read Augustine's *Soliloquies* three years before and had found it a wonderful book with passages of great power combined with tenderness and beauty.[32] The quoted passage may have come to his mind and suggested the poem, as he thought of the sad events of the winter.

The death of William Carruthers may have suggested the final stanzas of "The River Path." The scene was the same as "The Last Walk in Autumn," Pleasant Valley in Amesbury, overlooking the Merrimac River.[33] The setting sun, shining through an opening in the hills, symbolized Divine light coming through the hills of doubt by the river of death, while the beloved dead were God's angels beckoning from the opposite shore. The descriptive stanzas were good, showing Whittier's usual accuracy of observation and awareness of natural beauty; the interpretation, as in his other religious poems, was clear and detailed, as his readers would wish it to be.

Although he refused a request from Haverford College in April on the plea that his health compelled him to abandon as far as possible all intellectual exertion of that sort,[34] he found himself able to write a long poem, "The Quaker Alumni" for a meeting at Newport in June of alumni of the Friends' Boarding School at Providence. It was well suited for its purpose: easily understood from an oral reading, with a blending of the light touch, the sentimentality, and the serious thought that such an occasion demands.

Early in the year Ticknor and Fields suggested a volume of Whittier's recent poems. Whittier wished to dedicate it to Mrs. Howell but left the decision with her, knowing her "delicacy and unwillingness to invite any unnecessary display." She evidently did not make up her mind for several weeks, although she wrote to him in the meantime asking him to destroy her letters. Plans for the volume were being made, and he asked her again if she objected to the use of her name or her initial. He preferred to use her name and enclosed dedicatory lines which, he wrote, withheld much that he would like to say.[35] The volume would be divided into two parts; the first would contain ballads and the second would be loosely called "Poems and Lyrics." It was ready in July without any reference to Mrs. Howell and with a proem of six stanzas evidently addressed to his sister and applying only to the first section. It was put on sale in October. Everything in it except the proem and "The Quaker Alumni" had appeared in the *Atlantic* or the *National Era* within the past three years, since the "Blue and Gold Edition" of 1857.

Whittier was keeping in touch with public affairs. On June 4 Charles Sumner, now restored to his former health and vigor, made his first important speech in the Senate since he was assaulted by Preston Brooks. It was on the bill for the admission of Kansas as a Free State and was a reply to an assertion that slavery was a form of civilization and that ownership of slaves could not be prohibited by Congress. Whittier wrote to Sumner that it was all that he could wish. The civilized world would now see slavery as it really was.[36]

Sumner was back in the fight against slavery, but Whittier could only lament that he himself was too unwell to be of any use. Mrs. Howell gave him some advice, but he replied that he had only a small capital of strength to start with and only a limited amount of hope to supply the deficiency. He would do what he could, not to regain health and vigor, which he could not expect, but to get into a condition to be worth something to his friends and to the world. He was ashamed of seeming to complain and would try to imitate those who had borne pain and weakness cheerfully and bravely.[37]

His lament that he could not be active and useful found its way into a poem written in the summer and printed in the October *Atlantic.* "The

Summons" began with two stanzas of accurate and clearcut descriptions of summer sights and sounds outside the dusty village. Then his spirit heard a call for help from suffering humanity, and in an un-Quakerly metaphor he knew the place that he ought to occupy in the vanguard of Freedom and was ashamed that he could do nothing but write poetry while the battles of the Lord were being fought. He could only say Godspeed to those whose deeds could match their will; the summons came to him too late as he sank beneath the weight of his armor. A few weeks later he was ashamed of the tone of the poem, as he had been ashamed of the tone of his letter to Mrs. Howell. At first he thought that it was only "a little complaining" in its tone, but now he was sure that it was "too complaining" and hoped that he would never do such a thing again.[38]

The summer was an unhappy one. Elizabeth was feeble, unable to ride more than a few miles in a chaise without great fatigue, and consequently could not spend a few weeks, as they had hoped, with Harriet Minot Pitman in Reading and Harriet Winslow Sewall in Melrose. Whittier thought that he was not well enough to go to a welcome-home dinner to Hawthorne with Emerson, Lowell, Whipple, Fields, Longfellow and other distinguished guests and sent a letter of regret with some pleasant remarks about Hawthorne: the "weird and subtle beauty" of his legendary tales had early aroused Whittier's admiration and made him ashamed of his own. He did not feel able to attend a meeting of the Overseers of Harvard College and was rather nonchalant about it: "The College must take care of itself, and as for me I regard it as perfectly safe in our friend Felton's keeping." He was kept from seeing friends by visitors whom he had not learned to refuse to see. " 'If,' as the old song says, 'they would only let a body be,' " he lamented. "One hates to be stared at and put on exhibition."

But there were days when he evidently felt well — or found enough enjoyment in what he was doing to forget his discomfort. He went to William Ashby's Laurel Party, and a reporter observed that he seemed to be one of the happiest people there. He went to a reunion of former residents of Haverhill and spoke at some length in response to the toast "Old Haverhill," telling amusing incidents in his early recollections.[39]

In 1856 he had said that the Republican Party should nominate John C. Fremont again in 1860, but he did nothing to bring this about. He tried to write some political essays in August, but the effort brought on trouble with his head and eyes and he was obliged to give up most of his reading and writing. Still, he was able to help with plans for the local agricultural fair. He wrote to William W. Caldwell of Newburyport, a druggist and verse writer, to ask him for a poem for the occasion. Caldwell evidently declined, and Whittier asked Harriet McEwen Kimball, who sent a poem with which he was delighted and which he thought was the very finest harvest song that he had ever read. He felt, as Captain Cuttle in *Dombey and Son* would say, that he had "worked a good traverse" when he set her to writing it. He added a postscript: the entire poem was excellent, but he particularly liked the last three verses. If Whittier's admiration for this poem was sincere, and there is no reason to doubt that it was, one can only be thankful that he did not bring his own poetry down to quite that level.

The political essays that Whittier tried to write in August may well have been in support of Abraham Lincoln, who had been nominated for the Presidency at the Republican convention in June. A month later, when the campaign started on the local level, Whittier was ready and able to take part in it and to do some writing for it and even appear at a public meeting. It was easier for him to write to people of his own neighborhood, people whose attitudes and responses he could accurately gauge.[40]

Illustrations by Winslow Homer of "My Playmate" which appeared in *Ballads of New England*, **1870.**

XXI
1860 - 61

At a Republican Ratification meeting September 7 Whittier read a set of resolutions expressing perfect confidence in Lincoln and endorsing John A. Andrew, Republican nominee for governor, as a leader in the conflict between constitutional freedom and the aggressions of slavery. The reference to slavery aroused no opposition but it would have in many places where Republicans did not wish the party to be branded as Anti-Slavery. No farther away than Newburyport a newspaper editor had written, "A man may be a Republican and believe in the divine right of slave-holding. — There are grounds enough for opposition to slavery and for favoring the Republican Party without mixing politics with religious theories or abstract moral codes."[1] Whittier was practical enough to see that the best thing to do was to try to make clear that a Republican victory would be a victory for Anti-Slavery, as he would later keep the public reminded that slavery was the underlying cause of the Civil War.

Two weeks later he was unanimously nominated for Sixth District Elector at a Republican convention in Ipswich. On October 11 he was elected one of the vice-presidents of a Lincoln and Hamlin Club at a Republican demonstration in Newburyport. His "The Quakers Are Out," written for the occasion, was sung.[2] It was in the anapestic tetrameter which Whittier favored for campaign songs and asserted triumphantly that Lincoln would surely win, as evidenced by the Republican success in the Pennsylvania state election.

His first reaction to Lincoln's election was devout thankfulness. "I agree with thee that 'hallelujah' is better than 'hurra,' " he wrote to Lucy Larcom, and he was grateful to God for letting him live to see the slave power rebuked. Later in the month, declining an invitation to a Republican victory celebration in Haverhill, he remarked that he had voted for a successful Presidential candidate for the first time in his life, and then proceeded to a statement of the policy which he thought should be followed in dealing with the Slave States. The triumphant party could afford to be generous, and he repeated emphatically the position of Abolitionists, unchanged since 1833: the Federal government had no right to interfere with slavery in the states that chose to keep it, but outside of these states slavery had "no more legal right or constitutional guarantee than polygamy out of Utah." As for the threat of secession, he would not believe that it was serious. "Business men in the South will not long indulge in the childish folly of setting fire to the clothes on their back in the expectation that their neighbors' fingers will be scorched in putting it out."[3]

Privately he was not so sure. While he thought that Lincoln was conservative, cautious, and moderate and that if South Carolina seceded she would find herself alone, he also thought that it might be too much to expect that as great a wrong as slavery should die without a national convulsion.[4] In "Italy," written after Garibaldi had entered Naples, and published in the *Independent* November 22, there was a stanza that did not appear in later printings:

> And who am I whose prayer would stay
> The solemn recompense of time
> And lengthen slavery's evil day
> That outraged justice may not lay
> Its hand upon the sword of crime.

The slavery referred to was the slavery of the population of Naples before the coming of Garibaldi; "Naples," Whittier's poem of sympathy for Robert C. Waterston, whose daughter had died and was buried in Naples, said that added to the father's sorrow was the bitter thought that she was buried "where slaves must tread around that spot."

Whittier's satisfaction in a Republican victory and in Garibaldi's success was not matched by any happiness in his personal life. He had to go to Portland in October to assist in his brother's confused affairs. He returned to Amesbury tired, worried, and ill, and the unsettled weather, varying from autumn to winter, made him worse. He got behind with his correspondence and could not read as much as usual. However, he found time to read and enjoy a book by Henry Ward Beecher, probably *Thirteen Years in the Gospel Ministry,* which Edna Dean Proctor told him about. He read Beecher's sermons, now appearing weekly in the *Independent,* with interest and approval and thought that Beecher, like Tennyson's Galahad, had the strength of ten. He also read Oliver Wendell Holmes' *Elsie Venner,* which had been appearing serially in the *Atlantic* since January under the title of "The Professor's Story." It both fascinated and repelled him, like the evil influence of the snake that it described. He told Holmes that the conception of Elsie Venner was one of the most striking in all romance and the moral bearing of her case deeply suggestive.[5]

He was disappointed in not being able to visit Mrs. Howell, who was spending several months at Mount Wachuset in Princeton, Massachusetts. He went to Lynn, hoping that Mrs. Howell's sister Hannah would go to Princeton with him. When she could not make arrangements, he then thought of going with William Spooner but was sick and had to return to Amesbury. In the middle of September he thought of going and taking Ralph Waldo Emerson with him but caught a cold which settled in his lungs and made him "as hoarse as any raven that ever croaked." But his disappointment in not seeing Mrs. Howell was not related to any hope that she would return to the Society of Friends and thus remove one obstacle to their marriage. He looked quite objectively upon her conversion to the Episcopal church. He could not blame her for living as her own nature directed, with its love of beauty and harmony. He knew that she had a deeply religious nature which sought expression in other forms and symbols than the Quaker faith of her youth, and circumstances had made her somewhat uncharitable toward "plain Friends." But time would correct that and she would find that human nature was the same in Episcopal vestments as in Quaker garb.[6]

The November *Atlantic* contained further evidence that Whittier's place in American literature was assured for his own time with a prophecy of his future fame that is now proving to have been true. James Russell Lowell reviewed *Home Ballads and Poems,* finding Whittier the most representative poet that New England had produced; whatever he lacked, he was indigenous — including some of his rhymes, which must "march out with no honors of war." Even his too great tendency to metaphysics and morals was native, but Lowell was pleased to find less of it in the new volume and to find pictures filled with color and showing the "true eye for Nature which sees only what it ought and that artistic memory which brings home compositions and not catalogues." He approved of "Skipper Ireson's Ride" and "Telling the Bees" but did not like — and here he was giving an opinion that most readers at that time did not share — the conclusion of "The Garrison of Cape Ann;" putting a moral at the end of a ballad was "like sticking a cork on the point of a sword." The future would not fail to do justice to a man who had been so true to the present.

On New Year's Day 1861 Whittier called early on James and Annie Fields. He was well and was feeling the gaiety that comes from restored health. He insisted on blowing the fire, which was reluctant to burn as it should, and when the flames began to roar, he responded by rejoicing over Garibaldi's victory.[7] But he found little to rejoice over for the next two months.

He was back in Amesbury January 5, unwell and destined to be confined to the house most of the time until early March. His sister Mary Caldwell died January 7. She had left her husband shortly before his suicide and had been living near the Whittiers, at the end of the short street, now called Pickard Street, leading from Friend Street. Whittier and Elizabeth felt quite alone, and, he wrote to Hannah Lloyd Neall, "The cloud which rested upon poor E. is heavier now and darker, from the shadow of this new affliction."[8]

As an Anti-Slavery man, he felt the weight of a special responsibility for the course of public events. What he had hoped was an idle threat was now a fact. One state after another was seceding, and on February 4, delegates from six of them would meet in Montgomery, Alabama, to draw up a provisional constitution of the Confederate States of America. In the North there were two main lines of thought: war and compromise. Whittier wanted neither — at least no dishonest compromise which would surrender anything that was basically right. He made his position clear in a poem which was soon followed by prose articles and letters. "A Word for the Hour" was dated January 16 and was sent immediately to the *Boston Evening Transcript,* which printed it the next day. The firmament, the poem said, was breaking up, light after light going out in black eclipse. Why should we

. . . . . yield eternal right,
Frame lies of law, and good and ill confound?

We are safe on the vantage-ground of freedom, where, having tried honorable methods and having denied no just claim, we are sadly looking on at a suicide. Forcing the seceding states back into the Union by war would be lighting

The fires of Hell to weld anew the chain
On that red anvil where each blow is pain.

Many of the groups favoring compromise united in support of a proposed Constitutional Amendment introduced into the Senate December 18 by John J. Crittenden of Kentucky. It would prohibit slavery in all territory north of 36 degrees 30 minutes and would protect it south of that line, while new states would decide for themselves. Congress would have no power to abolish slavery in the District of Columbia as long as it existed in Virginia or Maryland and without the consent of its inhabitants and the compensation of non-assenting owners. Congress would be forbidden to abolish the interstate slave trade. Future amendments on certain provisions would be forbidden, including the return of fugitive slaves, and slavery could not be abolished in any state. Fugitive slave laws would be declared Constitutional and state legislatures would be asked to repeal or modify the Personal Liberty laws, which had been intended to nullify the existing Fugitive Slave Law. It also included a clause intended to please those who still believed in the aims of the American Colonization Society and Southerners who regarded free negroes as a potential danger: land would be bought in South America or Africa and free negroes sent there at public expense.

The Crittenden Compromise never got out of committee, but it had a good deal of popular support. Meetings were held and petitions signed. One such petition got nine hundred signatures in Newburyport — but none was circulated in Amesbury.

Anti-Slavery people were alarmed, and Sumner said in the Senate that the signers of such petitions did not know what they were signing.[9] When Whittier heard that it had been said that Massachusetts favored the Crittenden Resolutions, he wrote to Sumner that nothing could be more untrue; he had not found one Republican who favored them. As for returning fugitive slaves, Massachusetts simply couldn't do it: "The great body of our people can no more hunt slaves than commit cannibalism." But they would be ready to compensate the owners, which ought to satisfy anybody outside of South Carolina.[10]

Anti-Slavery people were also unhappy over a speech by William H. Seward in the Senate January 12, which emphasized moderation, forbearance, and conciliation on the part of the government and the first importance of preserving the Union. Sumner deplored the speech. Salmon P. Chase said that it gave new Constitutional guarantees to slavery in the states and, in direct violation of the most solemn pledges public men ever made to an honest people, would surrender the whole of New Mexico and Arizona to slavery as a peace offering. Chase also disapproved of Whittier's poem, "To William H. Seward," which appeared in the *New York Evening Post* January 28. The poem thanked Seward, and while Whittier had some reluctant dissent, he could not censure what he knew was said with a noble purpose. While he thought the preservation of the Union less important than liberty and truth and righteousness, he approved of Seward's

. . . . . Wise calm words that put to shame
Passion and party.

If Seward could save the Union from war without damaging the cause of Freedom and the Constitution, he would be forever blest as a peacemaker.

Even before receiving Chase's letter Whittier doubtless knew that his poem would not be well received by Anti-Slavery people, and perhaps on second thought he realized that he had implied more approval than was justified and more than he had intended. He sent word to Seward that the poem bound him to good behavior and that if he yielded the ground upon which the Republicans had won the election and consented to the further extension of slavery, he would compromise Whittier as well as the country and himself. As he explained to Francis H. Underwood, the poem was intended to be admonitory as well as commendatory: "I hoped to give him such a kindly hint that he could take it and profit by it, without offense or pride of opinion interfering to counteract it."[11]

Further evidence of Whittier's belief in the importance of local opinion — grass-root politics, as it would now be called — is a signed editorial in the *Villager* January 31, entitled "The Great Question." It would be useless, the editorial began, to attempt to bring the Slave States back by the surrender of every principle of justice and humanity, and unwise to attempt to force them back into the Union; he would not give much "for a Union the chain of which is welded on the red anvil of war" — a phrase evidently remembered from "A Word for the Hour." For the sake of the true Union men of the South, he would do anything for a temporary truce except a surrender of principle. The Personal Liberty Laws he thought might be repealed or modified if a great danger to the cause of Freedom and justice could be averted. But he thought that the repeal of these laws would have no effect upon the seceding states. Payment might be made for non-rendition of fugitive slaves, but the North could not hunt negroes for the South: "It is not business for gentlemen, to say nothing of Christians." As far as John Brown was concerned, the Republican Party platform had included a pledge that Slave States had the right of protection from lawless invasion by citizens of Free States. No more than this could be done. "We cannot give up our faith in the Declaration of Independence. We cannot deny the freedom of speech and press. We cannot disfranchise our colored citizens. We cannot permit the extension of slavery. To use the memorable words of Luther on his trial: 'Here stand we. We cannot otherwise. God help us!' "

He had now come to the point of recommending emancipation by compensation of slave owners. The thought may have been in his mind since Salmon P. Chase suggested it in a letter two months earlier. An editorial written for the *Villager* approved a plan proposed in Congress for buying the slaves in the border states, a plan which he said was in accordance with views expressed by Sumner and Seward. He would extend the offer to any state which adopted the policy of emancipation with compensation.[12]

His poor health in the late winter and early spring and his concern about the crisis in the life of the nation may have been the reason for his writing no poetry for several months. "Cobbler Keezer's Vision" in the February *Atlantic* had been written and sent to Fields earlier. Whittier called it an absurd ballad which he liked for its absurdity.[13] It was a pleasant picture of contemporary New England, with no shadow of war over it. He had earlier referred to Keezer and his light-hearted ways in "The Sycamores" and "The Border War of 1708."

It was reported by a Washington correspondent that President Lincoln had "put his foot down against all applicants for office of extreme abolition tendencies," and Whittier felt it necessary to exert himself to get government positions for his brother and others. Civil Service was far in the future, and appointments were made on the basis of personal judgments and recommendations — or as political rewards. Whittier was not above using the latter in an attempt to get his brother a clerkship in Washington or a consulate at Halifax. He was sure that his brother would perform his duties — and would continue to write in defense of the Republican Party, as he had been doing. He next asked Sumner to use his influence to get positions in the Boston Custom House for his brother and for Isaac Pitman. Office seeking, he told Sumner, was as repugnant to his brother as to him, but necessity compelled him to do it. Matthew Franklin Whittier was given the position in the Custom House and worked there twenty years.[14]

In late March the snow was still deep and Whittier longed for spring and the sounds of brooks and birds. He was worried about efforts to save the Union by compromises but still hoped that slavery, the "Great Nuisance," would fall off from the American people. It seemed to him that the current of events was toward separation of the Slave States. Better this, he thought, than "the sin and dishonor of bowing down yet lower to the Evil Spirit of Slavery."[15]

On April 12 Fort Sumter was fired on, and the Civil War began. Whittier's first reaction was not grief and alarm. There had been no major war within his lifetime to show him how bad war could be, and he had accepted the fact that it had been God's way of ending the slavery of the people of Italy. His first emotion now was a sense of reassurance. There was at last a United North, and he could hope and believe that God reigned and all was well. The old fires of Liberty seemed to be rekindled and all classes were showing a spirit of sublime self-sacrifice.[16]

One question now was, what should be the Quaker form of self-sacrifice? Whittier's first act was a small symbolic one: he declined the pay due him as a Presidential Elector, being unwilling "to add one farthing to the heavy pecuniary burdens of the Commonwealth." When this was magnified into a newspaper report that he had written a strong letter to Governor Andrew sustaining the Constitution and contributing to aid Volunteers, he felt obliged to write a letter of explanation. "No one who knows me," the letter concluded, "can doubt my deep sympathy with the United North and with those who, with a different idea of duty from my own, are making generous sacrifices of person and property; but as a settled believer in the principles of the Society of Friends, I can do nothing at a time like this beyond mitigating, to the extent of my power, the calamities and suffering attendant upon war and accepting cheerfully my allotted share of the privation and trial growing out of it."[17]

Not being sure that all Quakers would see their duty as he did, he wrote a circular letter addressed to members of the Society of Friends. They could not expect to be exempt from the chastisement which Divine Providence was inflicting upon the nation, and while maintaining their testimony against war, they should show that heroism and self-sacrifice were not inconsistent with peace principles. They should visit and help the sick and wounded and relieve the necessities of widows and orphans. They should do as well in war time as Quakers in Great Britain had done in the time of the Irish famine. They could support the work of Dorothea Dix in Washington. The Society of Friends was wealthy, "and of those to whom much is given much will be required in this hour of proving and trial."[18]

There was, as Whittier said, a United North, but it was united only in defense of the Union; it was anything but united on the subject of slavery. Mobs were breaking up Anti-Slavery meetings as they had a quarter of a century ago. Whittier saw that it was necessary to say again what he had said twenty-eight years earlier in a letter replying to the editors of the Richmond *Jeffersonian and Times*. "What shook the pillars of the Union," he had then asked, "when the Missouri question was agitated? What but a few months ago arrayed in arms a state against the Union, and the Union against a state? From Maine to Florida, gentlemen, the answer must be the same, slavery."[19] He now asked the same question and gave the same answer in "Ein Feste Burg Ist Unser Gott" (sub-title, "Luther's Hymn") in the *Independent* June 13:

> What gives the wheat-field blades of steel?
> What points the rebel cannon?
> What sets the roaring rabble's heel
> On the old star-spangled pennon?
> What breaks the oath
> Of the men o' the South?
> What whets the knife
> For the Union's life? —
> Hark to the answer: Slavery!

It was this stanza and others attacking slavery that attracted the most attention, not the stanzas related to the thought of Luther's hymn. The excitement that these lines caused the next winter is further proof that opposition to Anti-Slavery died slowly.

The Hutchinson Family Singers were then at their height of popularity. John Hutchinson went to Salmon P. Chase, now Secretary of the Treasury, to get help in obtaining a permit to sing at army camps. Chase sent him with a letter of introduction to Simon Cameron, Secretary of War, who gave him a permit dated January 14, 1862, good until February 1. Their first concert was in a church in Fairfax, Virginia. The church was crowded with soldiers of two New Jersey Regiments, and there was no trouble until the singing of "Ein Feste Burg Ist Unser Gott." As soon as the Hutchinsons had sung the stanza quoted above, there was a hiss from one corner of the church. The commanding officer, a major, announced that if it happened again the offender would be put out. A surgeon under his command said, "If there is to be any putting out, you had better begin with me." The Major replied, "I can put you out — and if I cannot, I have a regiment that will." The soldiers shouted, "Put him out." Order was restored, while the surgeon sent for pistols to defend himself. The Hutchinsons prevented further trouble by singing a number that they had found useful in softening an audience:

> No tear shall be in heaven; no gathering gloom
> Shall o'er that glorious landscape ever come;
> No tear shall fall in sadness o'er those flowers
> That breathe their fragrance thro' celestial towers.

The soldiers dissolved in tears.

The next morning the Hutchinsons were summoned before General Philip Kearny, who told them that he would not allow them to give further concerts. Next an order came that copies of their songs were to be sent to General William B. Franklin, who soon sent an order, evidently under instructions from General McClellan, revoking the Hutchinsons' permit.

When John Hutchinson returned to Washington he saw Salmon P. Chase, who asked for a copy of Whittier's poem and said, "I'm Secretary of the Treasury; Stanton is Secretary of War, and he thinks just as I do." (Edwin M. Stanton had replaced Cameron the day after the Hutchinsons received their permit.) Two days later Chase told Hutchinson that the poem had been read at a Cabinet meeting, where it had met unanimous approval, and Lincoln had remarked that it was just the kind of song that he wanted the soldiers to hear and that the Hutchinsons might go among soldiers wherever they were invited to sing. Lincoln later told a Civil War correspondent that the reading of the poem had influenced him to issue the Emancipation Proclamation.[20] The incident got a good deal of publicity, and when McClellan was a candidate for the Presidency in 1864, Lincoln campaign orators seldom missed the chance to say that while McClellan was unable to drive out the Rebels he did drive out the Hutchinsons. Whittier wrote a pleasant letter to the Hutchinsons, saying that he had of course no objection to their using his verses and would be pleased and gratified if they could get any music out of them. "Whatever General McClellan may do with my rhymes, I am thankful that Congress is putting it out of his power to 'send back' fugitive slaves as well as singers."[21]

In May of 1861 Whittier was ill and unable to write continuously for more than a short time. He declined to write a poem for an event at Haverford College on the plea that the effort would "seriously aggravate" his illness.[22] But in June he was well enough to write nine stanzas and — most unusual for him — read them at a public gathering. The event was William Ashby's Laurel Party on June 23, with one hundred thirty present — and they were not all staid old folks. There were young people who, according to an observant reporter, "strayed off and became very much scattered to find out the most romantic view, though two generally kept together and from appearances when they came back had enjoyed themselves as well as the married ones." There was speaking — plenty of it. When Whittier was introduced by Rev. James C. Fletcher he said that he was not a talking man but had prepared a few verses for the occasion which he would offer. The verses, which he read with his hat on, according to the Quaker custom, were "Our River."[23] It was little more than doggerel but was suited to the occasion in pleasant thought and light touch. The Civil War occupied one stanza but only to lead to the comforting thought that nature and God are still the same and that the message of the pine trees and the laurel blossoms was that God's love underlies all. Whittier thought "Our River" good enough to send to the *Atlantic,* which printed it in the August issue, without the present headnote.

This summer he did what he had tried to do the previous summer and fall. He visited Mrs. Howell at Princeton. He was there two or three days, including a Sunday when he and Mrs. Howell walked at sunset time to John Roper's farm on the north side of Mount Wachuset. She evidently let him enjoy the scenery, which he described in "Monadnock from Wachuset." He began by wishing that he were a painter, and the first part of the poem was an attempt to let the reader see a picture of the scene rather than the scene itself. In the second section there were simple, homely details showing that Whittier had still in middle age a lively enjoyment of the sights and sounds on a farm. The lines flowed smoothly, with a skillful — and probably instinctive — use of liquids to give the softened sounds of early evening:

    The bleat of sheep along the hill we heard,
    The bucket plashing in the cool, sweet well,
    The pasture bars that clattered as they fell,
    Dogs barked, fowls fluttered, cattle lowed ——.

Then, just as this tone would have begun to lose its effect, there was a change of note and a quickening of rhythm:

    . . . . . the gate
    Of the barnyard creaked beneath the merry weight
    Of sun-brown children.

The poem would not have been satisfactory either to Whittier or his readers if it had not had a lesson, drawn this time not from nature but from the remark of John Roper, who replied to their praise of his farm with Yankee simplicity and sincerity:

    "Yes, most folks think it has a pleasant look;
    I love it for my good old mother's sake,
    Who lived and died there in the peace of God!"

The poem might better have ended here, but Whittier never wished to take the risk of his readers' missing the point, and so he told them that man was more important than nature and that the life of John Roper's mother was an echo of the songs of angels and the harps of seraphim.

Whittier sent a copy of the poem to Mrs. Howell, who read it one morning in the woods where it derived new beauty from the soft air, and gratefully assured him that it would always commemorate the memory of their beautiful hour together that Sunday evening.[24] The poem was printed in the April *Atlantic:* their evening together was evidently not too sacred to share with the public — for fifty dollars.

The course of the war in the summer of 1861, although it did not touch Whittier or his relatives personally, brought sorrow and bitterness. Like most people in the North, he was, as one of his young friends said, "prostrated" when he heard of the Union defeat at Manassas (Bull Run) July 21. He was also disheartened by the continued insistence of Government and people that the war was not against slavery but was being fought for "the flag" and it saddened him to think of the brave young soldiers dying for "the Union with Slavery." The War — and he probably shared the Northern disappointment that it had not been easily and quickly won — had given a sting of hatred to his feelings which they did not usually have. "Would to God we were free of them [the Slave States] altogether!" he wrote; "the cruel and mean barbarians!"[25]

In April he longed for the repose of the mountains and the woods, and the need had become imperative by mid-summer. He went to the White Mountains in August in the hope of gaining a little of their strength, but they seemed to have forgotten the Scriptural injunction "to do good and communicate." He was not well enough to do any climbing but stayed in Centre Harbor like Coleridge before Mt. Blanc

> Upward from their base
> Slow travelling with dim eyes.[26]

As a result he wrote "Franconia from the Pemigewasset", which appeared in the March *Atlantic*. It was written in the autumn, sent to Fields, and revised after receiving the proof. The fourth line in the second section was changed at Fields' suggestion; it first read "Lapped clear of mist," and Whittier altered it to "Burned clear of mist." "I defer to thy judgment," he wrote to Fields. "I shrink from the feline suggestiveness of my figure of speech." Three lines were expanded into five.

> Tangling the dusky woods with silver gleams;
> And far below the dry lips of the streams
> > Sing to the freshened meadow lands again

became the present lines 10-14 in the second section.

The descriptive lines were clear and true. Whittier's eyesight was not failing, in spite of the implications in his letter and in the poem. However, the concluding analogy of the thunderstorm which had cleared the air and freshened the meadows and the storm of war that would pass and leave a greener earth and fairer sky, blown clear by the Northern wind of Freedom, mars the picture for readers today but doubtless appealed to the war-conscious readers of 1862.

Looking at the mountains became tiresome after a while, and not all of the summer guests came for peace and spiritual uplift; there was thrumming inside the hotel and the clatter of bowling balls outside, according to "A Legend of the Lake." This poem was written in the summer, published in the December *Atlantic,* and then, at the request of a relative of the hero, not included for many years in any collection.[27] Whittier was too swept away by his own emotional response to the story to notice that he was writing one of the worst poems of his mature years, with sentimental narrative, monotonous rhythm, numerous clichés, and prosaic lines.

On August 31 John G. Fremont, who had been appointed to the command of the Western District, issued a proclamation of martial law in

Missouri. One of its clauses was an order that the property, real and personal, of all persons in the state who took up arms against the United States or had been in any battle on the side of the enemies of the United States was confiscated to the public use and their slaves set free. This last provision aroused a storm of protest, and Lincoln was urged to remove Fremont from his command. The proclamation of course pleased Anti-Slavery people. Whittier saw it as a direct blow against slavery, the real cause of the war, and said again, "If the present terrible struggle does not involve emancipation partial or complete, it is at once the most wicked and the most ludicrous war ever waged." He hoped that Lincoln would not interfere and tie the hands of Fremont; that would be worse than a score of Bull Runs.[28] He wrote the first version of "To John C. Fremont" and sent it to the *Boston Evening Transcript* so that it might be printed immediately without the delay that would have occurred if he had sent it to the *Atlantic* or the *Independent*. It assured Fremont that he had simply acted a brave man's part without a statesman's tact and had followed common sense in striking at the cause as well as the consequence; God had spoken through him, and anyone who tried to recall his words might as well try to stop the northwest wind or roll the Mississippi back to its sources.

The poem did not keep Lincoln from countermanding Fremont's order but it gave great satisfaction to Fremont. Mrs. Fremont saw it in the *New York Evening Post* and read it to her husband as he stood dejectedly before an open fire, convinced that the Administration was determined to make him fail. The lines were "like David's harp of gold. His face lit up with such a different kind of look from the angry, baffled, resentful kind of face he had just had." He took the paper, bent over to read it by the light of the fire, and said, "He speaks for posterity. I *know* I was right. I want these words on my tombstone:

"God has spoken through thee,
Irrevocably, the mighty words, Be *free*:"[29]

"Thy Will Be Done" appeared in the *Independent* September 19. It expressed the resignation to Divine will that was quite necessary in those days, among the darkest of the Civil War, with the hope that present sufferings would lead to the eternal gain of Liberty.

The War was not yet having any restrictive effect upon Whittier's corner of New England. The mills in Amesbury were working overtime to fill contracts for Army goods and had recently paid a semi-annual dividend of five percent. The usual Agricultural Fair was held, and Whittier got Lucy Larcom to write a Hymn for it. There were no restrictions on travel, and Whittier complained that he was overrun with pilgrims. A gunboat was being built at George W. Jackman's ship-yard in Newburyport with oak timber supplied by a Quaker who asked Whittier if selling timber for a gunboat was consistent with the peace doctrines of the Society of Friends. Whittier's reply was, "If thee does furnish all of that oak timber thee spoke of, be sure that it is all sound." Whittier was doubtless amused by what he thought to be the pretended hesitation of his questioner, but he probably knew that sound oak timber was especially essential in any war vessel, which had to be strong enough to stand shell fire and ramming. The frames of a gunboat formed a solid body from stem to stern, caulked inside and out, so that it would be tight even if the planking was shot or torn off.[30]

In spite of Whittier's local prominence — or perhaps because of it — he was not exempt from fruit-stealers. His pear trees did especially well in 1861, although it was generally a poor fruit year, and were full of Beurres, Bartletts, and other favorite varieties. He must have suffered considerable vexation when one night every pear was stolen.[31] This may have been the beginning of a local juvenile custom. Stealing Whittier's pears came to be regarded by boys as an accomplishment of peculiar distinction to which every ambitious boy would aspire. The *Boston Transcript* found some humor in the 1861 theft and printed two stanzas entitled "To J. G. W. on learning that a thief one night broke into his garden and stole all his pears," inquiring if the poet suffered more from the theft of his pears or from the theft of a bright image or golden grain of thought from his poetry.

As to most Northerners, who had thought that the war would be a brief one and were impatient with McClellan's inaction, the war seemed to Whittier to drag along — and it was a sad war. "I long to see some compensation for its horrors in the deliverance of the slaves," he wrote to Hannah Newhall. "Without this, it is the wickedest war in the nineteenth century." He had abandoned the long-held position that slavery in the states which already had it could not properly be interfered with, and he would be ready to welcome the Emancipation Proclamation and the Thirteenth Amendment. "The Watchers" in the November 14 *Independent,* described two angels, Peace and Freedom, standing by a field where a battle had been fought. Freedom was ready to leave the fighters to their senseless brawl; both sides accepted slavery, the enemy of Freedom. Peace implored him to wait and watch and prepare the way where Peace might follow, but Freedom replied that it was too late. The conclusion of the poem was a rather weak evasion. The vision passed, but the poet heard a voice telling him that he should hope and trust and that all was possible with God.

Whatever great issues are heavy upon the minds of men, daily life with its satisfactions and problems goes on. Whittier wanted to get a shawl for his sister, and with a typical male helplessness in buying women's clothes appealed to a woman friend of the family, Hannah Newhall, in the same letter in which he lamented the sad and purposeless war. "Someone has said that 'friends are not worth having unless they can be made use of,' but without subscribing to that selfish theory, I am going to put it into practice. I want my sister to have a winter shawl, suitable to be worn without or instead of a cloak — one which a moderate sort of Friend of her age, and who wishes to keep the middle path between the rigid simplicity of the 'High seats' and the fashion-following occupants of the lower ones, can wear without misgivings. Could thee not, without too much trouble, find something of the sort in Philadelphia — at a price not exceeding $10 — and send it, with the bill for the same, by someone returning to Lynn or Salem?'' The shawl arrived, price nine dollars, and Elizabeth liked it very much.[32]

310

Mary Whittier (1806-1861), from a photograph of a now lost miniature.

XXII
1861 - 64

"A war with England would ruin us. It is too monstrous to think of. May God in his mercy save us from it!" was Whittier's prayer in December 1861. Indignation was running high in Great Britain over the removal of Confederate Envoys James M. Mason and John Slidell from a British mail steamer by Captain Charles Wilkes of the United States steamship San Jacinto and their confinement in Fort Warren. It seemed to Whittier that the United States could afford to make a handsome apology and that the government needed more wisdom than it had shown thus far to sustain the national honor and to avert a war.[1] Fortunately the government did better than Whittier expected, and the demand of the British ambassador that Mason and Slidell be released was complied with on the basis of Wilkes' failure to bring the British steamer into port for a decision on the legality of the seizure.

The danger of a war was over, but Whittier, like many thoughtful people in the North, was pained by the strong pro-Confederate sentiment in England. Before the War there had been a good deal of criticism of the United States in England because this country had not abolished slavery, as evidenced by an English cartoon showing a slave-holder with a cowhide whip and the motto "Haven't I a right to wallop my nigger?" Whittier's poem "To Englishmen" was in the *Independent* of January 30, with a reference to the cartoon in a footnote to the fourth stanza. The footnote was later included in the headnote, where it results in a curious contradiction; it seems to say that Englishmen were indifferent or hostile to abolition and at the same time were criticizing the treatment of slaves.

As a war drags on, civilians become used to news of defeats and are less excited than in the early weeks when the final outcome seems to them to be determined by every engagement. Whittier accepted the failure of the Burnside Expedition, as it was called, with more philosophy than Bull Run. Whittier found the news discouraging and supposed that the "priesthood of Secession" would think that the stars in their courses were fighting against the Union but decided that perhaps the North did not yet deserve success or perhaps God's way to success was not the same as theirs.[2]

There was one event in the autumn of 1861 for Anti-Slavery people to be happy about. After the capture of Port Royal, South Carolina, by Northern forces November 7, slaveholders on the coastal islands fled inland, leaving their slaves, who were thus for all practical purposes emancipated. They were given work on the abandoned plantations, and schools were opened for them. Soon other Negroes came from the mainland, having heard that the Northerners were not the monsters that their masters had described to them. Whittier, however, was not as jubilant as most Abolitionists. In "At Port Royal," published in the February *Atlantic,* he imagined that he was listening to the "Song of the Negro Boatmen" with a secret pain and a smile that was close to tears; with a prescience of what would happen a century later, he was frightened as he realized that the fate of the nation depended upon the black race:

> That laws of changeless justice bind
> Oppressor with oppressed;
> And, close as sin and suffering joined,
> We march to Fate abreast.

The public was less interested in this warning than in the "Song of the Negro Boatmen," which immediately became popular. There is obvious inconsistency between the dialect and the literary treatment of the last two stanzas, especially the reference to Paul and Silas in prison. But people who liked the song did not analyze it; they found it lively and singable. Seven musical settings appeared within a year. Government officials in San Francisco committed it to memory; the postmaster repeated a stanza every time Thomas Starr King went into his office.[3]

There was unqualified cause for rejoicing early in the spring. The Senate, soon followed by the House, passed a bill abolishing slavery in the District of Columbia. Whittier was so unwell that he had been forbidden to write, but he wrote an ecstatic letter to Sumner: "Glory to God! Nothing but this hearty old Methodist response will express my joy at the passage of the bill." He lamented that his poor health kept him from being more than a looker-on, but blessed God that he had been allowed to live to see the progress of the great cause.[4] He said the same thing in the poem celebrating the event, "Astraea at the Capitol." He had known that truth would crush the lie but had scarcely dared to hope that he would see it happen. The victory had not come in prayerful calm, as he had hoped it would, but he accepted God's ways, which were wiser than man's, and rejoiced in what had already happened and in hope for the future.

Late in May he offered to write an introduction — without pay — for Dora Greenwell's *The Patience of Hope.* This introduction is in Volume VII of the Riverside Edition. The essay seemed to him to be one of the books that have the "Divine seal and imprimatur" — like those of Thomas à Kempis, Augustine, Fenelon, and Luther — insisting upon faith and holiness of life, rather than rituals or modes of worship. He had hesitated to suggest the publication of the book at a time when people's minds were on quite other things, but decided that it was especially needed at such a time; the thought of things which were eternal would be welcome in the chaos of civil war.

He also knew that lighter touches were needed, as he explained at length in the dedication of "Amy Wentworth" to the artist William Bradford, entitled "In War Time":

. . . . . Milder keys
Relieve the storm-stunned ear.

Pleasant pictures should be hung on the walls and household melodies sung, while treason boasted its savagery. Like the average person in war time, he was ready to believe horrible stories about the enemy: the fine arts of Treason, the poem continued, included tanning human skins, carving pipebowls from human bones, and drinking whiskey from the skull of a Loyalist.

This introduction was longer than the poem to which it led. The theme of "Amy Wentworth" was the same as "Among the Hills," written five years later: the love of an upper-class woman for a good man socially and culturally below her. It was Whittier's recollection of an old story told him by his mother, and he was not sure that the woman's name was Wentworth; it might have been one of the other old Portsmouth, New Hampshire, names.[5]

The Whittiers were in Amesbury most of the summer. Their nieces (their brother's daughters) were with them. Their nephew Charles Whittier, whose father had ceased to be a Quaker at the time of his first marriage, had enlisted in the 13th Massachusetts Infantry and had been in camp for several months when he got a discharge for night blindness; Elizabeth hoped that he had profited from the severe discipline — which she underlined — of camp life.[6]

As fall came on, Whittier felt less anger and bitterness about the course of events and more acceptance and trust. In "The Battle Autumn of 1862" the emphasis was on Nature, which remained unchanged in war time and, close to God, shared the eternal calm and, more clear-sighted than man, saw the good that comes out of suffering. In a hymn which he wrote for the annual Agricultural Fair, the emphasis was on God, Who was unchanged. This hymn never appeared in any volume of Whittier's poems, and he probably forgot it when he was preparing *In War Time*. It was another example of Whittier's ability to say clearly and simply what common people were trying to think and feel:

Once more, Oh God, before our eyes
The fullness of Thy bounty lies,
And, shaming all our doubt and fear,
Again Thy goodness crowns the year.

On loyal homes, or rebel soil,
On slavery's task, on freedom's toil,
On good and ill Thy mercies fall,
For Thou, Oh Father, pitiest all!

> Yet must the debt of sin be paid,
> And justice come, though long delayed;
> The wrong must die, and good must be
> Joint heir of Thy eternity!
>
> Oh! hearts must break with pain and loss,
> And mourners bow beneath the cross,
> But well we know, whate'er befall,
> Thy love keeps watch above us all.

Early in October it became evident that Charles Sumner's re-election to the Senate would be vigorously contested. A "People's Convention" held in Faneuil Hall October 7 nominated candidates for State office who were opposed to Republican policies, including Abolition, and the nominations were adopted by the Democrats. Their candidates for the Legislature would vote against Sumner, and so the campaign centered on him. Campaign oratory was then quite unrestrained, and Sumner was described as, next to Jefferson Davis, worthy of the scaffold. Whittier came to Sumner's defense in a signed editorial in the *Villager* of October 16. The fact that Whittier sent it to a local paper when anything that he wrote would have been accepted by papers with national circulation is another evidence of his belief in the importance of the small town. Sumner, the editorial said, seemed to be hated for his virtues. His only crime seemed to be that he had stood by his principles and had sustained Lincoln in his Proclamation (the preliminary Emancipation Proclamation of September 22). Sumner's defeat would weaken the government at home and abroad. Whittier would vote for him as he would for any loyal and true man in this hour of the nation's peril, the conservative Governor William Sprague of Rhode Island or Orestes A. Brownson of New Jersey, a "Catholic Democrat." Two weeks later a signed editorial in the *Villager* bitterly attacked the People's Party, which he described as opponents of the State and National administrations who were trying to get control of Massachusetts: "Whatever can be done by personal hate, envy, and disappointed ambition, combined with timid conservatism seeking peace at the hands of radical democracy and secession sympathizers, we may be assured will be done." If all Republicans did their duty, Sumner and Governor John Andrew would be reelected.

Whatever Whittier believed to be the duty of Republicans, it evidently did not include willingness to accept a nomination. He was nominated for State Senator in the Fourth District. Alijah W. Thayer urged him to accept and offered to supply him with medicines to keep him well enough to perform his duties, but Whittier promptly declined.[7]

Charlotte Forten, following Whittier's advice, had gone to teach in the Oaklands School on St. Helena Island, near Port Royal. As a result she asked him to write a hymn for her pupils to sing at Christmas. He could not refuse, although he was not well enough to do much writing. It pleased the children to know that the hymn was written especially for them, and they learned it and sang it on Christmas day.[8]

In the letter enclosing the hymn Whittier hoped that Charlotte would make the acquaintance of Thomas Wentworth Higginson, who was now a colonel in command of the First South Carolina Volunteers, a negro regiment intended only for reoccupying islands and working on the plantations that the slaveholders had abandoned. It was unlikely that Higginson would be contented with no more action than that. Whittier was quite impressed by Higginson's heroic self-devotion, but trembled as he thought of the peril that Higginson had placed himself in: as a prominent Abolitionist he would be a marked man. But Whittier's simple, unquestioning faith in God, which was increasing with the years, reassured him; if Higginson had Divinely appointed work to do, his head would be covered in the day of battle. Whittier was, in fact, rather sentimental about Higginson: "How strange to think of him, so fresh, so beautiful in his glorious manhood, with his refinement, culture, and grace leading that wild African regiment to avenge the wrongs of two centuries of slavery!" Higginson would have been amused if he had known of Whittier's reference to his regiment as "Wild African." Negroes were used to obeying orders and proved more amenable to discipline than the Massachusetts farm boys in Higginson's previous command. When Whittier heard of the courageous conduct of the regiment in an expedition to Jacksonville he thought that twenty such regiments under men like Higginson and his friend Dr. Seth Rogers, now an Army surgeon, would give a new aspect to the war.[9]

Whittier was still interested and active in local affairs. The Civil War had caused a decline in circulation at the Public Library. People were spending their leisure time reading the newspapers, and the mills were so busy that few people had much leisure time. The Librarian's annual pay was reduced from fifty to thirty-five dollars. But new books were still being bought, and Whittier sent lists to Fields, asking for them at as low a figure as possible.[10]

The prosperity of mill workers in Amesbury and Salisbury had one pleasant result: there was a warm-hearted response to an appeal for the unemployed in Great Britain, who, thrown out of work by the decline in imports of cotton from the Southern states, still did not share the pro-Confederate sentiments of the British upper classes. Whittier wrote the Resolutions for a public meeting to raise a relief fund. A committee was formed to solicit subscriptions, and on January 1, 1863, Whittier sent two hundred and thirty-eight dollars to John Bright with a copy of the proceedings of the meeting and a letter concluding: "With a grateful appreciation of thy generous efforts to promote good feeling between the people of England and the United States, and of thy eloquent and truthful presentation of the great question involved in our terrible arbitrament."[11] Whittier was doubtless referring to

Bright's speech at Birmingham, December 18, in which he said, "I blame men who are eager to admit into the family of nations a State which offers itself to us based upon a principle, I will undertake to say, more odious and more blasphemous than was ever heretofore dreamed of in Christian or Pagan, in civilized or in savage times. The leaders of this revolt propose this monstrous thing that over a territory forty times as large as England the blight and curse of slavery shall be for ever perpetuated."[12]

"The Cry of a Lost Soul" appeared in the *Independent* of December 25. Whittier had read in *Exploration of the Valley of the Amazon under the Direction of the Navy Department* by William Lewis Herndon and Lardner Gibbon the story of how the tropical cuckoo in Brazil had been given the name "El alma perdido."An Indian woman left her child in the care of her husband while she went to get water. She had to go farther than expected, and her husband left the child and went in search of her. When they returned, the child was missing, and when they called to him they got no answer except the wailing cry of the little bird. The story suggested to Whittier the comforting thought that there is eternal good in Divine Providence and that the erring soul may be lost to itself but not to God. A number of translations were made into Portuguese, one of them by Dom Pedro II, Emperor of Brazil, who sent Whittier a copy of his translation and two stuffed cuckoos which were lost in transit. A second pair arrived safely and were kept for many years in the parlor.

Early in the year Whittier had written to Fields that if he could have one day of good health he hoped to write something better than he had yet written for the *Atlantic*. He may have already started work on "Andrew Rykman's Prayer," which he mentioned in a letter to Fields in June as a poem on which he had bestowed much thought and which he believed was in some respects the best thing that he had ever written. The poem was sent to Fields in November and returned with suggestions, one of which at least Whittier took rather lightly. He acknowledged that "pearl" and "marl" did not "jingle well together" but thought that they had a meaning and if the reader would roll his r's a little they would do. This attention to meaning and casual dismissal of style is another instance of the attitude that kept Whittier from writing as good poetry as he was capable of and it also explains his high opinion of "Andrew Rykman's Prayer," which can by no means be rated among his best. The trochaic tetrameter couplets become monotonous, and the thought could have been given in fewer lines. But it evidently appealed to Whittier himself because it said what was increasingly on his mind: his own unworthiness, which kept him from claiming as his right

> . . . . . the crowns of gold,
> Palms, and harpings manifold,

a thought which reappeared twenty years later in "At Last," and his prayer that he might be a servant of God assigned to the lowliest task.[13]

"Andrew Rykman's Prayer" has not been one of Whittier's more popular poems, but ninety years after it was written some lines from it favorably impressed the judge in a poetry contest in a Kansas prison. Whittier would have been amused to know that an inmate serving a term for forgery submitted them as his own and won the first prize, a carton of cigarettes. By the time it was discovered that the lines were plagiarized he had smoked the cigarettes.

The year 1863 began with constant company at the Whittiers',[14] in spite of which Whittier found time to write "The Proclamation." Lincoln, as he had promised in his preliminary proclamation in September, issued an absolute Proclamation of Emancipation January 1, by which slaves were declared free in states and parts of states recognized as in rebellion against the United States government. Whittier's poem, in the February *Atlantic,* was prefaced by a sentence from Lincoln's Proclamation including "I enjoin upon the people so declared to be free to abstain from all violence, unless in necessary self-defense." It counselled slaves to escape to freedom, heaping on their masters' heads only the coals of prayer, and to heal the land with freedom which had been cursed by their slavery. As of course Whittier knew, this was visionary, but vision and idealism were needed, as he continued to be aware throughout the War.

But the Northern public was at the moment more interested in a sensational event than in the dream of a perfect national future. Ben Butler was triumphantly returning to Massachusetts, having been relieved of his command in New Orleans after an administration during which there was never a quiet moment. He had the added distinction of having been declared an outlaw and a felon by Jefferson Davis, whom any Confederate officer might hang without a trial. Even Whittier was enthusiastic, not foreseeing his attitude toward Butler's politics twenty years later, and regretted that he could not go to a dinner at the Parker House, Boston, in Butler's honor. What pleased Whittier was not Butler's military success but his change of heart toward slavery, which he had once regarded "in the abstract with something more than Democratic tolerance," and the fact that in New Orleans he had "fraternized with loyal men irrespective of color or condition, rather than with slave-holding rebels."[15]

When he was writing "The Countess" in March, Whittier was sure that Fields would like it; if he himself was any judge, it was far better than "Amy Wentworth." But he wasn't so sure when he had completed it and was sending it to Fields; if Fields thought that its simplicity crossed the border line and became silliness, he was to say so. Three weeks later he was still making revisions, with apologies. Fields' patience he thought must exceed Job's: What if Satan had made the old patriarch a publisher at the mercy of importunate authors male and female? However, some of the changes may have been made at Fields' suggestion. Whittier told Lucy Larcom that Fields was an admirable verbal critic whose suggestions had been of more value than anybody else's.[16]

"The Countess" was another rather sentimental story of a marriage between people of different social position, but this time it was the man who
was above the woman. Francis Vipart was a titled Frenchman who had fled
from Guadeloupe during the French Revolution and married Mary Ingalls
of Rocks Village March 21, 1805.[17] She was beautiful but consumptive and
died on January 5, 1807 — not, as the poem said, within a year of her marriage. Whittier exaggerated the social difference between them. Mary Ingalls
was the granddaughter of Paine Wingate, who was pastor for sixty years
of the Second Church in Amesbury, and when one recalls the lofty position
of the Congregational clergy in early New England, it is obvious that her
position was at least equal to that of a poor, if cultured and charming young
exile, whose family came to Rocks Village in their search for a farm on which
to earn a living.

In writing "The Countess" and its introduction, Whittier's thoughts were
going back to his boyhood, on the way to "Snow-Bound." His father had
told him about Mary Ingalls and Francis Vipart and described her as a very
lovely girl and her husband as gallant and light-hearted. The immediate impulse may have been a photograph of Dr. Elias Weld, the Rocks Village physician who lent books to Whittier in his boyhood and is described in "Snow-
Bound." "The Countess" was dedicated to him. Whittier did not know
whether he was living or not and characteristically did not bother to find
out. A few weeks later Whittier learned that Dr. Weld had died at the age
of ninety-two without seeing Whittier's tribute to him.[18]

On the national scene it was still necessary to keep Abolition sentiment
alive. "Mithridates at Chios" in the *Independent* of May 7 told of the Chians
who were delivered into slavery to their own slaves as punishment for bringing the slave trade into Greece and concluded with the thought that the freed
slaves in the United States would not enslave their former owners but would
    . . . . . break, not wield, the scourge wet with
    their blood and tears.

Elizabeth was seriously ill in the spring and spent some weeks at Jamaica
Plain, a suburb of Boston, having medical treatment. On his way to visit
her Whittier saw the Fifty-fourth Massachusetts Regiment leave for the South
on May 28, the only regiment that he saw during the war. It was a negro
regiment commanded by a young white officer, Col. Robert G. Shaw.
Whittier became as emotional as when he pictured Thomas Wentworth Higginson with his regiment: "As he rode at the head of his troops, the very
flower of grace and chivalry, he seemed to me beautiful and awful as an angel
of God come down to lead the host of freedom to victory." Whittier wanted
to write a poem about his feelings but was afraid that he would indirectly
give a new impulse to war. After Shaw's death in the attack on Fort Wagner
July 18 Whittier felt for his parents "that reverence which belongs to the

highest manifestation of devotion to duty and forgetfulness of self, in view of the mighty interests of humanity."[19]

In late May he received a long letter from James Worthen of Paducah, Kentucky, who thought that the government should prohibit the shipping of all supplies into Tennessee. Roving bands of Rebels, he reported, were getting supplies through friends who had permits from officials in Paducah. Whittier evidently sent the facts to someone in Washington and wrote to Lucy Larcom that only God knew whether the North really deserved to win the War, when one thought of the rapacity of contractors and office holders.[20] He frugally used the back of Worthen's letter, as he did with many letters in his later years, for experimental lines and stanzas for a new poem. It was "Anniversary Poem," written for the Annual Meeting of the Alumni of the Friends' Yearly Meeting School at Newport June 15, the same group for which he had written "The Quaker Alumni" three years earlier. "Anniversary Poem" said substantially what had been said two years earlier in the circular letter to Members of the Society of Friends but added that the freed slaves were, by tradition, the wards of the Quakers

> . . . . . to cherish and uphold,
> And cast their freedom in the mould
> Of Christian grace.

A few days before the Alumni Meeting Whittier received a letter from Moses Cartland, who was struggling to write a speech for the occasion; he was tired from thirty weeks of school teaching and had little enthusiasm for orations.[21] Whittier was unable to go to the meeting but his poem was read and Cartland gave his address on "The Mission of Poetry."

A few days later Cartland became ill with pneumonia and died July 5. Whittier felt the loss deeply. In some ways Cartland had been closer to him than his own brother. He had kept to the Quaker faith, while Matthew Franklin Whittier had left it without any apparent regret. He had a zeal for reform, of which there is no evidence in Matthew Franklin Whittier's life. He and Whittier had walked

> In love surpassing that of brothers

according to the poem Whittier wrote about him entitled "A Memorial." It had such an intimate personal note that sending it to the *Independent* for publication was rather poor taste. The last three stanzas were the best part of the poem. They were another example of Whittier's sincere and graceful expression of the faith of his time in the survival of personality and the happy reunion of friends in the life after death.

It was probably the news of Cartland's illness that kept Whittier from the annual Laurel Party June 25, but he wrote a poem entitled "The River's Complaint," which was read after the dinner.[22] It was occasioned by a rumor that a hotel was to be built at the spot where the Laurel Parties were held.

It was not given to the newspapers at the time, nor did it appear in any edition of his poems. Whittier probably mislaid it and forgot it. Seven years after his death Samuel T. Pickard found the manuscript, copied it, with some difficulty in deciphering it, entitled it "The Plaint of the Merrimac," and sent it to the *Independent*. It was later printed in *Whittier-Land*.

Late in July Whittier was told of an incident which gave him a chance to write a poem that was patriotic without being warlike. Emma D. E. N. Southworth sent him the story of Barbara Frietchie and her flag as it had been told to her by a neighbor who was a relative of Barbara Frietchie and who had been in Frederick at the time. It did not occur to Whittier to question the facts, and he wrote "Barbara Frietchie" and sent it to Fields for the *Atlantic*. Fields liked it as he liked "few things in this world" and sent a check for fifty dollars, but "Barbara's weight should be in gold."[23]

Whittier handled the story with considerable skill. There was just enough introductory description to give a clear picture; the second couplet was evidently suggested by a paragraph in Oliver Wendell Holmes' "My Search for the Captain" in the December 1862 *Atlantic* which Whittier had read and admired.[24] The narrative moved swiftly enough so that the readers would not stop to notice the extreme acrobatic ability of the heroine in seizing the flag as it fell from the staff. Whittier wrote a moralizing conclusion in what is now the next to the last couplet but then, led by an instinct which for once was not submerged by his sense of duty, wrote a final descriptive couplet.

"Barbara Frietchie" was widely copied in Northern papers and has appeared in many anthologies. When Winston Churchill was riding through Frederick in 1941 with the Franklin D. Roosevelts he recited the whole poem when the President pointed to the attic window in Barbara Frietchie's house where the flag had hung.[25]

"Barbara Frietchie" became the topic of an extended controversy: how much of the story, if any of it, was true? Whittier received many letters on both sides of the question. He was not interested in separating the facts from the fiction but was content to say that Barbara Frietchie was a real person and his account of her heroism was substantially true.[26]

The Whittiers spent some time pleasantly at the Isles of Shoals in August, where Celia Thaxter told them of Star Island in such an interesting way that Whittier advised her to write it for the *Atlantic*. One evening Elizabeth walked out on the rocks to look at the sunset and fell. She did not appear to be seriously injured, and the fall may not have been the cause of her growing weakness and her death a year later.[27] When Mary Shepard and Charlotte Forten called at the Whittiers' on September 2 they found Elizabeth as lovely as ever but very frail. She urged them to come again, and they stayed over the weekend of September 12-14. They had a delightful visit; everything was cheerful, and either Elizabeth's health was temporarily better or she had learned not to let physical weakness or suffering affect her spirits as they had formerly. Whittier talked a good deal about his boyhood — "a rare thing for him to do" was Charlotte's comment;[28] it would be less rare as he got older, and in two years he would write it in "Snow-Bound."

During the last weeks of 1863 and the first weeks of 1864 Whittier was worried and unwell. Elizabeth was now seriously ill. He did not feel able to go to Philadelphia for the thirtieth anniversary of the American Anti-Slavery Society where he hoped to meet old friends of the Abolition days. But he wrote a letter to Garrison which showed that he was not in a mood of sentimental reminiscence but was quite aware of present and future problems. There were millions of freed slaves, uneducated, bewildered, and starving in the wild chaos of war. The accumulated wrongs of two centuries must be undone and the negro given a fair chance. Race prejudice must be overcome: "We must lift ourselves at once to the true Christian attitude where all distinctions of black and white are overlooked in the heartfelt recognition of the brotherhood of man."[29]

Late in November Fields sent three hundred forty dollars in royalties and an offer of a loan of five hundred dollars. Whittier gratefully declined the loan, saying that, as a bishop once said of strawberries, with God all things are possible and He might have made a better man and more generous publisher but He never did. The three hundred forty dollars was evidently more than he expected; from a "Shoddy" point of view the amount might be small, he said, but they hadn't cheated the government out of it and it made him as rich as Croesus. This happy feeling did not last. A month later he wrote to Fields that it was a matter of material consequence to him that his new volume of poems should sell and asked if someone could do for him "in a moderate and qualified degree" what George William Curtis had done for Longfellow in the *Atlantic*.[30]

The new volume was *In War Time*, and it was not reviewed in the *Atlantic*, probably because James Russell Lowell had already sent a review to the *North American Review* for the January number. Fourteen hundred copies were sold by April 30, 1865. There was only one new poem, the dedication to Samuel E. and Harriet W. Sewall, but there were changes and additions in others. The most significant change was in "Italy," in which the stanza implying approval of war as a way to end slavery was omitted and a stanza added prophesying the coming of peace. Whittier had found it easy to accept war as a means to an end when it was in Europe; he could think of it only as a prelude to peace when it was closer to home and its victims were men that he knew.

His concern about money came from his added family responsibilities. His niece must have been a great help in the household as Elizabeth grew weaker, but she was only eighteen and there was her education to be paid for. Her father could not be depended on for any substantial help; he was regularly employed at the Boston Customs House but had married again and was moving from one place to another with his customary frequency.[31] She later went to Ipswich Seminary — her uncle paying her expenses.

A few pleasant things happened. A telegraph line was installed from Newburyport to Amesbury, and on December 19, "a glorious winter morning" when nature had "put on all her jewels," Whittier received a message "flashing over the wire" from George J. L. Colby, editor of the *Newburyport Herald*. "The old settlers of the Powow," Whittier wrote in reply, "would have given Satan the credit of such a marvellous transmission, but we can gratefully recognize it as one of the good gifts of Providence."

Jean Ingelow's American publishers, Roberts Brothers, sent him the new volume of her poems. He liked them, and thought that "High Tide on the Coast of Lincolnshire" was the best ballad of the time. Whittier's choice of this poem agrees with that of most readers and critics; this poem has been included in numerous anthologies.

In January Elizabeth Lloyd Howell sent him a sermon by a high official of the Episcopal church which pleased him as "a noble and honest utterance on the Slavery question." He had often been critical of the attitude of the Episcopal church, as of other churches, toward slavery, and he was grateful to God for the marvellous change.[32] His reply to Mrs. Howell began "My dear Friend," not the "Dear Elizabeth" of his former letters.

He received the news in January that his hymn for the dedication of the Unitarian Church in San Francisco had been a success. He had been doubtful about it: "I have just sent what I *trust* is a hymn to T. S. King for the opening of his new 'steeple house,' " he wrote to Fields, and Elizabeth was afraid that it could not be sung. The hymn was in tercets, an unfamiliar form to hymn-singers, but the choir leader composed some music for it and it was "poured through" the choir and new organ with considerable success. Thomas Starr King had helped to raise money for the organ by giving a series of lectures,[33] and it would not be surprising if he and other contributors were not wholly pleased by one stanza:

Our puny walls to Thee we raise,
Our poor reed-music sounds Thy praise:
Forgive, O Lord, our childish ways!

But there were some good lines looking forward to a united nation free from slavery and a world united in one hope, one faith, and one love.

He was doing something practical to help freed negroes, whom he had described in his letter to Garrison in November as bewildered, ignorant, naked and foodless. He was collecting money and clothing for the New England Freedmen's Aid Society and was treasurer of the fund; within a year $793.25 was collected, and four boxes of clothing were sent to Port Royal.[34]

He was also writing a poem about practical deeds of mercy. He read a description by Charles Eliot Norton of the Brotherhood of Mercy in Florence[35] and wrote "The Brother of Mercy" about the dying porter who mourned that for the first time in forty years he could not go with the Brotherhood on their errands of mercy, and he could not contemplate an Eternity among the lazy saints wearing a white robe and a gold crown; a voice then told him that Heaven was love as God was love and that he might work in heaven as he had on earth, and he saw an angel's shining face. The theme and its treatment suggest Leigh Hunt's "Abou Ben Adhem and the Angel."

Thomas Starr King did not live long to enjoy his new church and its organ; he died March 4, and Whittier promptly wrote a memorial poem for the *Independent* of March 17. It was soon included in a volume entitled "In Memoriam" dated March 28 and sold at a Sanitary Fair in New York. This was not his only contribution to the Fair. Mrs. Fremont asked him to write "Barbara Frietchie" on a picture that she was having made to sell there, and he was asked for an autograph to be used in an album of photographs of the most distinguished authors of the nineteenth century.[36]

Whittier received two invitations in the spring, neither of which he accepted. One was to visit the Army of the Potomac, and it showed that poetry, especially Whittier's, meant a great deal to men in the nineteenth century. "Your loyal verse," Brigadier-General Rice wrote to him. "has made us all your friends, lightening the wearisomeness of our march, brightening our lonely campfires, and cheering our hearts in battle, when 'the flags of war like storm-birds fly!' "[37]

The other invitation was to the April Meeting of the Saturday Club in Boston. This Club was originally an informal group of fourteen who as early as 1857 had dinner together once a month at the Parker House. Other members were added later, and the meetings were pleasant affairs. James Russell Lowell said that he had never seen as good society elsewhere, and Oliver Wendell Holmes thought that there were never such agreeable meetings as theirs. Longfellow went once as a guest and immediately decided to join. Whittier became a member in 1858 and remained on the list as long as he lived but seldom if ever went to the meetings. In fact, the men on the committee that invited him to the April meeting, Emerson, Lowell, and Holmes, did not know that he was a member. It was to be a special meeting with a few "friends of Shakespere" as invited guests, including Governor John A. Andrew, Richard H. Dana Sr., William Cullen Bryant, and George Bancroft. Emerson added a note urging Whittier to come, and he thought at first that he would, but two days before the meeting wrote to Emerson that he could not, greatly to his regret because he regarded this as an exceptional occasion, although he was not in general a diner-out. Emerson had come to have a high regard for Whittier. A few days before the April dinner he wrote that Whittier was a "true poet . . . . . hid like a nightingale" and recorded succinctly in his Journal of that year, "Whittier is unspoiled."[38]

"The Wreck of Rivermouth" was in the April *Atlantic,* without the present introductory note but with a footnote explaining that Whittier got some of the historical background from the *New England Historical and Genealogical Register*. Joshua Coffin had also told him a good deal about Eunice Cole at the time he was writing "Margaret Smith's Journal." The story came into his mind as he was thinking about Celia Thaxter's sea stories and pictures, and he imagined himself writing it on Appledore Island looking toward the Hampton shore. It was the story of a party of happy young people who were drowned when their boat was hit by a squall returning from the Isles of Shoals. Present at the funeral was Rev. Stephen Bachiler of Hampton, the subject of scandal in his old age and of much controversy among historians. Whittier erroneously believed that Bachiler was an ancestor of his, but was no more concerned about it than most men are about the lives of their remote ancestors. He later rewrote the lines in "The Wreck of Rivermouth" referring to Bachiler and believed that Bachiler was a man of strong intellect and, for his time, remarkably tolerant of those who differed with him on matters of doctrine and was loved and respected by Oliver Cromwell but had his faults and indiscretions and "fell into the snare set for him by an evil woman."[39] Later research has seemed to indicate that the charges against Bachiler were part of a scheme by the Puritans of Massachusetts Bay Colony to discredit the authorities in New Hampshire and bring that colony under the control of Massachusetts.

Illness and suffering of members of their household and the death of old friends bear heavily on unmarried men, and the spring of 1864 brought both of these to Whittier. Elizabeth was sick during April and May, with occasionally a few days of comparative comfort and then a return of pain and illness. No one knew what the illness was; some thought that it was a disease of the spine, and it seems to have affected her brain. She was unnaturally cheerful and thought that she would soon be well, while Whittier could not throw off his depression as he saw her increasing weakness and suffering. His perceptions had become so sharpened, he said, that he could see what ought to be done far better than he could do it. There were no nurses with professional training, but Lizzie Hoxie of Lynn, who was regarded as a qualified nurse, took care of her for a time, and then Mary Esther Carter. Dr. Henry I. Bowditch came to see her and could only say that he hoped that she would recover if she could take nourishment enough. Whittier got Fields to send some grapes and a bottle of sherry wine. When it came time to pick mayflowers in Folly Mill Woods, there was a sunny day when Elizabeth felt well enough to ride in a carriage and to be lifted out and sit on a robe spread on the ground and watch while Whittier picked the flowers.[40]

The death of Joshua Coffin removed one of the few remaining links with his boyhood, and Thomas Starr King, Joshua Giddings, and Owen Lovejoy had been part of Whittier's Anti-Slavery years. Nathaniel Hawthorne had been part of what would later be called the Flowering of New England, and Whittier was at his funeral May 23, standing among a group of writers beside the path as the carriage passed with Hawthorne's widow — and in violation of his Quaker principles taking off his hat as the others did.[41]

A visit from Gail Hamilton was a pleasant relief and was followed by a typically amusing letter. She had meant to look into the closet in the Garden Room where he kept the firewood for the Franklin stove; she suspected that there was a perennial oak fountain bubbling up hard wood. He was continually going there and coming out laden with wood, but she never saw any wood going in or evidence of wood in any other part of the house. She and Whittier were both amused by an article about him by David Wasson in the March *Atlantic* in which Whittier was described as of the Saracenic or Hebrew prophet type. "I hope Wasson's unlucky word will not stick to me, but I see it will not be thy fault if it don't," he wrote to her. "I'm neither an 'Ebrew Jew' nor an Arab sheikh. Instead of buying and selling 'old clo,' I have given mine away to the contrabands, and I never could endure the tent life of an Ishmaelite on Salisbury Beach more than one day in the year."[42]

He went to the New England Yearly Meeting of Friends but was suffering so much from boils that he could not make his usual calls in Rhode Island and did not even visit Joseph and Gertrude Cartland; Job, he wryly said, did not make visits when afflicted "with sore boils from the crown of his head to the soles of his feet." They started with a large boil or abscess and spread to nearly forty small ones which caused such lameness that he could scarcely use his hands. He continued to suffer from them through the summer and into the fall. Harriet Minot Pitman cheerily wrote that he should be congratulated. She had been told at a water cure establishment that boils were very healthful and were worth at least a thousand dollars apiece. If he was run down he should take bark and wine and would then grow fat — she would like to see him in that condition.[43]

Whatever cheer could be brought by humorous letters from friends was needed in this summer of 1864. Elizabeth was now so sick that even Bayard Taylor and his wife had to be told to postpone their visit. She was suffering extreme pain and weakness and had to stay in a darkened room. But through all of this, Whittier was still aware of troubles outside his own household. When he heard that fourteen persons were in Maryland State Prison for violating the Fugitive Slave Law he wrote to Sumner asking if anything had been done for them. And he was deeply concerned about the coming Presidential election.

A national convention of "Radical Men of the Nation" had met in Cleveland May 31 and nominated John C. Fremont for the Presidency. The Republicans — who still preferred the safer term "Union" — met in Baltimore a few days later, June 7 — too early, Whittier believed.[44] The delegates were over-confident; it seemed at the moment that Grant's and

Sherman's forces had been having unqualified success and that Richmond and Atlanta were about to fall, bringing down the whole Confederacy with them. Lincoln was nominated unanimously on the second ballot, and the Convention dissolved with no doubts about his election. Then came a series of military reverses and the resignation of Salmon P. Chase as Secretary of the Treasury — he had resigned before, but this time Lincoln accepted his resignation, saying that they had reached a point of mutual embarrassment in their official relations which could neither be overcome nor continued consistently with public service. Public confidence in the Administration plunged downward, and Whittier saw that Lincoln's reelection was doubtful. Although Lincoln was no favorite of his, he tried to do the one thing that would unite the Republican Party. He made an appointment to talk with Fremont at his summer home at Nahant. Mrs. Fremont wrote that her husband would see him and invited him to stay overnight while she would go to Amesbury to see Elizabeth if she could leave her own sister, who was ill. But she made it clear that her husband saw his duty: Lincoln must not be re-elected. If he was, France, England, and Austria would recognize the Confederacy, and the West would separate from New England and form a new nation friendly toward the South; the Confederate government hoped for Lincoln's re-election as the quickest way to independence. All this prophecy of doom had no effect upon Whittier. He went to Nahant and said, "There is a time to do and a time to stand aside," and Fremont should sacrifice himself for the good of the greater number.

Fremont did not make any announcement at the time, and Whittier explained his own position in a letter to the *Liberator,* which Fremont would be sure to see. He had been sorry to see extracts from other papers criticizing Fremont and thought that Lincoln could not be re-elected if it could not be done without disparaging and sacrificing Fremont, who enjoyed a wide popularity as the chosen leader of the well-nigh successful effort in 1856 to place the Government on the side of freedom. His treatment by the Administration was something which Lincoln's best friends found it hard to justify. His admirers might regard his candidacy as an error in judgment without questioning his motives. While most of those who voted for Fremont eight years ago would now vote for Lincoln, they still believed in Fremont's integrity and were proud of his genius and his history.[45]

While Whittier was writing this letter, the Democratic Party was meeting in Chicago. If it had met a week later it might have acted differently. It adopted a platform with an immediate peace plank — which its nominee, General McClellan, virtually repudiated. Then, on September 3, the news came that Sherman had taken Atlanta and that Admiral Farragut had taken the defenses of Mobile, and Lincoln issued a Presidential proclamation of thanksgiving.

On the same day Elizabeth Whittier died. Although the disease, the pain, and the opiates had affected her mind, she had remained patient and cheerful. Neighbors and friends had helped to take care of her; one of them, Joan Colby, had taken care of Whittier's mother and sister Mary during their final illnesses. Whittier stayed alone in the room with her the night she died, while Mary Esther Carter lay outside the door to be at hand when needed.[46]

Although he had known that it was coming, Elizabeth's death was still a shock for which Whittier was not prepared. She had been closer to him than any other member of his family. They had the same literary tastes and interests. They both wrote poetry and each was interested in what the other wrote. They both loved the beauty of the countryside. They were both liberal but not evangelical Quakers. They shared a wide circle of friends. In recent months they had admired Fremont and had been less than enthusiastic about Lincoln.

After these months of care and anxiety Whittier suffered from the inevitable reaction and confusion. It seemed to him that his life had lost its chief motive. It would be strange to send a poem for publication without first showing it to Elizabeth. He missed her when he walked out to see the autumn woods. He could not seek relief by travelling and visiting; he was still suffering from boils and was not well enough to go more than a few miles from home. But he had the wisdom and the strength not to bury himself in selfish indulgence of sorrow. His religious faith, which in recent years had increasingly centered on unquestioning trust, now helped him to believe that what God willed was best, and he was determined that the home should not be a gloomy and forbidding place. Elizabeth would want it to be cheerful and would want old friends to come, friends whom she had loved and, as he was assured by his faith in life after death, still loved.

For many weeks he could not write but wisely found other things to do. He worked in his garden and did his duty as a member of the committee in charge of building the new schoolhouse. He helped with the local Agricultural Fair; he declined an invitation on the day of the Fair because he could not consistently leave it. A Seedling Grape which he entered received favorable notice of the committee as being a choice variety and entitled to much consideration.[47]

The Democratic Party's peace plank confirmed Whittier's resolution to vote for Lincoln, who, he felt bound to say, was not the man of his choice, but "between him and that traitor platform who could hesitate!" He was happy to see that all loyal men were rallying to Lincoln's support. On September 17, Fremont withdrew as a candidate — not, he said, to aid in the triumph of Lincoln but to do his part toward preventing the election of McClellan. How far Fremont had been influenced by the advice that Whittier had given him in August is hard to say. There had been overtures from the

Lincoln forces, and jobs had been promised to Fremont's friends. But whatever his motives, his withdrawal removed the last bit of doubt about Lincoln's election, which Whittier hailed as a "glorious result" and observed Thanksgiving in his heart before the Governor's official proclamation.[48]

XXIII
1864 - 65

In the months following Elizabeth's death, currents in Whittier's thoughts flowed toward the writing of "Snow-Bound." He was thinking increasingly about the past, and his faith in God and in the future life were part of his daily living. In this and in his interest in events and people he was close to the thoughts and feelings of his fellow-countrymen, and the "Flemish pictures" in "Snow-Bound" would be in colors familiar to his readers.

When he was still unable to write, a few weeks after Elizabeth's death, he sent Fields "The Vanishers," which had been written during her final illness and had, he said, beguiled many weary hours.[1] The "little vanishers" called "puckweedjinees" in *The Supernaturalism of New England* where they resembled the English variety of fairies now became the spirits of the beloved dead, whose beckonings showed that mortals were on the right path to an eternity where they and the spirits would meet. In "Snow-Bound" he would see Elizabeth's hand beckoning him, white against the evening star.

But now the world around him gave him something to be happy about. Slavery in the entire nation was about to end. The reelection of Lincoln had shown that the people of the North definitely wanted slavery abolished: "It is the voice of the people now, for the first time, heard upon the question," Lincoln said in his Annual Message when Congress reconvened early in December. "What glorious times we live in!" was Whittier's jubilant exclamation. "My heart is full of thankfulness. It is great to live now — to see and hear what will fill the horizon of history in all coming time, and sound in all earth's voices forever."[2]

The House of Representatives concurred January 31 in the vote of the Senate in April and adopted what became Article XIII of the Constitution. Lincoln signed the bill two days later, and as Whittier sat in Fifth Day meeting in the Friends Meeting House, "Laus Deo" wrote itself, he said, or rather sang itself to the rhythm of the church bells ringing in Amesbury, as everywhere in Massachusetts, by the order of the Governor.[3]

"Laus Deo" is one of Whittier's poems in which, as Howard Mumford Jones once justly said, he did not achieve "marmoreal perfection" and he had so exhausted his primitive vocabulary that he "fell back on the twentieth chapter of Job and the fifteenth chapter of Exodus for figure and speech." But Scriptural references carried an emotional effect when the Bible was a basic part of the average reader's being, and in spite of its failings, the poem reached people that would not have responded to marmoreal perfection, including an old Negro in a school for freed men in Georgia. When his teacher read "Laus Deo" to her pupils, Uncle Charlie fell upon his knees with streaming eyes and clasped hands, crying "Oh glory to God for what He has done for us wretched people."[4]

Plans were soon being made in Newburyport to celebrate Emancipation, and Richard Plumer, long-time Abolitionist and worker on the Underground Railroad, called on Whittier and asked him for a poem. Whittier replied that he would write something if he had the inspiration and if he felt better.[5] Inspiration and improved health evidently came, and he wrote "Hymn for the Celebration of Emancipation at Newburyport," which was printed in the *Newburyport Herald* with the suggestion that subscribers bring their papers and join in the singing. The celebration was at City Hall and the speaker was William Lloyd Garrison, who had been invited by twenty-eight leading citizens of Newburyport — times had indeed changed. The next morning Garrison, Gail Hamilton, and William Ashby called on Whittier. Garrison and Whittier reminisced and Gail Hamilton and Ashby listened.[6]

Whittier had not spent the entire autumn rejoicing over Emancipation. The war was by no means over, and in November a fair was held in Boston to raise money toward a National Sailors' Home. Whittier was one of a group of authors, including Oliver Wendell Holmes and James Russell Lowell, who served as Editorial Council of *The Boatswain's Whistle,* edited by Julia Ward Howe and published to be sold at the fair. Each member of the Council made at least one contribution; Whittier's was prose, "John Woolman in the Steerage."

Another prose piece written in the fall was "David Matson," which was printed in the February issue of *Our Young Folks.*[7] The first paragraph explained that it was in the main a true tale, similar to "Enoch Arden," which was "the story of a man who went to sea, leaving behind a young wife and little daughter" — Whittier did not go to the trouble of refreshing his memory of "Enoch Arden" and had forgotten that there were also two little sons. "David Matson" was popular enough to be worth stealing. A few years after it was first printed, it was published as an original story in a literary weekly in Baltimore.[8] It was later expanded into one hundred sixty-three pages of verse entitled "David and Anna Matson" by Abigail Scott Duniway, who modestly said in the dedication to Whittier that she rehearsed "in trembling, broken verse," the legend that he had so "quaintly, sweetly told."

In the fall he wrote tributes to two very different authors, William Cullen Bryant and Gail Hamilton. Bryant's seventieth birthday was celebrated November 5; Whittier did not attend but sent "Bryant on his Birthday," in which he said that Bryant was equalled only by Wordsworth in seeing "charms to common sight denied," but that in such times as those in which they were living, Bryant the man was more important than his poetry:

His life is now his noblest strain,
His manhood better than his verse.

"Lines on a Flyleaf" was written in a copy of Gail Hamilton's *A New Atmosphere*, which was published in late November. Whittier thought that the book would be a success without his endorsement and the author would laugh at any breaking of spears in her defense, but he liked her "electric words" in which he found "the tonic of the northwest wind" and thought that her wit was like summer heat lightning, which sharply outlines the hitherto dim trees and hilltops. He also liked his poem,[9] perhaps because it gave him a chance to say that there was no such thing as woman's sphere, and even the Apostle Paul, if living, would see the heroism in the lives of four women who had "cast their crowns at duty's feet": Lydia Maria Child, Sarah J. Clarke Lippincott, Anna E. Dickinson, and Harriet Beecher Stowe.

"Kallundborg Church" was written for the January, 1865, *Atlantic,* and he also found time in December to make corrections in a poem which Ann Wendell had written and sent to him from the Philadelphia Hospital.[10]

Joan Colby, who had taken care of Whittier's mother and Elizabeth, lived across the street from the Whittier garden and frequently called at the house. One day when she was there, Whittier came out of the Garden Room with Anna Brownell Jameson's *Legends of the Monastic Orders* in his hand. He read to Mrs. Colby the story of St. John de Matha, who used his white mantle with red and blue cross as a sail on his ship carrying Christians whom he had ransomed from slavery in Tunis, and remarked that it would be a good subject for a poem. Mrs. Colby replied that he was just the one to write it, and he wrote "The Mantle of St. John de Matha." When he sent it to Fields, he asked if it were a true ballad. He ought to have known that it was not; it had symbolic meaning, with the inevitable explanation. He confessed, as he did frequently, that he was often sadly mistaken about his pieces, but he thought that the feeling of this poem was genuine, whatever its expression might be.[11]

"The Eternal Goodness," in the March 16 *Independent,* was a summation and reaffirmation of Whittier's religious faith as it had been developing through the years and which was strongly on his mind at this time. "Through what a mystery are we passing into one still greater!" he wrote to Lucy Larcom. "But isn't it a blessed thought that we are in the hand of one who *can* have no motive or desire in respect to us but for our good! I cannot forego this child-like faith, for it is all I have."[12] This simple trust in God's goodness was his refuge from his sense of sin and his confusion. There are lines that clearly parallel passages in his earlier writings.

Not mine to look where cherubim
And seraphs may not see

and

> Forgive me if too close I lean
> My human heart on Thee!

are close to lines in "Follen";

> Where even seraph eyes have failed
> Shall mortal blindness seek to come?

> While with thy childlike faith we lean
> On Him whose dearest name is love.

The stanzas most frequently quoted and used in hymns are

> And so beside the Silent Sea
> I wait the muffled oar;
> No harm from Him can come to me
> On ocean or on shore.

> I know not where His islands lift
> Their fronded palms in air;
> I only know I cannot drift
> Beyond His love and care.

Their thought, without the imagery that gave them their success, was in "My Summer with Dr. Singletary:" "What He has in reserve for me hereafter I know not, nor have I any warrant to pry into His secrets. I do not know what it is to pass from one life to another; but I humbly hope that, when I am sinking in the dark waters, I may hear His voice of compassion and encouragement, 'It is I; be not afraid.' "

"The Eternal Goodness" said what an increasing number of people believed or at least wanted to believe. Some of them wrote to Whittier that it contained their creed.[13] There was little in the poem to give it any claim to literary excellence; the rhythm was monotonous, and many lines were nothing more than simple factual statements. But the Biblical imagery reached people whose thoughts and feelings were formed and colored by Bible memories and who could dream of Heaven as islands lifting fronded palms in air — a dream impossible to a later generation, to whom such islands were places of brutal warfare or the destination of luxury cruise ships.

Whittier's trust in divine goodness did not lead him to close his eyes to human depravity or to draw a veil over it. He was eager to point to slavery as human depravity in its most hideous form. On March 9 Charles C. Coffin, the Civil War correspondent, lectured at Music Hall in Boston and showed relics of slavery that he had brought back from Charleston, including the steps of a slave auction block. He read a vigorous letter from Whittier, commending him for bringing them; it was as if Dante "had torn the dreadful inscription, 'Hope enters not here' from the doors of Hell and borne it away with him to the upper world . . . Let these infernal hieroglyphics and symbols of the worship of Anti-Christ be carefully preserved. . . . Let them tell the generations to come of that most hideous form of human depravity, which, priding itself on its evangelical purity and with the name of Christ on its lips, bought and sold the image of God, and subjected body and soul to the base uses of lust and avarice."[14]

A few weeks later there was another reason for hating slavery. "How black and hateful slavery looks in the lurid light of this monstrous crime," he wrote when the news came of Lincoln's assassination. "We never yet hated it enough." He forgot his distaste for Lincoln and could think of him only as "our beloved President." But he did not like the fierce and revengeful tone of the public mind; bloodshed and cruelty on the part of the North would not bring Lincoln back to life. "The hanging of a score of Southern traitors will not restore Abraham Lincoln nor atone for the mighty loss," he wrote in an editorial for the *Villager,* and the misguided common people of the South should be forgiven and their returning loyalty welcomed and encouraged. It was slavery that should be blamed for Lincoln's death, and the Northern public should be eager to destroy every vestige of slavery and racism.

However, in proving the evil influence of slavery, he listed crimes that must have made it hard for the reader not to direct some of his wrath toward people rather than toward the institution: Brooks' assault on Sumner; violence in Kansas; the bones of Northern soldiers dug up and made into bracelets and brooches (a variation on the charge in the dedication of "Amy Wentworth" that pipe-bowls were carved from bones); starvation of prisoners at Andersonville; the plan to blow up Libby Prison; the massacre at Fort Pillow; hotels set on fire; obstructions placed on railroad tracks. And yet the North was about to leave the pro-slavery politicians in charge of Southern state governments.[15]

Whittier was not the only one to be concerned over the restoration of power and authority to Southern legislators who had led their states into rebellion. The assassination had stirred up public indignation against dangerous concessions to Rebels, who could be expected to restore slavery and to outlaw loyalists. General Godfrey Weitzel had permitted the Confederate Legislature of Virginia to reassemble at Richmond, and General William T. Sherman had included a similar clause in the terms of surrender by General Johnston in North Carolina. At a meeting in Faneuil Hall June 21 Whittier was appointed a vice president and placed on a committee to prepare an address to the people of the United States, which said that no state could absolve a citizen from his allegiance to the Union, and that slavery must be abolished by "paramount and irreversible law." The introduction said that in the arrangements made by General Weitzel and General Sherman the government barely escaped a serious if not fatal political defeat at the hands of a vanquished enemy. Whittier, with his usual good judgment, thought it unwise to mention the generals' names and thus alienate their friends and admirers, but he was willing to sign the document, which he hoped would help to save the nation "from the sin and shame of a reconstruction which shall at the same time give a premium to rebellion in the increase of political power and punish loyalty with outlawry."[16]

Whittier's thoughts were not wholly on public affairs in these history-filled spring months. He planted a flowering shrub which Lucy Larcom had sent him beside Elizabeth's grave in the Quaker section of the Union Cemetery, where an old white rose bush near the grave of his mother and aunt was getting ready to bloom. Leaf buds were opening on the trees, birds were singing, and everything looked as it had when he and Elizabeth had stood there in previous springs.[17]

The May *Atlantic* contained Whittier's "The Grave by the Lake." He had read an article about a skeleton of a man over seven feet tall that had been found many years earlier in a mound surrounded by stones near the Melvin River in New Hampshire.[18] Since the skeleton was supposed to be that of an Abernaki Indian, perhaps a chief, it would be expected that the poem would deal with history or legend, but instead its theme was immortality —

> But somewhere, for good or ill,
> That dark soul is living still.

The question the poet then asked himself was what happened to the numberless dead who had died without the Christian faith, and the answer was that God could be trusted to take care of them; Christ's love reached out to souls imprisoned in sin.

He thought of going to Yearly Meeting of Friends at Newport but could not find anyone to go with him and was advised by his doctor to go to northern New Hampshire rather than to the seashore; he had a cold and a pain in his head. He went by train to Alton Bay, where he wrote a letter to Gail Hamilton while waiting for the steamer to Center Harbor; he had seen that the "inevitable" Phoebe Hanaford had printed a book, *Our Martyred President.* "I hoped this could be spared him," Whittier commented, "but if there was any doubt about his martyrdom before, there is none now. She ought to be arrested and tried with the rest as auxiliary after the fact." From Center Harbor he went to Campton and stayed over night at Selden Willey's farm, where Mr. and Mrs. James T. Fields were boarding. He then went to Plymouth for a day or two and left June 14 for Amesbury by train through Dover.[19]

On June 27 he went to the annual Laurel Party. The guests — or at least the more important ones — had tea at William Ashby's at Newburyport, and then the party of three hundred went up the river in a steamer and two gondolas lashed to its sides. Whittier's "Revisited," written for the occasion, was read. He was always in good mood at Laurel Parties and when writing for them, and now, with the Civil War over, he could ask the river to sing songs of peace and home. With his recent visit to New Hampshire in mind, he asked the river to bring

The green repose of thy Plymouth meadows,
The gleam and ripple of Campton rills.

But the poem also mentioned the utilitarian functions of the river, which then turned mill wheels and typified the strength and glory of the North, freedom bringing beauty and grace to rugged labor. It was also a hint of Heaven

Where the rivers of God are full of water,
And full of sap are His healing trees.[20]

"The Changeling," in the July *Atlantic*, was a sentimental and improbable piece of fiction about Eunice Cole of Hampton, whom Whittier had written about in "The Wreck of Rivermouth." The mother, who was supposed to have been bewitched by Goody Cole into thinking that her child had been stolen by witches and a hideous imp left in her place, was cured by a prayer by her husband, and Samuel Sewall released Goody Cole from prison, something that would have been beyond the authority of a single judge. But the poem made good reading; Oliver Wendell Holmes read it with delight and found it sweet and tender.[21]

Whittier was kept at home most of the summer by poor health. One day in August he went to Ipswich to arrange for his niece Lizzie, who was keeping house for him, to go to Ipswich Seminary during the winter term, and drove from Ipswich to call on Gail Hamilton. She was not at home, and he wrote her a lively account of his disappointment; illness had not dulled his sense of humor. "I drove up to thy domicile; the blinds were tightly closed. I went round about it and pulled the bell handle — and nobody answered. 'I passed by the walls of Balclutha and they were desolate.' I wandered over to 'My Garden', and what with the drought and the weeds there was a mighty slim chance of 'sass and posies' there! In my bewilderment I heard somebody call me 'Cap'n!' (Do I look or behave like a military chieftain, that I should be so saluted?) I was then informed that Miss Dodge had left for some unknown and mysterious locality, only designated as 'the country.' I tore off a fragment of an Hon. M.C.'s letter in my pocket, with my name thereon and gave it to the young man who gravely announced that he stood in thy shoes as thy representative, took a last lingering look at the southwest chamber window, half fancying that thee was peering down on me through the blinds and enjoying my disappointment, and departed. My 'chariot wheels drove heavily.' "[22]

During the summer he was worried about money. He and his brother, he told Charles Sumner, had been made poor by the war which had made so many rich.[23] He was not listed as having an income large enough to pay a Federal tax in 1865; there was a six-hundred dollar exemption and there were numerous deductions such as house repairs, insurance, real estate taxes, and interest on debts, and the *Villager* remarked that when an income was less than one thousand dollars, there was little left to tax. Payments by Ticknor and Fields of two hundred dollars September 4, 1864, and nine hundred twenty-two dollars April 30, 1865, evidently covered all sales of various editions since December, 1863. Poems printed in the *Atlantic* and the *Independent* brought fifty or one hundred dollars, according to length. There had been no edition made up wholly of poems not in earlier volumes since *In War Time*, late in 1863, which had given Whittier one hundred forty dollars. *National Lyrics* was issued in August, 1865; it contained only two poems not in previous collections and was unlikely to be a best seller. His friends thought that he was living more economically than was pleasant or good for his health, and one of them, the son of John and Sarah Davis, for whose fiftieth wedding anniversary Whittier had written some verses in 1863, sent him a check for "some little health-giving and amusing trip of thy own choosing."[24] He did not take any trip and perhaps used the money for his niece's tuition at Ipswich Seminary. In spite of his restrictions, he gave ten dollars, probably about half a week's income, to the Amesbury and Salisbury Library Association.

He was still feeling the weariness and the loneliness that had come as one after another of his friends and relatives had died. He was too practical and too conscientious to bury himself in melancholy isolation; he had friends to enjoy and duties to perform. But in a deep inner recess were feelings that could not wither and disappear; as with most unmarried men, they could best be kept from poisoning the springs of thought and action by bringing back the past, with its bright lights and clear outlines softened by the haze of tenderness that comes through suffering and loss, if the soul has grown in love and faith.

Whittier began to write "Snow-Bound" as a labor of love, and the dead seemed to be overlooking his pages as he wrote. At first he was writing only for himself and his niece; he wanted Lizzie to know all the people that had been part of his boyhood and her father's. But, as had happened with so many of his very personal poems, he felt no restraint that would keep him from sharing it with the public — and he needed the money. He thought of making it a short poem suitable for *Our Young Folks*, but then decided to tell Fields about it. He called it "a homely picture of old New England homes" and hoped and trusted that it might be good, if he ever finished it. Fields was encouraging; he rejoiced to hear that Whittier was writing a "snow-piece."

The poem was completed and sent October 3 to Fields, who could do whatever he thought best with it. Whittier thought that Fields would like some parts of the conclusion and assured him that the portrait of Harriet Livermore was as close to life as he could make it. He knew that he would wish to make changes in the proof but was too unwell to do anything more at the time. Fields replied that he would use the poem as a book to be illustrated by F.O.C. Darley and offered to send an advance payment of two hundred dollars.

The proof came back with Fields' suggestions for various changes. Two of these were surely needed, but Whittier could not think of anything better: "mindless wind" is awkward in sound, "wind" having a long "i" to rhyme with "blind," and "womanly atmosphere" is colorless and prosaic. He changed "The woodchuck in his robes of gray," which gave a blurred picture; a woodchuck can hardly be thought of as robed.

Whittier told Fields not to send the revised proof lest he tear the poem to pieces with alterations, but Fields sent another proof and Whittier added several pages and then thought of an alteration in the description of the boys and girls when the road was being plowed, omitting two lines. He did not notice one curious error which surprisingly persisted through all editions until 1892: "wedding knell" instead of "wedding bell." Other changes were made as the first edition was being printed, and still others in later editions.[26]

Snow-Bound was published February 17, 1866, without illustrations by Darley but with two woodcuts of the farmhouse and a portrait of Whittier which he did not like: it was "a trifle harsh and severe — something of 'the Sword of the Lord and Gideon' in it." The poem was an immediate success. Ten thousand copies had been sold by April 2, when Fields wrote, "We can't keep the plaguey thing quiet. It goes and goes, and now, today, we are bankrupt again, not a one being in crib. I fear it will be impossible to get along without printing another batch."

In a reaction from the emotion under which "Snow-Bound" was written, Whittier was less enthusiastic about it than his friends; it was well enough, he thought, but still it was silly and had some "droll mistakes" into which he had been led by "the fatal facility of octosyllabic verse," and he had to shut his eyes to its faults and make himself believe that it was all right, as his friends told him. As its sales continued, he was afraid that it did not deserve the success that it was having.[27]

It continued to have that success, for a number of simple reasons. It was told with the same narrative skill that had appeared earlier in his prose fiction. Interest was sustained by skillful turning to a new topic just when the reader had received full satisfaction from a scene, incident, or character and was ready for the next. The scenes, indoor and out, were, as in everyday life, part of a canvas that included human figures. These were normal people, varied by one eccentric treated with humor and sympathy; they had enough individual qualities to avoid being stereotypes — in other words, they were like the readers and people that they knew.

The lines were easy and pleasant to read. Guided by instinct rather than by theories of verse, Whittier kept the iambic couplets from monotony by changing, at just the right point, to other rhyme schemes that heightened the emotional effect or gave final emphasis to a thought.

The strongest appeal of "Snow-Bound" was its theme and setting. To some readers who wrote to Whittier about it, the life described was like their childhood on a farm, but its appeal was not limited to them. Deep in the American mind was a real or imagined love for the farm, often strongest in those who had never lived on a farm nor had their ancestors since the settlement of North America. Sitting in their warm homes, in the new luxury of a hot-air furnace and flaring gas chandeliers, they let their imagination give them a nostalgic delight in a life that they had never known. They found this life in "Snow-Bound", as they found it in Currier and Ives farm prints, among the most popular products of that firm which knew how to please the public.

To Americans in the Nineteenth Century and the first generation of the Twentieth, death was a real part of life. Children were reminded of it in stories and poems written especially for them. Families went to cemeteries to put flowers on graves. Everyone was sure that the dead were living and was endlessly interested in the where and how of life and death. The references to the dead and to immortality which have been criticized in "Snow-Bound" as irrelevant gave the life described there a completeness without which readers would have turned from it with a feeling that something was lacking. When Paul Hamilton Hayne read "Snow-Bound" to his wife, mother, and son, remote as they were from New England farm life, their eyes filled with tears — and they were especially moved by the lines beginning

> Alas for him who never sees
> The stars shine through his cypress-trees![28]

"Snow-Bound" has been written about by reviewers, editors, and critics, each generation treating it according to the prevailing fashion. Some of the things that have been said about Whittier's esthetic and philosophical plots and purposes would surprise and amuse him. There is a good measure of truth in Gail Hamilton's comment on her conversations with Whittier: "And literary methods we never talked about. I suspected he never had any." It could not have occurred to him to use symbolism of which the interpretation would require techniques possible only to the academic mind. A discerning critic has recently pointed out the danger in "trying to force into a pattern of symbolization or imagery any poem not written with such a pattern in mind": to do this with "Snow-Bound" "effects a distortion of meaning, a muddying of otherwise clear waters."[29]

By midsummer the sales of *Snow-Bound* had reached twenty thousand; Whittier received ten cents a copy. With this $2000 and $1200 from a speculation of three hundred dollars, added to what he already had, there was enough for him to live on, to pay Lizzie's expenses at Ipswich Seminary, and to give one hundred dollars a year to charities. The fact that he had three hundred dollars to speculate with arouses the suspicion that he had not been in such need as his friends had been led to believe. Now he stopped worrying about money; more would be a burden, he thought. He was too old to display wealth or change his way of living — and, he said, when he died there wouldn't be much for his friends to quarrel about.[30]

Snow-Bound would ultimately bring him ten thousand dollars, and it became customary for editors to ask him to name his price when they wanted him to write for them. Money accumulated, and after his death his admirers were unhappy over the size of his estate; it destroyed the image that had been created by his poetry and his quiet, unostentatious personal life.

Photograph of Whittier in the 1850's by Harris.

Photograph of Whittier in the 1860's.

Daguerreotype of Whittier, c.1860 (Courtesy of Donald P. Wright)

Portrait of Whittier by Edgar Parker, originally done in 1874. (At Moses Brown School, Providence, RI)

Thomas Hill's painting of "Birthplace of John Greenleaf Whittier," 1868. (Courtesy of the Haverhill Public Library)

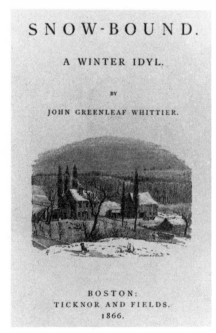

Title page of the first edition of *Snowbound*, 1866.

Photograph of Whittier, 1866, by F.K. Clarkson, Amesbury.

342

Kitchen of Whittier Birthplace, photograph c.1890.

Harry Fenn illustration of the Kitchen which appeared in *Saint Nicholas*, April 1893.

XXIV
1866 - 67

Whittier did not give all of his time and attention to "Snow-Bound" during the autumn and winter of 1865-66. As always, he was watching political developments and was happy over the Republican victories in New York and New Jersey and the prospect of a Republican working majority in the Massachusetts Legislature. But President Johnson was not acting at all as Whittier had expected. He vetoed the extension of the Freedman's Bureau February 19, and Whittier felt like railing at his folly and stupidity. His Washington's Birthday speech three days later was even worse, and Whittier could only hope that he was drunk at the time — better to suppose that than to think that the speech was deliberate "in cold blood."[1]

Whittier wrote "The Peace Autumn" to be sung at a meeting of the Essex Agricultural Society and then sent it to the *Atlantic* but a year later was doubtful about including it in *The Tent on the Beach*; it seemed to him that compared with "The Battle Autumn of 1862" it was hardly up to the mark. "The Worship of Nature" appeared in the *Christian Watchman and Reflector* in January. About half of the poem was a rewording of his early poem with the same title. Other stanzas followed the thought of lines in "Mogg Megone" beginning:

Is not Nature's worship thus,
Ceaseless ever, going on?

"The Maids of Attitash", as printed in the February *Atlantic*, did not have the wholly happy ending of the present form. The less beautiful sister who said that love in a cottage was better than wealth was overheard by a rich young man who decided that he preferred her to her beautiful sister who said that love which came to her must bring silk and diamonds with it. The girl who did not care about wealth had all the luck — she got both wealth and love, and her covetous sister got nothing. When Whittier revised the poem a year later, he added one of his favorite themes: the strong young farmer married the other sister, who found that love changed everything to gold. "Attitash" was the Indian name for huckleberry and had recently become the name of a lake in Amesbury which Whittier thought was prettier than St. Mary's lake that Wordsworth wrote about.[2]

Since Elizabeth's death the friendship of women had come to be, more than ever, a necessary part of his life. Gail Hamilton called one day in February and he assured her that she was on missionary ground; he was getting into the condition of a monk on Mount Atlas who did not know what a woman was like. He wrote frequently to Lucy Larcom. He was grateful for the crayon portrait of Elizabeth that she gave him, and that still hangs in the parlor, showing Elizabeth as she looked when comparatively well and happy.[3]

Although he knew that his friends would laugh at him, he was so saddened by the death of his parrot that he would cry if it would do any good. Charlie was an old friend, and Elizabeth had liked him. He had been a colorful member of the household. He had not forgotten some of the language that he had learned from sailors in his youth, and one Sunday morning he shouted it to church-goers as he danced on top of one of the chimneys. He danced there once too often and fell down one of the flues. When he was rescued several days later he was too weak to do anything but say faintly one of his favorite phrases, "What does Charlie want?" Whittier used these words as the theme of "The Common Question," which he sent to Lucy Larcom for *Our Young Folks*, although he was not sure that it was suitable.[4] Present day readers would share Whittier's doubts about it; the laborious moral lesson and some of the vocabulary and sentence structure must have made the poem difficult even for Nineteenth Century children.

Snow-Bound had brought an increase in fame and fortune, and now came the price of fame, a never-ending stream of letters and requests. Colonel Julius Allen asked him to write to Cassius Clay, ambassador to Russia, to try to secure the release of Colonel Allen's half-brother.[5] Schuyler Colfax, Speaker of the House of Representatives from 1863 to 1869, sent Whittier a speech for his inspection and asked for his autograph. Whittier sent in reply nineteen lines dated July 11, 1866, which later found their way into the *Independent*, commending Colfax' patience which had borne

> The weary toot of Bunkum's horn,
> The hissing of the Copperhead,
> And Folly dropping words of lead

and prayed that God would keep him wise, firm, and faithful.[6] Clara Barton also asked for his autograph on cards with a picture of Barbara Frietchie and lines from the poem.

Requests for help came frequently from writers. John B. Phillips sent some poems for him to forward to the *Atlantic* if he thought that they were good enough. Alice Cary asked him to send a favorable notice to some paper or magazine of her new book *Lyrics and Hymns*, if he could do so without violence to his conscience. The widow of John Pierpont wanted Whittier to write her husband's biography.[7]

Poems were written to him and printed in magazines and newspapers. One of them, in the *Newburyport Herald*, addressed him as a sweet harpist, urged him to continue his songs and to lead President Johnson, and assured him — not altogether a pleasant prospect — that brothers and sisters whom he had helped to escape from slavery would crowd his cottage door, grasp his hand, and flood his garden with their tears.

The success of *Snow-Bound* made it good business to get out a new book as soon as possible. Fields urged him to have a large edition of *The Tent on the Beach* on the market before the sea was chilled. It was to be a stringing together of poems, most of them previously published in periodicals, in a narrative of three men camping on Salisbury Beach. Whittier was slow about getting to work on it and thought of giving it up altogether. In August he wrote that "The Tent on the Beach" was not yet pitched — in fact, the cloth was not yet woven.[8] He gave illness as his excuse, but the truth is that he had allowed other things to crowd it out.

He read and enjoyed Bayard Taylor's novel, *The Story of Kennett*. He went to Boston to hear Emerson lecture. He wrote to *The American Freedman* commending an editorial which said that white children should not be refused admission to schools for Negroes.[9]

He wrote "Abraham Davenport" for the May *Atlantic*, the episode of the Puritan in the Connecticut Legislature who chose to perform his immediate task even if the end of the world was at hand. It was one of Whittier's best poems. It taught a lesson, but that lesson was so much a part of the Puritan inheritance which Whittier, like most Quakers, shared, that he could present it simply and naturally, without enlarging upon it or thrusting it at the reader. It had a quiet tone, with a touch of light humor but also with high points of intensity and emphasis. The metrical pattern, it has been pointed out, was so gently persistent that it could carry even the formal description of the threatening sky without melodrama.[10] There was skill, doubtless instinctive, in beginning three lines with verbs having their subjects to the preceding lines and then focusing upon the human response by beginning the next line: "Men prayed and women wept."

"Abraham Davenport" has been said to be a perfect picture of the Puritan attitude. Whether this attitude shows that the "Puritan civilization has carried the cult of the personal conscience into mere dutiolatry," as William Dean Howells expressed it a few years later,[11] is a question that would not occur to Whittier or his readers.

Whittier was concerned, however, about misunderstandings of his religious beliefs. When he read "The Theology of Whittier" by Henry Blanchard in the May issue of *The Friend*, he wrote a letter explaining his position. His hope for himself and humanity lay in the love of God as revealed in the life and teachings of Jesus.[12]

His attempt to correct false impressions also led to the writing of one of his most widely quoted poems, parts of which have been sung by millions of worshippers in Protestant churches. Whittier was working on this poem one summer day when William Dewhirst, a young man who lived nearby and did chores for him, dropped in on his way home from the center of the village. Whittier stopped writing to ask, "What are they saying in the village today?" Dewhirst replied, "They are saying you are a Unitarian." "But that is certainly not news," Whittier said, with a smile, and showed the paper on which he had been writing; it was the manuscript of "Our Master."[13]

He showed the manuscript to two others before sending it for publication: Rev. James C. Fletcher, who was building Hawkswood, a large Victorian house with gardens, stables, and a greenhouse, overlooking the Merrimac River, and Dr. Leonard Withington, pastor of the First Church, Newbury, whose preaching Whittier had mentioned in complimentary terms in "To My Old Schoolmaster." They called at Whittier's house and talked about "The Eternal Goodness." Whittier was surprised that it had been misunderstood and gave a clear explanation of his beliefs, indicating that in regard to the divinity of Christ he was as orthodox as the Wesleys. He then went to his desk and got the manuscript of "Our Master," which he had Fletcher read aloud.

He sent the poem to Fields in September, for Mrs. Fields, he said, who would like its theology if not its poetry; it presented his "view of Christ as the special manifestation of the Love of God to humanity."[14]

The success of "Our Master" came partly from its emphasis on Jesus as the center of faith. Jesus had been crowded out of many Protestant churches by disputes about the methods and rewards of the salvation of one's soul. An attempt to restore Him to his place and to give Him the emotional appeal that He had never lost in the Roman Catholic Church was often marred by sentimentality. In Nineteenth Century America, Protestant men still went to church, and sentimentality repelled them. Whittier avoided it and succeeded in making the figure of Jesus appealing to both men and women. Simple worship of Jesus as the personification of love was a practical impossibility in churches planned for more involved and elaborate procedures, but their members liked to think and sing about it and to regard it as their real belief, even if they were not ready to practice it. The stanzas of "Our Master" were easily read and understood. Where there was figurative language it was simple and clear: winds of God blowing away the mists of earth, the healing of His seamless dress.

There could also be no misunderstanding of the religious lesson added as an irrelevant but sincere conclusion — and to Whittier's readers, a welcome one — to "The Dead Ship of Harpswell," in the June *Atlantic*. A young woman at Orr's Island sent Whittier the story of a spectre ship that sailed into Maine harbors when a death was about to occur. He told the story well but felt that it should end on a note of faith: there was an angel at the helm of the Ship of Death.

Whittier's increasing prominence made him thought of again as political material. Richard P. Waters of Beverly, a former United States Consul, called one day to urge him to be a candidate for Congress. He would have had a good chance of election. Pre-Civil War Republicans had not yet been shelved as innocuous elder statesmen, and his personal character was regarded as above reproach: his youthful political machinations had been forgotten — if indeed they were ever widely known. But he was now beyond that kind of ambition and too old for such a radical change in his way of life.

Other events, unimportant in themselves but part of the fabric of his every-day life, kept him from working on "The Tent on the Beach." The Quarter-ly Meeting of Friends was now held in Amesbury annually in May, and local Quakers served dinner in their homes to out-of-town members. Whittier was the only Quaker living near the meeting house who could afford to have din-ner guests, and he had as many as could be seated in the dining room. As usual, he went to the Yearly Meeting of Friends in Newport.[15]

There was a large crowd at the Laurel Party a few days later, and Whittier kept in the background. Perhaps he was embarrassed by a rather silly poem addressed to him which referred to the laurel as Daphne and to Whittier as Apollo. The crowd kept calling for Whittier until Mrs. Lippincott stepped forward and said that she would speak for him to relieve him of his embar-rassment — and, according to Robert Rantoul, did so "most acceptably."[16]

Whittier invited James and Annie Fields to spend a weekend with him before they went to their summer home, promising them "passable provender and comfortable lodging." There is no record of their coming for a week-end, but late in July they came to Amesbury by train from Beverly, and Whit-tier was ready with an enthusiastic welcome.[17]

The affection between James and Annie Fields was so conspicuous and their manner toward their friends so pleasant that Whittier and Gail Hamilton amused themselves by pretending to believe just the opposite. Gail Hamilton had written to Whittier in the winter that he would have a dreadful time if he visited them: "They are so selfish and self-absorbed there. Annie is so brusque and violent in her ways, and Jamie is such a tyrant in the house that you will have no peace in your life." Whittier told Lucy Larcom about this letter in some amusement. He continued the subject in June and wrote to Gail Hamilton, "James and Annie Fields have gone and joined the Shakers at Enfield. Cause: domestic infelicity. Very sad, isn't it? All books are denied them except a copy of 'New Atmosphere.' Lucy Larcom saw them shut up in separate dormitories!"[18]

Whittier was at the Isles of Shoals for a short time and after his return to Amesbury was invited to be a member of a delegation of Massachusetts Republicans to meet a group of Southern Loyalists at Philadelphia September 3. He used his letter declining the invitation as a means of telling the South what he believed to be the attitude of Massachusetts people toward reconstruc-tion. They were not looking for revenge; they could not wholly forget, but they could forgive. They had sent aid to Southern cities suffering from plague or fire; and the same hands that had aided the hunted Loyalists of East Tennessee had been extended to feed the starving rebels of Savannah. They favored the restoration of Southern states to their place in Congress as soon as it could be done safely; in other words, as soon as "the monstrous inequality of representation growing out of slavery" had been corrected so that a rebel in South Carolina should not have "double the political power of a loyal man in one of the New England States."[19]

Fields was taking care of Whittier's interests while Whittier himself was neglecting them. Two volumes of his prose were published in October, with no help from the author. They contained only material that had appeared in earlier volumes. Whittier had said that he would prepare a third volume, but when he looked over the mass of material that might be included, he was appalled and decided to "let it remain in its limbo." In November, Ticknor and Fields published a new edition of "Maud Muller". Plans had been made for a cheap edition of the complete poems in one volume, called the Diamond Edition because it would be printed in diamond type. Fields offered Whittier three thousand dollars for the five years beginning in October, 1867, payment in advance. At the end of the fifth year ten cents would be paid on each copy sold thereafter. He assured Whittier that this edition would not interfere with the sale of the others and added the cheerful news that the sales of *Snow-Bound* were keeping up and that Whittier would receive a "handsome checque" the next month.

Whittier did not agree that the Diamond Edition would not interfere with the sales of other editions, but he thought that on the whole he would gain by Fields' proposition, which he regarded as liberal. He would need the money if he lived, he told Fields, and if he didn't it would be "comfortable for somebody else."[20] This remark about needing the money can have two explanations. He was far from being in immediate need; a list of his assets on the back of a letter dated October 16, 1866, totals eighteen thousand dollars.[21] But a man of fifty-eight would find it hard to get out of the habit of fearing that he might be in need, and in his uncertainty about his health he could hardly avoid thinking about an old age without income from writing. In the Nineteenth Century little thought was given to providing dignified charity for the elderly poor; children were expected to take care of their parents, and the unmarried and the childless must provide for themselves or become paupers without the softening verbiage of a later day.

But there was no immediate need for money, and Whittier continued to delay "The Tent on the Beach." Ticknor and Fields announced in October that it would be published in November, but Whittier's mind was on other things. He had company most of the time in the early fall, and his time was "frittered away." An early frost killed his tomatoes and his grapes. He went to Boston to the Republican State Convention, caught cold, and was sick for a while. On October 4 he was well enough to receive a visit from Governor Smyth of New Hampshire and several officers of the Amoskeag Veterans of New Hampshire. The companies with their military bands paraded in front of Whittier's house, the Amoskeag Veterans in Continental uniforms. When the Governor and the officers left, Whittier stepped out to see them, as he said, "civilly off," and he was given a grand military salute, with music and three cheers. "Was ever a Quaker in such predicament?" he asked Gail Hamilton. "I did, I fear, somewhat compromise myself by lifting, almost involuntarily, my hand to my hat — but I resisted the temptation, and only pulled my hat lower down over my brow, by way of testimony."[22]

Charles Sumner wrote that he was to be married, "and at the age of fifty-five, begin to live." Whittier himself had realized that even love doesn't make it possible for a man to begin to live when he is in the fifties, but he told Sumner to go ahead and he would support him in this crisis as he had in all others. He was amused when Sumner left for Washington; instead of simply taking his carpet-bag and going to the railroad station, he now rode to the station in a coach with Mrs. Sumner, Mrs. Sumner's child, Mrs. Sumner's child's nurse, and Mrs. Sumner's little dog.[23] It was a sight that would make any bachelor rejoice anew in his independence and prophesy matrimonial disaster, but Whittier refrained from any cynical comment, even to Gail Hamilton.

In spite of the vexation that Fields must have felt at Whittier's continued delay with "The Tent on the Beach," cordial relations continued, and Whittier was at Fields' house in November. He almost went to the theater with Mr. and Mrs. Fields to see Adelaide Ristori as Elizabeth, but his courage failed him at the last moment. He had never been inside a theater, and he did not feel like breaking a life-long rule — and, furthermore, he was afraid that the excitement would cost him many nights of sleep.[24]

Whittier was never cured of writing poems about events that someone told him about without verifying the facts. This time it was an account of a ship-wreck on Block Island. "The Palatine" made full use of horror and crime: the islanders lighted a false beacon to lead the ship to the rocks, the crew and passengers were murdered, the ship was pillaged and burned. A year later the burning ship reappeared, and still put in an appearance on moonless nights.

Correspondence and controversy followed. A man in his ninety-second year claimed to have seen the phantom when he was young, and a man in Newburyport sent Whittier a china plate recovered from the wreck. Others accused Whittier of misrepresenting the facts. He replied that he had not done so intentionally; the man that sent him the story was, he thought, "a gentleman of character and veracity," and doubtless told the story as he had heard it, perhaps following a tradition current on the mainland. Richard H. Dana's "The Buccaneers," which Whittier thought was a remarkable poem, was based on the same tradition.[25]

At long last, on December 28, Whittier sent "The Tent on the Beach" to Fields, not, even then, in the final form, and so badly written that he was afraid that it was not legible. He thought that Fields might object to the personal character of the narrative framework, which represented Fields, Bayard Taylor, and Whittier camping at Salisbury Beach as the Beach had been before the first hotel and cottages were built, with Whittier reading the poems. His first plan had been to have each man read his own, but he realized that this plan was hackneyed and as old as the *Decameron*, and he abandoned it in disgust. Fields replied promptly that he had no objection to being one of the characters. Whittier thought that he could improve the poem when he saw the proof, but that it was already better than "Snow-Bound." He was surprised — although he should not have been, since publication had been announced for November — that Fields wanted publication in the winter. The publishers were much prompter than Whittier had been, and the printing was completed by February 1. Whittier was pleased with the appearance of the volume but wished to make some corrections if there was a second edition — which he thought unlikely if, as had been reported in the *Transcript*, ten thousand copies had been printed. He under-estimated the sales appeal of a follow-up of a best seller; *The Tent on the Beach* sold at the rate of a thousand copies a day, and Whittier wrote to Fields, "The swindle is awful. Barnum is a saint to us. I am bowed with a sense of guilt, ashamed to look an honest man in the face."[26]

He was unable to do any writing for publication during the winter. He was in Boston for about two weeks, came home in a storm, caught cold, and for a month suffered from neuralgia and was unable even to go to Friends Meeting. He was not well enough to take care of company and "kept them off." His niece Lizzie was at Ipswich Seminary, Mary Esther Carter was going away for a time, and he thought that there would soon be nobody left in Amesbury. But there was a family across the street that he would enjoy and find useful as long as he lived. A distant cousin, Adelaide Purington, was married to Gustavus Cammett, who was a Congregationalist, and so Adelaide could no longer be a Quaker, but they both went to the Yearly Meetings. The first of their two daughters, Carrie Maude, was born December 14. Whittier rocked her cradle, and as soon as she was old enough to play with blocks he would build tall chimneys which she would push over and they would laugh together. He differed from most bachelors in liking little girls and playing with them easily and naturally. He did not like little boys, whose vigorous actions tired and irritated him.[27]

By mid-February the weather had become as mild as April. He was now well enough to be outdoors and to go to Friends Meeting. He was also well enough to think of having company and to be humorous about his neuralgia. He invited Gail Hamilton to spend Sunday with him; he had been unable to ask her earlier while

That horrible *tic*
Was piling the agony high and thick,
Like a wicked monk of St. Dominic
Turning the rack and putting through,
Hand over hand, an "Ebrew Jew" —
Screwing and stretching, from toe to finger,
The old clo' man, like a patent wringer.[28]

The burden of correspondence and requests was getting heavier. He had received hundreds of letters since the publication of *Snow-Bound*, and many of the writers wanted him to do something for them or for the world. Henry Ward Beecher asked him to write a poem about the old Stuyvesant pear tree, which had just been blown over. Lucy Stone asked him to use his influence with Wendell Phillips to change his attitude toward women's rights, which he thought ought to wait until Negroes had received theirs. Dorothy Wharton, a stranger to him, wanted him to write on behalf of the Indians. Richard S. Spofford of Newburyport, who had married Harriet Prescott, wrote that he hoped to be appointed Marshall of Massachusetts. Whittier thought that he was a genial and good-hearted fellow, although he was not approved by most of his wife's friends, and he wrote to Sumner and Fields in his behalf. Spofford was a Democrat, he said, but that wouldn't hurt anybody except himself.[29]

A letter that he wrote in March was read in Congress. A fund was being raised in Boston to send food to the South. Whittier sent a contribution and a letter to the editor of the *Transcript*. People in many places in the South, he wrote, were threatened with actual starvation. "There can be no doubt of our duty to relieve them to the extent of our ability." He was sure that this would be done cheerfully. Massachusetts felt no hatred toward the people of the South, and now a Providential opportunity had come to overcome evil with good: "to magnanimously overlook the insane hatred still manifested toward us; and, as far as any action of ours can do so, to convince the people of the South that while resolved, for their good as well as for our own, that slavery and treason shall have no possibility of resurrection, we have only kindness and good will for themselves; and that our hearts and purses are open to aid them in recovery from the evils resulting from civil war and social changes."

When F. E. Woodbridge of Vermont was speaking in the House in favor of an appropriation for the relief of the destitute in the South, a Representative from Indiana interrupted to ask him to give way for a moment to the reading of a letter from Whittier. Woodbridge replied that he presumed it was better than anything he could say. The letter was read and Woodbridge thanked the gentleman from Indiana "for causing to be read an article from the sweetest of all our poets, John G. Whittier, a citizen of Massachusetts and an early and earnest pioneer of the anti-slavery cause."[30]

Before the year was over, there was further evidence of the high regard in which he was held. James T. Fields asked him to write for the 1868 *Atlantic Annual*. He was asked to contribute to a new magazine, *The Broadway*. The Governor of Massachusetts offered to appoint him to the Board of Education. He was asked to be a Trustee of Brown University; he thought that his health made it unwise to accept but did not absolutely refuse, and he became a Trustee in 1869. When Bayard Taylor and his wife were in England they visited Tennyson. There was a Blue and Gold Edition of Whittier's poems on his desk, and he asked many questions about Whittier.[31]

Late in the winter Whittier wrote five stanzas, "To Eli and Sybil Jones." For the past seventeen years Eli and Sybil Jones had gone on various missionary journeys and before that had travelled and preached in this country. They were called "Quaker ministers," a term which meant volunteer travelling preachers and religious workers; Friends meetings then had no resident paid clergy. They had visited Amesbury several times in the 1840's and had been "present," which meant that one of them spoke, at Sunday and Thursday meetings at the Friends Meeting House and at other meetings at the home of Moses Huntington in Pleasant Valley. Whittier, his mother, and Elizabeth were at these meetings. Now, at about Whittier's age, they were soon to leave for the Holy Land, which was then a comparatively unknown country to Friends. Whittier would have liked to go with them and briefly thought of doing so. Just before they left, he sent them his poem, in which he compared himself to a man watching a lifeboat, too weak to do anything but send a faint cheer across the wave.[32]

It had become evident that a second printing of *The Tent on the Beach* would be needed, and Whittier began sending suggestions for changes. Fields was more patient than most publishers would have been, especially when Whittier sent changes to be made in changes sent a day or so before. He changed some of the stanzas in the connecting narrative following "The Grave by the Lake" because they seemed to him to have a note of self-praise, and in the fourth printing later in the year he changed the last two stanzas to their present form.[33]

A revision that he suggested in another stanza was never made. He thought that the last four lines in the twenty-third stanza of the introductory narrative should be changed to

And, when the darkness seaward sprung,
   Its arch of light the rainbow flung,
The beach-birds circled in a wilder flight
And the green buds of waves broke into
   bloom more bright.

He thought that "prismy hues" sounded like "prunes and prisms" — a phrase which he remembered from Dickens' *Little Dorrit*. Fields wrote that he had made all the changes that there was time for: "Please examine the edition sent and see if you demand others."[34] Whittier took this rather broad hint and made no further changes for this printing.

As one looks at *The Tent on the Beach* today, he shares Whittier's surprise that it was so popular. The first part, which gave the title to the volume, had only one new poem. The narrative introducing and connecting the poems was often pleasant and graceful but without the features that made "Snow-Bound" a success. There were no new poems in the second part of the volume, and the poems in both parts had been widely copied in newspapers. A possible explanation is that the volume was of convenient size to attract readers and buyers who wanted Whittier's recent poems to keep and re-read and did not want a complete edition. Many people, then as now, would always buy the next book by the author of a best-seller.

The warm weather was late in coming. In mid-April, nearly time for mayflowers, the snow still lay in Folly Mill Woods and there was a bitter east wind. In the mood of depression that such weather always caused, it seemed to him that he was living a poor life of idleness and that the life of a hard-working farmer or mechanic was more enviable than that of a writer or politician. He had many visitors, most of them strangers who, he said, come to look at him and make speeches to him — "a sort of thing to make one feel sadly mean and ridiculous." He had rather chop wood than talk poetry with strangers.[35]

George L. Stearns died April 9, and Whittier wrote a poem which he sent rather doubtfully to Fields for the *Atlantic*. He was right in his opinion that it was "ragged and unkempt." The first line, he said, was "all out of proportion as to length, but it says just what I wanted to say."[36] In fact, throughout the poem, as was so often lamentably true in his verse, he was thinking so much of what he wanted to say that he gave little attention to the way he was saying it. The worst stanza was later omitted: it rhymed "Cretan" and "beaten," and worse still, "provider" and "Ida." He was paid one hundred dollars for the poem, and his conscience should have troubled him.

When he heard that slavery was soon to be abolished in Brazil, he wrote "Freedom in Brazil" and sent it to Fields. It differed from the present version and contained some double rhymes that Fields objected to because they detracted from the dignified movement: environ — iron, curses — rehearses, ringing — swinging. Whittier changed them. Then, too late to prevent publication, he found that the report of emancipation in Brazil had not been confirmed.[37] Complete emancipation did not occur until 1888, and Dom Pedro did not find himself "begirt by grateful hearts," as Whittier had prophesied in the poem.

In a letter to Grace Greenwood, Whittier gave a touching report of his own condition: "Much of the time I can do little more than sit and think of old days and old friends." This was hardly true. He went to walk in the woods one Sunday and found what he called one of Emerson's "solid banks of flowers." He went to Friends Yearly Meeting. As usual, he had a tableful of dinner guests on the day of Friends Quarterly Meeting.[38]

He wrote to Gail Hamilton, "Don't fail to come to Mr. Ashby's junket. I shall be there if my head will let me." Of course it did — the thought of going to a Laurel Party would make him feel better. Ashby was eighty years old but showed no signs of weakening. He met his guests at the railroad station with carriages to his garden, where a "bountiful repast" was served. They then went up the river on a steam barge, passing Fletcher's estate of Hawkswood. Dinner was served on a rocky knoll. Among the speakers was the Brazilian Minister d'Azambuja, who was a guest of Fletcher; he had read Whittier's "The Cry of a Lost Soul" and had seen Dom Pedro's translation of it. Fletcher, who presided, read Whittier's poem for the occasion, probably most of the stanzas of "June on the Merrimac," which remained unpublished for ten years. The fourth stanza could not have been written in 1867. The last two lines —

Beneath whose century-woven shade
Deer Island's mistress sings

referred to Harriet Prescott Spofford, who did not live at Deer Island until 1874.[39]

During the summer he spent some time at the Isles of Shoals, which he enjoyed because it was cool — the only place where he could escape the dog-days — and because Celia Thaxter was a delightful talker and story teller. He spent two days at a cottage at Salisbury Beach with his nieces and then left them there and returned to Amesbury, where he kept bachelor's hall and had a woman guest who helped him make some currant jelly.[40]

One day Harry Fenn called to get help in preparing illustrations for an edition of *Snow-Bound*. He found Whittier in a bad mood; he had just had a woman visitor who had read his own poems to him and had asked for a lock of his hair. He told Fenn to climb Powow Hill and look at the view. When Fenn returned and enthusiastically described the river and the sky, Whittier was in better mood and read some lines of his own that resembled Fenn's description. He advised against visiting the Birthplace, which he said was guarded by a dragon, an untidy one at that; the fireplace had been replaced by a modern Yankee cookstove and the room had a commonplace air that would discourage the artist. Nevertheless Fenn went to the Birthplace, where he found conditions as Whittier had described them. The dragon was a woman who could barely understand English, but Fenn succeeded in getting her to have the cookstove and fireboard removed. Behind it were the cranes, hooks, and chains that had been used in Whittier's boyhood. After more persuasion she allowed him to go to the attic, where he found pieces of spinning wheels, chairs, and tables, which he took down to the kitchen. He got a fairly satisfactory sketch, made a few other sketches around the farm, and returned to Amesbury. Tears came to Whittier's eyes when he saw the sketch of the kitchen, which he said was just as he had known it a half-century ago.[41]

The 1860's were a time of revival in the Society of Friends, bringing new ways that Whittier did not like, but the revival enthusiasm did not leave him untouched, and it resulted in some serious thinking and questioning. His poem "The Answer" appeared in the September 26 *Independent*. He referred to it ten years later as containing his belief on the subject of Universalism. He was not a Universalist, he said, for he believed that the soul would be lost if it persistently turned from God in the next life as in this but that Divine love and compassion followed man in all worlds.[42] The poem said that man had freedom of the will and might be a willing captive in his own dark jail if he refused to see and turn toward the guiding lights of love.

He was not neglecting his everyday public duties. He continued to be active in the management of the Public Library, which in 1867 moved into a new building on Friend Street constructed and owned by the Salisbury Manufacturing Company. The Library had free use of the first floor, and there was more than enough room for its 2200 volumes. Whittier had done much of the book-selecting and buying, and the collection was a good, well-balanced one. There was evidence of a broad-minded attitude on the subject of religion: there were various religious histories including *Early Jesuit Missions*, and there was also Darwin's *Origin of Species*.

He was on a committee of School District No. 2 to recommend a location and design of a schoolhouse. He was working hard to raise money for the Freedman's Aid Society and was "boring and button-holing" everyone he met. He had "screwed out" four hundred fifty dollars and was sure that he would get the rest.[43]

His niece Lizzie was with him during the fall until she left to teach in a school for Negroes in Richmond, Virginia. Addie Caldwell was also with him for a time. He liked her and was sorry when she left. She was the wife of his nephew Lewis Caldwell, whom he did not like and whom he found irritating and boring but whom his sense of family obligation forced him to help frequently with money and with appeals to people to hire him or get positions for him. When Caldwell married, Whittier wrote to Lucy Larcom that Lewis had blundered into one good speculation; his wife was a very nice, practical, good-principled lady-like woman and Whittier felt better about him and less solicitous after seeing her.[44]

Charles Dickens was giving readings in Boston early in December and Fields got Whittier one of the coveted tickets for the first of the series, December 2. Whittier hoped that he could go, see Dickens, and shake his creative hand. He went to Boston on the day of the reading but sent a note to Fields in the afternoon that he was not well enough to be two hours in a crowded hall and another in the evening, telling him to give the ticket to "some poor wretch who dangled and shivered all in vain in your long queue the other morning.'' As far as Dickens was concerned, it was well that he could not go, he said; Dickens would have more than enough of meeting people. Whittier had dreamed the night before that he saw Dickens surrounded by a mob of ladies with scissors snipping at his hair. But when the day came for Dickens' last reading in Boston, Whittier made ''an effort'' (quoting Mrs. Chick in *Dombey and Son*) and found himself in the packed hall between Longfellow and Richard H. Dana Sr. He sent Celia Thaxter a lively picture of Dickens:

"We waited some half hour: a slight, brisk man tripped up the steps, sparkling with ring and chain, tight vested, wide bosomed short dress coat, white choker, tight pantaloons enclosing, as the Prairie girl said of Judge Douglass, 'a mighty slim chance of legs.' Somehow a reminder of his own Tim Tapertit in *Barnaby Rudge*. Face marked with thought as well as years — head bald or nearly so — a look of keen intelligence about the strong brow and eye — the look of a man who has seen much and is wide awake to see more. I don't think he shows the great genius that he is — he might pass for a shrewd Massachusetts manufacturer or an active New York merchant. But his reading is wonderful, far beyond my expectations. Those marvellous characters of his came forth, one by one, real personages as if their original creator had breathed new life into them. You shut your eyes and there before you are Pecksniff and Sairy Gamp, Sam Weller, Dick Swiveller, and all the rest.''[45]

XXV
1868 - 69

Everything that Whittier wrote would now find an eagerly awaiting public, and it is not surprising that the *Atlantic* used "The Wife" as the opening piece in the February number. Whittier made its purpose quite clear:

..... I fain would teach
In this light way the blind eyes to discern,
And the cold hearts to feel, in common things,
Beatitudes of beauty.

When it was rewritten as "Among the Hills," with many changes and additions, the purpose became less didactic; instead of teaching, Whittier would

Invite the eye to see and heart to feel
The beauty and the joy within their reach.

The story, like "Amy Wentworth," was the love of a girl for a man socially inferior to her, but unlike "Amy Wentworth," it followed through and told the reader that they married and lived happily ever after. However, in its rewritten form it was not all sentimentality; there was realism in the description of the effect of husband and wife upon each other. There was also realism in the Prelude. Whittier was not blind to facts, however much he chose to tell of the beautiful and the inspiring rather than the ugly and the depressing. He knew how hideous farm life could be. The picture of a farm of this sort was sharply etched, with every detail blending in the total impression, and the occupants fitted their background —

Saving, as shrewd economists, their souls
And winter pork with the least possible outlay
Of salt and sanctity.

Later in January, "Hymn for the House of Worship at Georgetown" appeared in the *Independent*. It was written for the dedication of a new and magnificent church building in Georgetown, Massachusetts, paid for by George Peabody as a memorial to his mother. The circumstances and the outcome show that in spite of Peabody's adroitness and discernment in finance and philanthrophy, he was naive and inept in church matters. There was already one Congregational church in Georgetown, and there was no need of a second one. The pastor of the First Church was Charles Beecher, a brother of Henry Ward Beecher, and, like other Beechers, fond of excitement and controversy. He was often in conflict with his parishioners and on three occasions handed in a resignation, which he knew would not be accepted. He was a liberal in theology and impatient with people who disagreed with him. In 1864 eighty-five conservatives left and formed the Orthodox Congregational Church, meeting in a small chapel. Then a sister of George Peabody, formerly a member of the First Church, visited Georgetown and being in sympathy with the Orthodox group, suggested to her brother that he build a Memorial Church. He readily agreed and paid one hundred thousand dollars to have the building so well constructed that it would not need repairs for a hundred years. In spite of the small membership, the church was built to seat six hundred. The interior was glorious in chestnut and black walnut, the outer walls were brick and freestone, and the tower was one hundred fourteen feet high.[1]

When Charles Beecher heard that Whittier had been asked to write a hymn for the dedication, he went to him and said, "You are a progressive and Mr. Peabody is a conservative, and of course you will not write a poem for conservatives." Whittier replied, "We need progressives and we need conservatives" and wrote the hymn. It was sung by a quartette at the dedication January 8, a pleasant winter day with perfect sleighing, and the church was filled. A letter from George Peabody was read containing one clause which, Whittier wrote in a note to the *Boston Transcript*, would have kept him from writing the hymn if he had known about it. Peabody restricted the use of the building to religious and strictly moral purposes, "excluding forever all lectures, discussions, or controversies on political or other subjects of whatever nature inconsistent with its object as the House of God and a memorial of the dead." This restriction and Whittier's note were the subject of so much discussion — the *Independent* called the restriction "a pious disgrace to a Christian age" — that Whittier wrote another note, this time to the Haverhill *Tri-Weekly Publisher*, explaining that he should not have commented on the terms of the gift if he had not written the hymn for the dedication; Peabody, a conservative, thought the restrictions wise and salutary, while Whittier, calling himself a Radical, thought otherwise but did not change his opinion of Peabody's "more than princely munificence wisely and worthily bestowed and the noble example which he is setting to the rich men of his own and all future times."[2]

The Orthodox Memorial Church did not last one hundred years, but there was adequate proof that the walls were well built. After forty years there were so few members left that they united with the First Church and gave their building to the town to be used as a Town Hall. A fire in 1920 burned out the interior but left the walls standing. They were so solidly constructed that they could not be pulled down, and every brick had to be taken out separately.

From the middle of December to the middle of January Whittier was sick, more seriously, he believed, than he had ever been before, with a fever that left him weak and without appetite. He could not write, and so sent to the *Atlantic* for its February number a poem that he had written early in

December. It was "The Meeting," which he said was his reason for faith, "not enough conservative or radical to suit either party."[3]

"The Meeting" told what Whittier found in the kind of Friends meeting that was still held in Amesbury, before the coming of the evangelistic type that was already a part of the Quaker revival and would later reach Amesbury, to Whittier's displeasure. The particular meeting described was a silent one, but he also liked the kind of speaking done by Avis Keene, who had recently died; she saw the Eternal beauty mirrored in the beauty of the earth. The phrasing here indicates, it has been pointed out, that Whittier was recalling Plato's doctrine regarding archetypal beauty. The part of the poem that Whittier thought would not be acceptable to conservatives said that the teachings of the past no longer fitted human needs:

> The manna gathered yesterday
> Already savors of decay.

The recent advances in astronomy and archeology had brought doubts unknown in an earlier and simpler age, and even the Bible was no longer clear and fixed in its teachings. The conclusion was a contemporary attitude but hardly a radical one: a feeling of closeness to spiritual mysteries came when people met together in earnest desire to find the truth and found that Christ lived, not a king in the sky, but on earth in work and prayer among the poor and unfortunate. Again Whittier was saying something that in its clarity and simplicity would confirm and strengthen a trend in Nineteenth Century Protestant thought.

This sympathy for the unfortunate would, Whittier believed, be part of the life after death. The thought had been haunting him for a long time when he wrote "Divine Compassion" and sent it to the *Independent*[4], and it would seem an important question to a generation which had little doubt about personal immortality. If he reached Heaven by God's grace, the poem said — and he accepted without question St. Paul's "By grace ye are saved" — he did not want a victor's crown or martyr's palm but only a survival of his human sympathies.

Whatever the nature of Whittier's illnesses, they did not have any dismal effect on his personality. As soon as he was able to write in late January, he could make a humorous comment: it might have been better if he had been forbidden to write twenty years earlier. When he first looked out on the snow it looked dreary, and he longed to see bare ground, but he knew that the winter world would look beautiful as soon as he felt better,[5] and that is exactly what happened. He wrote "The Clear Vision," and it seemed to him that he was seeing for the first time the sunset glow on snow-covered hills and the beauty in the lines of tree branches. He could praise the Divine love which had sent the sickness and suffering that opened his eyes; every year the natural world seemed more beautiful. This growing delight in the beauty of nature was one of the happiest features of Whittier's later years;

he mentioned it frequently in his letters, and two years after "The Clear Vision" it found expression in another winter poem, "The Pageant."

Two other poems in the spring of 1868 were also written under strong religious impulse. "The Two Rabbis" (later "The Two Rabbins") was completed by June 29. Whittier liked it better than most of his recent poems.[6] The story, which was Whittier's invention and not based on anything in rabbinical literature, was well told and led directly to the conclusion, without needless moralizing or explanation: sin can be cured only in the self-forgetfulness of love.

The story of "The Dole of Jarl Thorkell" was also Whittier's invention and not derived from any Norse saga — as, in fact, was rather obvious from the story itself, which imagined a Christian idealism in a pagan world: a young woman easily persuaded everyone that it would be better to divide what food there was in time of famine than to make human sacrifices to the gods.[7]

Poor health did not result in Whittier's being wrapped up in his own affairs. He was as interested as ever in young authors. He encouraged Celia Thaxter to write two poems, which appeared in the *Atlantic*, "Rockweeds" in March and "The Wreck of the Pocahontas" in April. Publication in the *Atlantic*, which still had some of the best-known names in American and English literature among its contributors, would seem to have been adequate recognition of a young writer, but Whittier thought that Celia Thaxter deserved more. He took a rather curious way to bring this about. He wrote to George J. L. Colby, editor of the *Newburyport Herald*, asking him to print "The Wreck of the Pocahontas" with a note calling it "a poem of singular power" and asserting that if the public could forget "what's in a name" and compare it impartially with a poem by the English Laureate in the January *Atlantic*, their verdict would be in favor of "the comparatively unknown and unpracticed writer, who has told with such strength and intensity the story of her child-experience." The English Laureate was Tennyson, and his poem was "The Victim." It was not Tennyson at his best, and Whittier was perhaps justified in placing it below "The Wreck of the Pocohontas."

Also in the March *Atlantic* was a story by twenty-three-year-old Elizabeth Stuart Phelps, "The Tenth of January." Whittier wrote to her as soon as he had read it, the first of his many letters to her over the years.[8] His enthusiasm for this story was justified. It was based on the collapse of the Pemberton Mill in Lawrence, Massachusetts, and while the plot had some of the stock features of Victorian sentimentality, the description of Lawrence and its mill workers and of the disaster itself was vivid and true, and — more surprising in 1868 than it would be a century later — there was a direct placing of the blame.

The impeachment trial of Andrew Johnson was going on in the spring of 1868, and Whittier received a ticket of admittance to the Senate Gallery. He stayed in Amesbury and followed the progress of the trial with some anxiety. He does not seem to have been deeply concerned over the issues involved but was worried about the effect on the Republican chances of success in the fall. He was opposed to impeachment at first, but he thought that the Senate vote on May 16 which meant its defeat would hurt the Republicans in the Presidential election.

The chief obstacle in the way of Grant's election was Salmon P. Chase, who might receive and accept the Democratic nomination. If he accepted it, Whittier believed, Chase would be giving the lie to "the profession and practice of his whole life." In a letter to the *Independent* he urged, "Don't give up Judge Chase yet . . . Wait and see: I believe in him. I wish the Democrats had the grace to come up with such a man; but there is no prospect of it, and I trust he won't go to them." He did, but on July 9 Horatio Seymour was nominated, and the *New York Herald* commented, "The die is cast. The Democratic Convention has decided that our next President shall be General Grant."9

In Amesbury there was a flag raising and a meeting in Washington Hall, where Whittier was one of the vice-presidents and introduced resolutions endorsing cordially and without reserve the nominations of Ulysses S. Grant and Schuyler Colfax. But he declined to write a campaign song, as he had done in other elections; more practical appliances, he thought, were needed. "Nothing short of the harp of Orpheus, which 'drew iron tears down Pluto's cheek' could exorcise or charm to sleep the evil spirits of Democracy."10 However, when he heard the news of Grant's election he wrote "After Election," a poem of triumph with a religious fervor which came from his belief that the Democratic Party was an evil force and that a Republican victory was a victory for freedom, for which God should be praised. He had not wholly got over his love of geographical lists, and he named the different parts of the country from which election returns came as he waited in the telegraph office, bracing himself for the worst and rejoicing as the good news came: "We have a country yet."11

The summer started pleasantly. Gail Hamilton found Whittier in good spirits when she visited him early in June and went with him to Friends Meeting, where, there being no windows open, there was what she described as "quite a Congregational air." Whittier's niece Lizzie was with him for the summer, and he had a good housekeeper. He went to the annual Laurel Party late in June and saw a good many people, including one of the Curson girls, now married, whom a later generation would know as the grandmother of John P. Marquand.12

The rest of the summer was an uncomfortable and unhappy time. Whittier planned to join James and Annie Fields at Plymouth, New Hampshire, but was kept in Amesbury by the serious illness of the husband of his niece Mary Caldwell. She had been married, less than a year earlier, at the age of twenty-three to Enoch Stevens, who was forty-six. He owned a small shoe factory and houses for his employees a short distance from Whittier's home. He had now suffered a stroke which left him paralyzed, unable to move or to speak beyond monosyllables, and with his mind affected. Although Mary was as old as Whittier's mother had been at the time of her marriage, she seemed like a child to Whittier. "I cannot leave his poor little child-wife alone if I can be of any service to her," he wrote to Celia Thaxter, and he was surprised that she did so well in caring for her husband with a patient energy and assiduity that Whittier had not expected of her.

Enoch Stevens died July 28. Whittier was now suffering from the effects of heat and too many visitors. On the Fourth of July the temperature was one hundred, and he sat barefooted by the piazza door, while a boy across the street languidly did his patriotic duty by exploding a fire cracker once in a while. The heat continued and the dust blew about. "We can't lay the dust of the street," he wrote to Lucy Larcom "for fear the water will turn to steam and blow up the cart." Dr. Sparhawk ordered him to go to the Isles of Shoals to break up a persistent headache, but the trip tired him, and he got home worse than before, just in time for another heat wave. He wanted to write something for the *Atlantic* but would have to wait until cooler weather.[13]

The hot weather did not dry up the stream of visitors. They came constantly, most of them strangers, "waifs from the seashore and mountains," Whittier called them. Besides his visitors there were his nieces' friends; Alice Whittier was spending the summer with her sister Lizzie at Whittier's, and the house was seldom quiet. Whittier felt tired in body and mind, and an unsettled homeless feeling came over him and a longing for rest. His thoughts often turned toward his sister Elizabeth, and time had not lessened his sense of loss.

Not all of his visitors, however, were waifs from the seashore and mountains. James Russell Lowell and two of his friends called, and Whittier took them to see the view from a bluff overlooking the Merrimac River.[14]

One day two women called. One was Sarah Bagley, who had been a friend of Elizabeth and a teacher when Whittier was a member of the District 2 School Committee. She was intelligent and interesting, and Whittier encouraged her to call frequently. On this day she brought with her a woman who was staying at her house studying, teaching, and writing, Mary B. Glover, later Mary Baker Eddy, one of whose poems, "Christ My Refuge," dated August 2, 1868, was printed in the *Villager*. Mrs. Eddy's account of their visit is in "Articles and Manuscripts" in the Archives of the Christian Science Mother Church in Boston. The writer was permitted many years ago to see but not to copy a typescript, and Mrs. Eddy's most recent biographer, Robert Peel, notes that he used this account. Mrs. Glover and Miss Bagley called on a warm, sunny day and found Whittier in the Garden Room, flushed and coughing, with the windows closed and a fire in the Franklin stove. He was in bad mood from too many visitors. Mrs. Glover sensibly suggested that he open the windows and admit some of the clear, warm air. The conversation is not fully recorded, but it must have been pleasant and helpful; when the visitors left, Whittier said to Mrs. Glover, "I thank you, Mary, for your call; it has done me much good." Mrs. Eddy later wrote that she had cured Whittier of "incipient pulmonary consumption" in one visit. She sent him an autographed copy of *Science and Health*, which was found with other books in the attic after his death. He recalled her visit many years later in conversation with members of his family.

Perhaps it was Mrs. Glover's visit that made Whittier think of his attitude toward his own health. "Don't suppose for a moment that as the country folks say I 'enjoy poor health'," he wrote to Gail Hamilton a few weeks later. "I don't at all. I bear it, as I ought to, without murmuring — but it isn't nice at all."[15]

The summer drought was finally broken late in August by heavy rain which cleared the air and made the earth green and beautiful. Cardinal flowers bloomed at the foot of Powow Hill, Whittier's pear trees were heavily loaded with fruit, and his grapes were "like those the Israelites found at Eschol." Lizzie went to teach in Gordonsville, Georgia.[16]

Whittier and his publishers were still profiting from the popularity of his poems. The Diamond Edition had sold better than had been expected, and Whittier received an additional check early in November. A new edition printed from the Diamond plates appeared in October. The pages were larger than in the Diamond Edition and had a red line border around the printing to break the awkwardly large margins. A few weeks later Ticknor and Fields' successors, Fields, Osgood and Company, brought out *Among the Hills*. Whittier was pleased with its appearance and liked the illustrations but was afraid that its contents would be "nicely cut up by the critics." He wished that the book were better, he told Harriet Minot Pitman, because it would probably be his last one — "an announcement which my friends ought to receive with satisfaction." However, the public was ready to buy it, even though it had only one poem which had not been previously printed; and one jobbing house ordered five thousand copies in advance.

Early in December the publishers sent a check for fifteen hundred dollars, which Whittier thought that he would use to help pay for the Birthplace if he could get it at a reasonable price. He evidently lost interest in the plan, which may have been a passing notion that in his boyhood home he would get rid of the unsettled homeless feeling that he had complained of in the summer.[17]

He showed more enthusiasm for Lucy Larcom's *Poems* than for either of his own books. When it was in preparation, he had made suggestions for rewriting "On the Beach," although he added that he ought to let criticism alone, as he was not able to correct his own verses. He sent Fields an enthusiastic notice to be used in advertising. He called it to the attention of his friends, including Harriet Minot Pitman, to whom he wrote that it was one of the best volumes of poetry ever written by a woman: even Jean Ingelow had written nothing better than some of the poems in it[18] — praise that meant a good deal at that time. He showed a copy to Richard Webb and pointed out some of the poems that he liked best.

This conversation with Richard Webb, who was visiting the United States with his daughter, was at the Marlboro House in Boston, where Whittier was staying during a woman suffrage convention. Deborah Webb had set her heart on seeing Whittier and Niagara Falls, and although she said that both were indescribable, she recorded various details. She noticed that Whittier was quick and graceful in his movements and that his face was one of extreme refinement, with a sad and sensitive mouth, a good deal fallen in, dark deep-set eyes and prominent dark eyebrows. His hair was gray. He had a sadness and earnestness of expression, and his manner was shrinking and gentle, but he had a good sense of humor and a sudden hearty laugh. He talked with the Webbs about poetry; he thought that Jean Ingelow was better than Adelaide Proctor, lamented the slovenliness of Mrs. Browning, did not care generally for Browning but admired "How They Brought the Good News from Ghent to Aix." He said that he and Emerson had once analyzed "Lochiel's Warning" and decided that it was not genuine and then tried the same test on "The Burial of Sir John Moore" and decided that it was. She concluded that he seemed to have read everything.

Whittier took no active part in the Woman's Suffrage Convention although his name was on the list of officers. He went to two of the meetings and found the Convention a very dignified body. He approved of woman suffrage, which to him meant welcoming women to the same rights that he enjoyed, but he had no intention of joining any organization. He was not by nature a "joiner," and after the abolition of slavery he felt relieved of the obligation to be a member of anything except the human race. A year later Julia Ward Howe sent him a notice of a convention at Newport to form the American Woman Suffrage Association and asked his advice. He wrote that he could not attend but was in sympathy with the movement; he could not foresee the consequences of giving the vote to women, but he was sure that it was always safe to do right, and — an echo of his 1833 "Justice and Expediency" — "the truest expediency is simple justice." Part of the opposition to woman suffrage at that time came from the belief that it would make women less "womanly" by Victorian standards, but Whittier believed that Nature would prevent that and would be "conservative of all that the true man loves and honors in woman." As usual, he was more practical than most reformers and did not believe that the voting privilege would be a remedy for all the evils of which women were justly complaining; it must be accompanied by "a more practical education, higher aims, and a deeper sense of the responsibilities of life and duty."[20]

When he was in Boston he had dinner with Sumner, Emerson, and Whipple. Sumner's marriage had broken up, but Whittier found him "in very good spirits notwithstanding his infelicitous marriage speculation" — like Mark Tapley in *Martin Chuzzlewit*, "jolly under creditable circumstances." Bachelors do not look upon the break-up of a marriage as anything very tragic; the husband is merely returning to the way of life that the bachelor has, by hard luck or good judgment, never left, and Whittier was probably not deeply touched when Sumner wrote to him a few days later, "There is little happiness for me. This is my lot and I try to bear it."[21]

Whittier hoped that as soon as Grant became President he would make Sumner Secretary of State.[22] As in other instances, he tried to influence a national issue by writing to the local newspaper. "Charles Sumner and the State Department" was a long signed editorial in the *Villager* December 10. It seemed to him that Sumner's whole life had been education for the position and that there was "a certain propriety in assigning to the man who struck the heaviest blows at secession and slavery in the national Senate the first place under him who, in the field, made them henceforth impossible." If Grant received Whittier's advice by some devious route he did not follow it. He appointed Elihu B. Washburne, who resigned five days later. His successor was Hamilton Fish, who served through both of Grant's terms.[23]

Whittier started the new year 1869 suffering more than usual from neuralgia. Lizzie was now teaching in Camden, South Carolina, and he was lonely, dwelling much on the past and thinking of his mother and sister Elizabeth. However, he was able to write a pleasant and graceful letter, as his letters of this sort increasingly were, to be read at a Burns festival in Washington January 26. He had, he wrote, although not Scottish by descent, "a Scotchman's love for the poet whose fame deepens and broadens with the years. The world has never known a truer singer. — In the shout of enfranchised millions, as they lift the untitled Quaker of Rochdale [John Bright] into the British cabinet, I seem to hear the voice of the Ayrshire poet,

> For a' that and a' that,
> It's coming yet for a' that;
> That man to man the world o'er
> Shall brothers be for a' that".[24]

The first of his poems to be published in 1869 was "Howard at Atlanta" in the March *Atlantic*. It was the story, true except for one word, of a visit by General Oliver Otis Howard, head of the Freedman's Bureau, to a school for Negro children in Atlanta. When he asked what he should tell the children in the North about them, one boy said, according to the poem, "Massa, tell 'em we're rising!" His words seemed to Whittier to have more meaning than the boy had intended; the master's chain as well as the slave's had been broken, and black and white were rising together. The boy was Richard R. Wright, and when he heard the poem he wrote a letter to Whittier saying that he liked the poem and was grateful for Whittier's interest in his people, but he objected to one word in the poem. He had not said "Massa," for he had "given up that word." Whittier accepted the correction and changed "Massa" to "General" in subsequent printings. When Richard wrote to Whittier, he described himself as a "little miller boy" and said that he would go to work later that week, but he did not remain a miller boy. He became president of the Georgia State Industrial College for Colored Youth, and after retiring from educational work started on a successful career in banking. At the age of ninety he was still active as president of the Citizens and Southern Bank and Trust Company of Philadelphia.[25]

Whittier continued unwell during the spring, with a cough and an almost continuous headache, but he was able to be in Boston in April and to have dinner at James T. Fields'. The only other guest was Oliver Wendell Holmes, and the talk was quite free and open. Holmes asked Whittier's honest opinion of Longfellow's "New England Tragedies." Whittier said with some hesitation that he liked them but was surprised to find that Longfellow had preserved almost word for word the text of old books that Whittier had lent him twelve years earlier. Both Holmes and Whittier liked "Evangeline," but Whittier wondered that Longfellow had no outburst of indignation against the treatment of the Acadians. He had thought for a long time of working up the story himself but was glad that he had not — still, he could not understand Longfellow's calm way of telling it.

He went to Providence but was too sick to go on to New York and Philadelphia. After he returned to Amesbury, he had one visitor who was more interesting than most of the "pilgrims." She was a graduate of a New York medical school and was on her way to Germany for a year's study in surgery. She told Whittier that she could cut up a body without a tremor of what he called her "delicate hand or long fringed eyelid." On her return from Germany she intended to go to Arizona where she thought she would find plenty of gun-shot wounds and knife stabs to experiment on.[26]

The May *Atlantic* had one of his now rare pieces of prose written for publication. He was often impressed by the heroism of everyday people in peace-time deeds, and in "The Heroine of Long Point" he told, simply and clearly, the rescue of a captain and crew of a ship wrecked near the Canadian shore of Lake Erie. The summer tourist to the Great Lakes, he wrote, should give the heroic woman who saved their lives unaided a place in his imagination along with Commodore Perry's battleline and the Indian heroines of Cooper and Longfellow.

"Norembega," in the June *Atlantic*, was the first of three poems written in 1869 based on early American history or legend. The second was "Marguerite," which may have come from his conversation with Holmes about "Evangeline." He had found in the Haverhill records the indenture of an Acadian girl as a servant in a family in Haverhill. The poem had the indignation that Whittier had been surprised to find missing in "Evangeline," but it was directed not at the British who forced the Acadians into exile but at the harsh treatment that he imagined the girl had received in a New England household and at the bigotry of her mistress. There was a sentimental scene at the girl's deathbed when the son of the household told her that he loved her in spite of his mother's scornful charge that he loved a Papist and beggar. The mother's attitude toward her son's love for a Catholic girl was one that many middle-class Protestant women would have had in Whittier's time, and by showing it in a character already pictured as cruel, Whittier was making them see their own attitude in an unpleasant light. He had dealt with the same theme in "Mary Garvin" thirteen years earlier. Whittier thought that "Marguerite" had real feeling in it when he sent it to Fields in November, but later in the month he was not satisfied with it and decided to keep it around and see if he could make something of it. He sent it to Fields again a year later,[27] and it was printed in the *Atlantic* for March 1871.

"Marguerite" may have been one of the "two or three little things" which he told Celia Thaxter that he might publish sometime. One of them was "Nauhaught, the Deacon," the story of an Indian deacon at Yarmouth.[28] It was told in blank verse, which Whittier had learned to handle well. In later printings lines were removed which probably caused vexation to some church people:

> . . . . . Up in heaven
> Would the good brother deacon grown so rich
> By selling rum to Indians laugh to see him
> Burn like a pitch-pine torch?

was replaced by

> . . . . . Would the saints
> And the white angels dance and laugh to see him
> Burn like a pitch-pine torch?

Whittier was still unwell in May, too sick for visiting, he told Bayard Taylor, who had invited him to his home in Chester County, Pennsylvania. The only way he could be comparatively free from suffering was to remain quiet at home and avoid exposure and excitement. He declined "going through the operation" of having a bust made by Millmore, who had just done Charles Sumner and Wendell Phillips.

In spite of his poor health he did his duty at the time of the Friends Quarterly Meeting in Amesbury. On the second day of the meeting he had forty guests at breakfast and twelve at dinner. It is not surprising that he felt tired afterward.[29]

In the middle of the summer he spent a short time at the Isles of Shoals and early in September went to Centre Harbor with Addie Caldwell and

Lizzie, and spent a week with the Pitmans and Lucy Larcom. He dreaded the dark, cold season more as he grew older, he wrote to Celia Thaxter, but added more cheerfully, "Nothing in the world is half so bad as we fear it will be."

An article in the September *Atlantic* by Harriet Beecher Stowe had aroused as much controversy as her *Uncle Tom's Cabin*. It was "The True Story of Lady Byron's Life" and had been prompted by the publication of Countess Guiccioli's *My Recollections of Lord Byron*. Mrs. Stowe's sympathy for Lady Byron had no reservations, nor did her condemnation of Lord Byron, whom she accused of incest. His half-sister, Augusta Leigh, was not mentioned by name, but readers of the article knew who was meant. There was strong feeling in this country and abroad that the article should not have been published. Whittier thought that some of the American papers treated Mrs. Stowe outrageously, but he was sorry that she had told the dreadful story and also sorry to feel that it was true: It was a "new horror introduced into the world."[30]

Whittier had continued to hope that Rome would become part of the kingdom of Italy in spite of the failure of Garibaldi and "Young Italy" to take the city. As a result of Garibaldi's attempt in 1867, Napoleon III had sent French troops to defend Rome, and they were still there in the autumn of 1869, when Whittier wrote "Garibaldi" for the October *Atlantic*. Whittier never lost his skill in selecting and presenting the high points in a scene which he knew only by reading about it, and he pictured Garibaldi

> . . . . . watching lone
> The hot Sardinian coast-line, hazy-hilled,
> Where, fringing round Caprera's rocky zone
> With foam, the slow waves gather and withdraw.

Mrs. Lucia G. Alexander sent a copy of the poem to Garibaldi, who acknowledged it, but whose hands were too swollen by rheumatism to write a letter.[31]

Whittier had some doubt about "The Hive at Gettysburg" and asked Oliver Wendell Holmes' opinion before sending it to the *Independent*, the first poem he had sent them, the editors complained, for eighteen months. The poem drew a parallel between the honey that Samson found in the carcass of a lion (Judges 14:8) and the hive inside a shattered drum on the field of Gettysburg; as in the riddle that Samson made, "Out of the strong came forth sweetness," union, peace, and freedom had been taken from "the rent jaws of wrong." Whittier was afraid that the parallel would seem forced and fantastic. Holmes did not think so, and it could not have occurred to either of them that a century later the English Bible would be so unfamiliar to many readers that they could not guess what Whittier was referring to or know where to look it up. Holmes made two criticisms which he called "hypercriticisms," trivial comments resulting from his "dyspeptic ear" which often insisted on liquids where "a better aural or acoustic digestion would like more solid substance." The two phrases which he thought unmusical were "flowery rounds" and "Danite athlete;" the two words in the latter "stuffed the mouth with consonants." Whittier changed it to "oldtime athlete."[32]

Two new volumes of Whittier's poems were printed in the fall. *Ballads of New England* contained ten poems, all of which had been previously printed in some collection. The attraction of this volume was its illustrations. Whittier thought that the poems were better suited for illustration than "Snow-Bound," being more varied and picturesque, and the publishers employed some of the most popular artists in the United States, including Winslow Homer. Whittier was pleased with the pictures, which he said made him almost ashamed of the verses that they illustrated.[33] The volume was favorably reviewed by Howells in the December *Atlantic*.

The only complete editions at this time were the two-volume Blue and Gold, in rather fine print, and the inexpensive one-volume Diamond Edition, in even finer type. The Merrimac Edition, issued in September, was in two volumes. The print was satisfactory and the plates were used eleven years later in the Cambridge Edition.

Three poems late in 1869 were not written for general publication. "To a Young Physician" was written for *The Fairy Leaf*, printed for a fair in Boston in aid of consumptives' and children's homes. It contained seven stanzas, five of which were included with slight alterations in "The Healer."

Whittier had a hand in arranging a surprise party for his neighbors J. Wells Colby and Joan Colby on their fortieth wedding anniversary December 13. Their house, across the street from Whittier's garden, was filled with friends and neighbors. "The interest of the occasion," the *Villager* reported, "was deepened by the consideration of Mrs. Colby's life-long and self-sacrificing services to the sick and suffering in the vicinity," among whom had been Whittier's mother and sisters. The gifts included seventy-five dollars wrapped in a paper on which were five stanzas that were read to the company. They had the happy combination of humor and sentiment that Whittier so often succeeded in achieving in verses of this sort.[34]

"To Alice and Phoebe Cary" was Whittier's inscription in a copy of his *Ballads of New England* which he sent to the Cary sisters at Christmas. They had called at his house and stayed over night on their first visit to the East. Numerous poems by them had been printed in *The National Era*. The next spring he saw Alice in New York for the last time, and after her death wrote "The Singer" for the August 1871 *Atlantic*.[35]

"In School-Days," which is still one of the best-known poems in American literature, was written when Whittier found that he could not write verses to go with some pictures that the publishers of *Our Young Folks* had sent him. He wrote to Lucy Larcom, then editing the magazine, that he was sending instead something which he was sure was childish if not childlike. He told her to be honest and not to print it if it seemed "too spoony for a grave Quaker."[36]

One of the reasons why "In School-Days" became immediately popular was that it reminded people of their childhood. They had gone to one-room schools which were like the one realistically described in the second and third stanzas, when the present-day theory had not developed, that school should be a joyful place where children would be unaware of the passage of time and would leave reluctantly. But more than that, the sentiment was simple and sincere, and the concluding lesson — which is not the part known and quoted today — was what Whittier's contemporaries liked and expected. After Oliver Wendell Holmes read the poem, he wrote to Whittier, "It melted my soul within me to read these lovely verses. . . . . . I had no sooner read them than I fell into such ecstasy about them that I could hardly find words too high-colored to speak of them to my little household. I hardly think I dare read them aloud. My eyes fill with tears just looking at them in my scrapbook, now, while I am writing." Matthew Arnold called it one of the perfect poems which must live. Eight years later Longfellow had not forgotten it. Writing to Elizabeth Stuart Phelps on the topic of co-education, he said, "Certainly there is something more in education than is set down in the school books. Whittier has touched this point very poetically in that little lyric of his called 'In School-Days.' "[37]

The girl referred to in the poem was probably Lydia Ayer, who died at the age of fourteen. It has been generally thought that the incident was not Whittier's own experience, but he was rather evasive on the question. In 1878 he visited an old red school-house in West Ossipee, New Hampshire, and listened while the class read "In School-Days." When the children asked him if it was true he replied that it was quite likely that there was some truth in it.[38]

XXVI
1870 - 72

In January Whittier went to a meeting of the Radical Club in Boston, that informal discussion group which had started three years earlier at John T. Sargent's and had come to be regarded as "the very inner temple wherein the gods forged their thunderbolts." Whittier kept quiet and listened to Thomas Wentworth Higginson, Wendell Phillips, Julia Ward Howe, and Lucy Stone. Mrs. Fields described the talk as the "unnatural and excited view of the inside ring" but conceded that it might result in a better understanding of one's own beliefs. It evidently had that effect on Whittier. His lines written a few days later for Mrs. Sargent (now, with the addition of the first two lines, "By Their Works") had as their central thought that whatever is done in the name of love is done to Christ. He revised and added to "My Triumph," which he had started work on in the fall, and which sounded a note of confidence: other men would do what he had failed to do, the Age of Gold would come, and he would be part of it.[1]

In spite of this confidence, he foresaw some problems in the religion of the future, especially the part that the Society of Friends would have in it. He did not approve of the Quakers' adopting the ways of other denominations, and he wrote a letter to the *Friends Review* in which he tried to explain his preference for the old ways without giving offense to those who thought otherwise and without denying that the Society needed spiritual renewal. He did not approve of a "hired ministry," which meant regular pastors for local meetings. If he became convinced that preaching was needed, he would prefer to listen to such men as Horace Bushnell and Henry Ward Beecher rather than to the products of a Quaker theological school. The letter of course resulted in letters to him; he answered at least one personally and others by a second letter to the *Friends Review*. The traditional Quaker trust in the Inner Light seemed to him to be the only efficient solvent of those doubts which came from the "searching eye of philosophy and the terrible analysis of science."[2]

In spite of Whittier's dislike of cold weather, he enjoyed winter scenery, and "The Pageant," sent to Fields February 24, was well done. Whittier himself could not guess whether it was good or not but thought that it was an accurate description of what he had actually seen. He later thought that it was the best "snow picture" that he had ever made — "a good deal more artistic than Snow-Bound."[3] It described the morning after an ice storm, and had no moral or religious lesson. There were some details that would be more pleasing to Whittier's contemporaries than to later readers: tree branches compared to chandeliers, a hemlock described as "Ethiopian." But others were vivid and clear:

How flash the ranked and mail-clad alders
    Through what sharp-glancing spears of reeds
    The brook its muffled water leads!

The clamor of some neighboring barn-yard,
    The lazy cock's belated crow,
    Or cattle-tramp in crispy snow.

During the winter he did a good deal of reading. He liked Henry Wilson's series of articles which were to be his *History of the Rise and Fall of the Slave Power in America*. He was reading the volumes of William Morris' *The Earthly Paradise* as they appeared, and his comment showed that he had the attitude of his time toward Chaucer; Morris, he said, was "Chaucer improved and made decent — wonderfully sweet and pleasant reading." He was more tolerant than many readers, however, toward Elizabeth Stuart Phelps' new novel, *Hedged In*, which shocked Harriet Beecher Stowe. Its heroine was what was then called a "fallen woman." In a rhymed letter to Lucy Larcom he asked her to review it for the *Atlantic*; it taught a lesson and helped people to treat a sinner with love, believing that she can be changed by God's love within her.[4] *Hedged In* was favorably reviewed in the June *Atlantic* but along quite different lines from Whittier's suggestions and probably not by Lucy Larcom.

He did not feel able to go to the final meeting of the American Anti-Slavery Society in New York in April, but a few weeks later was having a good time in the city as the guest of Col. Julian Allen. He was given a reception by the Union League Club. He went to a meeting of a clerical association at Theodore L. Cuyler's, where the clergymen dispensed with the program planned for the evening and listened to Whittier's lively and humorous talk. He amused them by describing the Quaker practice of speaking in meeting by anyone who felt called upon to do so and said that these voluntary remarks were not always edifying. He gave as an example a man whose exhortations became wearisome to his listeners, who passed a resolution that it was the sense of the meeting that he be advised to remain silent until such time as the Lord should speak to him more to their satisfaction and profit.

He called on various people, including Alice and Phoebe Cary. Horace Greeley called at the same time. Alice was seriously ill, but she turned the conversation from her own sufferings to happier topics.

He returned home tired from the excitement and seeing and talking with too many people. His housekeeper was away, but Mary Esther Carter and her niece Carrie Carter took her place.[5]

Whittier's "To Lydia Maria Child" appeared in the June 16 *Independent* but may have been written a number of years earlier. It was suggested by Mrs. Child's "Lines Written on the Anniversary of the Death of Ellis Gray Loring," dated May 24, 1859, but not published until after the abolition of slavery, as indicated by Whittier's fourth stanza. Whittier's poem asked why no whisper came from Loring on the spring air but concluded on a note of conviction that doubtless brought comfort and reassurance to Whittier's contemporaries as well as to himself: the yearning for a voice or sign from the darkness was itself the best proof that we shall meet our loved ones in a life after death. Mrs. Child wrote to Whittier that the lines were very tender and touching, and "the sunshine of your faith makes rainbows on the tears."[6]

Two occasional poems were written during the summer. "A Spiritual Manifestation" was read at the Brown University President's Levee on June 29. It had the light, humorous touch that Whittier could use sucessfully and which must have been enjoyed by the audience. It imagined Roger Williams speaking to the gathering and describing the motley group of settlers that came to Rhode Island, including one not mentioned in the present form of the poem:

> In rustled Madam Hutchinson
> Loud-voiced for rights of woman.

The concluding stanzas had just the right touch of reverence and sentiment. The poem had some poor rhymes, perhaps because it was not subject to the criticism of an *Atlantic* editor: taught her — daughter, catch them — fetch them, proud for — chowder, assorter, — water.

"To William Ashby and His Household" was written July 11 at the Isles of Shoals for the last of the Laurel Parties. Five of its stanzas, with minor variations, are now stanzas 1, 3, 4, 6, and 7 of "The Laurels." Samuel J. May read Whittier's poem, and Dr. Samuel Spaulding a poem by Lucy Larcom, and on the return trip down the river the two clergymen collected money for a Laurel Party for the poor children of Newburyport without regard to sect or color.[7]

Whittier returned to Amesbury but soon had reason to wish that he had stayed at the Isles of Shoals. The temperature rose to ninety-eight and went down only to ninety at night, and he spent the night going from one room to another and trying without success to sleep on sofas and floors. In spite of his discomfort he wrote a long letter to Celia Thaxter, whose letters and company he thoroughly enjoyed; her last letter had seemed to bring "the sweet breath of wild rose and mignonette" as if the cool sea air of the islands blew inland, bathing his "hot, aching brow for a moment in the dream of a milder atmosphere."[8]

Late in August he sent a short poem "The Sisters," which he thought that Fields might like, as it touched "a matter of universal interest" and had "a certain lyrical swing and freedom which we lose in labored and more pretentious poems."[9]

When he mentioned "labored and more pretentious poems," he may have been thinking of his "Miriam," which he had been working on during the summer. He sent it to Fields, explaining that it was wholly fiction, although consistent with the character of Akbar and his Christian wife. Fields suggested that it be published immediately in a volume with other poems. Publication was delayed until November, when the volume appeared with woodcuts, including a picture of Miriam in spite of Whittier's objection, "I rather shrink from seeing a pretty woman's face on my sober page, as thee suggested. It would be quite out of keeping." There was a dedication poem to Frederick A. P. Barnard, who had become president of Columbia University in 1864, and who had written to Whittier in 1868 reminding him of their Hartford days.[10]

The narrative in "Miriam" was well told and could have carried its meaning with a few brief lines of introduction or conclusion. The introduction, however, was almost as long as the story itself, much longer than necessary to make the point that truth, which to Whittier meant the teachings and example of Jesus, is to be found in all religions. The conclusion of the narrative had a paraphrase from the *BhagavadGita*, which Whittier had first read nearly twenty years earlier in a copy that Emerson had lent him. Whittier incorrectly implied that Christian forgiveness was the same as the Oriental desireless striving to attain Nirvana.[11]

Whittier so thoroughly disapproved of Napoleon III that his sympathies had been with the Prussians during the Franco-Prussian War. After the French defeat at Sedan September 2 and the capture of Napoleon III, his peace principles came to the fore, and he asked Sumner if the United States government couldn't do something to stop the War. The Prussians, he hoped, would now be as magnanimous as they had been brave.[12] But the War went on, and the Prussians were starving Paris into surrender when Whittier's "Disarmament" in the *Independent* January 5 appealed to mankind to "put up the useless sword" and included in the horrors of war

> . . . . . cities starving slow
> Under a rain of fire.

The poem used both Christian and Buddhist teaching. It was the voice of Christ that said, "Put up the sword," and the narrative to prove that unarmed peace conquers every wrong was the myth that when Buddha was threatened by a monster and said, "Poor fiend, even thee I love," the monster turned into a dove.

"The Prayer-Seeker," in the December *Atlantic*, was sure to appeal to readers in Whittier's own time but not to become a permanent part of religious literature. The first two stanzas were melodrama. A veiled woman in black glided like a ghost down a church aisle, put a paper with the words "Pray for me" on the preacher's desk, and glided back like a guilty thing — "ghost" perhaps having reminded Whittier of the ghost of Hamlet's father, who started "like a guilty thing." None knew the source of her grief or shame, and therein she was typical of all mankind; Heaven listens to the loving prayer for others of people with sorrows of their own who do not try to seek out the cause of others' sufferings, to learn, in a sadly sentimental phrase,

Why cheeks grow pale, why eyes o'erflow.

A poem about his birthday may have had considerable revision before its publication ten months later — and it is further proof of Whittier's popularity and importance that the *Atlantic* cared to use a poem in October that began

Beneath the moonlight and the snow
Lies dead my latest year;
The winter winds are wailing low
Its dirges in my ear.

"My Birthday" had the kind of sentimentality that was more acceptable to Whittier's contemporaries than it would be to later generations which found less delight in weeping:

My eyes are wet with thankful tears
For blessings which remain.

But the blessings listed were not peculiar to Whittier's time: the beauty of Nature, human love, freedom from the hate and clamor of party strife. The danger in old age was self-indulgence; the tumult of youth was better than that.[13]

When Whittier decided on the last day of the year that he could not go to a meeting of the Radical Club, where Mary Grew was to read a paper on Essential Christianity, he wrote "How Mary Grew" and sent it to Mrs. Sargent. A year later he had almost forgotten what he had written but was afraid that it was a "very sad jingle" — as indeed it was — and trusted that it would not "get any farther than M. G's pocket." Ten years later he changed his mind. He still supposed that the verses were not "very creditable in a literary point of view" but was very glad to let others know his estimate of a beloved friend and so was willing that Mrs. Sargent should use them in her *Sketches and Reminiscences of the Radical Club*.[14]

During the winter Whittier was working on a new edition of *John Woolman's Journal* and an anthology of poems for children.

The Introduction to the *Journal* was ready January 20. Whittier found it a labor of love. It was made easier — a fact which he did not mention — by including long passages from his "Quaker Slaveholding and How It Was Abolished," which he had written for the *National Era* in 1847, totalling about one third of the Introduction. The volume was issued in April. There were later printings, and the Introduction was used in a number of English and Scotch editions of the *Journal*.[15]

Of the literary friends whom he said he consulted about *Child Life*, the only one that he mentioned in the Preface was Lucy Larcom, who was also the only one who received part of the profits. She got three hundred dollars and a percentage, as she did later on *Songs of Three Centuries* and *Child Life in Prose.*

The Preface implied that Whittier did most of the actual selecting himself, and he evidently went about it seriously and conscientiously, trying to find pieces that combined simplicity with literary excellence and which neither descended to silliness nor were too difficult for children to understand; and he sometimes asked the opinion of children. He hoped that the poems of fancy and imagination would not cause children to confuse truth and error and, not forgetting his conviction that poetry should do good, thought that even nonsense verse such as Edward Lear's "The Owl and the Pussy Cat" might "not be without a certain moral value as a fitting caricature of the affectation of sentiment." As for poems about fairies, the schoolmaster and the newspaper had been busy with disenchantments, but there was still enough "beautiful wisdom" left to justify including a few.

Some of the poems in the collection are still popular, such as his "Barefoot Boy" and "In School Days," Clement Moore's "A Visit from Saint Nicholas," Thomas Hood's "I Remember, I Remember" — hardly a child's poem — William Cullen Bryant's "Robert of Lincoln," Tennyson's "The Brook", and Browning's "The Pied Piper of Hamelin." It was a time when children were told about death, and Whittier included poems about dead and dying children: James Russell Lowell's "The First Snow-Fall" and "The Changeling," Maria White Lowell's "The Morning Glory," Dirk Smits' "Death of an Infant."

During the winter months of 1870-71 he was too busy editing to write any poetry but not too absorbed to be aware of current events. He would have liked to go to the New York celebration on January 12 of the freedom of Rome and its inclusion in a united Italy. The Franco-Prussian War had forced Napoleon III to withdraw the troops that he had placed in Rome to maintain Papal rule, and Whittier rejoiced that the change of government had come without bloodshed. His religious feeling, he said, had not entered into the sympathy with which he watched "every effort for the deliverance of Rome from a despotism counting its age by centuries." He would have felt the same way if he had been a Catholic, occupying as he did "the standpoint of a republican radical," desiring that all men of all creeds should enjoy the civil liberty which he prized so highly for himself.[16]

He had mixed feelings toward the struggling new republic in France. His sympathies were with the men who were trying to establish it, but still — in spite of his wish that the United States government might stop the war and in spite of his appeal in "Disarmament" to "put up the sword" — the siege of Paris by the Prussian army seemed the logical sequence of the bombardment of Rome by Oudinot (the subject of his vigorous invective in "The

Pope and Saint Peter" in 1853) and he found significance in the fact that the chassepot, "which made its first bloody experiment upon the half-armed Italian patriots without the walls of Rome" had failed when used by the soldiers of the new French republic against "the inferior needle-gun of Prussia."

On the national scene he thought that Congress ought not to adjourn without doing something to protect Union men in the South; he had been reading about Ku Klux Klan activities. It seemed to him that one pretext for the disturbances, from which Negroes were the chief sufferers, would be removed if amnesty were extended to all who had served under the Confederacy, and that the government had gone so far in its leniency that there was no point now in making exceptions. The real difficulty in Reconstruction was that the states that had formed the Confederacy had been readmitted to the Union and had to be dealt with as states, contrary to Sumner's advice.

The local mills were important enough to justify an invitation by the Salisbury Manufacturing Company to the Massachusetts Legislative Committee on Labor to visit them and investigate health conditions, especially hours of labor. Whittier and the president of the local bank had been mentioned as disinterested persons who might take part in the investigation. A report in the *Boston Herald* implied that their opinion was already known to the Company representative who had given the invitation. Whittier wished it understood that this representative, John Gardner, had no knowledge of their opinion. He was sure that the agent in charge of the mills, Marquis deLafayette Steere, would have no reason to fear it. As for Whittier's opinion on hours of labor, he did not need to say to those who knew him that he would like to see a reduction as far as warranted by the interests of both capital and labor.

A week later he was more specific. Mill owners should give serious consideration to the recent hearing of the Massachusetts Legislative Committee on Labor on the working of the ten-hour day at the Atlantic Mills in Lawrence. There had been no corresponding decrease in wages, and at first there had been a slight decline in profits, which had now been overcome by the increased energy and activity of the employees. Employers, he continued, should give consideration to the health and well-being of employees, and "the poor man's capital of labor should be, at least, as carefully protected as the capital invested in mills and machines." He was convinced that the change would come by legislation if not by voluntary action by manufacturers. The latter seemed to him the better way: "The laborers, grateful for the hour or more of daily leisure thus afforded, would naturally seek by increased diligence and faithfulness in their work to make the diminution of profit as light as possible." He continued this note of idealistic optimism in his conclusion: "To all questions of this kind, the Golden Rule of our Divine Master may be safely applied. No system of labor contrary to it can be truly successful; none in accordance with it can ultimately fail."[17]

William Dean Howells had succeeded Fields as editor of the *Atlantic*. Whittier was afraid that he would now lose all interest in the magazine; he found it hard to adjust himself to changes, and Fields had been a true good friend for many years. Fields assured him that the *Atlantic* still wanted everything that he wrote, and during the remaining years of his life the *Atlantic* received the larger part of his poetry. His relations with Howells were pleasant, although they never became intimate. There was one incident which might have made trouble for Howells if Whittier had been less kind and tolerant. Howells saw clearly enough that Whittier's work was not all equally good, and he returned one poem, asking Whittier to send something else. Whittier sent the poem for publication elsewhere but gave no sign of resentment and sent Howells another. Whittier was at this time a much more important person than Howells, and the publishers were doubtless aware that the public wanted to read everything that he wrote. If he had stopped sending poems to the *Atlantic* and had sent them to other magazines that would have been glad to get them, Howells would have been in an awkward position. Fortunately Howells soon saw the light. He did not change his opinion of the poem that he had rejected, but he never again ventured to pass upon contributions from the writers who had made the *Atlantic* what it was; he accepted everything that they sent, printed it, and praised the gods.

When the "pilgrims" began to come in May, Whittier wished that he might have his choice of them. He would have enjoyed one who had hoped to come in the winter but was unable to. Bret Harte wrote that he wanted to talk with Whittier about Thomas Starr King, whom they both loved and who perhaps knew Whittier better but hardly admired him more than Harte himself did. Whittier met Harte in Boston and was "much pleased with him."[18]

His first published poem since January was "The Robin" in the June *Atlantic*, based on a Welsh myth told him by his neighbor Joan Colby. The concluding stanzas gave a rather far-fetched symbolic interpretation which had a lasting popularity. The final stanza was set to music and published in a song book thirty years later.[19] "The Singer" appeared in the August *Atlantic*, in time to be read to Phoebe Cary shortly before her death.

He was elected a delegate to the Republican State Convention at Worcester on an anti-Ben Butler ticket. Butler, now a Republican, was a candidate for the nomination for governor and was campaigning vigorously, attacking capitalists and editors. He won the support of such reformers as Wendell Phillips, who spoke at the annual Salisbury Beach Gathering September 13, concluding, "I for one when I hear in November as I hope to hear, that from Barnstable to Berkshire the people of the Commonwealth have strangled the press with one hand and the monied corporations with the other and have made Benjamin F. Butler governor of Massachusetts, I shall say, 'Amen! So be it! Glory to God!' " "Isn't Butler on a rampage!" was Whittier's comment; "I confess I don't like his style of doing things." But he did not go to the Convention to assist in the defeat of Butler by the conservatives.[20]

In October he was busy raising money for the aid of sufferers in the great Chicago fire and forest fires in Wisconsin and Michigan. The fire in Chicago caused a property loss which it was thought would approach two hundred million dollars; many insurance companies, including twenty in New York, became bankrupt. Temporary homes had to be built for thousands before winter. In Wisconsin and Michigan the forest fires swept into farming districts and villages, and thousands were left destitute and homeless. The telegraph and cable carried the news over the world, and there was a generous response, which Whittier wrote about in his poem "Chicago" in the December *Atlantic*. He wrote a letter to the *Villager* and succeeded in raising nearly a thousand dollars, contributing twenty dollars himself.[21]

Whittier's religious thinking now led him toward one of his most-quoted poems. Early in December he answered a letter from a woman who had asked him if he was a Unitarian, telling her that he was a member of the Orthodox part of the unhappily divided Society of Friends, but had a higher regard for practical piety than for doctrinal soundness and inclined rather to the old standards of Quakerism than to the "new lights." A letter a few weeks later to the Editor of the *Friends Review* questioned the efficacy of the protracted meetings and revivals that were coming into fashion among some groups of Friends. Whittier would not fight against it, not liking ecclesiastical quarrels, but he had an instinctive dread of noise and excitement in religious matters.[22]

The ideas in these two letters were combined in "The Brewing of Soma" in the April *Atlantic*. It started with an account, evidently from Max Muller's translation of *Vashista*, of the drink brewed by Hindu priests and drunk by worshippers, bringing "sacred madness" and "a storm of drunken joy." Then it led to the "sensual transports" in Christian churches and to the stanzas which appear in many Protestant hymnals, beginning:

> Dear Lord and Father of Mankind,
> Forgive our foolish ways!

"King Volmer and Elsie," in the March *Atlantic*, had been written the previous summer. A Danish friend had sent him a literal prose translation of Christian Winter's "King Volmer and Elsie," and Whittier thought that he had "made a nice thing of it."[23]

Whittier spent the month of February in Boston, staying at the Marlboro House, seeing a great many people and enjoying pleasant breakfasts at James T. Fields'. He thought that the weeks in Boston had been good for him, but he was still unwell, suffering from erysipelas in the face, and was not well enough when writing "The Pennsylvania Pilgrim" to do justice to the theme

— although he thought that the poem was better than "Snow-Bound." In late spring he was too ill to write more than a brief note to Sumner.[24]

The year was on the whole not a happy one. There was much to worry about in public events and in his own affairs. Charles Sumner had made enemies of President Grant's friends in Congress, especially Roscoe Conkling and Simon Cameron, and there was a threat that he would be read out of the Republican Party. It seemed to Whittier absurd that such men as Conkling and Cameron should read out of the Party the man who had made it, although he conceded that Sumner might have been wrong in some matters.[25]

He was afraid that the negotiations for the settlement of claims for damages by Confederate cruisers that had sailed from British ports during the Civil War would end in failure because of the folly of the United States in putting in claims which it did not expect would be admitted. Great Britain had objected to the American indirect claims of loss of maritime trade, increased marine insurance rates, and the expense of prolonging of the War. Whittier urged Sumner to do all in his power to save the treaty.[26] When the tribunal delegated by the Treaty of Washington to settle the claims reassembled in June, the indirect claims were not admitted, the case was continued, and a decision was given in September.

On May 31 Sumner spoke for three hours in the Senate against Grant's reelection. It was a phillipic of the classical sort, accusing Grant of founding a family by offices and endowments and of plotting against the peace and existence of the nation. In the midst of the excitement aroused by the speech, Sumner wrote to Whittier assuring him that it was honest and was inspired by a sense of duty. Sumner was doubtless hoping to retain Whittier's personal regard, but he must also have been aware that Whittier's opinion would become known to the public. It was. When a paragraph in the *Boston Evening Transcript* gave what were supposed to be Whittier's views, he wrote to the Editor in some vexation that he preferred to explain them himself. Before mentioning the speech, he said that he had not changed his opinion of Sumner; they had stood together for thirty years, and it would take more than a mistake to make him desert an old friend. He felt some impatience with Republicans who were grasping the spoils of a victory won by others and were displacing a man of Sumner's integrity and intellect. But he could grieve over the mistakes of men whom he loved and respected, and he regretted Sumner's speech because it exposed him to the charge of personal resentment and was unduly severe in its tone and temper.[27]

The next day he wrote to William Cullen Bryant about a statement in the *New York Evening Post*. Was it possible, he asked, that the *Post* condoned the "brutal language of Senator Carpenter?" If so, he had misunderstood the character of the *Post*. Matthew Hale Carpenter, Senator from Wisconsin, had replied to Sumner's speech with more vigor than decorum and had described Sumner as one of the objects seen by the writer of the Book of

Revelation along with the "great red dragon" and the "whore of Babylon." Whittier was also disturbed by the charge that Sumner had misquoted Edwin H. Stanton's opinion of Grant. No one who knew Sumner could doubt that he told the truth: "A truer man than Charles Sumner does not exist. He may err in judgment, but there is in his nature a moral impossibility of deliberate falsehood. All who know him intimately will echo the words of Ralph Waldo Emerson in reference to him, 'He has the whitest soul I ever knew.' "

The fact was that Sumner had been unwise in quoting Stanton's adverse opinion of Grant. Stanton had evidently said one thing in private and another in public and had commended Grant in a Republican campaign speech in 1868. Sumner, as Whittier said, had told the truth, but as Stanton had died, any quoting what he had said in private conversation was sure to raise questions that could not be answered.[28]

Whittier felt little interest in the election. He thought that the great issues of the past were not in it to any serious extent, and he could not believe that the country would go to Mr. Mantalini's "bow-wows" if either Grant or Greeley was elected; it would take a bigger man than either of them to spoil the "magnificent and successful experiment" of the American nation.[29] When some Negro voters, confused by a letter from Sumner telling them to vote for Greeley and a reply from Garrison telling them to vote for Grant, asked Whittier's advice, he told them to make their own decision. The Republican Party had been the chief instrument in overthrowing slavery, and now the Democrats had an abolitionist as their candidate. Grant, although not originally an abolitionist, had faithfully carried out the laws passed by Congress in behalf of the Negroes, and Greeley had always been an advocate of human rights regardless of race or color. The Negro had become the master of his destiny — and here Whittier's prescience failed him — no power on earth could deprive him of his civic rights.

Whittier himself voted for Grant, whom he had never liked in spite of his endorsement of Grant in 1868. He thought that Grant had not a particle of magnetism. He liked Greeley personally and — here his usual political shrewdness failed him — thought that he had a chance of winning; Greeley received the electoral votes of only six states, all in the South. Whittier's strongest feeling was such disgust with the bitter personalities of the campaign that he was ready to say "Let parties and politics be hanged." He thought that it was folly for Grant to run for a second term; he was grateful to Grant for what he had done in the Civil War — an unQuakerlike attitude that he mentioned only in a private letter — but wished that he could have been contented with four years in office. He thought that it was also folly for Greeley to be a candidate but defended him as a great and good man of whom his countryman, whatever their politics, might be proud; he was the most popular man in the United States and could afford to smile at the ridicule of his white great-coat.[30]

During these months Whittier had worries of his own. He was anxious about some of his relatives whom the hard times had perplexed, and he could not give sufficient attention to his own business affairs. He wrote to James R. Osgood in May that he had received no royalties for nearly two years except the copyright on the new volume and *Miriam*, and he asked if the *Blue and Gold Edition* could be kept up to date like the *Diamond Edition* by the addition of his recent poems. The publishers evidently approved, and the *Blue and Gold* was reissued later that year and again in 1875. A few weeks later he told Osgood that he needed money and asked if there was something due him on the *Journal of John Woolman* and *Child Life*. Before the year was over, his worries about money must have been reduced if not wholly removed when Osgood offered him one thousand dollars a year for ten years for the copyright of the *Diamond Edition* and ten cents a copy after that. It is pleasant to observe that in spite of his worries about money he was willing to accept as small an amount as fifty dollars from the *Independent* for a poem when the *Atlantic* was willing to pay one hundred dollars for everything that he could send. It is also pleasant to note that he entertained a good number of Friends at Quarterly Meeting; he bought two turkeys, beef, and tongue, he told Celia Thaxter, "to *meat* the exigency."[31]

The poem that he was willing to sell to the *Independent* for fifty dollars must have been "The Quaker Meeting. From 'The Germantown Pilgrim', an unpublished poem," which was printed June 6. Whittier's first suggestion was that "The Germantown Pilgrim" should be in a volume by itself, about the size of *Snow-Bound*, but he would not insist if Osgood preferred a larger volume to include other poems. Fields objected to "Germantown" and Whittier suggested "The Pennsylvania Pilgrim," which he thought "a rather pleasing sounding alliteration." He had seen the proof by June 19, and the volume was issued in September. It had the present introductory sketch of Francis Daniel Pastorius and twelve short poems, one of which, "The Three Bells," had just appeared in the September *Atlantic*, and another, "A Woman," had not been printed before. "A Woman" was on the same topic as Elizabeth Stuart Phelps' novel, *Hedged In*, which Whittier had asked Lucy Larcom in a rhymed letter to review for the *Atlantic*. The lines in the letter:

> For who shall see tarnish
> If He sweep and garnish?
> When He is the cleanser
> Shall we dare to censure?

were paralleled in "A Woman" by

> What lip shall judge when He approves?
> Who dare to scorn the child He loves?

The title poem of the volume, was, as Whittier's Introductory Note said, "a simple picture of a noteworthy man and his locality." It was a serious biographical study, amply documented by long footnotes. The volume was successful. Bayard Taylor liked "The Pennsylvania Pilgrim" because of the "warm, bright background of tolerance and mellow humanity upon which his figure is drawn like the ground of dead gold which the early Italian painters gave to the forms of their saints, only more luminous." Emerson and his wife and daughters read the entire volume. He made no comment on the title poem but liked "King Volmer and Elsie" the best "if only because the reader's voice broke suddenly at the summit of the story" — an indication that emotions in 1873 responded to very different stimuli from a century later.[32]

The summer of 1872 began pleasantly. The Public Library had received a gift from Gardner Brewer of Boston of six hundred forty-six volumes, which filled empty spaces on the shelves that Whittier had mentioned in the 1871 annual report. The gift was from Brewer personally and he assured Whittier that his sole object was to gratify the employees of the Salisbury Manufacturing Company and "agreeably occupy their minds." He evidently had a poor opinion of their mental powers and thought that it was better to give them light reading, provided that it was not objectionable from a moral point of view. He thought that he had better give one copy at least of all the novels and poems in the Tauchnitz Edition, printed in Germany to evade paying copyright, unless they had some "pernicious influence", and he asked Whittier to erase all such from the list; he himself had erased the novels of Fielding and Smollett. Whittier must have been amused; Fielding's *Amelia* and Smollett's *Humphrey Clinker* had been in the Library at least six years. He may have been other than amused when Brewer wrote that the books would have to be imported before Congress passed an International Copyright Law and he might have to get Congress to pass a special act to admit them. It evidently did not occur to Brewer than an author might resent a scheme to deprive authors of their just dues. Whittier made no comment in his note of thanks except to say that the binding was neat and strong.[33]

During part of July he and his niece Lizzie had a pleasant visit at the Isles of Shoals, where the weather was cool even when the thermometer was "on a rampage of ninety or one hundred" on the mainland. After he returned to Amesbury, there was a heat wave and he spent some time at Salisbury and Hampton Beaches.

He was in Amesbury August 13 and had a terrifying experience which might have been fatal. Two thunder showers, one from the southeast and one from the east, came together over Amesbury in the late afternoon. There was a deluge of rain and almost incessant thunder and lightning. A bolt struck Whittier's house, following the lightning rod down the chimney to the roof, entering the attic and splintering a beam, and then going to the first floor, where it burned a curtain just above Lizzie's head and broke a mirror above Addie Caldwell's. Whittier, who was at the door of the Garden Room, felt a crushing blow on his head and back and was thrown to the floor. He suffered badly from pain in his neck and along his spine during that night and the next day. Both of the women were paralyzed and deafened for a short time and Addie could not see.[34]

In August he wrote the lines "To Edward and Elizabeth Gove" for their fifty-fifth wedding anniversary. The Goves lived on a farm on the New Zealand Road in Seabrook and attended the Friends Meeting in Amesbury after the Seabrook Meeting was discontinued. Their son married Anna Maxfield of Amesbury, who had kept house for Whittier at one time.[35] The lines were regarded as too personal for publication, although "The Friend's Burial," written less than a year later, after Elizabeth Gove's death, was printed in the *Atlantic*.

"The Three Bells" in the September *Atlantic* had an explanatory note omitted from *The Pennsylvania Pilgrim* and later printings:

"Many readers will remember Captain Leighton of the English ship Three Bells, who some years ago rescued the crew of an American vessel sinking in mid-ocean. Unable to take them off in the storm and darkness, he kept by them until morning, running down often during the night, as near to them as he dared, and shouting to them through his trumpet, 'Never fear! Hold on! I'll stand by you!' " The last stanza differed from the present one but was an equally strained analogy:

As thine, in night and tempest
I hear the Master's cry.
And tossing through the darkness
The lights of God draw nigh!

During the fall there were numerous visitors, some old friends but mainly strangers. Several were from England, including George MacDonald. There were the usual items of business. He asked James T. Fields to open the Lyceum course. He got more requests for autographs than he could possibly answer. Nora Perry wanted him to help her to get her poems published: "If you will say to Mr. Osgood next time you see him something like this — 'Why don't you publish Nora Perry's poems?' "[36]

When Addie Caldwell returned to New York, Whittier went with her as far as Boston. An Amesbury man whom he described as a very intimate friend of his, Henry Taylor, went to Boston at the same time and died two weeks later of smallpox. There were four other cases in Amesbury, all traced to Boston, and Whittier was vaccinated.

There is little about Henry Taylor in Amesbury history and tradition. Whittier described him as an "unschooled mechanic." In the 1830's he played the violin at the First Church, and in 1851 he signed the constitution of the First Universalist Society, but his name is marked "withdrawn." Whittier had become acquainted with him twenty-five years earlier when he made some remarks that suggested the mysticism of Boehme and Spener and said something that sounded like a quotation from Plato. When Whittier asked him if he had not read Plato he replied that he had never heard of Plato. Whittier lent him a volume, which he soon returned with the comment that Mr. Plato had got hold of some of his ideas. Whittier watched the progress of his mind through the years. The only books that he ever referred to were a volume of Emerson, Alger's *Oriental Poetry*, and the New Testament. He expressed himself with careful precision, hesitating until he found the exact word, and when he found a depth of meaning beyond common language, he would make up words of his own. By degrees he reached a state of absolute quiet which to Whittier resembled that of the founder of Buddhism, Sakya Mouni, as described by Edward Hayes Plumptre. Yet he was not gloomy or ascetic and he had a quick sense of the ludicrous. Whittier wrote a tribute for the *Villager* and sent copies to Mrs. Fields and later to Emerson and regretted that Taylor had never visited Emerson.[37]

Of the two religious poems at the close of the year, one was strongly in the Quaker tradition and one was far from it. "In Quest" was partly from Whittier's own experience and partly from a study of what he called the phenomenon in which a clear answer comes in the "expectant silences of prayer."[38] The solution of the riddle of the world was the recognition that God is as good as He asks man to be and has a love for man that has nothing to do with that terrifying "caprice of will" which Whittier's readers would know referred to one of the tenets of Calvinism. "A Christmas Carmen" was very different from the Quaker ways of Whittier's boyhood and from the ways that he preferred for himself. It used metaphorically the things that he did not like in worship: music, choruses, hymns, bugles. The poem was a paean of praise for the world peace which Christians hopefully believed their religion was bringing about.

XXVII
1873 - 74

The wide range of Whittier's friendships — from a neighbor who did his washing to a United States Senator — appeared in the early months of 1873. He helped to arrange a house-warming for Kate Choate, who had saved enough money to build a house near Whittier's, attended the house-warming, made a speech congratulating Mrs. Choate, and read what he called "a paper of machine poetry which had been intrusted to him for the occasion."[1] He began a campaign to have the Massachusetts Legislature rescind its censure of Charles Sumner.

In the last two days of a special session called to act on measures connected with the Boston fire the Legislature had passed a resolution which in effect censured Sumner for a bill that he had introduced into the Senate to remove the names of Civil War battles from the Army Register and from the regimental colors. There was nothing radical in this, and there had been no excitement in 1862 when Sumner had objected to placing names of Northern victories on regimental colors and in 1865 to placing pictures of Civil War battles in the Capitol. The action of the Massachusetts Legislature, which Whittier called an act of "pitiful folly," was intended to please Union veterans and to punish Sumner for deserting Grant in the 1872 Presidential campaign.[2]

Whittier started his campaign by writing a petition to the Legislature which was signed by over five thousand Massachusetts citizens, including some of the most distinguished men in the state, among them Longfellow, Holmes, Agassiz, Wendell Phillips, William Claflin, Charles W. Eliot, and Vice-President Henry Wilson. With his usual political acumen, he knew that the strongest opposition to rescinding the resolution would come from men who thought that Union veterans would oppose it and from Republicans who had not forgiven Sumner for his attempt to prevent the reelection of Grant, and he proceeded to get the support of military men and of Grant's adherents. A petition signed by military officers in Amesbury was presented to the Legislature by the Amesbury Representative, Lieutenant Richard Briggs. Whittier got letters from various military officers including Thomas Wentworth Higginson and sent them to a Representative from Salem, Willard P. Phillips, with the suggestion that they be sent to Boston newspapers. He wrote a letter to the *Boston Daily Advertiser*; he had found no soldiers who considered themselves wronged or insulted by Sumner's proposal, which was a compliment to them and not an insult, as it implied that they had no vindictive hatred toward their fallen foes and were as magnanimous in peace and victory as they had been heroic and patient during the war. He got letters favoring rescinding from Frederick Douglass, who had headed the Republican electoral ticket in New York, and from Gerrit Smith, who had been a conspicuous and influential member of the Republican Convention which nominated Grant, and also from distinguished Massachusetts natives now living elsewhere, including William Cullen Bryant.

As usual, he wrote a letter to the *Villager*, although it is hard to see how a small local newspaper could have any effect upon the Massachusetts Legislature. He was sure that if the censure were not rescinded in the present Legislature, the question would keep coming up. He mentioned Sumner's "spotless character . . . brought into strong relief against the corruption and miserable dishonesty of too many of his colleagues"[3] — an obvious reference to the Credit Mobilier scandal.

He went to the committee hearing at the State House. His deafness was coming on, and he could not hear Garrison, whose remarks were quoted to him afterwards. Garrison opposed rescinding the censure. Whittier was at first "half-indignant" but got over it and was ashamed of himself. Then a letter from Garrison to the *Boston Journal* allowed him to think that he had been given the wrong impression of Garrison's remarks at the hearing. He longed "to see all the old advocates (how few of us remain!) cordial and kindly and forbearing toward each other." On the same day he was one of the signers of a letter to Garrison asking him to write an autobiography. However, a few days later he found it hard to be "cordial, kindly, and forbearing" toward Garrison. One word in Whittier's letter to the *Advertiser* had been misprinted, making it read that Sumner's proposal implied that Massachusetts soldiers cherished no vindictive hatred of fallen "heroes" instead of fallen "foes." Garrison dwelt on the words, "fallen heroes" in a letter to the *Advertiser* intended to excite soldiers against the rescinding of the censure. Whittier sent a correction to the *Advertiser* which was printed in the same issue as Garrison's letter.[4]

The movement for rescinding ended in failure, but it had succeeded in showing the public what Sumner's proposal really was and the high regard in which he was held by the people of Massachusetts. As Whittier had predicted, the matter came up again a year later and the censure was rescinded in February 1874, a few weeks before Sumner's death. Whittier was happy to write to Sumner that the record of the Bay State was now clear, and the folly of the extra session of 1872 was wiped out.[5]

He had come to Boston shortly before the hearing on the Sumner petition in spite of a smallpox epidemic which had kept him away earlier and his discomfort from erysipelas, and had spent two weeks at the Claflins' enjoying the luxury of hothouse flowers and wood fires. Lucy Larcom was also at the Claflins but found that Whittier's mind was so much on the Sumner censure that he could not think of much else, including *Child Life in Prose*. At last, late in March, he got down to business and began to write the preface.

He was concerned that the material was *not good enough*, by which he did not mean literary excellence. "We don't exactly want goodyness," he wrote to Lucy Larcom, "but we can't have too much of rational goodness." One piece that evidently seemed to him to meet that requirement was the passage from *Tom Brown's School Days* in which conscientious little Arthur on his first night at Rugby bravely faced the scorn of his dormitory mates by kneeling in prayer; this selection had the largest illustration in the book.

Lucy Larcom spent several days at Whittier's during the first week in April, while they finished work on the book, including the preface, which Whittier thought was dull, and he was glad to have the whole thing over with. "My head aches at the thought of it," he wrote. "What business have I to edit a book for children, as if I could say from experience with Mrs. Gamp 'Blessings on the man as has his quiver full of such'?"[6]

The preface explained that the book was *about* childhood as much as *for* it; the language and thought of some selections were beyond the comprehension of children. At this point he was astute in recognizing that children can feel what they cannot understand; in his own boyhood, he recalled, Gray's "Elegy" and Cowper's "Lament for the Royal George" had awakened faint echoes and responses, "vaguely prophesying of wonders yet to be revealed." Although he had aimed at simple and not unhealthful amusement, he had been glad to find "the light tissue of these selections occasionally shot through with threads of pious or moral suggestion" — the "rational goodness" which he recommended to Lucy Larcom. But he did not feel it right to sadden childreaders with gloomy narratives and painful reflections upon the life before them. Still, of the twenty-six narratives in the first section, "Stories of Child Life," the death of good children occurred in five, and another selection was a passage from Elizabeth Stuart Phelps' *The Gates Ajar* in which a little girl's mother returned from a visit to a doctor too tired and ill to play with her daughter and announcing that she was dying of cancer.

The volume had two other sections, "Fancies of Child Life" and "Memories of Child Life." Slovenly editing placed three selections in the first section that belonged in the third: Whittier's "The Fish I Didn't Catch," Celia Thaxter's "On White Island," and John Woolman's "The Robins."

Although Whittier was too busy to give much attention to his own affairs during the first months of 1873, he found time to encourage and help other writers. He wrote to Paul Hamilton Hayne that he had read Hayne's poem in the January *Atlantic* ("The Voice in the Pines") with sympathy and feeling, and told him that now that William Gilmore Sims and Henry Timrod had died, the South must look to him and John R. Thompson as its literary leaders. He wrote two introductory stanzas for Celia Thaxter's "Lars," which he thought might be mistaken for a foreign sketch. When he read the proof sheets of her volume of prose sketches *Among the Isles of Shoals* he thought that the book was admirable in matter and manner, and when he saw the volume he was even more enthusiastic. It seemed to him to have all the charm of Thoreau and of Gilbert White's *Natural History and Antiquities of Selborne*.[7] Most readers would not agree. Celia Thaxter's style often shows obvious striving for effect.

Two poems were published in June. "Conductor Bradley" has been justly criticized for its complete lack of everything that makes a true poem, but it was obviously sincere in its admiration of sense of duty rising above physical pain in an action which, Whittier clearly saw, made the self-consciousness of sick-bed dramas seem poor and noteless. "Hymn for the Opening of Plymouth Church, St. Paul, Minnesota" was dignified and suited to the occasion — and written in a steady rhythm which, if it can be criticized as monotonous, was readily singable.

Whittier was at the Isles of Shoals during the first week in July with his niece Lizzie and her friend Jettie Morrill. He reported that the young ladies had a good time; "they found *boys* there," and they horrified themselves by visiting the scene of the recent murder on Smutty-Nose Island. Paul Hamilton Hayne spent a day there with Whittier and assured him several months later, "As long as memory 'holds her seat,' I shall remember with the keenest delight that day spent in your society." It seemed to him that Whittier's "elastic spirit of youth" would never desert him. Annie Fields was at her best, and her husband was in high spirits, telling humorous stories. One afternoon the talk turned to religion. Whittier thought that Emerson had no faith in immortality, but Mrs. Fields disagreed; she had heard Emerson speak at Thoreau's grave and later speak expressly on immortality. At Whittier's request, Celia Thaxter read one of Emerson's essays, and Whittier quoted hymns and spoke of the beauty and necessity of childlike worship. Mrs. Fields thought that he was reproaching himself for not having spoken before on serious matters and was trying to breathe a new life into his hearers. He evidently tried too hard, brought on a nervous headache, and reluctantly gave up a plan of going to Portsmouth and the Pepperell House at Kittery with James and Annie Fields.

He arrived home, still with the nervous headache, and found an accumulation of letters at which he worked hard but hopelessly; for every letter that he answered, two came in the next mail. Summer pilgrims, mainly women, dropped in daily, and he could only hope that none of them were interviewers for newspapers. He did not feel well enough to go to the Isles of Shoals again but spent a few days at Salisbury and Hampton Beaches. In August he received the good news that a new contract with James R. Osgood and Co. would give him twenty-five hundred dollars a year and ten percent royalty for eight months on any new book; the contract was extended ten years in 1883 at three thousand dollars a year.[8]

Late in the summer he received and declined two invitations from Ralph Waldo Emerson. One was to visit him at Concord and the other, seconded by John Murray Forbes, was to spend a week with Emerson at Forbes' summer home on Naushon. Whittier gave as his reason for declining the second invitation that he was suffering from a cold "with feverish habit" and would be a guest to be tolerated and not enjoyed; he would get away from the sea and go to the White Mountains as soon as he could bear the fatigue of the journey. This may have been true, but a more important reason seems to have been that he did not wish to change his plans. He was in West Ossipee September 14, sending Mrs. Fields a description of the mountains.

Ben Butler was again trying to get the Republican nomination for Governor of Massachusetts. John Murray Forbes had warned Whittier that he would have to hear anathemas of Butler if he came to Naushon, and Whittier told Emerson to say that anathemas of "the irrepressible Benjamin" would not disturb him in the least. He would not be concerned if the anathemas of Dr. Slop (in *Tristram Shandy*) were poured out upon him: "Who pities a rhinoceros peppered with small shot?" But Whittier was seriously worried that Butler would be elected; the Administration was on Butler's side, or at least he would claim that it was and would not be contradicted. However, when the State Convention met in Springfield, Butler could not get enough votes for a resolution against bolters, and there had been so many threats of non-support if he was nominated that he withdrew at the last moment, greatly to Whittier's relief.[9]

Whittier was pleasantly reminded of the past by a letter in late August from Hannah Cox, wife of John Cox, inviting him to their golden wedding at Longwood, Chester County, Pennsylvania, on September 16. A few weeks later he was asked to write something for a memorial volume of the golden wedding and sent "The Golden Wedding of Longwood," which was printed in *Golden Wedding of John and Hannah Cox* and in the January 1874 *Atlantic*. When he sent it to the *Atlantic* he described it as not "learned nor graceful nor obscure with transcendentalisms, but plain homely verse, as befitted the subject and the occasion" and he liked it and thought that others would but told Howells to do as he thought best about publishing it. He might have added that it had a note of sincere admiration for the Anti-Slavery workers of the 1830's and 1840's and especially for John and Hannah Cox, who were keepers of an important station on the Underground Railroad.[10]

Whittier's habit of writing the first draft of a poem on scraps of paper resulted in the printing of "John Underhill" in the December *Atlantic* without the final stanza, which he omitted in copying.[11] This stanza was needed to round out the thought. John Underhill was banished from Boston with Anne Hutchinson and went to Dover, New Hampshire, confident in his own righteousness. There he sinned, confessed, and left in repentance to preach and to fight in frontier wars, and the people of Boston, as told in the last stanza, rejoiced to hear that he was guarding the land from which he had once been exiled.

Whittier's publishers were not pleased when he wrote a poem for a book to be published by another firm. He gave "Child-Songs" to a publisher for a collection, *Little People of God*, by Mrs. George L. Austin. In reply to James R. Osgood's protest, Whittier wrote that it had not occurred to him that so small a matter was of any possible consequence to anyone but himself. If he had anything to publish in book form he would give it to his regular publishers, as he had always done. "You have no idea what magnificent offers I have had from time to time," he told Osgood, "and how peremptorily I have set them aside to stand by my old publishers." Whittier evidently spent some time revising the first draft of "Child-Songs." He made changes in all but one stanza.[12]

A letter to Charles Sumner, which Whittier intended to be private, was published and led to his clearest and most complete explanation of his attitude toward Roman Catholics. The letter to Sumner commended his attitude toward the "Virginius" case. The "Virginius" was a steamer flying the American flag — with papers fraudulently obtained — which was captured by a Spanish vessel near Jamaica. The captain and some of the men on board were executed, on the ground that it was carrying men and arms to aid insurgents in Cuba. There were, as usual, many people who were ready to assist any insurrection in Cuba with the hope of ultimately annexing the island, and a public meeting was called in Steinway Hall in New York to arouse sentiment against Spain. Sumner was asked to be one of the speakers but instead sent a letter — which was not read — opposing the purpose of the meeting, urging considerate treatment of the new Spanish Republic, and disapproving war-like preparations going on in the navy yards. It was printed in the *New York Tribune* and *Boston Advertiser*, and Sumner received letters of approval from many prominent men including Richard H. Dana Jr., Caleb Cushing, and Henry Wadsworth Longfellow, as well as Whittier. Whittier's letter was printed in the *Villager*.[13] He conceded that the shooting of the passengers on the "Virginius" was shocking and unjustifiable, even though they were filibusterers, but it was regretted by the president of the Spanish Republic and by intelligent Spanish Republicans. Action by the United States against them would have the effect of aiding "Ultramontane Popery," the Spanish monarchists, and "the cruel priesthood who are fighting against Republicanism in Europe." Crushing out the Republic of Spain would be an act of atrocity paralleled only by the crushing out of the Roman Republic by the so-called French Republic of 1849.

A letter that Whittier received criticizing what the writer understood to be his attitude toward the Catholic Church would have been ignored by many men in as firm a position of popularity as Whittier, but he wrote a long, careful reply. He pointed out first that he had referred only to "Ultramontism" — the theory that political as well as ecclesiastical matters should be subject to papal control — and had not intended to reflect upon Catholics as such, "least of all upon liberty-loving members of that venerable church." He had spoken as strongly against oppressive and unjust acts on the part of Protestants as on the part of Catholics. He had vindicated Daniel O'Connell and his political friends in Ireland. When he was in the Massachusetts Legislature, he had denounced the mob that destroyed the Ursuline Convent in Charlestown and had tried to get indemnity for its owners. He had opposed the Know-Nothing movement. Like other Quakers, he had contributed to a relief fund for Catholics in Ireland during the famine. But he was not blind to the fact that leaders in the Catholic Church were hostile to republican forms of government and to religious and personal liberty, and he had seen bishops and priests oppose the abolition of slavery "while a large body of their people were persecuting and abusing the poor blacks in our cities." He had seen that the strength of Monarchists in Europe came from the active support and sympathy of the Catholic Church. He knew, however, that these things were deplored by many good Catholics such as Father Farrell and Orestes A. Brownson. He had nothing but Godspeed for such Catholics as the editors of some papers which his correspondent had sent him; they were not "ultramontane" but talked like republicans and freemen. His correspondent had mentioned his "To Pius IX" and "The Dream of Pio Nono." As a peace-loving Quaker and republican, he could say nothing less and had nothing to retract. But he asked his correspondent to look at other poems of his about Catholics, "The Female Martyr," "Marguerite," "The Men of Old," "The Gift of Tritemius," and "Mary Garvin," and believe what was really true, that he loved good men, whatever their creed, and honored nobleness and piety in Catholics as well as in Protestants.[14]

The death of Louis Agassiz December 14 gave Whittier a painful sense of loss and raised for him again the question of survival after death. "Where is he now? So much life and vigor and usefulness, can they be utterly lost?"[15] He did not give as definite an answer as might have been expected in "The Prayer of Agassiz," published in *The Christian Union* January 14, although it was implied in the phrase "Eternity's new year." The thought emphasized was that Agassiz would be remembered and his name heard in the voices of Nature.

Whittier was in Boston in late December and at a reception to Emerson at the Radical Club. It was a distinguished gathering, with Longfellow, Wendell Phillips, Vice-President Henry Wilson, Henry James, and foreign guests. Emerson read his "Boston" and there was lively discussion of whether Boston would act now with the same spirit that it had in the American Revolution.[16] He was in Boston at other times during the winter of 1873-74, and his activities did not appear to be restricted by poor health. He had a head-and-shoulders portrait painted by Edgar Parker. He was at the Claflins' the second week in February, and on the sixteenth was one of the guests at a farewell banquet to Wilkie Collins at the St. James Hotel. He was in Boston again early in March, called on Longfellow, and enjoyed meeting Robert C. Winthrop, whom he had first met when he was in the Legislature.[17]

When the news came on March 11 of the death of Charles Sumner, who had been in the Senate only the day before and had heard the report of the vote of the Massachusetts Legislature rescinding his censure, Whittier was in Amesbury, on the street, about to mail a letter to him. He returned home to write a long letter to Henry Wilson. He was crushed by the suddenness of Sumner's death. Massachusetts should thank God that she had "wiped out the stigma of ingratitude toward her illustrious son." Sumner's greatness was recognized at last: "Oh eloquent, just and mighty death!" He was a pall bearer at the funeral in Boston March 16. The morning was sunny, and Longfellow recorded in his journal that he heard the first bluebirds of the season, but there was plenty of time for the weather to change before the burial in Mt. Auburn Cemetery in Cambridge. The procession from King's Chapel did not arrive there until nearly six, and the sky had now "taken on a subdued gray tinge, through which the light of the setting sun shone but faintly over the city of the dead," according to the official report; Whittier, who doubtless suffered from the cold, said that there was a chill wind and a "leaden arch of sky."[18]

Ceremonies in Boston did not end with Sumner's funeral. There was a memorial service at the Radical Club with a gathering that Mrs. Sargent thought was the most brilliant ever seen there and which caused Edmund Clarence Stedman to say that while the literary center was being removed from Boston to New York, Boston had not yet been shorn of its glory. Rather surprisingly, Whittier spoke, and even more surprisingly, began with a humorous remark that seems out of place at a memorial service. "Had Sumner supposed while in life that I should attempt to talk of him in a memorial gathering, he would have exclaimed with the Scotch poet, when told that a certain militia company would fire a salute over his grave, 'Don't let that awkward squad fire over me!' " He then spoke a few words which Mrs. Sargent found eloquent in their beauty and simplicity, expressing his gratification that the vote of censure had been repealed by the Legislature before Sumner's death. The observance by the Legislature was in Boston Music Hall June 9, with a eulogy by George William Curtis and Whittier's poem "Sumner," which was read by J. W. Churchill, Professor of Homiletics at Andover Theological Seminary. The poem was praised by distinguished persons who heard it: Longfellow, Wendell Phillips, Garrison, Curtis, and others; but the best that Whittier could say for it was that he hoped that it was as good as could be expected under the circumstances. He did not want to write it but did want to say a word, some time in some way, of the friend that he had loved. He was unwell — any physical or mental effort caused difficulty in breathing and he had a pain in his left side, along with the usual headache — and he said later that he had no time for careful revision. Nevertheless there were at least two preliminary galley proofs with Whittier's revisions and additions before it was given to Professor Churchill; it had become Whittier's custom to have his poems printed from his manuscript on galley sheets which he corrected and revised. One curious typographical error appeared in the first published printing. In the second line of the seventh stanza "not" was misprinted as "hot," making the line read

"He saw hot Sinai's cloud and flame."

There was some newspaper controversy over the line, and Whittier wrote to the editor of the *Albany Journal* that he had seen the blunder but had not regarded it as important enough to correct. He thought that the *Journal* had made a good case for the incorrect printing but on the whole preferred his own version.[19]

Unlike most of Whittier's poems for special occasions, "Sumner" was much too long. As printed in the eight-page pamphlet and read at the commemorative exercises, it had forty-seven stanzas. Before it was printed in *A Memorial of Charles Sumner,* seven more were added. The "word" that Whittier wished to say about his friend was, to say the least, unduly expanded. The reason seems to be that he wanted to do a thorough and honest piece of character analysis. He admitted Sumner's pride, one of

The slight defects he never hid,

the natural pride in his own strength. One of the lines in the present nineteenth stanza,

The first to smite, the first to spare

was evidently an echo of the first line in William Cullen Bryant's "The Death of Lincoln":

Oh, slow to smite and swift to spare.

It would be pleasant to believe that it was the thoroughness and sincerity of the poem that led Longfellow, who was one of the trustees of Sumner's papers, to ask Whittier to write Sumner's biography. But Whittier was not the first choice. Longfellow had wished that George W. Greene were well enough to do it, and then the task was offered to John Lothrop Motley, who declined. Longfellow's letter to Whittier made an emotional appeal. "Will your love for Sumner and your regard for his memory, and the desire that nothing unworthy may be said of him, induce you to undertake his biography?" Whittier thanked them for asking him and suggested that Longfellow should do it himself. It was done, four substantial volumes, by Edward L. Pierce.[20]

While Whittier had approved of Sumner's resolution in the Senate, which would help to heal the wounds of the Civil War and had led the movement to have the censure by the Massachusetts Legislature rescinded, he was not ready to forget the Anti-Slavery conflict. The day before Sumner's death the Massachusetts Legislature passed resolutions on the death of Millard Fillmore, who as President had signed the Fugitive Slave Law, stating that he was entitled to the "affectionate remembrance of the American people and an honorable place in the long line of their illustrious public servants." William Lloyd Garrison wrote a letter of protest to the *Boston Journal*, which printed it March 20, and Whittier immediately wrote to Garrison to thank him for the letter: "I heartily endorse thy estimate of the man and his conduct and thy protest against the eulogy, formal and hollow and unmeaning as it was."[21]

Whittier's preference for the old ways in the Society of Friends, which he had explained in letters to the *Friends Review* four years earlier, had been confirmed by the attitude of several Congregational ministers who visited him in the early spring. Two of them went to Friends Meeting with him and were not pleased when they did not find the plain, quiet ways that they had expected. One of them told Whittier that Congregationalists ought to approach the ways of Friends, who, however, seemed to be moving toward them. Soon after, Whittier read an article by Augustine Jones which gave, he thought, the distinctive doctrines of Friends and was consequently unacceptable to Friends who liked to think that Quakerism was no different from other so-called Evangelical sects. It was evidently time to do something before the old ways were wholly lost, and he went to Boston and sent for Augustine Jones to meet him at the Marlboro House. Whittier wanted Jones to join him in publishing a new periodical for the Society of Friends which would give New England a stronger position in the affairs of the Society, New England Quakerism being much more conservative than the Western variety. Whittier's serious consideration of such a project when he felt unable to write poems for publication is proof of his intense devotion to the old ways which were passing, even in his own Amesbury Friends Meeting. Nothing came of the plan, fortunately. Whittier would have been unable, physically and temperamentally, to settle down to the routine editorial duties.

Two of Whittier's friends died in May. Lovesta Bailey, wife of Alton Bailey, was a member of Amesbury Friends Meeting. Whittier, to whom so many readers looked for religious inspiration, said that he went to her when his own faith faltered and that she was one of the most saintly women he had ever known. She had a long and painful illness, which she bore with patience; pain, she said, was all right because it came from God. Whittier's poem about her, "Vesta," was not published until fall — it was in the November *Atlantic* and in the new volume, *Hazel Blossoms* — but was probably written earlier.[22] Whittier's feelings about her were evidently so deep and strong that they swept away his critical faculties; there are lines which are typical of the religious sentimentality of the time:

> She leans from out our clinging arms
> To rest herself in Thine.

Dr. Thomas C. Sparhawk had been Whittier's physician as well as personal friend until he had become paralyzed about a year before his death.

Whittier organized a testimonial fund to pay for a monument in the cemetery. He talked to some of his friends, wrote to others, and sent a communication to the *Villager* with the heading "The Beloved Physician," the title of a poem about Dr. Sparhawk by Margaret Winslow in the Boston *Daily Transcript.* "There may be better men," Whittier wrote, "but for myself I am free to say I have never known them." A meeting was to be held at the Public Library, and Whittier hoped that there would be a hearty response. He led the subscription list with fifty dollars.[23]

However poor his health, he did not use it as a way to evade local obligations. He wrote a letter recommending one of his neighbors as a competent music teacher. He was chairman of a committee in charge of a fund for flood sufferers in Mississippi and Louisiana. He wrote the report of the committee appointed for the annual examination of the Public Library, although at the time he was scarcely able to speak, had a persistent headache, and had been forbidden by his physician to do any writing.[24]

The report contained some bad news. A lecture course intended to raise money for the Library had not done much more than pay for itself. The most popular of the scheduled speakers, Henry Ward Beecher, who had offered to lecture without pay, had been too busy with his own affairs and had cancelled all his lecture engagements. The charge that Beecher was guilty of adultery with the wife of Theodore Tilton was getting more publicity than any similar case in the history of the nation. Whittier believed in Beecher, who he thought had done good to thousands, and regarded him as a personal friend; if Beecher had fallen into temptation, Whittier would be grieved but would be ashamed of himself if he did not continue to be his friend. On July 20 Tilton appeared before a committee of Plymouth Church with a sworn statement, supported by documentary evidence, of Beecher's adultery, but Whittier still hoped that Beecher would have a good deliverance from the "wretched scandal." Two weeks later he still believed in Beecher and hoped he would withstand the onslaught, although Francis Moulton's last statement was an "ugly one." A month later the case seemed a "most mournful tragedy." "I have loved Beecher so much!" he wrote. "I *cannot* believe him guilty as charged, and yet it looks very dark. God pity him in any case!"[25]

There had been no poem by Whittier in the *Atlantic* since January and none published elsewhere except "Sumner." In the August *Atlantic* was "A Sea Dream," which he had first planned to send for the January number and had decided after a careful re-perusal was one that the world could do without. It was, he told Howells, more faultless in rhythm and construction than his ordinary style of pieces but lacked "excuse for being."[26] In quoting this phrase from Emerson's "Rhodora" Whittier was obviously not accepting Emerson's dictum "that beauty is its own excuse for being" but was thinking along his usual line, that a poem should do good in the sense of teaching a lesson or conveying a moral or spiritual truth. Since "A Sea Dream" did nothing of that sort, the only reason for his changing his mind and sending it to the *Atlantic* must have been that he was too unwell — or thought that he was — to write anything else. His headaches and other discomforts thus had the fortunate effect of bringing one of his best poems to the reading public and perhaps even of saving it from the waste basket.

The excellent part of "A Sea Dream" was the song. Its nostalgia was delicately done. The past was brought back to the singer by details in the scene by the seaside which had the color of youth: waves glad in breeze and sun, the ships off shore

> Rose red in morning's glow.

A quick focussing in the fourth stanza:

> The freshness of the early time
>> On every breeze is blown;
> As glad the sea, as blue the sky —

led to the contrast: they were no longer boy and girl. He was a world-worn man on whom the evil years had left their sign, which she, where the angels were, could wash out with tears of divine love. The poem as printed in the *Atlantic* did not have the present eighth stanza, and there were a jarring abruptness and a prosaic note in the opening lines of the next stanza, which then read:

> Oh turn to me that dearest face
> Of all thy sea-born town.

Whittier evidently noticed this defect, and the printing in *Hazel Blossoms* a few weeks later contained the present eighth stanza and changed the first two lines in the ninth to the present form so that they led from the picture of the angel to the human face that he remembered and which he asked might remain

> On memory's frescoed wall,
> A shadow, and yet all.

The last stanza did not have the effect of the fall of a curtain but of opening a window to the future, and the next to the last line, with a graceful touch that gave structural and artistic unity to the poem,

> Or by the blown sea foam

took the reader back to the first stanza.

Whittier's health was, according to him, "feeble" all the summer, and on the advice of the "Medicos" that he go to the country to get farther from the sea, he spent some time in North Conway and West Ossipee. The visit did him good, but he still could not write for more than an hour at a time and often for only a few minutes.[27] However, he succeeded in writing the prefatory note to *Hazel Blossoms* in September. The note referred wholly to his sister Elizabeth and her poems which were printed in this volume. It seemed to him that if her health, sense of duty and fitness, and self-distrust had permitted, she might have occupied a high place among the poets. The introductory poem, without title but in later collections entitled "*Hazel Blossoms*," was a rather strained analogy between the witch hazel and his verse.

The volume had only one other poem, "Kinsman," that had not already been published and one, "The Healer," that was expanded from "To a Young Physician," written five years earlier. "Kinsman" had probably been written soon after the death of Abbott Kinsman at the age of nineteen in the Philippine Islands July 4, 1864. The Kinsman family of Salem were Quakers, and Whittier knew them through the Salem Quarterly Meeting. Abbott Kinsman's letters and diary indicate that he was a somewhat livelier young man than Whittier may have supposed. He smoked cigars and experimented with opium. Some pretty girls taught him to dance, and he danced "like everything" all one Sunday evening.[28]

Hazel Blossoms was entered for copyright October 12, and on that day Whittier was busy with a philanthropic project in Amesbury. At a meeting of subscribers to a corporation which had been formed to establish a Home for Aged Women he was elected to a committee of five to bring in a plan of organization and a code of by-laws. At the next meeting the constitution and by-laws presented by this committee were adopted with some amendments.[29] This Home, and similar ones in many New England towns, met a real need. An elderly woman without resources or relatives able or willing to take care of her could escape the stigma of going to the poorhouse by paying a small admission fee — in Amesbury it was at first fifty dollars — and being cared for as long as she lived, in comparatively pleasant surroundings. Whittier continued his interest in the Home, making frequent contributions and leaving a legacy of ten thousand dollars. The Home functioned until 1972.

By the next month he was well enough to write some poetry. His publishers suggested an illustrated edition of "The Witch's Daughter" and Whittier agreed to add some eighty lines which would be "full of pictures" and as good as the original poem. When he saw the proof, he thought that there were too many illustrations but he was satisfied with the poem itself, which had been renamed "Mabel Martin": "As it now stands I regard it as the best poem of the kind I have ever written, and I am pretty sure I could not improve upon it in a new poem at this late day." Still, he made changes until on November 22 he told James R. Osgood to send no more proofs, lest he should go on disturbing what he thought very well as it was.[30]

The added lines numbered one hundred twenty-three instead of the eighty that he had promised. Seventy-eight of these constituted the Proem and the long introductory description of Pleasant Valley in Amesbury entitled "The River Valley." This was much longer than was needed for the narrative and had no relation to the characters or events. But it was well-organized and effective; Whittier still had the ability to see clearly and to choose the right details to make his readers see with equal clarity. Other stanzas added within the narrative amplified and intensified the mental suffering of the persecuted heroine. In the years since writing "The Witch's Daughter" Whittier had suffered enough loneliness to be able to enter more fully into her feelings.

He was now able to do more reading. He wrote with his usual enthusiasm to Howells about Lucy Larcom's *Childhood Songs*, a collection of her poems for children. "In the entire world of English child-literature," he told Howells, "I do not know of anything better." He told Lucy Larcom that her book was better than their *Child Life*. He was reading Thomas à Kempis. Emerson's recently published *Parnassus* — which contained seven of his poems — did not arouse his enthusiasm; he described it as Emerson's "old scrap book," containing many good things and some poor ones.[31]

XXVIII
1875 - 76

Whittier was in Boston much of the winter, part of the time at the Claflins'. Early in February he must have been feeling better than usual. He allowed Mrs. Sargent to give him a reception. Visitors came and went for an hour and a half, some stopping briefly on their way to a reception, others lingering in groups to talk.[1] Later in the month there was a fair in Boston for the benefit of the Society for the Prevention of Cruelty to Animals, and Whittier contributed a prose sketch, "Our Dumb Relations," to *The Ark*, issued in connection with it. It is proof of his breadth of reading and his memory of significant facts that he could call to mind so many references to affection between men and animals, ranging from the Hindu epic *Mahabharata* to Emerson's remarks at Thoreau's funeral.

The theme of "The Two Angels" in the April *Atlantic* seems sentimental to a later generation, but to people who had shuddered under the terrors of Hell fire there was comforting assurance in the angel Pity whose tear quenched flames in Hell, while the smile of Love brought hope, and the voice of God told the two angels that the sweetest song in heaven would be the song of sin forgiven.

In the fall, Whittier had been asked to write a poem for the one hundredth anniversary of the Battle of Lexington. It was a peculiar assignment for a Quaker. He later said that he had stretched his Quakerism to the full strength of its drab to write about the Lexington folks who were shot and did not shoot back, and refused to write about Bunker Hill, where the men did shoot back to some purpose. Furthermore, he thought that occasional verses were fatal to any poet except Holmes, who always managed to come off safely.

In spite of his doubts, Whittier usually came off safely with occasional verses, and he was successful with "Lexington"; if it had been a failure he would hardly have been asked to write for the Bunker Hill anniversary. However, it was not a typical American patriotic poem, and if the audience heard it when it was sung at the exercises on the morning of April 19 — there were one hundred thousand people in town, most of them probably interested in seeing President Grant plant an elm tree — they had something to think about. It hopefully prophesied world peace, the golden age of brotherhood.[2]

After returning to Amesbury in March he wrote to Daniel Ricketson that he had reread Thoreau's letters to Ricketson in *Letters to Various Persons*, published ten years earlier. His opinion of Thoreau was now very different from his hasty comment on *Walden* in 1854. "What a rare genius he was! To take up his books is like a stroll in the woods or a sail on the lake —

the leaves rustle and the water ripples along his pages." Ricketson was a wealthy New Bedford Quaker and Abolitionist who had built a cabin on the outskirts of New Bedford like Thoreau's at Walden Pond and spent much of his time there reading and writing.[3]

Early in the summer he did his annual chore of writing the report of the committee appointed to examine the Public Library and then went to the White Mountains, staying for a month at the Bearcamp River House in West Ossipee, a quiet, old-fashioned inn. A group of young people were with him, his nieces and some of their friends, but he wanted to see some of his own friends and went to the railroad station at train time hoping to see Edna Dean Proctor or Gail Hamilton, to whom he had written that it was the duty of every good Christian to visit the sick and he was little better than sick himself.[4]

He was sick and in a state of nervous discouragement when Lucy Larcom tried to talk with him one day about an anthology that they were preparing, to be called "Songs of Three Centuries" and to include English and American poetry of the last three hundred years. He had been worrying about it and about his brother's affairs and had been unable to sleep for the last two nights, and was in no mood to be patient when Lucy insisted — unreasonably, he thought — that the proofs need not be returned promptly. He said some things that hurt her feelings and of course was sorry later. Rather than feel that such a life-long friend was estranged, he would "prefer to have the unfortunate book in the Red Sea deeper than Pharaoh's chariot wheels."[5]

But there were days when he was in better mood. He often walked to the river and looked silently at the graceful sweep of the stream. "Sunset on the Bearcamp" was evidently forming itself in his mind; one day he watched the play of sunlight through the leaves and the figures that it made on the water and asked his companion if the shadow on the pool did not look like fingers on a hand. This picture is in the last two lines of the first stanza:

> The drowsy maple-shadows rest
> Like fingers on its lips.

Late in August he wrote three stanzas in the autograph album of the daughter of a friend of Lucy Larcom.[6] Parts of these stanzas appeared in "Sunset on the Bearcamp." The first stanza in the autograph was

> A gold thread in the purpling hem
> Of hills, the Bearcamp runs,
> And down the long, green valley falls
> The last of summer suns.

This, with a few changes in single words, became the first four lines of the poem. The second stanza was

> Beneath its light yon mountains seem
> No longer granite-browed.
> The rock that melts in rosy mist
> Is softer than the cloud.

This became part of the third in the poem:
>How changed the summits vast and old!
>>No longer granite-browed,
>They melt in rosy mist; the rock
>>Is softer than the cloud:

The third stanza was
>O life, that closes like the day,
>>Like it sink warm and still,
>With golden glory on the stream
>And rose-light on the hill!

"Golden glory of the stream" was simplified to "The golden water flows" in the last stanza of the poem. "Rose-light on the hill" became "The rose-light of perpetual hills."

The autograph had a Wordsworth-like simplicity and directness lacking in "Sunset on the Bearcamp." Not content with descriptive details which were adequate and effective because they were accurate and true, Whittier added that the flowers were as beautiful as those by the Yarrow or the Mulla and that the unseen altar imagined on the hills with heavenly figures above it confirmed the ancient Greek dream of gods on Mount Ida. The Yarrow may have come into his mind as he thought that the scene would stay in his memory, as Wordsworth said of the daffodils in "I Wandered Lonely as a Cloud." Whittier had said virtually the same thing in "Franconia from the Pemigewasset," but now he added a reference to the life after death — that topic of which his contemporaries never tired: the sunset glory that had entered into his soul would live eternally as his soul would live, and would blend with the slightly pagan scenery of heaven:
>Beside the mystic asphodels
>Shall bloom the home-born flowers.

He had returned to Amesbury by late September. Final selections were being made for *Songs of Three Centuries*; Whittier left some decisions to Lucy Larcom and entrusted most of the proof reading to her. The volume had grown far beyond the original plan of a small collection, and by late September Whittier thought that it was not worth while to hunt for more poems. It was issued in time for the Christmas trade and contained five hundred sixty poems in three hundred forty-two double-columned pages. A long preface explained that Whittier wanted the book to be thoroughly readable, not so much by the scholarly few as by the "general mass of readers" who would enjoy brief lyrical selections in their "snatched leisure." The number of selections from the less known writers and what he called "waifs and estrays of unknown authors" shows the wide range of his reading. He was not satisfied with the third section, "From Wordsworth to Longfellow"; he was not well enough and did not have enough time to give it the attention that he should have.[7] One poem was included which he had told Lucy Larcom not to use: Julia Ward Howe's "Battle Hymn of the Republic," which he rejected as too warlike. Two errors continued through all the printings and even in the Revised Edition in 1890; Augustus M. Toplady was given as the author of Charles Wesley's "Love Divine, All Loves Excelling," and William Byrd as the author of "My Mind to Me a Kingdom Is," the larger part of which was by Edward Dyer, with revisions and additions by Byrd.

Songs of Three Centuries was an immediate success. Within two weeks it was evident that all of the edition of five thousand copies would soon be sold. Demand for other Whittier volumes was also keeping up well. The year's royalty on *Hazel Blossoms* was $1057 and on all others was $675 for the quarter ending August 13 and $625 on November 13.[8]

Whittier was unwell during most of the fall, but he had come to realize that life could be good even when he was uncomfortable, and the autumnal changes had never seemed so sweet.

Few events in his life, Whittier said, gave him greater pleasure than a letter about one of his early poems, "The Vaudois Teacher," which, translated into French, became a household poem among the Waldenses, who did not know its origin. Rev. James C. Fletcher, when a student at Geneva, found that it was a favorite poem among them. Later, having found that it was by Whittier, he told him about its popularity there, and when he went to Italy in 1875 he wrote to the Moderator of the Synod, who informed the members at a pastoral banquet that the poem was by Whittier. They voted to send "a very warm Christian fraternal salutation to the author of 'The Vaudois Colporteur.'" Whittier wrote to the Moderator of the Synod, "I shall keep the letter amongst my most precious remembrances, and it will be a joy to me to know that in your distant country and in those sanctuaries of the Alps, consecrated by such previous and holy memories, there are Christians, men and women, who think of me with kindness, and give me a place in their prayers."[9]

"The Giver and the Taker," an early form of "Giving and Taking," was in the *Villager* October 14, "From the Waif." It was a versification of a prose translation of a poem by Tinnevaluva, a Hindoo poet. A sentence in the headnote, not in later printings, is another bit of evidence that Whittier was interested in Oriental literature and philosophy when they came closest to Christianity: "He was remembered for his hatred of idolatry and caste and for his almost Christian conception of God and human duty."[10]

Early in October Whittier was asked by James H. Carleton to write a poem for the dedication of Haverhill Public Library. The suggestion had come from Ezekiel J. M. Hale, who had started the movement to build the Library and had been the first and largest donor. The building, costing $47,665, was completed and stocked with over twenty-one thousand volumes. The dedication took place November 11, and Whittier's "The Library," set to music by B.

J. Lang, was sung by a quartet and printed in the Order of Exercises. It differed from the present form in the sixth stanza, the last two lines of which were

We hear the sage's word; we trace

The foot-prints of our human race.

"The Library" was dignified and suitable, in spite of Whittier's mistrust of his skill in occasional verses. It was the right length, it did no obvious teaching, and it led, with a touch of simple stateliness in rhythm and phrase, from God's first command "Let there be light" to the life thrilling along the Library alcoves where the lords of thought awaited the call of the reader. The second stanza reminded the public that Whittier was not among the still numerous embattled conservatives who accepted literally the first chapters of Genesis:

Faint was the light at first that shone

On giant fern and mastodon,

On half-formed plant and beast of prey,

And man as rude and wild as they.

When Vice-President Henry Wilson, whom Whittier regarded as an old and dear friend, died November 22, Whittier was again reminded how few early Abolitionists were left. However restricted he was by poor health, he was usually able to go to funerals, and he went to Wilson's in Boston on November 29. He sat, sad and thoughtful, beside the coffin in the Hall of Representatives, which was elaborately decorated with festoons of smilax, intertwined with white flowers. One of the clergymen taking part in the service was a young man of thirty-nine whose influence upon the religious life of Americans was, like Whittier's, to extend far beyond his own denomination. Phillips Brooks was in his sixth year as rector of Trinity Church. A few years later Whittier was reading his sermons with a great deal of satisfaction, "not always agreeing with him but liking his spirit and earnest convictions" and referring to him as a "rare man among the Episcopalians."[11]

Whittier paid for going to Wilson's funeral by a recurrence of erysipelas in his face brought on, he thought, by the cold weather on that day. In other ways the winter began pleasantly. A Christmas present that he received suggested a poem for *St. Nicholas*. The present was a fringed gentian between two pieces of glass, and he hung it in the window of the door at the north side of the Garden Room. The poem was "The Pressed Gentian." It was overloaded with preaching, which filled the last two stanzas — half of the poem. It is not easy to see in the poem anything that would appeal to children and that would encourage Mary Mapes Dodge, the editor of *St. Nicholas*, to tell Whittier to send more at his own price. The fact must be that Whittier's name would impress the adults who paid for the magazine, whatever their children or grandchildren might think of his writings.[12]

He was happy to have his cousins Joseph and Gertrude Whittier Cartland with him during the winter. They had sold their house in Providence and were hunting for a house in the country. Whittier had known and liked them for a long time. Joseph had taught at Haverford Friends School, now Haverford College, and had been superintendent there. Gertrude Whittier had taught at Moses Brown School and was principal of the girls' department from 1852 to 1855, when she and Joseph were married and he became principal of Moses Brown School, while she became assistant principal. Their marriage had been delayed by her poor health until she was thirty-three. One of her relatives, whom they visited on their wedding trip, remarked that she hoped that Gertrude would live for a few years to enjoy happiness. Twenty years later, when they spent the winter at Whittier's, she was evidently in good health, and she lived to be eighty-eight.

It was fortunate that Whittier had the Cartlands with him at this time. The approaching marriage of his niece, who had lived at his house since she was thirteen — she was now thirty — and his plans for living elsewhere than in his own home had turned his thoughts to the past and to his own loneliness. But still he felt that he was happier than he deserved to be; he had friends, and he received letters from them in almost every mail, with messages of love.[13] Not all the letters, however, were of that sort. After being in Boston at the Marlboro House for three weeks in January, he came home to find nearly one hundred letters waiting for him and got a sick headache trying to answer them. One was from a man who was preparing to write a life of Edgar Allan Poe and wanted to know if Whittier in his acquaintance with Poe — they never met — considered him a "confirmed sot."[14]

During the late winter and early spring Whittier was occupied with two quite different pieces of business: plans for moving to Oak Knoll and writing a hymn for the opening of the International Exhibition at Philadelphia, the celebration of the centennial of American independence.

The estate in Danvers, to which Whittier gave the name "Oak Knoll," had been bought by relatives with whom he planned to live much of the time after Lizzie's marriage. He went to Danvers to see it in October, but alterations were to be made and he would not go there to live until spring. He decided to take some of his parlor furniture, as he thought that the couple who were coming to live at his house would wish to use their own, but he rather surprisingly did not consider taking his mother's picture, which continued in its place over the parlor mantle. He hunted for bedroom furniture at lower prices than his cousins had expected to pay, and not having the Amesbury fondness for handsome and spirited horses, recommended a steady eight-year-old that could be bought for two hundred twenty-five dollars or a nine-or-ten-year old, good, strong, and kind one, for one hundred fifty.[15]

One day two callers, one of them General Joseph R. Hawley, President of the United States Centennial Commission, came to ask Whittier to write the ode or poem, Longfellow having decided not to do it. He declined, not feeling equal to the nervous strain. Bryant, Lowell, and Holmes also declined, and the committee decided to go to a younger man. Whittier and Holmes both suggested Bayard Taylor, who accepted the assignment which, he said, had come to him "through the failure of so many better men to accept it." He had already written a hymn for the Centennial, which he now withdrew. Whittier had now been asked to write the hymn, and Taylor urged him to do it. He forgave Whittier for not writing the ode, knowing the state of Whittier's health — Whittier outlived Taylor by fourteen years — but the public would be puzzled because the best poets in the country were doing nothing for the program. The hymn should come from New England: Taylor represented Pennsylvania, and the cantata was supplied by Georgia (Sidney Lanier). He appealed to Whittier "as a dear, old friend . . . and as a true American to help in this emergency."

Whittier replied immediately that he hadn't an idea in his head, and if he had, his head, being in the possession of the fiend Neuralgia, was in no condition to do anything with it. Would Taylor send a copy of his hymn? Whittier wanted something suggestive to look at before making a decision. Taylor sent his hymn immediately: "I shall be very glad indeed if I am able, in this way, to furnish kindling-wood for your fire." Whittier now, quite unenthusiastically, said that he would "try to fix up something," although he was discouraged when he saw Taylor's hymn, which was "too good." He asked permission to use two lines from it:

Yet unto later good ordain
The rivalry of hand and brain

which he would change to

And unto common good ordain
This rivalship of hand and brain.

Taylor of course said, "Take all you want and welcome!" and tactfully added "There are some expressions which any hymn for the occasion must include; and such should be considered common property."[16]

There were other lines in Whittier's hymn evidently suggested by lines in Taylor's and he adapted two of Taylor's lines to make a more effective and relevant conclusion. Taylor's lines were

And bless, through power and wisdom won,
The peaceful cycle here begun.

These became the final couplet in Whittier's last stanza:

And, cast in some diviner mould,
Let the new cycle shame the old!

Whittier included some ideas derived from his own thinking and his experiences. It seemed to him significant that the nation was now united and free, and it was the founders of this nation who spoke the divine word of liberty

Whose echo is the glad refrain
Of rended bolt and falling chain.

He had, like most of the thoughtful people of his time, what has been called "the moralist obsession of the liberal middle class," and wrote

> . . . . . We crave
> The austere virtues strong to save,
> The honor proof to place or gold,
> The manhood never bought or sold!

He sent the hymn with many misgivings, but it was a great success at Philadelphia. Set to music by John Knowles Paine, it was sung on May 10, the opening day of the Centennial, by a chorus of eight hundred, directed by Theodore Thomas. Applause and cheers broke out before the singers had finished the first line and were repeated at the close of each stanza. To what extent the enthusiasm was caused by the words or by the music is hard to say, but the audience probably agreed with the singers in preferring what a reporter called Whittier's "clean and shapely lines" to the "jagged strophes clothing still more jagged and misshapen thought" of Sidney Lanier's cantata, "The Centennial Meditation of Columbia." One member of the chorus said that when singing the cantata, he always felt as though he had seen some word wrong and had suddenly lost the connection and another was quoted as saying that a popular horse-car ballad of the day

> Punch, brother, punch with care,
> A three-cent hole for a six-cent fare

was more expressive of American spirit and sentiment than Lanier's "lofty musings on the 'weltering of long ago around about the moveless base of my final resting-place.' "[17] Most critics would doubtless rank Lanier's poetry above Whittier's, but Whittier, at the age of sixty-eight, was still thinking and feeling as the great majority of Americans did and could speak to them in words that they understood and could imagine to be their own.

Whittier thought that he would have liked to hear the singing of the hymn at Philadelphia but probably would not have understood it, because, quoting the first line of Charles Lamb's "To Clara K.," "The Gods have made me most unmusical." Had he gone to Philadelphia, he would have found a bust of himself by David M. French just inside the door of the Exhibition Hall. French, a sculptor and stone-cutter in Newburyport, sent Whittier a copy of the bust, which his friends regarded as an excellent likeness. Whittier did not think seriously of going to Philadelphia: "The very thought of that Ezekiel's vision of machinery and the nightmare of confusion of the world's curiosity shop appalls me, and I shall not venture myself amidst it."[18]

Except for the "Centennial Hymn," Whittier did no writing during the winter and spring, but as usual he was reading recent books. Early in the winter he read Howells' *Private Theatricals*, which he thought equal to anything that Howells had ever written; Mrs. Farrell seemed to him wonderfully well done, and he liked Howells' "half-relenting way of showing her up, like Izaak Walton's putting the frog on the hook 'as if you loved him.' "

When Sarah Bagley called on him early in March, he lent her John Fiske's new volume of essays, *The Unseen World*. The essay that gave its title to the volume could not have met with Whittier's full approval; he could not have shared Fiske's attitude toward life after death: "Could we but know that our present lives are working together toward some good and even an end in no wise anthropomorphic, it would be of less consequence whether we were individually to endure."[19]

Lizzie was married April 19 at Whittier's house at 11:15 by the local Episcopal rector. There were not many guests, ten or twelve friends of the bridegroom and a few others, but even so, the house "had to be stretched for the occasion." The small rooms and cozy nooks, Whittier observed, served better for courting than for weddings. The bride was "somewhat agitated" but bore up well and departed hopefully with her husband on the 11:40 train for Boston, where they were to stay a day or two at the Hotel Brunswick and then go to their new and elegantly furnished house in Portland, whose elegance would be further increased by over two hundred dollars' worth of silver received as wedding gifts. There were "spoons enough to tempt General Butler if he ever visits Portland," was Whittier's comment — a reference to the charge that Butler had stolen silver spoons in New Orleans.

Whittier went to Oak Knoll, April 29. For the next five years he spent much of his time there but kept his legal residence in Amesbury, returning occasionally for a few days or a few weeks. From 1880 to 1888 he was at Oak Knoll somewhat less, perhaps a little over half of the time, and in 1889 somewhat less than half.[20] He was there even less in the last two years of his life; conditions were not as pleasant as they had been at first.

Oak Knoll was less than a mile from the railroad station, which was about a half hour's train ride from Boston, and Whittier looked forward to more frequent visits by his Boston friends. The house and its surroundings were far more attractive than Whittier's home in Amesbury, where the neighborhood was becoming commercialized; within a few hundred yards of Whittier's home there were five carriage factories, a blacksmith shop, a cigar factory, and a saloon. The house at Oak Knoll had been built in 1842 and was rather impressive with its Greek Revival pillars. It was approached by a driveway that curved round the knoll that suggested the name. The original owner had been fond of nature and art and, in a time when landscaping was a new skill, laid out the grounds with deciduous and evergreen trees and a flower garden with a fountain.[21] Best of all, there was much to remind him of his boyhood: farm land with hayfields and orchards, and barns for cows, pigs, and horses. Crows built nests in the pine trees at the west of the house, quails came close to the house and even onto the piazza, and pheasants came to get the grain scattered for them in the winter.

The rooms were large and high-studded. The parlor was square, "rather stiff and prim" according to one visitor, but with a view over sweeping meadows. Whittier's study was on the first floor, with windows looking eastward over flower beds and southward across the veranda and through the trees. The house was heated by a furnace, but his study also had a stove with a wood fire in ordinary weather and a coal fire in extreme cold. Whittier never used the study in the evening; his eyes could not stand the strain of reading by gas light, and he spent his evenings in a room with other members of the household.

It was just the kind of household that Whittier would like; one elderly man, three bright and interesting women, and a lively little girl — a lively little boy would have spoiled everything. The man was Edmund Johnson, a widower, whose wife had been Phebe Whittier, daughter of Obadiah Whittier and hence first cousin of John G. Whittier. He had an honorary title of Colonel. The women were his daughters, Caroline, aged forty-nine; Abby, forty-eight; and Mary, forty-six. Caroline had founded and still directed Miss Johnson's School for Young Ladies on Bowdoin Street in Boston, for which, a year later, Whittier wrote "At School-Close." She had been a pupil of her cousin Moses Cartland at Clinton Grove Academy in Weare, New Hampshire, and he described her as "a most interesting and beloved pupil. There was always an intellectual sunshine in her presence; while her affectionate disposition and uniform kindness made it ever welcome." She was offered the presidency of Wellesley College by its founder, Henry Fowle Durant.[22] Abby, widow of Henry Woodman, had an adopted daughter, Phebe, seven years old.

Lucy Larcom told Lizzie Whittier Pickard that her uncle had a beautiful and fitting home at Oak Knoll. His cousins, she thought, were just the people for him to live with, and little Phebe the best companion he could have.[23] On this point she was unquestionably right. Whittier had a special genius for playing with little girls, and Phebe doubtless enjoyed his company more than that of her mother or her maiden aunts. They were strict disciplinarians and laid down rigid rules; Phebe was not allowed to go to parties where boys were to be present. Whittier left the discipline to the women, and he and Phebe enjoyed life together. They drove about the country roads in a pony chaise drawn by Jessica, the pony that replaced a recalcitrant donkey that Whittier was afraid might hurt Phebe. When Jessica had to be killed after she broke her leg kicking in her stall, Whittier wrote "Lament to Jessica," which ended:

> She kicked to right,
>   She kicked to left.
> The stable post she struck it.
>   She kicked and broke her ankle bone
> And then she kicked the bucket.

He got down on his knees and built Phebe a stone farm house and barn with stone animals going into it. They both enjoyed the numerous pets and the names that he gave them. The mocking bird was named David for King David of the Old Testament. His name perhaps suggested the name of the cat, Bathsheba; after her funeral Whittier gave Phebe an elegy that he had written:

> Bathsheba!
> Whereat
> None ever said "Scat."
> No worthier cat
> Ever sat on a mat
> Or caught a rat.
> Requiescat!

There were dogs, including Robin Adair, a shepherd, and a little dog named Jackanapes. A pet squirrel, kept in Whittier's study, was named General Gordon, and there was a Jersey calf, Phillippa.

Only a few days after going to Oak Knoll Whittier began to think of having his friends visit him there.[24] But first he had to return to Amesbury for the Quaker Quarterly Meeting, and for three days his house was, as he said, "overrun." The second day was the biggest one. A special train arrived in the morning soon after nine. It was Whittier's custom to open the gate in the fence and stand on the front step so that people walking from the railroad station to the meeting house could come up the path and shake hands. Then he would go to the meeting and return soon after twelve with the dinner guests — this year there were twelve. The dinner was always roast beef, asparagus — he was interested in having it tender —, potatoes, and, if they could be found, strawberries. After dinner the guests went again to the meeting house, while this year Whittier stayed at home; he was "too tired for preaching."[25]

The couple living in the house were Mr. & Mrs. George W. Cate, who remained there until Whittier's death. There was always a hired girl to help with the housework, and when Mrs. Cate, who suffered from headaches, was unwell, her younger sister, later the wife of the printer Frederick A. Brown, helped with the work. Mrs. Cate had the responsibility of the Quarterly Meeting dinners, and can hardly have accepted without inner protest Whittier's remark when he once came into the kitchen after the guests had left and said, "Thee has escaped it all."

Until the second story at the west end of the house was added in 1883-84, the Cates had the two rooms at the east end of the first floor, using one of them as a living room. They and Whittier both used the parlor, where most of the furniture belonged to the Cates. Whittier had the Garden Room and the bedroom over it that had been Elizabeth's.

The arrangement worked out well. Whittier had known Cate for ten years. He was an attorney and later judge in the Amesbury Police Court. He and his wife were people of refinement and intelligence, who lived quietly, had no children, and were willing that Whittier should come and stay as long as he wished and should have visitors.

Whittier was following national affairs and was favorably impressed by James G. Blaine's defense in the House of Representatives against charges brought by a Democratic committee — "ex-Confederates," Whittier called them. They accused Blaine, a candidate for the Republican nomination for President, of using his position of Speaker in 1869 to do favors for a railway company for which he had been indirectly rewarded. The charges were based on letters which Blaine now obtained and read in Congress with interpolations. Whittier thought that Blaine had cleared himself of the charges, but the ordeal that he had gone through led Whittier to say that the Presidency wasn't worth such a candle and to tell the story, which he later used in another connection, of the man who was well spoken of until he unwisely became a candidate for public office, when he was so abused that he had to call his dog to see if he was himself or somebody else.[26]

He was at Oak Knoll in early June and thinking about Dom Pedro's approaching visit to Boston. It seemed to him that the Emperor would enjoy a dinner at the Atlantic Club better than being "toted about" and shown the public buildings. As for himself, he would not try to get to him through "the double wall of Boston and court etiquette"; if only Dom Pedro could do as other people did, he might come to Oak Knoll with Mr. & Mrs. Fields and they could have him for an hour or two to themselves. Whittier was in Amesbury a few days later and received an invitation to a reception to Dom Pedro at the Radical Club too late to accept it, and furthermore, he wrote to John T. Sargent, he hardly thought that he would care to take any special pains to meet His Imperial Majesty — adding contritely, "Though to be sure Dom Pedro is a good deal more than an Emperor." But the matter did not drop there; Dom Pedro wished to meet Whittier, and the Sargents arranged an informal meeting June 14 at three o'clock, with only a few others present.

When Whittier stepped toward the Emperor to greet him, he found himself embraced in what he called "the style of Brazilian friendliness — a hug." He recovered from the slight shock and led the Emperor to a sofa where they talked for half an hour before joining in the general conversation. The Emperor left at five o'clock in an open barouche, standing and waving his hat. When some humorous comments were made about the embrace that he had received, Whittier turned to Mrs. Sargent and said, "That was meant for thee."[27]

During the larger part of the summer he was at Oak Knoll, quietly spending the hot days under the pine trees, convinced that the country could get along very well without him. When the heat got too bad in July, he went to the Isles of Shoals, where he found that too many people had the same idea; there were five hundred guests at the Appledore House and the dinner tables were crowded.[28]

After a few days in Amesbury in the third week in August he went to West Ossipee accompanied by Isabella Hume, one of the group of young women in Amesbury that he enjoyed being with and who evidently found no generation gap between him and themselves. His nephew's wife, Addie Caldwell, was already in West Ossipee, and others, including Mary Esther Carter and Jettie Morrill, were to go soon.

There was a pleasant company of boarders at Bearcamp River House, the weather and scenery were good, and Whittier felt refreshed and strengthened. Phebe sent some apples and pears from Oak Knoll, which he shared with the company — or rather, he told her, the inner circle of it. The "inner circle" included five young women who, with two boys and two guides, climbed Mr. Chocorua. The trip was planned one evening as Whittier and the group sat by the fireplace, Whittier as usual keeping the tongs in his possession and not letting anyone else touch the fire. The party drove in a four-horse coach to the foot of the mountain and climbed to the edge of the timber line, where they camped for the night. The guides cut trees for an enormous camp fire, and the party sat round it telling stories and, according to the lively account given by the young women the next day, listening to the growling of bears and other terrifying sounds. They started at daylight the next morning and climbed to the summit. The two boys, Adoniram Stockbridge, son of one of the guests, and Tip, the stable boy at Bearcamp House, went ahead of the others who, according to Whittier's rhymed account, followed "panting and straining." His poem did not mention that Tip had been drinking and had some difficulty getting over the ledge. They had lunch on the summit and then went down the mountain and returned to Bearcamp House in the evening. After Whittier heard the story of their adventures, he composed "How They Climbed Chocorua" and dictated it to Lucy Larcom. It was read to the group the next morning, and a few days later Whittier had Lucy Larcom read it as the work of an unknown author at a husking bee in the barn of the two guides, the Knox brothers.[29]

The next evening there was a good deal of fun, arranged by Lucy Larcom, with the reading of pretended telegrams from ridiculous persons and a poem by Lucy Larcom "To the Unknown and Absent Author of How They Climbed Chocorua," which said that the bear on the mountain had been frightened away by the poet's verses and the poet had been caught by the coattails in one of the traps. Whittier then said that the old poet ought to make a will and proceeded to dictate it; everyone in the group was mentioned, including the stage-driver and the stable boy looking on from the doorway. The next morning he added a codicil bequeathing his pencil to Samuel T. Pickard, who left for Portland the same day. After Pickard had gone, Whittier was afraid that he would print "The Last Will and Testament of the Man in the Bear-Trap" in the *Portland Transcript* and wrote to him asking him not to print the "foolish verses," which, he said, were hardly consistent with his years and "eminent gravity" and would make "the heathen rage and the people imagine vain things."[30]

Jettie Morrill had told Lizzie Whittier in the winter that George L. Osgood was writing the music of a song for her and wanted some words. "Do you think Mr. W. would be very much annoyed if you were to tell him of this? Do you suppose he would be willing to write some lines for me, choosing his own subject?" Lizzie had probably been too busy with plans for her wedding to carry on the negotiations, and now at Bearcamp House Jettie tried another approach. She said to Whittier, "You never wrote a love song. I do not believe you can write one. I would like to have you try to write one for me to sing." He wrote "The Henchman" "offhand," as he said when he sent it to Howells for the *Atlantic*, and gave it to Jettie the next day. It was, he wrote to Howells, quite out of his line and he doubted its being good enough for the *Atlantic*. It did not appear in the *Atlantic*, and Whittier did a good deal of work on it before sending it to the *Independent*. It was not, he said, "exactly a Quaker piece," it was not didactic, and it had no moral, but it was "natural, simple, and not unpoetical."[31] It was published in the *Independent* December 20, and three years later was published by Oliver Ditson & Co. as sheet music, dedicated to Jettie Morrill. It did not become one of Whittier's most popular poems. It was an intellectual exercise rather than an expression of warm human love, and it came painfully close to being didactic and to having a moral:

The love that no return doth crave
To knightly levels lifts the slave.

Whittier returned to Amesbury with a cold and faced with a bushel of letters to answer and the unhappy task of getting some pictures and other personal belongings ready to send to Oak Knoll. Lizzie stayed with him and helped him until he left for Oak Knoll feeling rather sad. He thought of himself as having no "fixed abiding place" and the newspapers had the same thought about him. He was reported as living in Peabody, buying a house in Portland, living in seclusion in a cottage that he was said to have bought at the Isles of Shoals, visiting Dr. H. A. Tucker — whom he had never heard of — at Martha's Vineyard, and being in Newburyport.[32]

For a few days after his return to Oak Knoll there was Indian summer weather. He could lie under the pines and beeches, and he found it pleasant to live once more in the country and come in close contact with outward nature. Then, before the leaves had fallen, there was an early snow storm and the trees seemed full of snowy blossoms — "strange and sadly beautiful." The leaves fell and the cold weather set in, but he still found it pleasant to walk through the bare-boughed woods, to play with the dogs, and to visit the horses and cows in the barn. It was cold enough to have a coal fire in his study. He could not read as much as he would like; however, before the month was over he was reading the two-volume *Memoir* of Norman Macleod and finding it "one of the most interesting of books — sweet, earnest, playful, full of love and good works, enlivened all along with poetry and Scotch humor."[33] Macleod was a Scottish minister active in various projects in Glasgow, including the establishing of refreshment rooms for working men and a mission church for the poor to which only people in working clothes were admitted.

He was pleased when the Cartlands at last found a house to their liking in Newburyport, on the corner of High and Broad Streets. This was the house in which Whittier would spend the last winter of his life. It had the advantage of being only a little over two miles from a Friends Meeting in West Newbury — which, however, was abandoned a few years later.

The 1876 Presidential election was approaching, and before Whittier left West Ossipee, he commented that New Hampshire was alive with political caucuses and flag raisings, but there was little real enthusiasm. The only hope of the Republicans, he thought, was to be found in the folly and "general cussedness" of the Democrats, which from present appearances was not likely to fail them. If there was little to arouse enthusiasm, however, there was much to cause alarm. Federal troops in Louisiana, South Carolina, and Florida were being used to support Republican administrations, and there were reports of intimidation and fraud. "If there must be fraud or intimidation to secure a victory I should prefer defeat," was Whittier's attitude. "And I hope if Governor Kellogg [of Louisiana] or any other Republican attempts to do evil that good may come, they may be exposed at once." As election day approached, however, he hoped that Hayes would be elected; Hayes would be a safer man than Tilden, who, however he might feel and wish, would not be able to control the Democratic party. By the day before election he had despaired of a victory for Hayes, and if it occurred he would be happily disappointed.

When the votes of several Democratic districts in Louisiana, Florida, and South Carolina were thrown out, thus giving Hayes a majority of one in the Electoral College, the election became for Whittier, as for the entire nation, "a long-drawn agony." He knew that Democrats had cheated and intimidated, but that was no reason Republicans should, and, as he said before the election, he did not want Hayes elected unless he could be elected fairly.

He took no part in the campaign, and his only political activity this year was a letter to the *Boston Journal* supporting William Claflin's candidacy for Congress.[34] Claflin was elected and served two terms.

Whittier spent a good deal of time on "The Witch of Wenham," which was completed by early November. At first it was a story improvised for Phebe; then he visited the scene of the story, the old Prince House not far from Oak Knoll, and wrote the poem. He thought that it was one of his best, although he admitted that he was not a good judge, and that the *Atlantic* should pay him one hundred fifty dollars for it; other magazines would pay two hundred, and he was afraid that his days of writing that sort of poem were about over. His income was less than it had been; railroad dividends were down as a result of ruinous competition.

The poem was printed in the February 1877 *Atlantic* and two years later in *The Vision of Echard*. Howells thought that it was the best poem in the volume, told "simply, picturesquely, with a sort of tremor of intense feeling in its music," and the "faint glimmer of archness in the young girl's character" seemed to him to give the "finest effect to the tale." The review continued, "Mr. Whittier has more than once realized the grim witch time in his verse, but we cannot recollect that he has ever brought it so vividly and pathetically to mind, while losing none of the love-charm proper to this particular theme." Readers a century later would not be likely to agree with Howells. Like "Mabel Martin," "The Witch of Wenham" gives anything but an accurate picture of the terrible days of witchcraft. No sane young woman, just rescued from imprisonment and almost certain death, would whisper to her lover and rescuer when a ferryman cried "God keep her from the evil eye and harm of witch,"

He does not know . . .

A little witch am I.

As an antiquarian once pointed out, "If there be a bit of historic fact at the bottom, the story of the charges preferred, the arrest, the escape and flight, fall far short of a true picture of those days of doom." No one could question that the story was simply told, but few would be likely to notice any "tremor of intense feeling in its music." Still, that tremor was felt by others besides Howells in Whittier's own time. When Oliver Wendell Holmes' wife asked him to read it to her, he refused because he knew he would break down before he got through it; it had made him tearful the first time he read it. There were two stanzas with good descriptive details: in the farmhouse attic where the heroine was imprisoned, swallows were moaning and stirring in the chimney and bats were wheeling round and round.

On Christmas day he received a check for one thousand dollars from sales of the illustrated *Mabel Martin*, which was more than he had expected and must have helped considerably to make up for reduced railroad dividends.[35]

Oak Knoll, Danvers, with Phebe Woodman on the front lawn.

Whittier's study at Oak Knoll.

Phebe Woodman (1869-1953). (Courtesy of Robert E. Caliga)

Elizabeth Whittier Pickard (1845-1902).

Samuel T. Pickard (1828-1915).

Bayard Taylor (1825-1878).

Celia Laighton Thaxter (1835-1894).

XXIX
1877 - 78

Whittier did not feel quite at home at Oak Knoll — home had been Amesbury with his mother and sister — but he liked his cousins and he enjoyed the winter scenery.

One day he watched from the window while Phebe, wearing a red hood, struggled through the snow to scatter nuts and corn for the squirrels and birds. Soon after she came back into the house, he handed her the manuscript of "Red Riding Hood" and asked her to make the last section of it part of her evening prayer. It was just the sort of thing adults wanted children to read; it told them to be good. It appeared in the May *St. Nicholas*.[1]

He was not confined to Oak Knoll, either in body or spirit. There were visits of a week or so at the Claflins', and during one of them he went to hear Elizabeth Stuart Phelps read a lecture on George Eliot to an audience of eighty women and four men. He had recently read and liked *Daniel Deronda*. He read accounts of Moody and Sankey's evangelistic campaign in Boston, disliking their theology and their methods but believing that they could reach and move men that James Freeman Clarke and Phillips Brooks could not. He was giving a good deal of thought to treatment of the South which would lead to its complete integration into national life, and through Mrs. Claflin advised President Hayes to conciliate the best of the Democrats by appointing Lucius Lamar to a Cabinet post and to rely no longer on carpet-baggers.[2]

He was reading new books as they appeared. Gail Hamilton's *What Think Ye of Christ* led him to re-define his own beliefs: the Divinity of Christ but Christ as a man through whom the Divine was made miraculously manifest. After he started to read her novel, *First Love is Best*, he could not stop until he had finished it. He read a volume of Samuel Johnson's *Oriental Religions* dealing with Chinese ethics and faith and, with typical Nineteenth Century enthusiasm for Confucius, was astonished to find that such a man could have made his appearance "amidst the dull and dreary commonplaces of his people." He read Sarah Orne Jewett's *Deephaven* three times and gave copies to his friends. It was her first book, and she was grateful for his enthusiastic letter to her, but, as often, he was too enthusiastic to be critical, and he failed to notice the mild Victorian snobbery in a condescending attitude toward the quaintness of natives in a decaying seaport town.[3]

There was no falling-off in popular demand for whatever he wished to write. "Fitz-Greene Halleck" was written for the unveiling of a monument, and said simply and gracefully what the occasion required, referring to poems which had appeared in school readers and must have been familiar to the audience. A request from Robert Rantoul for a poem for the dedication of a monument to Ferdinand Freiligrath arrived too late, but Whittier approved the project and sent twenty dollars, regarding Freiligrath as the leading liberal poet of his time and recalling his encouragement in the dark days of the Anti-Slavery movement.[4]

In his "Hymn of the Dunkers" in the May *Atlantic* Whittier imagined one of the sisters praising God for their escape from persecution and looking forward to the second coming of Christ to "make clean the world with fire." While the *Atlantic's* subscribers were reading the poem, Whittier, in similar mood of hope for the future, was seeing nature's resurrection in green grass and budding and blossoming trees as a promise of life and fulfillment to mankind.[5]

Also in May the *Youth's Companion* printed Whittier's first contribution to that highly successful magazine, "King Solomon and the Ants." Like other distinguished contributors, among whom were Tennyson, Gladstone, Mark Twain, Theodore Roosevelt, and Phillips Brooks, Whittier did not feel it necessary to restrict himself to thought and phrasing suitable for children.[6] "King Solomon and the Ants" taught a lesson for adults:

Happy must be the State
Whose ruler heedeth more
The murmurs of the poor
Than flatteries of the great.

Although he had found no inspiration in his own brief period of school teaching, he painted an idealistic picture of pupil-teacher relations in a poem for his cousin Caroline's school, entitled "At School-Close. Bowdoin Street, Boston 1877." The teacher's joy, it said, was like the sculptor's, whose clay model grew to the desired grace, and the pupil's joy would be like

The wakening sense, the strange delight
That swelled the fabled statue's breast
And filled its clouded eyes with sight.

The ideal of womanhood recommended to the pupils was doubtless more acceptable in 1877 than it would be a century later: woman should be pure, true, prompt in duty, obedient to conscience, gentle, pitiful; she should keep her faith in human nature and the goodness of God, and she should bless a world that needed

. . . . . Martha's helpful carefulness
No less than Mary's better part.

During part of August and September Whittier was at the Bearcamp House in West Ossipee, New Hampshire. He had a southeast room and boasted that he never missed a sunrise. He did no climbing and little walking, spending much of his time in a pine grove reading to the young people who gathered round him and watching them dance the Virginia reel in the evening. After a group of young people had failed to find a waterfall that he had told them about, he told them in some amusement that they had taken the wrong road. Then, after spending more time than usual in his room for the next three days, he read them "The Seeking of the Waterfall."[7] The poem was needlessly long, fourteen stanzas describing the climb up the mountain and fifteen preaching a sermon on the rewards that come from following visions leading toward goals that are never reached, but it appeared in the January 1878 *Atlantic*, whose readers still welcomed moral and religious lessons in verse.

The *Atlantic* was ready to take anything that Whittier sent, and within a few days after sending "The Seeking of the Waterfall" he was writing to Howells about a poem that would appear in the November number, "In the Old South." It told the incident in the Old South Church in Boston which he had transferred to the First Church in Newbury in "Margaret Smith's Journal," the young Quaker woman who interrupted a meeting by entering dressed in sackcloth, barefooted, with her face blackened and ashes on her head, and delivered a "warning from the great God of Heaven and Earth to the Rulers and Magistrates of Boston."

In the late fall he was at Oak Knoll, looking forward to his seventieth birthday. Like most bachelors, whose childhood memories stay with them through life, he was thinking about his boyhood. It seemed only a little while ago that he was driving the cows home from pasture with his pockets full of nuts and the leaves rustling under his feet.

He did not want a big birthday celebration; it was bad enough, in his opinion, to be old without being twitted about it, and he thought that he had put a stop to plans for a "fuss." But the fuss could not be stopped. It had begun in April when Hurd & Houghton asked him for a photograph from which to make a drawing. He sent his latest, which he thought was good in outline but, according to his friends, was too stern, "a little too much of the 'Sword of the Lord and Gideon' look." The expression was serious rather than stern and was what the public wanted; the vogue of smiling photographs was far in the future.[8]

The Literary World gave part of its December 1 issue to poetry and prose for Whittier's birthday. Some of the contributions were more notable for length than for quality. Edmund C. Stedman wrote fifty-one lines of blank verse and William Lloyd Garrison one hundred six. Holmes and Longfellow wrote sonnets. Whittier especially liked Longfellow's "The Three Silences of Molinos," which he said touched him too deeply for words; he evidently did not mind being addressed rather inaccurately as "Hermit of Amesbury." It is somewhat harder to understand what he found touching in Paul Hamilton Hayne's lines unless it was their sincerity:[9]

> From this far realm of Pines I waft thee now
> A Brother's greeting, Poet, tried and true;

So thick the laurels on thy reverend brow
We scarce can see the white locks glimmering through.

A politician's image was not damaged then as it would be today if it was known that he wrote poetry, and Israel Washburn, who had been governor of Maine and was now collector of the port of Portland, sent his poem to Whittier, at the suggestion of Samuel T. Pickard, for approval before sending it to *The Literary World*. Whittier changed one line. Washburn had written

. . . . . Notes which tell
Of hope of heaven to all mankind.

He evidently assumed that Whittier, like himself, was a Universalist. He was not; in answer to a question that he had been asked, he wrote: "I am not a Universalist, for I believe in the possibility of the perpetual loss of the soul that persistently turns from God in the next life as in this." (He later wavered in this opinion.) He changed the last line to read:

Of broader hopes for human kind.[10]

All these tributes demanded some kind of public acknowledgment, and Whittier asked if *The Literary World* would be willing to print one that he would write. This was just what the editor had hoped, and Whittier was told that he could have as much space as he wished and that the manuscript should be in the hands of the editor by December 20. Whittier's poem was entitled "Response" and was modestly and gracefully expressed: the praise that he had received made him half believe that he was somebody else, and as he looked at his life-work through the partial eyes of his friends, he thought that in over-valuing what he had done, they were reading, between the lines of what he had written,

The finer grace of unfulfilled designs.

"Response" was ready before the deadline. Whittier had another use for it: he sent it to Longfellow to read at the *Atlantic* dinner in his honor if, as he feared, he could not go. His physician had warned him to avoid all excitement, pleasurable and otherwise, as the only way he could be free from "severe suffering." Still, Longfellow urged him to come, and he couldn't make up his mind. He hated the thought of going, especially since he had refused to be at any observance of his birthday at Haverhill or Amesbury. He was beginning to be ashamed of the affair and would be glad when it was over.

He was still undecided on the morning of his birthday. Then three of the young women who had been with him at West Ossipee in the summer arrived at Oak Knoll, bringing flowers and a collection of sketches from a group of his friends — and one of them brought him a pair of sealskin gloves. He looked at his gifts, especially the gloves. The weather was cold but sunny, and he let the young women help him to get ready and to leave for a train which would get him to Boston in time for the festivities.[11]

The dinner would have come off about as well without its chief guest. It had other purposes besides honoring him. Like other *Atlantic* dinners, it was good advertising. But a shadow hung over it. James R. Osgood was in financial difficulties, and Charles Fairfield, one of the partners in the firm that was his chief creditor, had a plan of transferring Osgood's publishing interests to Harper and Brothers in New York. He and Osgood were at the dinner, and during the evening Henry O. Houghton found an opportunity for conversation which led a year later to the merging of James R. Osgood & Co. with H. O. Houghton & Co., forming Houghton Osgood & Co., later Houghton Mifflin and Company, thus keeping the publishing house of New England authors in Boston.

It is unlikely that Whittier knew anything about all this, and it is equally unlikely that he knew all the guests seated at a u-shaped table in the magnificent Hotel Brunswick's new east dining room, with marble-tile floors, walls of Pompeian red, and frescoed ceiling, dedicated on this occasion. It is still more unlikely that he partook of all the seven courses or of the different wines with each course.

He was seated between Houghton and Emerson. Next to Emerson was Longfellow, and beyond Houghton were Howells and Holmes. Houghton began the speech-making with a history of the *Atlantic* and, irrelevant as it was to the ostensible purpose of the gathering, a description of the speculative nature of the publishing business, with the enigmatic statement, "Publishing and authorship must necessarily keep pace with each other." Whittier must have wondered what application this had to him, and his perplexity doubtless increased his embarrassment when he was introduced and was greeted by a "tremendous ovation." He spoke briefly and hesitantly, and was not heard by the guests at the lower ends of the table: "You must know you are not to expect a speech from me tonight. I can only say that I am very glad to meet with my friends of the *Atlantic*, a great many contributors to which I have only known through their writings, and that I thank them for the reception they have given me. When I supposed that I would not be able to attend this ceremony, I placed in my friend Longfellow's hands a little bit of verse that I told him, if it were necessary, I wished he would read. My voice is of 'a timorous nature and rarely to be heard above the breath.' Mr. Longfellow will do me the favor to read the writing. I shall be very much obliged to him, and hope at his ninetieth anniversary some of the younger men will do as much for him." Longfellow introduced "Response" in a pleasant conversational manner, but his voice was no more powerful than Whittier's, and there was cupping of hands behind ears. Holmes did rather better; he read vigorously and clearly "For Whittier's Seventieth Birthday," fourteen stanzas, of which only four referred to Whittier. Emerson, whose mind was failing, read Whittier's "Ichabod," to the consternation of Longfellow and doubtless of as many others as heard it.

He could not have made a worse choice. A denunciation of Daniel Webster, who had been dead long enough to be a revered part of Massachusetts legend, was out of place at a festive gathering, even if none of the guests had suffered a horrible moment of wondering whether

The glory from his gray hairs gone
Forevermore

could refer to the guest of the evening. Emerson had simply chosen a poem that he liked, without thinking of the occasion at which he was to read it. He had included "Ichabod" in *Parnassus,* and once when William Henry Channing asked him to read some of his favorite poems, he chose "Ichabod" as his specimen of Whittier.

Howells, to whom Houghton delegated the introduction of the speakers, introduced Mark Twain as a humorist who never left you hanging your head for having enjoyed his joke.

Thirty years later Clemens remembered distinctly the men seated at the "grand table" — Clemens himself was not even near it: he was half way down on the right. He remembered Whittier as "grave, lovely, his beautiful spirit shining out of his face"; Emerson as "supernaturally grave, unsmiling"; Longfellow, "with his silken-white hair and his benignant face"; Holmes, "flashing smiles and affection and all good-fellowship everywhere."

He had prepared his speech with especial care, and he thought that he had something unusual and startling. It was an account of an imaginary visit to the lonely cabin of a melancholy miner who did not welcome him cordially, having had other literary visitors. One, he said, was Mr. Emerson, "a seedy little bit of a chap — redheaded." Another was Mr. Holmes, "as fat as a balloon — he weighed as much as three hundred and had double chins all the way down to his stomach." The third was Mr. Longfellow, "built like a prize fighter. His head was cropped and bristly like as if he had a wig made of hair brushes." They had been drinking, the miner said, and they kept on drinking. Between drinks they would "swell around the cabin and strike attitudes and spout." Then they played "cut-throat euchre at ten cents a corner on trust." Clemens said that he finally explained to the miner, "Why, my dear sir, these were not the gracious singers to whom we and the world pay loving reverence and homage; these were imposters."

There has been endless discussion about this speech. Was it laughed at and applauded, and if not, did the listeners disapprove of a burlesque of men who, as Howells said, were of extraordinary dignity and were held in a species of religious veneration, or were they, after the seven-course dinner, in no condition to be either startled or amused? Clemens himself thought that he had committed a terrible blunder. He sent notes of apology to Emerson, Holmes, and Longfellow. Emerson had not heard the speech; Holmes and Longfellow were not offended, and Longfellow added that he thought that Whittier had enjoyed the dinner very much, by implication including the speech, which, however, Whittier does not seem to have mentioned either publicly or in letters to his friends. He may not have heard it, but he must have read it in the newspapers the next day. Curiously, one obvious criticism of the speech did not apparently occur to anyone; it had no relation to the supposed purpose of the gathering. The only reference to Whittier or his writings was, "Emerson says, 'The bulliest thing I ever wrote was Barbara Frietchie'. ''

Clemens' speech was not the final one. The speaking went on and on, and the guests at the head of the table began to drift away. Richard H. Stoddard went to Whittier with a sonnet in his pocket but decided not to read it; he was tired, Whittier was tired, everybody was tired, and so he satisfied himself with shaking Whittier's hand. John Townsend Trowbridge had planned to read his "Story of the Barefoot Boy" based on the incident told him by Whittier's brother of the two boys trying to rise in the air by lifting each other, but when Whittier left, Trowbridge decided to do the same; it was eleven o'clock, and the speaking was still going on.[12]

After staying two days at the Adams House, Whittier returned to Oak Knoll and took up the task of answering some of the hundreds of letters and of acknowledging the gifts. To the three young Amesbury women who had come to Oak Knoll on the morning of his birthday he sent fifty dollars to be used to help unemployed persons. The mills that gave employment to the larger part of the population had not been operating for over a year; no one knew when they would re-open, although only five years earlier they had greatly increased their water-power reservoir by building the dam that formed Lake Gardner and had paid for it out of accumulated profits. A few of the help had tried to get work in other towns, but many were illiterate and could do nothing but stay in Amesbury and stand about the streets: "a miserable sight," Whittier called it, "these pinched, ragged, hopeless-looking people." Early in the year the Protestant churches had held a union meeting and had taken up a collection for the poor. But not everyone was making great sacrifices for the poor: enough people owned trotting horses to have a mile and a half race track on the ice at Lake Gardner.[13]

Whittier was grateful for the kindness in the letters and in the verses that were showered upon him as if he were a magazine editor, "some beautiful, some intensely absurd," so poor that they would be valuable as curiosities. But he also felt humbled rather than exalted, as if he were getting more credit than he deserved and were reading his own obituaries. By the middle of January he could trust that the "queer fuss" was over in this country, but he was still getting letters from England.[14]

He was growing old gracefully. Lyman Abbott visited him at Oak Knoll, and forty years later wrote an ecstatic description of his appearance. "No one would call his face handsome; it was better, it was beautiful. The features were homely, though the forehead was high and the eyes were luminous. The photograph but poorly represents him. For his face was a transparency; the spirit within lighted it up; and photographs rarely, the older photographs never, interpret the spirit. His illuminated face has made quite real to me the picture given in Exodus, of Moses when he descended from the Mount where he had talked with God and 'his face shone!' Whittier's was a shining face.''[15]

It is quite possible that in conversation with Lyman Abbott, who was sufficiently inspiring to be chosen to succeed Henry Ward Beecher at Plymouth Church, Whittier's face shone with an inner light, but there were times in the irritations of daily living when divine inspiration was less evident. One day when Jettie Morrill was playing a Beethoven sonata especially well, according to Elizabeth Hume, who was herself a skilled pianist and studied with Edward MacDowell and Tobias Mathay, Whittier left the room, without an apology. His bad manners can hardly be excused by his dislike of piano music or by his increasing deafness. But he was still kind and thoughtful to people who needed help. When he was detained at Oak Knoll most of the winter by poor health, he worried about James and Abby Squires; he had heard that Abby was unwell and he was afraid that she might be suffering and in need of the money that he had left for them with a neighbor. He wrote to the neighbor to give them whatever help they needed and he would pay for it. He offered to try to get Paul Hamilton Hayne a government position in South Carolina or Georgia, and when Hayne replied that he was not well enough to endure the confinement of office work, he asked Houghton about the possibility of publishing a small volume of Hayne's poems. He used his influence to get Bayard Taylor appointed ambassador to Germany. Like other friends of Charlotte Forten, Whittier was interested in her approaching marriage to Rev. Francis J. Grimke, a son of Sarah and Angelina Grimke's brother and a slave mother; he sent fifty dollars as a wedding gift.[16]

He spent most of the winter at Oak Knoll, doing no writing for publication. "William Francis Bartlett," in the March *Atlantic*, had probably been written a year earlier, soon after Bartlett's death December 17, 1876. William Francis Bartlett was the son of Harriet Plummer, one of Whittier's classmates at Haverhill Academy. Whittier's opposition to war did not keep him from admiring soldiers. Early in the Civil War, Bartlett became a Captain in the 20th Massachusetts Volunteers and lost a leg at Yorktown. A year later, as Colonel of the 49th Massachusetts Regulars, he led an assault on Port Hudson and was twice wounded. He was wounded again on the second day of the Battle of the Wilderness, and it was then that Whittier wrote, "I see that Harriet Bartlett's brave young hero is again wounded — I trust not seriously."[17] However, the poem emphasized Bartlett's peace-time activities rather than his war record.

Although Whittier was spending little time in Amesbury, he had not lost interest in its affairs. He was a director of the Amesbury and Salisbury Home for Aged Women. He gave twenty-four books to the Public Library. He attended the annual town meeting in March.

At Oak Knoll he enjoyed the spring beauty, "the emerald of the lawn, the pear and peach and cherry bloom, the yellow cluster of the sycamore maples and the white glory of the magnolia." As he often remarked, his love of natural beauty was growing stronger as he grew older. But he had other and livelier interests. He went to Horticultural Hall in Boston to see a demonstration of the phonograph; he confessed to an "awful curiosity" to see and hear that "strangest and most weird and uncanny of all inventions." Unhappily the instrument did not arrive.[18]

During May and early June Whittier was working on "The Vision of Echard," and was attending to various business matters, his own and some of his relatives'. It was a period of business depression, and in some parts of Massachusetts real estate was selling for three tenths of its previous value. Then there was the usual Quarterly Meeting, and since Whittier was the only Quaker except the aged Squires living near the meeting house, many duties, as well as entertainment of guests, came his way. There was the usual flood of letters, which he found it impossible to keep up with, especially since there were times when he could not write at all. But as usual he found time and strength to tell other poets that he liked their work. He wrote to Oliver Wendell Holmes that he liked "The School-Boy," which Holmes had written for the hundredth anniversary of the founding of Phillips Andover Academy; he wrote to Richard H. Stoddard praising "History," his recent Phi Beta Kappa poem; and he told J. S. Cutler of Danvers that there was "somewhat of poetic feeling and rhythmical felicity" in his verse. But he also gave this author some kindly criticism and advice. There were many errors in rhyme, a fault which Whittier thought could be easily corrected, and there was a "slight" grammatical error in the words "Thee, oh bells."[19]

He left the country for the ocean in July and went to the Isles of Shoals, where he probably enjoyed himself rather less than on other visits there. The hotel was full, and ninety people who came one morning had to be sent back on the noon steamer to Portsmouth without dinner. Whittier left at the same time, not, presumably, because of lack of food but from a surfeit of music. John Knowles Paine was playing Beethoven sonatas morning, noon, and night, "divinely," according to Celia Thaxter, who was lifted "right up out of the mud and dust of the way"; she had never experienced "such heaven on earth before." But it is unlikely that even John Knowles Paine's playing made Whittier regard piano music as anything other than something to escape from.[20]

He returned to Oak Knoll and to the endless flood of letters. Francis Parkman wanted Whittier's opinion of the character, tastes, disposition, and ability of a man who wished to marry his daughter. A Negro in Sioux Falls, who described himself as good looking and prosperous, offered to pay him if he could arrange correspondence leading to marriage with some "good lady of color," either half white or wholly black, at least five feet six inches, weighing one hundred fifty pounds or more "if not of the corpulent mould." A woman who had incurred a debt of one thousand dollars without her husband's knowledge asked Whittier to pay it for her, since he was a bachelor and had no wife's bills to pay. Another woman wrote that she would like seventy-five dollars but added a postscript that she would accept fifty.[21]

Whittier was at the Bearcamp House in West Ossipee during the first three weeks in September, with the usual young people, including Addie Caldwell, Jettie Morrill, and Horace Currier. A Gloucester ship captain, Seth Stockbridge, father of Adoniram Stockbridge, who had been in the party that climbed Chocorua, had a dory brought from Gloucester to use on the Bearcamp River. He named it "Jettie" and it was ceremoniously launched, with a solo by Mrs. Houston West. A party of young people boarded it, and Captain Stockbridge rowed it down the river to Ossipee Lake. Whittier looked on and then wrote "The Voyage of the Jettie" to amuse Horace Currier, who was slowly dying of tuberculosis.[22] The lines in which he spoke of himself as

> . . . . . Onlooking idly,
> Apart from all so widely

may have been intended to show that he shared his sick friend's forced remoteness from the gayety of the healthy young people. The last two stanzas in the poem would hardly seem likely to cheer an invalid. But whether Horace Currier was resigned to his fate or still believed that he would recover, if he was like most people of his time, he would not object to being told that people are voyagers under sealed orders and that the poet prayed that the Unseen Pilot — an echo of Tennyson's "Crossing the Bar" — would guide them safely into the port of peace. Many of the lines, however, have a light, playful tone that most men of seventy would not find it easy to achieve.

He returned to Amesbury and was there in late October, when a fire destroyed the house and barn second from his and spread to the house next to his. He took down his mother's picture as the only precious thing to be saved.

He was sending his friends copies of his volume of poems, *The Vision of Echard*, the first volume since 1874 to contain poems not previously printed in any collection. Whittier's popularity showed no sign of declining; two thousand two hundred eighty-two copies were sold by May 1 of the next year. Howells reviewed it in the December *Atlantic* with only one unfavorable comment; "The Two Angels" he thought "scarcely too energetic, but its danger is in that direction. Otherwise, this beloved poet's art, like that of Longfellow's, mellows from year to year; and ripening late after a long growth, in which some crude flavors mingled, his poetry now has a richness as uncloying as it is unstinted." Lafcadio Hearn, in the *New Orleans Item*, called it "the finest American book of the year." Oliver Wendell Holmes assured Whittier, "You write from the heart. Who has preached the gospel of love to such a mighty congregation as you have preached it? Who has done so much to sweeten the soul of Calvinistic New England?" Perhaps an even greater proof of Whittier's popularity came a few weeks later. A soap salesman asked him to write some "Poetry of a somewhat humorous style describing the merits of Old Country Soap as a strictly pure and superior article," which would be set to music and sent to his fifteen hundred customers.[23]

The poem that gave the title to *The Vision of Echard* had appeared a few weeks earlier in the September *Atlantic*. In it Whittier tried to express the beliefs of Fifteenth Century Roman Catholic mystics, which he called the "older Protestantism of the mystics before the days of Luther," a "purely spiritual religion independent of creed, ritual, or even the outward letter of the Scripture."[24] It was longer than necessary, and the reader of a later day finds himself hurrying through the forty-seven rather monotonous four-line stanzas. But it may have been stanzas in this poem that Holmes had in mind when he spoke of Whittier as preaching the gospel of love to a mighty congregation.

"At Eventide" was printed in the *Youth's Companion* a few days before the publication of *The Vision of Echard*. It can hardly have interested many of the juvenile readers of the magazine, but their grandparents probably read it and saw their own lives more clearly through Whittier's analysis of his own.

"The Problem" was also an old man's poem, very different from the vigorous reform poems of his young manhood. There was nothing in it that could provoke controversy; the answer to the problems of capital and labor was simply the Golden Rule, the interests of the rich and poor were the same, and there was no solution to be found in the catch-words of the "blind leaders of the blind."

There was still one cause that he could get excited about: preventing Ben Butler from becoming governor of Massachusetts. Butler had won the Democratic nomination after his followers used ladders to enter the convention hall in Worcester through the second story windows and take possession of the hall before his conservative opponents arrived. A few days later he was nominated at a Greenback convention in Boston. Whittier regarded Butler as a strong but evil man, whose policies would have a bad economic effect; he feared that his own income and his cousins' would fall even lower, below four percent, and might be wiped out altogether. He returned to Amesbury in the middle of October to help keep Republicans firm in their opposition to Butler. Whittier's district did even better than he had dared to hope, and he was greatly relieved when Butler was defeated.[25]

He was doing the usual amount of varied reading. In the spring he read Frederick William Farrar's *The Eternal Hope*, a collection of sermons, and agreed with the title of one of them: "Life is Worth Living." He read and recommended William Black's *Macleod of Dare*, Oliver Wendell Holmes' *John Lothrop Motley*, and Frederick Gustavus Burnaby's *On Horseback through Asia Minor*. He was delighted with Howells' *Lady of the Aroostock*. He liked Edwin Arnold's poem, "After Death in Arabia"; he knew of nothing ancient or modern so filled with a robust and satisfying faith as this poem, which looked to the spiritual intimations of immortality.[26]

It has been said that Whittier once met Arnold, who called his attention to certain Persian and Hindu translations. Whether this is true or not, Whittier had evidently been reading some of them. In May he had written an autograph beginning:

> Not vainly in the Persian clime,
> > In King Vitaspe's golden time,
> Did fair-haired girls, flower cinctured, cull
> > The altar's gift from field and wood.

He now wrote the first of three "Oriental Maxims," which he called paraphrases of Sanskrit translations, "The Inward Judge. From Institutes of Manu." In some of the lines he followed closely the wording of the prose translation, John Muir's *Religious and Moral Sentiments Metrically Rendered from Sanskrit Writers, with an Introduction and an Appendix Containing Exact Translations in Prose*.

This poem appeared in the *Independent* January 5, and "The Dead Feast of the Kol-Folk" must have been sent to the *Atlantic* for the January number about the same time. It resembled his "Song of Slaves in the Desert" in being a metrical rendering of a primitive song with a note of pathos, but had no bearing upon any religious or ethical principle. The primitive song was a Ho dirge which he read in the *Journal of the Asiatic Society, Bengal*. When the poem was printed in the *Atlantic*, it did not have the present introductory note quoting a passage from Edward Burnett Tyler's *Primitive Culture*, published in London in 1873, which Whittier read in 1874. This passage has no direct bearing on the poem, which would be clearer to the reader if the explanation in the *Journal of the Asiatic Society* were given.

"That same evening the ceremony is gone through of calling the spirit of the departed. All the company, except four people, the father, mother, and two women, or brother and sister and two women or men, sit outside in the back yard; some boiled rice and a pot of water is then placed within the inner room of the house, and ashes sprinkled from thence to the threshold; the father and mother, or brother and sister, as it may be, then go out, taking two ploughshares in their hands — the other two people are left in the house to watch. Those who have gone out proceed to the spot where the body was burned, and where (in some parts of the country) a clay horse and rider and an earthen pot on a tripod, with the mouth closed, are placed; round this spot the two relations walk, beating together the ploughshares, and calling out in a plaintive wild strain" (Here follows the dirge with an interlinear translation).[27]

Whittier's poem had details from both the chant and the introductory explanation and also descriptive details in a literary tone not in keeping with the native simplicity of the original; for example,

> Come from the shadow-lands
> From the dim meadow-lands
> Where the pale grasses bend
> Low to our sighing.

The numerous successive lines beginning with "Come" may have been suggested by Whittier's memory of lines in Scott's "Gathering Song of Donald the Black."

Whittier hailed Bayard Taylor's "Prince Deukalion" as a noble poem which placed the author in the first rank of the poets of his time. He wrote to Taylor that it resembled, in solemnity and power, the great dramas of the immortal Greeks. The letter reached Taylor shortly before his death and was the only praise of his poem that he received after its publication. Taylor died December 19, and there was a memorial meeting in Tremont Temple, Boston, January 10. Whittier was unable to go — he had not been in Boston for six months — and sent a letter to be read. What impressed Whittier the most was that Taylor had built up his reputation slowly by industry and patience under many disadvantages; "what he was he owed wholly to himself."[28] A similar point was made in "Bayard Taylor" in the March *Atlantic*:

> His task, beguiled with songs that shall endure,
> In manly, honest thoroughness he wrought;
> From humble home-lays to the heights of thought
> Slowly he climbed, but every step was sure.

As printed in the *Atlantic* the poem consisted of only the second and third sonnets, and began:

> For us he wandered through strange lands and old;
> We saw the world with him.

The concluding lines of each sonnet were typical of the time: tears were shed for the dead, who were pictured as living in a Heaven that would bring rapture to the senses.

XXX
1879 - 80

A snow storm kept Whittier from the inauguration of the Republican governor whom he had helped to elect, and except for two visits to Boston, each for two days, the weather kept him from leaving Oak Knoll during January and February. One of the visits was to his brother, who was still suffering from inflammatory rheumatism. He himself was too unwell to stay in Boston as long as he had hoped, and he called on no one but his brother and James T. Fields.[1]

While his poor health restricted his activities, it did not make him think about himself to the exclusion of everything else. He watched the progress of the freed slaves and found encouragement in the fact that they were buying land and their power was being felt and respected as their votes were sought by rival politicians.[2] He was interested in appointment of a new principal of Friends Yearly Meeting School in Providence and hoped that it would be a capable business man. Augustine Jones was appointed, and one of his first projects was to try to have a portrait of Whittier painted for the school by William Morris Hunt,[3] but a few months later Hunt committed suicide, and it was five years before the school acquired a Whittier portrait. He was keeping in touch with his friends and relatives. He heard once more from Elizabeth Lloyd Howell, who sent him a poem that she wanted him to send to the *Atlantic*; he sent it with some hesitation, and it did not appear in the *Atlantic*.[4]

Whittier's interest in the East and his concern for temperance were combined in a poem for the *Youth's Companion* of February 20. "The Khan's Devil" was doubtless highly approved by adults who believed that children should be warned of the dangers of drink — and the adults who read and subscribed to the *Youth's Companion* would be likely to feel that way.

A movement had been started to preserve the Old South Church on Washington Street in Boston, the congregation having moved to the so-called new Old South Church in Copley Square. Whittier's contribution was "The Landmarks," read at a public meeting and printed in the March *Atlantic*. An account of the heroic act of the young man who saved St. Michael's Church in Marblehead by swinging out from the tower on the bell rope and cutting away burning timbers had been sent to Whittier by Antoinette C. Devereaux with the wish that he "bless the hallowed pile and the hands that saved it."[5] He did this, and then asked, since life had been risked for St. Michael's, should not wealth be staked for the Old South?

Whittier was in Amesbury as usual in early March, Town Meeting time. One day as he was walking home from the Post Office, he stopped at the Congregational parsonage to talk with Rev. Pliny Boyd, who asked him to write something that could be printed in a four-page sheet, largely advertising, to be issued in connection with an entertainment and fair of the Ladies' Social Circle of his church. Whittier said that it was difficult to force the muse, but he had a partly written poem of local interest which he could finish in a short time.[6] "Abram Morrison" was in *The Social Banner*, which was dated March 6, and described the Amesbury eccentric whose remarks in Friends Meeting had amused Whittier in his boyhood. As printed in *The Social Banner* it had fourteen stanzas in place of the present twenty-five. It did not have the amusing stanza quoting Morrison in Friends Meeting after the visit of President Monroe to Amesbury in 1817 and the coming of a travelling menagerie. Another stanza not in *The Social Banner* was Whittier's thoughtful appraisal — and a lesson:

We have learned in later days
Truth may speak in simplest phrase;
That the man is not the less
For quaint ways and home-spun dress,
    Thanks to Abram Morrison!

Whittier returned to Oak Knoll in an unhappy state of mind about his health. His strength had been worn down by the long hard winter, and he complained of a new complication of old and new troubles and pains. His doctor said that a man of active brain ought to make a fool of himself occasionally, but life seemed to Whittier too serious for such treatment, and he had to make it a duty to ignore duty and to play with the dogs and talk nonsense. But the rhodora was blooming at Oak Knoll, and he was able to read, with a good deal of satisfaction, a volume of Phillips Brooks' sermons, not always in full agreement with him but liking his spirit and earnest convictions. Lyman Abbott called, and they talked on a topic that Abbott had asked him to write about the previous summer, the "Inner Light."[7] One of the two sonnets that Whittier wrote later in the year for Abbott's *Christian Union*, "The Word," was on the same theme: the voice of the Holy Spirit, the word of God within, gave early myths healthy meanings suited to human need. The other sonnet, "The Book," described the Bible as a gallery of sacred pictures and then, in a metaphor hardly to be expected from a man who worshipped in a plain Quaker meeting house, as

A minster rich in holy effigies,
And bearing on entablature and frieze
The hieroglyphic oracles of old —

oracles which could be understood only when a light came on them from above.

William Lloyd Garrison died May 24, and on the 27th Whittier sent his poem "Garrison" for use at the funeral if the arrangements permitted it, adding that he knew nothing of music and the verses might not be adapted to singing. The lines were singable as far as form was concerned, but their use by a congregation or choir would have been rather awkward, as they were an apostrophe to Garrison. They were read by Rev. Samuel Johnson at the funeral in the church of the First Religious Society in Roxbury. Whittier was present, in spite of his growing dread of trips to Boston, and was greatly impressed by the speaking of Wendell Phillips and Theodore Weld.[8] He sent "Garrison" to the *Independent* May 30, with a letter saying that the poem might be superfluous "after the surpassingly beautiful tribute of Wendell Phillips and the perhaps still more touchingly eloquent words of Theodore P. Weld." Still, something was due, he thought, to the intimate friendship of more than fifty years, "unbroken and undisturbed by any differences of opinion and action during the long anti-slavery struggle."

He said the same thing a few months later in his introduction to Oliver Johnson's *William Lloyd Garrison and His Times.*[9] "Our personal relations were undisturbed," he wrote, after mentioning his differing with Garrison on the question of voting. There had of course been several occasions when their relations were, by any ordinary definition of the word, at least briefly disturbed. But he may have forgotten them, and if he recalled them, he doubtless regarded them as not worth consideration. Instead of thinking of disagreements he preferred to recall the happiness of working with the "noble company of whom Garrison was the central figure" and his memories of Garrison as a young man.

There was the usual Friends Quarterly Meeting in May, and in June Whittier was at a Yearly Meeting in Portland, where he went to visit the Pickards; he had not seen his niece for two years. He returned to Amesbury and visited his birthplace in East Haverhill, which he was pleased to find had been bought by one of his old neighbors, now a retired shoe manufacturer. He walked around the farm and sat by the brook, wondering if he really was the same person who sixty years before had set water wheels in the brook and hunted eggs in the barn.[10]

He was at Oak Knoll three weeks in August and then at West Ossipee through the first part of September. It was not a happy holiday. Horace Currier evidently had not long to live, and Whittier was conscious that he himself had reached an age when the shadow of eternity was over all the pictures of the world. But his thoughts were still on the future. A letter in answer to an invitation to the twenty-fifth anniversary of the settlement of Kansas said that a state with such a record of peril, adventure, fortitude, self-sacrifice, and devotion to freedom would do all that it could to aid victims of prejudice and oppression, and a letter in answer to the twenty-fifth anniversary of the Republican Party said that the Party must be maintained "until the purity of the ballot-box everywhere is safe from violence and intimidation and the civil rights of every class of our citizens made secure beyond the possibility of suppression or infringement."[11]

On the return trip from West Ossipee a woman entered the car whom he knew at once; she always opened the windows. She did as usual, and as a result his cold got worse, and he suffered pains in his head, back, and legs. He was still suffering from them when Paul Hamilton Hayne and his wife arrived at Oak Knoll for a five-day visit, but he soon felt better and was able to enjoy his guests. He liked the company of women as much as ever, and he and Mrs. Hayne sat in his study near the Franklin stove and talked about the old and the new South, slavery and emancipation, Henry Ward Beecher, and Harriet Beecher Stowe. Mrs. Hayne was outspoken, and her husband believed that Whittier was eager to learn the truth about the South and had modified some of his early opinions. Hayne used this visit as the basis of his description of Whittier beneath his own tranquil roof in "The Snow-Messengers," a poem dedicated to Whittier and Longfellow. After he had sent the poem for publication in the March *Harper's*, Hayne was afraid that the stanzas describing Longfellow might imply that he regarded Longfellow more highly than Whittier and assured him, with underlining and double underlining, "No impression, however, could be more false, and only a rather luckless turn of expression of imagery, which I found it utterly impossible to change, without re-composing the whole poem, or at least the latter portion of it — can be viewed as responsible for the implication noticed, to which by the way my wife (among the most loyal of your friends) first drew my attention."

After the poem had appeared, Whittier sent reassurances. He was grateful for the kind allusions to himself and his surroundings, and Hayne must not dream that he could be jealous of any good words for Longfellow. That would be "too much like Dick when the cat gets noticed" — a reference to a stanza in "The Snow Messengers" describing Whittier with a cat on his shoulder.

> While terrier Dick, denied all words to rail,
> Snarls, as he shakes a short, protesting tail.[12]

Whittier was in Amesbury during the month before election helping in the local Republican campaign. His nephew Lewis Caldwell spent a week with him and bored him most of the time. Caldwell thought that he could write poetry and gave his uncle copies of some of his verses, which his uncle sent to Abby Woodman with the comment, "Was there ever such a mess!"[13] The comment is understandable if the verses were those that had been printed in the *Villager* — or resembled them. One was "The Old Willow" —

> The willow stood near cot and barn
> And gave to each a rural charm;

While in the glow of summer heat,
It cast its shade along the street.

In October there were two reminders of Abolition days. The mayor of Boston asked Whittier to write a poem for the unveiling of a statue in Park Square, a duplicate of the Freedman's Memorial statue in Lincoln Square, Washington, showing a near-naked muscular Negro kneeling before a frock-coated Lincoln. Whittier's poem, "The Emancipation Group", was read by a Negro boy, a graduate of Boston Latin School, at exercises in Faneuil Hall December 6, along with a prayer by Phillips Brooks and an oration by Mayor Frederick O. Prince. He returned the check of one hundred dollars and asked that it be sent to the treasurer of a fair for the Old South Church.[14]

On the last day of October the Fisk Jubilee Singers, who had returned from a money-raising tour in Europe, came to Amesbury to give a concert. They called on Whittier, who met them at the door and led them through the parlor and dining room to the Garden Room, being careful that Mrs. Cate should at no time be left alone in the room with any of them. They told of the good treatment they had received in Europe, and after their return to the United States, being forced to leave a hotel at midnight because they were black. They sang spirituals and left an autograph album to be called for the next morning. In it Whittier wrote the first, second, fourth, and sixth stanzas of "The Jubilee Singers," of which the last lines looked forward to the future —

Till Freedom's every right is won,
And Slavery's every wrong undone![15]

Whittier was at Oak Knoll November 11, a perfect Indian summer day, following a day of wind and snow. His poem, "St. Martin's Summer," showed that he could still see outdoor scenes as an artist would see them and put them in clear pictures drawn with a few quick lines:

. . . . . rose-red dawn
And thin moon curving o'er it.

. . . . . the birchen shadows,
Braiding in long, wind-wavered lines
The westward sloping meadow.

Oliver Wendell Holmes' birthday was August 29, an awkward time for a festival in Boston, and so Houghton, Osgood and Company had his birthday breakfast on December 3. Whittier was seated at the head table next to Mrs. Houghton, who was next to Holmes, but stayed only a short time and left before the speaking began — as was perhaps good judgment; the party did not break up until dinner time, long after the guests from the country had left to catch their trains. Whittier delegated James T. Fields to read "Our Autocrat" from a manuscript which he had sent when he thought that he would not be present. Whittier had worked hard on this poem. The manuscript had one sheet of paper pasted over another, with several stanzas rewritten and one with an awkward metaphor omitted. He had tried to strike the right note but had made too obvious an effort to show Holmes' deeper qualities as poet and man.

As a result of Whittier's early departure from the breakfast, he missed meeting Edmund Clarence Stedman, who had come partly for the purpose of meeting him and who now wrote to Whittier that he had loved and honored him from boyhood and that Whittier's poetry had given him hope and purpose when he "dreamed of yet doing some good work in life, or meditated upon the use and nobleness of the poet's art in the movement of this workaday world." He sent Whittier the first copy of his *Lyrics and Idylls*; the dedicatory poem was "Ad Vatem," which had been one of the verse tributes in the *Literary World* at the time of Whittier's seventieth birthday. Whittier replied with enthusiastic praise of the poems. He admired the elegiac poems and the war pieces but was charmed with the idylls. He thought "The Discoverer" had the stamp of immortality upon it and was one of the "most striking and powerfully suggestive poems" of the time.[16] Most readers of a later day would not have such a high opinion of "The Discoverer," which was about a three-year-old child who had died and was discovering how spirits fare and what angels look like and would not return to tell about them in spite of his relatives' wish:

Hush, does not the baby this way bring,
To lay beside the severed curl
Some starry offering
Of chrysolite or pearl?

Whittier's seventy-second birthday passed quietly. Holmes showed no resentment at Whittier's escape from his breakfast and sent a birthday note, to which Whittier replied that the four American poets surviving from an earlier day seemed to be garlanded as if for sacrifice, the world waiting to see which one would die first.[17]

The winter months were unhappy ones. Whittier's brother was still suffering intensely from what was called lung trouble and inflammatory rheumatism. Whittier had hoped that his brother would outlive him but was now very doubtful, and his affection for his brother was intensified. He was "one of the best fellows living" but his life had been "full of trial and suffering, an affectionate brother, unselfish and generous to a fault."

He was saddened by his inability to relieve the increasing amount of human suffering, even though he was giving more than could reasonably have been expected of him. Royalties from *Child Life, Child Life in Prose, Songs of Three Centuries*, and *The Vision of Echard* totalled only $436.60 in six months.[18] He explained to one woman, whose account of her troubles he had read with sympathy, that he had to care for those persons who had been providentially placed in his way and that he could not be of much service to her, but still he enclosed twenty dollars. He started a collection for Donald Grant Mitchell with an offer of two hundred fifty dollars when he heard that Mitchell was sick and his farm mortgaged for more than its sale value, but the project was dropped when Mitchell's brother reported that money was not desperately needed and a collection would be inadvisable.[19]

"My Trust," in the *Youth's Companion* for January 8, began with a memory of his childhood and his mother's gentle restraint of his selfish moods, and led from there to resignation to God's will and to trust that loss and lapse lead through pain to higher levels. But he was not satisfied with his adult life, as "My Trust" might be taken to imply. As he looked back he thought that he had longed for goodness but had found it hard to bring his imaginative and poetic temperament into subjection.[20] This dissatisfaction appeared in "A Name," a poem addressed to his three-year-old grandnephew, Greenleaf Whittier Pickard. It expressed the hope that his namesake would find the high ideals that had escaped him, would stand firm where he had been swayed by flights of fancy, and would see clearly where he had groped.

Thirty years after the writing of "Ichabod" and twenty-eight years after Daniel Webster's death, "The Lost Occasion" appeared in the April *Atlantic*. It had been suggested by a phrase used by Robert C. Winthrop. According to Phoebe Woodman Grantham, Webster's widow had begged Whittier to write a retraction of "Ichabod." But Whittier regarded "The Lost Occasion" as a complement to "Ichabod" rather than as a retraction; the two poems, he said, should be read together.[21]

Spring was late that year, and Whittier was glad to receive some flowers that Charlotte Forten Grimke sent him from Washington and which he acknowledged with twelve lines beginning:

> Long have I waited for the Spring's
> Slow opening buds and tardy bloom.

Then he found — or at least wrote a poem saying that he had found — trailing arbutus. Whether "The Trailing Arbutus" referred to April, 1880, or to his memory of another spring, it was evidently based on personal experience. The descriptive details were clear and accurate and could have been written only if he had found the flowers, tinted like a shell, in dry leaves and mosses under dead boughs, while the pines that sheltered them from the cold east wind moaned overhead. The application in the third stanza probably pleased Whittier's contemporaries more than later readers: the flowers in the leaves and moss suggested lowly people who in their restricted lives are able

> To lend a sweetness to the ungenial day
> And make the sad earth happier for their bloom.

The trailing arbutus had been better protected from the wind than the lawn at Oak Knoll, which had not been raked up at the end of the first week in May. Whittier's cousin Abby was in San Francisco, and Whittier reported to her on the happenings at Oak Knoll with the concern of a man brought up on a farm. The work somehow was never quite done, but potatoes and early corn and peas were planted, the garden was in good order, and the household was enjoying asparagus. In the way of most gentleman farmers, they were "practicing a rigid economy on the principle of saving at the tap and letting out at the bung."[22]

He was having less trouble with his eyes than in the winter and was reading Howells' *The Undiscovered Country*, which was appearing serially in the *Atlantic*. His interest increased as the story progressed. He thought that the characterization was admirable and that the story belonged to what he called "our Questioning Period" — a period of great interest in spiritualism: "The unquiet heart of today beats through it." By late June he was ready to say that the story was all that he could wish.[23]

He was worried about his niece Lizzie, whose husband wrote that she was no better. Whittier did not feel well enough to go to Portland and asked Mrs. Gustavus Cammett if she would go for a few days — and he scrupulously added that he would pay her expenses. Lizzie's illness was what was then called nervous prostration, and her uncle thought that she might be helped by spending some time at his home in Amesbury; she needed change, absolute rest, freedom from responsibilities, and to be among her old friends: "Of course the *boy* would stay at Portland."[24] Whittier may have suspected that his namesake was the chief cause of the nervous prostration. Greenleaf was doubtless already showing some of the energy, vigor, and unruliness that made his great-uncle once remark, "That boy isn't worth raising."

Whittier's suggestion was not followed, and he was well enough a few days later to go to Portland himself. He returned to Oak Knoll early in July, looking well and feeling a lively interest in the coming Presidential campaign. It was sure to be a bitter one, with effective use by the Democrats of James A. Garfield's involvement in the Credit Mobilier scandal. When he found that he could not be at a meeting in Amesbury to form a Republican Club, he wrote a letter to be read, describing Garfield as a man of "pure character, wise statesmanship, and lifelong fidelity to the principles of the Republican party, the Union of the States, and the security of the rights of person, property, and franchise." But his emphasis was on the party rather than the candidate; and while he intended no disparagement of the Democratic candidate, General Hitchcock, and knew that many of his supporters were sincere and patriotic, it seemed to him that the Democratic Party had not changed since the Civil War, and it would not be safe to entrust the financial interests of the country and the welfare of blacks to a party which compromised with the "Greenback heresy" and used fraud and violence to suppress the Negro vote in the South.[25]

He was at the Bearcamp House in West Ossipee two weeks in September — for the last time. The weather was perfect, and he thought the mountains had never been more lovely in their sunsets and sunrises. The hotel was burned to the ground shortly after he left. He had written "The King's Missive" and sent it to James R. Osgood, who had commissioned it for inclusion in *Memorial History of Boston*. From the list of events that Osgood sent him to choose from, Whittier selected the letter of Charles II which was sent to John Endicott by the Quaker Samuel Shattuck in 1661 and resulted in the release of Quakers in the Boston jail.[26]

"The King's Missive" was a lively narrative, told, as Whittier wrote in a later headnote, "with pardonable poetic license." The arrival of Shattuck just as Governor Endicott had exclaimed that he would hew the Quakers in pieces before the Lord, and Endicott's order to restore Shattuck's hat when he saw the King's seal, had an effective touch of drama and were of course fiction. The departure of the freed Quakers was well told, with good description of the autumn countryside, which could have been written only by one who was still close to rural New England.

A few months after the publication of the *Memorial History of Boston*, "The King's Missive" was criticized by George E. Ellis in a paper read before the Massachusetts Historical Society. Whittier took this more seriously than criticisms of other poems for deviations from historical fact and wrote a long defense of his poem and of the conduct of early Quakers, evidently based on considerable reading. The persecution of Quakers, Whittier believed, came from the fixed intention of the clergy and the leading men of Massachusetts Bay Colony to allow no differences of opinion on religion and not, as Dr. Ellis had said, from the intrusion, indecency, and effrontery of the persecuted. He conceded that the Quakers were obstinate, but their obstinacy and endurance served to protect other religious dissidents in England. The only excuse for the conduct of the Puritan authorities was, as he had said earlier, the spirit of the age in which they lived. Whittier believed that he had honestly tried to be fair to both Puritans and Quakers, and had gone to extremes in "Margaret Smith's Journal" to find excuses for John Norton.

This letter was sent to the *Boston Daily Advertiser* March 22 but was not printed until March 29, to allow Dr. Ellis time to write a reply to be printed the next day. Whittier was quite willing that Dr. Ellis should reply and was confident that Dr. Ellis could not refute his statements. Dr. Ellis' letter was printed, as planned, the next day, and Whittier immediately wrote a reply which was printed the day after that.[27] In this he reasoned that if there had been no prisoners in the jail when the letter came from Charles II, Endicott would have said so instead of consulting his deputy and assuring Shattuck that the King's order would be obeyed. The strong language of Seventeenth Century Friends was no worse than that of the magistrates and ministers who persecuted them: "It was a coarse, hard age, in which nobody was mealy-mouthed. The Puritan himself was scarcely the modern ideal of a saint.'' But, Whittier said in his concluding paragraph, he took no pleasure in dwelling on the story of Quaker persecution, and he was a warm admirer of all that was true and noble in the character of the Puritans. This, although he had probably forgotten it, was what he had said nearly fifty years earlier in an article entitled "New England" in the *New England Weekly Review*.

The October 1880 *Atlantic* had "The Minister's Daughter," which may have been the poem that Whittier sent to Howells in May with considerable doubt about its being suitable for the *Atlantic*. He might have gone farther and doubted that it was worth publishing anywhere except for the help that it might give to people who needed a simple, childlike story to relieve the strain of their break with Calvinism. It was written after a revival preacher had held meetings on the green at the corner of Friend and School Streets in Amesbury, near Whittier's home. From the porch of her house across the street, Sophronia Moody saw the penitents in their baptismal robes walking to the Powow River for immersion. The preaching was about the awful severity of the punishment for sin, and she and Whittier agreed that a theology based on fear had baleful effects. She suggested that he write something to help people understand that God is a God of love.[28]

The news of Lydia Maria Child's death October 20 came to him like a sudden and heavy blow. He went to the funeral, where the pall bearers were elderly farmers, and the funeral procession walked over the red and gold of fallen leaves. Just after the casket was placed in the ground, a rainbow appeared in the western sky. In Whittier's last conversation with her they had talked of the future life, and it now seemed to him that she was herself an evidence of immortality, since God's moral and spiritual economy would not suffer such light and love to be annihilated. The same thought appeared again in two stanzas in his poem about Mrs. Child, "Within the Gate," in the January *Atlantic*.[29]

But there were lighter moments. Daniel Neall and James Wright came to see him, and their talk about old friends of the Anti-Slavery days was pleasant reminiscence. Dom Pedro sent him some Portuguese translations that he had made of Whittier's poems. Charles H. Davis made a crayon portrait of him, which he gave to Amesbury High School. Davis was the son of Whittier's neighbor James H. Davis. When he was a boy he showed artistic skill, and Whittier would get down on his knees to look at the boy's drawings spread out on the floor. He was about to study in Paris, with his expenses paid, at Whittier's suggestion, by an Amesbury carriage manufacturer. When some of his work was exhibited in Paris the next summer, Whittier thought that he had already fulfilled his friends' promise in his behalf. He later achieved considerable success as a landscape painter; Whittier called him the best landscape painter in America.[30]

He did not look forward to the election with any enthusiasm; he longed for peace and kindly feeling. But he dutifully went to Amesbury to do what he could, especially to help the Republican candidate for Congress, Eben F. Stone, in whose behalf he wrote a letter to the *Boston Morning Journal*. On the national scene things looked favorable, but the Republicans were not yet out of the woods, and the "hoodlums of New York City" might, after all, "elect the President of the great Republic." Whittier was one of the vice-presidents of the local Republican Club, and his house was decorated and illuminated for a torchlight procession October 19. On another night there was a political demonstration, the greatest ever seen in Amesbury, according to the *Villager*. Houses and stores were decorated. A procession was reviewed at Whittier's house by Whittier and Eben F. Stone. James Squires stood on School Street with an immense pitch-pine torch. An "old lady of seventy years" stood at her door swinging a broom saturated with blazing kerosene. The gun club fired a salute of two hundred guns. Whittier privately called the affair "a silly parade and row," and the excitement kept him awake. He was glad when the election was over. Garfield, he thought, was a "cool, wise, honest man," and would know how to keep his popularity.[31]

Whittier returned to Oak Knoll and spent Thanksgiving there, thinking of the Thanksgivings at Amesbury with his mother and sister. On the day before his birthday he had a bad cold and described himself as unable to write or think — and then wrote a long, thoughtful letter to Augustine Jones, who had asked his advice on the question of permitting music instruction at the school. Whittier wrote that he had no scruples against music, although it might be misused, as in "sensuous compositions and songs and military matters." But he did not approve of it as a form of worship and was afraid that if it were taught to Quaker children in the school, they would return to their home meetings and sing "Hold the fort for I am coming" in the "Howling Dervish" style of conducting a meeting. Although he did not mention it in this letter, some members of Amesbury Friends Meeting wished to introduce singing there, and as he once said, turn the meeting into a Methodist camp meeting. His suggestion, which was followed, was that non-Quaker pupils, and even Quaker pupils if their parents wished it, should be allowed to have musical instruction by a teacher from the city, an "outside barbarian," who would come to the school and be paid by the pupils, thus avoiding the use of funds given by donors who would not wish their money spent for the teaching of music.[32]

His birthday passed quietly at Oak Knoll. A young people's group at the Universalist Church in Danvers invited him to attend a celebration of his birthday, and he declined in a pleasant letter; however numerous the occasions, he never wrote a merely perfunctory letter. His cold, he said, kept him from going out, but even if he could go out he would prefer to take part in the celebration of someone else's birthday rather than his own, which would require "something of the self-consideration of the old Spanish grandee who, when he heard his name spoken, always took off his hat and bowed to himself." But he was glad to know that his birthday was remembered in that beautiful section of his native country, and he repeated what he evidently wanted everybody to know, that he had reached an age when he regarded literary reputation as of small consequence compared with the consciousness that he had "honestly endeavored to subserve the best interests of humanity and to speak needed words for freedom and justice, Christian character, and faith in the Divine goodness."[33]

XXXI
1881 - 82

Whittier was in Amesbury in early January. The clear, cold weather, with sleighbells ringing and Mount Washington visible from the hills, instead of suggesting a winter poem, made him think of the great number of Negroes crowding into Kansas, barefooted and ragged and with no way of getting shelter and food. His thoughts then turned to the whole problem of sin and want and pain; was it all necessary? He found it a terrible and oppressive mystery, from which he could escape only by his faith in God's goodness and its ultimate triumph.[1]

He was at Oak Knoll most of the winter, confined to the house with a lame knee and having to use a cane. He was not sleeping well, and the nights were long and tedious. He found escape in thought by reading two travel books by Isabella Bird, *Life in the Rocky Mountains* and *Unbeaten Tracks in Japan*, but he could not read for long periods and not at all in the evening. When he could not read, he thought of the past and of friends who had died, and was often lonely. He was not well enough to go to Boston to see his brother, and most of the visitors who came to see him were strangers.[2]

There was a resulting note of pathos in the introductory poem of *The King's Missive*, published in February. He asked the few of his old readers that were left upon the border line to give him, in response to his slower, feebler measures, the sympathy of love which meant more to him than praise.

This volume was the first with previously uncollected poems since *The Vision of Echard* in 1878. It had three sonnets, pieces of religious instruction, not previously printed: "Requirement," "Help," and "Utterance." There were two "Oriental Maxims," both evidently derived, like "The Inward Judge," from John Muir's *Religious and Moral Sentiments Metrically Rendered from Sanskrit Writers, with an Appendix Containing Exact Translations in Prose*.[3] "Laying up Treasure" was from the *Mahabharata* and was much shorter than its source, omitting entirely the horrors of death which made up two thirds of the original. "Conduct" was the same length as its source but more specific in its command:

. . . . . Evermore restrain
Evil and cherish good.

Comments by Edwin P. Whipple and Oliver Wendell Holmes on this volume expressed the feelings of Whittier's readers and showed what Whittier's contemporaries were looking for in poetry. Whittier's hold on the public mind, said Whipple, was primarily moral, but his ethics were touched with or by emotion, sometimes wrath and sometimes tenderness and compassion, but always tending to move to tears. And his poetry was always pure: "In reading this last volume, I feel as if my soul had taken a bath in holy water." Holmes wrote that after reading Whittier's poems, he always felt the refreshment of their free and sweet atmosphere — "always the morning air of a soul that breathes freely, and always the fragrance of a loving spirit."

Whittier himself was less sentimental about his verse. He was not yet ready to write explanatory headnotes for his poems, as he did seven years later for the Riverside Edition. He was afraid that it would seem to be attaching too much importance to his writings, when he saw and felt their deficiencies so clearly that he sometimes turned from them in utter weariness.[4]

By April 2 he had written "Rabbi Ishmael" and sent it to the *Atlantic*. He thought that he might be the only one that would like it, but he was not concerned: he had written it to get it off his mind. The theme was from a passage in the Talmud, and he told the story with brevity and directness under the influence of strong emotion. Rabbi Ishmael, asking the blessing of God's mercy for mankind, saw God's face in smiling assent and told the throng waiting outside the temple that God was a God of love rather than of justice: a conclusion that would be pleasing to readers who were not wholly free from the fears of Calvinism.

The news of James T. Fields' death on April 24 came as a shock. It was only a few weeks since he had been assured by Mrs. Fields that Fields had wholly recovered from a recent illness. Whittier and Fields had been friends for forty years, and Whittier could not recall that any shadow had ever rested on the sunshine of their friendship. His faith in immortality assured him that this friendship was not ended, and this was the concluding thought in his poem about Fields, "In Memory," in the July *Atlantic*.[5]

He returned to Amesbury in May, still suffering from the shock of Fields' death and the strange feeling that came from having outlived so many of his friends. He was kept in the house by bad weather, and various irritations bothered him more than they would have if he had felt well. There were fences to be repaired and painting to be done, and he came to the conclusion that an old house was a constant nuisance.[6] He was vexed by a report that he had used his influence to get George P. Loring appointed to the Agricultural Bureau. Actually he had influenced the appointment without knowing it. He had written to Loring, who he erroneously thought had already been appointed, congratulating him and recommending Charles H. Brainard for a clerkship. This letter was shown to the President and was the deciding factor in Loring's appointment. Brainard, as would be expected, got the clerkship.[7]

He was at Oak Knoll late in June and went directly from there to Intervale, New Hampshire, staying a month at the Intervale House with the Cartlands and George W. Morrill and his family, and then visiting the Pickards briefly at their summer home at Fryeburg, Maine. Here he heard the news of the improved condition and probable recovery of President Garfield, who had been shot by a disappointed office-seeker July 2. Then a few hot days sent him back to Oak Knoll, "overcome," he said, "by the extreme heat." But he was well enough one day in August to go to Lynn and have dinner at Charles F. Coffin's. The sorrows and troubles of this unhappy year had not destroyed his sense of humor, and another guest, Augustine Jones, remembered twenty-five years later two hours of lively conversation which showed him the humorous side of Whittier's character as he had never seen it before.[8] He kept no notes of the conversation, but Samuel T. Pickard, who was at Oak Knoll for a short time in the winter when Whittier was worried and unhappy, recorded some of his amusing stories about Quakers and what they did when they felt like swearing. A Quaker sea captain called to his cabin boy, "Here, come on deck and use some of thy language." A Quaker was hauling apples when the tailboard of the wagon gave way and the apples rolled down the hill. He called a boy and said, "Boy, does thee swear sometimes? Here is a quarter. Talk to this matter."[9]

Early in August he was asked to write a hymn to be sung at a banquet in Boston given by the Massachusetts Horticultural Society to the American Pomological Society. He was now refusing numerous requests for occasional poems, but he did not refuse this one, and the "Hymn," renamed "Garden" for the Riverside Edition, was written promptly.[10] Whittier had evidently been reading of attempts to locate the Garden of Eden, and, with a light touch that probably displeased religious conservatives who still accepted the Book of Genesis as historical fact, suggested that instead of searching for the Garden it would be better to work, with God's blessing, to bring beauty to every part of the earth. The first stanza was taken from the fourth stanza of "A Song of Harvest," with the second and fourth lines shortened to six syllables. The public was still interested in everything that Whittier wrote, and four stanzas were quoted by John D. Long, Governor of Massachusetts, in his Thanksgiving Proclamation.

The early reports of President Garfield's condition had been over-optimistic, and Whittier was depressed by the news in late August of the President's sufferings; it was now evident that he had no chance of recovery. When Garfield died September 19, Whittier's feeling of depression gave way to the belief that Garfield's death was uniting the nation. The mourning for Garfield in all parts of the country by people of all political beliefs proved, it seemed to him, that the heart of the nation was sound and loyal, and he felt a new hope for the nation and had a firmer faith in its stability. On the day of the funeral he thought that the world seemed gathered round Garfield's grave: "History records nothing like it. The moral influence of his life and death must long be felt for good."[11]

Early in October he was pleased to hear from the president of Swarthmore College that the main building, which had been destroyed by fire, was to be rebuilt. He asked if he could help in replacing the library and thought that there were people in Boston who would also help. At his suggestion Oliver Wendell Holmes sent copies of his own books, some of which are still in the college library.[12]

He was now spending more time in Amesbury and was again selecting books for the Public Library. But in Amesbury as well as at Oak Knoll, "pilgrims" found him.[13] Many of them were bores, but not all. He enjoyed two women visitors from England, Caroline and Hannah Cadbury, who arrived on a rainy morning in November. After the usual talk about the weather and an early frost the conversation turned to books. He told them that Arthur Penrhyn Stanley, Dean of Westminster, was read a good deal in America; Dean Stanley, he said, held the Quaker doctrine — at least it used to be the old Quaker doctrine — that a measure of light was given to every man. He was also in sympathy with the views of Christian Karl Josias Bunsen and his wife, of Thomas Hughes, and of Matthew Arnold.[14] Whittier must have enjoyed his visitors; otherwise he would hardly have given them a note of introduction to Longfellow, who may not have been pleased to see them. He wrote in his diary October 28 that Whittier had written that he dreaded the coming winter. Longfellow did not; the thought of winter brought a sense of rest and seclusion.[15]

Two poems sent to magazines in the fall had the obvious intention of teaching lessons. "The Rock-Tomb of Bradore" concluded with a little sermon: love makes its own atmosphere, and its flowers bloom through Polar snows. The poem had a lamentable number of clichés and genteel phrases: a French-Eskimo girl was

A twenty summer's maid
Whose blood had equal share
Of the lands of vine and snow.

But the scenery was well described; Whittier could still picture places that he had never seen. He sent "Granted Wishes" to the *Youth's Companion*, calling it "a bit of rhyme which I hope may find a place in your admirable paper."[16] It had six stanzas which were extended to thirteen two years later for *The Bay of Seven Islands*, renamed "The Wishing Bridge," and localized in Marblehead. The added stanzas rounded out the story and justified the concluding lesson:

God gives the wishes of our youth
But in His own best way.

He had a quiet birthday at Oak Knoll. The day passed not unhappily, but he had reached an age where a birthday is a serious matter, a solemn reminder of the inevitable end, and he loved the world and familiar scenes and faces too well to be ready to leave them.

He was still thinking about the nearness of death when he wrote a birthday letter to Longfellow. They, along with Emerson and Holmes, were approaching the "inevitable end of Earth." A direct personal expression of this thought was "At Last," which he thought said what all must feel who were, like himself, near the border line. He later saw that it was not only old people who found their own belief in this poem. "I suppose," he once wrote, "the prayer is one which we all feel, if we do not utter. In this day of spiritual unrest and questioning (a condition of things which after all seems to me hopeful and full of promise of a newer if a shorter confession of faith) I think we must all fall back on the mercy and goodness of the Eternal Father."[17] Stanzas from "At Last" have been among the most popular of the hymns made from Whittier's poems. The Heaven to which he looked forward was close to popular belief, which had rejected the pearly gates and streets paved with gold; these had become too difficult to accept and, as more people lived in cities, less attractive. But green pastures, peaceful rivers, and holy music were not so sharply inconsistent with scientific knowledge and could be accepted by some as fact and by others as pleasing metaphor.

Longfellow was nearer the "inevitable end of Earth" than Whittier had supposed when he wrote the birthday letter. Whittier was at the Claflins' in March, and one day when Elizabeth Stuart Phelps was there, they decided to drive to Cambridge and call on Longfellow, who had asked Whittier to come to see him. When they got to Longfellow's home, Whittier went alone to the door. He did not go in but returned to the carriage in evident agitation and sprang in, hitting his hat on the door. "Longfellow is sick," he said, "very sick. They are very anxious." He was gloomy on the ride back to Boston and went to his room as soon as they got into the house. Longfellow died two days later.[18] He and Whittier had never been intimate friends and had not met for a long time, but Whittier was deeply affected by his death. A sense of loneliness again came over him as if he had outlived the world. The circle of writers of his generation — the "literary fellows," as a member of Grant's cabinet had called them — who had always been friendly and had appreciated each other, was now small and would soon cease to exist. He wrote "The Poet and the Children," a poem about Longfellow's last birthday, for the May *Wide Awake*, and then, oppressed by sorrow and loneliness, felt as if he could never write again. He declined Thomas Bailey Aldrich's request for a poem about Longfellow for the *Atlantic*. His appraisal of Longfellow, which would have been universally accepted then and which would cause a few smiles a century later, was in a letter to his niece: "The death of a man like Longfellow is a national loss. He has been an influence for good; all the Christian virtues his verse and his life exemplified. Pure, kindly, and courteous, he was never otherwise than a gentleman. There is no blot on the crystal purity of his writings. His fame is secure, and is likely to increase in the future. I cannot imagine a time when his songs shall cease to be loved and cherished."[19]

A few weeks later the news came of Emerson's death, and again there was an oppressive feeling of loneliness and isolation. The world could not be the same as it had been when Emerson and Longfellow were living. Emerson "had no mental superior," he wrote, and added simply, he "was a good man and friend."[20]

He was worried because he could not keep up with his correspondence. He still felt that he ought to answer every letter, and many of them required care and thought. New books and manuscripts by aspiring poets kept coming with appeals for criticism and help. Many people wrote to ask questions about his life. To save time he wrote an autobiographical sketch in the form of a letter, which he had Fred A. Brown print for him. He prepared it carefully, making corrections in the galley proof and added two sentences. But his memory was not always accurate, as his first authorized biographer would soon discover, and he wrote that he was working with his uncle when the news-carrier delivered the *Newburyport Free Press* containing his first poem; his uncle had died two years before Whittier's first poem was published.

He was helping and advising Harriet Winslow Sewall in preparing a volume of Lydia Maria Child's letters, for which he was to write the biographical introduction. This was to contain a sonnet by William P. Andrews, and Whittier suggested a change in one line. As for David Lee Child's love letters, they might be included unless they were silly: "Sensible people are sometimes silly in such epistles." Then he was worried about the effect of Mrs. Child's religious radicalism on the sale of the book. He thought that none of her private, unguarded remarks should be printed if they were more extreme than what she had chosen to publish and that the publication of anything that seemed like a sneer at religious opinions cherished by others would be contrary to her toleration and liberality.[21] In Whittier's introduction the only references to her radicalism were a quotation from her *Progress of Religious Ideas*, which he thought "should vindicate her from the charge of undervaluing the Christian faith or of lack of reverent appreciation of its founder," and the statement: "If she touched with no very reverent hand the garment hem of dogmas and held to the spirit of Scripture rather than to its letter, it must be remembered that she lived in a time when the Bible was cited in defense of slavery, as it is now in Utah in support of polygamy; and she may well be excused for some degree of impatience with those who, in the tithing of mint and anise and cummin, neglected the weightier matters of the law of justice and mercy." The points that he emphasized were her self-sacrificing commitment to Abolition and to other causes in aid of the wronged and the weak.

Francis J. Garrison called Whittier's attention to one error in the introduction. Whittier had referred to "raven down of darkness" as Shakespeare's. He evidently did not know "Comus" as well as he knew "Paradise Lost." He replied that the phrase might be Milton's, but he had trusted to Thomas Wentworth Higginson, who was usually accurate, and suggested that "the poet's" be substituted for "Shakespeare's."[22] In the *Works* it is "Milton's." He went to Amesbury May 16 to be ready for the Quarterly Meeting. He enjoyed being at home, in his study with pictures of his mother and sister, Emerson, Longfellow, Thomas Starr King, and Garrison. His old neighbors came in to see him, and he could do some reading. But the east wind was blowing, he was "groaning (inaudibly) with neuralgic pains", and there was the usual great pile of unanswered letters, which could not be expected to grow smaller.[23]

After the Quarterly Meeting he returned to Oak Knoll, and on June 14 he was one of the two hundred guests at the *Atlantic's* seventieth birthday party for Harriet Beecher Stowe at the Claflins' estate in Newtonville — it was actually her seventy-first. There was music by the Germania Band, the Beethoven Club, and a soloist, and refreshments without wine, which had been suggested by Henry O. Houghton and rejected by Mrs. Claflin. Whittier thought that Mrs. Stowe bore herself very quietly and modestly, and Garrison thought that Whittier's poem for the occasion was excellent and was well read by Frank Sanborn.[24] Whittier's poem, "A Greeting," hardly deserved this praise; it was undistinguished except for the acquaintance that it showed with Mrs. Stowe's books.

He was at the Isles of Shoals for a few days in late June and early July with Mrs. Gustavus Cammett and his Oak Knoll cousins. Phebe rowed and sailed and had such a good time that it was a pleasure to see and hear her, and Whittier and Celia Thaxter talked about Spiritualism. In the middle of July he went to Center Harbor with the Cartlands, but after a few days a heat wave drove them to the Asquam House at Holderness, on a hill surrounded by two lakes and with a mountain horizon on all sides.[25]

One day Whittier stood on the piazza watching a thunder storm and a rainbow. In spite of his seventy-four years he saw the pictorial possibilities and wrote "Storm on Lake Asquam" in which the details were handled with no diminution of his perceptive and appreciative skill:

> Thunderous and vast, a fire-veined darkness swept
> Over the rough pine-bearded Asquam range.

And over all the still unhidden sun
Weaving its light through slant-blown veils of rain.
To present-day readers, however, the poem is marred by the simile in the next line; the sun

> Smiled on the trouble, as hope smiles on pain.

When Whittier thought about nature, instead of looking at it and telling others what he saw, he wrote less vividly and succinctly. "A Summer Pilgrimage," sent to the *Atlantic* November 16, told sincerely but diffusely what a vacation in the mountains meant to him, with specific references to these days at Holderness.

When Whittier thought that the hot weather was over, he returned to Amesbury and then to Oak Knoll, where he encountered the worst heat of the summer. The temperature was higher in Boston than in Savannah or Pensacola. He had four sleepless nights, but there were letters to be answered. He sent a firm but kindly note to a young poet. He was too ill to do more than say that he did not advise publishing at present. "Without depending on writing for support, one can enjoy the pleasant gift of verse, until there is a real demand for more permanent publication in verse form."[26]

The hot weather and illness may have made Whittier unusually sensitive to criticism. He resented a statement by the editor of the *Friends' Review* that he wished that Whittier were as sound in religious matters as Longfellow. Whittier wrote to him that he knew of nothing in his life that could make the editor wish that he were as sound "as a very decided Unitarian and non-meeting attendant" and went on to an exposition of his own faith. His hope and reliance were "in the mercy and goodness of God as revealed in Christ in his earthly manifestation and in his spiritual evidence in the souls of men." While he was not in accord with the new methods and doctrines in the Society of Friends, he had nothing but kindly feelings for those who differed from him.[27]

Tolerance of others' belief and worship was also the theme of "The Mystic's Christmas" in the *Youth's Companion* December 21. The Mystic did not join in the Christmas festivities in the monastery. When the other monks asked him why he sat apart, he replied that they might keep the holiday in their own way. But he himself had found a clear inward sight, and for him the outward symbols had disappeared, and he said to the other monks:

. . . Judge not him who every morn
Feels in his heart the Lord Christ born.

Whittier was in Amesbury early in September. Addie Caldwell was there for a few days, "happy on being entirely free of her wretched husband." Whittier's brother resigned his position at the Boston Custom House. There would now be more expenses for Whittier to pay, and he sent only half as much for a friend's golden wedding as he would have sent had it not been for his brother's illness and the needs of other relatives.[28]

One Saturday seven women teachers from Lawrence came to Amesbury to see its two chief objects of attraction, Whittier and the view from Powow Hill. They called on Whittier in the morning and were received, according to the local paper, "as everybody else is by him, in a kindly manner." But Whittier was now to pay a higher price for fame than being visited by school teachers. He had realized for some time that he would be a subject for biography, and in March he had, if James R. Osgood understood him correctly, virtually asked Francis H. Underwood to write one. Underwood's impression eleven years later was that he had met Whittier in a horse-car and that Whittier had commended his sketches of Lowell and Longfellow, adding "I hope thee will continue and make similar sketches of all our poets." But his enthusiasm soon dwindled. Elizabeth Stuart Phelps evidently hinted that she might write a "memorial" if she outlived him, as she had done for James T. Fields. Whittier told her that he hoped it would be "brief and dry," but there was little or nothing to say of his life, and his poor rhymes spoke for themselves. He added that he had told Underwood that he was welcome to everything in which the public would "reasonably feel an interest" — a point on which he and Underwood would soon find themselves in disagreement — but he would like to think that someone more closely in sympathy with him would feel like "saying a kind and tender word" for him after his death, and he trusted she would do it, "And then let the great silence fall."[29]

He made a real effort to help Underwood, who went about his task conscientiously, sending a list of questions which Whittier tried to answer with Gertrude Cartland's help. Underwood later said that Whittier's memory was wholly gone. This was an over-statement; Whittier had forgotten many details of early publications but not more than would be expected of a man nearly seventy-five looking back over a half-century of writing. He was unable to answer some of Underwood's questions and answered others incorrectly.

A still greater source of vexation, "one of the miseries of notoriety," was a surprise biography by William Sloane Kennedy. He had called on Whittier in the summer, stayed about an hour, and then had gone to Haverhill and elsewhere asking questions about Whittier and cautioning people not to let Whittier know. Whittier knew nothing of the book until James R. Osgood told him about it, and he told Osgood that Underwood, and Underwood only, had been authorized to write. He thought that the book would not amount to much and would not interfere with the sale of Underwood's book, and his advice to Underwood was to let Kennedy alone and have Osgood issue a simple statement; the matter was not worth quarreling about. When the book appeared Whittier called it "caricatures" without reading it.[30]

As the fall elections approached, Whittier was regarded as good political advertising. He was asked to preside at the Seventh Congressional District Republican Convention and of course declined but took the chance to say that he was a warm personal and political friend of Eben F. Stone, "a man of tried ability and integrity, whose whole life is a guarantee of his faithful and efficient performance of every duty." Whittier's letter was read and Colonel Stone was nominated. Whittier went to the State Republican Convention, where Robert S. Rantoul, acting under orders from the chiefs, gave him a conspicuous seat near the front of the platform. The proceedings had hardly started when Whittier's chair was observed to be vacant. He had withdrawn to a less conspicuous seat, where he could see and hear without being observed.[31]

After the election Whittier joined the Oak Knoll family at Hotel Winthrop in Boston, where they had been since September. The hotel was on Bowdoin Street, and Whittier's room was up one flight on the corner looking out on the tower of the Church of St. John the Evangelist. A door was cut through to the rooms occupied by the family from Oak Knoll. The hotel was small and informal — like Amesbury, Whittier said, where people were neighborly and dropped in without knocking. He liked the fact that he was not overwhelmed by the service, as in the big hotels where he was not allowed to wait on himself as he was used to doing. The boarders liked to call themselves "the family." They would gather in a little reception room on the street floor, Whittier sitting on a sofa. For several weeks he seldom went out except to see his brother, who was at the Maverick House in East Boston, very ill, Whittier thought, but cheerful.[32]   Whittier had a bad cold when he came to Boston, which got better and then worse again as his birthday approached. He did not want any great demonstration on that day and would be glad if he could "get out of the way of all these things." He was grateful for his friends' good feeling and kindness, but he dreaded a scene. There was nothing on the day resembling a scene, but there were many callers, the majority of them personal friends, most of them women. Governor John D. Long sent a letter of congratulation, and someone sent a bottle of rare old Andalusian wine, which Whittier promptly acknowledged, saying that he was not accustomed to tarrying long at the wine but in this case would remember Paul's advice to Timothy.

Before Whittier could have more than started answering his birthday mail, he was besought to write some lines for a child named for his sister Elizabeth. "May I again implore you, Mr. Whittier, with all the earnestness of a devoted Father in behalf of his darling child to grant this courtesy . . . In the name of everything that you hold sacred, Mr. Whittier, I beseech you, grant us this request." His answer is not recorded, but he may well have replied as he did to another importunate person earlier in the year: "I have been compelled by thousands of demands like thine to decline most of them. My health has greatly suffered by their pouring in upon me daily: and with strong desire to oblige everybody I can no longer do it. . . . My friend Longfellow was driven to death by these incessant demands."[33]

XXXII
1883 - 84

After his brother's death on January 7, Whittier went to Amesbury to rest and avoid company. In Boston he had more callers than he wanted, and yet he was lonely, with that especial form of loneliness that comes to the last surviving member of a family: there was no one to talk with about boyhood memories. But there was an important matter to be attended to without delay. Underwood must be kept from using the early poems and even told to stop work on the book if he persisted in digging up all that schoolboy nonsense.[1]

It is easy to see why Whittier disliked his early poems. His outlook on life and poetry was quite different from what it had been when he was writing a poem a week or composing "Mogg Megone." But his determination to keep Underwood from doing what any conscientious biographer would feel an obligation to do was selfish and unreasonable.

He made his wishes quite clear. "For mercy's sake, let the dead rest. . . I see no use in setting all the literary ghouls to digging for something I have written in my first attempts at rhyme. I detest the whole of it." It seemed to him quite sufficient to say that he wrote occasionally prose and poetic pieces which he had not thought worthy of preservation. The public would have no interest in these "abortions" or, if they had, they would have no right to know them. As for "Mogg Megone," he wished it were in the Red Sea.

Underwood was disappointed and distressed. He had gone through the files of the *Liberator*, *New England Magazine*, *Democratic Review*, and *New England Weekly Review*, only to have Whittier "angry to the last degree" at having the early poems rediscovered. He told Whittier that if he didn't use them, others would and his book would be criticized as superficial. Neither he nor Whittier could convince the other, and Underwood continued his work with little help from Whittier — who, however, did not carry out the threat of stopping him.

Whittier made a final appeal when he received the proof sheets in June. "Could not the enumeration of my wretched first appearances in the newspapers and magazines be omitted? Why not say, in brief, that I wrote a good many rhymes not worth recalling? I detest the stuff — and hoped it was buried in oblivion, fathoms deep." With good reason he objected to one chapter heading: "Beginning of Fame." The term "fame" was hardly applicable at that period in his life, and he thought it could be safely said that there were ten thousand boys and girls in the United States who could write better verses than he wrote at their age.

This was his last protest; he now accepted his fate and made the best of a bad business. He told Underwood that he might use the recent "What the Traveler Said at Sunset," and when he found that Nora Perry had got hold of some "album nonsense" and used it in a monograph in the *Boston Home Journal*, he sent Underwood the lines beginning "Words Butter No Parsnips," written after receiving a jar of butter from Ruth Jones Challis of Pond Hills, Amesbury. He was afraid that the critics would not agree with Underwood's opinion of his writings and thought that it would be best to anticipate them by admitting obvious faults and limitations, which none saw more clearly than himself. "Touch upon my false rhymes and Yankeeisms. Confess that I sometimes 'crack the voice of melody and break the legs of Time.' Pitch into Mogg Megone. That 'big Injin' strutting around in Walter Scott's plaid has no friends and deserves none. Own that I sometimes choose unpoetical themes. Endorse Lowell's 'Fable for Critics,' that I mistake occasionally simple excitement for inspiration. In this way we can take the wind out of the sails of ill-natured cavillers. I am not one of the master singers. I don't *pose* as one. By the grace of God I am only what I am, and don't wish to pass for more."[2]

After Whittier's death Underwood complained bitterly that Whittier had not helped him, had not given him one document, letter, or memorandum, and had seemed to think that a biography was to be evolved out of the writer's inner consciousness. Worse still, he said, Whittier did nothing in his defense when Frank B. Sanborn attacked the book as inaccurate and untrustworthy.

On this last topic Underwood was unfair. A man seventy-five years old could hardly be expected to engage in a controversy about his own life. However, Underwood probably did not know that Whittier wrote to Thomas Bailey Aldrich when the book appeared, asking that it be treated kindly if it was mentioned in the *Atlantic*; he would have preferred that it should not have been written, but he thought that Underwood had been painstaking and careful and had worked long and hard for his material, and he hoped that the book would sell. He told Underwood that his friends seemed quite satisfied with it, and it was remarkably free from errors. Underwood had made a lively book for "such a dull subject."

The book was not a success, and Underwood had a nervous breakdown. James R. Osgood lent him one hundred dollars for a trip to Florida, and the royalties had not reached that amount several years later.[3]

Whittier spent most of the winter in Boston, not too happily. He could not, in his phrase, "get about much," but unfortunately for him, other people could. He had not acquired the technique of avoiding lion-hunters, and was beset by strangers with albums and curiosity to see what a Quaker poet was like. He seems to have done no writing for publication and to have written fewer letters than usual. One letter, however, it was evidently a pleasure to write. A school in Georgia appointed a day to be observed in honor of

Whittier, and he wrote to one of the teachers, "Say to the dear young people under thy charge that while I loved liberty and hated slavery I had never any but the kindest feelings toward the people of the South. I believed that they would be more prosperous and happy if slavery should cease, and I think it is already evident that the South has now started on the road to a higher degree of prosperity than it has ever known, and no one can more heartily rejoice in your welfare than myself."[4]

Just before returning to Amesbury he let the Claflins give him a reception and evidently enjoyed it. It was largely a gathering of old Anti-Slavery people and reformers, in rooms hung with portraits of Abolition leaders. Whittier received his guests cordially, and a reporter observed that his "strong, serene, spiritual face seemed illuminated with a new light."[5]

Whittier went to Amesbury a few days later. Compared with Boston, the town was quiet, and he found it refreshing, although a long-lasting cold, or a series of colds, kept him largely confined to the house. He was thinking much of the past. He wished that he could visit Folly Mill Woods to see if the mayflowers were in bloom and to find them under the leaves of the pine slopes where he and Elizabeth used to find them. One evening as he sat by the fire thinking sadly of old friends who had died, letters arrived from Mrs. Fields and Sarah Orne Jewett with the proof-sheets of Miss Jewett's "Landless Farmer." The shadows vanished from his thoughts as he read the story, which he found "true as a sun-picture to the life and atmosphere of a farming neighborhood."[6]

Mrs. Fields had told him that Sarah Orne Jewett was reading the recently published three volumes of *Letters and Memorials of Jane Welsh Carlyle*, and he asked her to send them to Oak Knoll. When he returned there, he began to read them and was soon convinced that they were "a strange, sad revelation! What a tone of desperation in these letters, thinly disguised by the common phrases of 'Dearest' and 'O my dear husband'! There is no sincerity in these professions. They did not love each other so much as they loved and pitied themselves. Carlyle loved nobody and nothing and I do not find that Mrs. C. was much different." Some of the letters he thought were bright and witty and "canny," and Mrs. Carlyle's expletives were "more forcible than pious." He suspected that she and her husband swore at each other sometimes. Two weeks later he had read the letters again and decided that his first judgment had been too severe, and that Jane Carlyle was " 'cut out' for a very noble woman. Her wit and humor are simply marvelous. If she had married a man she really loved she would have been a happier and better woman. There is no excuse for Carlyle's shaking his fist in the face of the divine providence that had given him such a woman."[7]

Two poems, the first since January, appeared about the same time, "What the Traveller Said at Sunset" in the *Independent* May 17 and "How the Women Went from Dover" in the June *Atlantic*. The first of these began as an extended metaphor of a traveller at nightfall leaving lighted hearths and crossing as a boundary line into the darkness, uncertain of what he was to find and shrinking from it. He represented the person approaching death, and then the metaphor was lost in Whittier's direct statement of what he wanted to find in the future life. The poem impressed Whittier's contemporaries. Oliver Wendell Holmes read it with deep emotion and thought that perhaps he ought to have selected it as his favorite in *The Bay of Seven Islands* instead of "How the Women Went from Dover," which he described as "alive all over" and which gave him the "old thrill" as he read it.[8]

Most readers would agree with Holmes that "How the Women Went from Dover" was alive until they came to the little sermon to women in the last two stanzas. Whittier worked hard on it. He made many changes in the manuscript and in the proof printed by Fred Brown and still other changes before publication in the *Atlantic*.[9] He removed one apocryphal detail in the proof, a reference in the fifteenth stanza to Stephen Bachiler, but he had no reason to question the commonly accepted legend that Robert Pike of Salisbury prevented the whipping of the Quaker women as they passed through the town. Robert Pike, as Whittier explained in the headnote, was far in advance of his time in advocating religious freedom and opposing ecclesiastical authority. The women were rescued by a quite different person, Walter Barefoote, who has been described as an unscrupulous, ruthless schemer and, on occasion, a tavern brawler, but able, energetic, and resourceful, and who, as has been said, gave one of the finest demonstrations of mercy and decency in the history of the North American provinces. He did not stop the whipping of the women; that had been completed when he arrived on the scene. He persuaded the constable to appoint him as a deputy to take the women across the Merrimac River to Newbury. He then put them on a vessel and sent them to a Quaker friend of his in Kittery.[10]

Early in May Whittier replied to a request from George William Curtis for a poem for the December *Harper's*. He promised to send it by July 1, and then went on to a vigorous complaint about an article in the February *Harper's*, "The Local Associations of Whittier's Poems" by George M. White, which, he said, was full of misrepresentations and distortions and a "coarse familiarity which would have made anybody but a Quaker use expletives more forcible than pious."[11]

White's article was a rambling miscellany, but there was only one detail that could be called "coarse familiarity." White described Whittier's black coat as "seedy" and worn white on the back seams. Perhaps Whittier resented a reference to his deafness and the publication of statements made in what he had supposed was a friendly private conversation. Several items about Whittier's boyhood later appeared in *Whittier-Land*; Pickard evidently assumed that Whittier would not object to their use.

Part of Whittier's wrath came from his having expected that sketches made the previous year by Harry Fenn would be used to illustrate an article by Harriet Prescott Spofford for *Harper's*, which had been delayed because an article about Whittier had appeared in the *Century* on the day when Mrs. Spofford's article was accepted by *Harper's*. The editors' intention to use it was not affected by their using White's article, and it led off the January 1884 number. It was a thorough and orderly survey of Whittier's life and work. She received a good deal of help in biographical details from Samuel T. Pickard, including a description of Oak Knoll, much of which he later quoted verbatim in his *Life and Letters of John Greenleaf Whittier*. Everything that Mrs. Spofford said of course pointed out something commendable, and there was not the slightest suspicion of a shadow of adverse criticism.

The poem that Whittier promised by July 1 had arrived at the editorial office by May 31, and Whittier was asked to name his price.[12] The poem was "St. Gregory's Guest," printed in the December *Harper's* entitled "Supper of St. Gregory" with two sentimental illustrations showing the Saint handing his silver cup to Christ disguised as a beggar and Christ blessing a woman who was apparently doing a good deed to a poor woman and child. The poem told its story simply and clearly but had three unnecessary final stanzas emphasizing the moral.

"Our Country" was written for a Fourth of July celebration at Woodstock, Connecticut. It was longer than necessary; Whittier failed to use the art of compression that he had often used in poems for occasions. He said a good deal to show his faith in the nation. Immigration was beginning to bring its problems, but Whittier was confident that in a wide-spread country which needed labor, even the outcasts from the old world would be moulded into the national plan. The same force that ended slavery would end the mistreatment of Indians, stop the evil of drink, bring justice to the working man, elect the right people to public office, and give women equal rights and duties. After the poem was first printed, he thought of a few other things and added a stanza:

> Give every child his right of school,
>> Merge private greed in public good,
> And spare a treasury overfull
>> The tax upon a poor man's food.

Whittier worked hard on the poem, making many changes for the better in the manuscript and the proof.

Whittier made a brief visit to Amesbury late in June to vote for a contract with a water company to supply water to the town from a reservoir on Powwow Hill, and then went to the Asquam House in Holderness with Joseph and Gertrude Cartland. They spent much of the time reading under the pine

trees. Whittier found Sarah Orne Jewett's *A Country Doctor* "charming."
One Sunday morning he read Francesca Alexander's *Story of Ida*,[13] a story
about a poor, virtuous Italian girl, who to most readers of a later generation
would seem colorless and uninteresting. Her love for a man unworthy of
her, and her illness and death, were told in wearisome detail and in a tone
of kindly condescension that women writers of the time seldom avoided when
writing about women of lower "condition," as they called it. But John Ruskin
had liked the story and supplied an introduction and comments that appeared
as footnotes. Whittier was so impressed by it that he wrote a sonnet which
he sent to the author after she had sent him a copy of the book. The sonnet
had some effective lines criticizing some of the religious tendencies of the time.

The weather at Holderness was pleasant and cool, and the food at the Asquam House was good, with blueberries and raspberries from the nearby
hill. Among the guests were some girls of Phebe's age, and he wished that
she were there — perhaps a hint that he thought that she was not seeing
enough young people. The hotel was full, and he wrote that if anybody else
came the guests would be

> Crammed just as full as h-ll is crammed,
> All crowded and all damned.

He thought that this "rather startling comparison" was in Wordsworth's
"Peter Bell."[14] Whittier, however, was responsible for the startling part of
the comparison. Wordsworth had written:

> Crammed just as they on earth were crammed
> All silent and all damned.

Before leaving Holderness he wrote "Sweet Fern," which was not published
until January and may have had considerable revision. It was evidently based
on an experience at Holderness. He was slowly climbing a hill when the
fragrance of sweet fern brought the memory of a boyhood incident, which
the poem told briefly and simply. The concluding lines had the simple
excellence of which Whittier was capable when he forgot that a poem should
do good.

He left Holderness early in August. On the way to Oak Knoll he visited
Haverhill, but except for the Academy and a few houses on Water and Main
Streets he found little to remind him of the town as it had been in his early
days. Trees that he remembered as young and vigorous were now old and
decaying, and he found only a few people that he knew. He called on one
of them, Dr. John Crowell, who lived on Winter Street, within sight of the
Common, and pointed out the site of the old meetinghouse, schoolhouse,
engine house, and hay scales which had been there in his boyhood. He gave,
as usual, an appearance of health and vigor, with elastic step and erect form.[15]

He continued to complain about the pains and infirmities of age, but he
seldom let illness keep him from doing anything that he really wanted to do.
On one warm day, although he was what he called "quite ill," he started

for Boston and Somerville to visit Harriet Minot Pitman. The train was hot and crowded, and when he got to Boston, he did not feel well enough to go to Somerville. He went to a hotel, had a sleepless night, stayed in bed nearly all the next day, and had another sleepless night. The next day he took a carriage to the Republican State Convention, to which he had been elected a delegate, stayed only long enough to vote for George D. Robinson to oppose Butler's reelection, and returned to Oak Knoll. He sent for a Salem physician and at last got some sleep.[16]

The Republicans nominated Robinson and started a vigorous campaign. They worked hard and collected and spent plenty of money. Whittier felt a deeper interest than in any election for many years. In spite of his seventy-six years and the "pains and limitations of age and its infirmities" and the likelihood that he might lose a chance to meet Matthew Arnold in Boston, he went to Amesbury to help in the campaign. Amesbury now had a large Irish population, and Butler still kept his hold on their loyalty and affection. Whittier referred privately to the "Irish-ridden-town" and to the "great number of Irish here, all Butlerites, and kept so by twenty rum shops."[17]

When he heard that some of the Negroes in Boston were inclined to vote for Butler, he wrote a letter to the *Boston Journal* urging them to reconsider. Massachusetts, he said, had been vilified and scoffed at for her adherence to the cause of the colored man, and now Southern newspapers were exulting over the attacks upon her reputation by the man whom they intended to vote for, whose reelection would be taken as an endorsement of the calumnies. Whittier did not mention them specifically, but everyone knew that he was referring to charges in a pamphlet published by the Democratic State Committee that inmates of the asylum for the poor at Tewksbury, which Butler had made a campaign issue, were eaten by rats, dead babies sold to Harvard Medical School, and sandals made from the skin of dead inmates.

Butler was defeated by nine thousand votes. In Amesbury Robinson received ninety-one votes more than the Republican candidate in 1882.[18]

Whittier was also busy raising money for Lucy Larcom, who was sick and unable to work. Money came promptly, including five hundred dollars from Mrs. Fields, and by early November there was eleven hundred dollars for the annuity and one hundred fifty dollars for her immediate needs. Her illness was now so serious that Whittier hesitated to put the money into an annuity, but he was soon assured by his former neighbor, Dr. Maria Dowdell, that Lucy would recover. More money came in, and he was finally able to present her with the annuity and $221. She accepted it gratefully and could not guess where it came from, Whittier told Mrs. Fields: "Thinks the Lord did it." Later George W. Childs sent one hundred dollars and promised to send that amount every year.[19]

Whittier sent her a check for her help in preparing a new edition of *Songs of Three Centuries.* He told her when he was at Holderness that there were no books there to consult and left her to decide what poems should be added. He named one that should be taken out, "The Blackbird" by Frederick Tennyson, which "ought to have his neck wrung as a useless bird and a better singer put in his place." "The Blackbird" survived even into the 1890 edition, probably because removing it would have meant making new plates. This check, Lucy Larcom told Whittier, meant more to her than any other sum that she might receive, since it stood for the generosity and friendship of years. She hoped that he had not given her more than a fair share of the spoils.[20]

If he did give her more than a fair share of the expected profits, he could well afford to do so. The income from his investments alone must now have been adequate for his own living expenses. His contract with his publishers, first drawn up at twenty-five hundred dollars a year in 1873, had been renewed in April for another ten years at three thousand. In addition he received ten percent of the retail sales of each new volume for the first eight months.

A new volume, *The Bay of Seven Islands*, was published in October. It had been in preparation since May, and by August he had read and returned the proof.[21] There were only four poems that had not been previously published. One of these was the first thirty-five lines of the title poem, "To H.P.S." Harriet Prescott Spofford's house could then be seen from Whittier Hill, as told in the first nine lines. Two of these lines:

> I see thy home, set like an eagle's nest
> Among Deer Island's immemorial pines,

were evidently from Whittier's memory, perhaps subconscious, of lines in Macaulay's "Horatius":

> From many a lonely hamlet,
>> Which, hid by beech and pine,
> Like an eagle's nest, hangs on the crest
>> Of purple Apennine.

The volume sold well enough to require another printing the next year. Whittier sent a copy to Oliver Wendell Holmes, who found so much hope and sweetness and human sympathy in it that his eyes filled with tears, and one tear even ran down his cheek.[22]

One result of Whittier's prosperity was his spending six hundred fifty dollars to add a second story at the west end of the house, making two new bedrooms. These rooms must have made living conditions much pleasanter for the Cates, who up to this time had only a small bedroom on the first floor. No architect was employed, and Whittier worried a good deal about the plans. On one point he was adamant. He would not have a second gable projecting over the bay window above the front door, as the carpenter, Jason Todd, a neighbor, had advised. It would look too pretentious and would be out of keeping "like a fashionable girl's bonnet on an old lady." He wanted "plain, substantial work but no nonsense for the newspaper reporters to ridicule." Whittier was at the house for a few days in January but found it cold, in spite of four fires, after the comfort of a furnace at Oak Knoll, and returned to Oak Knoll for the rest of the winter.[23]

He did not lose his chance to meet Matthew Arnold by being in Amesbury at election time. He not only met Arnold in Boston late in the fall but had dinner with him and found him "an able but very positive Englishman." He described Arnold as "one of the foremost men of our time, a true poet, and a brave, upright man to whom all English-speaking people owe a debt of gratitude." He was pleased to know that Arnold thought that "In School Days" was one of the perfect poems that would live.[24]

Whittier also met a rising young American writer, George W. Cable. He heard one of Cable's readings in Creole dialect and called on him at the Adams House. A reporter was present to interview Cable, and he included Whittier in a two-column account in the *Boston Herald*. Whittier strode into the room, stretched out his hand and said, "I am glad to see thee, friend. I have read all thy stories, and I like them very much. Thee has found an untrodden field of romance in New Orleans, and I think thee the writer whom we have so long waited to see come up in the South. I did not expect to see so young a man as thee." He told Cable that the publishers would now urge him to write continually, and commended Cable's reply that he did not "believe in forcing the growth of the young tree." Too many writers, Whittier thought, had exhausted themselves in the first flush of success. Whittier was a good listener and seemed interested in Cable's account of his life and the works that he had in progress.[25]

Whittier failed to see Protap Chunder Mozoomdar, one of the leaders of the Brahmo Somaj, whom he wanted to see in Boston. The Brahmo Somaj had been founded in Calcutta in 1828 and two years later proclaimed Christianity as the only true religion: a Christianity, however, which included features of Hinduism and Mohammedanism. The branch of the church of which Mozoomdar was one of the leaders abolished all caste restrictions and Brahmanism. Whittier was greatly impressed by the movement; it was "the Lord's doing — the blade before the full corn in the ear," the "greatest event in the history of Christianity since the days of Paul."[26]

"How the Robin Came," sub-titled "An Algonquin Legend," was, with the usual disregard for the calendar, printed in the December *St. Nicholas*; it began

> Happy young friends, sit by me
> Under May's blown apple-tree.

It was a myth rather than a legend, and the conclusion was a sermon in which the young readers were instructed to find a lesson rather remote from the story:

> Unto gentleness belong

Gifts unknown to pride and wrong;
Happier far than hate is praise, —
He who sings than he who slays.

Whittier's seventy-sixth birthday was a quiet one at Oak Knoll. Many people thought that he was at the Hotel Winthrop and called there instead. The mail was heavy as usual; his writing desk was loaded down with letters. He was happy to receive many from the South as an indication that the old quarrel about slavery was nearly over.

At Christmas and New Year there was another flood of letters, and on January 18 he was too busy to write a letter about the proposed international copyright law, but told Francis J. Garrison simply to add his name to the petition. His correspondence had grown "enormous." Especially bothersome were manuscripts, which he had at last come to realize must, more often than not, be returned without reading. One man wrote, with at least the virtue of directness, "Now what I wish is this. Your opinion of my talent (or lack of it)." Another wrote that he could not approach his request with circumlocution — after two finely written pages: "But if, confiding in my honor as an Irish gentleman and, might I dare say so, as a fellow artist likewise, you would, *not give* but *lend* me five dollars."[27]

Whittier remained at Oak Knoll in spite of competition for his visits elsewhere. Mrs. Claflin was going through a nervous breakdown and was staying at the Claflins' country home in Newtonville to avoid the noises of the city, but Whittier received a cordial invitation from William Claflin to their Boston house, where he could go, sleep, eat, write, and have his friends visit "as independently as Robinson Crusoe on his island." Mrs. Fields invited him for a week or so; then, she wrote, "Perhaps dear Mrs. Claflin will be well enough to see you, and with the promise of your coming, she will not wonder at your pausing here for a brief visit."[28]

Wendell Phillips was "a great orator but not a wise man," Whittier wrote in a private letter after Phillips' sudden death February 2. He said the same thing in more detail to a newspaper interviewer. Phillips, he said, was the greatest orator of the country, perhaps of the world, and ranked with Demosthenes, Castellar of Spain, and Kossuth. His ideas were pronounced and his invective strong. His sincerity was proved by his throwing himself into the Anti-Slavery movement and making a great sacrifice, including social position, for principle. But his judgment was not equal to his rhetoric, as was shown by his joining Garrison in opposition to political action.

It was now expedient to say good things about Phillips, and numerous politicians were doing it who had once abused him for pleading the cause of the slave. Whittier, like other old Abolitionists, found it hard to listen to them patiently as they eulogized him extravagantly. He found it refreshing to hear a really sincere tribute, from a Negro. It was a eulogy in Tremont Temple, Boston, by Archibald H. Grimke, a nephew of the Grimke sisters

Sarah and Angelina, a graduate of Harvard Law School and editor of a paper in Boston devoted to Negro welfare.[29]

Whittier received a request from the *Andover Review* for a tribute to Phillips. He did not write the tribute, but he approved of the *Review* and sent "Adjustment," which appeared in the October number. The *Andover Review* was a monthly magazine recently founded by some of the new and liberal faculty members at Andover Theological Seminary, with a policy as stated by the president of the Seminary in its first number: "We seek to promote large-minded, large-hearted discussions of Christian truth."[30] "Adjustment," consisting of two stanzas in sonnet form, was in accord with this policy and was a courageous affirmation of faith for a man in the mid-seventies.

Whittier's popularity as an author showed no signs of decline. He was asked to write a poem to accompany a double-page picture from a painting by Edwin A. Abbey in *Harper's Weekly*. Abbey was one of the popular artists of his time, and *Harper's Weekly* was the leading illustrated magazine in the country. The poem as it appeared in the March 15 issue was the present first, second, and fourth stanzas of "Banished from Massachusetts"; a proof copy, preceding the publication of the magazine, had all four stanzas.

Further proof of Whittier's popularity appeared in a plebiscite of the readers of the New York *Critic* to find who were regarded as the greatest living American authors. Whittier was given third place, preceded only by Holmes and Lowell. Mark Twain was fourteenth on the list, and Walt Whitman twentieth.[31] The range of his popularity is suggested by two requests in 1884 for poems for occasions: he was asked to write the Harvard Phi Beta Kappa poem and, by the Catholic Young Men's National Union, to write a poem for the two hundred fiftieth anniversary of the settlement of Maryland.

It was children, however, who especially pleased Whittier when they liked his poetry. A little girl two and half years old could recite "The Barefoot Boy," and a remark of hers quoted to Whittier led to the writing of another poem published in a magazine for children. She said to her mother as they were going through a dark hall, "Mamma, take hold of my hand, so it will not be so dark." When Whittier heard of her remark and of her fondness for his poetry, he wrote to her mother that the little girl's opinion of his verses meant more to him than that of a learned reviewer, and he enclosed "a rhymed paraphrase of her own beautiful thought."[32] The poem was "The Light That Is Felt," which was printed in the December *St. Nicholas*. Although it was in a children's magazine, it was a poem for adults rather than children: it asked God to take the hands raised to him in prayer

And let us feel the light of Thee!

He was as usual in touch with political events and was interested in the choice of a Republican candidate for President. The Democratic Party had now recovered much of the strength which it had lost as a result of the Civil War, but it was badly divided, and the Republicans had a good chance of keeping possession of the White House if they nominated the right man. William Claflin wrote to Whittier that George T. Edmunds might be elected if nominated but would wreck the Republican Party in the same way John Adams had: he was a pessimist and wanted to do nothing as long as there was a way to avoid it. James G. Blaine would be dangerous if nominated and dangerous, but less so, if not. Whittier thought otherwise, but was willing for the sake of harmony that the votes of the Massachusetts delegation to the Republican Convention should be given to Edmunds. After the Illinois delegation changed from General John A. Logan to Blaine and thus ensured Blaine's nomination, he thought that the Massachusetts delegation should vote for Blaine. Apart from the results of the Convention, Whittier was interested in its personnel, especially the Negro delegates from the South, how they would look, act, and appear. He was also curious about the acts and general appearance of William Mahone, a former Confederate soldier, now boss of the Republican Party in Virginia, short and thin, with a long beard and always wearing a slouch hat and peg-top trousers.[33]

Whittier went to Amesbury as usual in March. The work on his house had evidently been completed, or if not, it was a lesser evil than the spring cleaning and painting at Oak Knoll, the "annual house overturning," he called it. A basement was being built under the Friends Meeting House containing a kitchen and dining hall for Quarterly Meeting attendants. The cost would be six hundred dollars, most of which Whittier thought unnecessary, but he was resigned to the fact that he would have to help pay for it. When he returned to Oak Knoll for a few weeks, he wrote to Mrs. Cate that he supposed they would have to get a Quarterly Meeting dinner "notwithstanding the cellar under the Meeting House," though they would probably have fewer guests. In spite of this apparent lack of enthusiasm, he really found much to enjoy in Quarterly Meetings. He met old Quaker friends, and enjoyed hearing the Quaker speech and seeing the costume. They reminded him of the older generation of Friends, and it seemed to him that there was now no quiet to get into: everyone was hurried, excited, and afraid of "Mrs. Grundy."[34]

After Quarterly Meeting he returned to Oak Knoll. He was in Amesbury in late June and early July, when an Abolition reunion in New York gave him a chance to say something about the coming election. Negroes, he wrote in a letter to be read at the semi-centennial of the Anti-Slavery meeting of 1834, did not yet have full civil rights in all parts of the country, and the time had not yet come when it would be safe to entrust the Government to those who had "persistently denied them the rights and privileges of citizenship." But he was happy that the state of public opinion in the South was improving, and optimistically trusted that before the centennial of emancipation the Negroes, educated and self-respecting, would have no reason to complain of uncivil treatment and political disabilities. When he heard of Cleveland's nomination, he thought that Blaine was likely to win; he did not foresee the effect that the Prohibition Party, aided by the Woman's Christian Temperance Union, would have. Nor was he yet fully aware of the strength of the opposition to Blaine by some important Republicans, especially advocates of Civil Service reform, who supported Cleveland. But he knew that the result was not certain, and he sent a letter and check to Henry Cabot Lodge for the Republican State Committee: "I am not prepared to abandon Republicanism and go over to a party whose principles and measures I have constantly opposed for the last quarter of a century." Whittier in 1884 was still an ally who was a tower of strength, and the Committee sent the letter to the press.[35]

Whittier was at the White Mountains during part of July and August. He could walk a little and enjoy looking at the mountain horizon at dawn and sunset, but he felt the limitations of old age and illness and was, he said, beginning to understand that he was "as they say of town paupers, 'past my usefulness'." He returned to Amesbury without feeling that his health and strength had been improved by his weeks in New Hampshire.[36]

There were letters that had to be written in spite of fatigue and illness. One was an answer to a list of questions about his habits of writing. He wrote that he preferred to write in the morning; he used no outline, his verses being made as the Irishman made a chimney by holding up one brick and putting another under it; he used no stimulants when writing; he had no particular habits of writing; for many years he had not been able to write or study more than half an hour without suffering. He did not add an important point that was not included in the list of questions, but which he mentioned in a letter two years later: he thought that he owed much to afterthought in revising the proofs, and that a French bishop was half right when he said that the Devil suggested one's first thoughts.[37]

Then there was a letter to be written to *The Critic and Good Literature* for its symposium of tributes to Oliver Wendell Holmes on his seventy-fifth birthday, and as usual, Whittier wrote a good letter. If Holmes did not hold first place in American literature in popular sentiment, it could be only because of his versatility. He was "Montaigne and Bacon under one hat."[38]

For weeks there was not a day free from visitors — thanks to the country's railroad system, which was approaching its peak — and most of them were people that Whittier could not avoid seeing. There were Haverhill Academy schoolmates, old Anti-Slavery friends, and a group of English visitors, "each with his or her scientific or other hobby."[39]

Somehow he found time to write "Birchbrook Mill," which he called a "weird New England ballad" and thought might be worth printing, although he wasn't sure. It appeared in the November *Atlantic* in the same form as in the *Works* except that the date "1750" was under the title. The weirdness was rather feeble, but the pictures of the New England countryside were good. Whittier still had his ability to choose the right details from his memory of what he had seen and to present them with simplicity and clarity.

As election day approached he declined a nomination as candidate for Presidential Elector but allowed his name to be used as one of the vice-presidents of the Massachusetts Blaine and Logan Club.[40] He was not unaware of the corruption in the Republican Party, but he could not follow the reasoning of the Independents, or "Mugwumps," who were supporting Cleveland. "Why did they not stay in our party and reform it, instead of joining one so much more corrupt?" was his question, and he was pained that Samuel E. Sewall, James Freeman Clarke, James Russell Lowell, Thomas Wentworth Higginson, George William Curtis, and the sons of William Lloyd Garrison had, as he phrased it, "gone over to the enemy."

Even more fatal to the chances of a Republican victory were the votes drawn from the Republican Party by the Prohibition candidate, John P. St. John. Until this election the Prohibition Party had never received more than ten thousand votes, but now women came to its aid. There were many women delegates at its convention, and its platform included woman suffrage. It was endorsed by the Woman's Christian Temperance Union, which thus took, as its president phrased it, "a position for God in politics," against the advice of Whittier, who wrote to Frances Willard begging her not to take this position. He could not vote for St. John "at the risk of aiding Cleveland and the *Liquor interest*," and he thought that the cause of Temperance could be best promoted in the states. The Prohibition candidates received 151,809 popular votes. Whittier thought the campaign "a very unpleasant one" — a rather mild statement — and was glad when it was over. He was of course vexed with the result and wished that a "cleaner" man than Cleveland had been elected.[41]

There was one practical matter to be attended to immediately after the election. Whittier's nephew, the bothersome Lewis H. Caldwell, might lose his position in the New York Custom House to some deserving Democrat. Whittier appealed to George William Curtis, one of the Mugwumps who had "gone over to the enemy" and to Richard S. Spofford, who had been an unsuccessful Democratic candidate for Congress, to use their influence to help Caldwell keep his position, but Caldwell was soon out of work and once more on his uncle's hands. "I think Uncle Sam is better able to carry him than myself," was Whittier's resigned comment, "but there's no help for it."[42]

The election had not stopped the current wave of interest in Spiritualism. Mrs. Fields was amazed at the "new people and the new kinds of mind engaged in solemn consideration of the subject" — perhaps this was a gentle reproof to Whittier, who had made a rather light comment when a woman arrived just as he was mentioning her in a letter: "An amazing coincidence which the Psychical Researchers might make a note of." But he listened to what people had to say about it and read current articles, including one by James R. Nichols in *Science News and Journal of Chemistry* and the Reports of the British Society for Psychical Research. An English woman called to see him and told him that she hoped that the investigation of occult phenomena would help to explain Spiritualism. Isabelle Beecher Hooker came to Amesbury to lecture on Spiritualism and spent the night at Whittier's. He made no comment on the lecture, which he probably did not attend, but said of Mrs. Hooker, "She is a Beecher and rather cranky, I imagine . . . She is not like Mrs. Stowe." Celia Thaxter was going to seances and receiving messages. Whittier himself said that he longed to get some message from his loved ones but felt that he must wait God's time. He believed, however, that there was such a thing as communion with the dead and that there was a prophecy of a coming revelation in spiritualistic phenomena.[43]

In the spring, Edgar Parker, who had done a head-and-shoulders portrait of Whittier ten years earlier, was commissioned by Charles F. Coffin to paint a life-size, seated portrait for the Friends' School (Moses Brown) in Providence. Whittier did some posing, and the artist evidently made some use of the earlier portrait. Although Parker had no formal training, he did excellent work, and this portrait of Whittier has been described as "the least known and yet the finest painting ever made of the poet." Parker worked on it during the summer, and the dedication took place October 24. Whittier declined an invitation and wrote that if the portrait had the miraculous power of locomotion attributed to medieval pictures, it would feel constrained to walk out of its frame and seek a humbler place than its position between busts of John Bright and Elizabeth Fry.

It was well that he declined the invitation. He would have found the exercises fatiguing. They occupied most of the day, beginning at 10:30 with an oration by Thomas W. Chase, president of Haverford College. There was adjournment until 2:30, when the school sang "Mark, the Merry Elves of Fairy Land," the relevance of which to the occasion is not clear, and the portrait was accepted by Augustine Jones. Whittier's letter was read, followed by letters from a long list of distinguished persons including Matthew Arnold and Charles W. Eliot. John Bright wrote that he felt it an honor that his bust should stand near Whittier's portrait. Oliver Wendell Holmes held no living countryman in higher esteem. John Boyle O'Reilly revered Whittier as a man and a poet. James Russell Lowell sent a sonnet, "To J. G. Whittier."

When it was decided to print the proceedings, Chase sent a copy of his oration to Whittier and asked for suggestions and corrections, "with a view to historical accuracy and a desire to hand down to after days a juster view both of thy aims and thy achievements.'' It may have been this zeal for accuracy along with the tone of the oration that led Whittier to think eight years later of asking Chase to write his biography.[44]

Whittier was at Oak Knoll in the late fall and early winter. Among the usual numerous callers was Edmund Gosse, whom Whittier described as a ''bright, modest young man, handsome and genial.'' Whittier might have spoken of him less pleasantly if he had foreseen that the visit would be the subject of an article in *The Bookman* in 1899. Gosse found the Danvers railway station dismal and the winter landscape of a most forbidding bleakness. Oak Knoll looked ''distinctly sinister,'' an impression strengthened by the reception he and his companion received. They rang the bell, and after a long pause the door opened, an unprepossessing dog came out, and the door closed. They rang again, the door was opened slightly, and a voice ''of no agreeable timbre'' asked what they wanted. They explained that they had come by appointment to see Mr. Whittier, and the door was closed. Finally a hard-featured woman admitted them, growling, into the parlor. Then their troubles were over, for Whittier appeared, ''with all the report had ever told of gentle sweetness and dignified cordial courtesy.'' Gosse saw no sign of age or feebleness. He noticed the large and luminous black eyes, fringed with thick black eyelashes that curved inward, and black eyebrows, making a vivid black bar that contrasted with the white hair and beard. Whittier's face did not have the immobility often seen in old people; ''waves of mood were often sparkling across his features.'' He told Gosse that he had enjoyed his *Life of Thomas Gray*, whose life was so quiet and sequestered that it was Quakerly and whose career had fullness and significance although to the outward world it would have seemed without movement.[45]

On Whittier's birthday a heavy snow storm kept many callers away. It also furnished a contrast to the seventy-seven roses sent by the Junior Class of the Girls' High School of Boston, which Whittier acknowledged in six lines of verse:

> The sun of life is sinking low;
> Without a winter's falling snow,
>   Within your summer roses fall.
> The heart of age your offering cheers,
> You count in flowers my many years,
>   God bless you, one and all!

Forty letters came from abroad, and a few days later a characteristically lively letter from Gail Hamilton. It began, ''Dear Angel. Is it your birthday? Thank heaven you were born! Thank Heaven a thousand times that you will never die, for the Kingdom of Heaven is within you.''[46]

Portrait of Matthew Franklin Whittier (1812-1883), painted c.1850. (Courtesy of Whittier Home, Amesbury)

Whittier Home, Amesbury, showing addition of 1884, and as it appears today.

Illustration by Edwin A. Abbey for which Whittier wrote "Banished from Massachusetts," which appeared in *Harper's Weekly*, March 15, 1884. (Courtesy of Lawrence Public Library)

XXXIII
1885 - 86

Whittier was beginning to feel lonely at Oak Knoll. He longed to see old friends and neighbors, especially those who had known Elizabeth, and to feel the nearness to her and his mother which came from being in their home. He planned to spend more time in Amesbury and had bought the next house to his on Friend Street, separated from his by a narrow street. In spite of missing the comfort of the furnace at Oak Knoll, he went to Amesbury in December and stayed through the first two weeks in January. As he should have known, there were not many of his old neighbors left, and he was pleased to get letters, in old familiar handwriting, from people whom he had long known and loved. He was getting quite enough from strangers and new acquaintances, at least twenty a day.[1]

One letter was from P. T. Barnum, who wanted Whittier's signature. Whittier did more than he was asked and wrote a letter which Barnum promised to hand down to his descendants. He thought that he and Whittier had something in common; his chief pleasure was to give the public, especially young people, instruction and pleasure, with the poison left out, as Whittier had always done.[2]

Whittier returned to Oak Knoll in the third week of January and stayed until April. He was, as he described himself with an old Yankee word, "miserable" and under a doctor's care. He did not feel able to write an ode to the memory of Charles George Gordon, which had been requested by Charles C. Reed of London. He greatly admired General Gordon, whose journal of experiences in the Soudan he had read a year earlier, and he liked the picture of him in Edna Dean Proctor's "El Mahdi": "brave, generous, and self-sacrificing, against the background of vacillating English and cruel and cowardly Egyptians." In the letter declining to write the ode, General Gordon was a "Providential man" and "his mission in an unbelieving and selfish age revealed the mighty power of faith in God, self abnegation, and the enthusiasm of humanity. For centuries no grander figure has crossed the disk of our planet." If he had the opportunity he would urge Tennyson to write a threnody about General Gordon, by which he meant something like Tennyson's "Ode on the Duke of Wellington." Reed sent this part of the letter to Tennyson, who wrote a four-line epitaph, which he sent to Whittier and later altered.

The publication of the part of Whittier's letter praising General Gordon brought out letters of protest from John Bright to Whittier and to Reed, to whom he wrote, "I am astonished and disturbed that my friend Whittier should for a moment have thought of writing anything in his [General Gordon's] honor, for such writing must be in direct contrast or opposition to all his admirable poems in which justice and mercy are held up for the acceptance of mankind." Whittier now regretted that his letter had been published, but only because it had disturbed Bright. Gordon was a "better man than David or Joshua — he was humane and never put his prisoners into brick-kilns nor under hammers," and he wrote to Reed: "He was born a soldier as I was a Quaker. I wish I could feel that I have been as true to my conception of duty as he has been to his."[3]

George Cable came to see him, and Whittier was as favorably impressed as he had been two years ago: "Ten righteous men like him would save the South." Another Southern writer also came to see him, Mary Murfree, who, under the pen name of Charles Egbert Craddock, had been writing popular local color stories. Whittier did not like her *Where the Battle Was Fought*, but he thought, as did most reviewers of that time, that *The Prophet of the Great Smoky Mountain* was excellent; still, on the whole he preferred Sarah Orne Jewett's stories, which were "charmingly written, natural, and restful." He wished that he might meet Edith Thomas, who he thought had a divine gift; *A New Year's Masque and Other Poems* had just been published and seemed to him more than a promise, an assurance.[4]

Whittier visited the Pickards in Portland and then returned to Amesbury too unwell to go about much in the beautiful June weather, which he welcomed after the long and to him bitter winter and spring. There was writing to be done and there were requests and invitations to be declined. He was invited by the Collector of the Port of Boston to join a group of James Russell Lowell's friends who were going out in a Revenue Cutter in Boston Harbor to meet him on his return from England. Whittier of course replied that illness kept him from accepting the invitation, and he could only express the joy which all shared as Lowell came back bringing from the Old World "such honors as were never before bestowed upon a representative of our country." He was also asked to write, on short notice, a poem to be printed with others in *The Literary World*. He wrote what he called "some hurried lines" which he thought had no value beyond the good will which prompted them.[5] Whittier had warned Lowell two years earlier that if he didn't return soon — he had been in England since 1880 and in Spain three years before that — he would find no one but strangers to welcome him. In "Welcome" he said that he was speaking for those who had died during Lowell's absence: Bayard Taylor, Emerson, Longfellow, and Fields. Stanzas added later for the Riverside Edition referred to Wendell Phillips and Lydia Maria Child.

An invitation to the two hundred fiftieth anniversary on June 10 of the settlement of Newbury was declined in a long letter which showed Whittier's acquaintance with Newbury and Newburyport people, history, and legends.

Age, illness, and his imagined nearness to death cast no tinge of gloom or weakness over his prose style. This letter succeeded in being lively and amusing without implying disrespect for the early settlers of the town, whom Whittier described as the "best and selectest of Puritanism." In Newbury, as elsewhere, Puritanism had its humorous side. The minister at the First Church in Newbury, Leonard Withington, who had recently died in his ninety-sixth year and whom Whittier called a "Puritan of the Puritans," once startled and shamed his brother ministers who were advocating the enforcement of the Fugitive Slave Law by giving them a form of prayer to be used while catching runaway slaves.[6]

"The Two Elizabeths" was written for the unveiling of the marble bust of Elizabeth Fry by William Theed of London at the Friends' School in Providence. When Whittier sent the poem to the *Atlantic* he supposed that the unveiling would take place before the magazine was issued, but there was delay in the shipment and the poem was seen by the public before it was read at the ceremony.[7]

In July Whittier went to the Asquam House in Holderness with the Cartlands and Addie Caldwell. He enjoyed it less than the two previous summers when Mrs. Fields had been there — at least he told her so in a letter which showed that he had not lost his youthful skill and pleasure in writing affectionate letters to women. "I wonder whether I have not asked too much of thee, dear friend — whether I have any claim upon the love and friendship which have made my life in its late autumn beautiful as its spring time."[8]

One day four college students on a hiking trip, loaded down with camping equipment, came up the driveway and stood in front of the hotel admiring the view. Whittier came out, chatted with them, and asked where they were going. One of them had a hunting knife with a broad shiny blade. Whittier asked to look at it, and as he turned it over in his hand he said, "This reminds me of the knives that Norwegians are said to use when they fight duels. The two men are tied together around the waist. Knives are given them and they slash at each other." It was not the kind of remark that the young men expected of a Quaker poet.[9] They could not know that Whittier was remembering the account of a fight in Bayard Taylor's "Lars," which he had read twelve years earlier.

Late in July Whittier and the others went to the Sturtevant Farm on a hill overlooking Center Harbor to stay until the middle of August or later if the Cates had not returned to Amesbury from their summer home at Rye Beach. On a hill a short walk from the house was a huge white pine tree with a wooden seat built around it. Whittier often sat there looking at Squam Lake and the Sandwich Mountains and Red Hill in the background.[10] One evening when the guests were talking about the big tree, Whittier said that he had just written "a little ditty" about it. Gertrude Cartland asked if they might hear it, and he read "The Wood Giant" in a voice deeper and fuller than his conversational tones. The thirteenth stanza, following a description of the sound of the wind in the branches, he read with especial emphasis:

Was it the half-unconscious moan
Of one apart and mateless,
The weariness of unshared power,
The loneliness of greatness?

"The Wood Giant" was printed in the *Independent* September 13. The editor, William Hayes Ward, had sent Whittier a check soon after Ulysses S. Grant's death, asking him to write a tribute to Grant or, if he did not, to keep the check and send verses on some other topic at his leisure, and this check paid for "The Wood Giant." The editor of the *North American Review* also asked for a tribute to Grant. Whittier did not write a tribute for either magazine but wrote a letter to George W. Cate to be read at a memorial service in Amesbury. Grant, he said, was a "silent, modest, unselfish man" who never boasted, but at the call of duty "he gave to his country all he had to give," and it was largely due to his "patriotic devotion, skill, and indomitable will" that the nation was now united. Later, Whittier presented an engraving of Grant to the Amesbury Grand Army Post.[11]

He returned to Amesbury in late August and went to Oak Knoll a few days later to face a pile of unanswered letters. Before answering them he wrote a birthday letter to Oliver Wendell Holmes, who thought that it was so good that he sent it to the *Boston Transcript*. "My father," Whittier wrote, "used to tell of a poor innocent in his neighborhood, who, whenever he met him would fall to laughing, crying, and dancing. 'I can't help it, sir. I can't help it. I'm so glad you and I are alive!' And I, like the poor fellow, can't help telling thee that I am glad thee and I are alive — glad that thy hand has lost nothing of its cunning and thy pen is still busy. And I say in the words of Solomon of old, 'Rejoice, O young man in thy youth and let thy heart cheer thee in the days of thy youth,' but don't exult over thy seniors who have not found the elixir of life and are growing old and past their usefulness!"[12]

Plans being made for a reunion of students at Haverhill Academy 1827-1830 were another reminder that he was old. Whittier would not have started the affair, which he thought would give as much pain as pleasure; those who went would miss so many whom they had known and would find it hard to connect their aged selves with their boyhood and girlhood. He explained this to Evelina Bray Downey, whom he was evidently delegated to notify. He obviously did not want her to come, although he properly said that he wished she might. It is easy to guess that he did not want to see an old woman whom he remembered as an attractive girl that he had almost fallen in love with and whom he had immortalized in "A Sea Dream."

Mrs. Downey came to the reunion, in spite of Whittier's hint. Mary Emerson Smith Thomas sent a letter. At the reunion ceremonies September

10, which began at two o'clock and lasted three hours, Whittier was the center of attention. A poem of welcome was addressed to him and he responded with "The Reunion," which he had brought Abby J. Woodman with him to read. It lacked the light touch and tender humor that Holmes could have given it, but there were perceptive lines about old age and, inevitably, concluding stanzas about the life after death, which, it may be hoped, did not interfere with anyone's enjoyment of the collation which immediately followed. Then the invited guests arrived, each of whom had to be presented to Whittier. One of them, Dr. John Crowell, read "My Psalm." It was now five o'clock, too late for Whittier to visit the Academy building. Mrs. West sang "Auld Lang Syne," with nearly all — presumably not Whittier — joining in the chorus, and the party was over. He had given a signed photograph to each of the schoolmates and had agreed to let one of them, Harrison Plummer, paint his portrait for the Public Library.

The reunion was more exciting than he had wished or expected, and he spent a sleepless night, and was tired and ill the next day. Part of his fatigue probably came from his increasing deafness. When he was in a group it was a painful effort to try to understand and to make the right replies when he was not sure that he had heard right.[13]

Demands for help and sympathy were now incessant. He was supporting Lewis Caldwell, "that uncomfortable nephew" who had lost his position in the Custom House. He was also helping Lewis Caldwell's sister, Mary Patten, with her business affairs. He sent a check for fifty dollars to Hampton Normal and Agricultural Institute.[14]

One gift that he made, after some hesitation, soon caused him considerable annoyance. He was asked, as other prominent persons were, to contribute not more than ten dollars toward the purchase of a horse and buggy for Walt Whitman. When *Leaves of Grass* had first appeared thirty years earlier, he had not been especially interested in it and had made no public comment. He now consulted Oliver Wendell Holmes, who regarded some of Whitman's poems as cynical examples of indecent exposure but recognized that Whitman had served well in the cause of humanity, and comparing the situation to the parable of the Good Samaritan, thought that Whitman, who stood "stark naked before the public in 'Leaves of Grass,' " could be, not set on an ass, but "put in a go-cart of some kind or other, which is nearly the same thing." Whittier had come to a similar conclusion and sent his contribution before receiving Holmes' letter, saying that he was sorry to hear of the physical disabilities of the man who had tenderly nursed the wounded Union soldiers and had as tenderly sung the dirge of their great captain. "I have no doubt, in his lameness, that a kind, sober-paced roadster would be more serviceable to him than the untamed, rough-jolting Pegasus he has been accustomed to ride without check or snaffle." The letter concluded, "I need not say perhaps that I have been pained by some portions of W. W's writings, which for his own sake, and that of his readers, I wish could be omitted." Whittier wrote "Confidential" on the letter, intending that his contribution should not be given publicity, but it appeared on a list with the thirty-one others and resulted in newspaper reports that he approved passages in Whitman's poetry that had what he called an "evil tendency." He wrote an indignant letter for publication in the *Boston Evening Transcript* and then evidently changed his mind, perhaps wisely deciding that the less said the better. In this letter he said that he did not know Whitman personally and had very slight knowledge of his writings, "which, while indicating a certain virile vigor and originality" seemed to him often "indefensible from a moral point of view." He had heard of Whitman's work as a nurse in Union hospitals during the Civil War and had read "his tender tribute to the memory of President Lincoln," and had sent his contribution without expecting it to be publicized. "With no wish to sit in judgment upon others, and making all charitable allowance possible for differences of temperament, education, and association," he confessed that he strongly disliked what was called "the sensual school of literature and art." Dr. Holmes wished him to say that his gift was also solely "an act of kindness to a disabled author, implying no approval whatever of his writings."[15]

One of the persistent Whittier myths is that he threw *Leaves of Grass* into the fire. It evidently was started by a remark that Whitman made to Horace Traubel in 1888. "I know from Sanborn, I think, that Whittier years ago started to read the *Leaves* and when he came to what are called the indelicate passages threw the book into the fire."[16] This is rather flimsy evidence to prove the truth of a story inconsistent with Whittier's habits and temperament. He was neither impetuous nor theatrical, and he was too interested in good fires — he would never let anyone touch the Franklin stove in the Garden Room — to spoil a fire by throwing a book into it.

He delayed returning to Amesbury until Mrs. Cate could find a new hired girl, telling her that she would have quite enough to do to take care of one man.[17] He was in Amesbury on November 10 when he replied to an invitation to a meeting of the Essex Club, a Republican group. His letter included shrewd political comment and an eloquent and idealistic description of an America in which the Republican Party would not be needed. "Then may the language which Milton addressed to his countrymen two centuries ago be applied to the United States, 'Go on, hand in hand, O peoples, never to be disunited; be the praise and heroic song of all posterity. Join your invincible might to do worthy and god-like deeds; and then he who seeks to break your Union, a cleaving curse be his inheritance.' "[18]

He dreaded the long dark winter more and more as he grew older — an attitude hard for a later generation, which scarcely knows what darkness is, to understand. But he could still do a good deal of reading and get enthusiastic about it. He read a book for children by Jane Andrews, who conducted a private school in Newburyport far in advance of its time in relating the individual to the world at large. Whittier thought that there was nothing in juvenile literature equal to *Ten Boys Who Lived on the Road from Long Ago to Now*, which told the story of past centuries in a style which a child could not fail to understand and in which adults would find an irresistible charm. A few weeks later he found Elizabeth Stuart Phelps' "Madonna of the Tubs," in the December *Harper's*, an admirable story "in spite of some of her peculiar mannerisms."[19] It was a sentimental story of a fisherman supposed lost at sea who reappeared on Christmas Eve when a rich young society woman had just arrived at his house with gifts for his impecunious wife and children and who miraculously found her estranged lover — and who learned the lesson of love from the fisherman's wife, the Madonna of the Tubs.

Soon after returning to Oak Knoll he sent "Requital" to the *Independent*. He hoped that it was an adequate return for the one hundred fifty dollars that he had already received. He described it as an Oriental legend which he greatly admired, and he was sure that its lesson must be good.[20] Whittier's intention of teaching a lesson was so obvious that only a generation which liked to be preached to would find that the poem had anything to say to them.

Whittier's seventy-eighth birthday was cold and stormy, but there were many visitors — perhaps not as many as if the weather had been better, for he had time in intervals to think of friends who had died and to feel lonely. Then he wondered if he could be the little black-haired boy on the old Haverhill farm. The inevitable reporter came and found him in the parlor before a wood fire. There was the usual question about his health and the usual answer; it was not the best, and he had pains in his head. He was receiving thirty letters a day, most of which should be answered, and two thousand requests annually for autographs, which he could refuse if he wished. Among the birthday letters was one from a Southern woman who cursed him along with all "mean, hateful Yankees." But there was a telegram from the Southern Forestry Association telling him that in remembrance of his birthday a live oak tree had been planted in his memory, which like the leaves of the tree would be forever green.[21]

The year 1886 began with sundry troubles. The gas lighting system at Oak Knoll failed one night and only some candles which Mrs. Fields had sent saved the household from having to go to bed in the dark. He went to Amesbury early in January and was there when an ice storm did heavy damage to his six elm trees, nearly ruining two and stripping the others of many of their branches. During the night it seemed to him that he heard the crash of falling branches every moment. But he was able to enjoy the scenery the next morning with youthful enthusiasm. The pine woods on a nearby hillside were a sight that the oldest inhabitant had never seen. The branches swept smoothly down, "every twig and needle encrusted and glistening — a vast, glass forest, such as might have been seen by Vathek in the underworld of Eblis."

There were all sorts of visitors. One day a Mormon woman came, whom he found intelligent on all subjects but Mormonism, on which she was a "sheer fanatic." She had "the sixth part of a husband in Bishop Wells of Utah and an undivided part of his thirty-two children." She told him that everyone in Salt Lake City was reading Elizabeth Stuart Phelps' "The Gates Ajar," which he thought was having a deservedly large sale although it was not wholly to his taste.[22]

"The Homestead," in the February *Atlantic*, was a lament for the past and an impractical appeal for the future. It was the result of the painful impression that he had received the past summer from deserted farmhouses in New Hampshire. The description of the present dreariness was well done; nobody but Whittier, as Sarah Orne Jewett told him, would have thought of the lines

His track, in mould and dust of drouth
On floor and hearth the squirrel leaves.

As in Oliver Goldsmith's "The Deserted Village," the effect was heightened by contrasts with a happy past reminiscent of Whittier's own boyhood. The last six stanzas were an appeal to young men who had left New England farms to return and never mind the low income; they would have fields, trees, fresh air, and flowers. He told them to

Reclaim the waste and outworn lands
And reign thereon as kings.

This was more poetic than practical. The "skill" that would spare their "toiling hands" and the "chemic aid" of science, perhaps suggested by James R. Nichols' experiments at Haverhill, had not reached the point of making life kingly on a one-family farm. Whittier at this time really believed that the farmers of New England were better off on their poor soil than those on the rich lands of the West; he thought that they lived comfortably and had no mortgages on their farms. However, four years later he advised his cousins at Oak Knoll against farming: "It doesn't pay at all. More than a thousand Vermont farmers have run away and left their homes and farms to the squirrels and woodchucks."[23]

He returned to Oak Knoll, where a lame knee, which forced him to carry a cane, kept him confined to the house most of the time. Before leaving Amesbury he had got Fred Brown to print a new poem, "Revelation," to save the trouble of copying it, but then he made so many changes that correcting it was even more trouble, and he wasn't sure that it was legible when he sent it to the *Atlantic*. He had crossed out entire stanzas and made five changes in wording.

He was more satisfied with "Revelation" than with some of his poems that have proved more popular, thinking that it might be interesting as an expression of his deepest religious feeling, and, in accord with his usual way of evaluating poetry, might help some inquiring spirit.[24] It was suggested by a passage in the *Journal of George Fox*, who, overcome by the thought that Nature was the source of all things, rejoiced when a voice within told him that there was a living God who made all things. Similarly in "Revelation," belief in Nature as the source brought fear because Nature did not care about man and unpitying energy could not be reached by prayer, but a voice within said that God was near and that His Spirit moved the Universe. "Revelation" has never been one of Whittier's more popular poems, but it must have brought comforting assurance to thoughtful people in a time when discoveries of laws and forces of Nature seemed to throw a shadow over religious faith.

The winter was a long, hard one which left him so unwell that he began again to think about his biography. He would have preferred that none should be written — "Why should I not be left in peace?" — but that could hardly be expected. The constant stream of articles about him in periodicals, along with the books by Underwood and Kennedy, was conclusive and painful evidence that his life was public property. Before choosing a writer he determined that Ticknor and Co. should be the publisher; William D. Ticknor had published his *Lays of My Home* in 1843, when Abolitionists were unpopular and their books unprofitable. He also decided to turn over all his papers to Samuel T. Pickard, who would select whatever he thought suitable for use with some supervision from Whittier himself. The biographer would thus be badly handicapped. He would not be able to study Whittier's early work, as Underwood had tried to do, and he would not be given the materials necessary for complete and impartial treatment of Whittier's life and work. Another handicap would be lack of source material before 1860. Whittier had destroyed a great mass of letters without looking them over. Many were private and confidential, and the easiest way was to make a bonfire of them all. Unauthorized use of letters seemed to him a breach of trust, and he wished that his own letters to thousands of correspondents might also be disposed of.

He now thought of several possible writers and decided on William Dean Howells, who, however, was under contract to write for the Harpers. Deferring until later the question of who would do the writing, he then decided to bequeath his papers to the Pickards and to let Pickard start working on them while Ticknor would try to find a writer to "reinforce" him. The final decision was not made until five years later, and it was one that could not be carried out.[25]

By the last of March his lame knee seemed to be getting better, and he went to Amesbury, thinking that by the time the trailing arbutus was in bloom he would be able to go out and pick some as usual. But early in April there was a northeast storm with high wind, there was no sign of green in the fields or dooryards, and he had a bad cold. He was quite aware that he was getting to be an "old boy;" if he lived until December he would be in his eightieth year.[26]

Alice Freeman, now in her last year as president of Wellesley College, wrote to him that he had been mentioned frequently at the College during the past week. A new dormitory was to be named "Norumbega Cottage" in honor of Eben H. Hosford, Chairman of the Board of Visitors and one of the most generous benefactors of the College, who had published an article about his discovery of the site of the mythical city of Norumbega, the subject of Whittier's poem by that name in 1869. There was to be a housewarming, and the thirty girls living in the dormitory wanted him to be there. He of course replied that he could not attend and sent a sonnet for the occasion, "Norumbega Hall," with a note explaining that he had no time to copy or improve it; it was dated April 16, two days later than the date of Alice Freeman's letter. The handwriting was as poor as his usual handwriting at the time, and in the seventh line "beautiful" had been crossed out and "marvellous" written above it. Nevertheless Alice Freeman had facsimiles printed to distribute to the guests. She herself lived in the dormitory, and the sonnet referred to her as a Princess like the heroine of Tennyson's "The Princess," a comparison often made at that time.[27]

St. Gregory's Guest and Recent Poems, the last volume with previously uncollected poems before the seven volumes of poetry and prose in 1888, was entered for copyright April 28, dedicated to General Samuel C. Armstrong. Most of the poems in the volume had been printed previously. Among those that had not were "Hymns of the Brahmo Somaj." Whittier had missed seeing Mozoomdar, the prophet of the Brahmo Somaj, in 1883, but had evidently read some of his writings and speeches containing hymns which he now paraphrased. These show that his enthusiasm for the movement, "the Lord's doing — the blade before the full corn in the ear"[28] — did not come from new truth that he found in it but from its rephrasing and reinforcing of Christian belief.

He hoped that Houghton Mifflin would not lose by publishing the book "in so elegant a dress" — wrappers of white vellum paper with title in gilt within an elaborate gilt frame. He thought that if he didn't buy copies himself, they would remain on the publishers' shelves.[29] The book sold well; there was a second printing two years later.

Whittier returned to Oak Knoll late in April. He was still lame and making use of the dozen canes that had been sent him at various times but, he assured Gail Hamilton, he was using only one at a time. He had now had, he said, two of Mrs. Thrale's "three warnings": he was deaf and lame. But he was grateful every day that he still had his eyesight and that life and nature were still sweet and beautiful.[30]

He was in Amesbury in early July to witness with some amusement the festivities when parts of Salisbury, including Salisbury Point and the Salisbury section of the Mills Village, were annexed to Amesbury. He had favored the change and had helped to bring it about. His name headed a petition to the Legislature in January, and when he could not be in Amesbury in February to meet a committee from the Legislature, he wrote a letter pointing out that the change would be an improvement for the library, post office, roads, schools, police department, and business and industries. His judgment on this point was sound. The library served one town and part of the other and could get municipal support from neither. There was a Salisbury High School with forty pupils and an Amesbury High School with forty-one. Market Square, the business and industrial center, was half in Amesbury and half in Salisbury. The Legislature was slow in acting, but the bill was finally passed and signed by the governor June 16. A telegram came at 1:30, and a few hours later a crowd had gathered in the square near the railroad station to welcome the committee that had represented the town. The chairman was put on a horse and paraded through the streets with a brass band. This was merely a spontaneous affair; the planned celebration was July 5, and Whittier wrote the previous day, "We are going to have a grand celebration here tomorrow. West Salisbury and Salisbury Point are annexed to Amesbury and we feel bound to burn powder and make a great deal of noise about it. We are now almost large enough for a city, but I am not fat enough for an alderman." The celebration, announced in the form of a wedding invitation, "at home July 5," was a success, with sports, band concerts, and parade, including antiques and horribles, one of them a reference to President Cleveland's honeymoon.[31]

During the late summer and fall, Whittier was feeling the discontent that comes to old people because life isn't what it used to be. He went to the White Mountains, staying first at the Asquam House in Holderness, where he was lonely in spite of some of his friends' being there and begged Mrs. Fields to come and occupy the one vacant room. When she did not come, he thought that he would not stay long; he felt that he was living idly and uselessly and was ashamed of being only a looker-on when there was so much to be done. After a few weeks he went to Sturtevants' at Center Harbor and resigned himself to the steady stream of pilgrims.[32]

By this time he had written "Samuel J. Tilden," which was printed in the *Boston Transcript* August 4 and the present revised form in the *Portland Transcript* two weeks later. It was more of a character analysis than one would expect in verses immediately after the subject's death, but the emphasis was on Tilden's good qualities.

He lamented that he was not younger or a millionaire when he heard of the illness of General Armstrong, who he thought had been working beyond his strength and should have a rest. His friends must redouble their efforts to maintain the school. He did so himself, sending one hundred dollars to the Hampton Fund, and later, just before Christmas, fifty dollars in payment, he said, for a barrel of pitch pine kindlings which he sorely needed in Amesbury.[33] When he read in *The Southern Workman* that Rain-in-the-Face, an Indian chief who had been one of the leaders in the attack on Custer at Little Big Horn, had applied for admission to the school, he was deeply moved by the fact that only ten years after the massacre, one of the fiercest chiefs should wish to learn the ways of peace and the arts of civilization. He wrote "On the Big Horn" as a supplement to Longfellow's "The Revenge of Rain-in-the-Face," in the same meter and with the same rhyme scheme.

He spent most of the autumn at Oak Knoll. He was increasingly sensitive to the beauty of nature, and the Oak Knoll woods had never been more beautiful, but he had a series of colds, he was saddened by realizing that his life had not been what he had dreamed when he was young, and he was lonely: his world seemed at times to consist of only a few dear friends. One of them was of course Mrs. Fields, and when he did not find her at home when he called at her house in Boston, he wrote five stanzas[34] which she published after his death in her *Whittier. Notes on His Life and His Friendships*, although their intimacy would suggest that he did not intend them for the public:

> I missed the love-transfigured face,
>> The glad, sweet smile so dear to me,
>> The clasp of greeting warm and free:
> What had the round world in their place?

"The Bartholdi Statue" was written for the dedication of the Statue of Liberty on October 28. Like most of Whittier's poems for an occasion, it was suitable in tone and in length. He intended to change one line in the proof, which was the result of "the exigency of rhyme" but the proof never came, and the poem as read at the dedication, printed in the *Independent*, and copied widely in newspapers had a factual error. It referred to the flag of France as the fleur-de-lis, which had been the flag of the monarchy. He intended to change

> In peace beneath thy fleur de lis

to

> In peace across the severing sea.

In the Riverside Edition the line was changed to refer to the flag of the French Republic:

> In peace beneath thy Colors Three.

Whittier planned to go to Amesbury early in November to vote, but he declined to go to Cambridge to receive an honorary degree of Doctor of Laws at the two hundred fiftieth anniversary of Harvard College. He did not refuse to accept the degree, as he might have done, on the same ground as President Cleveland who said that he had only a scanty education and could not figure as an eminent lawyer. He simply refused to be present and evidently regarded the matter as relatively unimportant. It was still Quaker practice to avoid the customary titles of honor, as it had been from the time of George Fox. Harvard's Charles W. Eliot is said to have preferred Whittier's poetry to Homer's, and he thought that Whittier's presence to receive an honor as a representative of literature would add greatly to the occasion. Whittier was assured, through Harriet Minot Pitman, that he need not be in Sanders Theater more than half an hour, that he would not be expected to speak, that he would have a reserved seat, and that he could leave quietly whenever he wished without attracting attention. "Harvard *cannot* accept your refusal."

Harvard accepted his refusal and gave him his degree in absentia, the only one of the honorary degrees so conferred and the one that received the most enthusiastic applause. Men leaped to their feet and shouted approval, and the cheers died away only to rise a second and third time.

The enthusiasm was unquestionably sincere and can have caused no surprise. James Russell Lowell was expressing popular sentiment when he wrote to Whittier a week later, "I was thoroughly glad that Harvard honored herself by putting you on her roll of honor." M. A. DeWolfe Howe came to Harvard from Lehigh University in 1886. As he looked back fifty years later he wrote, "It was starting in an afterglow from genuine lights to begin an acquaintance with Boston while Holmes and Whittier and Lowell were still living and Emerson and Longfellow had but recently quitted the scene. . . The embers of a great tradition had by no means lost their warmth and light."[35]

Two letters on November 22 show quite different moods on the same day. In one letter he hoped that there was nothing ominous in the recent marriage of a seventy-two-year-old neighbor in a thunder storm. In the other he described the beauty of a summer-like day when he managed "to creep into the woods with the squirrels and the belated birds, thankful for this respite from the rigors of winter." He dreaded the coming months of darkness and cold, "but, after all, nothing is really as bad as our fears."[36]

It was a day like this that he described in "A Day," dated November 29. The warmth and beauty made such an impression that it quite shut out his conscientious concern to do good. That he could see so clearly and with such appreciative selectivity at the age of seventy-nine makes one again wish that he had spent more of his life trying to write well, and less trying to give useful instruction. The pictures in the poem were true and blended into a unified whole. The last two stanzas, however, were marred by sentimental exclamations, which were obviously sincere expressions of Whittier's feelings but which kept the reader from his own emotional response.

His seventy-ninth birthday was a quiet one. Whittier sat in front of a fireplace, while his presents were on display in the next room. He gave no impression of infirmity and talked amiably with a reporter from the *Boston*

Journal. He mentioned his recent visit to Boston, where he missed the faces of Whipple, Longfellow, Phillips, Garrison, and a host of friends.

He answered letters from people who sent poetic tributes. Elizabeth Cavazza's was "too beautiful for its subject." J. S. Cutler, whose poetry he had kindly but firmly criticized eight years earlier, sent him a poem with a "tender and Christian spirit," and again he wrote that he did not deserve the praise and appreciation: "The poem is better than its subject."[37]

Then Christmas came and two hundred letters.

XXXIV
1887 - 88

Whittier's cousins were in Bermuda most of the winter of 1887 while he was at Oak Knoll, shut in by the cold and snow. When they sent him some jasmine blossoms, he sent some to Frances C. Sparhawk and a letter lamenting that he scarcely knew what was going on in the literary, political, or theological world and that while he sometimes felt that he had something to say that needed to be said, he was not strong enough to write.[1]

It was true that he was doing no writing for publication, but he was not unacquainted with current affairs. He was, among other interests, following the conflict between faculty and Board of Visitors at Andover Theological Seminary, where some of the faculty, including the President, were being accused of unfaithfulness to the Andover creed of 1808. Whittier's sympathy was with the faculty and President; he did not see how they could hold to Calvinism and the doctrine of eternal punishment. He himself no longer tried to answer the question of life after death[2] — the same attitude that he took toward psychical research, which was now getting a good deal of public attention. He read the Reports of the Society for Psychical Research which Mrs. William James sent him and also the reports of the British Society and hoped that some clue might be found to the mystery of life, death, and the hereafter, but hardly expected it: "We shall still have to trust and wonder."

Celia Thaxter was being swept along by the wave of interest in Theosophy and sent Whittier a picture of Mohini, whose face, Whittier thought, was a fine one but not strong and gave the impression that he might be cheated by Helena Blavatsky. He revised his opinion and now found all the marvel and mystery of the Orient in the face, which was almost like one's idea of Christ's. But his suspicions of Madame Blavatsky were confirmed when he read Richard Hodgson's article in the *Journal of Psychical Research*, which told of an elaborate system in the official headquarters of the Theosophists by which letters were dropped through cracks in the ceiling or handed through a hidden opening in the wall.[3]

He was still interested in the Temperance cause, which he believed could best be promoted by state rather than national action. His name led the list of signers on a petition to the Massachusetts Legislature for a state constitutional amendment.[4]

He went to Amesbury as usual for Town Meeting in early March and stayed long enough to pick out forty or fifty books to give to the Y.M.C.A.[5] He returned to Oak Knoll and wrote a tribute to Henry Ward Beecher for a memorial volume. The proper thing to say was fortunately Whittier's sincere opinion: "Of Henry Ward Beecher as a reformer and orator, and as a great moral and political force in his day and generation, no words of mine are needed. Our country owes him a deeper debt of gratitude than it has paid or ever can pay him for his noble services in the dark days of the Rebellion. One of the bravest of men, he proved the truth of the adage that the bravest are the tenderest. Apart from his unequalled pulpit successes, his bold and efficient advocacy of temperance and the abolition of slavery entitle him to the grateful remembrances of the nation and of all mankind." But he also knew the other side of Beecher's character and wrote to Mrs. Fields: "He had faults, like all of us, and needed forgiveness; and I think he could say, with David of old, that he would rather fall into the Lord's hands than into the hands of man." [6]

There were two signs of spring early in April. Whittier found the first wild flowers on the south side of an embankment, and he sent a check to the tailor who had made his coats ever since he was editor of the *Pennsylvania Freeman*. [7] As long as he lived, he was neat in appearance, and since he kept an erect posture and did not gain weight, his coats were made with only a slight variation in measurement over forty years.

Perhaps if he had been obliged to struggle against overweight or, like Oliver Wendell Holmes, had enjoyed exercise and admired the athletes in gymnasiums, he might have been more enthusiastic when an athletic field at Swarthmore College was named for him. He appreciated the honor and thought that the Greeks were wise in combining physical with mental culture and that recreation was as necessary in a Friends' school as in any other — but he counselled moderation. "Life is a very earnest thing: and the time allotted to us is too precious to be wasted in idle sports and that unnecessary 'bodily exercise which profiteth nothing'." [8]

He was doing less writing this year than at any time since his boyhood, but requests for poems for occasions continued to come. The Council of the New England Society of Pennsylvania asked for a poem to be read at the next Forefathers' Day dinner. A check for one hundred dollars was enclosed and promptly returned. A few days later a more challenging task was offered. The president of the Constitutional Centennial Commission wanted a poem which could become a new national hymn. [9] This was beyond Whittier's powers in his eightieth year nor is it likely that he could ever have done what no one else has succeeded in doing.

He was in Amesbury during most of May, attending to the business affairs of his niece Mary Patten, who was slowly dying of tuberculosis, and then went to Portland to visit the Pickards at the time of the Friends' Yearly Meeting, where he found much that was uninteresting and distasteful. There was little of the old quiet and reverence, and there was a "melancholy attempt at singing by a woman who had no music in her soul." Many of the speakers, especially those from the West, ignored what had been the fundamental Quaker belief in the Divine Immanence. He was now convinced that it would be impossible to reconcile the differences within the Society of Friends.[10]

He came to Amesbury about the middle of June, was at Oak Knoll briefly late in the month, and went to the White Mountains with the Cartlands early in July. They stayed for a short time at the Senter House but fortunately left before it was burned and went to Sturtevants'. He enjoyed the blueberries and wild raspberries but was disappointed in the weather. There was rain nearly every day, and the ground was too wet to lie on. Still, the rain made the rough, rocky countryside beautiful with fields greener than June and woods with abundant tender green foliage. The mountains were softly outlined and all their harshness gone.[11]

He soon had to think about other things than weather and scenery. His niece Mary Patten died July 26, and he was worried about the future of her children. Then alarming news came from Oak Knoll. On the afternoon of July 28 Phebe rode her horse through the town and then suddenly turned and galloped to the Putnamville railroad station, one of the passenger stations in Danvers, where she tied her horse to a tree and boarded a train to Boston. She could not be found in Boston and no one knew whether she was dead or alive until a telegram came from Mrs. Woodman's cousin, Joseph A. Whittier, that she had arrived at his home in East Saginaw, Michigan. Her mother and one of her aunts went to Michigan and brought her home seated between them lest she attempt another escape.

Mrs. Woodman tried to keep the story out of the newspapers, but after Phebe's return a reporter for the *Boston Globe* came to Danvers and even had the temerity to call at Oak Knoll. First, however, he talked with a local clergyman — not the minister of the church that Phebe attended — who told him all that he knew and perhaps a little more. He said that Phebe was well treated but saw few visitors and only a very few girls whom her mother and aunts — "well-meaning old ladies" — chose for her companions. (Her mother was fifty-nine, her aunt Caroline sixty, and Mary fifty-seven). He thought that she was sensitive about her position as an adopted child. He said that she had been born in New Orleans. She had been left an orphan; her father was an English gentleman who lost his property in the Civil War. (This does not agree with what Mrs. Woodman told the reporter.) Phebe's character was above suspicion.

The reporter then went to Oak Knoll. Mrs. Woodman did not wish him to publish any account of the affair but was evidently glad of the opportunity to reply to the town critics. Phebe's action, she said, was solely the result of outside influences which were "unwisely if not unduly used." If Phebe had not been allowed the liberty of other girls, it was because they (Mrs. Woodman and her sisters) thought that it was for her good. She might have explained that rules had been relaxed: Phebe at one time had not been allowed to go to children's parties if boys were to be present, but in Bermuda the previous winter she had danced with at least one man: Herbert Ward, the future husband of Elizabeth Stuart Phelps. Mrs. Woodman would not tell the name of Phebe's parents nor where she had lived before adoption but said that she came from one of the best families in New England. She was at times sad about her past, which was seldom mentioned at home in her presence, and disparaging references to it by outsiders caused her much grief. Mrs. Woodman finally told the reporter to talk with Rev. Charles B. Rice, the minister of the First Congregational Church, which Phebe attended.

According to him, Phebe's departure was due to a complication of causes, and he believed that it would not have happened if Whittier had been at Oak Knoll. Phebe went to Whittier with all her troubles.

The reporter tried to make a sensational story out of this rather colorless material, and he added a hint of a love angle: it was rumored that her mother favored a "matrimonial alliance" which was distasteful to Phebe.[12]

Whittier was of course much disturbed by Phebe's action. He said that he did not know its "immediate cause," perhaps implying that he knew of some deep-seated trouble. When he saw the article in the *Boston Globe* he wrote a letter to the *Boston Transcript* which he hoped would do no harm even if it did no good. The simple facts of the matter, he wrote, were that his "much-loved young friend" had made, without the consent or knowledge of her family, a visit to her mother's and his cousin, a well known and prominent citizen of East Saginaw, where she had been warmly invited. She now deeply regretted the circumstances of the visit. The letter concluded, "It is only justice to state that from my personal knowledge no other relations than those of mutual affection and regard have ever existed, or still exist, between her and the family where she has lived an exceptionally happy and beautiful life."

Kind letters and offers of assistance had come from his friends, and he was now able to assure them that Phebe was at home again and ashamed of her "flitting." He was pleased to get a note from her, and he wrote to Mrs. Woodman that he hoped that all would settle down and peace and quietness would reign at Oak Knoll. Lucy Larcom thought, as did many people in Danvers, that Phebe had only wanted to "break away and do something sensational."[13] Whatever her motive, she did nothing of the kind again, and Whittier seemed no less fond of her.

After his return to Oak Knoll in September, Whittier made a decision that became controversial. It is evidence of his continuing importance that Howells asked him to use his influence to prevent the hanging of eight anarchists. A bomb had been thrown which killed a number of workingmen and policemen after a meeting in Haymarket Square in Chicago to protest police brutality when strike-breakers were attacked by strikers at the McCormick

Reaper Works. Howells believed that the conviction was unjust; no witness could be found who could connect the defendants with the bomb throwing, and the prosecution based its case on the argument that the defendants, by preaching hatred of policemen and other law-enforcement officials, had in effect caused the death of the policemen for whose murder they were indicted.

Since Whittier had been opposed to capital punishment, his refusal to do what Howells asked has been called negligence and cowardice and part of a reactionary attitude that had come with old age. Whittier, according to Howells' biographer, lacked the courage to speak out against the prevailing mood of vindictive hysteria. His reply to Howells was that he was opposed to capital punishment and had striven to have the death penalty abolished but had never interfered with the law in individual cases. He could see no reason for making the case of the anarchists an exception. This reply was honest and logical. It seemed, however, to suggest that he might make an exception in cases other than that of the anarchists, although he had never done so. But this does not prove that he shared or feared the nation's "mood of vindictive hysteria." Opposition to violence was part of his Quaker faith, and no group that made it part of their creed and practice could conceivably have his sympathy.

Howells appealed to Whittier again November 1, enclosing a paper about the anarchists by a young Chicago minister, which reached the same conclusion that Howells had reached several months earlier: the defendants should have been indicted for conspiracy and not for murder. Howells' appeal did not make use of Whittier's opposition to capital punishment, although Howells himself was opposed to it and referred to the crime as one "which our barbarous laws punish with homicide." He asked Whittier to write to the Governor of Illinois, who he thought was leaning toward clemency, and do "what one great and blameless man may to avert the cruelest wrong that ever threatened our fame as a nation." A letter from Whittier would have great influence. "Write to the Governor I beg you and sign your honored and beloved name strong and full to the letter."[14]

Whittier did not write the letter, but the matter remained in his mind. He referred to it twice in conversations that were reported inaccurately. One was what he called a desultory conversation with a writer for the *New York Times*, and the resulting article seemed unfair to Howells in giving the impression that he thought the crime less detestable and awful than Whittier did. Whittier took the blame upon himself and said that there had been a lack of explicitness on his part. Several years later, in what was evidently another desultory conversation, he was reported as saying that he was not sure that capital punishment was in accord with the New Testament but that at times public order demanded an explicit sacrifice and that he had finally written to Howells that he could not interfere with conditions that he did not understand.[15] It is unlikely that he said that he was not sure that capital punishment was in accord with the New Testament; he had always been sure that it was not.

To the promoters of a new town in southern California named for him he wrote one of his usual graceful letters, with some sound advice. The directors of the Pickering Land and Water Company had voted unanimously May 5 to name their town "Whittier" and one of them, Hervey Lindley, had agreed to write to Whittier for his approval. When the sale of lots began May 19, one lot was reserved for him. The southern California land boom was approaching its peak, and lots soon sold at greatly advanced prices. Lindley was evidently too busy during the spring and summer to write to Whittier, who had just received his letter when he replied October 13, saying pleasant things about the southern California climate and soil and prophesying that the great tide of immigration to that region would fill the vacant lots and outlying farms of the "Quaker City." But he added that he did not use the term in a sectarian sense. He saw good in all denominations and hoped that all would be represented. He also hoped that the Quakerism would be of the "old practical kind" and would not waste its "strength and vitality in spasmodic utterances," and would rely, not on creed and dogma, but on "faithful obedience to the voice of God in the soul." He did not doubt that the evil of intemperance would be kept from fastening itself on the new settlement; he probably knew that remnants of the Wild West still could be found in some of the older California towns. In a postscript he acknowledged the deed of the lot, which at that time was worth perhaps three thousand dollars. A few weeks later he received a copy of the first issue of the town newspaper, printed on white satin.

Early the next year his Oak Knoll cousins were in California with fifteen hundred dollars that he had commissioned them to use to build a house on the lot, but he was beginning to have doubts. He wrote to Mrs. Woodman that if building a house seemed impracticable, she could have a fence put around the lot and a few trees planted. Land values were falling rapidly, and a few weeks later he had begun to suspect that "Whittier" was a "humbug." If it seemed so to Mrs. Woodman she could use the money in any way she wished — spend it in "riotous living" or visiting places worth seeing.[16] Nothing was done with the lot, and it was listed in the inventory of his estate as of no particular value.

Stained glass memorial windows were being installed in St. Margaret's Church, London, with inscriptions by contemporary poets. A Milton window was being made, to be paid for by George W. Childs. Archdeacon Frederick W. Farrar thought that Whittier should be the one to write the inscription, since he "would feel the fullest sympathy for the great Puritan poet," and suggested that Childs make the request of Whittier. Childs sent the letter to Whittier, who wrote the lines and sent them to Childs in their present form. The lines compared favorably with the inscriptions in other windows by Lowell, Tennyson, and Browning, but they did not perfectly fit the scenes in the window, which did not include anything about Milton's prose in defense of a republican form of government. It was this aspect of Milton that Whittier had always admired. Forty-two years earlier he had said in "The Training" that blind Milton approached nearly to his conception of a true hero and quoted from "The Ready and Easy Way to Establish a Free Commonwealth," written when it was clearly evident that the Commonwealth was doomed and the monarchy about to return.[17]

"The Brown Dwarf of Rugen" was sent to *St. Nicholas* before November 3. The editor, Mary Mapes Dodge, had asked Whittier for a poem a year earlier, offering one hundred fifty dollars or any price that he might name. The price paid was two hundred dollars, which Whittier evidently hesitated to accept. "As for its not being worth two hundred dollars," Mrs. Dodge wrote, "I can only say that, in our private estimation, you have won high rank as a humorist by the mere suggestion of such an idea!"[18] Adults were doubtless pleased by a note with the poem warning young readers that bad companions and evil habits, desires, and passions were more to be feared than the elves and trolls told about in the poem, which had frightened children in the past.

It was known by the middle of November that Whittier would be at Oak Knoll on his eightieth birthday. Preparations for its observance began early, and it was soon evident that it would get wide-spread and enthusiastic attention. Whittier made no objection. He welcomed a young writer who came to get material for an article in a Whittier Souvenir Number of the *Newburyport Herald*. Whittier entered the room, his interviewer reported, "tall and straight as a young pine, with the elasticity of youth but blended with the dignity of age." His hair, abundant on the back of his head but not elsewhere, was white, his beard white and carefully trimmed, his eyebrows thick and almost black. He talked a good deal, as deaf people often do; said, as usual, that his health was not good and declined, as usual, to tell which was his favorite among his poems.

December 17 was clear and cold. Whittier, buoyed up by the excitement of the occasion, showed no signs of invalidism. Plenty of guests arrived, including Oliver Ames, Governor of Massachusetts, who came with other politically important persons in a special train of parlor cars provided free of charge by the Boston and Maine Railroad. Whittier mingled with his guests and led them into the dining room, where there was a huge birthday cake flanked by fruit and flowers, including a basket edged with eighty roses and sprays of fern and containing an open book made of white roses with a pen made of violets lying across it with a white satin bookmark on which was inscribed the last stanza of "My Triumph." The Governor cut the cake and was busy at this task for half an hour, while Whittier helped to distribute pieces to the guests.

Whittier got through all this excitement better than he had feared but caught cold and had blinding headaches and neuralgic pains that kept him awake at night. It was impossible to answer the hundreds of letters which, he said, brought his friends' goodwill down upon him like an avalanche. One of them was from Samuel F. Smith, author of "America," who perhaps best defined one reason for all the birthday excitement: "Few men, treading the quiet paths of life and away from the bustle of contending elements, have had so large a share in fashioning public opinions, as that which has fallen to your lot." Whittier's paths had not always been quiet, but the public was beginning to enjoy thinking that they had.[19]

An address of congratulation with hundreds of signatures arrived late. It was started by the Essex Club after a speech by George F. Hoar at a banquet November 12. A letter to Whittier from the Club was written in a bound book, signed by the club members, and taken to Washington, where it was signed by Senators, Representatives, Supreme Court Justices, and many prominent citizens. Whittier wrote a graceful acknowledgment. He was deeply moved by the fact that political and sectional differences seemed to have been set aside by the signers and that the men with whom he had differed in the past had joined with personal and political friends "in this tribute of respect to a private citizen, who loves his whole country and is devoutly thankful that the sun of his closing day shines upon a free and united people."[20]

He was equally moved by an account of the celebration of his birthday by Negroes in Washington and by the resolutions passed there, which seemed to him to be the voice, once dumb in slavery, of millions of his fellow-Americans. He believed, with an optimism which history has not justified, that the time was not far distant when Negroes would have the "free, undisputed rights of American citizenship in all parts of the Union" and their "rightful share in the honors as well as the protection of the government."[21]

The *Boston Daily Advertiser* published a Whittier Birthday Number with letters, poems, and articles by people well-known at that time. James Russell Lowell sent four lines, and Oliver Wendell Holmes sent a sonnet. But the only contribution that would attract the notice of critics of a later day was Walt Whitman's. He evidently felt no resentment over Whittier's reported disapproval of some of his lines.

> As the Greek's signal flame, by antique records told,
> (Tally of many a hard-strained battle, struggle,
>   year — triumphant only at the last),
> Rose from the hill-top, like applause and glory,
> Welcoming in fame some special veteran, hero,
> With rosy tinge reddening the land he'd served,

So I aloft from Mannahatta's ship-fringed shore,
Lift high a kindred brand for thee, Old Poet.

Whitman also wrote "expressly for *Munyon's Illustrated World*" the following which printed it in facsimile:

This the start — the blessed babe, then here
    was born,
This is the house — these the environment, the hills
    and fields, the poplars tall,
Fit stamp of birth — the sense of Sabbath calm, the
    concrete soil, the pure New England air,
Ever maintain'd in songs of thine — maintain'd in
    thee thyself,
Thrice blessed now, Old Poet!

A year passed before Whittier wrote anything for publication. He had acquired what was in those days a comfortable fortune — he had totalled up his assets and found that they came to eighty-five thousand dollars — and he was helping in preparing the Riverside Edition. He read proofs, he replied to Horace Scudder's suggestions and sometimes followed them, and — when he could — answered Scudder's questions. Scudder was doing a thorough and scholarly piece of editing. The headnotes on many poems were written or altered at his suggestion. Some of the awkwardly long titles were changed, and other titles were made more specific. Scudder tactfully suggested verbal changes in some lines where there was poor rhythm or grammatical errors such as "God be judge 'Twixt thee and I" in the third stanza of "Calef in Boston." "Perhaps the tradesman used this form, but is it necessary to translate his expression into a solecism?" Scudder inquired, and Whittier changed the line and also the fourth line, which rhymed with it. The eighth stanza of "The Wishing Bridge" read:

. . . . . The great world lies
Beyond me as it laid."

"Cannot some change be made in the fourth line so that *lay*, the proper form, can be substituted for *laid*?" Scudder wrote, and Whittier made the correction and wrote "Thanks!" in the margin. He hoped that he was correcting "a little of the bad grammar and rhythmical blunders" which had annoyed his friends who had "graduated from Harvard instead of a district country school" — evidently choosing to forget his months at Haverhill Academy.

Scudder failed on two points, through no lack of effort. He hoped to include a bibliography of Whittier's poems, and his notes show that he looked up many items, but the task was much greater than he had supposed. The best that he could do was to list the poems by year of composition or publication, and there were numerous errors; had he depended on Whittier's memory there would have been many more. Whittier had warned him that he did not remember dates, and Scudder asked help from Samuel T. Pickard and did a good deal of research. Scudder also failed to get Whittier to allow the publication of many of his early poems. Whittier thought as he read the proofs that there were too many poems anyway, and he wished that many of them had not been written or had been written better. He had a strong desire to drown some of them like so many unlikely kittens, but the publishers said that there was no getting rid of them — they had more than nine lives. But he was firm about the early poems. When he received the proofs of the section in the Appendix to be called "Early and Uncollected Verses" he wrote to Scudder, "I am horrified by the strange array of the ghosts of rhymes thee marshall before me. I do not know them. I have named on the other page all the poems which I care to have republished. I cannot consent to any more." All but three on his list, "Paulowna," "Suicide Pond," and "Lines on a Portrait" were included in the Appendix. When he sent back later proofs in July, at the same time he sent "Isabel," which he thought "a little better than most of the early pieces and in a different strain" — and which probably was not his. He also sent "The Drunkard to His Bottle" and "The Exile's Departure." When he sent a copy of his portrait by Robert Peckham, he suggested that it might head the early pieces: "It looks about as green and homespun as the verses themselves."

Work had also started on the three volumes of prose, although they were to be published two months later than the poetry. Scudder did the arranging. Whittier was able to give somewhat more help than with the poems. He supplied copy and sent lists of items which he could not find, suggesting where Scudder might look for them.[22]

By the middle of April he was thinking of going to Amesbury for a few days or perhaps a fortnight as soon as Mrs. Cate had finished the spring cleaning. He supposed that there was not much to be done in the rooms that he used, but there was no telling what folks would do in the craze of house cleaning. Mrs. Cate evidently reassured him, and he went to Amesbury a few days later. The winter had seemed long and bitter; there had been a three-day blizzard in the middle of March, and from the hills in Amesbury snow could be seen not far to the north. But by the last of April grass was beginning to turn green in low places and arbutus was blooming among pine needles. He was thankful that he had lived to see another spring, to watch the "slow, beautiful resurrection of Nature," and he was not too deaf to hear the birds.[23]

When he returned to Oak Knoll, he found the countryside "wonderfully beautiful," with miles of apple blossoms stretching away in all directions. He read a best-selling novel by a young woman who would be an important figure in the literary world of the next half-century; Margaret Deland's *John Ward, Preacher*, seemed to him a book of real power with well-drawn characters. Charles R. Lanman, professor of Oriental Languages at Harvard, and still remembered by elderly Harvard men for his brilliance, kindness, eccentricities, and caustic comments on his colleagues, sent a painting of marshes which reminded Whittier of his boyhood, "summer afternoons — the interminable levels of green broken by gleams of water, and the picturesque haycocks burning in the distance," the "low, green prairies of the sea," as he had called them in "Snow-Bound."[24]

As summer came on he had little strength and doubted that he would be able to go to the White Mountains. He no longer tried to keep up with his correspondence; he had not been able to answer a quarter of the letters that he had received during the past year. But he wrote a reply to a notice of a reunion of members of the Free Soil Party June 28 on the fortieth anniversary of the first Free Soil convention, which gave him a chance to say some good things about the Republican Party. That party had saved the Union and abolished slavery. If it had made mistakes incidental to fallible humanity, it had kept faithful to its original doctrines of human equality and civil rights, regardless of color or condition. Whittier was not well enough to "dine out," as he said, but he went to the reception at the Parker House in Boston preceding the dinner to meet some of his old friends, stayed half an hour, and left before the dinner.[25]

He went to Amesbury as usual for the Friends Quarterly Meeting and had a houseful of company, but only a few of his old friends of fifty years ago were there. He soon returned to Oak Knoll, and was wavering on the question of going to Amesbury before July 4, when a statue of Josiah Bartlett, a native of Amesbury and a signer of the Declaration of Independence, was to be unveiled. Whittier had been asked to write a poem for the occasion and had started working on it in March. It was finished and revised by June 12. It was to be read by Professor J. W. Churchill of Andover Theological Seminary, who had read Whittier's "Sumner" at the memorial service in Boston Music Hall. He wanted to be sure that Professor Churchill was paid; twenty-five or thirty dollars should be handed to him in an envelope, and if the committee didn't supply the money, Whittier would. By June 22 it developed that the committee had no money left, having spent it on other parts of the day's program — a "mere Fourth of July row," he called it — and he sent twenty-five dollars and a note to Professor Churchill.

It is surprising that Whittier even toyed with the idea of being in Amesbury on July 4. He foresaw that it would be a noisy time, a "big fuss," as he called it; he was having headaches, and he had been told by his Salem physician that he must be absolutely quiet and must avoid excitement. He made his final decision only on the day before the event — a wise one, as events proved — to stay at Oak Knoll. He still thought that he might have gone to Amesbury if he could have stayed quietly at home, but it had been announced that he would be seated on the platform with the speakers and dignitaries for perhaps two hours, and that was out of the question.[26]

If Whittier had gone to Amesbury, he would not have found it quiet even if he had stayed at home. On the evening before the Fourth a band serenaded

Jacob R. Huntington, the carriage manufacturer who had paid for the statue, and if Whittier had been at home it would doubtless have serenaded him. Boys fired torpedoes and crackers, and, according to the newspaper account, "all night the sounds of the celebration were heard on every hand." The Amesbury Drum Corps, which had not been invited to take part in the ceremonies, had a parade of its own shortly after midnight. If Whittier had fallen asleep from sheer exhaustion, he would have been awakened at sunrise by a salute fired by Battery C of Lawrence.

So much was planned for the day that it was well that everyone was awakened early. Horse cars from Newburyport started arriving at five o'clock and made ninety-five trips during the day, crowded and with passengers on the roof. The great military and civic procession was scheduled to start at ten, but the Eighth Regiment arrived late and the start was delayed until 11:20. If Whittier had been at home he could have seen the parade as it passed his house; it took thirty minutes to pass, and he was not too deaf to hear two bands and a drum corps.

The route was five miles long and the day intensely hot, and the military marchers complained that no one gave them anything to drink along the way. Many of them were overcome by the heat and were revived on the lawn of the Main Street Congregational Church, where the Woman's Christian Temperance Union sold refreshments, presumably not the kind that the marchers had craved. The line had thinned considerably by the time it arrived at the square where the statue awaited unveiling. The exercises started at half past one and included, along with other speeches, one oration which filled nearly four newspaper columns. Whittier's "One of the Signers" came last and probably received little attention; dinner for three hundred guests was waiting in the Opera House. It was inconspicuously placed in the newspapers the next day. It was also read at the Fourth of July celebration at Woodstock, Connecticut.[27]

"One of the Signers" was, like most of Whittier's verses for occasions, simple and dignified and suited to the occasion and to the audience. It looked beyond the event to its larger significance. The signers of the Declaration of Independence, it said, had started a force that went over the whole world and whose course was marked by broken chains. The last stanza looked toward the future; Josiah Bartlett would be remembered when Freedom needed someone to speak in its defense.

Whittier had worked hard to write a good poem, but he did not get sentimental about it or about himself. In the quiet of Oak Knoll he wrote a humorous poem, "My Double," about the dedication of the statue and his imaginary part in it. He would certainly have forbidden its publication if it had occurred to him that Samuel T. Pickard would use it in *Whittier-Land*.

Whittier came to Amesbury two days later and described himself in a letter to Edna Dean Proctor as so ill and weak that he was hardly able to enjoy the visit of dear friends. But he was at Center Harbor with the Cartlands a week later, staying at the new Senter House, a large gambrel-roofed wooden hotel, with a tower, gables, piazzas, porches, and porticos, which was very fine, Whittier said, but a little too much so; he liked an old hotel better than such a "genteel" one, where there was too much fashion and ceremony. After three weeks he went to Sturtevants', where he stayed four weeks. He had a pleasant summer, on the whole, although the ground was damp most of the time — "a 'moist body' like Mantalini's" — and he couldn't lie on it. But the dampness kept the countryside as fresh and green as in June.[29]

He returned to Amesbury September 3 with a cold that he thought he had caught on the Lake Winnepesaukee steamboat. There were important matters to be attended to immediately. Wilbur Berry, the husband of Whittier's niece Alice, was going into business as a grocer and was buying a house. The Berrys had lived on a farm until the house had burned. Whittier sent some practical advice about repairs, painting, water supply, and drainage. Interest charges would be one hundred sixty dollars a year, of which he would pay one hundred. He wrote to Francis J. Garrison to suggest that "The Heroine of Long Point" be included in one of the volumes of prose in the Riverside Edition. He thought that it had been published a dozen or more years ago; it had been published nineteen years earlier in the May 1869 *Atlantic*. He wrote to Scudder to give his approval to the arrangement of the prose volumes.[30]

There was another important matter that he felt unable to do anything about. He had been asked to write a poem for the Centennial Celebration of the Inauguration of Washington, and he firmly declined. (He reconsidered later.) The mere thought of writing such a poem tired him, and he had no reason for hoping that he would ever be equal to it. He thought that he saw what the poem ought to be, but someone else must write it, perhaps Edmund C. Stedman or Richard H. Stoddard.[31] News of the death of Evelina Bray Downey's husband led him to write a kindly, solicitous letter. He had heard recently from Mary White Smith, who was well, but Harriet Minot Pitman was near death. Whittier had been kept informed of her condition. In July her daughter had hoped that she would partially recover, but by early October all that could be hoped for was a quiet release. She died October 28, and Whittier wrote an obituary for the *Boston Evening Transcript* describing her as a "friend and supporter of every movement which promised to benefit her fellow beings," including Anti-Slavery and Woman Suffrage. "Her friendship was a benediction, and she never lost a friend except by death."[32]

Mary White Smith's husband, Samuel F. Smith, had his eightieth birthday October 21, and Whittier wrote a kind and complimentary letter referring to "America." A few days later he wrote to Celia Thaxter, who had told him that she had been reading Miguel Molinos. He had read some of Molinos' writings — one begins to wonder if there was anything that he had not read — and had felt their truth and beauty. He had also read *John Inglesant* by Joseph Henry Shorthouse, which he considered a "wonderful novel," in which Molinos was one of the characters. His eyes were troubling him and he had not yet read Mrs. Humphrey Ward's *Robert Ellsmere*. He read it later and found it "unsettling," as did many others, doubtless as Mrs. Ward had intended.[33] She had the hero say, "I can no longer believe in an incarnation and resurrection . . . Christ is risen in our hearts, in the Christian life of charity. Miracle is a natural product of human feeling and imagination; and God was in Jesus preeminently, as He is in all great souls, but not otherwise in kind than He is in me or you."

A Presidential election was approaching, and Whittier was as firmly Republican as ever. He was also as firmly pro-tariff and thought that the Republican nominees, Benjamin Harrison and Levi Morton, would "sustain the great principle of protection to American industry." But as election day approached and he heard reports of suppression of the Negro vote in Southern states, he became convinced that the vital issue was civil rights, "the Constitutional right of citizenship, a free ballot and fair count." He was still an important enough public figure so that a letter of his on this topic was read at a meeting of the Harvard Republican Club in Tremont Temple in Boston. He was also important enough to be beset by office seekers soon after the election, who wanted him to say a good word about them to President Harrison.[34]

The marriage of Elizabeth Stuart Phelps on October 20 caused a good deal of surprise and some amusement to Whittier, as to many others. She was forty-four and her husband, Herbert Ward, was twenty-seven. When they had called together at Oak Knoll, Whittier had been pleased with Ward's delicate attentions to Elizabeth, which she seemed to enjoy, but it had evidently not occurred to him that they had any thoughts of marriage. "If Elizabeth had been announced as a star actress in the theatre, I should not have been more surprised," he wrote to Mrs. Fields, but checked his amusement by realizing that there was a serious side to the matter. "It is very strange, but how do we know it is not best for both? Love seems to have cured her. She had an intense longing for it, and it was better than homeopathy or 'Christian Science' or 'mind cure' for her case." He sent Mrs. Ward a letter of congratulation, assuring her that she had his best wishes for her happiness and, quoting the last two lines of his Prelude to "Among the Hills," the full realization of "the one great purpose of creation, Love, the sole necessity of Earth and Heaven". When he heard that she and her husband were to spend the winter in Hampton, Virginia, where a cottage had been offered them by General Armstrong "to have their love in," he was afraid that they might find it a little lonely there before spring, and that the young husband might yearn for the fashion and folly of the hotel on the mainland and be tempted by the sight of dancers crossing the lighted windows. Nothing of the sort seems to have happened, and when they called on Mrs. Fields and Sarah Orne Jewett in the spring, Miss Jewett reported, with perhaps a touch of spinster cynicism, that they were "very happy together, poor dears" and "about of an age, as far as that goes."[35]

But there were also serious things to think about in the autumn of 1888. Richard S. Spofford had died August 11, and Whittier was writing a sonnet to be printed and given to his friends. Spofford and his wife, Harriet Prescott Spofford, had lived since 1874 at Deer Island in the Merrimac River between Newburyport and Amesbury. He was a corporation counsel with an office in Boston — daily commuting to Boston was now possible. In spite of his being a Democrat and even a supporter of Ben Butler, Whittier liked him, called him a "genial, good-hearted fellow," and tried to get him appointed Marshall of Massachusetts in 1867: "His Democracy won't do any hurt to anybody but himself." The sonnet was written with care, as is evidenced by numerous changes in the manuscript and two printed proofs before the final copy, which was dated Amesbury, November 9. In the eleventh line "for friends alone he had" become "who friends in all men had," still a rather strong statement describing a man active in party politics.[36]

He returned to Oak Knoll, feeling the weight of his years but thankful that life was still worth living. He still loved nature and his friends, and was still interested in current affairs. He told a visitor that he found it hard to understand the new type of labor leaders; he knew that there could be no improvement without agitation, but agitation should not include strikes and lockouts: "You can't get far with strife and hatred." He followed current developments in psychical research. In the spring he had urged Oliver Wendell Holmes to read the two-volume *Phantasms of the Living* published by the British Society for Psychical Research. He now sent Edna Dean Proctor tickets for a meeting of the American Society, with the comment that she might be interested or amused. He had heard that Professor Josiah Royce of Harvard would have some ghost stories to tell and thought that a ghost that had "safely passed the competitive examination of the Cambridge Mugwumps must be worth seeing."[37]

Mrs. Claflin invited him to spend his birthday at her home in Boston, but he did not feel equal to the effort of leaving Oak Knoll. He felt better than on his last visit to Boston and hoped that he would so continue if he did not have too many visitors on his birthday.

There were not many birthday callers — perhaps a dozen or two — but Whittier had a cold and even that number tired him. After the guests had been led into the dining room and told to help themselves — fruit, candy, coffee, water, and no alcoholic drink — he withdrew to his study with William Claflin and Douglas Sladen, an English novelist and editor. They talked about England, which Whittier said was the only really civilizing power in the world, the only nation in which policy seemed to be shaped by duty. He hoped that England and America, joined in political alliance and friendship, would solve social and economic problems together and abolish war.[38]

The day closed happily — at least he told a new friend that it did. A box of flowers from Mrs. Lucy Kilham of Boston arrived just at sunset, and he wrote to her the next day. He had not lost his youthful skill in writing the kind of letters that women liked, and his letter to Mrs. Kilham had just the right proportion of description, emotion, and personal regard: "I received on my birthday many letters and tokens of interest and friendship from all parts of the country but still there was a want — a half confessed feeling of lack — a looking for something that had not come. And so the bright winter day waned; and just as the sunset blazed through the pines and left the blazon of gold and wood-tracery on our western windows, the expressman brought thy box of flowers. As soon as I saw it I said, 'That is from dear Mrs. Kilham!' I know that I did not deserve it and had no right to expect it, but I was very glad and grateful. I have outlived most of those dear to me in early life, and the feeling of loss, loneliness and isolation sometimes rests heavily upon me but God has been good in giving me new friends, like thyself, whom I have learned to love and reverence, the thought of whom is a happiness, and whose words and kindly remembrance are a benediction. And so, thanks to thee, my day closed in peace and gratitude."

A letter to Elizabeth Whittier Pickard a few days later sounded a wholly different note: "I had about a hundred letters for the birthday fuss. I don't like such occasions."[39] But a few days after this he received a post-birthday letter which gave him real pleasure. It brought the congratulations and best wishes of the Essex County Agricultural Society, and he wrote a long letter in reply, recalling his own youth on the farm and giving a high opinion of farmers and farming in Essex County — an opinion closer to the sentiment in "The Homestead" than to his privately expressed opinion to his Oak Knoll cousins that farming didn't pay at all. Matthew Arnold, after a visit in Essex County, had asked him where the tenants or working people lived and had been surprised to learn that the tenants were the landlords and the workers were the owners.[40]

In late December and early January the weather was unusually mild. Christmas Day was a "summer-miracle in our winter clime" and resulted in "The Christmas of 1888," one of the last three of Whittier's poems to be printed in the *Atlantic*. Old age had not reduced his susceptibility to sense impressions. He still saw clearly and could still tell what he saw in effective detail. He was also still close to the thoughts and feelings of his readers, to whom, as to him, Christmas was first of all the day when Jesus was born. After the cold of early dawn with no "herald of the One," the warmth and brightness were a reminder of the first Christmas, the near and far were blended, and

> Our homestead pine-tree was the Syrian palm,
> Our heart's desire the angels' midnight psalm,
> Peace, and good-will to men.

Chapter XXXV
1889 - 90

The "dream of summer," as Whittier called it, lasted into January. He got out of doors and observed that the pussy willow, lilac, and cherry buds were swelling. The mild weather also encouraged callers. He had not had a day free from visitors for nine months, and they took something from his vitality and left him exhausted. On the day before New Year's he had no respite until nine in the evening.[1]

He went to Amesbury for a week or two and had returned to Oak Knoll by the last of the month. "The Christmas of 1888" had been sent to the *Atlantic* by January 23, and he was at work on a poem for the Centennial Celebration of the Inauguration of Washington — which he had said in September that he was too feeble in health to write. He worried a good deal about this poem and wished that he had not been over-persuaded to write it. He always distrusted his judgment of his own poems, and there were lines in "The Vow of Washington" that he was especially doubtful about; he was not sure that the poem was equal to the occasion and told the Committee that if they had any doubts he would be satisfied to let the whole matter drop. Clarence W. Bowen, the secretary of the committee in charge, may well have wished that he had accepted this offer. Whittier sent five letters at intervals of a few days with additions and corrections. He dismissed as absurd a newspaper report that he would read the poem at the exercises; he didn't care who read it, and if critics found fault with it, he would join them, as Charles Lamb hissed his own play.[2]

"The Vow of Washington" was dignified and suited to the occasion, but as might be expected from Whittier's struggles with it, gave an effect of thought and labor rather than of inspiration. Bowen read it to the audience at the Sub-Treasury building on Wall Street. The elite were not among those present; President Harrison and his cabinet were at a religious service in St. Paul's, the church that Washington attended.

In spite of a vow to write no more verses for occasions, he did not give a positive refusal to a request from the Haverhill Board of Trade. Plans were in the making for a celebration of the two hundred fiftieth anniversary of the settlement of Haverhill in the spring. He wrote that he would be happy to do what he could to make the celebration a success, but the time was far off, and he was warned by age and illness not to make any promise for the future.[3]

He was staying in the house most of the time, idling the hours away by the fireside. He did not feel able to go to the Tavern Club's dinner on James

Russell Lowell's birthday, although Charles Eliot Norton assured him that his presence would be all that was needed to make the occasion memorable. But he wrote a letter with a pleasant blend of humor and sentiment. As headmaster of the *Atlantic*, Lowell had him as a pupil and sat in lenient judgment on "doubtful grammar, lisping lines, and incompatible rhymes." Lowell's name should be on the list of those who saved the Union. Before the guns of Grant and Sherman knocked the Slave Confederacy in pieces, it was already "badly shaken by a continental explosion of laughter, the train of which was fired by the bard of Jaalem."

He had already written his contribution to *The Critic's* Lowell birthday number. Lowell, he wrote, was not too old to add to his already "splendid reputation as a poet and critic, and as a representative man whose worth and genius are acknowledged wherever our language is spoken." Whittier had just reread Lowell's description of the New England spring in the "Bigelow Papers," which he thought had never been so well told before, nor had the wit and wisdom of country life ever been so admirably rendered.[4]

Although Whittier said that his eyes did not allow him to do much reading and that he seemed quite outside the literary world, he was doing enough reading to be not wholly outside the world of contemporary events and causes. He read the first published proceedings of the American Society of Psychical Research, which had "some striking instances of dreams and phantasms." He approved the object of a meeting of the Prison Association to protest an attempt by organized labor to prohibit prison labor. Enforced idleness, he believed, would result in filling prisons with maniacs. His sympathies were with the laboring class in their just demands, and he would favor every legitimate measure which promised to help them, but the suppression of labor in prisons would bring them too small a gain "to be purchased by the transformation of prisons into madhouses."[5]

Believing, as he had often said, that the liquor problem could best be solved on a state rather than a national level, he approved a proposed amendment to the Massachusetts constitution prohibiting the manufacture and sale of intoxicating liquor; he had signed a petition for the amendment in 1887. He went to Amesbury in time to vote on the amendment at a town meeting April 24, but was in the minority in both the town and the state.[6]

When he was told that a street in a California town was named for him while another was named for the English actress Lilly Langtry, he observed cheerfully that he could stand the incongruity of the association if Mrs. Langtry could; she might have as much objection to a Quaker as he had to an actress. His objection to actresses was evidently to their profession rather than to themselves. A young actress, Ullie Akerstrom, who was playing at the Amesbury Opera House with "a carefully selected company," with "rich and handsome costumes, new and effective scenery, calcium light and mechanic effects," called on Whittier and gave him her portrait, a volume of her poetry entitled "Toot Yer Horn and Other Poems," and some flowers. He thought afterward that he should have looked at the flowers before she left and should have thanked her more warmly for them. He read some of the poems and found some of them really fine — an opinion in which a less kindly critic would hardly concur. He sent her an autographed picture and a note concluding, "That through all the trials and temptations of thy life thee may be kept by the All-loving Father is the wish of thy friend."[7]

He was not feeling well, with palpitation of the heart and difficulty in breathing, and the Quarterly Meeting and some not wholly welcome visitors did not make him feel any better. In spite of the discomfort resulting from much reading or writing, he wrote three lines for the dedication of a library at Gammon Theological Seminary in Atlanta, and a few weeks later a long letter to the *Boston Journal*, stating emphatically his confidence in Hampton Institute and in General Armstrong. Both were under attack — as proof of his faith in General Armstrong and the Institute he doubled his annual subscription of fifty dollars.[8]

He was in Portland in June for Yearly Meeting and a visit to the Pickards. Poor health did not keep him from noticing the beauty of his surroundings: flowers were blooming everywhere and lawns and parks were a vivid green. There was another pleasant feature in Portland: his grandnephew Greenleaf Whittier Pickard's manners were somewhat improved. As a small boy he had been much too energetic and active to please an elderly man whose preference was for little girls. The Pickards were frequent visitors to Amesbury, where Greenleaf's conduct once caused his great-uncle to remark to his mother that the boy wasn't worth raising. At meals he would reach for something that he wanted, shouting "Give me that." One day when the Pickards and Whittier were riding in an open carriage, Greenleaf threw his hat into the street and the carriage had to stop and wait until it was retrieved. When they started out to ride the next day, Whittier pulled Greenleaf's hat down with such force that it could be removed only with adult assistance.[9]

Whittier went to Conway, New Hampshire, in July and stayed at the Conway House. There were people there that he liked, and the mountains were looking their best. Rains had made the countryside greener even than in June.

On July 29 he wrote to Robert Bonner Sons, publishers of the *New York Ledger*, gratefully accepting one thousand dollars for "The Captain's Well." This amount, he was aware, was beyond the real value of the poem, but it would make it possible for him to do some good which he otherwise could not have done. The poem was printed with illustrations by Howard Pyle as a supplement to the *Ledger* January 11, 1890. It was well received. The *Independent* described it as "one of the strongest, most beautiful, and finished productions that ever came from his pen." James Russell Lowell thought that it was in Whittier's happiest vein, a vein peculiarly his own, and tears came into his eyes as he read it.[10]

The story had been used by Harriet Prescott Spofford in a poem for the dedication of the Simpson Annex to Newburyport Public Library in 1882. Whittier had written to her that the story could not be better told, and now in the headnote to "The Captain's Well" he wrote, "To the charm and felicity of her verse, as far as it goes, nothing can be added; but in the following ballad I have endeavored to give a fuller detail of the touching incident upon which it is founded." His reason for telling the story again is said to have been to arouse interest in cleaning out and reopening the well, which had been filled with rubbish.[11]

Whittier had known the story since childhood and had probably read the account of Bagley's shipwreck and sufferings in Arabia in a book published before his return to America, *A Journal of the Travels and Sufferings of Daniel Saunders, Jr., a Mariner on Board the Ship Commerce of Boston, Captain Samuel Johnson, Commander, which was Cast Away Near Cape Morebet on the Coast of Arabia, July 10, 1772*. As usual, Whittier did not bother to check factual details. The second couplet had an error:

Back to his home, where wife and child,
Who had mourned him lost, with joy were wild.

Bagley was not married until several years after his shipwreck. This couplet was changed to the present form in a reprinting of the poem "with authorized corrections" in the *Portland Transcript* January 29. Another error was never corrected. The thirty-fifth couplet has Bagley's neighbors say "The poor old captain is out of his head." Bagley was only nineteen at the time of his shipwreck. He made several voyages before returning to Amesbury, but if, as Whittier told the story, he began to dig the well the day after his return, he was not old nor was he a captain.[12]

If Whittier's purpose was to get the well reopened, he must have felt some disappointment when nothing was done about it. Two years after Whittier's death a letter to a local paper appealed to the public-spirited people of Amesbury to put the well in condition to be used; it was filled with mud and debris. Three years later, in 1897, a canopy was built over the well and a pipe installed connected with the town water system. Wells at a nearby pumping station had drained the water away from the spring that had supplied the Captain's Well.

Whittier left Conway August 14 because of what he called serious illness and went to Newburyport to be taken care of by the Cartlands. He had hoped to visit the Isles of Shoals, but that was now out of the question. Every physical or mental effort caused suffering, his eyesight was failing, and reading and writing were difficult. But he did not refuse a request from the *Boston Daily Advertiser* for something for Oliver Wendell Holmes' birthday. He was not given much time; the request came only six days before the birthday, and he mailed "O. W. Holmes on His Eightieth Birthday" to the *Advertiser* four days later, on the morning of August 27. Later in the day a copy made by Gertrude Cartland was mailed to Mrs. Fields to be given to Holmes on the twenty-ninth. The poem was a sonnet, and if it seems sentimental to readers of a later day who do not care for such lines as

And love repeat with smiles and tears thereat
His own sweet songs that time shall not forget,

it was direct and true to Whittier's own thought and the thought of his time, that life in old age, when one is waiting the call to a higher life, is not diminished, but the heavens have come nearer. His illness had convinced him that his own end was near, and he was in a calm state of mind. He said again, "I believe in God and the immortal life and calmly await and trust."

While Whittier's chief thought during his illness was on the future life, he had learned some practical adjustments that must have made him easier to care for. He wrote to one of his relatives, who suffered from dyspepsia and insomnia, that dyspepsia could not be cured by medicine and that the will had more control over it than anything else. He read *Pickwick Papers* and other pleasant books before going to bed and found that filling the mind with droll images was conducive to sleep and made aches and pains less burdensome. [13]

A pleasant event in September was a visit of John Wallace Hutchinson and his sister Abby Hutchinson Patton. They sang "Ein Feste Burg Ist Unser Gott," and Whittier told them that if they sang that song to the soldiers with the unction and spirit with which they had just sung it, he did not wonder that they had their "expulsion." [14]

A few days later there was another reminder of earlier days. Simeon Dodge of Marblehead was nominated as Republican candidate for the State Senate. He had been an active worker on the Underground Railroad, keeping fugitive slaves in his home for weeks until they could safely be sent farther north. In those days he was unpopular with his neighbors, but after Anti-Slavery became fashionable, he was elected to various town offices and was Collector of Customs for many years. He was now seventy-four but vigorous and active. Whittier wrote to him that the Republicans could not have made a better choice. Whittier's support still had publicity value, and the letter was printed in the newspapers with the explanation that it had been sent voluntarily and unexpectedly. Dodge was elected. [15]

The demands on his sympathy and on his purse continued at the usual rate. The construction costs of the Home for Aged Women in Amesbury had used up most of the capital, and an attempt was being made to raise one thousand dollars to add to the invested funds; Whittier gave one hundred dollars. Two days before Thanksgiving a fire in Lynn destroyed buildings worth more than a million dollars and left many poor families homeless. On Thanksgiving Day Whittier sent a check for fifty dollars and hoped that on that day all hearts and purses would be open.

He paid the Town of Amesbury a tax of $119.60 — poll tax $2.00, personal property $33.60, and real estate $84.00. A rumor still persists that he evaded paying taxes. The receipted bill for 1889 shows that the tax was paid on time, and the assessment seems to be adequate. While there is no way of knowing the value of that part of his personal property which was subject to local taxation, it probably did not exceed two thousand dollars, many of his securities being tax-exempt. The valuation of his house at fifteen hundred, land at fourteen hundred, and wood-house at one hundred, and of the house that he owned on the corner of the street at one thousand and land at one thousand seems adequate in the light of real estate values at the time.[16]

Whittier was at Oak Knoll for Thanksgiving, but he now spent less time there than in former years. One reason may be that Abby, Caroline, and Phebe travelled a good deal, and, in the opinion of some of Whittier's friends, he did not enjoy Oak Knoll when they were not there. Other friends in Amesbury heard that there was disagreement about money and that after his death there was some question about the ownership of some bonds in a safe. Sarah Orne Jewett thought that he did not enjoy Oak Knoll during the last five years of his life: "It came out in many ways and made him sad and troubled." She had heard many people wonder about it, since he had been so happy in the earlier years there. On the day of the Whittier memorial service in Amesbury she rode on the train with Phebe, who talked of "their fancied wrongs." Francis J. Garrison told her that Phebe had been in Houghton Mifflin's office "behaving badly."[17] There is no reference to trouble of any kind in Whittier's letters, but legacies to the Woodmans and Caroline Johnson were smaller than one might expect. In the absence of any knowledge of business arrangements between the Oak Knoll family and Whittier, one can only guess that his cousins expected him to act toward them with more generosity than seemed necessary or right to him.

Whittier decided to spend his eighty-second birthday in Amesbury, and the reason that he gave may have been an attempt to remove any suspicion that he was unhappy at Oak Knoll. "As life draws nearer the close," he wrote to Mrs. Fields, "one feels desirous to be near the old home and the unforgotten landscape of youth, and to muse by the same fireside where our dear ones used to sit" — which would apply to his birthplace rather than to his home in Amesbury.

Early in November he began to dread his birthday and decided to have a notice printed in the newspapers. He prepared it with care and tried to be firm without hurting anyone's feelings. In the first draft he wrote "He would be glad to see all the friends who wish to see him," but wisely changed it to read "No one more heartily enjoys the presence of his friends, and he would be glad to welcome them all, but he is scarcely able to bear the excitement of a large company, however pleasurable it would be under other circumstances."[18] This notice reduced the number of visitors; William Claflin and Edward P. Pierce gave up their plan of coming when they read the notice. His old neighbors called, as well as reporters who were hard to get rid of, and one hundred fifty pupils marched to his house, after a flag-raising at the Whittier School, but all that he had to do was appear at a window and wave to them. Mrs. Fields came on the noon train and stayed three hours, making his birthday, he later told her, a very happy one. There were of course baskets and boxes of flowers, one from the Haverhill Whittier Club having eighty-two roses, and a picture of a golden Greek vase in a portfolio of red Levant morocco leather which was described in detail by Grace Greenwood in the *New York Tribune*: "On the whole, no devout monkish old illuminator could have done much better for his patron saint."

He could not sleep that night. The next day he overlooked the happiness that Mrs. Fields had given him and decided that the "row" had been very trying.[19]

During the late fall and early winter Whittier had the usual number of varied interests. He highly approved a translation of the medieval Latin hymn "Veni Sancte Spiritus" by Richard H. Thomas, a prominent Quaker minister who had a strong influence over young Friends by a broad and constructive approach to Christianity which joined faith and knowledge. Whittier, like Dr. Thomas, opposed the pastoral system which was making its way into Friends meetings and, along with the increasing use of music, was making them like other Protestants, especially the Methodists. "Quakerism has run into Methodism," Whittier wrote, "and the Quaker singing is dolefully bad. I am too old-fashioned to bear it with patience; but I suppose the singers mean well, and perhaps like the speakers of 'unknown tongues' in Paul's day they 'edify themselves.' "[20]

The death on December 12 of Robert Browning, whose poetry Whittier had never learned to like, brought out the comment, "A great strong man has left us in Robert Browning — but he was not Wordsworth"[21] — an opinion that Browning societies would endorse with a quite different interpretation.

"Burning Driftwood" was printed in the *Independent* of January 2. Copies had previously been sent to Whittier's friends, one of whom sent a barrel of driftwood as acknowledgment. Whittier worked hard on the poem. The manuscript has numerous lines crossed out and rewritten, and the eighteenth stanza is on a slip pasted over an earlier form. A proof printed from this manuscript has many changes in Whittier's writing. He added the first stanza and rewrote the sixth, seventh, and ninth.[22]

The strength of the poem came from its sincerity and its effective use of metaphors. It followed the line of thought of an old man, evidently Whittier himself, who saw in the burning driftwood the fragments of early hopes and dreams, ships which gave him distant glimpses of delights but which did not reach the harbor of contentment; only those ships which were piloted by Duty sailed safely. The tone was not that of a lament for pleasures never attained. The wrecks of passion and desire were fitly burning and warming the chill hands of age. Whatever had been lost, the best remained, and a song of praise was on his lips; more had come to him than he had dared to dream, the wonders of invention, the progress of social justice, the end of slavery.

He complained of having to be idle and, as he could read only a little, knowing hardly anything of what was happening in the world. It really wasn't that bad. He knew what was happening in Congress, where the Speaker of the House, Thomas B. Reed, had substituted the "counted quorum" for the "voting quorum." Previously a member had to vote in order to be recorded present, and the Republican majority was so small that Democrats could keep the House from transacting business by simply failing to vote. Reed proceeded to declare a quorum by counting Democrats who were present but not voting. Whittier had some fear that Reed's stand was not a safe one, but he thought that Reed showed pluck and "grand self-control under rebel yells and insults."

He was doing more reading than could be called "only a little," and as usual it was widely varied. An article in the *Friends Review* described the Alaska mission which his Oak Knoll cousins were interested in and told of a plan to organize a stock company to build a canning factory where Indians might work and be kept from contaminating influences. Lucy Larcom sent him her *A New England Girlhood*, which he read twice. He read a volume of Louise Chandler Moulton's poems, a book "of which any poet might well be proud." Oliver Wendell Holmes' "Over the Teacups," appearing serially in the *Atlantic*, seemed to him to have the fine flavor of "The Autocrat of the Breakfast Table" and "The Professor at the Breakfast Table." He read a few of George Woodberry's poems and thought him a writer of much promise, his style a little affected and imitative but showing originality and power.[23]

In late February Whittier went to the Cartlands'. He had recovered from a light case of grippe but now had a relapse and was seriously ill for a few days. His Newburyport physician, Dr. Howe, was out of town, and Dr. Douglass came from Amesbury to see him. When he felt better, he sat in the front window, where he had something exciting to watch. The cold weather and the sleighing lasted into the middle of March, and High Street, broad and two miles long, was perfect for driving and racing. One afternoon there were five hundred sleighs going up and down the street, some of them racing six abreast. One sleigh tore by empty and in splinters. It was a great scene, but Whittier's headaches kept him from watching it long at a time. The Cartlands did not own a horse and would not have enjoyed sleigh riding any more than Whittier would have. Joseph Cartland felt the cold as much as Whittier did. He wore black velvet ear-caps into the summer and put them on again early in September, and he wore kneepads to keep his knees warm.[24]

By March 10 Whittier was well enough to write a kindly and humorous autograph for a neighbor of the Cartlands, Mrs. William H. Swasey. When she was a young girl, Susan Babson lived in Amesbury, but her father forbade her to ask Whittier to write in her autograph album. Her husband now told Whittier of her disappointment, especially when her teacher took her class to a wedding at the Friends Meeting House and she saw Whittier standing at a small table in charge of the book in which the witnesses signed their names. He now wrote twenty lines, concluding

> I trace a name, then little known,
> Which since on many winds has blown,
> Glad to make good, however late,
> Her loss at such an early date,
> For which even now I almost pity her,
> By the best wish of
> John G. Whittier.[25]

He started another poem, writing, as was his custom, on the back of a letter. He never published it, although he probably intended it for publication. The editor of the *Youth's Companion* wrote to him in January asking for a poem and offering five hundred dollars for an autobiographical sketch of his boyhood. He could have used a little extra money at this time. He was sending an annual contribution to Tuskegee Institute, and Booker T. Washington wrote to him that help must be asked from friends or the students would have to be sent home. Then a school at Hampton Institute named for him was burned, and on March 9 he sent a check for fifty dollars, all, he said, that he could do at that time. The eighteen lines that he wrote and never revised or used were entitled "A Song of Praises" and were probably developed from the thirteenth stanza of "Burning Driftwood", expanding the two ideas in that stanza: the wonders of the world coming to him and the righting of the wronged and the poor.[26] Four lines referred to world peace:

> For the world-step forward taken;
> For an evil way forsaken
>
> For the tools of peaceful labor
> Wrought from broken gun and sabre.

These may have come to him from thinking about an International American Conference. He had written a letter urging that the Conference take measures to secure peace among all the nations represented: "If in the spirit of peace the American Conference agrees upon a rule of arbitration which shall make war in this hemisphere well nigh impossible, its sessions will prove one of the most important events in the history of the world." James G. Blaine was president of the Conference, and Whittier's letter was too complimentary to him to be read publicly but was quoted by Andrew J. Carnegie in his closing address.[27]

Whittier stayed at the Cartlands' through the spring. In spite of whatever caused his unhappiness at Oak Knoll, he continued to write friendly letters with no note of displeasure or distrust. Now that Phebe was grown up, he wrote more frequently to her than to her mother.[28]

Although his worries about "The Vow of Washington" had made him resolve never to write another poem for an occasion, he wrote "Haverhill" for the two hundred fiftieth anniversary of his native city. The poem was not worth all the trouble that it caused. It was, as Whittier himself, said, mechanical and unpoetical, and it was too conscientiously thorough in saying all that Whittier thought ought to be said: the early settlement, its growth, a description of the city and its surroundings, a reminder that work is good in a democratic society, and an appeal to the people of Haverhill to combine the old and the new in their religious thinking and to do some good in the world. When he sent it to Col. Jones Frankle, chairman of the committee, he asked that Professor Churchill, who had read "One of the Signers," should be engaged to read it so that its "faults and failings" should be forgotten in the "fine elocution of the Professor." He cautioned Col. Frankle not to let it get into the hands of reporters, not, as he has been accused, for the purpose of publishing it elsewhere and getting paid for it but to keep it out of the papers until it was read at the exercises July 2. On June 20 he sent forty or fifty copies for reporters and guests, with the suggestion that one be given to Albert L. Bartlett, who was to read it.

Horace E. Scudder had just become editor of the *Atlantic* and had written that he hoped Whittier still regarded himself as a contributor (nothing of his had appeared in the *Atlantic* since "The Christmas of 1888" in March 1889) and wished that Whittier would send him a poem so that he might send out his first number of the magazine "well freighted." He now asked Whittier for "Haverhill." Whittier was willing if Col. Frankle and the committee had no objection; reporters might be satisfied with slips containing a few stanzas. If Col. Frankle and the committee had the slightest objection to this arrangement, he would prefer to have the whole poem given to the reporters: "I don't think it will be much loss to the Atlantic." If the *Atlantic* was to have the poem, the copies that he had sent to Col. Frankle were of course to be kept out of sight until the *Atlantic* appeared. Scudder wrote to Col. Frankle that the use of the poem in the *Atlantic* was dependent on its not appearing in any newspaper and promised to select stanzas to be printed as extracts and given to reporters with the explanation that the entire poem was withheld for publication in the *Atlantic* "by the wish of Mr. Whittier" — a misleading statement, to call it nothing worse — who would receive a "liberal sum, as for any contribution which he is in the habit of making to our pages.'' Whittier wanted to hear the poem read, not having the faith in Bartlett's reading that he would have had in Churchill's, and asked Bartlett to come to Oak Knoll and read it to him. Bartlett came on a very hot day and found Whittier with a headache and tired from visitors but insistent that he should read the poem. In spite of his deafness Whittier proved to be an agreeable listener, complimented Bartlett on his reading, and said, ''The lines sound very well; doesn't thee think so?'' He may have thought that the reading did not bring out the rhythm as much as he would like; he talked about rhythm and said, ''We poets might as well write prose if the melody of our lines is not kept.''

Everything now seemed to be satisfactorily arranged. Whittier's poem was already in type for the *Atlantic*, which would be issued July 25. Slips with twelve stanzas were ready for the newspapers.

At the exercises July 2 Bartlett read the poem — if his memory forty years later was correct, from a printed copy without manuscript corrections, probably the same form as in the *Atlantic*. On the same day the *Haverhill Gazette* printed the twelve stanzas prepared for the papers and also what it believed to be the entire poem with a triumphant announcement: ''Notwithstanding the fact that the poem was disposed of to the *Atlantic Monthly*, and it was only intended that a portion of it should be published in the newspapers, the *Gazette* takes great pleasure in printing for the edification of its readers this evening the full context of the lines by Whittier, which we feel confident they will fully appreciate.'' An editorial explained that the *Gazette*, along with many people, had been greatly disappointed when it was announced that the poem had been promised to the *Atlantic*. ''It felt that this tribute of affection from the Quaker poet to the city of his nativity belonged to the people, and not to a high priced magazine.'' Evidently no one from the paper listened to the reading at the Academy of Music. The poem as printed in the *Gazette* did not have the second or twenty-first stanzas, and there were differences in the first and ninth stanzas. The next day the poem appeared again in the *Gazette*, this time in the form in which it was being printed in the *Atlantic*. The *Gazette* printed it at the request of Albert L. Bartlett, who wished the correct version published.

By this time the poem as first printed in the *Gazette* had been copied in other papers, and Horace E. Scudder saw it in the *Boston Post*. He wrote immediately to Col. Frankle with quite understandable indignation. ''You can readily understand how dismayed we are to find in the morning papers (the *Post* is the one I have seen) Mr. Whittier's poem practically in full. We do not see how after your distinct public anouncement of Mr. Whittier's wishes in this particular, the papers could have had the face to publish more than the extracts furnished.''[29]

Rather better than ''Haverhill'' were four stanzas written for Grace Gurteen, daughter of the delegate from Haverhill, England, who came to see Whittier at Oak Knoll. They said something that he really wanted to say: there was lasting friendship between Old and New England.

He spent part of the summer at the Green Acre House in Eliot, Maine, on the banks of the Piscataqua River. The Cartlands were there and other people that he liked: Harriet McEwen Kimball, Grace Greenwood, Rev. Julius Atwood, Mrs. Ole Bull. It was too far from the railroad station to be crowded, although some "pilgrims" found their way there.[30]

Whittier returned to Oak Knoll late in August, and on the last day of the month wrote "The Last Eve of Summer." When he sent it to the *Independent*, he hoped that it would not be considered dismal; he did not like dismal poems although he thought that it had a solemnity of feeling more natural to age than to youth. Its chief interest to later readers is in what it reveals about Whittier himself. He still found delight in the sights and sounds of nature and could still see pictures to be presented in verse. There was a wistfulness in his asking if this would be the last summer of his life but there was his usual faith in immortality.[31]

He was still interested in politics. On September 7 he wrote to the *Boston Evening Transcript* supporting the candidacy of Edward L. Pierce for Congress. The letter was thought important enough to print in a political pamphlet a few weeks later. Further proof that he was still looked upon as able to influence elections came a month later. He was asked to write a letter to the *Philadelphia Inquirer* advocating the tariff and Republican principles. He evidently did not write the letter, and when the Republican party was badly defeated in the Congressional elections, he wrote that he had expected this "avalanche"; making the tariff the sole issue had invited defeat.[32] He was right; the McKinley Act of October 1 aroused much public resentment, especially a clause which gave a bounty to sugar producers in the United States. He spoke of James G. Blaine with his old-time ardor. Blaine, he said, might have been elected in 1888 as easily as Harrison if he had allowed his name to be presented to the Republican convention.

Two volumes were in preparation. One was a new edition of *Songs of Three Centuries*. It had an added section entitled "Later Poems," the first poem being Philip Freneau's "The Indian Burying-Ground." A footnote was necessarily added: "This poem and a few others are included to supply omissions in the early sections." The introduction to the first edition was retained and a new introductory note added, dated November, 1890, explaining that the third section in the first edition, "From Wordsworth to Longfellow," had not been wholly satisfactory to the compiler and in the haste of its preparation some items that would have added to the value of the volume were overlooked. Some that were added have become popular classics: Francis William Bourdillon's "Light" ("The night has a thousand eyes"), John Henry Newman's "Lead, Kindly Light," Phillips Brooks' "O Little Town of Bethlehem," and Edward Rowland Sill's "The Fool's Prayer." Two poems by Emma Lazarus were added, one of them "The Crowing of the Red Cock," which Whittier considered her best. He had said of her soon after her death, "With no lack of rhythmic sweetness, she had often the rugged strength and verbal audacity of Browning." Lucy Larcom helped, as she had in preparing the first edition.[33]

"At Sundown" was being prepared for a private printing by Riverside Press. It contained twelve poems, all of which had been previously printed except the dedication, "To E. C. S." (Edmund Clarence Stedman). Stedman's copy reached him the day after Whittier's birthday. His wife handed it to him with "tears in her eyes and a smile on her face," and before he had finished reading the dedication, he wrote to Whittier, "what with weakness and surprise and gratitude and a rush of tender feelings," he was crying like a child.

The volume was printed mainly for Whittier to give to his friends. However, it was advertised by Houghton Mifflin as for sale at one dollar and a half. If this advertisement was intended to protect Whittier from a flood of requests, it failed in its purpose. Whittier wrote to Francis J. Garrison in February that he would like twenty copies. He was "beset on all sides with requests for them," but he could give them only to old friends.[34]

Whittier was in Amesbury in November and thought that he would stay there over his birthday, but warm weather made him change his mind and go to Oak Knoll. He let it be known that he did not feel equal to a general reception, and Mrs. Woodman explained to a caller the previous day that the birthday would be celebrated only by a little family dinner and a few friends calling. Rather more than a few friends called, and the dinner was not restricted to members of the family. Among the guests were Mrs. Fields, Charles F. Coffin and his family, and a twenty-six-year-old poet, Allen Eastman Cross, who became known for his popular religious poems and hymns.

Hundreds of letters and telegrams came from all parts of the United States and from England, Scotland, Ireland, Australia, and the Hawaiian Islands.[35] There was one letter that, he assured the writer, was most welcome of all. It was from ten-year-old Helen Keller. Their correspondence had started a year earlier when she wrote that she was joyful all the day long because her mind could see all the lovely things which she could not see with her eyes, and she loved him dearly because he had taught her so many lovely things. He replied that he was happy to know that she had been pleased with his poems and he thought that her teacher, Miss Sullivan, must be a good and noble young woman. He wrote again in the summer, and she now wrote that the children at Perkins Institute for the Blind were planning an entertainment with readings from his poems. She was sorry at first that the day was cloudy, but then she thought that the sun had hidden himself because he knew that Whittier liked to see the world covered with snow and kept back his brightness so that snow crystals would form and then softly fall and tenderly cover every object. Whittier's reply described the day at Oak Knoll. He was not surprised that she thought eighty-three years a long time, but to him it seemed only a little while since he was a boy no older than she, playing on the old farm at Haverhill.[36]

516

CHAPTER XXXVI
1891 - 92

Whittier stayed at Oak Knoll through Christmas and New Year's and then went to the Cartlands'. High Street, which runs two miles from the south to the north end of Newburyport, was then bordered with elm trees. Whittier was still a keen observer, and after an ice storm he saw the prismatic colors tangling the trees with rainbows.

He was doing little reading, barely glancing at the newspapers but somehow keeping aware of what was going on: General Nelson Miles' attempt to pacify the Sioux and Cheyennes, Grover Cleveland's courageous "silver letter" which might cost him the Presidential nomination, studies of the British Society for Psychical Research. He wished that something might be done to check the evil of intemperance; he had come to believe that the "rum seller" controlled politicians as slavery once had done.[1]

He had an attack of grippe but was well enough in late March to welcome a delegation of women temperance advocates from England led by Lady Somerset. They tried to keep Whittier from getting tired by amusing him with anecdotes and recitals, but like most deaf people he found it easier to talk than to listen, and when he got a chance he talked about the progress of temperance, the Woman's Christian Temperance Union, and himself: he loved the world and he had friends whom he would be sorry to leave, but he was waiting in serenity and peace for the end which he knew would come soon.[2]

Among the many callers were Alice Freeman Palmer, who later sent him her husband's new translation of the *Odyssey*, and Phillips Brooks, for whom Gertrude Cartland provided the strongest chair in the house — which collapsed under his weight. There was soon a more important crisis in Brooks' affairs, and when he was elected Episcopal Bishop of Massachusetts it seemed to Whittier that the very air of Massachusetts had become more free and sweet.[3]

He signed, with some misgiving, a proposal already signed by Thomas Wentworth Higginson, Julia Ward Howe, Samuel L. Clemens, and William Lloyd Garrison, for a Society of American Friends of Russian Freedom to help Russian patriots get political freedom and self-government. It seemed to Whittier impertinent to admonish Russia when seven million black Americans were being denied their civil rights. But he changed his opinion a few months later when Francis J. Garrison sent him a picture of Russian exiles in Siberia and letters of some who had escaped and of George Kennan, who had been sent by *Century Magazine* to investigate conditions in the mines, prisons, and penal colonies. These convinced him that all civilization and Christianity should cry out against the monstrous cruelty of Russian despotism.[4]

Whittier was at Oak Knoll in April, returning to the Cartlands' in early May. He was still unable to do much reading, but he read Sarah Orne Jewett's "A Native of Wimby" in the May *Atlantic* and could imagine that he was the rich Senator Joseph K. Laneway trying to find his lost youth in the old homestead pastures.[5]

His chief concern now was to make definite and final arrangements for his biography. He talked it over with Gertrude Cartland one morning, and later in the day she wrote to Thomas Chase, who had retired in 1886 at the age of sixty-three from the presidency of Haverford College. She told him that Whittier had planned to leave his papers to the care of Samuel T. Pickard but wished to have "some competent *Friend*" ready to assist in the writing if his friends thought that a biography was advisable.[6] The emphasis on having a Friend was probably intended as an excuse for not leaving the whole matter in the hands of Samuel T. Pickard. The death of Thomas Chase less than a month after Whittier's death resulted in having the writing done wholly by Pickard.

Whittier was in Amesbury as usual during Quarterly Meeting time, when he had a youthful but distinguished visitor, eleven-year-old Helen Keller. Luckily he had a volume of his poems in raised print from which she read "In School Days." She recited "Laus Deo," and he placed in her hands a statue of a crouching slave from whom the fetters were falling, probably a copy of the Freedman's Memorial for which he had written "The Emancipation Group."[7]

In mid-July Whittier and the Cartlands went to the Elmwood Inn in Wakefield, New Hampshire. The Inn was on the top of a hill with a view of hills in Maine and New Hampshire. Whittier still had his country habit of getting up early, and he would walk around the grounds and visit in the barn. In the evening he would walk to a spot near the barn where he could see the western sky.[8]

After two weeks at Wakefield he did not feel well enough to stay longer and returned with the Cartlands to Newburyport. When he gained a little strength, he was able to walk out into the Cartlands' garden. He was still good newspaper copy, and after a neighbor told a Boston reporter that he had seen Whittier there, a newspaper headline announced: "At Cartlands' Garden." Whittier could only wish that the "miserable newspapers" would let him alone.[9]

The death of James Russell Lowell on August 12 brought Whittier and Oliver Wendell Holmes closer together. They were now the only survivors of the group that had once made eastern Massachusetts the literary center of the country. As soon as he heard of Lowell's death, Whittier longed to see Holmes, and Holmes, who was at Beverly Farms, was eager to see Whittier; they were, he said, no longer on a raft but on a spar. Whittier went to Oak Knoll about the first of September, in time to enjoy the late season hay-making and the early apple-gathering, and Holmes came to see him there. They had a pleasant hour of talk, a "little" saddened by memories of the friends who had left them so much alone but only a little; old men have become used to losses. A week later Whittier wrote to Holmes, extravagantly praising his "James Russell Lowell"; "As a work of artistic beauty and fitness it has no rival in our literature."[10]

In spite of his poor health in the summer, Whittier worked hard on "Between the Gates" for the September 10 *Independent*. The manuscript and three advance printings have many variations. The present seventh stanza, in the *Independent* and in the present form, was not in the earlier forms, and its addition suggests one reason why young people liked Whittier, a man of their grandparents' generation. He wanted it understood that he knew that old age was not always pure and holy:

> Not always age is growth of good;
>   Its years have losses with their gain;
> Against some evil youth withstood
>   Weak hands may strive in vain.

The present final stanza is direct and clear, and replaced two diffuse and rambling stanzas.

An offprint from the *Independent* may have been made for Whittier and his friends or perhaps for his admirers who could not get copies of the *Independent*. He still had a wide following and sentimental worshippers. "Noble soul, I revere, I love you," one ecstatic woman in Scotland wrote to him. Two books with his autograph brought one hundred dollars each at a Methodist fair, and a letter sent with them brought two hundred dollars — much to his surprise.

In spite of trouble with his eyes he was reading Howells' "An Imperative Duty," which was appearing serially in *Harper's*. The September installment ended where Dr. Olney, who knew that the girl he loved was one-sixteenth Negro, believed that neither she nor a young minister who was about to propose to her knew it. Whittier was anxious to see how Howells solved "the terrible problem which socially as well as politically confronts us," the problem of the place of the Negro in American life and specifically interracial marriage. At this point Whittier misunderstood Howells' purpose, which was to present the problem of the application of the Puritan sense of duty to involved situations. What was the right thing for Dr. Olney to do? And was Mrs. Meredith right in telling her niece, on the edge of marriage, of her racial ancestry? "Duty with her," Howells wrote, "could mean but one thing, and she had done her duty." He left to the reader "the question of how far the Puritan civilization has carried the cult of personal conscience into mere dutiolatory."[11]

Whittier was in Amesbury during most of October and part of November. He was confined to his room for several weeks by a cold which made it hard for him to talk. Visitors annoyed and tired him; one day he had ten at one time, and he then began to refuse to see some. When six came one afternoon, he saw only three of them. He was able to do some reading and to write letters. He found Charles Paul Mackie's new book about Columbus, *With the Admiral of the Sea*, "a noble work." He liked the new edition of *Snow-Bound* except the picture "intended to be" his mother's. He sent the usual one hundred dollars to General Armstrong.[12] He was able to leave the house long enough to vote. It would not occur to him to register a protest by not voting or by voting against Republican candidates, but he strongly disapproved of the conduct of the Harrison administration in its dealings with Chile. The sympathy of the United States with the Liberal president Jose Manuel Balmaceda had been made evident by the seizure of a vessel sent by the Conservative rebels to get arms at San Diego. After the Liberal government was overthrown, a group of American sailors on shore leave at Valparaiso were attacked and two of them murdered by a mob thought to include Chilean sailors and the police of the new Conservative government. The United States' ultimatum and demand for an apology showed a warlike attitude that seemed wholly wrong to Whittier, who had never given up hoping for world peace and, especially, harmony in the Western Hemisphere.[13]

Soon after election day he went to the Cartlands' for the winter. He was in a calm state of mind, with no solicitude about himself and with trust in the Divine Goodness. Perhaps it was this calmness that suggested the use and revision of lines written some time ago which he had recently found. On November 27 he sent a badly written manuscript to Fred Brown, asking him to put it in type and send a proof. This was done promptly. The lines included, with some variations, all but the last eighteen of "An Outdoor Reception." The concluding lines were:

> On easy terms with law and fate,
> For what must be I calmly wait,
> And trust the path I cannot see, —
> That God is good sufficeth me.

The proof with corrections was returned to Fred Brown December 4 with a request for five or six copies on narrower paper which could be better enclosed in an envelope. Whittier sent a copy to Mrs. Fields, calling it "rhymes hastily pencilled years ago" and adding that he had tried "to mend some of its lines." The copy for publication was sent to *St. Nicholas* December

15, but the poem did not appear until the following November. In the meantime it was printed in the enlarged edition of *At Sundown*, the publication of which was delayed to let the poem appear first in *St. Nicholas*.[14]

Preston Powers wrote to ask for an inscription for a bas-relief to be carved in a red sandstone rock in Perry Park, Denver, called "The Closing Era" and showing an Indian and a dying buffalo. Whittier at first thought that he could not write any suitable lines because he could not clearly visualize the figures or the surrounding scenery. Then he saw a photograph of "The Dying Lion" carved on the side of a grotto in Lucern, and wrote "Inscription. For the bas-relief by Preston Powers, carved upon the huge boulder in Denver Park, Col., representing the Last Indian and the Last Bison." The editors of the Riverside Edition assumed that the plan was carried out, but it was abandoned late in 1891 or early in 1892. A group of women raised enough money to have Powers' model cast in bronze to be shown at the Chicago World's Fair and then placed on the grounds of the Colorado State Capitol. The fourth line in the inscription:

Their graven semblance in the eternal stone

was obviously inapplicable, and the inscription was not used.[15]

Whittier did not expect a crowd on his birthday but hoped that Mrs. Fields and Sarah Orne Jewett would come. They did and also many others. The event was too well advertised. On December 12, the Saturday before the birthday, the *Boston Journal* had a Whittier page with letters from authors and others who had been asked to tell what their favorite poem was. Most of them evaded the question, but Richard Malcolm Johnston of Baltimore, himself an author, chose one that didn't exist, "A Firelight Interior" — perhaps lines from "Snow-Bound."[16]

The day before the birthday Gail Hamilton called, as she said, "to tone him up." The next morning the first visitors arrived at nine, and there was a constant stream until evening. Newburyport people thought that the kindest thing to do was to stay away, and the *Newburyport Herald* said, evidently on its own authority, that visitors would be limited to the members of Haverhill Whittier Club, who were among the first arrivals. Fifty-six of them came on the 8:15 train. Whittier, still erect, looking, one of them recorded, fragile but not decrepit, greeted them, accepted eighty-four pink roses tied with a broad pink ribbon, listened to a speech by the president of the Club, and replied that it could not be said of him that he was a prophet without honor in his own country and his own house, for he had been signally honored by his own dear townspeople.

The roses from the Club were not the only massive flower gift. There were also eighty-four roses from a girls' school in New York, eighty-four carnations from Mrs. James R. Nichols, and a box of carnations from the Whittier Club of Leavenworth, Kansas, which arrived "unchilled and unfaded" — good evidence of the progress of transportation. A reporter noted that the parlors were "filled with the fragrance of roses, pinks, orchids, and rare flowers." There was also a wreath of pine cones and swamp berries from Mrs. Fields, which would be the subject of one of Whittier's last four poems.

There was fruit — plenty of it. In the bay window on Broad Street was a gilded basket four feet high filled with a variety of fruits, and there were big dishes of fruit on the dining table. There were other gifts, including a blotter marked "Absorbing Thoughts," and a footstool covered with dyed yellow lambskin that he acknowledged in verse a week later. He seemed interested in everything. He greeted guests cordially and did not seem tired. When the last guest had left, he joined the family at the tea table, remarking that he had never had a more comfortable and happy birthday.

There was a reaction the next morning. He was tired, he had a headache, and he thought that he had evaded as many guests as he could and had lain down half the day. But he felt better before long. Gail Hamilton came "to tone him down." It was the last time she would see him. He gave her one of his birthday pinks to send to a little girl in Honolulu whose birthday was also on December 17. Then she showed him two pictures of Florence Chandler Maybrick, who had been convicted in England of murdering her British husband and sentenced to life imprisonment. Gail Hamilton had believed that injustice had been done and had worked to obtain Mrs. Maybrick's release. One of the pictures showed Mrs. Maybrick before the trouble began, "a piquant young face with a toss of curly hair above it"; in the other "only an infinite trouble and bewilderment looked out from the large eyes with the amazement and *incomprehendingness* of a child." Whittier looked from one picture to the other with a murmur of pity and sympathy, and gave Gail Hamilton a spray of ivy to send to Mrs. Maybrick with the message that she should be

. . . . . strong
In the endurance that outwearies wrong.

He had now quite forgotten his early morning fatigue and depression and seemed eager to meet more people. While he was talking with Gail Hamilton in the parlor, the daughter of the Episcopal rector and some of her friends — "common mortals," she called them — were in the library. They had come to see the flowers and did not expect to see Whittier, but he evidently wanted to see them, and as they went into the dining room, they heard a quick firm step in the hallway, and to their surprise Whittier came to greet them.

On December 29 he was still well enough to write to Mrs. Fields and — quoting a phrase from *Pickwick Papers* — to "let himself down to poetry," three stanzas about the wreath of pine cones and swamp berries which had outlasted the birthday flowers. These, with minor changes and the addition of two stanzas, became "The Birthday Wreath."[17]

He did no more writing for a month. Early in January he had a serious attack of grippe which he thought would be fatal. He felt only the peace that came from trust and love, and he had no cares or anxieties. He did not even have to worry about being a burden to Gertrude Cartland; his niece Lizzie and Sally Weeden, a young niece of Gertrude Cartland and a cousin of Whittier, who was living with the Cartlands, took care of him. Dr. Howe called twice a day for eight days. It was late in the month before Whittier could sit up several hours a day, and he gained strength slowly. By the middle of February he was able to spend half the day downstairs. His appetite improved, and he ate some eggs sent from Oak Knoll. However, letter writing was still a burden. On February 29 Gertrude Cartland wrote a letter about John Bright at his dictation and he signed it. Whittier's illness had not affected his mental powers, and the letter was vigorous in thought and expression. Bright, it said, had no equal in his time as an orator. As a statesman he believed that righteousness alone exalted a nation and that justice was always expedient. Americans owed him a debt of gratitude for advocating the cause of the Union during the Civil War; but for him the Confederacy might have been recognized by the British government.[18]

General Armstrong sent some pussy willows, which perhaps suggested "The Wind of March," Whittier's last nature poem, written a few days later. In these lines there was the usual accurate and sensitive recording of the sights and sounds of nature and the consequent thought and feeling. The emotion was not the impress of "the sky's gray arch," "the shaken elm-boughs," and the "roar of storm" but was a trustful gratitude for what these told him of the nearness of spring. There was also, in the last two stanzas, the usual familiarity with the Bible and adeptness in using it.

As soon as he was able to go out, about the middle of April, he went to Oak Knoll. He was still weak and was surprised that he had lived to see another spring. But he was gaining strength and he enjoyed the beautiful opening of spring. Nature never disappointed him. Every season seemed more beautiful than when he was young, and in "this glorious flower time" the world seemed almost too fair and sweet to leave. Still, he hoped that when his time came he would be as willing to go as he had been during his attack of grippe.

He was sadly vexed, he wrote to Celia Thaxter, by a "fellow" who was going around trying to collect his early poems and to find anecdotes and incidents for a biography. The "fellow" was W. Sloane Kennedy, who had published what Whittier called a "sort of biography" in 1882. He now even had the temerity to write to Whittier, who sent the letter to Houghton Mifflin. He could not understand what Kennedy meant to do or could do without infringing on copyrights. It was all a forerunning, he feared, of what would come after his death. He had destroyed letters from his friends and hoped that his friends would destroy his. He wrote to Celia Thaxter that he wanted her to destroy his letters if she had not already put them out of the reach of "these prowling literary ghouls." (Mrs. Thaxter fortunately did not obey this order; and some of the letters to him that Whittier tore in half and threw into the wastebasket at Oak Knoll were salvaged and are now in Essex Institute.)

Whittier went to Amesbury as usual at Quarterly Meeting time. He was not able to go to the meetings but had old friends at dinner as he had for half a century. He thought of going to Portland when the Yearly Meeting was held there, chiefly to talk with Thomas Chase about the biography that he had agreed to write with Samuel T. Pickard's help. Whittier would have preferred that none should be written but was resigned to the fact that it was inevitable — as was further emphasized by Kennedy's forthcoming book.

When he heard how hot the weather was at Portland, he was glad that he had not gone there. But it was hot in Amesbury, and he wished that he were at Oak Knoll, where it would seem cooler because there would be fields and trees to look at. He stayed in Amesbury through June. It was still hot when he went to Oak Knoll early in July, and mosquitoes made the night unbearable, although he found some compensation for his deafness in the fact that he couldn't "hear the wicked little tormenters singing."[19]

He thought longingly of the Isles of Shoals and Center Harbor but felt able to go only a few miles from Amesbury to a house at Hampton Falls. He had visited there with his mother many years before but did not know much about it now and only hoped that it would be comfortable and that "pilgrims" wouldn't find it. The owner, Sarah Abby Gove, attended Amesbury Friends Meeting, and one Sunday Whittier asked her if she had a room or two at her house. She had, and Whittier and some of his friends went there July 17, thinking that they would go to Center Harbor in the late summer or early fall if he gained enough strength.

The house, named "Elmfield" from the two big elms on the lawn, was a large square colonial house with a small gambrel-roofed ell much older than the main house. It was near the road — a quiet road, like most country roads at that time. Freight and people that had once been carried over this road in carts and carriages were now carried by the Boston and Maine Railroad, and the trolley car line, which would advertise itself as the only line passing the house in which Whittier had died, was not yet thought of. Whittier's room was on the second floor, the south front corner, opening on a piazza from which he could see the marshes, Hampton Beach, and the ocean.

The weather became pleasantly cool, and there was always a breeze around the house from one direction or another. Whittier soon felt better and enjoyed the food at the hotel next door, where Elmfield lodgers got their meals. The Pickards, the Cartlands, Sally Weeden, and Mrs. Henrietta Osgood were at Elmfield, and others lodged nearby, but they had not let it be known that Whittier was there, and one day he said to Sarah Gove, "I haven't had such a rest in forty years — not a pilgrim for three weeks.'' The Cartlands had a carriage, and Whittier went twice with them to places that he had visited with his mother and sister, but more often he preferred to walk to the post office or along a path by the river or to the Meschech Weare house, where Washington had once been a guest. Here he examined with interest the paneling and the wall paper with hunting scenes. He spent a good deal of his time sitting on a bench under one of the big elm trees on the Elmfield lawn. He reread Helen Hunt Jackson's *Ramona*.

On July 26 he sent "To Oliver Wendell Holmes" to Horace E. Scudder. It was written in a great hurry, he later told Holmes, when the thought came to him that he might get it into the September *Atlantic*. He was afraid that the magazine was already made up but was confident that Scudder would squeeze it in if he could so that Holmes, whose birthday was August 29, might see it in the magazine to which they had so long been contributors. The next day he sent a corrected form of the fourth stanza — the present form — and later, too late to be used, the ninth stanza, which had been omitted by whoever copied the poem for him, to his vexation.[20] Its omission gave the poem a quite different emphasis from what Whittier intended. The preceding stanza was meant to be a background of gloom for the ninth, which read:

Sorrow is real, but the counterfeit
    Which folly brings to it,
We need thy wit and wisdom to resist,
    O rarest Optimist!

The last two stanzas could not have better described his own feelings toward death even if he had known that he had only a few weeks to live:

The hour draws near, howe'er delayed and late,
    When at the Eternal Gate
We leave the words and works we call our own,
    And lift void hands alone

For love to fill. Our nakedness of soul
    Brings to that Gate no toll;
Giftless we come to Him, who all things gives,
    And live because He lives.

But he was still attentive to the world around him. He wrote two letters July 28. One was to the officer of the Amesbury Bank who bought securities for him and had suggested certain bonds. Whittier was somewhat suspicious of Astoria bonds, which paid rather too well for the times, but was willing to buy them or bonds of Port Huron. The other letter was to the Governor of New Hampshire, answering an invitation to the unveiling of a statue of John P. Hale at Concord. Whittier was still thrilled by Anti-Slavery memories, and he wrote a good letter. No one knew better than himself, he wrote, how bravely and wisely Hale acted "in the revolt and conflict which placed his state permanently on the side of freedom. He broke the chains of party and set free the best and worthiest of the Jefferson Democrats to speak and vote as their better instincts and consciences inclined them. His victory made all the after successes possible which culminated in the abolition of human slavery and the establishment of the Union on an immovable basis."[21]

He declined another invitation two weeks later to the two hundred fiftieth anniversary of the incorporation of Gloucester, Massachusetts. His letter was a thoughtful and gracious tribute to the city and to the occasion:

"I acknowledge with thanks your letter of invitation. No son of New England, certainly no son of Massachusetts, whose State House holds over the heads of her legislators the emblem of one of her great industries; no antiquarian, who recalls the romantic story of the Cape's discovery and settlement, can be indifferent to the proposed celebration of the two hundred and fiftieth anniversary of Gloucester.

"Your city has long been the nursery of brave, hardy, and patriotic men, whose skill and daring have made the ocean their tributary and field of harvest. You are to Massachusetts what Bergen is to Norway. Your situation and surroundings on one of the most picturesque capes of our Atlantic coastline suggest beauty as well as utility, and pleasure as well as profit. The salt odors of flake and store house are overblown by inland breezes, laden with the fragrance of wild roses and magnolias; and Gloucester has attractions for the summer tourist and pleasure seeker as well as for the man of business.

"I regret that I am unable to testify by my presence my interest in the coming celebration. With all good wishes for the continued prosperity of your city, I am

Very sincerely your friend
John G. Whittier"

About the middle of August Joseph Cartland asked him if he wanted to go to Center Harbor. Whittier replied, "We are finding everything so enjoyable here that I think we might as well give up Center Harbor."

For another week everything continued to be pleasant. The "pilgrims" had not found him, and he enjoyed the friends who were with him or who came to see him. He liked to talk about religion and willingly answered a question that an Amesbury Quaker, Charles H. Jones, asked him about Universalism and Unitarianism. He believed in the divinity of Christ, he said, and the necessity and efficacy of the Atonement, but Universalism had some claim on him because he had always leaned toward the concept of God as love: "I can't help feeling that those poor creatures that never have half a chance in this world will have a better chance in the next. *How* they will get it is God's business, not mine."

Another Amesbury Quaker, Susan L. Brown, came to stay for two weeks at Elmfield. She intended to keep in the background but found that Whittier, like many deaf people, liked to talk to one listener in a quiet corner, and he often talked to her about religion. He spoke indignantly of rigid creeds and of the sterner points of Calvinism. One day he suddenly asked her if she knew the meaning of eternity and seemed pleased when she replied that she did not expect to in this life. He quoted Horace Bushnell: "Sin is suicidal, it will end itself, it has no place in the eternity of God."

At times when the women had been talking by themselves, Gertrude Cartland would suggest that they go to find what Whittier and Joseph Cartland were talking about, and it would often be the Woman Suffrage movement and stories of evenings at the Radical Club.[23]

Whittier was helping in the preparation of the enlarged edition of *At Sundown*, which, he explained in a prefatory note written in July, was to be issued because there was a persistent demand and there were no copies left of the two hundred fifty printed in 1890. Fred Brown was printing copies of the poems to be added, and on August 20 Whittier sent him the stanza of "To Oliver Wendell Holmes" which had been omitted in the *Atlantic*.

He felt well through most of August. Then there was cold and damp weather, and worse still, "pilgrims" and reporters found him. One woman asked him for a lock of his hair and he replied, "I should think thee could see I have none to spare."

As Oliver Wendell Holmes' birthday approached, the editor of the *Boston Journal* asked for a poem for the occasion. Whittier replied that he had only time and strength to write a single verse, which he enclosed, dated August 26.[24] It appeared in the *Journal* the next day, and was his last poem:

Beloved physician of an age of ail,
When grave prescriptions fail,
Thy songs have cheer and healing for us all
As David's had for Saul.

Also on August 26 Whittier wrote to Holmes, sending a copy of "To Oliver Wendell Holmes" but not mentioning the lines sent to the *Journal*, which may have been written later in the day. About this time he sent his last letter to Evelina Bray Downey, who had sent him on August 12 a rambling letter with quotations from hymns.

On August 30 he wrote to Elizabeth Stuart Phelps Ward, beginning "I write no letters now," although he wrote two other letters on that day. He told her that he liked her "strong and noble" poem in the September *Atlantic*.[25] It was an account of an attack on a mountain stronghold of outlaws by a regiment that had been deprived of its colors as punishment for a mutiny. This was hardly a theme to be commended by a consistent Quaker, but it obviously pleased Whittier because the concluding stanzas sought to teach a lesson by an analogy: the great Commander, God, was told that human hearts would storm any height to win back the colors lost by rebellion and cowardice.

These letters were the last writing that he did. The next day he had an attack of diarrhea, as he often did in the summer. When home remedies had no effect, Dr. Douglass was sent for, and under his treatment Whittier was well enough after three days to leave his room, walk across the hall, and talk of going to Newburyport. But the next morning he had a stroke which left his right side paralyzed and made it hard for him to talk or to take food or medicine. His mind remained clear, and he realized his condition. He was quite resigned to the fact that he did not have long to live, and his only worry was that he was making so much trouble for the others at Elmfield, especially Sarah Gove. Three physicians were attending him, Dr. Douglass, Dr. Howe, and a woman doctor, Sarah Ellen Palmer, a native of Exeter, New Hampshire, who had recently begun to practice in Boston and who later had a distinguished career in medicine and surgery. Whittier thanked them for what they were doing for him but told them that it would not do any good and that he was worn out. He weakened steadily, and when he could say only a few words he said frequently, "I love all the world."

In spite of the Lizzie Borden trial and the approaching Corbett-Sullivan fight, Whittier's final illness got a good deal of public attention. Telegrams came from all over the country and a cable-gram from Frances Willard and Lady Somerset: "Love, reverence, gratitude." Newspaper reporters were keeping their papers informed.

On the morning of September 6 a nurse started to pull down the window shades so that he could sleep but he gestured with his left arm and said "No." He wanted to see the sunrise. It was the last time. His condition grew worse in the afternoon, and Dr. Howe came to stay through the night. Before sunrise it was evident that Whittier was dying. Gertrude Cartland recited "At Last" by the bedside, and the end came at half past four.[26]

A nurse placed a lighted lamp in a window as a signal to a reporter for the *Boston Globe* who had waited through the night concealed in some bushes in the yard. The *Globe* printed the first report of Whittier's death, but other papers had received a telephone dispatch the evening before which began, "I have just left the death bed of John G. Whittier," and stated that Whittier would be dead when the next day's papers were printed. The reporter was in Amesbury and had not been to Hampton Falls. He had returned late from supper, and the other reporters with whom he shared carriage fare, each putting the whole fare into his expense account, had gone to Hampton Falls without him.

In his latest will, signed February 11, 1890, Whittier had directed that his funeral should be in the "plain and quiet way of the Society of Friends." He could not foresee the public demonstrations or guard against them. It was a time when people thoroughly enjoyed mourning. On the day of the funeral, September 10, Whittier's birthplace was draped in black, and in the city of Haverhill flags were at half mast, bells were tolled, city offices closed, and school teachers were instructed to stop teaching during the hours of the funeral and tell their pupils about Whittier and his writings. In Danvers a memorial service was held in the Town Hall. In Amesbury the weather cleared in the morning and plans for the funeral were changed from the Friends Meeting House to the garden behind Whittier's house. A crowd was already gathering. The Haverhill city officials and the Haverhill Whittier Club came on a special train, and others came on the regular morning trains from Boston. Mr. & Mrs. William Claflin, Edmund C. Stedman, Harriet Prescott Spofford, Francis J. Garrison, Horace E. Scudder, Elizabeth Stuart Phelps Ward, Robert Treat Paine, Gail Hamilton, Sarah Orne Jewett, and Phebe Woodman came on one of the early trains; Phebe took the chance to narrate her wrongs to Sarah Orne Jewett. Samuel May, Parker Pillsbury, Caroline Healey Dall, and Edna Dean Proctor, who came on a later train, found the square near the railroad station a sea of heads. The town was having a holiday from work. Flags were at half mast, public buildings were draped in black, and pictures of Whittier were in store and house windows surrounded by flowers. One of Whittier's neighbors turned the first floor of his home into a lunch room.

Whittier's body was in an open casket in the parlor of his home, under his mother's portrait. A mass of flowers reached to the ceiling. From ten o'clock until the funeral, men, women, and children, estimated at five thousand, trooped through for a last look.

By noon people were already gathering in the garden, and by the time the service began a little after three, a half hour behind schedule, there were probably a thousand people there. Every seat was occupied, boys were sitting on the fence and in the trees, and men and women were standing in the rear. Among them was Francis H. Underwood, who could not get near enough to hear the speakers but could see "certain literary men (at a distance) in places of honor"; he left before the service was over.[27] There were also literary ladies in places of honor: Celia Thaxter, Harriet Prescott Spofford, and Gail Hamilton. Whittier would not have been pleased to know that the "fellow," William Sloane Kennedy, was there and was to write an account, with a list of the larger floral tributes and their senders, for his Revised and Enlarged Edition of *John Greenleaf Whittier*.

The service was opened by an elderly Quaker minister, William O. Newhall of Lynn, who announced that it would follow the Quaker tradition, and that Whittier had wanted it to be simple. "Quaker tradition" meant that anyone might speak who felt an urge to do so, and the reference to the service being simple may have been a hint that not too many should speak. There were eight speakers before the most distinguished of them, Edmund C. Stedman, who had not planned to speak but did so partly on impulse and partly because some of the Friends near him wished him to. Whittier, he said, "will be his own successor, and belongs to our time as well as to that earlier time to which he is linked by his work. We may say of him that the chariot swung low and he was translated, dividing the waters of truth, beauty, and religion with his mantle.'' Then there was music, contrary to the Quaker tradition, but Whittier would at least have tolerated it, since the singers were John Hutchinson and his sister Abby, who was singing for the last time in public. They sang George H. Boker's "Dirge for a Soldier," beginning "Close his eyes, his work is done." Hutchinson had written two new stanzas to replace those which specifically referred to a dead soldier.

The casket was left in the parlor long enough for everyone to have a last look, and then it was taken with the flowers to the Friends section of the Union Cemetery, followed by fifteen hacks. The Haverhill Whittier Club walked to the cemetery and past the open grave, each member dropping a cluster of roses to make a carpet for the casket to rest on. The funeral flowers were arranged as they had been at the house, and the casket was lowered at 5:20. The next day two thousand people visited the grave, and so many of them wanted a flower or at least a leaf that watchmen had to be placed on guard.[28]

There was of course a spate of memorial services, reminiscent articles, and tributes. There was an undercurrent of disillusion, however, which did not get into the newspapers. Whittier had been richer than the public supposed, and his image was blurred when his estate was appraised at $133,729.39. His money had been well invested; $83,500 was in municipal, county, and railroad bonds. The only item listed as of "no particular value" was the house lot in Whittier, California.

Some of Whittier's friends thought that he did not know how much money he had, and they believed that he would have left more and larger specific bequests if he had known how much the residue would be. When final distribution was made July 18, 1894, the residue was $59,486.52, of which the Amesbury and Salisbury Home for Aged Women, the Anna Jaques Hospital in Newburyport, and Hampton Institute each received one-sixth. The other half was divided among members of the family in proportion to their specific legacies. Among them was Louis Caldwell. Whittier had a strong sense of family obligation, and Caldwell's specific legacy was four thousand dollars. Although Whittier liked and pitied Caldwell's former wife, her legacy was a thousand dollars less. Lucy Larcom had not expected anything beyond the copyrights of *Child Life in Prose* and *Songs of Three Centuries*, and was grateful for an added five hundred dollars.[29] It might have been expected that Whittier would leave a substantial sum to Amesbury Public Library. He was the only remaining Trustee of the Library who had been a Trustee of the collection of books given by Joshua Aubin when the Library was opened in 1856, and at the time of his death he was still Chairman of the Book Committee. But he did not approve making the Library free to the public, as had been done in 1889. He was afraid that people would abuse books if they did not care enough for them to pay the fee of one dollar a year, although he had not openly opposed the change and probably thought that decisions should be made by the younger and more active Trustees. Three months before his death he visited the Library for the last time. He walked to the Library, then on Friend Street, to see a picture of himself which had been presented two days before and the flowers that were there in honor of the occasion.[30] But the Library was not mentioned in the will.

Neither was there a legacy to Amesbury Friends Meeting. Friends Meetings in New England had little need of money. They did not have the expense of a resident pastor or an elaborate house of worship.

Interest in Whittier and his poetry lasted, with no perceptible decline, for a generation after his death. There were impressive observances in 1907 of the hundredth anniversary of his birth, along with a flood of articles by men of importance in the literary world: Francis B. Gummere, Edward Everett Hale, Thomas Wentworth Higginson, Paul Elmer Moore, Bliss Perry, William Lyon Phelps. But not long after this a cleavage occurred between critics and other readers, and as this widened, new schools of criticisms found Whittier's poetry hardly worth mentioning — except, perhaps, as an amusing example of what an earlier age in its simple ignorance mistakenly took to be poetry. Whittier can not be expected to reach critics who believe with Susan Sontag that the poet's "principal means of fascinating is to advance one step further in the dialectic of outrage. To make his work repulsive, obscure, inaccessible; in short, to give what is, or seems to be, *not* wanted," or with Wallace Stevens, who said of poetry that "it resists understanding almost successfully."

Not all readers, however, wish to be repelled or puzzled or feel that it is their duty to be; if they are repelled or puzzled, they stop reading. They do not think of themselves as critics, and they do not care to analyze their motives in reading. They simply read what they like, and many of them still like Whittier's poetry and would not be in the least disturbed if critics told them that they ought not to. It may safely be said that what they enjoy is certain permanent values, which do not include two features that especially pleased readers in Whittier's time: the obvious instruction and the reiterated assurances that life exists after death. They do include a keenly observed and clearly presented view of outward nature, a direct and sincere appreciation of the best in the hearts and souls of men, a hatred of wrong and oppression, and a confident approach to a God of love — these in familiar words, figures, and rhythms. Until human nature or the English language changes completely, it seems likely that Whittier's poetry will be read.

Photograph of Whittier, 1877, by Mora of New York City.

Photograph of Whittier, 1880, by Notman of Boston.

Painting of Whittier, 1885, by Harrison Plummer of Haverhill. (Courtesy of Haverhill Public Library)

Photograph of Whittier, 1889, by Lamson of Portland, ME.

532

Dr Holmes.

Beloved physician of an age of ail'
When grave prescriptions fail
Thy songs have cheer and healing for us all.
As David's had for Saul.

John G Whittier

Hampton Falls N H
Aug 26 1892

The above fac-simile of the last verse written by Mr. Whittier, is kindly loaned us by the "Boston Journal." The following letter was sent with the verse:

HAMPTON FALLS, *August.*

Facsimile of "Doctor Holmes."

Sarah Abby Gove's house.

Whittier's funeral service.

The Whittier family burial lot in Union Cemetery, Amesbury.

Notes
Key to Abbreviations

APL	Amesbury Public Library
BPL	Boston Public Library
EI	Essex Institute
HCL	Harvard College Library
HEH	Henry E. Huntington Library and Art Gallery
HPL	Haverhill Public Library
Hav. CL	Haverford College Library
LC	Library of Congress
MHS	Massachusetts Historical Society
SC	Friends Historical Library, Swarthmore College
Albree	John Albree, Ed., *Whittier Correspondence from the Oak Knoll Collections 1830-1892*. Essex Book and Print Club, 1911.
Anderson Sale	*Catalogue of Manuscripts, Books, and Autographs from the Library of the Late John Greenleaf Whittier*. John Anderson, Jr., 1903.
Currier	Thomas Franklin Currier, *A Bibliography of John Greenleaf Whittier*. Harvard University Press, 1937.
EIHC	*Essex Institute Historical Collections*.
Pickard	Samuel T. Pickard, *Life and Letters of John Greenleaf Whittier*. Houghton Mifflin and Company, 1894.
Pollard	John A. Pollard, *John Greenleaf Whittier, friend of man*. Houghton Mifflin Company, 1949.
Shackford	Martha Hale Shackford, Ed., *Whittier and the Cartlands*. The Montrose Press, 1950.
Works	*The Works of John Greenleaf Whittier. Standard Library Edition*. Houghton Mifflin and Company, 1892.

Chapter I

1. JGW to Samuel T. Pickard, March 11, 1881. HPL.
    John J. Doak, "Reminiscences of the Poet Whittier." Manuscript, July 6, 1896. Owned by the writer.
2. Charles Arthur Hawley, "John Greenleaf Whittier and His Middle Western Correspondents." *Bulletin of Friends Historical Association*, Spring 1939.
    JGW to ? — February 8, 1884. Copy, HCL.
3. The land was bounded on three sides by land already owned by the Whittiers. It was bought for twenty dollars in the name of John Greenleaf Whittier. Deed formerly in collection of Carroll A. Wilson.
4. Pickard, p. 36.

5. Pollard, pp. 587-88.
   Pickard, pp. 27-28.
   Doak, op. cit.
   Margaret Sydney, *Whittier with the Children*. D. Lothrop, 1893. p. 1
   Emily B. Smith, *Whittier*. Whittier Press, Amesbury, 1935. pp. 27-28
   "Yankee Gypsies." *Works* V 339-40.
   Lillian Whiting, *Louise Chandler Moulton, Poet and Friend*. Little, Brown and Company,
      1910. p. 36.
   Susan L. Brown, untitled article, typescript. Owned by the writer.
6. "Snow-Bound." *Works* II 145-46.
   "The Fish I Didn't Catch." *Works* V 325.
7. Pickard, pp. 33-34. Whittier told Pickard that Aunt Mercy thoroughly believed this story.
   John F. Kellett, "Elizabeth Whittier and Greenleaf a Century After." Typescript. APL.
   Letter of William Bachelder Greene, quoted in manuscript note of Samuel T. Pickard. HCL.
8. "Snow-Bound." *Works* II 139.
   JGW to Horace Currier, July 9, 1879. Albree, p. 212.
   JGW to Lucy Larcom, May 22, 1867. MHS.
   Pickard, p. 25.
   JGW to Mary Abigail Dodge, quoted in letter of Mary Abigail Dodge to George W. Cate.
      Whittier Memorial Services. Fred A. Brown, 1893, p. 47.
   George M. White, "The Local Associations of Whittier's Poems."
      Harper's Magazine, February, 1883.
   "The Fall." *American Manufacturer*, February 26, 1829.
   JGW to Mary C. Brown, 1884. Copy, HCL.
   Haverhill Gazette, July 13, 1860.
   JGW to Annie Fields, June 22, 1886. HEH.
   "Sweet Fern." *Works* II 90. Manuscript dated "Asquam Lake, August, 1883." HEH.
   "The Quaker Poet at Amesbury." *Haverhill Weekly Bulletin*, October 18, 1884.
   American Manufacturer, July 30, 1829.
   Samuel T. Pickard, *Whittier-Land*. Houghton Mifflin Company, 1904. pp. 30, 32.
   "Magicians and Witch Folks." *Works* V 406.
   "Visits to Danvers." Letter signed "JGW, 10th mo. 15th, 1877" *Danvers Mirror*, November
      3, 1877. "From Salem Village Gazette."
9. Emily B. Smith, "Some Old Church History of Amesbury."
      Newburyport Daily News, October 17, 1901.
   Samuel T. Pickard, Manuscript note. HCL.
   JGW to Harry Fenn. HCL.
10. JGW to Ann Wendell, January 25, 1881. Hav. CL.
    Introductory note to "The New Wife and the Old." *Works* I 75
    Forster wrote to Joseph John Gurney, October 1, 1822, dating the letter "New
       Hampshire."
    Rufus M. Jones, *The Later Periods of Quakerism*. Macmillan and Company 1921. p. 649.
    Joseph Bevan Braithwaite, *Memoirs of Joseph John Gurney*. Lippincott, Grombo and
       Company, 1854. I 551.
    "William Forster." *Works* IV 88.
11. Samuel T. Pickard, *Whittier-Land*. p. 66.
    JGW to Elizabeth Neall, March 16 and April 6, 1840. Columbia University Library.
    Catherine E. Weld to Samuel T. Pickard, August 25, 1903. HCL.
    Sally Weld Tracy to JGW, July 20, 1863. HCL.
12. "The elder readers of the *Herald* will comprehend the vigorous and just portraiture of
       the mysterious guest — for they will recall Harriet Livermore." *Newburyport Herald*,
       March 19, 1866. "I am more inclined to the belief that you were just and fair in
       what you said about her [Harriet Livermore] in 'Snow-Bound' ". Charles C. Chase
       to JGW, November 13, 1887. Albree, p. 248.

JGW to Rebecca Davis, August 9, 1880. HPL.

JGW to Emily Wright, May 13, 1881. SC.

JGW to ?, September 18, 1879. Middlebury College Library.

Essex Gazette September 29, 1827. Quoted from *New York Commercial Advertiser.*

Harriet Livermore, *A Narration of Religious Experiences. In Twelve Letters.* Concord, N.H., 1826.

Pickard, p. 35.

Interview at age seventy-seven. Unidentified news clipping.

Harriet Webster Marr, *Atkinson Academy, The Early Years.* p. 90.

Manuscript note of Samuel T. Pickard. HCL.

13. Roland D. Sawyer, "A Visit with Whittier Eighty Years Ago." *Amesbury Daily News*, December 3, 1949. Quotation from interview in *Yonkers Stateman* 1869.

Henry Wadsworth Longfellow to Elizabeth Stuart Phelps, August 21, 1878. Samuel Longfellow, *Henry Wadsworth Longfellow.* Houghton, Mifflin and Company, 1893. III 287.

Diary of Horace Currier. Formerly owned by T. Franklin Currier.

14. JGW to James P. Nesmith, June 30, 1873. HEH.

"Burns." *Works* IV 93.

Samuel T. Pickard, *Whittier-Land.* p. 24: a corrected version is in "A Whittier Autograph," *Harvard Alumni Bulletin*, November 17, 1933.

Statement of Gertrude W. Cartland, quoted in "Biographical Sketch" by Albert L. Bartlett in *A Memorial of John Greenleaf Whittier from His Native City.* Haverhill, Massachusetts.

15. "The Training." *Works* V 346.

"The Agency of Evil." *Works* VII 251.

16. "Snow-Bound". *Works* II 144.

"Chalkley Hall." *Works* IV 37.

17. Earl T. Griggs, "John Greenleaf Whittier and Thomas Clarkson." *American Literature*, VII 456-60, January 1936.

18. *Journal of Charlotte L. Forten.* Notes and introduction by Ray Allen Billington. Dryden Press, 1953. p. 200.

JGW to Edith F. Glines, January 14, 1881. Haverhill Historical Society. Donald C. Freeman, "John Greenleaf Whittier," EIHC Vol. LXXXVI No. 4, October 1950.

Typewritten note of Samuel T. Pickard, based partly on a visit to East Haverhill with Whittier in 1881. HCL.

Manuscript, HPL, Pollard p. 501.

Interview. Unidentified news clipping.

Pickard, pp. 34, 35.

JGW to William Lloyd Garrison, February 14, 1859. HCL.

"Old Newbury." *Works* VI 312.

Pollard, p. 24.

"Old Newbury." *Works* VI 315.

JGW to William Lloyd Garrison, February 14, 1859. HCL.

C. Marshall Taylor, *John Greenleaf Whittier, The Quaker.* Friends Historical Society, London 1954.

Anderson Sale, p. 4.

19. JGW to Mrs. Charles Washington Coleman, February 26, 1877. In Mary Holdane Coleman, "Whittier on John Randolph of Roanoke." *New England Quarterly* VII 551, December 1935.

20. JGW to ?, August 11, 1888. *The Fete*, Eliot, Maine. Vol. I No. 1, p. 3. August 21-22, 1888.

Until recently it was assumed that Dr. Weld was the attending physician when Whittier was born, in spite of the fact that a guest at a meeting of Haverhill Whittier Club in 1894 said that it was her grandfather. Mr. Donald Wright believes this to be

Dr. Daniel Brickett, son of Brig. Gen. James Brickett, also a physician, and brother of Dr. John Brickett of Newburyport.

Statement of Miss Moody, a native of Haverhill, whose mother knew Dr. Weld in Rocks Village. Manuscript note of Samuel T. Pickard. HCL.

JGW to Mary Abigail Dodge, May 15, 1863. Copy, HCL.

JGW to Elias Weld, March 5, 1828. *A New Year's Address to the Patrons of the Essex Gazette, 1828. With a letter hitherto unpublished, by John G. Whittier.* Charles E. Goodspeed, 1903.

21. Preface to *Child Life in Prose.*
   "To J.P." *Works* IV 34.
   "The Training." *Works* V 346.
   EIHC. Vol. XCI No. 2, April, 1955.

22. "Robert Dinsmore." *Works* VI 248.
   JGW to William Plumer Jr., May 22, 1849. New Hampshire State Library.

23. Pickard, pp. 17-18.
   Joseph Merrill, *History of Amesbury and Merrimac.* Haverhill, Mass. 1880. pp. 305, 313.
   "Abram Morrison." *Works* II 185.
   Interview reported by P. De Jean. *Newburyport Herald*, December 17, 1887.

24. JGW to Daniel Roberts, July 29, 1877. Quoted in Currier, page 50. See "A Song of Peace."
   "Lines on the Death of Alexander I, Emperor of Russia." *The Free Press*, July 6, 1826.
   "The Sun." *Essex Gazette*, February 17, 1827.
   "The Quaker." *Essex Gazette*, March 17, 1827.

25. Pickard, pp. 50, 51.
   Whittier-land, p. 37.
   JGW to William Lloyd Garrison, February 14, 1859. Copy, HCL.
   Pickard, p. 53.
   "Haverhill Academy." *Newburyport Herald*, April 3, 1827.
   Nelson H. Grover, "Shoemakers Who Became Famous. John Greenleaf Whittier." *Illustrated Footwear Fashion*, Holiday number, 1900. Issued by Oran McCormick, Boston. p. 34.
   John Hoit to JGW, February 14, 1882. HCL.
   A. J. Huntress, "Reminiscenses of His Youth." *Newburyport Herald*, December 17, 1887.

26. Nathan Crosby, "Reminiscences of Distinguished Men of Essex County". Salem, 1880. EIHC Vol. XVII Part 2.
   Fred French of South Hampton, New Hampshire, former school teacher and local historian, told the writer that he saw Whittier making shoes about 1866 "somewhere up Birch Meadow way."

27. One of Evelina Bray Downey's letters to Samuel T. Pickard mentioned that when Whittier's father brought him back to the Thayers' after a week-end on the farm he also brought a joint of mutton.

28. A. L. Bartlett, *The Haverhill Academy and the Haverhill High School.* Haverhill, 1890.
   Robert K. Cheney, *Maritime History of the Merrimac: Shipbuilding.* Newburyport Press, 1964. Chapter XVII.
   JGW to Alpheus Currier, November 10, 1875. HPL.

29. *Haverhill Gazette*, April 28, 1827. The church was not the present First Church. The original First Church, of which Dudley Phelps was the minister, became a casualty of the Unitarian controversy. The meetinghouse was on Winter Street.

30. JGW to ?, October 7, 1890. HPL.

31. A. L. Bartlett, op. cit.
   Leverett Saltonstall's Reminiscences of Salem. Written in 1885. EIHC, Vol. *LXXXII* No. 1, January 1946.
   Arethusa Hall. A Memorial, edited by Francis Ellingwood Abbott. Cambridge, 1892.
   JGW to Mary Emerson Smith, July 2, 1829. Copy, HCL.

32. "Schoolday Remembrances." *Works* VI 316.
   Catalogue of the Officers and Students of Haverhill Academy. Haverhill, Mass. July 1828.
   John L. White to JGW, Haverhill Historical Society.
   Donald C. Freeman, "*John Greenleaf Whittier and his Birthplace*." EIHC. *Vol. LXXXVI*
      No. 4, October 1950.

33. JGW to Harriet Minot Pitman, April 24, 1877. SC.
   Evelina Bray Downey to Samuel T. Pickard. HCL.
   George Allard to Roland H. Woodwell, September 18, 1961; information given him by
      Mary White Smith's granddaughter, Mrs. Bramhall.
   Samuel T. Pickard, Manuscript note. HCL. The poem is "The Veil," *Haverhill Gazette*,
      November 24, 1827.
   Letter August 1832. Copy, HCL.
   Quoted by Nora Perry. Unidentified newspaper clipping at Whittier Home, Amesbury.

34. Harriet Minot Pitman to Samuel T. Pickard, August 9, 1882. HCL.
   JGW to Harriet Minot Pitman, January 7, 1882. SC.
   "Memory of Whittier to be Honored Tomorrow." *Boston Post*, December 16, 1945.

35. Copies, HPL.

36. JGW to Edwin Harriman, June 26, 1829. Copy, HCL.
   Mary Emerson Smith Thomas to Samuel T. Pickard, November 16, 1894. HCL.
   Sarah Thayer to Samuel T. Pickard, January 20, 1893. HCL.

37. The Friend was Charles Jones, and the statement was quoted to the writer by Charles Jones'
      granddaughter, Ruth Osborne.

38. JGW to Harriet Minot Pitman, March 6, 1880. HCL.

39. Said to Caroline Carter, who quoted it to the writer.

40. Typewritten article by Samuel T. Pickard, HCL.
   Eveline Bray Downey to Samuel T. Pickard. HCL.

41. Record Book of West School District of Amesbury.
   JGW to Abijah W. Thayer, November 28, 1828. Pickard, p. 71.
   American Manufacturer, February 5, 1829.
   Amesbury and Salisbury Villager, October 8, 1885.
   Rhymed epistle to Abijah W. Thayer. Copy, SC.
   JGW to James P. Nesmith, October 31, 1826. HEH.

42. JGW to Francis J. Garrison, March 27, 1888. SC.

43. Introductory note to "To Pius IX". *Works* III 329.

44. "Lines on the New Year." *Essex Gazette*, January 19, 1828.

45. "The Seaman's Funeral." *Essex Gazette*, June 16, 1827.

46. Manuscript formerly owned by Carroll A. Wilson.

47. "To the Merrimac." *National Philanthropist*, June 6, 1828.

48. Manuscript dated 1825. EI
   Editorial Note with "Life's Pleasures." *Boston Statesman*, July 21, 1827.

Chapter II

1. JGW to Elias Weld, March 5, 1828. HPL.
   JGW to James Nesmith, October 31, 1828. SC.

2. JGW to William Lloyd Garrison, October 11, 1828. *Journal of the Times*, October 24, 1828.
   Haverhill Gazette, November 15, 1828.

3. JGW to Abijah W. Thayer, November 28, 1828. Pickard, pp. 70-72.
4. Rufus Rockwell Wilson to Samuel T. Pickard, December 20, 1903. HCL.
    JGW to Abijah W. Thayer, February 6, 1829. Pickard, pp. 75-76.
    JGW to ?, June 24, 1878. EI.
5. Joseph Merrill, *History of Amesbury and Merrimac*, Haverhill, 1880. p. 348.
6. JGW to Francis J. Garrison, October 21, 1885. SC.
7. *National Era*, November 1, 1852.
8. March 14, 1829. Whittier stated that the poem was suggested by a passage in the first volume.
    The passage is in the second volume, p. 90.
9. "The Drunkard to His Bottle" is in the Riverside Edition, but the only evidence that it
    was written in 1829 is the date in this edition, in which many poems are incorrectly
    dated.
10. Willis Gaylord Clark to JGW, July 17, 1829. Anderson Sale, p. 6.
11. JGW to Mary Emerson Smith, July 2, 1829. HCL.
    George D. Prentice to JGW, June 8, [1829]. Formerly owned by Robert W. Lull. Copy,
    HCL.
12. JGW TO James P. Nesmith (?), January 2, 1860. SC.
13. JGW to Edwin Harriman, May 18, 1829. HCL. Part of this letter is in Pickard, pp. 93-94,
    incorporated with another letter to Harriman June 6, 1829, copy HCL.
14. JGW to Mary Emerson Smith, May 23, 1829. Copy, HCL.
15. JGW to Mary Emerson Smith, June 6, 1829. Copy, HCL.
16. "Have You Forgotten?" *Boston Courier*, June 9, 1829. Later entitled "To My Cousin."
17. JGW to Mary Emerson Smith, July 2, 1829. Copy, HCL.
18. Mary Emerson Smith to Samuel T. Pickard, December 13, 1892. HCL.
19. Mary Emerson Smith to Samuel T. Pickard, November 16, 1894. HCL.
20. Note 15.
    Pickard, p. 78.
    Samuel T. Pickard's record of papers in his file. HCL.
    Genius of Universal Emancipation, September 2, 1829.
21. JGW to John Neal, October 1829. John Neal, *Wandering Recollections of a Somewhat
    Busy Life*, Boston, 1869. pp. 337-38.
    Pickard, p. 77.
    John L. Brown to JGW, January 1, 1886. HPL.
22. *Legends of New England (1831) by John Greenleaf Whittier. A Facsimile Reproduction
    with an Introduction by John B. Pickard. Scholars' Facsimiles and Reprints*, 1965.
    p. X.
23. *Boston Courier*, September 7, 1829. *New Hampshire Statesman and Concord Register*,
    October 17, 1829. *New York Amulet and Ladies' Literary and Religious Chronicle*,
    May 15, 1830.
24. Pickard, p. 79.
    The office was on the second floor of a brick building at the corner of Main and Water
    Streets. *Haverhill Gazette*, December 17, 1945.
25. *New York Amulet and Ladies' Literary and Religious Chronicle*, July 2, 1830, Number
    12 in a series of "Moral Tales."
26. "New Year's Address to the Patrons of the *Essex Gazette*," January 5, 1828.
    Essex Gazette, February 20 and May 15, 1830.
27. *Proceedings of the American Anti-Slavery Society*. New York 1864.
28. *Newburyport Herald*, February 24, 1865.
29. JGW to *Boston Transcript*, March 14, 1864. *Boston Transcript*, March 16, 1864.
    JGW to William L. Garrison, January 17, 1864. BPL.
    Life of Arthur Tappan. Hurd and Houghton, 1870. p. 163.

30. *Ladies' Magazine*, February 1830.
    There are numerous minor changes which Whittier made on pages from *Legends of New England*, formerly owned by Carroll A. Wilson.
31. There are variations in six lines.
32. Mentioned in the 1835 version of the poem but not in the Riverside Edition.
33. Currier, p. 368.
    American Manufacturer, January 15, 1829.
    Essex Gazette, May 29, 1830, quotation from *Dublin Literary Gazette*.
34. Currier, p. 20.
35. Letter of Mary Abigail Dodge to a friend, later sent to Samuel T. Pickard. HCL.
    Whittier thought many years later that the position was offered because he had supported Clay in the *American Manufacturer*.
    JGW to *Boston Transcript*, March 14, 1864. Note 29.
    George D. Prentice to JGW, June 8, [1829]. Note 11.
36. Preface to *Legends of New England*.
    New England Weekly Review, July 2, 1830.
    A letter from Mrs. Sigourney to Whittier, dated January 16, 1856, is at Central Michigan University. She remembered him as "an interesting young man, who some lustrums of years since . . . occasionally, tho ' seldom, called at my abode."
    JGW to Charles Dudley Warner, January 12, 1885, in *Memorial History of Hartford County, Connecticut*, p. 614. Copy, HCL.
    JGW to Jonathan Law, February 4, 1832. Copy, HCL.
37. JGW to Abigail Whittier, October 9, 1830. Central Michigan University. This letter is incorrectly dated September 9. It mentions an apology to be in the *Review* the next day for lack of editorial material. Apologies appeared October 4 and 11, while the next issue after September 9 contained "The Spectre," "The Quilting Party," "To the Memory of J. G. C. Brainard," and three editorials evidently by Whittier.
    Pickard, p. 87, Note.
    JGW to Jonathan Law, February 4, 1832. University of Florida.
38. The statement was made to secretary of the Treasury Samuel D. Ingham and quoted in Ingham's account of his conversation with Col. Richard M. Johnson. James Parton, *Life of Andrew Jackson*. Mason Bros., 1861, Vol. III p. 306. It was in this same account that Ingham quoted Johnson as saying that Jackson "was so much excited that he roared like a lion." p. 304.
39. C. Marshall Taylor, "Whittier vs. Garrison." EIHC Vol. LXXXII No. 3 July 1946.
40. JGW to Louisa C. Tuthill, April 24, 1831. HCL.
41. This comment of Whittier's is in the *Review*, February 7, 1831, in a note asking that he be given credit for it by an editor who had copied it. Currier questioned Whittier's authorship.
42. JGW to Abigail Whittier. Note 37.
43. JGW to Charles Dudley Warner. Note 36. What chapters or pages were written by Whittier is a matter of conjecture. Currier discusses the question thoroughly on pp. 13-15.
    JGW to Jonathan Law, January 2, 1831. EI.
    Pennsylvania Freeman, September 6, 1838.
44. JGW to Jonathan Law. "At sea, ½ past 3 o'clock," December 31, 1830. Yale University Library.
45. JGW to ?, April 21, 1880. Colgate University Library.
    JGW to Charles Dudley Warner. Note 36.
    JGW to Jonathan Law. Note 43.
46. JGW to Jonathan Law January 15, 1831. Copy, HCL.
    Pickard pp. 85 and 94.
    "To the Friend in His Editorial Chair." *New England Weekly Review*, March 14 and March 21, 1831.

47. The facts have been told by Roland D. Sawyer in "Amesbury-Salisbury in Olden Days." *Amesbury Daily News*, May 4, 1957.

48. Lilly G. Warner to JGW, September 7, 1866. EI.
   JGW to Abigail H. Whittier, May 18, 1831. EI.
   New England Weekly Review, June 6, July 18, July 25, 1831.

49. JGW to Eli Todd, September 20, 1831. Yale University Library.
   Eli Todd, 1789-1833, practiced medicine in Hartford and was noted for his work with the mentally ill. He was the first superintendent of the Connecticut Retreat for the Insane.

50. The letter was printed in *The Century*, May 1902, in an article by William Lyon Phelps, "A Noteworthy Letter of Whittier's." It is now owned by Connecticut Historical Society.

51. JGW to Jonathan Law, undated. Noted by Law as received October 27, 1831. Copy, HCL.
   Aesculapius was the Roman god of medicine. "Sangrador" is Spanish, "phlebotomist." There is a physician in *Gil Blas* named "Dr. Sangrado," whose sole treatment was bleeding the patient and having him drink warm water.

52. Whittier's certificate of appointment, signed by John Russ, Chairman of the Central Committee for Connecticut, is in Harvard College Library.
   JGW to Mary Emerson Smith, August 1832. Copy, HCL.
   JGW to Alonzo Lewis, December 13, 1831. HCL.

53. Manuscript note of Samuel T. Pickard. HCL.
   Pollard, p. 515.
   JGW to Mary Emerson Smith, August 1832. Copy, HCL.
   Typewritten note of Samuel T. Pickard. HCL.

54. JGW to Charles Dudley Warner, January 13, 1885. Note 36.
   JGW to *Boston Evening Transcript*, September 19, 1887. *Boston Evening Transcript*, October 5, 1887.
   JGW to Louisa C. Tuthill, April 16, 1831. Copy, HCL.

55. JGW to Elizabeth Whittier Pickard. Anderson Sale, p. 40.

56. Richard M. Dorson, *Jonathan Draws the Long Bow*. Harvard University Press, 1946.

57. JGW to Jonathan Law, January 5, 1832. Copy, HCL. A letter to Lydia H. Sigourney February 2, 1832, tells a different story: he had handed the poem to a friend who had "threatened to publish it." Letter owned by Connecticut Historical Society.
   JGW to Sarah Josepha Hale, January 24, 1832. University of Virginia.

58. Sidney Perley, "Moll Pitcher," *Essex Antiquarian* Vol. III No. 3, March 1899.
   Richard N. Dorson. Op. cit.

59. JGW to ?, November 13, 1886. University of Indiana.

60. *London Atheneum*. Quoted by Oliver Wendell Holmes, *A Mortal Antipathy*. Introduction.

61. JGW to Gideon Welles, July 26, 1831. Connecticut Historical Society.

Chapter III

1. JGW to Sarah Josepha Hale, January 24, 1832. University of Virginia.

2. In a letter at the Essex Institute dated May 5, 1832, Whittier was urged to accept a position which he had been previously offered as head of the editorial department of the *Cincinnati American*.

3. JGW to Sarah Joseph Hale. Note 1.

4. JGW to Lydia H. Sigourney, February 2, 1832. Connecticut Historical Society.

5. JGW to J. T. and E. Buckingham, December 12, 1832. EI.

6. "Mr. Clay and the Tariff." *Haverhill Iris*, January 31, 1832.
   Essex Gazette, June 16, March 17, September 8, 15, 29, October 6, 1832.

7. Whittier sent Lawson's "Epicidium" to Thayer for publication in the *Essex Gazette*, February 11, 1832.

8. Claude M. Fuess, *Caleb Cushing*. Harcourt, Brace and Co., 1923. p. 129.
   JGW to Mary Emerson Smith, August, 1832. Copy, HCL.
   Pickard, pp. 168-169.

9. JGW to Jonathan Law, September 13, 1832. Copy, HCL.

10. Fuess, op. cit. p. 130.

11. JGW to Caleb Cushing, October 31, 1832. SC.

12. JGW to I. A. Rockwell, July 28, 1832. Yale University Library.

13. JGW to Mary Emerson Smith. Note 8.

14. JGW to Jonathan Law. Note 9.

15. JGW to Lydia H. Sigourney, January 1833. Connecticut Historical Society.

16. "Confessions of a Suicide" begins on page 287 of *Works V*: "I saw her wedded to another."
    JGW to James T. Fields, August 21, 1849. HEH.

17. JGW to Edwin Harriman, February 2, [1833]. HCL
    JGW to Mary Emerson Smith, March 2, 1833. Copy, HCL.

18. William Lloyd Garrison to JGW, March 22, 1833. Central Michigan University.

19. *William Lloyd Garrison: The Story of His Life as Told by His Children*. Houghton, Mifflin and Company, 1889. I 332.

20. *Newburyport Herald*, December 17, 1887.
    Fred Laurence Knowles, "Whittier's Advice to a Boy." *The Writer*, October 1888.

Chapter IV

1. JGW to Lewis Tappan, May 2, 1870. LC.
   Arthur Tappan to JGW, June 13, 1833. EI.
   Arthur Tappan to Lewis P. Laine, March 26, 1833. *Life of Arthur Tappan*, Hurd and Houghton, 1870.
   Pickard, p. 124.

2. These are printed with the title "The Abolitionists, Their Sentiments and Objects." *Works VII* 58.

3. JGW to Robert Cross, August 1, 1933. Privately owned.

4. *Essex Gazette*, July 13, 1833.

5. Currier, pp. 49-53.

6. JGW to William Lloyd Garrison, November 12, 1833. BPL. The latter part of the article was in the *Iris*, Methuen, April 4, 1834, and presumably an earlier part on March 28. The first four pages as printed in *Works* VI, 321 were added when the article was reprinted in the *Pennsylvania Freeman*.

7. See Robert D. Cross, "The Changing Image of Catholicism in America." *Yale Review*, Summer 1959.

8. *Essex Gazette*, September 14, 1833.

9. JGW to Jonathan Law, October, 1833. Copy, HCL.

10. *Essex Gazette*, November 11 and 16, 1833.

11. JGW to Isaac Knapp, September 26, 1833. JGW to William Lloyd Garrison, November 12, 1833. BPL. Whittier had evidently forgotten what he had said in these letters when he wrote "The Anti-Slavery Convention of 1833" for the *Atlantic Monthly*, February, 1874. (*Works* VII, 171.)

12. At a special meeting of the Board of Managers of the New England Anti-Slavery Society in Samuel E. Sewall's office November 18, 1833, eight delegates were chosen, among them Garrison and Sewall, with the power to appoint others. Joshua Coffin was added at a meeting November 29. *Records of New England Anti-Slavery Society*, II 269. BPL. Whittier was evidently appointed by the delegates, perhaps at Garrison's suggestion.

13. Pickard, p. 133.
    "Samuel E. Sewall," *Essex Transcript*, November 17, 1845.
    "The Anti-Slavery Convention of 1833." *Works* VII 171.
    Letter from correspondent to Editors of *National Intelligencer*, December 6, 1833. Quoted in *Essex Gazette*, December 14, 1833.
    JGW to ?, April 9, 1870. *Newburyport Herald*, April 15, 1870.
    "The Anti-Slavery Convention of 1833." *Works* VII 171.
    Letter of J. Miller McKim in *Proceedings of the American Anti-Slavery Society in Its Third Decade*. New York, 1864.
    JGW to J. Miller McKim, November 30, 1853. BPL.
    "Lewis Tappan." *Works* VI 279.
    Abridged account from full report in *New York Emancipator* of National Anti-Slavery Convention at Philadelphia, December 4, 5, 6. *Essex Gazette*, January 4, 1834.

14. JGW to William Lloyd Garrison, November 24, 1863. BPL. *Works* VII 145.
    JGW to Samuel J. May, November 3, 1871. *Memoir of Samuel Joseph May*, Boston 1873. p. 152.
    A note on the inside front cover of the original draft of the Declaration of Principles in Oberlin College Library reads: "This draft is in the handwriting of William Lloyd Garrison. I was on the committee with him for drafting it, and furnished some outlines brought with me from New York. I was requested by the Committee to write out my plan, but being quite exhausted, it was committed to Mr. Garrison, (signed) W. Goodell." C. Marshall Taylor, "Whittier vs. Garrison." EIHC Vol. LXXXII No. 3, July 1946.

15. Ann Wendell to Samuel T. Pickard. HCL. The letter (Pickard p. 219) gives the winter of 1836-37 as the time of Whittier's first visit to the Wendells. The letter was written after Whittier's death and therefore sixty years after his visit to Philadelphia in 1833. The reference to Christmas gifts precludes 1836 or 1837. He was not in Philadelphia before Christmas in those years.

Chapter V

1. JGW to Elizur Wright, February 25, 1834. University of Texas.
   Lists of sums paid by John Russell to Abigail Whittier and by Abel Page to John Whittier 1833-34. HPL.

2. Letter of James Neall, August 10, 1892. HCL.

3. Interview reported in *Pall Mall Gazette* and quoted in various American papers, including *Danvers Mirror*, January 23, 1886, and *Amesbury and Salisbury Villager*, February 11, 1886.

4. *Works* VII 87.
    Introductory note to "Follen". *Works* IV 29.
    JGW to Editor of *Essex Transcript*, March 31, 1843; in this letter Whittier corrected
    a statement in the *Transcript* that Follen had been converted to Abolition by his
    letter.
    Introductory Note to "Expostulation." *Works* III 24.

5. JGW to Elizur Wright. Note 1.

6. *Essex Gazette*, March 29, April 5 and 26, 1834.
    Letter signed "Eustis," March 1, 1834. Probably by Whittier. See Currier, p. 567.

7. *Essex Gazette*, June 7 and June 14, 1834.

8. Sarah L. Forten to Elizabeth Whittier, February 11, 1834. EI.
    Theodore E. Weld to James Gillespie Birney, June 9, 1834. *Letters of James Gillespie
    Birney*. Ed. Dwight L. Dumond. D. Appleton-Century Co., 1938. I 119.
    Mary Whittier to JGW, November 15, 1834. EI.

9. William Goodell, "An Appeal in Behalf of the American Anti-Slavery Society. Ad-
    dressed to the people of the City of New York." *Essex Gazette*, September 6, 1834.
    Essex Gazette, July 12, 1834.
    Essex Gazette, August 16, 1834.

10. *Life of Arthur Tappan*. Hurd and Houghton, 1870. p. 204.

11. JGW to Caleb Cushing, October 25, 1834. SC.
    The Colonization Society was not as near death as the Abolitionists hopefully sup-
    posed. Nine years later it was still active and highly respectable in Newburyport
    when it held its annual meeting at the Savings Bank a few days after the County
    Liberty Convention was held in a much humbler place, the Methodist Meeting
    House in the Joppa section of Newbury (now Newburyport).
    JGW to Caleb Cushing, November 3, 1834. SC.
    Caleb Cushing to JGW. Central Michigan University. In George Rice Carpenter, *John
    Greenleaf Whittier*, Houghton Mifflin 1903. pp. 202-03.

12. *Essex Gazette*, November 15, 1834. *The Iris*, November 21, 1834.
    JGW to William Lloyd Garrison, November 12, 1833. BPL.
    JGW to Elizur Wright. Note 1.

13. Journal of the House of Representatives, 1835. Unless otherwise noted, references to
    votes and motions are from this source.

14. *Essex Gazette*, September 11 and February 24, 1835.

15. *New England Magazine*, May 1, 1835.
    Louisa Whitney, *The Burning of the Convent*. James R. Osgood and Company, 1877.

16. The writer's grandmother, born in 1825, still spoke about it in a tone of sorrow when she
    was very old — she died in 1930.

17. JGW to ?, December, 1873. St. John's Seminary.

18. *Daily Evening Transcript*, February 26, 1835.

19. One of these, not mentioned in the House Journal, is reported in the *Columbian
    Centinel*, October 2, 1835.

20. "Dr. Channing on Slavery." *Essex Register*, December 17, 1835.

21. *Records of the New England Anti-Slavery Society*. II 295-303. BPL.
    Liberator, May 30, 1835.

22. *Essex Gazette*, August 1, June 13, and August 15, 1835.
    JGW to Elizabeth H. Whittier, August 27, [1835]. New York Public Library.
    Henry Benson to Amos A. Phelps, August 27, 1835. Copy in Samuel T. Pickard's
    handwriting. HCL.
    Pickard, p. 149.
    "Nathaniel Peabody Rogers." *Works* VII 220.

23. Whittier's own account of the events was in the *Essex Gazette*, September 12, 1835.
    Other details are in Pickard, pp. 149-53, derived from "conversations with Mr.

Whittier and other sources." Some of Whittier's statements were called false in an editorial in the *New Hampshire Statesman*, September 19, 1835.

24. William A. Kent married the widow of Beza Tucker; her daughter was the wife of Ralph Waldo Emerson.

25. Editorial, "Lucia Ames Kent." *Pennsylvania Freeman*, March 22, 1838.

26. William Tallack, *Friendly Sketches in America*. London, 1861. p. 220.
    JGW to Elizabeth Neall, March 16, 1840. Columbia University.
    "The Anti-Slavery Convention of 1833." *Works* VII 172.

27. Albert L. Bartlett, *Some Memories of Old Haverhill in Massachusetts*, Haverhill, 1915. p. 18.
    JGW to Thomas J. Mumford, November 3, 1871. Thomas J. Mumford, ed., *Memoir of Samuel Joseph May*, Boston, 1873. p. 152.

28. Pickard, p. 152.

29. "The halter has got around my father's neck again instead of being coiled around his body." Francis J. Garrison to Samuel T. Pickard, commenting on Carpenter's *John Greenleaf Whittier*, October 13, 1903. HCL.

30. Pickard, p. 143.
    "William Lloyd Garrison." *Works* VII 191.

31. *Records of New England Anti-Slavery Society*. II 317-18. BPL.

32. Sarah Lewis to Elizabeth H. Whittier, October 1, 1840. HCL.
    Sarah L. Forten to Elizabeth H. Whittier, March 23, 1835. Central Michigan University.

33. *Essex Gazette*, November 7, 1835.

34. JGW to Jonathan Law, August 24, 1835. Copy, HCL.

35. Both letters are in Albree, Cushing's December 24, 1835, page 38; Phillips' December 11, 1835, page 41.

36. JGW to Caleb Cushing, December 28, 1835. LC.

37. JGW to Abijah W. Thayer, November 29, 1835. Pickard, p. 156.

38. Note of Samuel T. Pickard in copy of *History of Saco and Biddeford*. HPL.

39. October 24, 1877. Yale University Library.
    JGW to Francis H. Underwood, July 21, 1883. SC.

40. JGW to John Langdon Bonython, September 15, 1881. *Century Illustrated Monthly Magazine*, June 1882.

Chapter VI

1. JGW to Abijah W. Thayer, January 10, 1836. SC.

2. JGW to Caleb Cushing, February 10 and 18, 1836. LC.
   JGW to Caleb Cushing, February 20, 1836. SC.

3. JGW to Robert C. Waterston, January 27, 1865. HCL. *Works* VI 274-77.

4. JGW to Jeremiah Spofford, November 23, 1836. EI.

5. Matthew Franklin Whittier was disowned from the Society of Friends in Seabrook Monthly Meeting, November 3, 1836.

6. *Newburyport Herald*, July 2, 1858.

7. Elizabeth Nicholson to Elizabeth H. Whittier, undated. HCL.

8. JGW to Ophelia Underwood July 8, 1852. *A Succinct Account of the Late Difficulties in the Salisbury Corporation*. Currier & Gerrish, 1852.
   Emily Binney Smith, *Whittier*. The Whittier Press, 1935. p. 34.

9. Record Book of Amesbury and Salisbury Anti-Slavery Society. Whittier Home, Amesbury.

10. *Morning Chronicle.* September 2, 1836.

11. John Hayward, *New England Gazeteer*, Concord and Boston, 1841.

12. There was no house on the lot when it was sold October 21, 1829, to Lydia C. Allen, wife of Thomas Allen. Samuel Morrill bought the property from Mrs. Allen, January 23, 1836, for eight hundred dollars and sold it to John Whittier, "gentleman," and Abigail Whittier, widow, May 21, 1836, for twelve hundred dollars. The increase in value may have come from rapid rise in real estate near the Mills, or Morrill, a shipwright, may have made improvements or completed the construction of the house which Allen had built. Charles I. Pettingell to Roland H. Woodwell, April 5, 1937. APL.

13. *Essex Gazette*, June 6, 1836.

14. "Parson" Milton was finally dismissed in the spring of 1837 and died two months later.

15. JGW to Jeremiah Spofford, August 27, 1836. EI.

16. JGW to Jeremiah Spofford, December 1, 1836. Copy, EI.

17. *Essex Gazette*, November 5, 1836.

18. *Essex Gazette*, September 10 and October 15, 1836.

Chapter VII

1. Pickard pp. 195-96.
George Rice Carpenter, *John Greenleaf Whittier*, Houghton Mifflin, 1903. pp. 158-60.
JGW to Caleb Cushing, January 16, 1837.

2. *Haverhill Gazette*, February 18, 1837.
JGW to Elizabeth H. Whittier, February 3, 1837. Albree, pp. 46-49.

3. JGW to Elizur Wright, February 8, 1837. University of Texas.

4. JGW to Edward M. Davis, February 26, 1837. HCL.

5. JGW to Robert Rantoul, March 31, 1837. EI.

6. Amesbury and Salisbury Anti-Slavery Society's Record Book, Whittier Home, Amesbury, Mass.

7. JGW to Abijah W. Thayer, March 31, 1837. Pickard, p. 157.
Carpenter, pp. 160-61.
JGW to Caleb Cushing, April 14, 1837. SC.

8. Receipt. BPL.

9. *Fourth Annual Report of the American Anti-Slavery Society.* New York, 1837.

10. *Proceedings of the Fourth New England Anti-Slavery Convention Held in Boston May 30, 31, June 1 and 2, 1837.* Boston, 1837. p. 122.

11. JGW to Elizabeth H. Whittier, June 14, 1837. Pickard p. 206.

12. *Letters of James Gillespie Birney.* Ed. Dwight L. Dumond. D. Appleton-Century, 1938. I 382.

13. JGW to William J. Allinson, June 17, 1837. Cornell University Library.
JGW to Elizabeth H. Whittier, July 18, 1837, and to Mary Whittier Caldwell, undated. Albree, pp. 50-53.

14. JGW to Elizabeth H. Whittier, July 4, 1837. Formerly owned by C. Marshall Taylor.
JGW to Lucy Hooper, August 17, 1837. Yale University Library.
JGW to Lucy Hooper, August 21, 1837. Pickard, pp. 211-12.

15. JGW to Henry Clay, "New York, 5th, 6th mo. 1837, 143 Nassau Street." Carpenter, pp. 153-156.

16. JGW to Harriet Minot, June 5, 1837. HCL.
Benjamin S. Jones to Mary C. Pennock, June 4, 1838.
Sarah P. Sellers, *David Sellers, Mary Pennock Sellers. By Their Daughter*. Innes & Sons, 1928. p. 51.
Clarkson Dearborn, "Seabrook Sketches." *Granite Monthly*, December 1893.
JGW to Harriet Minot, July 31, 1837. Central Michigan University.
JGW to "My Dear Sisters," August 14, 1837. Catherine N. Birney, *The Grimke Sisters*. Lee and Shepard, 1885. p. 203.

17. *Minutes of the General Association of Massachusetts at Their Session in North Brookfield, June 28, 1837*. Boston, 1837.
Alice Stone Blackwell, *Lucy Stone, Pioneer Woman Suffragist*, Little Brown, 1930, p. 25.

18. JGW to John Farmer, June 6 [?] 1837. BPL.
JGW to David Laing, July 5, 1837. SC.
JGW to Samuel Sewall, August 8, 1837. MHS.

19. Currier, pp. 32-39.

20. JGW to Harriet Minot, August 6, 1837. Boston Atheneum.

21. Amos A. Phelps to JGW, August 17, 1837. BPL.
JGW to Amos A. Phelps, August 21, 1837. BPL.

22. Stanton wrote in *Random Recollections* (quoted in Albree, p. 86): "Only those who know my shy friend [Whittier] well are aware how talkative, genial, witty, and humorous, sarcastic and entertaining he is in bright hours with two or three companions."

23. *Letters of James Gillespie Birney*, I 408.

24. First printed in "Whittier and Lucy Hooper" by Albert Mordell. *New England Quarterly*, June, 1934.

25. JGW to Lucy Hooper, August 27, 1837. HCL.

26. Told by Dr. Van Ness of the Second Church in Boston to Samuel T. Pickard. Scrapbook at Whittier Home, Amesbury.

27. Letters to Amos A. Phelps, September 18 and October 22, 1837. BPL.

28. Claude M. Fuess, *Life of Caleb Cushing*, Harcourt, Brace and Company, 1935. I 237.

29. *Newburyport Herald*, November 7, 1837.

Chapter VIII

1. JGW to George Bancroft, January 25, 1838 and February 5, 1838. MHS.

2. Edward M. Davis to JGW, January 31, 1838. Central Michigan University.
JGW to Harriet Minot, March 13, 1838. HCL.
JGW to Harriet Minot Pitman, April 24, 1877. SC.

3. Manuscript note of Samuel T. Pickard. HCL.

4. JGW to Elizabeth Nicholson, February 2, 1841. Hav. CL.
Hannah Lloyd Neall to JGW, November 19, 1856. HCL.
Elizabeth Nicholson to JGW, December 28, 1882. EI.

5. This book is described by Edward D. Snyder in *Pennsylvania Magazine of History and Biography*, April, 1938.

6. JGW to Samuel Allinson, March 13, 1843. Hav. CL.
    Elizabeth Lloyd to JGW, September 8, 1849. Thomas Franklin Currier, *Elizabeth Lloyd and the Whittiers*. Harvard University Press, 1939. p. 121.
    JGW to Elizabeth Neall, March 16, 1840, and August 28, 1841. Columbia University.
7. Sarah P. Sellers. *David Sellers, Mary Pennock Sellers.*
    Rachel W. Healey to JGW, March 21, 1843. EI.
8. JGW to Elizabeth Lloyd, July 14, 1859. Marie Denervaud, ed. *Whittier's Unknown Romance*, Houghton Mifflin Company, 1922, p. 34.
9. Mary Otis Willcox to Samuel T. Pickard, December 1, 1904. HCL.
10. JGW to Williams and Everett. Copy, HCL. The picture was lost for many years, but turned up in 1887. It was painted on wood, which cracked, and Whittier had it repaired and framed. His friends suggested using it in *Stedman's Library of American Literature*. JGW to Edmund Clarence Stedman, September 18, 1888. Copy, HCL.
11. *William Lloyd Garrison* II 211.
    JGW to Moses A. Cartland, pencilled date 1847. HCL.
12. *David Sellers, Mary Pennock Sellers.*
13. Joseph Sturge, *A Visit to the United States in 1841*. Hamilton, Adams & Co., 1842. p. 46. Robert Purvis was the son of a Moorish-Negro mother and an English father. He was wealthy and socially prominent and lived in a country home fifteen miles from Philadelphia which was a gathering place of Abolitionists. He was a son-in-law of James Forten.
14. Testimony of Samuel Webb. *Pennsylvania Freeman*, September 26, 1839.
    Pennsylvania Freeman, May 24, 31, 1838. From the *Pennsylvanian*.
15. Martha H. Shackford, "Whittier and Some Cousins." *New England Quarterly*, September 1942.
    JGW to Moses A. Cartland. Note 11.
    William Lloyd Garrison II 216-17.
16. Pickard, pp. 225-26.
17. Letter May 31, 1838. *Pennsylvania Freeman*, June 7, 1838.
18. *Pennsylvania Freeman*, May 28, June 14, August 9, 1838.
19. JGW to Caleb Cushing, July 3, 1838. SC.
20. "Chalkley Hall," Headnote note. *Works* IV 35.
    JGW to Elizabeth H. Whittier, August 3, 1838. SC.
    William J. Allinson to Samuel Allinson, July 18, 1838. Copy, HCL.
21. JGW to Elizabeth H. Whittier, August 3, 1838. Note 20.
22. *Pennsylvania Freeman*, October 11, 1838.
    JGW to Theodore D. Weld, October 21, 1838. St. John's Seminary.
23. JGW to Charles C. Burleigh, October 26, 1838. *Pennsylvania Freeman*, November 15, 1838.
24. Amesbury and Salisbury Anti-Slavery Society Record Book. Whittier Home, Amesbury.
25. Pickard, p. 183.
26. *Newburyport Herald*, November 12, 1838. From *Lowell Courier*.
27. JGW to Caleb Cushing, November 9, 1838. LC.
28. JGW to Elizabeth H. Whittier, November 24, 1838. Albree, p. 58.
29. JGW to Elizabeth Neall, February 10, 1839. Columbia University.
    Pennsylvania Freeman, February 14, 1839.
30. *Pennsylvania Freeman*, February 7, 1839.
31. Sarah ? to JGW, March 13, 1839. HCL.
32. JGW to Elizabeth Neall, February 26, 1839. Columbia University.
33. *Pennsylvania Freeman*, March 21, 1839.

34. JGW to Caleb Cushing, April 4, 1839. SC.
35. JGW to Theodore Weld, April 10, 1839. Copy owned by John B. Pickard.
36. Editorials May 16 were signed "E". There were no editorials May 23.
37. JGW to "Dear Mother and Sister and All," June 10, 1839. Albree, p. 60.
38. *Pennsylvania Freeman*, July 7, 1839.
    JGW to Moses Cartland, July 8, 1839. *Pennsylvania Freeman*, July 11, 1839.
    JGW to Elizabeth Neall, July 8, 1839. Columbia University.
    JGW to Mary Caldwell, July 17, 1839. Albree, p. 63.
    JGW to Moses A. Cartland, August 6, 1839. *Pennsylvania Freeman*, August 15, 1839.
39. JGW to Elizabeth Neall, August 8, 1839. Columbia University.
40. *Pennsylvania Freeman*, September 5, 1839.
41. JGW to Elizabeth Neall, August 26, 1839. Columbia University.
    Lucy Hooper to her sister Harriet, August 19 and 20, 1839. Albert Mordell, "Whittier
    and Lucy Hooper," *New England Quarterly*, June 1934, p. 318-19.
42. JGW to Caleb Cushing, August 23, 1839. LC.
43. *Pennsylvania Freeman*, September 5, 1839.
    Elizabeth H. Whittier to Abigail Whittier, evidently incorrectly dated September 8,
    1839. HCL.
44. *Pennsylvania Freeman*, November 7, 1839.
    JGW to Moses A. Cartland, March 15, 1840. Shackford, p. 8.
    JGW to Moses A. Cartland, October 31, 1839. Shackford, p. 9.
45. JGW to Hannah Gould. SC.
    H. J. Raymond to Rufus W. Griswold, July 30, 1839. *Passages from the Correspondence, and Other Papers*. W. M. Griswold, 1898, p. 30.
46. Whittier often forgot his own poems, but four lines of "The World's Convention"
    stayed in his mind twenty years. These lines, with variations as if written from
    memory, are in an autograph album of Helen N. Collins of Salisbury, dated 13th,
    10th mo. 1860. APL.
47. JGW to Fanny M. Macy, mounted in *The Poetical Works of John Greenleaf Whittier* 1870. Aldis Collection, Yale University Library.
    A Sketch of the History of Newbury, Newburyport, and West Newbury from 1635 to 1845. By Joshua Coffin A.B.S.H.S. Samuel G. Drake, 1845.
48. *Pennsylvania Freeman*, February 6, 1839.
    Pickard, p. 254.
49. *Newburyport Herald*, September 18, 1841. It was in the *Haverhill Gazette*, September
    11, 1841, "By John G. Whittier," and is so listed in Currier.
    JGW to Rufus M. Griswold, October 19, 1841. HCL.

CHAPTER IX

1. JGW to Elizabeth Neall, February 24, 1840. Columbia University.
2. JGW to Moses A. Cartland, March 15, 1840. HCL.
   JGW to Elizabeth Neall, March 16, 1840. Columbia University.
   J. Miller McKim to JGW, March 18, 1840. HCL.
   JGW to Elizabeth Neall, April 6, 1840. Columbia University.
   JGW to James Gillespie Birney, April 16, 1840. University of Michigan.
   JGW to Elizabeth Neall, April 19, 1840. Columbia University.
   JGW to Elizabeth H. Whittier, May 4, 1840. Central Michigan University.

Sarah Lewis to Elizabeth H. Whittier, July 5, 1840. HCL.
JGW to Elizabeth Whittier, May 30, 1840. John B. Pickard, "John Greenleaf Whittier and the Abolitionist Schism of 1840." *New England Quarterly*, June 1964.

3. JGW to Elizur Wright, March 14 and 25, 1840. University of Texas.
   Elizur Wright to JGW, April 6, 1840. Albree, p. 65.
   JGW to James Gillespie Birney, April 16, 1840. University of Michigan.
   JGW to Gerrit Smith, August 30, 1840. Syracuse University.

4. JGW to Samuel J. May, March 27, 1840. Pierpont Morgan Library.

5. JGW to Elizabeth H. Whittier, May 30, 1840. Note 2.
   JGW to Joshua Leavitt, June 24, 1840. *Emancipator*, July 2, 1840.
   American and Foreign Anti-Slavery Reporter Vol. 1 No. 1, June 1840.
   JGW to Moses A. Cartland, July 2, 1840. HCL.

6. *Anti-Slavery Standard*. Quoted in George Rice Carpenter, *John Greenleaf Whittier*. Houghton Mifflin, 1903. pp. 200-01.
   Lydia Maria Child to Abby Hopper Gibbons, May 13, 1840. Sarah Hopper Emerson, *Life of Abby Hopper Gibbons*, p. 94.
   Elizabeth Neall to Elizabeth H. Whittier, November 18, 1840. HCL.

7. JGW to Moses A. Cartland, March 15, 1840. HCL.
   JGW to Elizabeth H. Whittier, May 4, 1840. Albree, p. 68.
   JGW to Moses A. Cartland, July 2, 1840. Shackford, p. 14.
   Liberator, February 22 and March 8, 1839. Walter M. Merrill, *Against Wind and Tide*. Harvard University Press, 1936. p. 151.
   JGW to Elizur Wright, March 14, 1840. University of Texas.

8. JGW to Charles Burleigh, July 6, 1840. *Pennsylvania Freeman*, July 30, 1840.
   Village Transcript, July 3, 1840.
   JGW to Moses A. Cartland, July 2, 1840. Shackford, p. 14.

9. JGW to Ann E. Wendell, July 13, 1840. Pickard, pp. 261-62.

10. JGW to Ann E. Wendell, June 14, 1840. University of Virginia.
    JGW to Elizabeth Lloyd, July 13, 1840. *Elizabeth Lloyd and the Whittiers*, p. 12.
    JGW to Ann E. Wendell. Note 9.

11. Currier, p. 47. Copies were sent to Ann Wendell, Theodore D. Weld, and Rowland Greene, a Quaker who, according to *Centennial History of Moses Brown School*, often took part in religious meetings at the school.

12. JGW to Ann Wendell, July 24, 1840. University of Virginia.

13. Howard Mumford Jones, "Whittier Reconsidered." EIHC. Vol. XCIII No. 4, October 1957. p. 236.

14. Note 12.

15. John G. and Elizabeth H. Whittier to Elizabeth Lloyd, July 13, 1840. *Elizabeth Lloyd and the Whittiers*, p. 13.
    Pickard, p. 260.
    JGW to Elizabeth Lloyd, August 14, 1840. *Elizabeth Lloyd and the Whittiers*, p. 22.

16. Martha A. Shackford, "Whittier and Some Cousins." *New England Quarterly*, September, 1942.
    JGW to Elizabeth Lloyd, August 14, 1840. *Elizabeth Lloyd and the Whittiers*, p. 21.
    Note 12.

17. Elizabeth Lloyd to JGW, July 1840. *Elizabeth Lloyd and the Whittiers*, pp. 7, 8.
    JGW to Elizabeth Lloyd, July 13 and August 14, 1840. Ibid. pp. 10-11, 17-19.

18. Elizabeth Lloyd to JGW, before December 25, 1840. Ibid. pp. 55-56.
    JGW to Rufus W. Griswold, October 19, 1841. HCL.

19. JGW to Elizabeth Lloyd, November 2, 1840. *Elizabeth Lloyd and the Whittiers*, pp. 35-36.
    Moses A. Cartland to Joseph Cartland, October 22, 1840. Shackford, p. 18.

20. JGW to Richard Mott, November 15, 1840. HCL.
21. JGW to Ann Wendell, November 1840. Pickard, pp. 266-67.
22. For a time Charles Burleigh refused to publish the letter. JGW to Elizabeth Lloyd, November 2, 1840. *Elizabeth Lloyd and the Whittiers*, p. 37.
23. Sarah Lewis to JGW, July 27, 1840. HCL.
    James Gillespie Birney to Lewis Tappan. July 23, 1840. *Letters of James Gillespie Birney*. I 584.
    Sarah Lewis to Elizabeth Whittier, August 16, 1840. HCL.
24. Whittier continued to believe that Lucretia Mott and the other women were excluded because of the simple fact "that they were females." Letter to Richard Mott, November 15, 1840, Note 20. C. Marshall Taylor thought that Whittier was mistaken and said that "nearly all accounts published in connection with the Congress leave no doubt that the exclusion was really on the basis of religious bias." "Whittier vs. Garrison," EIHC. Vol. LXXXII No. 3, July 1946.
25. "A correspondent from Bradford informs us that at a recent meeting of the Lyceum in that town, a piece of Aboriginal Statuary was exhibited. 'It is,' says our correspondent, 'a leg from the calf down, together with the foot — formed from a deep grey stone.' " "Indian Relics," *Essex Gazette*, May 1, 1830.
26. JGW to Elizabeth Nicholson, February 2, 1841. Hav. CL.
    The account that Whittier read was probably Rev. Samuel Lee's translation of Ibn Batuta's *The Travels of Ibn Batuta*, Oriental Translation Committee, London 1809. Arthur Christy, "Orientalism in New England: Whittier." *American Literature*, January, 1930, I 372-92.
27. Elizabeth H. Whittier to Harriet Minot, January 4, 1841. Annie Russell Marble, "Elizabeth Whittier and the Whittier Home." *Outlook*, September 7, 1907.
    JGW to Annie Fields, January 6, 1890. HEH.
    JGW to Moses A. Cartland, January 2, 1841. HCL.
    JGW to Harriet Minot, March 24, 1841. Boston Atheneum.
28. JGW to Caleb Cushing, January 6, February 8, and February 24, 1841. LC.
    The postmaster was replaced by John Walsh, son of Michael Walsh, who had been Caleb Cushing's schoolmaster. Albree, p. 77.
29. JGW to Abby Kelly, March 18, 1841. American Antiquarian Society.
30. Sarah Lewis to Elizabeth Whittier, August 16, 1840. HCL.
    Ann Wendell to JGW, October 25, 1840. HCL.
    Elizabeth H. Whittier to JGW, June 16, 1841. Formerly owned by Robert W. Lull.
    Samuel Webb to JGW, February 8, 1841, with manuscript note by Samuel T. Pickard. Whittier Home, Amesbury.
    Joseph Sturge to JGW, February 9, 1841. Albree, pp. 69-71. Money was so badly needed that Elizabeth was teaching in the one-room school a short distance up Friend Street. She did not enjoy teaching any more than her brother had, and it is rather surprising that Whittier, whose affection for Elizabeth was later deep and sincere, was evidently willing that she should do work which he had found disagreeable.

Chapter X

1. Elizabeth Lloyd to Elizabeth H. Whittier, April 30, 1841. *Elizabeth Lloyd and the Whittiers* pp. 70-75.
    Unless otherwise noted, the account of Whittier's travels with Joseph Sturge is from Sturge's *A Visit to the United States in 1841*, Hamilton, Adams, & Co., 1842.

2. JGW to Moses A. Cartland, May 12, 1841. SC.
   JGW to Harriet Minot, May 26, 1841. Boston Atheneum.

3. "The Great Slave Market," *Essex Transcript*, November 13, 1843. This later appeared as "The Slave Market at Washington" in *Voices of the True Hearted*, probably March, 1845.

4. Ibid.

5. Tappan's reply June 12 outlining his letter to the Executive Committee and the terms on which he would return and the Committee's virtual rejection of this offer is in the Library of Congress. On the margin of page 1, in Whittier's writing: "I would affectionately caution you against unduly impeaching the motives of Friends who differ from you; — I beseech you to cultivate on all occasions feelings of charity and brotherly love. The beautiful example of John Woolman in this respect is worthy of your imitation. His labors were for years, as little encouraged as yours now by the leading influences of the Society, yet we find in reading his invaluable memoirs no traces of bitterness or uncharitable feeling."

6. Mary C. Pennock to Elizabeth Pennock, June 13, 1841. *David Sellers, Mary P. Sellers*, p. 65. The date of the letter is incorrectly given as 1840.

7. JGW to Thomas W. Dorr, June 19, 1841. Brown University.

8. John F. Kellett, *Elizabeth H. Whittier and Greenleaf a Century After*. Typescript. APL.

9. JGW to Frederick Palmer Tracy, June 1841. Owned by Frank Tracy Swett. Copy, EI.
   JGW to Elizur Wright, July 12, 1841 (?). University of Texas.
   JGW to sisters of Lucy Hooper, August 6, 1841. Pickard, pp. 274-75.

10. "The Factory Girls", *Middlesex Standard*, August 15, 1844.

11. Joseph Sturge to Lewis Tappan, July 30, 1841. HCL.

12. Pickard quotes a letter of Tappan to Whittier, March 14, 1842, asking his advice about the four hundred dollars left in this fund. There seems to be no reason to suppose, as Pickard did, that this was the same thousand dollars that had been left for Whittier's use. Tappan's letter to Whittier has the phrase "for the furtherance of the anti-slavery cause."

13. JGW to Caleb Cushing, August 28, 1841. LC.

14. JGW to Samuel E. Sewall, August 10, 1841. MHS.
    "Liberty Party Petition," August 8, 1841. Albree, p. 79.

15. JGW to sisters of Lucy Hooper. Note 9.

16. Albert Mordell, "Whittier and Lucy Hooper". *New England Quarterly*, June 1934.

17. JGW to Harriet Winslow, August 12, 1841. MHS.
    JGW to Moses A. Cartland, August 12, 1841. HCL.

18. JGW to Elizabeth J. Neall, August 28, 1841. Columbia University. *Whittier-Land*, p. 62.

19. Owned by Gladys M. Castle, Newburyport, Massachusetts. It is not mentioned in Currier.

20. JGW to Elizabeth Lloyd, August 28, 1841. *Elizabeth Lloyd and the Whittiers*, pp. 78-80.

21. *Village Transcript*, November 19, 1841.

22. John L. O'Sullivan to JGW, April 5, 1843. EI.

23. Edgar Allen Poe, "A Chapter on Autography." *Graham's Magazine*, November 1841. *Complete Works* 1902, XV 245.

24. Elizabeth Whittier to Hannah Cox, May 13, 1842. SC.
    Lucretia Mott to Hannah Wells, February 25, 1842. *William Lloyd Garrison* III 35.

25. JGW to Joseph Sturge, January 21, 1842. Friends Reference Library, London.
    Manuscript account by Albert L. Bartlett. HPL.
    Haverhill Gazette, June 22, 1940. The original petition is owned by Haverhill Historical Society.
    Samuel Fogg Bemis, *John Quincy Adams and the Union*. Alfred A. Knopf, 1956. pp. 427-436.

26. JGW to Samuel E. Sewall, March 31, 1842.
    Lewis Cass had published a pamphlet in Paris, February 1, entitled *An Examination of the Question, Now in Discussion, between the American and British Governments concerning the Right of Search, by an American.*
27. *The Narrative of Amos Dresser* was published by the American Anti-Slavery Society in 1836. Dresser was tried by a Vigilance Committee and given twenty lashes with a cowhide whip for being a member of an Anti-Slavery Society in Ohio, having in his possession periodicals published by the American Anti-Slavery Society, and, they "believed," having circulated these periodicals and advocated their principles.
28. JGW to Samuel E. Sewall, March 26 and June 17, 1842. MHS.
29. JGW to Harriet Minot, May 5, 1842. Pickard, p. 278.
30. JGW to Ann E. Wendell, February 8, 1842. University of Virginia.
    JGW to William Allinson, November 19, 1842. Copy, Hav. CL.
    JGW to Harriet Winslow, May 25, 1842. MHS.
    JGW to Thomas Tracy, June 12, 1842. American Art Association, *Illustrated Catalogue of the Literary Treasures of Walter Thomas Wallace of South Orange, New Jersey*, 1920.
31. JGW to Ann E. Wendell, July 2, 1842. Pickard, pp. 277-78.
    Margaret Wendell to Elizabeth Whittier, September 8, 1842. HCL.
    Joseph Cartland to Elizabeth H. Whittier, October 20, 1842. HCL.
    Ann Wendell to Elizabeth H. Whittier, November 2, 1842. HCL.
    Hannah Lloyd to Elizabeth H. Whittier, December 1842. HCL.
    Gail Hamilton, *Divine Guidance. A Memorial of Allen W. Dodge*, 1881. p. 285.

Chapter XI

1. JGW to J. W. Hayes, Luther Lee, E. R. Dike, October 10, 1842. *Newburyport Herald*, October 25, 1842.
   JGW to Samuel T. Pickard, November 14, 1880 [?] SC.
   Essex Transcript, February 10, 1843. The *Village Transcript* had been renamed the *Essex Transcript* and had become the organ of the Liberty Party in Essex County, from which it received some financial aid.
2. JGW to Ann E. Wendell, July 2, 1842. Pickard, p. 277.
3. Introductory note to "Raphael," *United States Magazine and Democratic Review*, December 1842.
4. Pickard, pp. 289-290.
   Albree, pp. 84-85.
   Horace E. Scudder, *James Russell Lowell*. The Riverside Press 1901, I 105.
5. *Newburyport Herald*, November 23, 1842.
   JGW to Matthew Franklin Whittier, February 7, 1843. Whittier Home, Amesbury.
6. JGW to James T. Fields, April 20, 1843. New Hampshire Historical Society.
7. JGW to Henry I. Bowditch, November 14, 1842. Vincent Y. Bowditch, *Life and Correspondence of Henry Ingersoll Bowditch*. Houghton Mifflin, 1902, I 140.
   JGW to William J. Allinson, November 19, 1842, Copy, Hav. CL.
   Essex Transcript, January 6, 1843. "Massachusetts to Virginia" was printed in this issue, three weeks earlier than the printing in the *Liberator* recorded in Currier. It did not contain the present fourth and fifth stanzas, which were sent to Fields for inclusion in *Lays of My Home and Other Poems*. Note 6.

8. Letter of A. J. Huntress. Undated. HCL. The *Essex Transcript* reported that the reading was by Henry I. Bowditch. See also Bowditch, op. cit. p. 139.

9. For best evaluation of Whittier's Anti-Slavery poetry, see "Whittier's Abolitionist Poetry" by John B. Pickard in *Memorabilia of John Greenleaf Whittier*, Edited by John B. Pickard. The Emerson Society, 1968.

10. Pickard, p. 291.
    William Tallach, *Friendly Sketches in America*. A. W. Bennett, 1861.

11. Part of this review is "The Bible and Slavery." *Works* VII 96.

12. *Essex Transcript*, September 8, 29, October 5, December 22, 1843.
    Newburyport Herald, September 25, 1843.

13. *Essex Transcript*, July 28, 1843. *Newburyport Herald*, July 29, 1843.

14. *Essex Transcript*, August 4 and 11, 1843.
    JGW to James Russell Lowell, October 18, 1843. HCL.
    JGW to David P. Harmon, October 22, 1843. HPL. Harmon was active in Abolition, and his house at the corner of Summer Street and Maple Avenue is said to have been an Underground Railroad Station.
    JGW to Matthew Franklin Whittier. Note 5.

15. JGW to Samuel Allinson, March 22, 1843. Hav. CL.
    "Thomas Wilson Dorr." *Essex Transcript*, December 30, 1842.

16. Introductory Note, "To the Reformers of England." *United States Magazine and Democratic Review*, January 1843. Curiously, the note in the Riverside Edition refers to quite other reforms; Whittier had evidently forgotten what he had in mind when he wrote the poem.

17. JGW to Ann E. Wendell, August 22, 1843. University of Virginia.

18. Rufus M. Jones, *The Later Periods of Quakerism*, Macmillan and Co., 1921. p. 522-23.
    JGW to Joseph Sturge, June 12, 1843. Friends Reference Library, London.

19. C. Marshall Taylor, *John Greenleaf Whittier the Quaker*. Friends Historical Society, 1954. p. 34.

20. William Sewel, *The History of the Rise, Increase and Progress of the People Called Quakers*. Third Edition. Isaac Collins, 1774. pp. 255-56.

21. The General Moulton House has been restored and moved to the west side of Route 1 (the Lafayette Road). Its original location was also on the west side of that road, but in the 1920's the road was straightened and ran behind the house, while the trolley car line continued to run in front of it.

22. *The Friend*. July 3, 1841. Vol. XIV No. 40. Formerly owned by C. Marshall Taylor. Not in Currier.

23. JGW to Amos A. Phelps, March 30, 1843. BPL.
    JGW to James T. Fields, January 24, 1842. SC.
    JGW to Elizabeth Lloyd, January 28, 1841. *Elizabeth Lloyd and the Whittiers*. p. 57.
    JGW to James T. Fields, March 30, 1843. Historical Society of Pennsylvania.
    JGW to James T. Fields, April 6, 1843. HEH.

24. Charles H. Brown, *William Cullen Bryant*. Charles Scribner's Sons, 1971. p. 288.
    JGW to James T. Fields, October 30, 1850. HEH.
    The Cost Books of Ticknor and Fields and Their Predecessors. Edited with an Introduction and Notes by Warren S. Tryon and William Charvat. Bibliographical Society of America, 1949. p. 57.
    JGW to J. Miller McKim, October 12, 1843. Cornell University Library.

25. Enoch W. Pearson, "It Might Have Been." *Yankee*, December 1949, pp. 44-47. T. Franklin Currier, "The Epping Oak" and communication to *Exeter News-Letter*, June 14, 1942. Pearson believed that Whittier was in love with Rowena and was thinking of her when he wrote in "Maud Muller".
    For all sad words of tongue or pen,
    The saddest are these: "It might have been!"

Gertrude Whittier Cartland was certain that the lines were written by Elizabeth H. Whittier, who signed her brother's name and placed the paper on the breakfast plate of Jonathan Cartland, who was much interested in Rowena. This account is given in Martha Hale Shackford's *Whittier and the Cartlands*, p. 33. Pearson, who found a manuscript of the poem dated "Lee, N.H. 1843," was sure that it was Whittier's writing, because it was the same as the writing in a letter which he received from Whittier in 1886. However, Whittier's writing changed through the years. Better evidence is T. Franklin Currier's statement that the manuscript that he found at the Essex Institute was in "Whittier's characteristic handwriting." If, as is possible, Whittier did not write the verses but copied them, Rowena believed that he wrote them. A letter from her son Herman T. Shepard to the writer July 11, 1935, contains this statement: "I was told long ago that my mother was a personal friend of Whittier and that a poem of his referred to her."

26. *Village Transcript*, October 21, 1842.
Newburyport Herald, February 14 and June 26, 1843.
Essex Transcript, February 17, March 2, September 22, November 10, November 17, November 20, 1843.
JGW to Amos A. Phelps, March 30, 1843. BPL.
Newburyport Herald, January 2 and 4, 1844.
Essex Transcript, January 5, 1844.
There is no reason to doubt that Whittier meant what he said and considerable reason to doubt Pickard's explanation (pp. 285-86) that Whittier withdrew because he thought that he would be elected. The Democratic candidate also withdrew — surely not because he wished to assure the election of Whittier, who was more nearly Whig than Democrat. If Whittier had thought that there was a chance of electing a Liberty Party man he would have said so and offered to support some other candidate, as he had promised to do in his letter of acceptance.
Abbott was elected January 20. Scattering votes, most of them probably for Gardner Perry, the Liberty Party candidate, were ten percent of the total.

Chapter XII

1. Maria S. Porter, *Recollections of Louisa May Alcott, John Greenleaf Whittier, Robert Browning*. Published for the Author, 1893. p. 32.
"Edwin Percy Whipple." *Works* VI 318.
2. Joseph Merrill, Manuscript notes. APL.
3. "Letter from John G. Whittier," January 15, 1844. *Essex Transcript*, January 19, 1844.
4. Henry B. Stanton to JGW, February 3, 1844. Albree, pp. 86-87.
Essex Transcript, March 1, 1844.
5. There is a file of the *Village Transcript* and *Essex Transcript* from December 7, 1840, to August 23, 1847, in Amesbury Public Library.
6. JGW to James Russell Lowell, April 17, 1844. HCL.
7. Currier thought that Whittier probably did little for the *Transcript* from July, 1844, to March, 1845, because of his being in Lowell editing the *Middlesex Standard*, but Whittier was in Amesbury part of the time.
8. Statement of Stephen Lamson, a compositor in the *Transcript* office, to Samuel T. Pickard. Pickard, p. 304. Lamson was recalling what had occurred nearly fifty years earlier, and may have thought that something occurred frequently which perhaps occurred only occasionally or even only once.

9. "The Sentence of John L. Brown"
   The first printing recorded in Currier is *Haverhill Gazette*, May 4. The volumes of the *Essex Transcript* were owned by J. M. Pettengill's daughters and were inaccessible until after the publication of the *Bibliography*.

10. JGW to Elizur Wright, April 28, 1844. University of Texas.

11. Joseph Sturge, *Visit to the United States in 1841*, pp. 166-67.

12. JGW to Samuel E. Sewall, March 31, 1842. MHS.

13. Pickard, p. 297.
    JGW to James Russell Lowell, April 14, 1844. HCL.
    JGW to James Russell Lowell, April 17, 1844. HCL. Lowell's introduction is printed in Pickard, pp. 297-98.

14. Pickard, pp. 298-99.

15. JGW to Thomas Tracy, April 13, 1844. HPL.

16. "Henry Clay". It was dated May 20 and was printed in the *Essex Transcript*, May 24.

17. The poem was probably "To Henry Clay." *Haverhill Iris*, August 25, 1832.

18. Report by George J. L. Colby. *Essex Transcript*, June 21, 1844.

19. The poem has six stanzas and two choruses. The fourth stanza is an earlier form of the second stanza of "Seed-Time and Harvest," and the fifth is an earlier form of the third stanza and is identical with the stanza in Whittier's manuscript dated October 22, 1849, in Yale University Library (Currier, p. 338). On the fourth page is "Written for a Liberty Party meeting at Prospect Hill near Boston. July 4, 1844." Manuscript formerly owned by Carroll A. Wilson.

20. JGW to James Russell Lowell, July 14, 1844. HCL.

21. JGW to Thomas Clarkson, July 10, 1844, in Earle Leslie Griggs, "John G. Whittier and Thomas Clarkson." *American Literature*, January, 1936, Volume 7, pp. 458-60.

22. JGW to James Russell Lowell, September 3, 1844. SC.
    JGW to Ann Wendell, October 18, 1844. Copy, Hav. CL.

23. JGW to Amos B. Merrill, September 1, 1844. SC.

24. John Kemble Laskey, "John G. Whittier". *Portland Transcript*, March 15, 1845.

25. Pollard, pp. 184, 321, 322.

26. Frederick W. Coburn, "John Greenleaf Whittier, Lowell Editor." *Lowell Courier-Citizen*, November 3, 1934.

27. JGW to David P. Page, August 29, 1844. EI.

28. Samuel Longfellow, ed. *Life of Henry Wadsworth Longfellow, with Extracts from His Journals and Correspondence*. Houghton, Mifflin and Company, 1893, II 20.

29. For Whittier's change in attitude toward Carlyle, see Roland H. Woodwell, "Whittier and Carlyle". *Memorabilia of John Greenleaf Whittier*. Edited by John P. Pickard. The Emerson Society, 1968. pp. 42-45.

30. *Middlesex Standard*, August 1 and 8, 1844.

31. Lucy Larcom, *A New England Girlhood*. Houghton, Mifflin and Company, 1892, pp. 254-55.

32. JGW to William Lloyd Garrison, September 10, 1844. BPL.

33. JGW to Ralph Waldo Emerson, September 12, 1844. HCL.
    JGW to James Russell Lowell, September 3, 1844. SC.

34. JGW to Ann Wendell, October 18, 1844. Note 22.

35. JGW to Robert C. Waterston, October 10, 1844. Yale University Library. A letter from Waterston about this case, December 7, 1844, is in Essex Institute.

36. *Emerson's Journals*. Houghton Mifflin Co., 1909 VI 537.
    Anderson Sale.

37. Harriet Nelson Greeley was born in Salisbury, November 25, 1818, the daughter of Rev. Stephen Nelson and Rhoda (Wadleigh) Greeley. The manuscript of Whittier's poem is owned by Arthur L. Bartlett Jr.; there is a photostat in Yale University Library. See also John F. Kellett, "Whittier and Harriet Nelson Greeley." *Newburyport News*, January 14, 1964.

38. *Newburyport Herald*, November 12, 1844. *Essex Transcript*, November 8 and November 15, 1844.
   Unidentified newspaper clipping.

39. *Essex Transcript*, November 15, 1844.

40. Frederick W. Coburn, "Hon. C. L. Knapp." *Lowell Courier-Citizen*, November 16, 1934.

41. Pollard, p. 222.

42. *Proceedings of a Convention of Delegates, Chosen by the People of Massachusetts, without Distinction of Party, and Assembled at Faneuil Hall in the City of Boston.*

43. Chauncey L. Knapp to JGW, February 18, 1845. HCL.

44. This editorial was reprinted as Whittier's in the *Essex Transcript*, March 14, 1845.

Chapter XIII

1. *Prudential Committee's Book, School District No. 2.* Whittier Home, Amesbury.

2. Moses Cartland to JGW, April 7, 1845. HCL.

3. *Essex Transcript*, August 22, 1845.

4. *Essex Transcript*, April 18, 1845.

5. Two numbers of the *Middlesex Standard* are missing, but these are February 20 and March 6, and none of the series appeared after January 23.

6. *Essex Transcript*, May 23, 1845.

7. Note in *Voices of the True-Hearted*. "The facts in this note are from Walker's *Trial and Imprisonment of Jonathan Walker*." Other details are in an article in the *New England Magazine*, November, 1898.

8. JGW to Ebenezer Hunt, July 2, 1845. Brown University Library. The reference to the *Emancipator* seems to indicate that Whittier's part-time editorial work on that paper, of which virtually nothing is known, may have continued longer than has been supposed. Currier, pp. 468-69.

9. Henry I. Bowditch to JGW, August 18, 1845. Central Michigan University.
   Elias Nason and Thomas Russell, *The Life and Public Services of Henry Wilson*. B. B. Russell, 1876. p. 63.
   JGW to Ralph Waldo Emerson, September 20, 1845. *Essex Transcript*, October 3, 1845.

10. JGW to Daniel Weed, September 24, 1845. *Essex Transcript*, September 26, 1845.

11. *Essex Transcript*, October 10 and 17, 1845.

12. JGW to Elizur Wright, October 19, 1845. University of Texas.

13. JGW to Elizur Wright. Note 12.
    Nason and Russell, op. cit. p. 65.
    Pickard, p. 328. Pickard is in error in referring to the Convention as a Liberty Party Convention.

14. JGW to Elizabeth H. Whittier, October 26, 1845. Elizabeth was visiting Harriet Minot Pitman, who had been married in 1844 and was living in Boston. Pickard, pp. 308-09.

15. *Essex Transcript*, October 31 and November 7, 1845.

16. *Essex Transcript*, November 7, 1845.

17. *Essex Transcript*, November 14, 1845.

18. JGW to John P. Hale, January 24, 1845. Pickard, p. 306.
    JGW to William E. Chandler, July 28, 1892, in *The Statue of John P. Hale* by William E. Chandler, Concord 1892.

19. JGW to John Farmer, June 6, 1837. Copy. BPL.
    "Of course you know that those noble lines 'God bless New Hampshire &c.' were inspired by Mr. Whittier's admiration for Mr. Hale's course at the time of his revolt from the Democratic party on the question of the admission of Texas to the Union." Lucy H. Hale to Samuel T. Pickard, February 10, 1893. HCL.

20. *Essex Transcript*, November 21, 1845.

21. Charles A. Dana to JGW, July 3, 1845. Albree, pp. 94-95.

22. JGW to Jonathan G. Chapman, April 14, 1846. SC.

23. JGW to Thomas Tracy, November 8, 1845. Yale University Library.

24. Joseph Sturge to JGW, November 3, 1845. HCL.

25. JGW to Frederick Palmer Tracy, January 18, 1846. Copy. EI.

26. Ida Russell to Elizabeth H. Whittier, May 30, 1846. HCL.
    Moses Cartland to Elizabeth H. Whittier, May 30, 1842. HCL.

27. JGW to Elizur Wright, December 1, December 15, December 16, 1845. University of Texas.
    JGW to Ann Wendell, January 6, 1846. Copy. Hav. CL.
    David Sellers. Mary Pennock Sellers p. 77.

28. JGW to Henry I. Bowditch, January 26, 1846. LC.
    JGW to Joshua Leavitt, January 24, 1846. *Emancipator*, January 28, 1846.

29. *Essex Transcript*, February 2, 1846.

30. *Essex Transcript*, March 12, 1846.

31.   "And Baker dreamed that Father Hill,
           The one whose head was addle,
        Sat singing, 'Baby, hush! be still'
           A-rocking Hibberd's cradle."
    A note explained that Harry Hibberd, a candidate for the Senate at the late election, lacked, it was said, the age qualification required by the Constitution. "Harry, with all his radicalism, is a young man of fine talents." In the line now printed "Gray H----d heard o'nights the sound" the name was printed with the note: "Ex-Gov. Hubbard's peculiar notions of the rights of individuals and corporations in respect to railroad routes are well known."

32. *Essex Transcript*, June 11, 1846.
    Speech of Amos Tuck in *Reunion of the Free-Soilers of 1848, at Downer Landing, Hingham, Massachusetts, August 9, 1877*. Boston, 1877.
    JGW to Henry I. Bowditch, July 31, 1846. Yale University Library.

33. "Methodists and Slavery." *Essex Transcript*, May 7, 1846.
    "Questions for the Clergy of the United States." *Essex Transcript*, June 25, 1846.
    Essex Transcript, July 2, 1846.

34. "The Slave Pauline" was unsigned in the *Essex Transcript*, but was printed as Whittier's in the *Democratic Standard* June 23 (Currier, p. 421) and in *The Friend of Virtue* published by the New England Female Moral Reform Society, August 15. In a letter to Elizabeth H. Whittier, August 9, Ida Russell sent her thanks for a copy of the Baltimore *Visitor* that Whittier had sent her: "I could not help laughing at the mention in the Visitor of his article about Pauline, could you?" HCL.

35. About one third of this article is in *Works* VI 271, entitled "The Funeral of Torrey."

36. JGW to Henry I. Bowditch, undated. SC.
    Henry I. Bowditch to JGW, May 30, 1846. EI.
37. JGW to Henry I. Bowditch, undated. SC.
    Letter June 13, 1846. *Essex Transcript*, July 23, 1846.
38. The poem and Whittier's letter February 9, 1884, acknowledging the authorship, along
    with the entire account of the supposed Mexican poet-patriot, are in Currier,
    pp. 318-20.
39. *Essex Transcript*, July 9, 1846.
40. Samuel Flagg Bemis, *John Quincy Adams and the Union*. Alfred A. Knopf, 1956,
    pp. 492-94.
    JGW to Joseph Sturge, June 15, 1846. SC.
41. JGW to Moses A. Cartland, "7th day My" [1846]. HCL.
42. Ida Russell to Elizabeth H. Whittier, April 24, 1846. HCL.
43. *Philadelphia Citizen*. Quoted in *Essex Transcript*, August 20, 1846.
44. *Essex Transcript*, August 6, 1846.
    JGW to Charles Sumner, September 8, 1846. HCL.
    "The Democracy of Freedom," *Essex Transcript*, September 17, 1846.
45. JGW to John P. Hale, September 16, 1846. Pickard, pp. 311-12.
46. *Essex Transcript*, September 10 and 24, October 1, 1846.
47. JGW to Charles Sumner, September 26, 1846. HCL.
48. *Essex Transcript*, November 12 and December 3, 1846.
49. Information given to the writer by J. Albert Davis, a nephew of Rebecca Davis.
50. JGW to William J. Allinson, November 10, 1846. Copy. Hav. CL.
    Whittier-Land p. 76.
    The Whittier, published by a school in Whittier, California. HCL.
    Joseph Sturge to JGW, November 18, 1846. EI.
51. Henry Peterstone to JGW, May 19, 1846. EI.
52. JGW to John P. Hale, December 18, 1846. Pickard pp. 317-18.
53. *Essex Transcript*, December 25, 1846.

Chapter XIV

1. JGW to Ann E. Wendell, February 21, 1847. University of Virginia.
2. *National Era*, January 21, 1847.
   Essex Transcript, January 28 and February 4, 1847. *National Era*, January 28, 1847.
3. JGW to Moses A. Cartland. Undated. HCL.
   Note 1.
   National Era, April 22, 1847.
   Longfellow, who met Bailey four years later through Charles Sumner at Whittier's
   suggestion, recorded in his Journal (II 215) that Bailey was "quite eveille and amiable."
   JGW to Francis J. Garrison, October 4, 1888. SC.
4. Note 1.
5. *National Era*, March 11, 1847.
6. *National Era*, February 11, 1847.
7. The seventh stanza was later updated. The original form was as follows:
       Lo! threescore years have passed; and where
       The Gallic timbrel stirred the air,

> With Northern drum-call, and the clear,
> Wild horn-blow of the mountaineer,
> While Britain grounded on that plain
> The arms she might not lift again,
> As abject as in that old day
> The Slave still toils his life away.

8. *Works* VII 115-19 The only change is in the tense of a verb.

9. Lewis Tappan to JGW, April 21, 1847. HCL.

10. *Newburyport Advertiser*, October 12, 1847.

11. *National Era*, March 11, May 20, June 3, June 17, July 1, July 22, 1847.

12. *National Era*, April 22, May 17, July 8, 1847.

13. JGW to Samuel Fessenden, July 26, 1847. SC.
    JGW to John P. Hale, July 30, 1847. Pickard, pp. 319-21.

14. *National Era*, August 19, 1847. The same analogy appeared in "The Panorama," 1855.

15. *National Era*, October 28, 1847.
    JGW to John P. Hale, November 2, 1847. Pickard, pp. 321-23, incorrectly dated October 2.
    JGW to John P. Hale, November 8, 1847. Pickard, pp. 323-24, incorrectly dated August 11, 1847.

16. Bayard Taylor to JGW, September 16, 1847. Pickard, p. 326.

17. *National Era*, September 9 and October 7, 1847.

18. "A letter from Amesbury to the *Philadelphia Press* thus quotes Mr. Whittier: 'Evangeline is a favorite with me,' said he. 'I think it one of the most beautiful of the poet's productions. Longfellow had an easy life and superior advantages of association and education, and so had Emerson. It was widely different with me, and I am very thankful for the kind esteem that people have given my writing. Before, Evangeline was written I had hunted up the history of the banishment of the Acadians and had intended to write upon it myself, but I put it off, and Hawthorne got hold of the story and gave it to Longfellow. I am very glad he did, for he was the one to write it. If I had attempted it I should have spoiled the artistic effect of the poem by my indignation at the treatment of the exiles by the colonial government.' "
    Newburyport Herald, November 21, 1883.

19. JGW to James T. Fields, undated. HEH.

20. JGW to Gamaliel Bailey, December 3, 1847. University of Texas.
    W. L. Chaplin to James Gillespie Birney. *Letters of James Gillespie Birney*, II 1092.
    JGW to Charles Sumner, February 23, 1848. HCL.
    "M. Cremieux, the Israelite." *National Era*, April 13, 1848.

21. Mrs. E. D. E. N. Southworth, *Reminiscences of the Poet Whittier*. Typescript. HCL.

22. JGW to Henry Wadsworth Longfellow, March 8, 1848. HCL.
    National Era, February 10, 1848.

23. JGW to Gamaliel Bailey, March, 1848. Copy. HCL.

24. *National Era*, April 6, 1848.

25. JGW to Charles Sumner, March, 1848. HCL.
    "Labor — the French Revolution." "Peace with France." *National Era*, April 27, 1848.

26. JGW to Charles Sumner, March 21, 1848. HCL.

27. Thomas F. Waters, "Whittier the Poet, as Historian." *Massachusetts Magazine* Vol. I, pp. 3-10, June, 1908.
    The First Parish, Newbury, Massachusetts 1635 — 1935. Newburyport, 1935. pp. 17, 25-26.

28. James S. Pike to JGW, April 23, 1878. Whittier Home, Amesbury. Pike's book was *The New Puritan; New England Two Hundred Years Ago; Some account of Robert Pike, the Puritan Who Defended the Quakers, Resisted Clerical Domination and Opposed the Witchcraft Persecution*. Harper, 1879.

29. JGW to James T. Fields, February 18, 1849. HEH.
30. " 'Tis Good to Live. A Thanksgiving." *National Era*, June 29, 1848.
31. "Liberty or Death." *National Era*, June 8, 1848.
32. Bayard Taylor to Mary Agnew, August 11, 1848. *Letters of Bayard Taylor*. Edited by Marie Hanson Taylor and Horace E. Scudder. I 128.
    Lewis Tappan to JGW, August 22, 1848. Albree, pp. 108-110.
33. John F. Kellett, *Elizabeth H. Whittier and Greenleaf a Century After*. Typescript, APL.
34. Told to the writer by the little girl, Caroline Carter, niece of Mary Esther Carter.
35. Thomas Wentworth Higginson, *Cheerful Yesterdays*. Houghton, Mifflin and Company, 1898. pp. 132-134.
36. *Newburyport Herald*, September 7, 1848.
37. JGW to Charles Sumner, June 20, 1848. HCL.
    JGW to Charles Sumner, June 23, 1848. Albree, pp. 97-100.
    JGW to Henry I. Bowditch, July 31, 1848. Yale University Library.
    "The Buffalo Convention." *National Era*, July 20, 1848.
38. "1840 and 1848." *National Era*, November 5, 1848.
39. The headnote in the Riverside Edition indicates that Whittier forgot that he had written the song in 1848. It was printed in the *National Era* October 19, 1848.
40. "Massachusetts Free Soil Convention." *Newburyport Advertiser*, September 8, 1848. *National Era*, September 14, 1848.
    Newburyport Herald, October 6, 1848.
    Letter October 24, 1848. *The Beacon of Liberty*, October 28, 1848.
41. "The Election in Massachusetts." *National Era*, November 16, 1848.
42. *National Era*, August 3, 31, September 7, 14, October 12, 1848.
    "Hirst's Endymion." *National Era*, November 30, 1848.
43. Charles Sumner to JGW, December 6, 1848. Albree, p. 111.
44. Lewis Tappan to JGW, December 22, 1848. EI.
45. Account of B. B. Mussey & Co., per B. S. Holt, January 28, 1850. HCL. This includes the sixteen additional pages in the second edition. The statement in Kennedy and Pickard, quoted by Currier, p. 63, that Mussey offered five hundred dollars for Whittier's copyrights, seems to have no basis in fact. The account lists the two-and-a-half percent as the copyright.
46. JGW to James T. Fields, December 15, [1848].
47. JGW to James T. Fields [December 12, 1848], December 13, 1848. HEH.
    JGW to James T. Fields, December 15, [1848]. SC.
    JGW to James T. Fields, January 3, 1849. Pickard, p. 341.
    Cost Books of Ticknor and Fields and Their Predecessors 1832-1858.
48. *National Era*, January 11 and February 8, 1849.
49. *National Era*, March 1 and April 5, 1849. The two are now combined as "England under James II," *Works* VI 348-67. The long note on page 366 is part of "Gilbert Burnett," *National Era*, May 17.
50. Lewis Tappan to JGW, November 18, 1848. Whittier Home, Amesbury.
51. *National Era*, January 25, 1849.
52. "The Reform School of Massachusetts." *National Era*, February 22, 1849. In *Works* it is part of "Peculiar Institutions of Massachusetts".
53. Emily B. Smith, *Whittier*. The Whittier Press, 1935. p. 31.
54. Mary Esther Carter to JGW. EI.
    John F. Kellett, "Whittier and Mary Esther Carter." Typescript, APL.
    Information given to the writer by Mary Esther Carter's niece, Caroline Carter, and by friends and neighbors of Mary Esther Carter.

55. JGW to Sarah J. Clarke, May 10, 1849. Pickard, pp. 335-36.
    Charles Sumner to JGW, April 11 [1849]. Edward L. Pierce, *Memoirs and Letters of Charles Sumner*. Roberts Brothers 1877-1893, III 73.
56. JGW to Lewis Tappan, July 14, 1849. Pickard, pp. 336-39.

Chapter XV

1. Letter December 1873. St. John's Seminary.
2. Elizabeth Lloyd to JGW, September 8, 1849. *Elizabeth Lloyd and the Whittiers*, pp. 120-25.
3. "The Tactics of Slavery." *National Era*, September 13, 1849.
4. *Villager*, November 8, 1849.
   Newburyport Herald, November 14 and December 20, 1849.
5. Record book of Sarah Little, a pupil in Putnam Free School, Newburyport, 1849. *Newburyport Daily News*, March 30, 1937.
6. JGW to James T. Fields, August 20, 1849. HEH.
7. *Essex Transcript*, October 20, 1843.
8. There are some variations from the form in the Riverside Edition and one additional stanza. It lacks the headnote telling Elizabeth's part in writing it. This is stated in a manuscript note by Whittier in Fred Brown's copy of the *Complete Poetical Works*, 1876. The poem was also printed as a broadside, not mentioned in Currier; Carroll A. Wilson had a copy.
9. Fredrika Bremer to JGW, December 14, 1849. Anderson Sale, p. 3.
   Fredrika Bremer, America of the Fifties: Letters of Fredrika Bremer Selected and Edited by Adolph Benson. The American Scandinavian Foundation, 1924. p. 54.
10. JGW to James T. Fields, July 30, 1849. HEH.
    The Cost Books of Ticknor & Fields and their Predecessors, pp. 147-48.
11. G. L. Phillips, "Transatlantic Interest in Elliott." *Centenary Commemoration of Ebenezer Elliott*.
12. Samuel Longfellow, *Henry Wadsworth Longfellow* II 174.
13. JGW to Emma B. Cochran, February 8, 1884. New York Public Library.
14. Horace E. Scudder, *James Russell Lowell*, Houghton Mifflin and Company, 1901 I 201.
15. JGW to Rufus W. Griswold, June 21, 1850. EI.
16. Lowell, 1850. Whittier's letter is dated March 8, 1850. The letter and the statistics were printed in the *Villager*, May 16, 1850.
17. JGW to James T. Fields, April 6, 1850. HEH.
18. Roland H. Woodwell, "Whittier and Carlyle." *Memorabilia of John Greenleaf Whittier*. Edited by John B. Pickard. pp. 42-46. Whittier's essay is in Volume VII of the *Works* with the title "Thomas Carlyle and the Slave Question." The date "1846" is careless editing; on page 141 there is a reference to a paper published January 2, 1850.
19. JGW to James T. Fields, May 23, 1850. Historical Society of Pennsylvania.
20. *National Era*, June 20, 1850.
    Villager, March 6, 1851.
21. Pickard, p. 680.
22. *The Cost Books of Ticknor and Fields and Their Predecessors 1832-1858*. pp. 166, 174.
23. JGW to Nathaniel Hawthorne, February 22, 1850. HEH.

24. David Donald, *Charles Sumner and the Coming of the Civil War*. Alfred A. Knopf, 1960. pp. 187-89.
Henry Adams, *The Education of Henry Adams*. Houghton Mifflin and Company, 1930. p. 49.
Pickard, p. 351.
For a study of Whittier's relations with Sumner, see J. Welfred Holmes, "Whittier and Sumner: A Political Friendship." *New England Quarterly* Vol. XXX, No. 1, March 1957, pp. 58-72.

25. JGW to Elias Nason, August 1874. Elias Nason, *The Life and Times of Charles Sumner*. B. B. Russell 1874. p. 142.
JGW to Sarah J. Clarke, May 18, 1851. Pickard, pp. 355-56.
"To Charles Sumner." *Works* IV 91.

26. Edward L. Pierce, *Memoir and Letters of Charles Sumner*. III 229.
Samuel Longfellow, *Henry Wadsworth Longfellow* II 186.
JGW to Henry Wadsworth Longfellow, August 22, 1850. HCL.

27. Sarah P. Sellers, *David Sellers, Mary P. Sellers*, p. 89.

28. JGW to Editors of the *Bay State*, October 4, 1850. New York Public Library.
Albree, pp. 113-14.
Newburyport Herald, May 29, 1850.

29. *Emerson's Journal* VIII 179.
Nathaniel Hawthorne to Henry Wadsworth Longfellow, May 18, 1851. Samuel Longfellow, *Henry Wadsworth Longfellow* II 209.

30. Anderson Catalogue, p. 42.

31. "Massachusetts." *National Era*, October 31, 1850.

32. "The Election in Massachusetts." *National Era*, November 21, 1850.
Donald, op. cit., p. 189.
JGW to Henry Wilson, November 18, 1850. New York Public Library.

33. Gamaliel Bailey to JGW, January 8, 1851. EI.

34. *National Era*, August 7, 1851.

35. JGW to Charles Sumner, January 16, 1851. HCL.
Donald, op. cit., pp. 189-204.
Pierce, op. cit., III 234-43.
Charles Sumner to JGW, March 25, 1851. EI.

36. *Villager*, March 13, 1851.
JGW to Charles Sumner, March 28, 1851, and undated. HCL.
Pickard, p. 354.

37. JGW to Sarah J. Clarke, May 18, 1851. Pickard, pp. 355-56.
JGW to Charles Sumner, May 20, 1851. HCL.

38. The two volumes are in Amesbury Public Library.

39. Howard Mumford Jones, "Whittier Reconsidered." EIHC. XCIII No. 4, October, 1957.

40. Address by John P. Marquand before the Whittier Home Association, June 16, 1949.
Amesbury Daily News, June 17, 1949.

41. JGW to Charles Sumner, August 20, 1851. HCL.

42. Record Book of the Washington Lyceum. APL.
JGW to Charles Sumner, September 14, 1851, October 16 [1851], and November 17, 1851. HCL.
JGW to Ralph Waldo Emerson, November 8 and December 27, 1851; January 8, February 18, February 23, 1852. HCL.

43. *National Era*, October 16, 1851.
Philip Magnus, *Gladstone: A Biography*, E. P. Dutton, 1954. pp. 99-100.
Charlotte Bronte to Elizabeth C. Gaskell, August 6, 1851. E. C. Gaskell, *Life of Charlotte Bronte*. Thomas Y. Crowell & Company. p. 337.

44. Frances C. Sparhawk, *Whittier at Close Range,* Riverdale Press, 1925. p. 76.
45. JGW to Rufus W. Griswold, October 10, 1851. BPL.
46. JGW to Charles Sumner, September 14 and October 16, 1851. HCL.
    Charles Sumner to JGW, September 11, 1851. Albree, pp. 117-18.
    Charles Sumner to JGW, October 7, 1851. Pickard, p. 363.
47. Ben: Perley Poore, *Perley's Reminiscences of Sixty Years in the National Metropolis.* Hubbard Brothers. I 404-05.
48. JGW to Samuel G. Howe, April 30, 1852. HEH.
    JGW to Charles Sumner, undated. HCL.
49. *National Era,* September 18, 1851. No cheap edition was printed until the Diamond Edition in 1867.

Chapter XVI

1. JGW to Ralph Waldo Emerson, December 12, 1852. HCL.
2. *National Era,* October 7, 1852.
3. JGW to Harriet Beecher Stowe, October 8, 1852. Chicago Historical Society.
4. George W. Bungay, *Crayon Sketches and Off-Hand Takings of Distinguished American Statesmen, Orators, Divines, Essayists, Editors, Poets, and Philanthropists.* Stacy and Richardson, 1852. pp. 38-42.
5. JGW to William S. Robinson, July 14, 1852. *Villager,* July 22, 1852. *National Era,* August 5, 1852.
6. *The Labor Movement: The Problem of Today.* Edited by George E. McNeill. A. M. Bridgman and Company, 1887. Chapter IV, "The Labor Movement in America," by the Editor. pp. 118-120.
   Newburyport Herald, June 11, 1852.
   Elizabeth F. Hume, "Newell Huntington." *Newburyport News,* April 2, 1942.
   Villager Extra, June 5, 1852.
7. Thomas Franklin Currier, "Whittier and the Amesbury-Salisbury Strike." *New England Quarterly* Vol. VII No. 1, 1935. pp. 105-109.
   JGW to Thomas Wentworth Higginson, July 13, 1852. HEH.
8. John F. Kellett, "Pioneer Irish-Catholics of Amesbury and Salisbury, Massachusetts." Typescript. APL.
   Letter, December, 1873. St. John's Seminary.
   "Henry Wilson." *National Era,* February 8, 1855.
9. James T. Fields to JGW, January 9, 1853. EI.
   JGW to Harriet Beecher Stowe, January 30, 1853. Chicago Historical Society.
   Currier, pp. 73-74.
   The Cost Books of Ticknor & Fields and Their Predecessors, 1832-1858. pp. 236 and 245.
10. Manuscript formerly owned by Carroll A. Wilson.
11. JGW to Gamaliel Bailey, December 8, [1852]. SC.
    John Wallace Hutchinson, *Story of the Hutchinsons Compiled and Edited by Charles E. Mann.* Lee & Shepard, 1896. I 315.
    Receipt signed by John B. Nichols, guardian of Lewis H. Caldwell, and note by Whittier, March 24, 1853. SC.
12. JGW to William J. Allinson, March 16, 1853. Copy. Hav. CL.
    JGW to Ralph Waldo Emerson, March 12 and March 16, 1853. HCL.

13. JGW to Gyles M. Kelley, December 3, 1853. HPL. Kelley was a member of the School Committee.
14. "New Mexico and the Indian Marauders." *National Era*, March 24, 1853.
15. "The American Slave Code." *National Era*, April 7, 1853.
16. "Official Piety" cannot be the "jingle" referred to in a letter to James T. Fields quoted in Pickard, p. 369. It had been published before that letter was written and surely could not be called a "jingle." The reference is more likely to "Letter from a Missionary of the Methodist Episcopal Church South."
17. S. J. Newton to JGW. (Undated) HCL.
    S. J. Newton to JGW, October 21, 1863. EI.
18. Laura E. Richards, *Samuel Gridley Howe*. Appleton-Century 1935. p. 18.
19. JGW to J. W. Stone, May 5, 1853. SC.
20. "New Hampshire". *National Era*, September 15, 1853.
21. Mary Rogers Kimball to Samuel T. Pickard. Pickard, p. 378.
22. JGW to Mary Russell Mitford, January 1, 1854. *The Friendships of Mary Russell Mitford*. Edited by A. G. L'Estrange. Harper and Brothers, 1882. p. 316.
23. JGW to E. A. Stansbury and others, September 23, 1853. New York Public Library.
    JGW to J. Miller McKim, November 30, 1853. BPL.
24. William J. Robinson to JGW, October 7, 1853. HCL.
    JGW to Ralph Waldo Emerson, October 24 and October 26, 1853. HCL.
25. JGW to James T. Fields, [January 1, 1854]. HEH.
26. JGW to James T. Fields, July 8, 1853. Yale University Library.
    JGW to Lucy Larcom, September 3, 1853. Daniel Dulany Addison, *Lucy Larcom, Life, Letters and Diary*. Houghton, Mifflin and Company, 1895. pp. 67-68.
27. Claude M. Fuess, *The Life of Caleb Cushing*, Harcourt Brace & Co., 1925, II 139-43.
28. JGW to Charles Sumner, November 15, 1853. HCL.

Chapter XVII

1. JGW to Julia Ward Howe, December 29, 1853. Laura R. Richards and Maud Howe Elliott, *Julia Ward Howe*. Houghton, Mifflin and Company, 1915. pp. 138-39.
   National Era, January 25, 1854.
2. This poem, with seven added stanzas and changes in two stanzas, is now "The Ranger."
3. JGW to James T. Fields. [January 1, 1854] HEH.
4. *Villager*, February 23 and March 2, 1854.
   George H. Mayer, *The Republican Party 1854 - 1964*. Oxford University Press, 1964. p. 26.
5. JGW to Charles Sumner, March 9, 1854. HCL.
6. Charles Sumner to JGW, March 17, 1854. HCL.
7. "A Miracle Needed." *National Era*, April 15, 1854.
8. *National Era*, June 1, 1854.
   Thomas Wentworth Higginson, *Cheerful Yesterdays*. Houghton, Mifflin and Company, 1898. pp. 151-57.
9. JGW to Henry I. Bowditch, May 26 and May 29, 1854. Vincent Y. Bowditch, *Life and Correspondence of Henry Ingersoll Bowditch*. Houghton, Mifflin and Company, 1902. I 269-271.
   JGW to Samuel E. Sewall, May 29, 1854. MHS.
   JGW to Editor of the *Times*, May 29, 1854. Boston *Daily Times*, May 30, 1854.

10. JGW to Mary R. Curzon, May 31, 1854. HCL.

11. JGW to Samuel E. Sewall, July 2, 1854. MHS.

12. JGW to Robert C. Winthrop, June 10, 1854. MHS.
    "A Word in Earnest." *National Era*, June 28, 1854.

13. There is also good authority in a statement by Edward Everett Hale, quoted in a note
    in the *Cambridge Edition*. The Kansas State Historical Society has a manuscript
    copy of the poem in Whittier's writing on the back of a half sheet of discarded
    manuscript of Edward Everett Hale's which was found among the papers of the
    New England Emigrant Aid Society. Cora Dolbee, "Kansas and 'The Prairied
    West' of John G. Whittier." EIHC, April 1946. pp. 171-72.

14. JGW to James T. Fields, August 14, [1854.] EI.
    A reference to *Literary Recreations and Miscellanies* places this letter in 1854. The
    passage quoted was erroneously included by Pickard in a letter April 7, 1851.
    Pickard, p. 359.
    Mrs. James T. Fields, *Whittier. Notes of His Life and His Friendships*. Harper and
    Brothers, 1893. p. 10.
    JGW to Daniel Richetson, March 17, 1875. SC.

15. Note 3.

16. JGW to Alice M. Kellogg, January 14, 1880. SC.
    Pickard, p. 368.

17. Review of *The Diary of George Templeton Strong*, Edited by Allen Nevins and Milton
    Halsey Thomas. EIHC, January, 1953.
    Curtis Guild to JGW, November 11, 1878. HCL.

18. Pickard, p. 703.

19. Cornelius Conway Felton to JGW, June 26, 1855. Albree, pp. 122-23.

20. Copy sold at American Art Association sale of collection of Stephen H. Wakeman.
    He also sent a copy to Goold Brown with a long inscription:
    "To Goold Brown. So honorably known for his successful devotion to that
    important department of Learning, which, in its promotion of precision of lan-
    guage and accuracy in the expression of thought, may be regarded as the handmaid
    of Truth, this little volume is offered by his friend The Author."
    Amesbury 24th, 5th mo., 1855.
    Volume formerly owned by Carroll A. Wilson. Brown was the author of three books on
    grammar. See Jones, *Later Periods of Quakerism*, p. 674 note.

21. Nathaniel Hawthorne to William D. Ticknor, September 30, 1854. New York Public
    Library.
    The Cost Books of Ticknor and Fields and Their Predecessors 1832-1856 p. 291.

22. Martha A. Shackford, "Whittier and Some Cousins." *New England Quarterly*, Sep-
    tember 1942.
    Elizabeth Lloyd Howell to the Whittiers, November 21, 1853. *Elizabeth Lloyd and
    the Whittiers*. pp. 125-26.
    Elizabeth Nicholson to Elizabeth Whittier, September 1, 1854. HCL.

23. JGW to Elizabeth Lloyd Howell, February 4 [1855]. *Whittier's Unknown Romance*,
    pp. 12-13. Currier (*Elizabeth Lloyd and the Whittiers*, pp. 125-26) thought that
    this letter should be dated 1853. The correct date is obviously 1855, as evidenced
    by the reference to the death of Mary R. Mitford, which occurred January 10,
    1855. The present writer pleads guilty to failure to detect the error when he read
    the proof of *Elizabeth Lloyd and the Whittiers*.

24. JGW to James Russell Lowell, February 4, 1855. SC.
    W. Sloane Kennedy, "In Whittier Land." *New England Magazine*, November 1892.

25. *Villager*, May 3, 1855.
    Elizabeth H. Whittier to Moses A. Cartland, May 16, 1855. Shackford, pp. 44-45.
    JGW to Charles Sumner, April 18, 1855. HCL.

26. JGW to Yearly Meeting of Progressive Friends, May 12, 1855. *Proceedings of the Pennsylvania Yearly Meeting of Progressive Friends, Longwood 1855.* New York, 1855.

27. JGW to William Lloyd Garrison, February 14, 1859. HCL.

28. "New Hampshire Senators." *National Era,* June 21, 1855. Also in *Facts for the People,* July 1, 1855.

29. Thomas Starr King to JGW, November 30, 1855. Pickard, pp. 375-76.

30. JGW to ?, November 24, 1855. SC.

Chapter XVIII

1. JGW to William Allinson, January 20, 1856. Copy, Hav. CL.

2. JGW to James T. Fields, January 6, 1856. HEH.

3. *The Cost Books of Ticknor and Fields and Their Predecessors 1832 - 1858.* pp. 352, 375. Josiah Quincy to JGW, April 4, 1856. EI.

4. Cora Dolbee, "Kansas and the 'Prairied West' of John G. Whittier." EIHC, Vol. LXXXI, October 1945. pp. 307-347.

5. JGW to Lucy Larcom, May 1856. MHS.
   JGW to James Freeman Clarke, March 25, 1856. HCL.

6. *John Greenleaf Whittier. A Profile in Pictures.* Compiled by Donald Prescott Wright. Haverhill, 1967.
   JGW to Charles H. Brainard, April 13, 1856. HCL.
   Newburyport Herald, March 18, 1856.

7. Quoted in Frank Luther Mott, *A History of American Magazines,* 1850-1856. Harvard University Press, 1957. p. 168.

8. *Villager,* April 17, 1856.

9. Roland H. Woodwell, *Amesbury Public Library 1856-1956.* Amesbury, 1956.

10. Pickard, p. 391.

11. *Recent Speeches and Addresses by Charles Sumner.* Higgins and Bradley, 1856. p. 595.

12. JGW to Charles Sumner, June 13, 1856. HCL.

13. William Lawrence, *Memories of a Happy Life.* Houghton Mifflin, 1926. p. 7.

14. JGW to John A. Douglass, June 2, 1856. Owned by Miss Alice D. Wells, Amesbury, Massachusetts.

15. JGW to Moses A. Cartland, July 15, 1856. Shackford, p. 50.
    George L. Mayer, *The Republican Party 1854-1964.* Oxford University Press, 1964. p. 43.
    JGW to ?, June 20, 1856. BPL.

16. *Villager,* July 10, 1856.

17. JGW to Moses A. Cartland. Note 15.
    JGW to Lucy Larcom, August 10, 1856. MHS.

18. Charles A. Dana to JGW, June 8, 1856. Pickard, pp. 384-85.
    Helen Clarkson to Samuel T. Pickard, July 15, 1893. HCL.

19. Frances Campbell Sparhawk, *Whittier at Close Range.* Riverdale Press, 1925. p. 39.
    JGW to Francis H. Underwood [?], July 28, 1883. SC.

20. JGW to George William Curtis, September 19, 1856. SC.
    JGW to Richard H. Dana Jr., October 20, 1856. MHS.
    Richard H. Dana Jr. to JGW, October 23, 1856. Central Michigan University.

21. *Newburyport Herald*, October 3, 4, 8, 1856.

22. JGW to Charles Sumner, November 12, 1856. HCL.

23. The present headnote is of course incorrect; it was the Republican and not the Free Soil party, which made great gains in 1856 and was successful in 1860.

24. JGW to William J. Allinson, August 7, 1856. Copy, Hav. CL.

25. Jones, *Later Periods of Quakerism*, p. 852.
    "Friends in Kansas." *National Era*, September 4, 1856.

26. "Aid for Kansas." *Villager*, October 23, 1856.

27. Jones, op. cit. p. 727.
    Albree, p. 128.

28. JGW to James T. Fields, January 4, 1857. HEH.
    Interview in *Yonkers Statesman* 1869. Quoted in "A Visit to Whittier Eighty Years Ago" by Roland D. Sawyer. *Amesbury Daily News*, December 3, 1949.

29. JGW to James T. Fields, January 4, 1857. EI.
    James T. Fields to JGW, January 2, 1857. Whittier Home, Amesbury.

30. *The Cost Books of Ticknor and Fields and Their Predecessors 1832-1858*, p. 401.
    James T. Fields to JGW, February 21, 1857. EI.

31. JGW to James T. Fields, March 5 and 11, 1857. HEH.

32. Elizabeth H. Whittier to Lucy Larcom, March 23, 1857. HCL.
    Record Book of the Officers and Committees of the Amesbury and Salisbury Library Association. APL.

33. JGW to James T. Fields, May 1, 1857. Pickard, p. 395. The reference is to Burns' comic "Epitaph on Captain Grose, the Celebrated Antiquary." When Satan came to get Grose and saw the bedposts groaning under their burden —
    Astonished, confounded, cried Satan: "By ---- ,
    I'll want 'im, ere I take such a damnable load."
    Pickard, p. 395.

34. JGW to James T. Fields. Undated. HPL.
    JGW to Samuel E. Sewall, May 5, 1857. MHS.

35. Pickard, p. 395-96.
    J. A. Tappan to Samuel T. Pickard, April 14, 1893. HCL.
    Augustine Jones, "Reminiscences of John G. Whittier". *American Friend*, December 12, 1907.

36. John F. Kellett, "Whittier and Mary Esther Carter." Typescript, Amesbury Public Library.
    "What of the rappings in these days? have they yet passed the forbidden threshold and made themselves at home among your Penates?" Mary E. Tenney to JGW, December 20, 1857. EI.
    Journal of Charlotte Forten. Ed. Ray Allen Billington. Dryden Press, 1953. p. 93.

37. Pickard, pp. 397-402.

38. *Newburyport Herald*, September 17, 1857.

39. JGW to Lucy Larcom, November 15, 1857. Anderson Sale, p. 37. Pickard, p. 370, incorrectly dated 1855.

Chapter XIX

1. James Russell Lowell to JGW, August 10, 1857. Albree, p. 130.

2. James Russell Lowell to JGW, November 4, 1857. *Letters of James Russell Lowell*, Edited by Charles Eliot Norton, II 18-19.

3. "The Original Version of Skipper Ireson Ballad." Letter of Samuel T. Pickard to *Boston Evening Transcript*. When Pickard asked Evelina Bray if she gave the story to Whittier, she replied, *"No* assuredly *No!"* Manuscript note of Samuel T. Pickard. HCL.

4. JGW to James Russell Lowell, November 5, 1857. HCL.

5. James Russell Lowell to JGW, December 30, 1857. Central Michigan University.

6. JGW to James Russell Lowell, December 1857. HCL.

7. James Russell Lowell to JGW, December 30, 1857. Central Michigan University.
   James Russell Lowell to JGW, January 23, 1858. Albree, pp. 131-32.
   JGW to James Russell Lowell, January 1, 1858. HCL.

8. JGW to Charles Sumner, January 11, 1858. HCL.
   JGW to William J. Allinson, January 12, 1858. Copy, Hav. CL.
   Frederick W. Coburn, "Thomas Bayley Lawson. Portrait Painter." EIHC LXXXIV, January 1948. p. 48.

9. JGW to Francis H. Underwood, January 20, 1858. Copy, HCL.

10. JGW to James Russell Lowell, February 16, 1858. HCL.
    Joseph Parish to JGW, January 28, 1858. EI.
    JGW to James Russell Lowell, Feburary 22, 1858. HCL.

11. Pollard, p. 355.

12. "Report of Amesbury and Salisbury Library Committee, John G. Whittier, James H. Davis, Benjamin Evans." *Villager*, June 10, 1858.
    JGW to James T. Fields, November 21, 1858. University of Kansas.

13. JGW to J. B. Gale, September 30, 1858, and October 16, 1858. *Villager*, October 7, 1858, and October 21, 1858.

14. Currier, pp. 343-44.

15. *Newburyport Herald*, December 20, 1858.

16. Samuel Longfellow, *Henry W. Longfellow* II 348.
    JGW to Francis H. Underwood, July 5, 1858. HCL.
    JGW to Francis H. Underwood, June 25, 1858. SC.

17. JGW to James Russell Lowell. [May 1858] HCL.

18. *Newburyport Herald*, August 5, 1858. The portrait was on exhibit at the drug store of W. W. Caldwell, Newburyport.

19. The vessel struck on Crackwood's Ledge, off Rockport, about three hundred feet from Thacher's Island, not on Avery's Rock. "The Great Storm of 1635." *Essex Antiquarian*, June 1897.

20. "The Blessed Damozel" had appeared in the Pre-Raphaelite paper, *The Germ*.

21. *Villager*, September 2, 1858.
    Letter September 11, 1858. *Atlas and Daily Bee*, September 13, 1858.

22. JGW to James Russell Lowell, August 10 and August 28, 1858. Copies. HCL.

23. Theodore Tilton to JGW, December 11, 1858. Central Michigan University.
    JGW to Francis H. Underwood, August 28, 1858. Copy, HCL.

24. JGW to James Russell Lowell, December 29, 1858. HCL.

25. Joseph Sturge to JGW, December 23, 1858. Central Michigan University.

26. Typed copy of fragment of early draft. HCL.

27. Pickard, pp. 419-20, 757-58.
    Ernest A. Blaw to JGW, January 27, 1891. HCL.

28. JGW to John S. Tyler, January 22, 1859. *Newburyport Herald*, January 27, 1859.
    Celebration of the Hundredth Anniversary of the Birth of Robert Burns, by the Boston Burns Club, January 25, 1859. Boston, 1859.

29. Hannah Lloyd Neall to JGW, January 4, 1858. *Elizabeth Lloyd and the Whittiers*, pp. 127-28.
    Lucy Chase to JGW, March 3, [1859]. Privately owned.

Chapter XX

1. JGW to Elizabeth H. Whittier, April 18, 1859. Owned by John B. Pickard.

2. JGW to Elizabeth Lloyd Howell, May 2 [1859]. Marie V. Denervaud, *Whittier's Unknown Romance*, Houghton Mifflin, 1922. p. 15. This letter is obviously May, not November 2, as printed in *Whittier's Unknown Romance*. The whole story of Whittier's love for Elizabeth Lloyd, when they were younger and he was in Philadelphia editing the *Pennsylvania Freeman*, and in 1859, three years after the death of her husband, Robert Howell, will never be known. She refused to help Samuel T. Pickard when he was preparing his biography, saying that she had no letters, and "I could not — if I *would*, add anything worth preserving to your proposed memoir of him". (Elizabeth Lloyd Howell to Samuel T. Pickard, February 25, 1893. HCL) According to her niece, Marie V. Denervaud, the letters were left to her sister, Hannah Lloyd Neall, who told Pickard that Elizabeth had destroyed many letters. (Hannah Lloyd Neall to Samuel T. Pickard, March 3, 1893. HCL) Whittier evidently destroyed many of her letters, as she asked him to do.
   JGW to Elizabeth Lloyd Howell, undated, and May 18, 1859. *Whittier's Unknown Romance*, pp. 16, 17, 18.

3. JGW to Elizabeth Lloyd Howell, May 14, 1859. *Elizabeth Lloyd and the Whittiers*, p. 128.

4. JGW to Elizabeth Lloyd Howell, May 17, 1859. *Whittier's Unknown Romance*, p. 17.
   JGW to Hannah J. Newhall, May 17, 1859. Westtown School.
   JGW to Elizabeth Lloyd Howell, June 2, 1859. *Elizabeth Lloyd and the Whittiers*, pp. 130-33.

5. JGW to Elizabeth Lloyd Howell, May 18, 1859. *Whittier's Unknown Romance*, pp. 18-20.

6. JGW to Elizabeth Lloyd Howell, June 2, 1859. *Elizabeth Lloyd and the Whittiers*, pp. 130-33.

7. JGW to Elizabeth Lloyd Howell, June 9, 1859. *Whittier's Unknown Romance*, pp. 20-21.
   JGW to Elizabeth Lloyd Howell, June 12, 1859. Ibid, pp. 21-23.
   JGW to Elizabeth Lloyd Howell, June 24, 1859. Ibid, pp. 23-27.

8. JGW to Elizabeth Lloyd Howell, June 29, 1859. Ibid, pp. 27-29.

9. Roland H. Woodwell, "William Ashby and His Laurel Parties." EIHC Vol. LXXXIV No. 1, January 1948.

10. JGW to Elizabeth Lloyd Howell, June 31, 1859. *Whittier's Unknown Romance*, p. 30.
    JGW to Elizabeth Lloyd Howell, July 9, 1859. Ibid, p. 31.

11. Elizabeth K. Halbeisen, *Harriet Prescott Spofford*. University of Pennsylvania Press, 1935. p. 57.
    Harriet Prescott Spofford a quarter of a century later recalled the brilliant talk by Longfellow, Lowell, Holmes, and Thomas Wentworth Higginson, which "made the hours sparkle" while she, "a shy and silent-suffering young woman" looked occasionally at Whittier, who was across the table from her, believing that he was the only one there who felt as uncomfortable as she did. Harriet Prescott Spofford, "The Quaker Poet." *Harper's New Monthly Magazine*, June, 1884.

12. Samuel Longfellow, *Journal of Henry Wadsworth Longfellow* II 387.
    JGW to Elizabeth Lloyd Howell, July 9, 1859. *Whittier's Unknown Romance*, pp. 31-32.

13. Lloyd M. Griffin, "Matthew Franklin Whittier, 'Ethan Spike.' " *New England Quarterly* Vol. XIV No. 4, December 1941.
    JGW to Elizabeth Lloyd Howell, July 14, 1859. *Whittier's Unknown Romance*, pp. 33-35.

14. Lewis Tappan to JGW, August 1, 1859. Albree, pp. 133-34.
    JGW to Elizabeth Lloyd Howell, August 22, 1859. *Whittier's Unknown Romance*, pp. 43-45.
15. *Newburyport Herald*, September 30, 1859.
    JGW to Elizabeth Lloyd Howell, September 28, 1859. *Whittier's Unknown Romance*, p. 47.
16. JGW to Elizabeth Lloyd Howell, July 14, 1859. Ibid, pp. 33-35.
17. JGW to Elizabeth Lloyd Howell, July 25, 1859. *Elizabeth Lloyd and the Whittiers*, pp. 133-35.
18. JGW to Elizabeth Lloyd Howell, August 3, 1859. *Whittier's Unknown Romance*, pp. 36-41.
19. Hannah Lloyd Neall to JGW, October 23, 1888. HCL.
20. Mary A. Dodge to Sarah Jane Clarke, Lippincourt, September 25, 1859. H. Augusta Dodge, *Gail Hamilton's Life in Letters* Lee, Shepard, 1901 I 246. Whittier had written to Gamaliel Bailey, "Who is Gail Hamilton? That last poem of hers ["Terra Incognita"] was a very fine one."
21. JGW to Elizabeth Lloyd Howell, July 30, 1859. *Whittier's Unknown Romance*, pp. 35-36.
22. JGW to William C. Clarke, November 30, 1859. *Tri-Weekly Publisher*, December 3, 1859.
    JGW to Elizabeth Lloyd Howell, November 6, 1859. *Whittier's Unknown Romance*, pp. 49-51.
    Lydia Maria Child to JGW, November 16, 1859. Formerly owned by Robert W. Lull.
    JGW to Charles Sumner, December 8, 1859. HCL.
23. Manuscript privately owned.
24. JGW to Theodore Tilton, December 11, 1859. SC.
    Alexander Milton Ross, *Memoirs of a Reformer (1832-1892)*. Hunter, Rose and Company. p. 174.
25. Nathaniel Hawthorne, "Chiefly about War Matters. By a Peaceable Man." *Atlantic Monthly*, July, 1862.
26. "Whittier on John Brown". *Liberator*, January 13, 1860.
    JGW to William Lloyd Garrison, January 15, 1860. *Liberator*, January 27, 1860.
27. JGW to Lucy Larcom. Pickard, p. 422.
    JGW to Ralph Waldo Emerson, December 12, 1852. HCL. The passage in the BhagavadGita is quoted in "The Orientalism of Whittier" by Arthur Christy, *American Literature*, November, 1933, Vol. 5, pp. 247-257. Whittier wrote to Celia Thaxter October 25, 1888: "I have long been familiar with the Bhavagad Gita, as translated under the care of Warren Hastings." HCL.
28. JGW to Elizabeth Lloyd Howell, December 14, 1859, and February 29, 1860. *Whittier's Unknown Romance*, pp. 51-55.
29. JGW to Elizabeth Lloyd Howell, March 20, 1860. Ibid, pp. 56-59.
30. JGW to Horace E. Scudder, February 25, 1888. Formerly owned by Carroll A. Wilson. Copy. EI.
31. JGW to James Russell Lowell, January 9, 1860. HCL.
    JGW to James Russell Lowell, January 10, February 3, and February 18, 1860. HCL.
    Maria S. Porter, *Recollections of Louisa May Alcott, John Greenleaf Whittier and Robert Browning*. New England Magazine Corporation, 1893.
32. JGW to ?, September 23, 1857. Cornell University Library.
33. Note in Cambridge Edition.
34. JGW to Thomas Chase, April 28, 1860. Hav. CL.
35. JGW to Elizabeth Lloyd Howell, February 29 and March 20, 1860. *Whittier's Unknown Romance*, pp. 53-55 and 56-59.
36. JGW to Charles Sumner, June 6, 1860. HCL.

37. JGW to Elizabeth Lloyd Howell, March 20, 1860. Note 35.
38. JGW to Elizabeth Lloyd Howell, September 19, 1860. *Whittier's Unknown Romance*, pp. 61-63.
    JGW to Lucy Larcom, October 1, 1860. Pickard, p. 431.
39. JGW to Elizabeth Lloyd Howell, August 9, 1860. *Whittier's Unknown Romance*, pp. 59-61.
    Newburyport Herald, June 30 and July 14, 1960.
    JGW to James T. Fields, July 16, 1860. HEH.
40. JGW to Elizabeth Lloyd Howell, Note 39.
    JGW to William W. Caldwell, September 3, 1860. Formerly owned by Daniel A. Goodwin.
    JGW to Harriet McEwen Kimball, September 11, 1860. "John Greenleaf Whittier to Harriet McEwen Kimball, Eight Letters." Edited by Lewis E. Weeks Jr. EIHC, January 1959. Vol. XCV. No. 1. pp. 41-51.
    Villager, September 27, 1860.

Chapter XXI

1. *Villager*, September 13, 1860.
   Newburyport Herald, September 2, 1860.
2. *Villager*, September 27, 1860.
   Newburyport Herald, October 13, 1860.
3. Pickard, p. 432.
   JGW to Hannah Lloyd Neall, November 8, 1860. *Whittier's Unknown Romance*, pp. 66-68.
   JGW to Edward G. Frothingham, November 21, 1860. *Villager* November 29, 1860. Frothingham was a native of Newburyport. He bought the *Haverhill Gazette* six years after Whittier was editor and frequently called at the *Gazette* office. Garrison was often a guest at his home when on a lecture tour.
4. JGW to Elizabeth Lloyd Howell, November 22, 1860. *Elizabeth Lloyd and the Whittiers*, pp. 138-40.
5. Elizabeth H. Whittier to Mary E. Shepard, November 5, 1860. Formerly owned by C. Marshall Taylor.
   JGW to Edna Dean Proctor, November 10, 1860. New Hampshire Historical Society.
   JGW to Oliver Wendell Holmes, August 2, 1860. LC.
6. JGW to Elizabeth Lloyd Howell, September 19, 1860. *Whittier's Unknown Romance*, pp. 61-63.
   JGW to Hannah Lloyd Neall. Note 3.
7. Mrs. James T. Fields, *Whittier. Notes of His Life and of His Friendships*. Harper and Brothers, 1893. p. 49.
8. JGW to Hannah Lloyd Neall, March 24, 1861. *Elizabeth Lloyd and the Whittiers*, pp. 140-41, incorrectly headed "To Elizabeth Lloyd Howell."
   JGW to Lucy Larcom, April 27, 1861. MHS.
9. *Newburyport Herald*, January 29 and February 14, 1861.
10. JGW to Charles Sumner, January 26, 1861. HCL. The comparison with cannibalism was from a letter of Salmon P. Chase, November 23, 1860. Albree, pp. 136-39.

11. Charles Sumner to JGW, February 5, 1861. Albree, pp. 140-41.
    Salmon P. Chase to JGW, February 1, 1861. EI.
    JGW to W. S. Thayer, February 1, 1861. Pickard, p. 435.
    JGW to Francis H. Underwood, February 7, 1861. Copy. HCL.

12. Salmon P. Chase to JGW, November 23, 1860. Albree, pp. 136-39.
    "Emancipation and Compensation." *Villager*, February 7, 1861.

13. JGW to James T. Fields, Pickard, p. 430. Joseph Merrill, author of *History of Amesbury and Merrimac*, thought that Cobbler Keezar was the John Cazar who was "denyed" by the Quakers in 1706 for not paying his debts.

14. *Newburyport Herald*, March 20, 1861.
    JGW to Anson Burlingame (?), March 2, 1861. EI.
    JGW to Charles Sumner, March 13, 1861. HCL.
    Lloyd W. Griffin, "Matthew Franklin Whittier, 'Ethan Spike.' " *New England Quarterly*, Vol. XIV No. 4, December 1941.

15. JGW to Hannah Lloyd Neall. Note 8.
    JGW to Lydia Maria Child, April 1, 1861. Pickard, pp. 436-37.

16. JGW to Lucy Larcom, April 27, 1861. MHS.

17. JGW to the Editor of the *Herald*, May 15, 1861. *Newburyport Herald*, May 18, 1861.

18. Pickard, p. 441. The circular is dated "Amesbury, 18th 6th mo. 1861."

19. *Letters of Lydia Maria Child*, Houghton, Mifflin and Company, 1883. p. 147.

20. Lecture by Charles C. Coffin at Whittier Birthplace, October 7, 1892. Quoted in *Rare Whittieriana at the Whittier Homestead*, October 1 and 2, 1938.

21. JGW to John H. Hutchinson, March 6, 1862. The letter and Hutchinson's account of the incident are in John Wallace Hutchinson, *Story of the Hutchinsons*, Lee & Shepard, 1896. pp. 381-97.

22. JGW to ?, May 10, 1861. EI.

23. *Newburyport Herald*, June 28, 1861.
    Frances C. Sparhawk, *Whittier at Close Range*. Riverdale Press, 1925. p. 117.

24. JGW to Hannah Lloyd Neall, January 24, 1862. University of Kansas.
    Boston Transcript, December 23, 1905. "Notes and Queries," Item 3928.
    Elizabeth Lloyd Howell to JGW, September 19, 1861. *Elizabeth Lloyd and the Whittiers*, pp. 142-44.

25. Frances C. Sparhawk, Op. cit., p. 38.
    JGW to Mrs. Samuel E. Sewall, July 31, 1861. MHS.

26. Note 16.
    JGW to James T. Fields, August 31, 1861. BPL.

27. JGW to James T. Fields, December 20, 1861. HEH.
    Pickard, p. 444. This is not in the letter to James T. Fields, December 20.

28. JGW to George L. Stearns, September 13, 1861. Pickard, p. 467, incorrectly dated September 19.

29. Pickard, pp. 462-63.

30. *Newburyport Herald*, July 9 and July 11, 1861.
    Lucy Larcom to JGW, September 8, 1861. Daniel Dulany Addison, *Lucy Larcom, Life, Letters, and Diary*. Houghton, Mifflin and Company, 1895. p. 152. The hymn was "Harvest Song," *Villager*, October 3, 1861.
    Newburyport Herald, September 11, 1861.
    Robert K. Cheney, *Maritime History of the Merrimac: Shipbuilding*. Newburyport Press, 1964. pp. 77-78.

31. *Newburyport Herald*, October 14, 1861.

32. JGW to Hannah J. Newhall, November 22 and December 4, 1861. Westtown School.

Chapter XXII

1. JGW to James T. Fields, December 20, 1861. HEH..
2. JGW to Lucy Larcom, January 30, 1862. MHS.
3. Thomas Starr King to JGW, February 27, 1862. Albree, pp. 142-45.
4. JGW to Charles Sumner, April 11, 1862. HCL.
5. JGW to Thomas Wentworth Higginson, September 30, 1872. University of Texas.
6. Elizabeth H. Whittier to ?, July 3, 1862. Whittier Home, Amesbury.
7. *Villager*, October 30, 1862.
   Alijah W. Thayer to JGW, October 27, 1862. EI.
8. JGW to Charlotte Forten. Charlotte Forten Grimke, "Personal Recollections of Whittier." *New England Magazine*, June, 1883.
9. JGW to Mary Curzon, December 24, 1862. HCL.
   Anna Mary Wells, *Dear Preceptor, The Life and Times of Thomas Wentworth Higginson*. Houghton, Mifflin, 1963. pp. 159-63.
   JGW to Charlotte Forten. *Journal of Charlotte Forten*, p. 173.
10. JGW to James T. Fields, June 6 and December 2, 1862. HEH.
11. *Villager*, December 18, 1862 and March 12, 1863.
12. Quoted in Rufus Jones, *Later Periods of Quakerism*, p. 645.
13. JGW to James T. Fields, December 2, 1862. HEH.
14. Elizabeth H. Whittier to Mary Shepard, January 5, 1863. Formerly owned by C. Marshall Taylor.
15. JGW to Edward L. Pierce, January 14, 1863. HCL.
16. JGW to James T. Fields, March 6 and March 29, 1863. HCL.
    JGW to James T. Fields, undated. HEH. C. Marshall Taylor owned a copy of the poem in Whittier's handwriting with only the first ten and last seventeen lines, with numerous variations in the wording.
    JGW to Lucy Larcom, March 16, 1863. Anderson Sale.
17. Charles E. L. Wingate, "The Countess." *Exeter News Letter*, January 5, 1934. From *Haverhill Sunday Record*.
    Rebecca I. Davis, *Gleanings from the Merrimac Valley*. Hoyt, Fogg, and Donham, 1881. pp. 35-36.
18. JGW to Charles E. Wingate, April 15, 1886. Charles E. Wingate, *Life of Paine Wingate*, II 470.
    Whittier-Land, pp. 50-51.
    JGW to H. Bogart, June 1, 1863. Wells College.
19. JGW to Lydia Maria Child. *Letters of Lydia Maria Child*. Houghton and Mifflin Company, 1883. pp. 240-41.
20. James Worthen to JGW, May 21, 1863. Formerly owned by C. Marshall Taylor.
    Report from United States Treasury Department. HCL.
    JGW to Lucy Larcom, 1863. Pickard, p. 469.
21. Moses A. Cartland to JGW, [June 10, 1863]. Shackford, pp. 54-55.
22. *Newburyport Herald*, June 30, 1863.
23. Pickard, pp. 454-56.
    James T. Fields to JGW, August 24, 1863. Pickard, p. 458.
24. The source of the description was called to the writer's attention by Dr. J. McDonald Ernest.

25. Eleanor Roosevelt, "Churchill at the White House." *Atlantic*, Vol. 215 No. 3, March 1965. p. 78.

26. JGW to ?, February 15, 1873. SC.
JGW to ?, June 11, 1881. *Dedication of the Barbara Frietchie Monument in Frederick, Maryland, September 9, 1914.*
JGW to Francis F. Browne, November 15, 1885. Francis F. Browne, *Bugle Echoes.* White, Stokes, & Allen, 1886. p. 123.
JGW to ?, October 19, 1890. Pickard, p. 458.

27. JGW to Celia Thaxter, January 1, 1864. HCL.
Whittier-Land, p. 92.
Celia Thaxter to Elizabeth H. Whittier, November 15, [1863]. HCL.

28. *Journal of Charlotte Forten*, p. 200.

29. JGW to Elizabeth Lloyd Howell, January 13, 1864. *Whittier's Unknown Romance*, p. 63.
JGW to William Lloyd Garrison, November 24, 1863. BPL. *Works*, VII. 145-47.

30. JGW to James T. Fields, November 28, 1863. HEH. The royalty of three hundred forty dollars was probably not, as Pickard believed, on *In War Time*, which was not entered for copyright until November 9. Whittier's royalty was ten cents a copy, and it is most unlikely that 3400 copies were sold in two weeks. Pickard incorrectly dated the letter January 28, 1864. It referred to the Hymn sent to Thomas Starr King, which was sung January 17 and printed in the *Independent* January 21, as having just been sent. Whittier had asked in the spring if his royalty on the Blue and Gold Edition could be increased to ten percent.
JGW to James T. Fields, December 25, 1863. HEH.

31. Lloyd Wilfred Griffin, "Matthew Franklin Whittier, 'Ethan Spike' " *New England Quarterly*, Vol. XIV, No. 4, 1941.

32. JGW to George J. L. Colby, December 19, 1863. *Newburyport Herald*, December 21, 1863.
JGW to Thomas Niles, December 31, 1863. SC.
JGW to Elizabeth Lloyd Howell. Note 29.

33. JGW to James T. Fields, November 28, 1863. Note 30.
Thomas Starr King to JGW, [January 18, 1864]. Copy. HCL.
Thomas Starr King to JGW, October 29, 1862. Central Michigan University.

34. *Villager*, March 2, 1865.

35. JGW to James T. Fields, January 2, 1864. HEH.

36. Jessie B. Fremont to JGW, February 14, 1864. HCL.
William L. Alger to JGW, March 17, 1864. HCL.

37. J. C. Rice to JGW, March 1864. Pickard, p. 476.

38. Edward W. Emerson, *Early Years of the Saturday Club.* Boston 1918.
M. A. DeWolfe Howe, *Holmes of the Breakfast Table.* Oxford University Press, 1939. p. 93.
Samuel Longfellow, *Henry Wadsworth Longfellow*, II 328.
Ralph Waldo Emerson, James Russell Lowell, Oliver Wendell Holmes to JGW, April 8, 1864. Central Michigan University.
JGW to Ralph Waldo Emerson, April 21, 1864 (incomplete) HCL.
John Murray Forbes, *Letters and Recollections*, ed. Sarah Forbes Hughes. Houghton and Mifflin Company, 1899, II 87-88.
Emerson's Journal, X 65.

39. *New England Historical and Genealogical Register*, II 192 and IV 323.
Joshua Coffin to JGW, July 2, 1848. EI.
JGW to Celia Thaxter, August 24, 1868. HC.
Whittier believed that he was a descendant of Christopher Hussey, whose wife was a daughter of Stephen Bachiler. Whittier was a descendant of Richard Hussey.

JGW to David Worth Dennis, August 11, 1888. Owned by Mr. and Mrs. William Dennis.

JGW to Committee on the Celebration of the 250th Anniversary of Hampton, August 4, 1888. *Exeter News-Letter*, August 19, 1938.

Roland H. Woodwell, "The Hussey Ancestry of the Poet Whittier." EIHC, Vol. LXX, January, 1934. pp. 58-68.

40. JGW to Mary Abigail Dodge, April 5, 1864. EI.
JGW to James T. Fields, April 1864. HEH.
JGW to Annie Fields, May 5, 1864. HEH.
JGW to Harriet Minot Pitman, May 12, 1864. SC.
Mary Abigail Dodge to George Wood, May 6, 1864. H. Augusta Dodge, *Gail Hamilton's Life in Letters*. Lee and Shepard, 1901. p. 402.

41. JGW to Harriet Minot Pitman, June 1864. Boston Atheneum.
JGW to Charles Sumner, June 1864. HCL.
Julian Hawthorne, *Hawthorne and His Wife*. Houghton and Mifflin Company, 1885, II 348.

42. Mary Abigail Dodge to JGW, May 9, 1864. Central Michigan University.
JGW to Mary Abigail Dodge, June 1864. Samuel T. Pickard, "A Merry Woman's Letters to a Quiet Poet." *Ladies' Home Journal*, December, 1899.

43. JGW to Harriet Minot Pitman, Note 40.
Harriet Minot Pitman to JGW, July 21, 1864. HCL.

44. JGW to Bayard Taylor, August 30, 1864. Pickard, p. 479.
JGW to Charles Sumner, August 20, 1864. HCL.

45. Horace Greeley, *The American Conflict*, II 660.
Thomas Graham Belden and Marva Robins Belden, *So Fell the Angels*. Little-Brown, 1956. p. 125.
Jessie B. Fremont to JGW, August 22, [1864]. Central Michigan University.
Jessie B. Fremont to JGW, November 11, 1889. Pickard, p. 487.
JGW to William Lloyd Garrison, August 29, 1864. *Liberator*, September 2, 1864.

46. John F. Kellett, "Whittier and Aunt Joan Colby." Typescript. APL.
Emily B. Smith, *Whittier*. Whittier Press, 1935. p. 25.

47. JGW to Lucy Larcom, September 3, 1864. Pickard, p. 480.
JGW to James T. Fields, September 27, 1864. Pickard, pp. 480-81.
JGW to Lucy Larcom, October 1864. Pickard, p. 481.
JGW to Sarah Jane Lippincott, October 1864. Pickard, pp. 481-82.
Villager, October 13, 1864.

48. JGW to Theodore Tilton, September 10, 1864. Northwestern University.
JGW to Lydia Maria Child, November 15, 1864. New York Public Library.

Chapter XXIII

1. JGW to James T. Fields, September 27, 1864. Pickard, pp. 480-81.

2. JGW to Mary Shepard [?], December 19, 1864. Copy. EI.

3. JGW to Lucy Larcom, February, 1865. Pickard, p. 489.
Newburyport Herald, February 3, 1865.

4. Howard Mumford Jones, "Whittier Reconsidered." EIHC. Vol. XCIII, No. 4, October 1957.
Mary S. Battey to JGW, February 17, 1867. EI.

5. Richard Plumer to William Lloyd Garrison, February 12, 1865. BPL.

6. *Newburyport Herald*, February 22, 1865.
   William Lloyd Garrison, The Story of *His Life as Told by His Children*, Houghton Mifflin & Co. 1889, II 130.
   H. Augusta Dodge, *Gail Hamilton's Life in Letters*. Lee and Shepard, 1901, I 480.

7. JGW to Lucy Larcom, November 29, 1864. Pickard, p. 482.

8. Phineas P. Whitehouse to JGW, January 9, 1869. Whittier Home, Amesbury.
   JGW to Phineas P. Whitehouse, January 12, 1869. Whittier Home, Amesbury.

9. Pickard, p. 539.

10. Ann Wendell to JGW, December 4, 1864. Formerly owned by C. Marshall Taylor.

11. Frances Campbell Sparhawk, *Whittier at Close Range*, The Riverdale Press, 1925. p. 47.
    JGW to Charles H. Brainard, November 18, 1870. SC.
    JGW to James T. Fields, 1864. Pickard, p. 488.

12. JGW to Lucy Larcom, May 11, 1865. SC.

13. Maria S. Porter, *Recollections of Louisa May Alcott, John Greenleaf Whittier, and Robert Browning*. New England Magazine Corporation, 1893.

14. JGW to Charles C. Coffin, March 1, 1865. *Boston Transcript*, March 10, 1865.

15. JGW to ?, April 14, 1865. HCL.
    JGW to Hannah J. Newhall, April 20, 1865. Westtown School.
    JGW to William J. Allinson, April 20, 1865. Copy. EI.
    "The Lesson and Our Duty." *Villager*, May 11, 1865. *Works* VII 148.

16. JGW to George L. Stearns, July 3, 1865. Pickard, pp. 492-93.

17. Note 12.

18. JGW to H. D. Young, February 5, 1890. SC.
    A marker was placed on the supposed site of the grave August 25, 1955. An account of the exercises was in the *Boston Herald*, August 31, 1955.

19. JGW to Mary Abigail Dodge, May 29 and June 11, 1865. EI.
    JGW to Lucy Larcom, June 13, 1865. American Antiquarian Society.

20. *Newburyport Herald*, June 29, 1865.
    Mary Abigail Dodge to George Wood, June 30, 1865. *Gail Hamilton's Life in Letters* I 513.
    Manuscript note of Samuel T. Pickard. HCL.

21. Thomas W. Waters, "Whittier the Poet as Historian." *Massachusetts Magazine*, Vol. I, January, 1908. pp. 3-10.
    Oliver Wendell Holmes to JGW, August 1, 1865. Albree, pp. 154-55.

22. JGW to Harriet Minot Pitman, November 8, 1865. SC.
    JGW to Mary Abigail Dodge, in Samuel T. Pickard, "A Merry Woman's Letters to a Quiet Poet." *Ladies' Home Journal*, December, 1899.

23. JGW to Charles Sumner, August 20, 1865. HCL.

24. *Villager*, June 15 and 21, 1866.

25. Account. HCL.
    Christy Davis to JGW, July 30, 1865. HCL.
    Emily Binney Smith, *Whittier*. Whittier Press, 1935, pp. 25-26.
    Caroline Carter. Unidentified news clipping.
    JGW to James T. Fields, August 28, 1865. HEH.
    James T. Fields to JGW, September 5, 1865. EI.

26. JGW to James T. Fields, October 3, 1865. HEH.
    James T. Fields to JGW, October 5, 1865. EI.
    JGW to Lucy Larcom, October 9, 1865. Pickard, pp. 497-98.
    JGW to James T. Fields, undated. HEH.
    JGW to James T. Fields, November 3, 1865. Pickard, p. 498.
    Currier, p. 100.

27. JGW to ?, April 28, 1878. Hav. CL.
    James T. Fields to JGW, April 2, 1866. EI.
    JGW to Mary Abigail Dodge, February 21, 1866. EI.
    JGW to Lucy Larcom, February 26, 1866. Pickard, p. 503.
    JGW to ?, April 2, 1866. Middlebury College Library.
28. Paul Hamilton Hayne to JGW, November 21, 1873. HCL.
29. Mary Abigail Dodge to Samuel T. Pickard, August 25, 1893. HCL.
    Elizabeth Vasson Pickett, " 'Snow-Bound' and the New Critics." *Memorabilia of John Greenleaf Whittier*, Edited by John B. Pickard. The Emerson Society, 1968.
30. JGW to Margaret Burleigh, July 14, 1866. Pickard, pp. 504-05.

Chapter XXIV

1. JGW to James T. Fields, November, 1865. HEH.
   JGW to Mary Abigail Dodge, February 21, 1866. EI.
2. JGW to James T. Fields, January 6, 1867. EI.
   JGW to James T. Fields, undated. HEH.
3. JGW to Lucy Larcom, January 27, 1866. Pickard, p. 502.
4. *Whittier-Land* pp. 97-98.
   JGW to Lucy Larcom, February 7, 1866. Pierpont Morgan Library.
5. Albree, pp. 156-58.
6. Currier, p. 225.
7. Clara Barton to JGW, June 30, 1866. EI.
   Alice Cary to JGW, September 22, 1866. EI.
   Ben: Perley Poore, *Reminiscences*, II 198.
8. James T. Fields to JGW, April 2, 1866. EI.
   JGW to James T. Fields, August 18, 1866. HEH.
9. JGW to Bayard Taylor, April 10, 1866. New York Public Library.
   JGW to Edmund C. Stedman, April 15, 1866. Marie Hanson Taylor and Horace E. Scudder, *Life and Letters of Bayard Taylor*, Houghton Mifflin, 1884. p. 457.
   JGW to Celia Thaxter, May 10, 1866. HCL.
   The American Freedman, May 1866, Vol. 1, p. 23.
10. Howard Mumford Jones, "Whittier Reconsidered." EIHC, Vol. XCIII, No. 4, October 1957.
11. *An Imperative Duty*. Harper & Bros., 1892. p. 132.
    JGW to the Editor of *The Friend*, May 7, 1866. *The Friend*, June, 1866.
13. John F. Kellett, *Whittier and William Henry Harrison Dewhirst*. Typescript. APL.
14. James C. Fletcher, "Whittier's Christian Belief." *New York Evangelist*, December 29, 1892.
    JGW to James T. Fields, September 30, 1866. HEH.
15. JGW to Harriet Minot Pitman, June 4, 1866. SC.
    JGW to Sarah Orne Jewett and Mrs. James T. Fields, June 19, 1866. HEH.
16. *Newburyport Herald*, June 23, 1866.
    Address of Robert Rantoul at Whittier Home, Amesbury 1899. Unidentified news clipping. HCL.
17. JGW to James T. Fields, June 1, 1866. HEH.
    M. A. DeWolfe Howe, *Memories of a Hostess*. pp. 68, 70.

18. Mary Abigail Dodge to JGW. Central Michigan University.
   JGW to Lucy Larcom, February 7, 1866. Pierpont Morgan Library.
   JGW to Mary Abigail Dodge, June 30, 1866. Copy. HCL.
19. JGW to William S. Robinson, August 24, 1866. *Villager*, September 6, 1866.
20. Currier, p. 100.
   James T. Fields to JGW, September 27, 1866. EI.
   JGW to James T. Fields, September 30, 1866. HEH.
21. HPL.
22. *Villager*, October 11, 1866.
   JGW to Mary Abigail Dodge, October 10, 1866. Copy. HCL.
23. Charles Sumner to JGW, October 17, 1866. EI.
   JGW to Mary Abigail Dodge, December 30, 1866. EI.
24. M. A. DeWolfe Howe, *Memories of a Hostess*, p. 222.
25. Joseph P. Hazard to JGW, November 3, 1866. EI.
   Benjamin Congdon to JGW, Pickard, p. 527.
   M. E. Hale to JGW, July 29, 1867. Privately owned.
   JGW to ?, October 21, 1876. SC.
     Recent research has shown that the story as Whittier told it was wholly fictitious.
     See John Kobler, "The Mystery of the Palatine Light," *Saturday Evening Post*,
     June 11, 1960, and Edward Rowe Snow, "Whittier: More Poet than Historian,"
     Boston Herald, March 7, 1971.
26. JGW to James T. Fields, December 28, 1866; January 2, 6, February 1, 18, 28, 1867.
   HEH.
27. JGW to Elizabeth Whittier, January 6, 1867. SC.
   JGW to Annie Fields, February 8, 1867. HEH.
   JGW to Anna Maxfield, February 17, 1867. Privately owned.
   JGW to Lucy Larcom, February 17, 1867. Yale University Library.
   Juliet P. Coombs, "Whittier and His Child Friends. Carrie Maude." *Little Folks*,
   June, 1907.
28. JGW to Mary Abigail Dodge, February 15, 1867. "Ebrew Jew" refers to David
   Wasson's phrase describing him as resembling a Hebrew prophet. The phrase
   "Ebrew Jew" is in *Henry IV* Part I, Act II, Scene 4.
29. Henry Ward Beecher to JGW, February 17, 1867. Central Michigan University.
   Lucy Stone to JGW, January 15, 1867. Albree, pp. 159-60.
   Dorothy Wharton to JGW [March 1867]. Copy. HCL.
   JGW to Charles Sumner, February 27, 1867. HCL.
   JGW to James T. Fields, February 28, 1867. HEH.
30. JGW to Daniel N. Haskell, March 4, 1867. *Boston Evening Transcript*, March 6, 1867.
   *Bread for Our Starving Countrymen. Speech of Hon. F. E. Woodbridge of Vermont
   in the House of Representatives.* Congressional Globe Office, 1867.
31. JGW to James H. Duncan, December 11, 1867. Brown University Library.
   Bayard Taylor to JGW, March 19, 1867. Anderson Sale.
32. Rufus M. Jones, *Later Periods of Quakerism*, II 893-96, 905.
   Rufus M. Jones, *Eli and Sybil Jones, Their Life and Work*. Porter and Coates, 1889.
   pp. 185-91.
   John F. Kellett, *Whittier and Eli and Sybil Jones*. Typescript, APL.
   Sybil Jones to JGW, March 4, 1867. HCL.
   Richard M. Jones to Samuel T. Pickard, December 28, 1895. HCL.
33. Currier, pp. 102-04.
34. JGW to James T. Fields. Undated. HEH.
   James T. Fields to JGW, April 17, 1867. HEH.
35. JGW to Lucy Larcom, April 16, 1867. SC.
36. JGW to James T. Fields. Pickard, p. 526.

37. James T. Fields to JGW, May 15, 1867. HEH.
    JGW to James T. Fields, undated. HEH.
38. JGW to Sarah J. Clarke Lippincott, June, 1867. Pickard, p. 524.
    JGW to Lucy Larcom, May 22, 1867. MHS.
    JGW to Mary Abigail Dodge, June 22, 1867. Copy. HCL.
39. *Newburyport Herald*, July 1, 1867.
    Unidentified newspaper clipping, Historical Society of Old Newbury.
    JGW to Mary Abigail Dodge, June 22, 1867. EI.
40. JGW to Annie Fields, August 18, 1867. HEH.
    JGW to Celia Thaxter, August 8, 1867. HCL.
    Newburyport Herald, August 5, 1867.
41. Currier, p. 108.
    JGW to James T. Fields, August 1867. HEH.
    Harry Fenn, "The Story of Whittier's Snow-Bound." *St. Nicholas*, April, 1893. Fenn's memory was at fault when he thought that the sketches were made for the first edition of *Snow-Bound*.
42. JGW to Mary Abigail Dodge, June 22, 1867. Copy. HCL.
    JGW to David Worth Dennis, November 23, 1877. Owned by Mr. & Mrs. William C. Dennis. The larger part of this letter was printed in Chauncey Hawkins' *The Mind of Whittier*, Thomas Whittaker, 1904, p. 108.
43. JGW to Moderator of School District No. 2, September 15, 1867. Whittier Home, Amesbury.
    JGW to Celia Thaxter, December 14, 1867. HCL.
44. JGW to Lucy Larcom, February 17, 1867. Yale University Library.
    JGW to James T. Fields, December 2, 1867. HEH.
45. JGW to Celia Thaxter. Note 43.

Chapter XXV

1. *The Peabody Memorial Church in Georgetown, Mass. Its Origin, the Exercises Connected with the Laying of the Cornerstone, The Dedication, and the Ordination of Its Pastor.* Georgetown, 1869.
2. C. Julian Tuthill to Samuel T. Pickard, April 14, 1899. HCL.
    Newburyport Herald, January 8, 1868.
    Boston Evening Transcript, January 24, 1868.
    Currier, p. 109.
3. Pickard, p. 529.
    JGW to Celia Thaxter, December 14, 1867. HCL.
    Martha H. Shackford, "Whittier's 'The Meeting' ". Shackford, pp. 62-70.
4. JGW to Editor of the *Independent*, June 28, 1868. Pierpont Morgan Library.
5. JGW to Lucy Larcom, January 28, 1868. Pickard, p. 529.
6. JGW to James T. Fields, June 29, 1868. HCL.
7. One other religious poem, "My Creed," which Currier was inclined to accept as Whittier's, was by Alice Cary. It was printed as Whittier's in the Haverhill *Tri-Weekly Publisher* September 5, 1868, and in various Iowa newspapers. *Bulletin of Friends Historical Society*, Autumn, 1939.
8. Celia Thaxter to JGW, January 28, [1868]. Central Michigan University.
    Elizabeth Stuart Phelps, *Chapters from a Life*. Houghton and Mifflin Company, 1896. p. 92.

9.   JGW to Horace Greeley, May 16, 1868. New York Public Library.
     JGW to Celia Thaxter, August 24, 1868. HCL.
     JGW to Editor of the *Independent*. Note 4.
     Thomas Graham Belden and Marva Robins Belden, *So Fell the Angels*, Little Brown,
        1956. p. 216.

10. *Villager*, July 30, 1868.
     "Campaign Songs." *The Nation*, September 24, 1868.

11. Oliver Wendell Holmes to JGW, December 15, 1868. Central Michigan University.

12. *Gail Hamilton's Life in Letters*. II, 612.
     Mary Abigail Dodge to JGW, June 9, 1868. EI.
     JGW to Celia Thaxter, July 4, 1868. HCL.
     Unidentified newspaper clipping. Historical Society of Old Newbury.

13. JGW to Harriet Minot Pitman, July 8, 1868. HCL.
     JGW to Lucy Larcom, August 23, [1868]. SC.
     JGW to James T. Fields, August 20, 1868. HEH.

14. JGW to Harriet Minot Pitman, August 24, 1868. HCL.
     Letters of James Russell Lowell. Edited by Charles Eliot Norton. I 404.

15. Diary of Sarah Bagley. Quoted in Mary Beecher Longyear, *The History of a House*.
        Brookline, 1959.
     Robert Peel, *Mary Baker Eddy: The Years of Discovery*. Holt, Rinehart, and Winston,
        1966. pp. 222-23.
     Mary Baker Eddy, *Pulpit and Press*. Christian Science Publishing Society, 1923. p. 54
        Note.
     Unidentified newspaper article in Edward A. Brown's scrapbook. APL.
     Mary Abigail Dodge to JGW, September 5, 1868. EI.

16. JGW to Celia Thaxter, August 2, 1868. HCL.

17. JGW to James T. Fields, December 6, 1868. Boston Atheneum.
     JGW to Harriet Minot Pitman, November 24, 1868. HCL.
     Villager, December 7, 1868.

18. JGW to Lucy Larcom, August 22, 1868. MHS.
     JGW to James T. Fields, undated. HEH.
     JGW to Thomas Wentworth Higginson, October 30, 1868. EI.
     JGW to Apphia Howard, November 28, 1868. HPL.
     JGW to Harriet Minot Pitman, November 30, 1868. HCL.

19. Deborah Webb to a friend, November, 1868. Owned by John B. Pickard.
     JGW to Deborah Webb, December 21, 1868. Owned by John B. Pickard.
     JGW to Apphia Howard. Note 18.
     JGW to Harriet Minot Pitman, November 24, 1868. HCL.

20. Julia Ward Howe to JGW, August 5, 1869. EI.
     JGW to Julia Ward Howe, August 12, 1869. *Works* VII 227.

21. JGW to Harriet Minot Pitman. Note 19.
     JGW to Apphia Howard. Note 18.
     Charles Sumner to JGW, November 13, 1868. Albree, p. 169.
     Charles Sumner and Alice Mason Hooper were married October 17, 1866. They were
        separated in June, 1867, and divorced in 1873. See *Henry James' Letters*, Ed. Leon
        Edel. Harvard University Press, 1984. II 33.

22. JGW to Apphia Howard. Note 18.

23. Ben: Perley Poore, *Reminiscences*. II 253.

24. JGW to Harriet Minot Pitman, January 20, 1869. HCL.
     JGW to Burns Club of Washington, January 18, 1869. *Newburyport Herald*, January 28,
        1869.

25. JGW to Secretary L. F. A., April, 1869. *Newburyport Herald*, May 18, 1869.
    Richard R. Wright to JGW, March 9, 1869. *Newburyport Herald*, May 18, 1869.
    Richard R. Wright to JGW, December 8, 1891. HCL.
    Richard R. Wright to Roland H. Woodwell, June 13, 1945.

26. JGW to Celia Thaxter, April, 1869. HCL.
    M. A. DeWolfe Howe, *Memories of a Hostess*. pp. 39-40.

27. Unidentified newspaper clipping.
    Pickard, pp. 547-48.
    JGW to Annie Fields, November 15, 1870. HEH.

28. JGW to Celia Thaxter, September 27, 1869. HCL.

29. JGW to Bayard Taylor, May 6, 1869. Pickard, p. 541.
    Charles H. Brainard to JGW, May 15, 1869. HCL.
    JGW to Charles H. Brainard, May 18, 1869. HCL.
    JGW to Harriet Minot Pitman, May 30, 1869. HCL.

30. Note 28.

31. Lucia G. Alexander to JGW, March 16, 1870. HCL.

32. Oliver Wendell Holmes to JGW, October 17, 1869. Albree, pp. 171-72.

33. JGW to James T. Fields, April 2, 1868. HEH.
    JGW to James T. Fields. Pickard, p. 543.

34. JGW to Thomas C. Sparhawk. Frances C. Sparhawk, *Whittier at Close Range*. Riverdale
    Press, 1925. p. 46.
    John F. Kellett, *Whittier and Aunt Joan Colby*. Typescript, APL.

35. Mary Clemmer, *The Poetical Works of Alice and Phoebe Cary, with a Memorial of Their
    Lives*. Hurd and Houghton, 1877. p. 19.

36. Pickard, pp. 545-46.
    JGW to Houghton Mifflin and Company, May 15, 1890. Formerly owned by T. Franklin
    Currier.

37. Mrs. James T. Fields, *Whittier. Notes of His Life and of His Friendships*. Harper and
    Brothers, 1893. p. 64.
    Oliver Wendell Holmes to JGW, March 15, 1870. Anderson Sale.
    Henry Wadsworth Longfellow to Elizabeth Stuart Phelps, August 21, 1878. Samuel
    Longfellow, *Henry Wadsworth Longfellow* III 287.

39. Diary of Horace Currier. Formerly owned by T. Franklin Currier.

Chapter XXVI

1. JGW to Elizabeth Whittier, January 22, 1870. SC.
   Lillian Whiting, *Louise Chandler Moulton, Poet and Friend*. Little Brown, 1910. p. 59.
   M. A. DeWolfe Howe, *Memories of a Hostess*, p. 114.

2. JGW to Editor of the *Review*, February 1870. University of Virginia.
   JGW to *Friends' Review*, March 1870. *Friends' Review*, March, 1870.
   JGW to ?, February 26, 1870. Albree, pp. 173-74.
       In a letter October 12, 1869, Whittier said that he wished that all Quakers could "come
       together, in the exercise of mutual charity at least, if not merging their respective
       meetings in one." SC.

3. JGW to James T. Fields, February 24, 1870. HEH.
   JGW to Helen Burt, January 16, 1885. Helen Burt, "Reminiscences of the Poet Whittier." *The Bookman*, May - June, 1885.

4. JGW to Charles Sumner, March 9, 1870. HCL.
   JGW to Celia Thaxter, March 5, 1870. HCL.
   JGW to Lucy Larcom, March 22, 1870. Pierpont Morgan Library.
5. JGW to ?, April 9, 1870. *Newburyport Herald*, April 15, 1870.
   Newburyport Herald, May 17, 1870.
   Theodore L. Cuyler, *Recollections of a Long Life*, p. 122.
   "The Singer," stanzas 13-16.
   JGW to Celia Thaxter, June 10, 1870. Pickard, p. 565.
   JGW to Harriet Minot Pitman, May 16, 1870. HCL.
6. *Letters of Lydia Maria Child with a Biographical Introduction by John G. Whittier and an Appendix by Wendell Phillips.* Houghton and Mifflin Company, 1883. pp. 101-02.
   Lydia Maria Child to JGW, June, 1870. Copy, HCL.
7. *Newburyport Herald*, July 16, 1870.
8. JGW to Celia Thaxter, July 28, 1870. HCL.
9. JGW to James T. Fields, August 28, 1870. SC.
10. Pickard, p. 568.
    Frederick A. P. Barnard to JGW, March 11, 1868. EI.
11. Arthur Christy, "The Orientalism of Whittier." *American Literature*, November, 1933, Vol. 5, pp. 247-257.
12. JGW to Charles Sumner, September 10, 1870. HCL.
13. Manuscript. SC.
14. Mrs. John T. Sargent, *Sketches and Reminiscences of the Radical Club.* James A. Osgood, 1880, p. 128.
    JGW to Mrs. John T. Sargent, January 15, 1871. SC.
    JGW to Mary Grew, August 12, 1880. SC.
15. Currier, p. 117.
16. JGW to Theodore Roosevelt, January 4, 1871. *Villager*, January 19, 1871.
17. JGW to Charles Sumner, March 21, 1871. HCL.
    JGW to Editor of the *Villager. Villager*, March 9, 1871.
    "Hours of Labor." *Villager*, March 16, 1871.
18. JGW to Annie Fields, April 18, 1871. HEH.
    James T. Fields to JGW, June 30, 1871. EI.
    William Dean Howells, *Literary Friends and Acqauaintances.* Harper and Bros., 1901. p. 136.
    Bret Harte to JGW, February 26, 1871. Anderson Sale.
    JGW to Thomas Wentworth Higginson, September 24, 1871. HEH.
19. John F. Kellett, *"Whittier and Aunt Joan Colby."* Typescript, APL.
    Music by W. M. Gilchrist. *The Laurel Song Book.* C. C. Birchard & Co., 1901.
20. JGW to Harriet Minot Pitman, September 27, 1871. HCL.
    Villager, September 21, 1871.
21. *Villager*, October 19, 1871. *Newburyport Herald*, October 31, 1871.
22. JGW to Mrs. Sallie Stalker, December 15, 1871. Owned by Medora M. Bybee.
    JGW to Editor of *Friends' Review*, January 17, 1872. *Friends' Review*, February 3, 1872.
23. JGW to Lucy Larcom, August 23, 1871. MHS.
24. JGW to James T. Fields, 1872 (?). HEH.
    JGW to Rebecca Allinson, February 12, 1873. Copy. EI.
    JGW to Celia Thaxter, May 21, 1872. HCL.
    JGW to Charles Sumner, May 20, 1872. HCL.
25. JGW to Mary Abigail Dodge, March 1, 1872, Copy. HCL.
26. JGW to J. A. Dugdale, May 22, 1872. SC.
    JGW to Charles Sumner, May 20, 1872. HCL.

27. Edward L. Pierce, *Memoir and Letters of Charles Sumner*. Roberts Brothers, 1893, IV, 518, 526.
   JGW to Editor of the *Transcript*, May 6, 1872. Albree, pp. 282-83.
28. JGW to William Cullen Bryant, June 6, 1872. SC.
   Pierce, op. cit., pp. 524, 526.
29. JGW to ?, August 3, 1872. SC.
30. JGW to Miles L. Newton, Joseph Disbrow, Robert Hubbard, September 3, 1872. *Works* VII 161-66.
   JGW to Harriet Minot Pitman, July 10, 1872. HCL.
   JGW to Mary Abigail Dodge, August 17, 1872. EI.
   JGW to James T. Fields, September 4, 1872. HEH.
   JGW to Thomas Wentworth Higginson, September 30, 1872. University of Texas.
   JGW to Josiah G. Holland, October 21, 1872. SC.
   JGW to Edwin Morton, May 10, 1872. *Springfield Republican*, May 17, 1872.
31. JGW to Edna Dean Proctor, December 5, 1872. New Hampshire Historical Society.
   JGW to James R. Osgood, May 24, 1872. SC.
   JGW to James R. Osgood, June 10, 1872. University of Texas.
   JGW to C. F. Richardson, June 18, 1872. Copy, HCL.
   JGW to Celia Thaxter, May 21, 1872. HCL.
32. JGW to James R. Osgood. Note 31.
   JGW to Lucy Larcom, June 19, 1872. MHS.
   JGW to Rebecca Allinson. Note 24.
   Marie Hansen Taylor and Horace E. Scudder, *Life and Letters of Bayard Taylor*. Houghton and Mifflin Company, 1885. II 610-612.
   Ralph Waldo Emerson to JGW, August 22, 1873. Pickard, p. 577.
33. JGW to Gardner Brewer, March 10, 1872. BPL.
34. JGW to Celia Thaxter, July 22, 1872. HCL.
   JGW to Elizabeth C. Kinney, July 20, 1872. Copy. HCL.
   JGW to Lucia Alexander, November 18, 1872. Yale University Library.
   Villager, August 15, 1872.
   JGW to Mary Abigail Dodge, August 17, 1872. EI.
35. John F. Kellett, "*Whittier and the Goves of Seabrook, New Hampshire*," Typescript. APL.
36. JGW to James T. Fields, September 4, 1872. HEH.
   Nora Perry to JGW, October 26, 1872. EI.
37. JGW to Harriet Minot Pitman, January 7, 1873. HCL.
   "Tribute to Henry Taylor," *Villager*, November 28, 1872.
   JGW to William Aikman, January 29, 1877. *Independent*, January 22, 1903.
   Annie Fields to JGW, December 1, 1872. Central Michigan University.
   JGW to Ralph Waldo Emerson, August 23, 1873. HCL.
   Edward Hayes Plumptre, "Sakya Mouni at Bodhaimanda." *The Contemporary Review* V, 114-16 (May-August 1867). Quoted in Arthur Christy, "The Orientalism of Whittier." *American Literature* 1933, Vol. 5, p. 250.
38. JGW to Henry Marford, January 25, 1873. SC.

Chapter XXVII

1. *Villager*, January 16, 1873. The house was the present 65 Thompson Street.
2. Edward L. Pierce, *Memoir and Letters of Charles Sumner*. Roberts Brothers, 1893, IV, 550-53.

3. JGW to Jones Frankle, February 26, 1873. HPL. Frankle was a colonel in the 2nd Massachusetts Heavy Artillery.
    JGW to Willard P. Phillips, March 7 and March 13, 1873. HCL.
    JGW to *Boston Daily Advertiser*, March 8, 1873. *Boston Daily Advertiser*, March 10, 1873.
    Villager, March 13, 1873.
4. JGW to Charles Sumner, March 5, 1873. HCL.
    Pierce, op. cit., p. 554.
    JGW to Harriet Minot Pitman, March 9, 1873. HCL.
    JGW to William Lloyd Garrison, March 10, 1873. SC.
    William Lloyd Garrison to *Boston Journal*, March 10, 1873. *William Lloyd Garrison*, IV 25.
    JGW to *Boston Advertiser*, March 16, 1873.
5. Pierce, op. cit., p. 554.
    Willard P. Phillips to JGW, March 20, 1873. HCL.
    JGW to Charles Sumner, February 17, 1874. HCL.
6. JGW to Rebecca Allinson, February 12, 1873. Copy. EI.
    JGW to Edna Dean Proctor, April 7, 1873. New Hampshire Historical Society.
    JGW to William J. Allinson, April 1, 1873. Copy. Hav. CL.
    Lucy Larcom to Harriet Minot Pitman, undated. Formerly owned by C. Marshall Taylor.
    JGW to Lucy Larcom, February 27 and March 29, 1873. MHS.
7. JGW to Paul Hamilton Hayne. February 5, 1873. Duke University Library.
    JGW to Celia Thaxter, February 14, 1873. HCL.
    JGW to James T. Fields, February 13, 1873. Davis Library, Phillips Exeter Academy.
    JGW to Annie Fields, March 30, 1873. HEH.
    JGW to William Dean Howells, May 12, 1873. HCL.
    JGW to Celia Thaxter, February 14, 1873. HCL.
8. JGW to Lucy Larcom, July 14, 1873. St. John's Seminary.
    JGW to Celia Thaxter, July 14, 1873. HCL.
    JGW to Edna Dean Proctor, July 22, 1873. New Hampshire Historical Society.
    JGW to Harriet Minot Pitman, August 10, 1873. HCL.
    M. A. De Wolfe Howe, *Memories of a Hostess*, pp. 129-31.
    Max L. Griffin, "Whittier and Hayne: A Record of Friendship." *American Literature*, March, 1947. p. 43.
    Paul Hamilton Hayne to JGW, November 21, 1873. HCL.
    Ellen B. Ballou, *The Building of the House*. Houghton, Mifflin, 1970. p. 241.
    Manuscript dated Boston, October 7, 1902. Owned by the writer.
9. JGW to Ralph Waldo Emerson, August 23 and September 2, 1873. HCL.
    JGW to Annie Fields, September 14, 1873. HEH.
    JGW to Ralph Waldo Emerson, August 23, 1873. HCL.
    JGW to Edna Dean Proctor, September 21, 1873. New Hampshire Historical Society.
10. Hannah Cox to JGW, August 16, 1873. Anderson Sale.
    JGW to William Dean Howells, undated. HCL.
    Rufus M. Jones, *The Later Periods of Quakerism*, p. 578.
11. JGW to Edna Dean Proctor, November 16, 1873. New Hampshire Historical Society.
12. JGW to James R. Osgood, November 8, 1873. SC.
    The first draft, or at least an early draft, is in SC.
13. Pierce, op. cit., IV 374-75.
    Villager, November 27, 1873.
14. JGW to ?, December, 1873. St. John's Seminary.
15. JGW to Mary Abigail Dodge, December 19, 1873. Copy. HCL.
16. Mrs. John T. Sargent, *Sketches and Reminiscences of the Radical Club*, James R. Osgood, 1880. pp. 293-97.

17. Anderson Sale.
    JGW to Edna Dean Proctor, February 16, 1874. New Hampshire Historical Society.
18. Mary Abigail Dodge to ?, March 13, 1874. H. Augusta Dodge, *Gail Hamilton's Life in Letters*, p. 745.
    George W. Cate, "Address on John G. Whittier." Typescript. Owned by the writer.
    JGW to Henry Wilson, incorrectly dated March 10, 1874. SC.
    Edward L. Pierce to Samuel T. Pickard, November 30, 1894. HCL.
    A Memorial of Charles Sumner. Boston, 1874. pp. 67-89.
19. Mrs. John T. Sargent, *Sketches and Reminiscences of the Radical Club*, p. 306.
    A Memorial of Charles Sumner. Note 18.
    Willard P. Phillips to JGW, June 9, 1874. HCL.
    JGW to Edna Dean Proctor, May 15, 1874. New Hampshire Historical Society.
    JGW to New York *Evening Post*, quoted in *Newburyport Herald*, June 19, 1874.
    Currier, pp. 123-26.
    JGW to ?, June, 1874. *Newburyport Herald*, July 3, 1874.
20. John Lothrop Motley to Henry Wadsworth Longfellow, May 16, 1874. Samuel Longfellow, *Henry Wadsworth Longfellow*, pp. 225-27.
    Henry Wadsworth Longfellow to JGW, August 7, 1874. Albree, p. 190.
    JGW to Henry Wadsworth Longfellow, August 8, 1874. HCL.
    JGW to Harriet McEwen Kimball, December 20, 1874. Pickard, p. 486, incorrectly dated 1864. The error was called to Pickard's attention by Edward L. Pierce in a letter November 30, 1894. HCL.
21. *William Lloyd Garrison*, IV. 249.
    JGW to William Lloyd Garrison, March 20, 1874. SC.
22. JGW to Gertrude W. Cartland, April 1874. Shackford, p. 60.
    Augustine Jones, "Reminiscences of John Greenleaf Whittier." *American Friend*, December 12, 1907.
    Nathan S. Wright, "Whittier's Poem 'Vesta.' " *Congregationalist and Christian World*, December 14, 1907.
    John F. Kellett to *Haverhill Gazette*. *Haverhill Gazette*, April 6, 1963.
23. *Villager*, May 28, 1874.
    JGW to Agnes Aubin, May 22, 1874. SC.
    List of papers in Samuel T. Pickard's file. HCL.
24. JGW to ?, April 8, 1874. Formerly owned by Joseph Trombla.
    Villager, May 14 and June 4, 1874.
    JGW to Celia Thaxter, June 26, 1874. HCL.
    JGW to Mary Abigail Dodge, June 6, 1874. Copy. HCL.
25. Henry Ward Beecher to JGW, October 6, 1873. Anderson Sale.
    JGW to Elizabeth Stuart Phelps, July 14, 1874. SC.
    Paxton Hibben, *Henry Ward Beecher: An American Portrait.* The Press of the Readers Club, 1942. p. 267.
    JGW to Oliver Johnson, August 9, 1874. SC.
    JGW to Annie Fields, August 22, 1874. HEH.
    JGW to Lydia Maria Child, September 20, 1874. SC.
26. JGW to William Dean Howells, undated. HCL.
27. JGW to Celia Thaxter, June 26 and September 26, 1874. HCL.
    JGW to Lydia Maria Child, September 20, 1874. SC.
28. "Excerpts from the Diary and the Letters of Abbott Kinsman from San Francisco, the Pacific, Hong Kong and the Philippines." Contributed by Mrs. Rebecca Kinsman Munroe. EIHC, January and April, 1953.
29. *Amesbury Daily News*, April 4, 1935.
30. JGW to James R. Osgood, November 11, and 22, and November 1874. Pickard, pp. 598-99.

31. JGW to William Dean Howells, November 24, 1874. HCL.
    JGW to Lucy Larcom, November 25, 1874. MHS.
    JGW to Louise Chandler Moulton, November 9, 1874. LC.
    JGW to Celia Thaxter, December 25, 1874. HCL.

Chapter XXVIII

1. Mary B. Claflin, *Personal Recollections of John G. Whittier*. Thomas Y. Crowell, 1893.
   pp. 71-72.
   Villager, February 4, 1875.
2. Edward G. Porter to JGW, November 5, 1874. EI.
   JGW to James R. Osgood, May 1, 1875. New York Public Library.
   JGW to James R. Osgood, March 20, 1875. SC.
   Proceedings at the Centennial Celebration of the Battle of Lexington.
3. Walter Harding, *The Days of Henry Thoreau*, Alfred A. Knopf, 1965. pp. 343-45.
   JGW to Daniel Ricketson, March 17, 1875. SC.
4. JGW to Mary Abigail Dodge, August 24, 1875. EI.
   JGW to William J. Linton, September 13, 1875. Yale University Library.
5. JGW to Lucy Larcom, undated, and September 22, 1875. MHS.
6. J. Warren Thyng, *Reminiscences of the Poet Whittier*. Granite State Publishing Co., 1908.
   Charles F. Carter, "A Footnote on Whittier." *New England Magazine*, June, 1906.
7. JGW to Lucy Larcom, September 22, 1875. Note 5.
   JGW to Edna Dean Proctor, December 5, 1875. New Hampshire Historical Society.
   Note to Revised Edition, November, 1890.
8. JGW to Harriet Minot Pitman, December 18, 1875. HCL.
   JGW to James R. Osgood, December 18, 1875. Copy, formerly owned by T. Franklin
      Currier.
   Whittier's receipt, October 23, 1875. Formerly owned by Carroll A. Wilson.
   Note by Samuel T. Pickard. HCL.
9. JGW to Edna Dean Proctor, October, 1875. Pickard, p. 305.
   J. D. Charbonnier to JGW, September 13, 1875. Pickard, pp. 607-08.
   J. Bevan Braithwaite to JGW, September 15, 1875. HCL.
   JGW to J. D. Charbonnier, October 21, 1875. Pickard, pp. 608-09.
10. The prose translation that Whittier used was probably Rev. W. H. Drew's, *The Cural of
    Tiruvalluvar, First Part; with the Commentary of Parimelarager*, American Mission
    Press, 1840. Arthur Christy, "Orientalism in New England." *American Literature*
    January, 1930, Vol. I, pp. 383-84.
11. JGW to Mary Esther Carter, April 7, 1879. EI.
    JGW to James G. Palfrey, November 26, 1875. Wellesley College Library.
    JGW to Edna Dean Proctor, December 5, 1875. New Hampshire Historical Society.
    Elias Nason and Thomas Russell, *The Life and Public Services of Henry Wilson*. B. B.
       Russell, 1876. pp. 436-48.
12. JGW to Edna Dean Proctor, December 15, 1875. New Hampshire Historical Society.
    Mary Mapes Dodge to JGW, January 28, 1876. EI.
13. JGW to Moses Cartland, March 12, 1841. SC.
    Rayner Wickersham Kelsey, *Centennial History of Moses Brown School*, 1919. p. 91.
    Mary Jones Smith to John F. Kellett, May 28, 1968. Privately owned.
    JGW to William Lloyd Garrison, February 10, 1876. SC.
    JGW to Harriet Minot Pitman, February 21, 1876. Boston Atheneum.

14. JGW to Edna Dean Proctor, February 16, 1876. New Hampshire Historical Society.
    JGW to James R. Osgood, (?) February 1, 1876. Formerly owned by Carroll A. Wilson.
    William A. Lewis to JGW, January 2, 1876. EI.
15. JGW to Abby J. Woodman, September 3, 1875, and February 28, 1876. EI.
    Unsigned manuscript note of one of Whittier's cousins. EI.
    JGW to Lucy Larcom, October 16, 1875. MHS.
16. JGW to Harriet Minot Pitman, March, 1876. Pickard, p. 612.
    Bayard Taylor to JGW, March 21, 1876, Pickard, pp. 617-18; undated, Pickard, pp. 618,
        620.
    JGW to Bayard Taylor, March 22, 1876. Pickard, p. 618.
    JGW to Bayard Taylor, undated. Hav. CL.
    The Centennial Liberty Bell, Philadelphia, 1876, p. 140.
17. Unidentified newspaper clipping.
18. *Villager*, September 14, 1876.
    JGW to David M. French, May 31, 1876. *Newburyport Herald*, June 14, 1876.
    JGW to Annie Fields, May 22, 1876. HEH.
19. JGW to William Dean Howells, December 19, 1875. HCL.
20. JGW to Harriet Minot Pitman, April 22, 1876, HCL.
    JGW to Lucy Larcom, April 23, 1876. Owned by John B. Pickard.
    JGW to Celia Thaxter, April 26, 1876. HCL.
    JGW to Mary Esther Carter, May 3, 1876. EI.
    Manuscript notes, probably by Abby J. Woodman. EI.
21. JGW to James T. Fields, June 8 and July 26, 1876. HEH.
    JGW to Abby J. Woodman, September 8, 1876. EI.
22. Martha H. Shackford, "Whittier and Some Cousins." *New England Quarterly*, Septem-
        ber, 1942.
23. Lucy Larcom to Elizabeth W. Pickard, April 19, 1877. HCL.
24. Manuscript notes on Oak Knoll. EI.
    Charles B. Rice, "Mr. Whittier in His Home." *Congregationalist*, October 6, 1892, Vol.
        7, p. 3222.
    Margaret Sidney, "Whittier with the Children." *Wide Awake*, January, 1893.
    Phoebe Woodman Grantham, "Whittier Lived in My Home." *World Horizons*, March,
        1938.
    Pickard, pp. 614-16.
    JGW to ?, May 3, 1876. SC.
25. JGW to Annie Fields, May 22, 1876. Pickard, p. 613.
26. JGW to Mary Abigail Dodge, June 6, 1876. Copy. HCL.
27. JGW to James T. Fields, June 8, 1876. HEH.
    JGW to Mary E. Sargent, June 13, 1876. Formerly owned by C. Marshall Taylor.
    JGW to Louise Chandler Moulton, June 16, 1876. LC.
    Mrs. John T. Sargent. *Sketches and Reminiscences of the Radical Club*. James R. Osgood,
        1880, pp. 301-03.
    Frances C. Sparhawk, "Whittier the Poet and the Man.' *New England Magazine*, No-
        vember 1892, Vol. VII, p. 297.
28. JGW to Harriet Minot Pitman, November, 1876. Boston Atheneum.
    JGW to Edna Dean Proctor, July 9, 1876. New Hampshire Historical Society.
29. JGW to Elizabeth W. Pickard, August 20, 1876. SC.
    JGW to Elizabeth W. Pickard, August 30, 1876. Owned by John B. Pickard.
    JGW to Abby J. Woodman, Undated. EI.
    Whittier-Land, pp. 110-14.
    Information given to the writer by Adoniram J. Stockbridge.
30. *Whittier-Land*, pp. 115-18.
    JGW to Samuel T. Pickard, September 12, 1876. EI.

31. Jettie Morrill to Elizabeth Whittier, February 22, 1876. Copy. HCL.
    JGW to William Dean Howells, February 6, 1877. HCL.
    JGW to William Hayes Ward, November 30, 1877. SC.
32. JGW to Abby J. Woodman, October 3, 1876. EI.
    Elizabeth W. Pickard to Samuel T. Pickard, October 10, 1876. HCL.
    JGW to Mary Abigail Dodge. Note 26.
    JGW to Elizabeth Stuart Phelps, September 22, 1876. SC.
    Newburyport Herald, August 10, 1876.
    JGW to Celia Thaxter, October 30, 1876. HCL.
33. JGW to Celia Thaxter. Note 32.
    JGW to Harriet Minot Pitman, October 1876. HCL.
    JGW to Harriet Minot Pitman, October 30, 1876. Boston Atheneum.
34. JGW to Abby J. Woodman, October, 1876. EI.
    JGW to Mary Abigail Dodge, September 10, 1876. EI.
    JGW to Harriet Minot Pitman, October 1876. HCL.
    JGW to Edna Dean Proctor, November 4, 1876. Pickard, p. 628.
    JGW to Lucy Larcom, November 6, 1876. Anderson Sale.
    JGW to Edna Dean Proctor, December 16, 1876. New Hampshire Historical Society.
    JGW to the Editors of the *Boston Journal*, November 2, 1876. *Boston Journal*, November 3, 1876.
35. Abby J. Woodman, *Reminiscences of John Greenleaf Whittier's Life at Oak Knoll, Danvers, Mass.* Essex Institute, 1908. p. 23.
    Harriet Fowler, Manuscript note. EI.
    JGW to William Dean Howells, November 18, 1876. HCL.
    JGW to Annie Fields, December, 1876. Pickard, p. 610, incorrectly dated 1875.
    "Recent Literature." *Atlantic Monthly*, December, 1879, pp. 775-76.
    Thomas F. Waters, "Whittier, the Poet, as Historian." *Massachusetts Magazine*, January 1908, Vol. I, pp. 3-10.
    Oliver Wendell Holmes to JGW, October 10, 1878. Pickard, p. 644.
    JGW to James R. Osgood, December 25, 1876. Currier, p. 130.

Chapter XXIX

1. Phoebe Woodman Grantham, "Whittier Lived in My Home." *World Horizons*, March, 1938.
2. JGW to Edna Dean Proctor, February 6, 1877. Copy. EI.
    JGW to Edna Dean Proctor, February 22, 1877. New Hampshire Historical Society.
    JGW to Elizabeth W. Pickard, January 22, 1877. SC.
    JGW to Mary B. Claflin, February 18, 1877. Hayes Memorial Library.
        Lucius Quintus Cincinnatus Lamar, elected to the Senate from Mississippi January, 1876, had supported the electoral compromise that resulted in Hayes' being declared President.
3. JGW to Mary Abigail Dodge, July 15, 1877. Copy. HCL.
    JGW to Elizabeth Stuart Phelps, July 6, 1877. SC.
    JGW to Sarah Orne Jewett, July 24, 1877. HCL.
    Sarah Orne Jewett to JGW, July 27, 1877. EI.
4. JGW to James Grant Wilson, March 3 and April 9, 1877. Copies. HCL.
    JGW to James Grant Wilson, May 14, 1877. *A Memorial of Fitz-Green Halleck: A Description of the Dedication of the Monument Erected to His Memory at Guilford, Connecticut.* New York, 1877. p. 41.

JGW to Annie Fields, March 7, 1877. HEH.
JGW to Robert S. Rantoul, March 5, 1877. EI.

5. JGW to Harriet Minot Pitman, April 24, 1877. SC.

6. M. A. DeWolfe Howe, *A Venture in Remembrance.* Little Brown, 1941. Chapter 5.

7. Elizabeth F. Hume, "Summers with a Poet." EIHC. Vol. XXV No. 4, October, 1939.
   JGW to William Dean Howells, September 25, 1877. HCL.

8. JGW to Mary Abigail Dodge, October 31, 1877. Copy. HCL.
   Newburyport Herald, November 13, 1876, January 2 and 25, 1877.
   JGW to Elizabeth Pickard, November 28, 1877. SC.
   JGW to Francis J. Garrison, April 16, 1877. SC.

9. JGW to Henry Wadsworth Longfellow, December 5, 1877. Formerly owned by Carroll
   A. Wilson.
   Paul Hamilton Hayne to JGW, January 10, 1878. Albree, p. 199.

10. JGW to David Worth Dennis, November 23, 1877. Owned by Mr. and Mrs. William C.
    Dennis.
    Anderson Sale, p. 30.

11. Edward Abbott to JGW, December 6, 1877. Whittier Home, Amesbury.
    JGW to Henry Wadsworth Longfellow, December 14, 1877. HCL.
    JGW to Lucy Larcom, December 16, 1877. MHS.
    Elizabeth Hume, "Neighbor to a Poet." EIHC, October, 1940.

12. Esther B. Ballou, *The Building of the House.* Houghton Mifflin, 1970. pp. 218-23.
    King's Handbook of Boston. Moses King, 1878, p. 42.
    Pickard, pp. 635-36.
    Caroline Ticknor, *Glimpses of Authors.* Houghton Mifflin, 1921.
    Octavius Brooks Frothingham, *Memoir of William Henry Channing.* Boston, 1886. p.
    402.
    Albert Bigelow Paine, *Mark Twain, A Biography.* Harper & Brothers, 1912. II, 603-09.
    Villager, January 3, 1878.
    Richard Henry Stoddard, "John Greenleaf Whittier," *Lippincott's Monthly Magazine,*
    June, 1899.
    John Townsend Trowbridge, *My Own Story with Recollections of Noted Persons.* Hough-
    ton, Mifflin and Company, 1903. pp. 425-26.

13. JGW to Harriet Winslow Sewall, December 19, 1877. MHS.
    JGW to Harriet Minot Pitman, December 27, 1877. SC.
    JGW to Jettie A. Morrill, Mary E. Bagley, and Elizabeth Hume, December 20, 1877.
    Newburyport Herald, December 29, 1877.

14. JGW to Harriet Minot Pitman, December 27, 1877. SC.
    JGW to Celia Thaxter, January 22, 1878. EI.
    JGW to Julia A. Hodgdon. Pickard, p. 639.
    JGW to Mary Esther Carter, January 18, 1878. Wellesley College Library.

15. Lyman Abbott, *Silhouettes of My Contemporaries.* Doubleday, Page, 1921. p. 129.

16. JGW to Adelaide P. Cammett. Formerly owned by Mrs. Carrie Ellis.
    Paul Hamilton Hayne to JGW, January 10, 1878. Albree, pp. 199-201.
    JGW to Paul Hamilton Hayne, February 1, 1878. Duke University.
    Paul Hamilton Hayne to JGW, February 8, 1878. Albree, pp. 202-05.
    JGW to Paul Hamilton Hayne, November 12, 1878. Duke University.
    Paul Hamilton Hayne to JGW, November 17, 1878. Central Michigan University.
    Bayard Taylor to JGW, February 20, 1878. Pickard, pp. 644-45.
    JGW to Thomas Wentworth Higginson, March 28, 1878. HEH.

17. JGW to Harriet Minot Pitman, May 12, 1864. SC.

18. *Villager,* January 3, March 21, April 4, 1878.
    JGW to Horace Currier, April 2, 1878. Copy formerly owned by T. Franklin Currier.
    JGW to Harriet Fowler, 1878. EI.
    JGW to Harriet Minot Pitman, May 12, 1878. HCL.

19. JGW to Cornelia M. Trimble, June 10, 1878. SC.
    Oliver Wendell Holmes to JGW. Pickard, p. 640.
    JGW to Richard H. Stoddard, June 29, 1878. New York Public Library.
    Richard H. Stoddard to JGW, July 6, 1878. Central Michigan University.
    JGW to J. S. Cutler, June 28, 1878. SC.
20. Rosamond Thaxter, *Sandpiper*. Marshall Jones Company, 1863. pp. 129-30.
21. Francis Parkman to JGW, July 29, 1878. EI.
    Letter, illegible signature. EI.
    Haverhill Weekly Gazette. December 13, 1878.
22. JGW to Harriet Minot Pitman, September 12, 1878. HCL.
    Unidentified newspaper clipping.
    Currier, p. 379.
    Jettie Morrill to Frank Morrill, September 4, 1878. Copy. APL.
23. JGW to Mary Abigail Dodge, October 30, 1878. Copy. HCL.
    JGW to George W. Cate, September 16, 1878. Privately owned.
    Currier, p. 136.
    JGW to Harriet Winslow Sewall, October 14, 1878. MHS.
    Oliver Wendell Holmes to JGW, October 10, 1878. Pickard, pp. 643-44.
    Letter, signature illegible, HCL.
24. JGW to William Dean Howells, June 2, 1878. HCL.
    JGW to Lyman Abbott, September 4, 1878. Lyman Abbott, *Silhouettes of My Contemporaries*. Doubleday Page, 1921. p. 130.
25. Hans L. Trefousse, *Ben Butler*. Twayne Publishers, 1957. p. 240.
    JGW to William L. Claflin, November 6, 1878. SC.
    JGW to William Lloyd Garrison, October 17, 1878. SC.
    JGW to Abby J. Woodman, September 16, 1878. EI.
26. JGW to Elizabeth Stuart Phelps, April 7, 1878. SC.
    JGW to Harriet Minot Pitman, December 15, 1873 and February 12, 1879. HCL.
    JGW to William Dean Howells, November 18, 1878. HCL.
    JGW to Gertrude Cartland, December 16, 1878. Pickard, p. 646.
27. Arthur Christy, "Orientalism in New England." *American Literature*, Vol. I, January 1930, pp. 372-392.
    Currier, p. 206.
    JGW to Edna Dean Proctor, May 15, 1874. New Hampshire Historical Society.
28. JGW to Annie Fields, December 18, 1878. EI.
    Pickard, p. 645.
    JGW to R. H. Conwell, *Works*, VI, 281-82.

Chapter XXX

1. JGW to Caroline C. Cate. Privately owned.
2. JGW to William Lloyd Garrison, February 11, 1879. BPL.
3. JGW to Gertrude Cartland, February 9, 1879. Formerly owned by Miss Ruth Osborne.
   Augustine Jones to JGW, March 27, 1879. EI.
4. JGW to William Dean Howells, February 23, 1879. HCL.
5. Antoinette Devereux to JGW, June 10, 1878. HCL.
   JGW to ?, February 22, 1879. BPL.
6. Edward Boyd to Herbert W. Boyd, August 1, 1940. APL.

7. JGW to Elizabeth Stuart Phelps, March 7, 1879. SC.
   JGW to Harriet Minot Pitman, April 4, 1879. HCL.
   JGW to Harriet Minot Pitman, May 7 and 16, 1879. SC.
   JGW to Mary Esther Carter. Frances Campbell Sparhawk, *Whittier at Close Range.*
   Riverdale Press, 1925. p. 156.
   JGW to Lyman Abbott, May 6, 1879. Central Michigan University.

8. JGW to Francis J. Garrison, May 3 and 27, 1879. SC.
   JGW to Harriet Minot Pitman, May 7, 1879. SC.
   JGW to James T. Fields, June 5, 1879. HEH.

9. *Whittier's Complete Poetical Works*, Cambridge Edition, p. 524, note. *Works* VII, 189-92.

10. JGW to Harriet Minot Pitman, May 7, 1879. SC.
    JGW to Adelaide Cammett, June 9, 1879. EI.

11. JGW to Lucy Larcom, August, 1879. Pickard, pp. 653-54.
    JGW to J. C. Emery, R. Morrow and C. W. Smith, August 29, 1879. EI.
    JGW to ?, September 13, 1879. *Danvers Mirror*, September 27, 1879.

12. JGW to Abbie J. Woodman, September 13, 1879. EI.
    Max L. Griffin, "Whittier and Hayne. A Record of Friendship." *American Literature*,
    March, 1947. pp. 43-45.
    Paul Hamilton Hayne to JGW, December 17, 1879. Central Michigan University.
    Paul Hamilton Hayne to JGW, January 13, 1880. EI.
    JGW to Paul Hamilton Hayne, January 29 and February 26, 1880. SC.

13. JGW to Abbie J. Woodman, October 27, 1879. EI.

14. Frederick O. Prince to JGW, October 6, 1879. Anderson Sale.
    JGW to Frederick O. Prince, December 8, 1879. *Newburyport Herald*, December 11, 1879.
    Bronze Group Commemorating Emancipation. City Document no. 126, Boston, 1879.

15. George W. Cate, "Curiosity." Manuscript owned by the writer.
    Visit of the Jubilee Singers to the Poet, John G. Whittier. HCL.

16. Daniel Dulaney Addison, *Lucy Larcom, Life, Letters, and Diary.* Houghton, Mifflin and
    Company, 1895. p. 185.
    Frank Foxcraft, "Mr. Whittier and the 'Autocrat', with Some Hitherto Unpublished
    Verses by Mr. Whittier," *The Congregationalist and Christian World.* December 14,
    1907.
    M. A. DeWolfe Howe, *Holmes of the Breakfast Table.* Oxford University Press, 1939.
    p. 143.
    Edmund Clarence Stedman to JGW, December 21, 1879. Albree, pp. 216-17.
    JGW to Edmund Clarence Stedman, December 31, 1879. Columbia University Library.

17. JGW to Oliver Wendell Holmes, December 17, 1879. Pickard, pp. 654-56.

18. JGW to Harriet Minot Pitman, March 3, 1880. SC.
    JGW to Mary Shepard, January 18, 1880. University of Virginia.
    JGW to Helen L. Colcord, January 11, 1880. SC.
    Account of Houghton, Osgood & Co., May 1, 1879. HCL.

19. JGW to James T. Fields, March 17 and June 17, 1880. HEH.
    Charles Dudley Warner to JGW, July 6, 1880. Central Michigan University.
    Pickard, p. 658. Note 1.

20. JGW to Harriet Minot Pitman, March 3, 1880. SC.
    JGW to Elizabeth Stuart Phelps, February 20, 1880. SC.

21. Robert C. Winthrop to Samuel T. Pickard, January 25, 1893. HCL.
    Address of Phoebe Woodman Grantham. EI.
    JGW to Emma B. Cochran. Copy. EI.

22. Charlotte Forten Grimke, "Personal Recollections of Whittier." *New England Magazine*,
    June, 1893.
    JGW to Abbie J. Woodman, May 7, 1880. EI.

23. JGW to William Dean Howells, May 21, 1880. Central Michigan University.
    JGW to William Dean Howells, June 19, 1880. HCL.
24. JGW to Adelaide Cammett, June 5, 1880. EI.
25. Lucy Larcom to Elizabeth Pickard, July 6, 1880. HCL.
    JGW to Harriet Minot Pitman, March 6, 1880. HCL.
    JGW to George W. Cate, July 5, 1880. Privately owned.
    Villager, July 8, 1880.
    Danvers Mirror, September 18, 1880.
    JGW to Helen Burt, October 20, 1880. Helen Burt, "Reminiscences of the Poet Whittier."
    The Bookman, June, 1895, Vol. I, p. 310.
26. JGW to James R. Osgood, July 22, 1880. Pickard, pp. 658-59.
    JGW to James R. Osgood, September 17, 1880. HEH.
27. JGW to Gertrude Cartland, (March) 28, (1881). Whittier Home, Amesbury.
    The letter March 22, 1881, entitled "The Friends in New England" is in Essex Institute. The second letter, with many variations from the printed form, is in Henry E. Huntington Library. Both are in Pickard, pp. 775-85. In addition to the volumes mentioned, Whittier may have used an article by Nathan Kite on persecution of Friends in New England, mentioned in an undated letter to Joseph Cartland. In the Whittier Home, Amesbury, is *A Call from Death to Life, Being an account of the Sufferings of Marmaduke Stephenson, William Robinson, and Mary Dyer in New England, in the year 1659. Printed by Friends in London 1660. One hundred copies privately reprinted. Providence, R.I. 1865*. Mary Dyer's letter written on the day before her expected execution was printed in the *National Inquirer*, February 8, 1838. It had been sent to the *Inquirer* by Joshua Coffin.
28. JGW to William Dean Howells, May 21, 1880. Central Michigan University.
    John F. Kellett, *Whittier and Sophronia Moody*. Typescript, APL.
    Typewritten note by Samuel T. Pickard. HCL.
29. JGW to ?, October 24, 1880. MHS.
    JGW to Annie Fields, October 28, 1880. EI.
    Biographical Introduction to Letters of Lydia Maria Child. Houghton, Mifflin and Company, 1883. pp. XXII - XXIII.
30. JGW to Sydney Howard Gay, September 24, 1880. Columbia University Library.
    JGW to Rowland Johnson, January 7, 1881. SC.
    Newburyport Herald, October 9, 1880.
    Villager, October 14, 1880.
    Weekly News, June 11, 1881.
    Pickard, p. 605.
31. JGW to Paul Hamilton Hayne, October 11, 1880. Duke University.
    JGW to ?, October 24, 1880. MHS.
    JGW to Abby J. Woodman, undated. EI.
    JGW to Annie Fields, October 28, 1880. HEH.
    JGW to Editors of *The Boston Journal*, October 23, 1880. *Boston Morning Journal*, October 25, 1880. This letter was copied in other papers, including the *Villager*, October 28, 1880, and the *Danvers Mirror*, October 30, 1880.
    Newburyport Herald, October 20 and 21, 1880.
    Villager, November 4, 1880.
    JGW to Abby J. Woodman, November 5, 1880. EI.
    JGW to Samuel T. Pickard, November 14, 1880. SC.
32. JGW to Elizabeth W. Pickard, November 29, 1880. Pickard, p. 661.
    JGW to Augustine Jones, December 16, 1880. *Providence News*, December 17, 1892.
33. JGW to C. H. Shepard, December 16, 1880. *Danvers Mirror*, December 25, 1880.

Chapter XXXI

1. JGW to Charlotte Fiske Bates, January 3, 1881. Scripps College.
   JGW to Harriet Minot Pitman, January 17, 1881. Boston Atheneum.
2. JGW to Elizabeth Neall Gay, January 27, 1881. Pickard, pp. 666-67.
   JGW to Phebe Woodman, February 2, 1881. EI.
   JGW to Ann Wendell, January 25, 1881. Hav. CL.
3. Arthur Christy, "Orientalism in New England: Whittier." *American Literature*, Vol. I, January, 1930. pp. 380-82.
4. Edwin P. Whipple to JGW, March 3, 1881. Albree, pp. 224-25.
   Oliver Wendell Holmes to JGW, June 6, 1881. Pickard, pp. 667-68.
   JGW to John W. Chadwick, March 5, 1881. Formerly owned by Carroll A. Wilson.
5. JGW to Elizabeth Stuart Phelps, May 9, 1881. SC.
   JGW to Frances C. Sparhawk, April 2, 1881. SC.
6. *Weekly News* May 7, 1881.
   JGW to Lucy Larcom, May 5, 1881. SC.
   JGW to Frances C. Sparhawk, May 12, 1881. Colgate University Library.
   JGW to Abby J. Woodman, May 18, 1881. EI.
7. *Boston Journal* May 24, 1881.
   JGW to Charles H. Brainard, May 12, 1881. HCL.
   Francis A. Walker to JGW, February 23, 1881. HCL.
8. JGW to Joseph Cartland, June 23, 1881. Whittier Home, Amesbury.
   JGW to ?, June 24, 1881. SC.
   Weekly News, June 25 and July 9, 1881.
   JGW to George W. Cate, July 12, 1881. Privately owned.
   Pickard, p. 669.
   Augustine Jones, "Reminiscences of John Greenleaf Whittier." *American Friend*, December 12, 1907.
9. Manuscript note of Samuel T. Pickard, February 1881. HCL.
10. Marshall P. Wilder to JGW, August 4 and 17, 1881. HCL.
11. JGW to W. H. B. Currier, September 24, 1881. *Works* VI 284-85.
    JGW to George William French, September 26, 1881. *Danvers Mirror*, October 1, 1881.
    JGW to ?, September 26, 1881. HEH.
    JGW to Rebecca Magill, September 27, 1881. SC.
12. JGW to Edward H. Magill, October 4, 1881. SC.
    Oliver Wendell Holmes to JGW, October 18, 1881. *Friends Intelligencer*, January 22, 1955.
    JGW to Abbie Kite, November 9, 1881. Hav. CL.
    Currier, p. 586.
    JGW to Mary C. Moore, December 12, 1881. *Works* VII 236-37.
13. JGW to George W. Cate, November 27, 1881. Privately Owned.
14. Whittier wrote to Annie Fields, September 4, 1886, that Matthew Arnold was "one of the foremost men of our time, a true poet, a wise critic, and a brave upright man to whom all English-speaking peoples owe a debt of gratitude." HEH.
15. "A Visit to Whittier in 1881." Edited by Henry J. Cadbury. *Bulletin of Friends Historical Association*.
    Samuel Longfellow, *Henry Wadsworth Longfellow*. III 319.
16. JGW to Perry Mason Co., November 28, 1881. Formerly owned by C. Marshall Taylor.
17. JGW to Elizabeth S. Jones, December 19, 1881. Pickard, p. 676.
    JGW to Charles H. Brainard, January 12, 1882. HCL.
    JGW to Edna Dean Proctor, February 18, 1882. New Hampshire Historical Society.

JGW to Sarah Orne Jewett, February 1882. Pickard, p. 676.

JGW to Abby J. Woodman, February 14, 1882. EI.

JGW to Henry Wadsworth Longfellow, February 25, 1882. HCL.

JGW to Charles R. Lanman, May 30, 1888. Formerly owned by Carroll A. Wilson.

18. JGW to Abby J. Woodman, March 14, 1882. EI.

Lucy Larcom to Samuel T. Pickard, March 20, 1882. HCL.

Elizabeth Stuart Phelps, *Chapters from a Life*. Houghton, Mifflin and Company, 1896. p. 158.

19. JGW to Edna Dean Proctor, March 28, 1882. New Hampshire Historical Society.

JGW to ?, March 28, 1882. University of Virginia.

JGW to Dorothea Dix, April 7, 1882. Copy. HCL.

JGW to Thomas Bailey Aldrich, March 28, 1882. HCL.

JGW to Elizabeth W. Pickard, March 1882. Pickard, p. 677.

20. JGW to Caroline C. Cate, April 28, 1882. Privately owned.

JGW to Edward H. Magill, May 7, 1882. SC.

21. JGW to Harriet Winslow Sewall, May 10 and July 1, 1882. MHS.

22. JGW to Francis J. Garrison, December 20, 1888. SC.

23. JGW to Elizabeth Stuart Phelps, May 18, 1882. SC.

JGW to Ann Wendell, May 22, 1882. SC.

24. JGW to Annie Fields, June 30, 1882. HEH.

Ellen Ballou, *The Building of the House*, Houghton, Mifflin and Company, 1970. p. 392.

Forrest Wilson, *Crusader in Crinoline*, Lippincott, 1941. p. 615.

25. JGW to Annie Fields, June 30, 1882. HEH.

JGW to ?, July 2, 1882. SC.

JGW to Annie Fields, July 14, 1882. HEH.

JGW to Caroline C. Cate, July 16, 1882. Privately owned.

Gertrude Cartland to Elizabeth W. Pickard, July 19, 1882. Formerly owned by C. Marshall Taylor.

JGW to Annie Fields, August 15, 1882. HEH.

JGW to Francis J. Garrison, July 26, 1882. SC.

26. JGW to Annie Fields, August 15, 1882. HEH.

JGW to Milton J. Kendell, August 12, 1882. SC.

27. JGW to ?, August 29, 1882. Hav. CL.

28. JGW to Harriet Minot Pitman, September 6, 1882. SC.

JGW to Abby J. Woodman, September 10, 1882. EI.

JGW to Francis J. Garrison, September 5, 1882. SC.

29. *Weekly News*, September 22, 1882.

James R. Osgood to Francis H. Underwood, March 22, 1882. Formerly owned by C. Marshall Taylor.

Francis H. Underwood to Samuel T. Pickard, January 7, 1893. Whittier Home, Amesbury.

JGW to Elizabeth Stuart Phelps, May 18, 1882. SC.

30. JGW to Francis H. Underwood, September 2, 1882. University of Texas.

JGW to Francis H. Underwood, September 28, 1882 (?). HPL.

JGW to ?, December 30, 1882. SC.

JGW to ?, May 23, 1883. SC.

31. JGW to W. H. Coates, September 30, 1882. *Newburyport Herald*, October 11, 1882.

Robert S. Rantoul, *Some Personal Recollections of the Poet Whittier*. EIHC, April, 1901. p. 132.

32. *Danvers Mirror*, September 30, 1882.

Unidentified news clipping. Whittier Home, Amesbury.

JGW to Harriet Minot Pitman, November 26, 1882. SC.

JGW to Samuel T. Pickard, November 13, 1882. SC.

33. JGW to George W. Cate. December 11, 1882. Privately owned.
Newburyport Herald, December 19, 1882.
JGW to ?, December 17, 1882. Frank Preston Stearns, *Sketches from Concord and Appledore*, G. P. Putman's Sons, 1895, p. 264.
L. C. Obregon to JGW, December 22, 1882. EI.
JGW to ?, April 12, 1882. Princeton University Library.

Chapter XXXII

1. JGW to Adelaide Cammett, January 4, 1883. EI.
JGW to Gustavus Cammett, January 7, 1883. Owned by John B. Pickard.
JGW to Ann Wendell, January 20, 1883. Central Michigan University.

2. JGW to Samuel T. Pickard (fragment). Owned by the writer.
JGW to Francis J. Underwood, January 20, June 14, and July 21, 1883. SC.
JGW to Francis J. Underwood, July 20, 1883. University of Texas.
Francis J. Underwood to Samuel T. Pickard, January 22, 1883. HCL.
Francis J. Underwood to Samuel T. Pickard, January 7, 1893. Whittier Home, Amesbury.

3. JGW to Thomas Bailey Aldrich, October 27, 1883. HCL.
JGW to Francis J. Underwood, December 25, 1883. SC.
Francis J. Underwood to Samuel T. Pickard, January 7, 1893. Note 2.

4. JGW to Charlotte Fiske Bates, April, 1883. "Whittier Desultoria," Charlotte Fiske Bates. *Cosmopolitan*, January, 1894.
JGW to a teacher at Dallas Academy. *Newburyport Herald*, March 8, 1883.

5. *Newburyport Herald*, March 12, 1883.
H. B. Blackwell, "The Whittier Reception." *Woman's Journal*, quoted in *Danvers Mirror*, March 24, 1883.

6. JGW to Harriet Minot Pitman, April 13, 1883. Formerly owned by C. Marshall Taylor.
JGW to Sarah Orne Jewett, April 11, 1883. HCL.

7. JGW to Annie Fields, May 5 and 18, 1883. HEH.

8. Oliver Wendell Holmes to JGW, November 4, 1883. Albree, pp. 232-33.

9. Manuscript and proof privately owned.

10. Charles I. Pettingell, "Walter Barefoote." *New England Historical and Genealogical Register, July, 1941.*

11. JGW to George William Curtis, May 9, 1883. HCL.

12. H. M. Alden to JGW, May 31, 1883. HCL.

13. *Villager*, June 28, 1883.
Danvers Mirror, July 7, 1883.
JGW to Harriet Minot Pitman. Pickard, p. 688.
JGW to Francesca Alexander, August 21, 1883. Lucia Gray Swett, *Ruskin's Letters to Francesca and Memoirs of the Alexanders*.

14. JGW to Abby J. Woodman, July 25, 1883. EI.

15. *Newburyport Herald*, August 6, 1883.
John Crowell, "The Poet 'on His Native Heath.'" *Haverhill Weekly Bulletin*, August 11, 1883.

16. JGW to Harriet Minot Pitman, September 22, 1883. SC.

17. *Weekly News*, October 19, 1883.
JGW to Sarah Orne Jewett, October 20, 1883. HCL.

JGW to Mary B. Claflin, October 20, 1883. Owned by John B. Pickard.
JGW to Annie Fields, October 22, 1883. HEH.
JGW to Thomas Bailey Aldrich, October 27, 1883. HCL.

18. JGW to Editor of the *Journal*, November 3, 1883. HCL.
Hans Louis Trefousse, *Ben Butler*. Twayne Publishers, 1957. p. 249.
JGW to Harriet Winslow Sewall, November 8, 1883. MHS.
JGW to Harriet Minot Pitman, November 8, 1883. SC.

19. JGW to Annie Fields, September 22, October 13, 22, 26, 1883, and undated. HEH.
JGW to Harriet Minot Pitman, November 8, 1883. SC.
Annie Fields to JGW, September 19, 1883. HCL.
George W. Childs to JGW, January 31, 1887. HCL.

20. JGW to Lucy Larcom, July 23, 1883. Yale University Library.
JGW to Lucy Larcom, August 24, 1883. Anderson Sale, p. 39.

21. JGW to Francis J. Garrison, May 30 and August 16, 1883. SC.

22. Oliver Wendell Holmes to JGW, November 4, 1883. Albree, p. 232.

23. JGW to Elizabeth Pickard, December 14, 1883. SC.
JGW to Caroline C. Cate, November 30, December 1, 5, 13, 15, 1883; January 8, 22,
28, February 5, 14, 1884. Privately owned.
JGW to George W. Cate, December 10, 12, 15, 1883. Privately owned.

24. JGW to Charlotte Fiske Bates, December, 1883. Charlotte Fiske Bates, "Whittier Desultoria". *Cosmopolitan*, January, 1894.
Mrs. James T. Fields, *Whittier*. Harper & Brothers, 1893. pp. 63-64.

25. Arlin Turner, "Whittier Calls on George W. Cable." *New England Quarterly*, March, 1949.
JGW to Mary B. Claflin, October 20, 1883. Owned by John B. Pickard.

26. JGW to Annie Fields, October 13, 1883. HEH.
Arthur Christy, "Orientalism in New England: Whittier." *American Literature*, Jan-
uary, 1930.
Danvers Mirror, December 22, 1883.
JGW to ?, December 17, 1883. HEH.

27. JGW to Sarah Orne Jewett, January 18, 1884. HEH.
JGW to ?, January 13, 1884. EI.
JGW to Francis J. Garrison, January 18, 1884. Formerly owned by C. Marshall Taylor.
JGW to Edna Dean Proctor, January 26, 1884. New Hampshire Historical Society.
Charles W. Russell to JGW, January 8, 1884. EI.
Frank Waters to JGW, February 7, 1884. EI.

28. William Claflin to JGW, February 4, 1884. Albree, pp. 234-36.
Annie Fields to JGW, January 20, 1884. HCL.

29. JGW to Caroline C. Cate, February 5, 1884. Privately owned.
Newburyport Herald, February 5, 1884.
JGW to William H. Dupree, April 7, 1884. *A Eulogy on Wendell Phillips by Archibald
H. Grimke Delivered in Tremont Temple, Boston, April 9, 1884*. Boston, 1884.
William J. Tucker to JGW, October 23, 1884. Whittier Home, Amesbury.

30. Annie E. Johnson to JGW, February 7, 1884. EI.
Frank Luther Mott, *History of American Magazines*. Harvard University Press, 1951.
IV 395.

31. Frank Luther Mott. Op. cit.

32. Mrs. George A. Palmer to Samuel T. Pickard, undated. HCL.
JGW to Mrs. George A. Palmer, April, 1884. HPL.

33. William Claflin to JGW, February 4, 1884. Note 28.
George W. Cate, Address on *John G. Whittier*. Typescript. Owned by the writer.

34. JGW to Abby J. Woodman, March 20, 1884. EI.
JGW to Caroline C. Cate, April 28, 1884. Privately owned.

JGW to Charlotte Fiske Bates, May 1884. Charlotte Fiske Bates, "Glimpses of Whittier's Faith and Character Through Extracts from Unpublished Letters." *McClure's Magazine*, January, 1894.

35. *Newburyport Herald*, June 25 and July 26, 1884.
Amesbury and Salisbury Villager, July 10, 1884.
JGW to Henry Cabot Lodge, *Newburyport Herald*, August 7, 1884.
Henry Cabot Lodge to JGW, August 6, 1884. HCL.
Henry Cabot Lodge, *Early Memories*. Charles Scribner's Sons, 1913. p. 342.

36. JGW to Dorothea Dix, July 24, 1884. HCL.
JGW to Celia Thaxter, July 20, 1884. HCL.
JGW to ?, August 17, 1884. SC.

37. JGW to Hugo Ericksen, August 14, 1884. University of Michigan.
JGW to ?, October 31, 1886. EI.

38. JGW to the *Critic*, August 18, 1884. Pierpont Morgan Library.

39. JGW to ?, September 12, 1884. Phillips Exeter Academy.

40. JGW to D. L. Withington, September 13, 1884. SC.
Amesbury and Salisbury Villager, September 18, 1884.

41. Maria S. Porter, *Recollections of Louisa May Alcott, John Greenleaf Whittier, and Robert Browning*, New England Magazine Corporation. p. 40.
Mary Earhart, *Frances Willard: From Prayers to Politics*. University of Chicago Press, p. 243.
JGW to ?, October 9, 1884. SC.
JGW to Mary Abigail Dodge, November 28, 1884. Copy. HCL.

42. JGW to George William Curtis, November 9, 1884. HCL.
Richard S. Spofford to JGW, March 6, 1885. HCL.
JGW to ?, September 24, 1885. Formerly owned by C. Marshall Taylor.

43. Annie Fields to JGW, October 9, 1884. HCL.
JGW to Annie Fields, October 29, 31, December 1, 1884. HEH.

44. Donald P. Wright, quoted in *Haverhill Journal*, December 12, 1957.
Danvers Mirror, April 19, 1884.
Villager, October 2, 1884.
JGW to Augustine Jones, October 13, 1884. Central Michigan University.
Proceedings at the Presentation of Portrait of John Greenleaf Whittier to Friends School, Providence, R.I. Tenth Month, 24th, 1884. Riverside Press.
Pickard, pp. 704-05.
Thomas Chase to JGW, November 4, 1884. Albree, pp. 237-38.
Albree, pp. 284-85.
JGW to Phebe Woodman, June, 1892. Albree, pp. 257-58.

45. Edmund Gosse, "A Visit to Whittier." *The Bookman*, January, 1899, Vol. 2, pp. 459-62.

46. *Amesbury and Salisbury Villager*, January 1, 1885.
Newburyport Herald, December 19, 1884.
Mary Abigail Dodge to JGW, December 17, 1884. HCL.

Chapter XXXIII

1. JGW to Lucy Larcom, December 12, 1884. Pickard, p. 699.
JGW to Abby J. Woodman, December 27, 1884. EI.
JGW to ?, November 2, 1884. EI.
JGW to Harriet Winslow Sewall, January 6, 1885. MHS.
JGW to Harriet Minot Pitman, January 24, 1885. SC.

2. Phineas T. Barnum to JGW, March 11, 1885. Central Michigan University.
3. JGW to Edna Dean Proctor, April 5, 1884. New Hampshire Historical Society.
   JGW to Charles C. Reed, March 4, 1885. Pickard, pp. 705-07.
   Alfred Tennyson to JGW, May 4, 1885. Anderson Sale.
   JGW to John Bright, March 31, 1885. New York Public Library.
   JGW to Charles C. Reed, April 2, 1885. Copy. HCL.
4. JGW to Annie Fields, March 24, 1885. HEH.
   JGW to Evelina Bray Downey, April 9, 1885. Hav. CL.
   JGW to Elizabeth Pickard, April 4, 1885. Formerly owned by George F. Whicher.
   JGW to Harriet Minot Pitman, May 16, 1885. SC.
   Richard Cary, *Mary N. Murfree.* Twayne Publishers, 1967. pp. 80, 115.
5. JGW to Frances C. Sparhawk. Frances C. Sparhawk, *Whittier at Close Range.* Riverdale
   Press, 1925, p. 105.
   JGW to Collector of Port of Boston, June, 1885. SC.
   JGW to Francis J. Garrison, June 22, 1885. Formerly owned by C. Marshall Taylor.
   Manuscript, Bowdoin College Library.
6. JGW to Samuel J. Spalding, June, 1885. EI.
7. Currier, p. 323.
8. JGW to Annie Fields, July 29, 1885. HEH.
9. William Stetson Merrill, "We Talked with Whittier." EIHC. April, 1958.
10. JGW to Mrs. George W. Cate, July 30, 1885. Privately owned.
    JGW to Harriet Minot Pitman, July 27, 1885. SC.
    Frederick W. Fowler, "John Greenleaf Whittier." *The New Hampshire Troubadour*, Vol.
    X No. 9. December, 1940.
    Pickard, p. 711.
11. JGW to George W. Cate, August 6, 1885. *Amesbury and Salisbury Villager*, August 13,
    1885.
    Newburyport Herald, February 3, 1886.
    Amesbury and Salisbury Villager, March 1, 1886.
12. JGW to Oliver Wendell Holmes, *Boston Transcript*, August 27, 1885.
13. JGW to Evelina Bray Downey, September 1, 1885. Copy. HCL.
    Newburyport Herald, September 11, 1885.
    *Reunion of the Schoolmates of John Greenleaf Whittier at St. John's Rectory, Haver-
    hill, Mass. September 10, 1885.* Chase Brothers.
    JGW to Harriet Minot Pitman, September 11, 1885. SC.
    JGW to Charles Wingate, December 24, 1885. HPL.
    JGW to Annie Fields, October 2, 1885. HEH.
    "The Whittier Reunion." Unidentified newspaper clipping.
14. JGW to Frances C. Sparhawk, September 24, 1885. New York Public Library.
    JGW to Samuel T. Pickard, September 1885. HPL.
    Samuel C. Armstrong to JGW, September 7, 1885. EI.
15. Thomas Donaldson, *Walt Whitman the Man.* Francis P. Harper, 1896.
    Oliver Wendell Holmes to JGW, September 7, 1885. Albree, pp. 241-42.
    JGW to Thomas Donaldson, September 5, 1885. New York Public Library.
    Albree, pp. 243-44.
16. Horace Traubel, *With Walt Whitman in Camden, March 28, 1888 - January 20, 1889.* I 217.
17. JGW to George W. Cate, October 31, 1885. Privately owned.
18. JGW to Edward H. Haskell, November 10, 1885. *Works* VII 240-41. The quotation is
    from the first and last sentences in Milton's "Of Reformation in England. The Sec-
    ond Book."
19. JGW to Abby J. Woodman, November 18, 1885. EI.
    JGW to ?, November 22, 1885. *Newburyport Herald*, December 18, 1885.

Ned Brown, "One World Idea Taught in This City Century Ago." *Newburyport Daily News*, May 3, 1961.

JGW to Annie Fields, December 19, 1885. HEH.

20. JGW to Harry C. Bowen, December 7, 1885. SC.

21. JGW to Annie Fields, December 19, 1885. EI.

22. JGW to Annie Fields, January 2 and February 3, 1886. HEH.
JGW to Caroline C. Cate, January 4, 1886. Privately owned.

23. JGW to Harriet Minot Pitman, January 27, 1886. HCL.
JGW to Harriet Minot Pitman, February 21, 1886. Boston Atheneum.
Sarah Orne Jewett to JGW. (Undated). HCL.
JGW to Phebe Woodman, April 13, 1890. EI.

24. JGW to ?, February 21, 1886. Boston Atheneum.
JGW to Rose Hollingsworth, March 25, 1886. SC.
JGW to Thomas Bailey Aldrich, February 6, 1886. HCL.

25. JGW to ?, March 13, 1886. Goodspeed Catalogue 254 (1936), lot 472.
JGW to George Woodberry, February 5, 1886. SC.
JGW to William Dean Howells, March 18 and 23, 1886. HCL.
Benjamin H. Ticknor to JGW, February 17, 1886. HCL.
JGW to *The Brooklyn Magazine. The Critic*, April 3, 1886.
Caroline Ticknor, *Glimpses of Authors*. Houghton Mifflin Company, 1922. pp. 75-79.
JGW to Annie Fields, April 2, 1886. HEH.

26. JGW to Rose Hollingsworth. Note 24.
JGW to ?, April 8, 1886. SC.

27. Alice Freeman to JGW, April 14, 1886. HCL.
JGW to Alice Freeman, April 16, 1886. Wellesley College Library.
George Herbert Palmer, *Alice Freeman Palmer*. Houghton Mifflin Company, 1910.

28. JGW to Mary B. Claflin, October 20, 1883. Owned by John B. Pickard.

29. JGW to Francis J. Garrison, May 4, 1886. SC.

30. JGW to Mary Abigail Dodge, May 14, 1886. EI.

31. *Amesbury and Salisbury Villager*, January 14, 1886.
JGW to George W. Cate, February 5, and 15, and May 10, 1886. Privately owned.
JGW to Annie Fields, July 4, 1886. HEH.
Newburyport Herald, June 17 and July 7, 1886.
Amesbury News, September 17, 1886.

32. JGW to Abby J. Woodman, July 14, 1886. EI.
JGW to Annie Fields July 21 and 27, 1886. HEH.
JGW to Sarah Orne Jewett, August 8, 1886. HEH.
JGW to Annie Fields, September 4, 1886. HEH.
JGW to George W. Cate, September 4, 1886. Privately owned.

33. JGW to Annie Fields, November 6, 1886. HEH.
JGW to ?, December 22, 1886. Copy. HCL.

34. JGW to ?, September 21, 1886. SC.
JGW to Sarah J. Clarke Lippincott, October, 1886. Pickard, p. 716.
JGW to Annie Fields, October 12, 1886. HCL.

35. Harriet Minot Pitman to JGW, October 26, 1886. HCL.
Francis B. Gummere, "The Poetry of Whittier." *American Friend*, Vol. 14., December 12, 1907. pp. 800-02.
James Russell Lowell to JGW, November 11, 1886. Albree, p. 246.
M. A. DeWolfe Howe, *A Venture in Remembrance*. Little Brown & Co., 1941. p. 103.

36. JGW to George W. Cate, November 22, 1886. Privately owned. The neighbor was George Turner, a trial justice in the Amesbury Police Court, who died three months later, February 24, 1887.
JGW to ?, November 22, 1888. MHS.

37. *Newburyport Herald*, December 20, 1886.
Boston Journal, December 18, 1886.
JGW to Elizabeth Cavazza, December 18, 1886. Pickard, pp. 716-17.
JGW to J. S. Cutler, December 31, 1886. EI.

Chapter XXXIV

1. JGW to Frances C. Sparhawk, February 16, 1887. Whittier Home, Amesbury.
2. JGW to Harriet Minot Pitman, January 19, 1887. Boston Atheneum.
JGW to Annie Fields, June 11, 1887. HEH.
3. JGW to Annie Fields, February 2 and 28, 1887. HEH.
JGW to Elizabeth Neall Gay, February 22, 1887. Pickard, pp. 719-20.
JGW to Abby J. Woodman, February 14, 1887. EI.
4. JGW to Rev. S. H. Emery, January 30, 1887. *Annual Reunion of the Emery Family*,
Taunton, 1888. p. 5.
Amesbury and Salisbury Villager, February 3, 1887.
5. *Newburyport Herald*, April 6, 1887.
6. *Beecher Memorial. Contemporaneous Tributes to the Memory of Henry Ward Beecher.*
Compiled and edited by Edward W. Bok. Brooklyn, 1887. p. 6.
Mrs. James T. Fields, *Whittier*. Harper & Brothers, 1893. p. 63.
7. JGW to Edna Dean Proctor, April 13, 1887. New Hampshire Historical Society.
Check to Gustavus Golze, Amesbury National Bank, April 11, 1887.
8. JGW to Ralph Stone, May 1, 1887. SC.
9. John A. Kasson to JGW, May 30, 1887. HCL.
10. JGW to Annie Fields, June 18, 1887. HEH.
JGW to John Bright, July 16, 1887. New York Public Library.
11. JGW to Abby J. Woodman, July 22, 1887. EI.
JGW to Phebe Woodman, July 23, 1887. EI.
JGW to Caroline Carter, August 2, 1887. Wellesley College Library.
12. Phebe was born in New Orleans, October 8, 1869. Her name was Nellie May Eaton. Her
parents died in an epidemic in 1874.
Richard P. Zollo, "Family Life at Oak Knoll: The Poet Whittier and His Cousins."
EIHC Vol. 119, No. 2, April 1983.
"Gone from Oak Knoll." Boston Daily Globe, August 6, 1887.
JGW to Annie Fields, October 21, 1887. EI.
Information given to the writer by Harriet Tapley.
13. JGW to Editor of the *Transcript*. *Boston Evening Transcript*, August 11, 1887.
JGW to Mary B. Claflin, August 3, 1887. Hayes Memorial Library.
JGW to Abby J. Woodman, August 15, 1887. EI.
Lucy Larcom to Elizabeth W. Pickard, August 11, 1887. HCL.
14. JGW to William Dean Howells, September 24, 1887. HCL.
William Dean Howells to JGW, November 1, 1887. EI.
Kenneth S. Lynn, *William Dean Howells. An American Life*. Harcourt Brace Javonich,
1970. pp. 282-92.
15. JGW to William Dean Howells, December 19, 1888. HCL.
William Hale Bickford, "A Reminiscence of Whittier." *Book News Monthly*, September
1914.

16. Charles W. Cooper, *Whittier. Independent College in California.* Ward-Ritchie Press, 1967. pp. 3-16.
    JGW to ?, December 3, 1887. Privately owned.
    JGW to Abby J. Woodman, January 16 and February 6, 1888. EI.
    JGW to ?, October 21, 1887. EI.
17. Frederick W. Farrar to JGW, October 27, 1887. Pickard, pp. 728-29.
    Thomas Wentworth Higginson, "The Place of Whittier Among Poets." *The Reader Magazine*, February 1905. pp. 368-72.
    JGW to George W. Childs, November 28, 1887. LC.
18. Mary Mapes Dodge to JGW, October 11, 1886. EI.
    Mary Mapes Dodge to JGW, November 3, 1887. Central Michigan University.
19. *Newburyport Herald*, December 17 and 22, 1887.
    Pickard, pp. 727-28.
    Boston Traveller, December 18, 1887.
    W. Sloane Kennedy, *John Greenleaf Whittier. His Life, Genius, and Writings.* D. Lothrop Co., 1892. pp. 314-15.
    JGW to Francis J. Garrison, Decmeber 29, 1887. SC.
    JGW to Gertrude Cartland, January 6, 1888. Whittier Home, Amesbury.
    Samuel F. Smith to JGW, December 16, 1887. EI.
20. George F. Hoar to JGW, January 20, 1888. Albree, p. 249.
    Danvers Mirror, December 17, 1887. The book is in the Whittier Home, Amesbury.
    Pickard, p. 727.
21. JGW to R. H. Terrell and George W. Williams, January 9, 1888. *Works* VII 196-97.
22. Eleanor N. Tilton, "Making Whittier Definitive." *New England Quarterly*, Vol. XII, June, 1939. pp. 281-314.
    JGW to Celia Thaxter, March 2, 1888. HCL.
    JGW to Annie Fields, April 30 and May 22, 1888. HEH.
    JGW to ?, April 5, 1888. SC.
    JGW to Horace E. Scudder, June 13, 1888. SC.
    JGW to Francis J. Garrison, July 27, 1888. SC.
    Currier, pp. 272-74.
    Horace E. Scudder to Samuel T. Pickard, March 29, 1888. HCL.
    JGW to George W. Cate. Privately owned.
23. JGW to Caroline C. Cate, April 12, 1888. Privately owned.
    JGW to Edna Dean Proctor, April 17, 1888. New Hampshire Historical Society.
    JGW to Annie Fields, April 30, 1888. HEH.
24. JGW to Abbie J. Woodman, May 13, 1888. EI.
    JGW to Rose Hollingsworth, June 11, 1888. SC.
    JGW to Annie Fields, May 22, 1888. HEH.
    JGW to Charles R. Lanman, May 30, 1888. Formerly owned by Carroll A. Wilson.
25. JGW to Ann Wendell, June 19, 1888. SC.
    JGW to ?, June 27, 1888. *Newburyport Herald*, June 29, 1888.
    Edward L. Pierce to Samuel T. Pickard, November 30, 1894. HCL.
    JGW to Caroline C. Cate, July 3, 1888. Privately owned.
26. JGW to ?, March 27, 1888. SC.
    JGW to George W. Cate, June 12 and 26, 1888. Privately owned.
    JGW to Caroline C. Cate, June 16, 1888, and July 3, 1888. Privately owned.
    JGW to Ann Wendell, Note 25.
27. *Newburyport Daily News*, July 5, 1888.
    Newburyport Daily Herald, July 5, 1888.
    Boston Daily Globe, July 5, 1888.
    JGW to Henry C. Bowen, June 10 and 14, 1888. American Antiquarian Society.
28. *Whittier-Land*, pp. 122-126. A preliminary draft was formerly owned by C. Marshall Taylor.

29. JGW to Edna Dean Proctor, July 11, 1888. New Hampshire Historical Society.
JGW to Annie Fields, July 23, 1888. EI.
JGW to Abby J. Woodman, July 18, 1888. EI.
JGW to Sarah Orne Jewett, September 12, 1888. HEH.

30. JGW to Samuel T. Pickard, September 5, 1888. SC.
JGW to Francis J. Garrison, September 4, 1888. SC.
JGW to Horace E. Scudder, September 6, 1888. Formerly owned by Carroll A. Wilson.

31. JGW to Clarence W. Bowen, September 10, 1888. American Antiquarian Society.

32. JGW to Evelina Bray Downey, October 19, 1888. Owned by Miss C. F. Andrews.
JGW to Francis J. Garrison, June 30, July 18 and 22, October 4, November 4, 1888. SC.
"Harriet Minot Pitman," October 31, 1888. *Boston Evening Transcript*, November 1, 1888.

33. Samuel F. Smith to JGW, October 26, 1888. HCL.
JGW to Celia Thaxter, October 25, 1888. HCL.

34. JGW to Mary Abigail Dodge, August 14, 1888. Copy. HCL.
JGW to Lewis H. Caldwell, *Newburyport Daily Herald*, July 12, 1888.
JGW to Annie Fields, October 29 and November 2, 1888. HEH.
JGW to Francis J. Garrison, November 4, 1888. Formerly owned by C. Marshall Taylor.

35. JGW to Annie Fields, October 21, 1888. HEH.
JGW to Elizabeth Stuart Phelps Ward, October 22, 1888. Pickard, p. 733.
JGW to Annie Fields, October 29 and December 14, 1888. HEH.
Sarah Orne Jewett to JGW, May 15, 1889. Central Michigan University.

36. Currier, pp. 328-29.

37. JGW to Mary Emerson Smith Thomas, December 10, 1888. Copy. HCL.
William Hale Bickford, "A Reminiscence of Whittier." *Book Review Monthly*, September, 1914. pp. 13-14.
JGW to Oliver Wendell Holmes, April 17, 1888. EI.
JGW to Edna Dean Proctor, December 8, 1888. New Hampshire Historical Society.

38. Douglas Sladen, "Whittier at Home." *Illustrated News of the World*, October 1, 1892.

39. JGW to Lucy A. Kilham, December 18, 1888. HCL.
JGW to Elizabeth W. Pickard, December 23, 1888. Formerly owned by C. Marshall Taylor.

40. JGW to David W. Low, December 30, 1888. SC.

Chapter XXXV

1. JGW to Gertrude Cartland, January 1, 1889. Whittier Home, Amesbury.
JGW to Edna Dean Proctor, January 23, 1889. New Hampshire Historical Society.

2. JGW to ?, February 26, 1889. HEH.
JGW to Clarence W. Bowen, January 31, February 6, 20, 21, March 7, 13, 17, April 9, 19, 1889. American Antiquarian Society.
Clarence W. Bowen to JGW, April 9, 1889. HCL.
JGW to Frederick A. P. Barnard. Pickard, p. 741.

3. JGW to Board to Trade, February 3, 1889. *Amesbury and Salisbury Villager*, March 21, 1889.

4. JGW to Annie Fields, February 21, 1889. HEH.
Charles Eliot Norton to JGW, February 20, 1889. EI.
JGW to George H. Monks, February 18, 1889. Central Michigan University.

5. JGW to William M. F. Rounds, April 5, 1889. *Danvers Mirror*, April 15, 1889.

6. JGW to E. H. Haskell, April 16, 1889. *Danvers Mirror*, April 20, 1889. *Amesbury and Salisbury Villager*, April 25, 1889.

7. JGW to W. D. Taylor, February 28, 1889. Copy. EI.
   JGW to Ullie Akerstrom, April 23, 1889. Whittier Home, Amesbury.
   Amesbury and Salisbury Villager, April 18, 1889.

8. JGW to ?, June 3, 1889. Formerly owned by C. Marshall Taylor.
   JGW to Abby J. Woodman, May 21, 1889. EI.
   Currier, p. 164.
   JGW to Annie Fields, July 5, 1889. HEH.
   JGW to Editor of the *Journal*, June 22, 1889.

9. JGW to Elizabeth W. Pickard, June 8, 1889. Formerly owned by C. Marshall Taylor.
   JGW to Phebe Woodman, postmarked June 17, 1889. EI.
   Newburyport Herald, May 28, 1889.

10. JGW to Robert Bonner Sons, July 29, 1889. *New York Ledger*, January 4, 1890. Currier,
    p. 189.
    James Russell Lowell to JGW, December 16, 1890. Horace E. Scudder, *James Russell Lowell*. II 400.

11. Frances Campbell Sparhawk, *Whittier At Close Range*. Riverdale Press, 1925. pp. 132-33.

12. Charles I. Pettingell, "History of Warren Lodge," *Warren Lodge A F and A M Centenary Celebration*. Amesbury, 1925. pp. 27-36.

13. JGW to Annie Fields, August 23, 1889. HEH.
    JGW to ?, October 29, 1889. University of California.
    JGW to Editor *Boston Daily Advertiser*. Formerly owned by Carroll A. Wilson.
    Note by Samuel T. Pickard, HCL.

14. JGW to Elizabeth W. Pickard, October 5, 1889. SC.
    JGW to Frances J. Garrison, October 4, 1889. SC.
    Abby Hutchinson Patton to JGW, December 4, 1889. HCL.
    John Wallace Hutchinson, *The Story of the Hutchinsons*. Compiled and edited by Charles E. Mann. Lee & Shepard, 1896. II 157-58. The date of the visit is incorrectly given as 1888.

15. *Marblehead Messenger*, August 24 and 31, 1900.
    Wilbur H. Siebert, "The Underground Railroad in Massachusetts." Proceedings of the American Antiquarian Society (New Series Vol. 45) 1935.
    JGW to Simeon Dodge, October 7, 1889. *Amesbury and Salisbury Villager*, October 17, 1889.

16. JGW to A. T. Newhall, November 28, 1889. *Newburyport Herald*, November 30, 1889. *Amesbury and Salisbury Villager*, October 31, 1889.
    Tax bill September 1, 1889, receipted by R. O. Bailey. Privately owned.

17. Sarah Orne Jewett to Samuel T. Pickard, January 7, 1893. HCL.
    Sarah Orne Jewett to Samuel T. Pickard, fragment. HCL.

18. JGW to Annie Fields, November 7, 1889. HEH.
    JGW to Francis J. Garrison, December 9, 1889. SC.
    Manuscript with note by Samuel T. Pickard, Whittier Home, Amesbury.
    Newburyport Daily News, December 10, 1889.

19. Edward L. Pierce to Abby J. Woodman, December 23, 1889. EI.
    Newburyport Herald, December 14, 1889.
    JGW to Phebe Woodman, December 18, 1889. EI.
    JGW to Edna Dean Proctor, December 21, 1889. New Hampshire Historical Society.
    Newburyport Herald, December 18, 1889.
    JGW to Celia Thaxter, January 11, 1890. HCL.
    JGW to Annie Fields, January 6, 1890. HEH.
    Unidentified newspaper clipping.

20. Currier, p. 164.
   Rufus M. Jones, *The Later Periods of Quakerism*. Macmillan & Co., 1921. pp. 922 and 970.
   JGW to ?, October 29, 1889. University of California.
21. JGW to Annie Fields, December 13, 1889. EI.
   On the ground of illness Whittier declined an invitation to attend a Browning Memorial Meeting in Boston January 28, 1890, and said that he was unable to write a letter fitting the occasion. *In Memoriam. Memorial to Robert Browning, under the Auspices of the Browning Society of Boston*. Cambridge [1890]. p. 58.
22. Manuscript and proof privately owned.
   Currier, p. 591.
23. JGW to Samuel T. Pickard, February 1, 1890. SC.
   JGW to Annie Fields, February 14, 1890. EI.
   JGW to Abby J. Woodman, February 17, 1890. EI.
   JGW to Lucy Larcom, February 25, 1890. HCL.
   Anderson Sale, p. 17.
   JGW to Louise Chandler Moulton, February 11 and 29, 1890. LC.
24. JGW to Phebe Woodman, March 6 and 13, 1890. EI.
   Newburyport Herald, March 10, 1890.
   "Mr. Babbitt," in Edmund L. Pearson's *The Believing Years*, (Macmillan Co., 1912) is Joseph Cartland.
25. "Whittier and a Girl's Album." *Youth's Companion*, January 23, 1896. The author, whose name is not given, was Ethel Parton, a daughter of James Parton and a neighbor of the Cartlands.
26. William H. Rideing to JGW, January 13, 1890. HCL.
   Booker T. Washington to JGW, January 21, 1890. HCL.
   JGW to Samuel C. Armstrong, March 9, 1890. Copy. HCL.
   Whittier-Land, pp. 153-54.
27. T. Jefferson Coolidge to JGW, February 28, 1890. EI.
   George W. Cate, *Address on John G. Whittier*. Typescript. Privately owned.
   Mary Abigail Dodge to JGW, May 1, 1890. Central Michigan University.
28. JGW to Phebe Woodman, April 13, 1890. EI.
29. JGW to Jones Frankle, May 24, June 20 and 23, 1890 HPL.
   JGW to Annie Fields, June 3, 1890. HEH.
   Horace E. Scudder to JGW, June 19 Whittier Home, Amesbury.
   JGW to Horace E. Scudder, June 23, 1890. HPL.
   Horace E. Scudder to Jones Frankle, June 23 and 30, 1890. HPL.
   Albert L. Bartlett, *Some Memories of Old Haverhill in Massachusetts*. Haverhill, 1915. p. 104.
   In Whittier-Land. Compiled by Charles W. Clancey. Whittier Press, 1930.
   Haverhill Gazette, July 2, 1890.
   Currier, pp. 166 and 258.
30. JGW to Mr. Clark, July 18, 1890. Dartmouth College Library.
   JGW to ?, July 20, 1890. EI.
   JGW to Elizabeth Neall Gay, August 1, 1890. Columbia University Library.
   JGW to Lucy Kilham, July 24, 1890. HCL.
31. JGW to ?, October 2, 1890. SC.
32. JGW to *Boston Evening Transcript*, September 27, 1890. *Boston Evening Transcript*, October 1, 1890.
   Currier, p. 627.
   Isaac R. Pennypacker to JGW, October 25, 1890. Albree, pp. 252-54.
   JGW to Editor of *Independent*, November 7, 1890. Formerly owned by Carroll A. Wilson.
33. Lucy Larcom to Solomon Solis-Cohen, October 18, 1890. Daniel Dulany Addison, *Lucy Larcom, Life, Letters, and Diary*, Houghton, Mifflin and Company, 1895. p. 260.

34. Edmund Clarence Stedman to JGW, December 18, 1890. Albree, p. 255.
    Currier, pp. 167-68.
    JGW to Francis J. Garrison, February 23, 1891. SC.
    Edna Dean Proctor to JGW, December 17, 1890. EI.
35. *Amesbury and Salisbury Villager*, December 18, 1890.
    Newburyport Herald, December 15, 17, and 18, 1890.
    JGW to Annie Fields, December 22, 1890. HEH.
36. JGW to Helen Keller, November 27, 1889. Anderson Sale.
    JGW to Helen Keller, December 1, 1889. SC.
    Pickard, pp. 748-50.

Chapter XXXVI

1. *Newburyport Herald*, January 10, 1891.
   JGW to Annie Fields, January 23, February 17, and March 6, 1891. HEH.
   JGW to Phebe Woodman, February 3, 1891. EI.
   JGW to Abby J. Woodman, March 21, 1891. EI.
2. Unidentified newspaper clipping.
3. Alice Freeman Palmer to JGW, March 28, 1891. EI.
   JGW to Alice Freeman Palmer, April 8, 1891. Wellesley College Library.
   JGW to Annie Fields, April 30, 1891. HEH.
4. Laura E. Richards and Maud Howe Elliott, *Julia Ward Howe* II 187.
   JGW to Francis J. Garrison, April 22 and July 3, 1891. SC.
   Circular, "To the Friends of Russian Freedom." SC.
   Oliver Jensen, Ed. *America and Russia: A Century and a Half of Dramatic Encounters*.
   Simon and Schuster, 1966, pp. 93-121. Kennan's articles were published in the *Century*
   and in his *Siberia and the Exile System*.
5. JGW to Sarah Orne Jewett, May 6, 1891. HEH.
   JGW to Lucy Larcom, May 9, 1891. Pickard, p. 751.
6. Gertrude Cartland to Thomas Chase May 5, 1891. Amesbury Public Library. Chase
   died October 5, 1892.
7. Helen Keller, *Story of My Life*. Doubleday Doran 1951, p. 136.
8. Lucy Larcom to Elizabeth W. Pickard, June 9, 1891. HCL.
   JGW to Phebe Woodman, July 17, 1891. EI.
   Ella Shannon Bowles, *Let Me Show You New Hampshire*. Alfred A. Knopf, 1938. p. 144.
9. JGW to Phebe Woodman, August 9 and 23, 1891. EI.
   JGW to Annie Fields, August 12, 1891. HEH.
   Newburyport Herald, August 15, 18, and 22, 1891.
10. JGW to Oliver Wendell Holmes, August 18, 1891, LC; September 8, 1891, Pickard p.
    752; September 21, 1891, LC.
    Oliver Wendell Holmes to JGW, September 3, 1891. Pickard, p. 752.
    JGW to Annie Fields, September 12, 1891. EI.
11. Manuscript and advance printing with manuscript corrections. HEH.
    Currier, pp. 169, 592.
    Katherine Jeffrey Finlayson to JGW, September 2, 1891. EI.
    JGW to Annie Fields, September 12, 1891. EI.
    JGW to Phebe Woodman, November 20, 1891. EI.

12. JGW to Phebe J. Woodman, October 12 and 21, 1891. EI.
JGW to Abby J. Woodman, October 25, 1891. EI.
Newburyport Herald, October 20, 1891.
JGW to Sarah Orne Jewett, October 22, 1891. HCL.
JGW to Francis J. Garrison, October 29, 1891. SC.
Samuel C. Armstrong to JGW, October 9, 1891. HCL.

13. Robert Samuel Rantoul, "Some Personal Reminiscences of the Poet Whittier." EIHC, Vol. 37, p. 136, April, 1901.
Maurice N. Hervey, *Dark Days in Chile*. MacMillan & Co., 1891. pp. 306-09.

14. JGW to Fred A. Brown, November 21, 1891. APL.
Proof and letter, JGW to Fred A. Brown, December 4, 1891. Privately owned.
JGW to Annie Fields, December 10, 1891. EI.
Currier p. 317.
JGW to Mary Mapes Dodge, July 23, 1892. SC.

15. Abby J. Woodman, *Whittier at Oak Knoll*, p. 21.
John A. Henderson, "The Indian and Buffalo Statue on the State Capitol Grounds." *The Colorado Magazine*, September 1936, Vol. XIII, No. 5, pp. 183-86.
Rocky Mountain News, March 6, 1892.

16. JGW to Annie Fields, December 10, 1891. EI. There were letters from Oliver Wendell Holmes, Sarah Orne Jewett, Celia Thaxter, Julia Ward Howe, Lucy Larcom, Rose Terry Cooke, Robert C. Winthrop, Harriet Prescott Spofford, Richard Malcolm Johnston, Donald G. Mitchell, Edna Dean Proctor, "S. F. M." of Charlestown, W. T. W. Ball. Holmes' letter was addressed to Whittier and is in Pickard, pp. 735-56.

17. *Newburyport Herald*, December 17 and 18, 1891.
Albert Le Roy Bartlett, "John Greenleaf Whittier: Biographical Sketch." *A Memorial of John Greenleaf Whittier from His Native City, Haverhill, Massachusetts*. Haverhill, 1893, pp. 19-20.
Pickard, pp. 753-54.
JGW to Mrs. A. L. Nichols, December 18, 1891. Cora Dolbee, "Kansas and the 'Prairied West' of John G. Whittier." EIHC. Vol. LXXXII No. 2, April, 1946. p. 160.
JGW to Abby J. Woodman, December 18, 1891. EI.
Mary Abigail Dodge to George W. Cate, December 6, 1892. *Memorial to John Greenleaf Whittier by the Citizens of Amesbury*. Fred A. Brown, 1893, p. 48.
Janice Goldsmith Pulsifer, "Gail Hamilton". EIHC, Vol. CIV, No. 3, July, 1968. p. 190.
JGW to Annie Fields, December 29, 1891. Pickard, p. 759.

18. JGW to Annie Fields, January 29, 1892. Yale University Library.
Check to Francis A. Howe, April 6, 1892. Owned by the writer.
Edith Howe to Donald P. Wright, March 3, 1952. Owned by Donald P. Wright.
JGW to Phebe Woodman, February 14, 1892. EI.
Newburyport Herald, February 2, 1892.
JGW to W. Walter Jubb, February 19, 1892. SC.

19. *Danvers Mirror*, April 16 and May 28, 1892.
JGW to Celia Thaxter, May 8, 1892. HCL.
JGW to Phebe Woodman, June 1892. Albree, pp. 257-58.
JGW to Elizabeth W. Pickard, July 12, 1892. HPL.

20. Pickard, pp. 760-61.
John F. Kellett, "Whittier and the Goves of Hampton Falls." *Newburyport News*, September 21, 1963.
JGW to Horace E. Scudder, July 26, 1892. Formerly owned by Carroll A. Wilson.
JGW to Horace E. Scudder, July 27, 1892. Formerly owned by T. Franklin Currier.
Information given to the writer by Sarah Abby Gove.

608

21. JGW to ?, July 28, 1892. Owned by William C. Taylor.
    JGW to Hiram A. Tuttle, July 28, 1892. *The Statue of John P. Hale, Erected in front of the Capitol, and Presented to the State of New Hampshire by William E. Chandler of Concord.* Concord, 1892.

22. JGW to J. J. Somes and Edward Dolliver, August 14, 1892. *Memorial of the Celebration of the Two Hundred and Fiftieth Anniversary of the Incorporation of the Town of Gloucester, Massachusetts.*

23. Mary Jones Smith to John F. Kellett, August 20, 1967. Owned by John F. Kellett.
    Untitled article by Susan L. Brown. Typescript. Owned by the writer.

24. JGW to Fred A. Brown, August 20, 1892. Privately owned.
    JGW to Caroline Johnson, August 28, 1892. University of Virginia.
    JGW to Charles E. L. Wingate, August, 1892. W. Sloane Kennedy, *John Greenleaf Whittier. His Life, Genius, and Writings,* D. Lothrop Company, 1892. p. 374.
    JGW to Oliver Wendell Holmes, August 26, 1892. LC.
    Evelina Bray Downey to JGW, August 12, 1892. HCL.

25. JGW to Elizabeth Stuart Phelps Ward, August 30, 1892. SC.

26. Pickard, pp. 765-68.
    Gertrude Cartland to Editor of *On Duty.*
    Edith Howe to Donald P. Wright, March 3, 1952. Owned by Donald P. Wright.

27. Francis H. Underwood to Samuel T. Pickard, January 7, 1893. Whittier Home, Amesbury.
    Amesbury Daily News, September 10, 1892.

28. *Amesbury Daily News,* September 16, 1892.
    Pickard, pp. 768-71.
    Kennedy, pp. 335-47.
    Caroline Healy Dall, "At Whittier's Funeral." *New England Magazine,* January, 1893.
    Edmund C. Stedman to Fred A. Brown, September 23, 1892. Privately owned.
    Newton Irving Jones, "An Account of Whittier's Funeral." *Boston Public Library Bulletin,* June 1936.
    John Wallace Hutchinson, *Story of the Hutchinsons: compiled by Charles E. Mann.* Lee and Shepard, 1892. pp. 191-93.

29. Lucy Larcom to Elizabeth W. Pickard, September 20, 1892. HCL.

30. The picture was an enlarged photograph by William C. Thompson, dated 1888, colored by Mrs. Thompson. It is now in Amesbury Public Library. The present Library building was opened in 1901.

INDEX

616

624

Milton, Charles 87
Milton, John 9, 10, 18, 38, 64, 179, 195, 223, 253, 276, 284, 361, 448, 490
"The Minister's Daughter" (JGW) 440
Minot, Harriet 15, 77, 96, 99, 132 (See also Pitman)
Minot, Stephen 15
"The Minstrel" (JGW) 19
"Miriam" (JGW) 374
Mirick, B.L. 40
"Mirth and Medicine" (JGW) 210
"The Missionary" (JGW) 79
Mississippi 396
Missouri Compromise 179, 253
Mitchell, Donald G. 437, 607
"Mithridates at Chios" (JGW) 318
Mobile, Alabama 326
"Modern Magic" (JGW) 170
"Mogg Megone" (JGW) 89; "not calculated to do good" (JGW) 100; 161 "poor taste . . . objectionable from moral point of view" (JGW) 265; 343, 453. See Bonython, John
Mohammedanism 461
Mohini 485
Molinos, Miguel 498
"Moll Pitcher" (JGW) 41, 52
"Moloch in State Street" (JGW) 229
"Monadnock from Wachuset" (JGW) 305
Monks, George H. 603
Monroe, James E. 85
Moody, Dwight 418
Moody, Sophronia 440, 593
Moore, Clement 376
Moore, Mary C. 544
Moore, Paul Elmer 530
"The Moral Warfare" (JGW) 112
Mordell, Albert 549
"A Mormon Conventicle" (JGW) 167
Mormons and Mormonism 167, 223, 478
"The Mormons and Their City of Refuge" (JGW) 223
Morrill, Frank 591
Morrill, George W. 444
Morrill, Jettie A. 389, 412, 413, 425, 427, 590, 591
Morrill, Samuel 546
Morris, William 372
Morrison, Abram 11, 432
Morrow, R. 492
Morton, Marcus 147
Moses Brown School 405
"The Mother's Revenge" (JGW) 51
Motley, John Lothrop 394, 586
Mott, Frank L. 567, 597

Mott, Lucretia 123, 129
Mott, Richard 125
Moulton, Francis 396
Mouni, Sakya 385
Mount Wachuset 297
Mozoomdar Protap Chunder 461, 480
"Mrs. Choate's House-Warming" (JGW) 386
Muir, John 429, 443
Mulla 402
Muller, Max 379
Mumford, Thomas 545
Munroe, Rebecca K. 586
"The Murdered Lady" (JGW) 38, 51
Murfree, Mary N. (Charles Edward Craddock) 472
Mussey, B.B. 56
"My Birth-Day," 1830 (JGW) 43
"My Birthday," 1871 (JGW) 375
"My Double" (JGW) 496
"My Dream" (JGW) 254
"My Playmate" (JGW) 291
"My Psalm" (JGW) 286, 475
"My Soul and I" (JGW) 184
"My Summer with Dr. Singletary" (JGW) 227, 228, 230, 233, 235, 246, 332
"My Triumph" (JGW) 371
"My Trust" (JGW) 437
"The Mystic's Christmas" (JGW) 450
Nahant, Mass. 224, 326
"A Name" (JGW) 437
"Naples" (JGW) 297
Naples 231, 227, 297
Napoleon III 287, 374, 376
Narrative of James Williams (JGW) 98
Nason, Elias 224, 557, 587
"Nathaniel P. Rogers" (JGW) 200
National Era; JGW Corresponding Editor 193; becomes property of Gamaliel Bailey 203
National Republican Party 65
"Nauhaught the Deacon" (JGW) 367
Nayler, James 9
Nayson, Jonathan 239
Neal, John 27, 34, 126
Neall, Daniel 107, 108, 115, 266, 440
Neall, Elizabeth 105, 123
Neall, Hannah 252, 278, 297, 298
Negroes 44; JGW's maturing attitude toward them 66; 71, 92, 165, 196, 200, 220, 221, 222, 223, 311, 315, 318, 321, 351, 355, 365, 381, 435, 443, 459, 462, 463, 465, 492, 516, 518
Nelson, Jeremiah 59
"The Nervous Man" (JGW) 57
Nesmith, Mary 18

220, 221; publication of *Songs of Labor and Other Poems* 221-223; election of Charles Sumner to Senate 224, 228, 229; interest in Amesbury Lyceum 231, 244; attitude toward labor and Amesbury-Salisbury strike 238, 239; religious conviction 254; attitude toward new Republican Party 254, 260; founding of Amesbury Public Library 257, 258; Fremont campaign 260-262; poems with Essex County background 266-268; contributor to early *Atlantic Monthly* 270, 271; Overseer of Harvard College 272; contributor to *Independent* 276; renewed acquaintance with Elizabeth Lloyd Howell 281-287; attitude toward Abraham Lincoln 297, 327, 333; suggestions for compromises with the seceding States 300-301; defense of Fremont's proclamation of martial law and freeing of slaves 307; death of his sister Elizabeth 327; the writing of "Snow-Bound" 336-337; the success of *Snow-Bound* 337-338; relief from worry about money 338-339; the success of "Our Master" 346; popularity of *The Tent on the Beach* 350; burden of correspondence 351, 405, 452; interest in young authors 360, 388; attitude toward woman suffrage 364-365; disapproval of new ways of Quakers 379, 395, 508; opinion of Ulysses S. Grant 381; rescinding the Legislature's censure of Charles Sumner 386-387; attitude toward Roman Catholic Church 391, 392; "A Sea Dream" 397; at Oak Knoll 408-523 passim; "Centennial Hymn" and its success at Philadelphia 405-407; seventieth birthday observance and Mark Twain's speech 420-424; "The King's Missive" and criticism 439-440; humorous side of his character 372, 445; reunion of students of Haverhill Academy 474-475; attitude toward Walt Whitman 475, 476; degree of Doctor of Laws 482-483; Chicago anarchists and capital punishment 488-490; arrangements for biography 451-468, 479, 517, 523; final illness and death 527.

Whittier, Joseph A. 487
Whittier, Leonard 72
Whittier, Mary, sister of JGW 1, 12. See also Caldwell, Mary
Whittier, Mary, cousin of JGW 70
Whittier, Matthew Franklin 1; marriage to non-Quaker 84; in Baptist Church 126; separating from his wife 284; 297

employed at Boston Custom House 301; 424, 431; JGW's affection for him 436; resigns from Custom House because of illness 450; death 453
Whittier, Moses 1, 2, 3, 448
Whittier, Nathaniel 5
Whittier, Obediah 103, 409
Whittier, Phebe 409
Whittier School, Amesbury 508
Whittier, Thomas 1
"The Wife of Manoah to Her Husband" (JGW) 179
Wilberforce, William 25
Wilbur, John 151
Wilde, John 245
Wilder, Marshall 594
Wilkes, Charles 311
Willard, Frances E. 466, 527, 598
Willcox, Mary O. 548
Willey, Selden C. 334
"William Forster" (JGW) 251
"William Francis Bartlett" (JGW) 425
Williams and Everett 548
Williams, George W. 602
Williams, Roger 373
Willis, Nathaniel P. 38, 158
Wilmington, Md. 133
Wilson, Forrest 595
Wilson, Henry 180, 182, 185, 228, 253, 372, 386, 392, 393
Wilson, James G. 589
Wilson, Rufus R. 539
"The Wind of March" (JGW) 522
Wingate, Charles E. 574
Wingate, Charles E.L. 574, 608
Winslow, Harriet 138, 143 See also Sewall, Harriet Winslow
Winslow, Margaret 396
Winter, Christian 379
Winthrop, Robert C. 250, 393, 437, 607
Wisconsin 379
"The Wish of Today" (JGW) 209
"The Wishing Bridge" (JGW) 446, 493
"The Witch of Wenham" (JGW) 414, 415
"The Witch's Daughter" (JGW) 267, 399
Witches and Witchcraft 4, 267, 415
"Within the Gate" (JGW) 440
Withington, D.L. 591
Withington, Leonard 218, 346, 473
Wolfeboro, N.H. 243
"A Woman" (JGW) 382
Woman's Suffrage 364, 365, 526
Wood, George 577
"The Wood Giant" (JGW) 473, 474
Woodbridge, F.E. 351